SPECIAL EDITION

USING

Microsoft®

Office
PowerPoint®
2003

Patrice-Anne Rutledge

Jim Grey

Tom Mucciolo

800 East 96th Street
Indianapolis, Indiana 46240

Special Edition Using Microsoft® Office PowerPoint® 2003

International Standard Book Number: 0-7897-2957-1

Library of Congress Catalog Card Number: 2003103662

Printed in the United States of America

First Printing: September 2003

05   04   03   4   3   2

Trademarks

Warning and Disclaimer

Bulk Sales

Que Publishing offers excellent discounts on this book when ordered in quantity for bulk purchases or special sales. For more information, please contact

U.S. Corporate and Government Sales
1-800-382-3419
corpsales@pearsontechgroup.com

For sales outside the U.S., please contact

International Sales
1-317-428-3341
international@pearsontechgroup.com

Associate Publisher
Greg Wiegand

Acquisitions Editor
Stephanie J. McComb

Development Editor
Kevin Howard

Managing Editor
Charlotte Clapp

Project Editor
Tonya Simpson

Copy Editor
Rhonda Tinch-Mize

Indexer
Chris Barrick

Proofreader
Paula Lowell

Technical Editor
Dennis Teague

Team Coordinator
Sharry Lee Gregory

Multimedia Developer
Dan Scherf

Interior Designer
Anne Jones

Cover Designer
Anne Jones

Page Layout
Julie Parks

CONTENTS

I PowerPoint Basics

III Making Presentations

IV Working with Graphics, Charts, and Multimedia

V Working with PowerPoint on the Web

TROUBLESHOOTING TABLE OF CONTENTS

About the Authors

Patrice-Anne Rutledge is the best-selling author of more than 20 computer and business books. In addition, Patrice has contributed to numerous international publications, developed the columns "Global Business Today" and "eCommunicate," and currently manages a large global communications department for a leading Internet software company near San Francisco. She has used—and has trained others to use—PowerPoint for many years, designing presentations for meetings, seminars, trade shows, and worldwide audiences. She can be reached at patrice@patricerutledge.com or through her Web site (www.patricerutledge.com).

Jim Grey, longtime Microsoft Office power user, has made a career communicating technical information plainly. A 14-year veteran of the software industry, he now manages a software quality assurance department for a large Medicare customer-service and claims-processing contractor.

Tom Mucciolo, founder and president of MediaNet, is an accountant turned actor turned author and an acclaimed speaker on presentation skills. He is an expert at enhancing the key components of communication, including the message (scripting), the media (visual design), and the mechanics (delivery). His seminars and workshops have been rated as "exceptional" and "entertaining," and many consider Tom one of the country's top presentation specialists. His one-to-one coaching sessions, ranging from basic to advanced, develop individual style and prepare a person for presenting in a very visual world.

Dedication

To my family, with thanks for their love and support.

—PR

To my wife, Joan, and my son, Peter. They tolerate my travel, inspire my creativity, and motivate my performance. Their love, their patience, and their willingness to let me spend valuable weekend hours writing made my efforts on this book so much easier.

—TM

ACKNOWLEDGMENTS

PATRICE-ANNE RUTLEDGE

I'd like to thank everyone who contributed to the creation of *Special Edition Using Microsoft Office PowerPoint 2003*: Stephanie McComb, Susan Hobbs, Nick Goetz, and Jim Grey for their organizational and editorial contributions and Tom Mucciolo for creating many great chapters on real-world presentation techniques. And special thanks to my mom, Phyllis Rutledge, for both her editorial expertise and her encouragement throughout the creation of this book.

JIM GREY

I thank Stephanie McComb for offering me this writing job, Kevin Howard for his feedback, and Tonya Simpson, Rhonda Tinch-Mize, and Dennis Teague for their closer look. I'm also grateful to Patrice-Anne Rutledge for laying a solid foundation and to my wife for working around me. And most importantly, I thank Sharry Gregory for always remembering me when there's work to do.

TOM MUCCIOLO

I'd like to thank my brother, Rich, for his support and advice, along with his creative talents in designing, capturing, and printing all the figures used in my chapters. My thanks to Patrice-Anne Rutledge for shaping the main content of this book and to the editorial team, from copy to technical to production, in being so adept at bringing this project to fruition.

On the personal side, I want to thank my mom and dad for always supporting everything I attempted, regardless of success or failure. On the technical side, I owe a debt of gratitude to my notebook computer for accepting every keystroke throughout the entire project without complaint. A really important thank you goes to my friend, the Backspace key, without which my words would loofk ljke thyss. Oh, and finally, I want to thank everyone on the island of Crete, mainly because no one ever thanks those people for anything, and this has to stop right now!

WE WANT TO HEAR FROM YOU!

As the reader of this book, *you* are our most important critic and commentator. We value your opinion and want to know what we're doing right, what we could do better, what areas you would like to see us publish in, and any other words of wisdom you're willing to pass our way.

As an associate publisher for Que Publishing, I welcome your comments. You can email or write me directly to let me know what you did or didn't like about this book—as well as what we can do to make our books better.

Please note that I cannot help you with technical problems related to the topic of this book. We do have a User Services group, however, where I will forward specific technical questions related to the book.

When you write, please be sure to include this book's title and author as well as your name, email address, and phone number. I will carefully review your comments and share them with the author and editors who worked on the book.

Email: feedback@quepublishing.com

Mail: Greg Wiegand
         Associate Publisher
         Que Publishing
         800 East 96th Street
         Indianapolis, IN 46240 USA

For more information about this book or another Que title, visit our Web site at www.quepublishing.com. Type the ISBN (excluding hyphens) or the title of a book in the Search field to find the page you're looking for.

INTRODUCTION

In this chapter

Microsoft PowerPoint 2003 is the latest version of this powerful presentation graphics software program and is part of the Microsoft Office 2003 family. Using PowerPoint, you can create a basic slideshow quickly or you can delve into sophisticated features to create a customized presentation. Because it's part of the Microsoft Office suite of products, you'll find PowerPoint intuitive and very familiar if you already use any other Office applications, such as Word or Excel.

Because creating a successful presentation is more than just becoming a PowerPoint power user, we've included a special section in this book on presentation skills. After you master PowerPoint, you can master presentation techniques, such as creating a script, evaluating the use of multimedia and color, reaching your audience, rehearsing your speech, speaking in public, and dealing with the technicalities of presentation. This information combines with a thorough discussion of all PowerPoint's many features to create a complete reference manual for anyone who makes presentations using PowerPoint.

WHY YOU SHOULD USE THIS BOOK

Special Edition Using Microsoft Office PowerPoint 2003 is for experienced computer users who want to be able to use PowerPoint's more sophisticated features, as well as its basic ones. This book gets you up and running quickly and then spends more time exploring the advanced features PowerPoint has to offer—customization, Web interface, animation, and multimedia. If you want to become a PowerPoint power user, this book is for you.

HOW THIS BOOK IS ORGANIZED

Special Edition Using Microsoft Office PowerPoint 2003 is divided into seven parts.

Part I, "PowerPoint Basics," introduces the fundamentals of using PowerPoint, such as navigating, using views, getting help, creating a basic presentation, and saving and opening files. If you're an experienced computer user but are new to PowerPoint, these chapters will get you up and running quickly. If you've used PowerPoint extensively in the past, they can serve as a quick review and introduce you to the new, exciting features of PowerPoint 2003.

In Part II, "Editing and Formatting Presentations," you continue on to the most essential, and universally used, features of PowerPoint—formatting, organizing, and adding content to your slides. You'll learn to work with text and tables, organize with Outline view, and customize and format your presentation. PowerPoint's collaboration and speech tools are also introduced.

Part III, "Making Presentations," takes you to the logical next step—the actual delivery of a presentation. You'll learn how to easily set up a slideshow, customize it to work with a particular projector, create timings and narrations, preview your work, and even create portable PowerPoint presentations to display from another computer. Finally, you'll learn how to create a variety of printed material, such as notes and handouts, to go with your slideshow.

Next, you can start exploring some of PowerPoint's more advanced capabilities. Part IV, "Working with Graphics, Charts, and Multimedia," introduces you to techniques that you can use to make your slideshows more creative. For example, you can add charts—including organization charts—to provide additional information in a presentation. Or you can add clip art, photos, movies, sounds, and animation for a complete multimedia effect. For a finishing touch, you can format, customize, and add a variety of special effects to these multimedia objects.

From here, you can check out PowerPoint's Web capabilities in Part V, "Working with PowerPoint on the Web." From saving PowerPoint presentations as Web pages to designing Web scripts to creating online broadcasts and meetings, you can integrate all the latest Web technologies with your PowerPoint presentation.

Part VI, "Advanced PowerPoint," explores other sophisticated uses of PowerPoint. You can embed and link Office objects, create macros to automate procedures, use the power of VBA (the programming language Visual Basic for Applications), and extensively customize PowerPoint's features and interface. And finally, this part covers areas such as troubleshooting and using PowerPoint's foreign language features.

Part VII, "From Concept to Delivery," takes you out of PowerPoint and into the world of presentation design. Written by a presentations expert, this section offers detailed information and advice about actually creating a presentation specifically for PowerPoint. It covers topics such as scripting a concept, choosing a visual design, developing presentation skills, and using technology in your presentation.

CONVENTIONS USED IN THIS BOOK

Special Edition Using Microsoft Office PowerPoint 2003 uses a number of conventions to provide you with special information. These include the following elements.

The New icon makes it easy to find discussions of features new in PowerPoint 2003.

TIP

Tips offer suggestions for making things easier or provide alternative ways to do a particular task.

NOTE

Notes provide additional, more detailed information about a specific PowerPoint feature.

CAUTION

Cautions warn you about potential problems that might occur and offer advice on how to avoid these problems.

Cross-references refer you to other sections of the book in which you find more detailed explanations of a particular function, such as the following.

→ To learn more about preparing yourself to present, **see** Chapter 27, "The Mechanics of Function—Developing Internal Presentation Skills."

Most chapters end with two specific elements: "Troubleshooting" and "Design Corner." The "Troubleshooting" section provides tips on common problems you might encounter using the PowerPoint features presented in the chapter. "Design Corner" provides a before-and-after look at a specific feature explained in that chapter. "Design Corner" takes you one step further than the typical example in this book by showing you common design tasks you might perform and their end results.

POWERPOINT BASICS

CHAPTER 1

INTRODUCING POWERPOINT 2003

In this chapter

by Patrice-Anne Rutledge and Jim Grey

1

POWERPOINT OVERVIEW

PowerPoint is powerful, easy-to-use presentation software that is part of the Microsoft Office suite of products. You can use PowerPoint to create presentations for a wide variety of audiences and for a wide variety of purposes. A presentation communicates information, and a good presentation can truly convince, motivate, inspire, and educate its audience. PowerPoint offers the tools both to create a basic presentation and to enhance and customize it to meet its goals.

UNDERSTANDING WHAT POWERPOINT CAN DO

One of PowerPoint's strengths is its flexibility. Using wizards and other automated features, you can quickly create a basic presentation even if you have little or no design skills. If you are a designer, PowerPoint's advanced features and customization options give you complete creative control. With PowerPoint, you can

- Create a presentation using a wizard, using a design template, or from scratch.
- Add content to your presentation with text and tables.
- Use task panes to create new presentations; search for documents and clip art; and apply design templates, layouts, transitions, and animation.
- Format a presentation by customizing color schemes, background, and templates.
- Make a presentation onscreen using a computer, with overheads and a projector, or via the Web.
- Create and print notes and handouts for you and your audience.
- Add content with charts, pictures, clip art, and other shapes or objects.
- Bring multimedia into the picture using sound, video, and animation.
- Use PowerPoint's powerful Web features to create online broadcasts, Web discussions, online meetings, Web scripts, and even complete Web pages.
- Explore advanced features such as linking, embedding, and macros to create customized PowerPoint applications.

EXPLORING NEW POWERPOINT 2003 FEATURES

PowerPoint 2003 includes many new features that users of previous versions will enjoy. This new version of PowerPoint focuses particularly on user productivity and integration with the Web. Some new features that might interest you include the following:

- **Smart tags**—PowerPoint now offers smart tags, which let you do things in PowerPoint that you would normally use other programs to do. PowerPoint recognizes certain information in your text—such as names, telephone numbers, or stock ticker symbols— and makes smart tags from them. The smart tag links to a program that lets you do something with the information, such as create a contact in Microsoft Outlook, or see a graph of a stock's performance.

→ For more information about smart tags, **see** Chapter 3, "Working with Text," **p. 63**.

- **More task panes**—The Research task pane puts a host of reference books and Web sites at your disposal, including dictionaries, thesauruses, translation services, an encyclopedia, and business and financial research sites. The Shared Workspace task pane helps you work on presentations you're developing with others in a central location called a document workspace.

→ For more information about task panes, **see** "Using Task Panes" later in this chapter, **p. 15**.

- **Improved viewer**—Microsoft has updated the PowerPoint Viewer, a program you can use to display a presentation on a computer that does not have PowerPoint. The Viewer is now freely distributable and, unlike earlier versions, can show animation.

→ For more information about the PowerPoint Viewer, **see** Chapter 9, "Presenting a Slideshow," **p. 175**.

- **Package to CD**—If your computer includes a CD writer, you can use Package to CD to make CDs of your presentations so that you can easily carry them with you. Package to CD also places the PowerPoint Viewer on the CD so that you can give your presentation on a PC that doesn't have PowerPoint. Package to CD replaces the Pack 'n Go feature in previous versions of PowerPoint.

→ For more information about Package to CD, **see** Chapter 9, "Presenting a Slideshow," **p. 175**.

- **Integration with Windows Media Player**—When your presentation includes audio and video clips, PowerPoint now uses Windows Media Player to play them within the presentation. You get a panel of controls that let you stop the clip, replay it, adjust its volume, and more.

→ For more information about the integration with Windows Media Player, **see** Chapter 9, "Presenting a Slideshow," **p. 175**.

- **Document workspaces (collaborative authoring)**—A document workspace makes it easier to work with others to create, edit, and review a presentation. The presentation is stored in the document workspace, which everybody accesses. The document workspace is a Microsoft SharePoint Services site, so you need SharePoint installed on a server to use document workspaces.

→ For more information about document workspaces, **see** Chapter 7, "Collaborating on Presentations," **p. 135**.

Other new PowerPoint features and enhancements include the following:

- Access to Word's thesaurus
- Office Web services, including online training, the Clip Art and Media site, the Assistance Center site, and the Template Gallery
- New user interface skin that matches the Windows XP color scheme you choose
- Improvements to slide-show navigation
- Improved support for tablet PCs, especially their use of ink

USING MENUS AND SHORTCUT MENUS

You use PowerPoint menus to perform specific actions. The PowerPoint menu bar includes nine menu categories, each displaying a list of related commands. Figure 1.1 shows the menu bar.

Figure 1.1
Use menus to
navigate PowerPoint.

Menu bar

In PowerPoint, only the most commonly used menu commands are displayed when you first install the program. To see additional menu commands, click the double down arrows at the bottom of the list. After you use a menu command, it becomes part of the regular menu, and you don't need to select the down arrows to locate it.

To open a menu using the keyboard, press the Alt key plus the underlined letter in the menu category you want to open. For example, pressing Alt+D opens the Slide Show menu. This is called a *hotkey*.

To customize how menu commands display on menus, choose Tools, Customize and go to the Options tab of the Customize dialog box (see Figure 1.2).

Figure 1.2
Choose how to
display menu
commands.

Select the Always Show Full Menus check box to display all menu commands rather than personalized menus. If you select this option in PowerPoint, it also affects menus in other Office programs.

Select Show Full Menus After a Short Delay to display the entire menu after you hover the mouse over an open menu for a few seconds.

→ To learn how to add, delete, and modify menu commands as well as create your own menu, **see** "Customizing Menu Commands" in Chapter 21, "Customizing PowerPoint," **p. 429**.

Several PowerPoint menus include submenus, identified with a right arrow next to the menu command itself. Figure 1.3 illustrates a submenu.

Figure 1.3
A submenu is a second-menu level of navigation in PowerPoint.

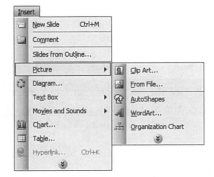

PowerPoint also includes shortcut menus, specific menus that are context sensitive and relate to a selected object. To view a shortcut menu, right-click the mouse. Figure 1.4 displays a shortcut menu.

Figure 1.4
To see specific menu options, right-click the mouse.

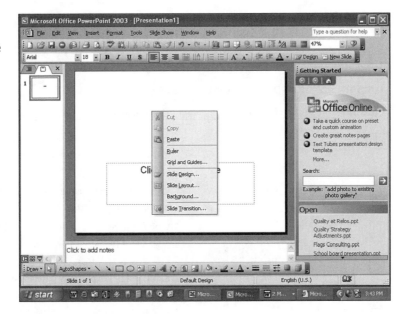

USING TOOLBARS

A toolbar is similar to a menu because it categorizes related commands to make it easier for you to perform a specific task. Toolbars use a graphical representation, or button, rather than a menu-based text representation. Even though toolbars use buttons rather than text, you can still display a text description of what the button does by pausing the mouse over it. A *ScreenTip* appears, identifying the button's function. Figure 1.5 illustrates a ScreenTip.

Figure 1.5
ScreenTips identify
toolbar buttons.

 ScreenTips don't appear? See the "Troubleshooting" section near the end of the chapter.

The Standard and Formatting toolbars are the two most commonly used PowerPoint toolbars. Table 1.1 describes the buttons on the Standard toolbar, which you'll use frequently in PowerPoint.

NOTE

You can switch between displaying the Standard and Formatting toolbars on either two rows or one with the Show Standard and Formatting Toolbars on Two Rows check box on the Options tab of the Customize dialog box. Open this dialog box by selecting Tools, Customize. Although it's usually easier having access to all these buttons on two rows, you might want to combine these toolbars if you want to save screen space.

→ To view a table of the buttons on the Formatting toolbar, **see** "Using the Formatting Toolbar" in Chapter 3, "Working with Text," **p. 67**.

TABLE 1.1 STANDARD TOOLBAR BUTTONS

Button	Name	Description
	New	Creates a new presentation and opens the New Slide dialog box in which you can choose from a variety of slide layouts.
	Open	Opens the Open dialog box from which you can open an existing presentation.
	Save	Opens the Save As dialog box in which you can save your open presentation.
	Permission	Lets you control who can open or change the document and set expiration dates to end their access.
	E-mail	Creates an email message with your presentation attached as a file.
	Print	Prints the presentation on the default printer.
	Print Preview	Displays the current presentation in Print Preview.

Button	Name	Description
	Spelling	Checks the spelling and style of the open presentation.
	Cut	Cuts the selected text or object, which is deleted from the presentation, and places it on the Clipboard.
	Copy	Copies the selected text or object, which remains on the presentation, and places it on the Clipboard.
	Paste	Pastes the selected Clipboard object into the location in the presentation you specify. If you haven't selected an object, the most recently cut or copied object is pasted.
	Format Painter	Copies the format of the selected text or object and applies this formatting to the next object you click.
	Undo	Undoes the last action.
	Redo	Does the previous action again.
	Insert Chart	Activates Microsoft Graph, with which you can insert a chart in your presentation.
	Insert Table	Displays a palette in which you can choose the size of table you want to insert.
	Tables and Borders	Displays the Tables and Borders toolbar.
	Insert Hyperlink	Opens the Insert Hyperlink dialog box, from which you can insert a hyperlink to a Web page, email address, or another document or presentation.
	Insert Microsoft Excel Worksheet	Places an Excel worksheet in the current slide.
	Expand All	Expands the content of the Outline tab in Normal view to display all titles and body text for each slide. Click the button again to contract the outline.
	Show Formatting	Displays text formatting in the Outline pane.
	Show/Hide Grid	Displays and hides a grid on your presentation, which you can use to more accurately position objects on your slides.

continues

TABLE 1.1 CONTINUED		
Button	**Name**	**Description**
▣	Color/Grayscale	Opens a menu that lets you preview your presentation in color, grayscale, or pure black and white.
47% ▾	Zoom	Lets you select a zoom percentage from the drop-down list from 25% to 400%, or enter your own percentage from 10% to 400%.
◉	Microsoft PowerPoint Help	Opens the Help task pane.

DISPLAYING TOOLBARS

To open and close toolbars manually, choose View, Toolbars and then select or deselect toolbars from the list of available options. Figure 1.6 shows this menu and the available toolbars.

Figure 1.6
Select a toolbar from this menu to display it.

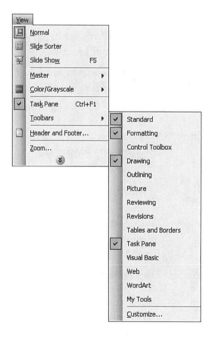

→ To learn how to customize and modify PowerPoint toolbars to fit your needs, **see** "Customizing Toolbars" in Chapter 21, **p. 430**.

MOVING TOOLBARS

You can easily move a toolbar to a new location. How you do this depends on whether the toolbar is *docked* or *floating*. Figure 1.7 illustrates both types of toolbars.

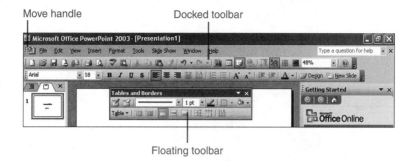

Figure 1.7
You can move PowerPoint toolbars to make the program easier to use.

To move a docked toolbar, drag the move handle on its left side to a new location. To move a floating toolbar, drag its title bar. You can easily switch a toolbar from docked to floating and vice versa. To float a docked toolbar, drag it to another location on the screen. To dock a floating toolbar, drag it to the edge of the window.

> **TIP**
>
> You can resize a floating toolbar by dragging on any side. This way, you can display the buttons straight across in one row or in several rows, depending on which way you like best.

 Can't find a toolbar button you've used before? *See the "Troubleshooting" section near the end of the chapter.*

USING TASK PANES

A task pane is a window inside PowerPoint that lets you do common PowerPoint tasks without covering your presentation. PowerPoint has 12 readily accessible main task panes and several others that appear only under certain conditions (such as the Revisions pane for reviewing and collaborating). These task panes are

- **Getting Started**—Lets you open a presentation you recently edited and get information from Microsoft Office Online that helps you use PowerPoint more effectively. This task pane, which Figure 1.8 shows, appears when you start PowerPoint.

- **Microsoft PowerPoint Help**—Lets you search for information when you need help using PowerPoint and provides links to selected topics, assistance, training, newsgroups, and software updates on Microsoft Office Online. Choose Help, Microsoft PowerPoint Help to see this task pane.

Click to switch to another task pane

Figure 1.8
Open a presentation, get tips for working with PowerPoint, or search for help in the Getting Started task pane.

- **Clip Art**—Lets you search for clip art images and provides links to the Clip Organizer and to the Clip Art and Media page at Microsoft Office Online. Choose Insert, Picture, Clip Art from the menu bar to open this task pane.

→ For more information about using clip art and the Media Gallery, **see** Chapter 13, "Exploring Clip Art, Pictures, Movies, and Sound," **p. 258**.

- **Research**—Lets you look up definitions and synonyms, translate short phrases into other languages, perform Web, news, and encyclopedia searches, and find financial information about companies. To open this task pane, choose Tools, Research.

- **Clipboard**—Offers the ability to collect and paste up to 24 different items. Choose Edit, Office Clipboard to open this task pane.

- **New Presentation**—Lets you create a new presentation in a variety of ways. Choose File, New from the menu bar to open this task pane.

→ To learn how to use the New Presentation task pane, **see** Chapter 2, "Creating a Basic Presentation," **p. 41**.

- **Shared Workspace**—Lets you collaborate with others in real time on presentations. To use this feature, you need a server that runs SharePoint. To open this task pane, choose Tools, Shared Workspace.

- **Basic File Search**—Provides both basic and advanced search capability on both your own computer and a network. Choose File, File Search to open this task pane.

- **Slide Layout**—Lets you apply up to 31 different layouts, each with its own additional design flexibility. Choose Format, Slide Layout from the menu bar or click the New Slide button on the Formatting toolbar to open this task pane.

- **Slide Design**—Lets you choose a design template for your presentation, set its color scheme, and apply animation schemes. Choose Format, Slide Design or click the Design button on the Formatting toolbar to open this task pane.

→ For more information about slide layouts and design, **see** Chapter 2, **p. 4**.

- **Custom Animation**—Lets you apply sophisticated animations to your slides or objects on your slides. Choose Slide Show, Custom Animation to open this task pane.

- **Slide Transition**—Offers the ability to apply animated transitions as you move from slide to slide. Choose Slide Show, Slide Transition to open this task pane.

→ For more information about the Custom Animation and Slide Transition task panes, **see** Chapter 15, "Working with Animation," **p. 319**.

You can also choose View, Task Pane from the menu bar to open the task pane. The most recently viewed pane opens, but you can easily change to a different task pane. To do so, click the down arrow on the upper-right side of the task pane to open a menu of all available panes.

Located below the task bar's name are back and forward arrows that you can click to go back to the previously viewed task panes in the order in which you opened them and then forward again, as well as a Home button that opens the Getting Started task pane. To close a task pane, click the Close button in the upper-right corner or choose View, Task Pane again.

To customize when task panes appear, choose Tools, Options and go to the View tab of the Options dialog box (see Figure 1.9).

Figure 1.9
Customize how to display task panes in PowerPoint.

Remove the check mark by the Startup Task Pane check box if you don't want a task pane to appear when you start PowerPoint. Remove the check mark by the Slide Layout task pane when inserting new slides check box if you don't want the Slide Layout task pane to open when you click the New Slide button.

You can also make the task pane wider or narrower. To do so, pause the mouse pointer over the left edge of the pane until the pointer becomes a two-headed arrow. Click the mouse and drag the left edge to either the left or right until the task pane is the width you want.

USING THE CLIPBOARD TASK PANE

PowerPoint shares its Clipboard task pane with other Office applications such as Word and Excel. This collect-and-paste feature lets you copy multiple items and then paste them selectively, rather than simply copying and pasting a single item. You can collect up to 24 items—text, objects, graphics, documents, Web pages, and so forth—and then selectively paste them as needed. The Clipboard task pane lets you view and manage the 24 items you have most recently copied. To open this task pane, choose Edit, Office Clipboard. If you already have a task pane open, click the down arrow in the upper-right corner and choose Clipboard from the menu that appears. Figure 1.10 illustrates this task pane.

Figure 1.10
You can easily manage and share information using the Clipboard task pane.

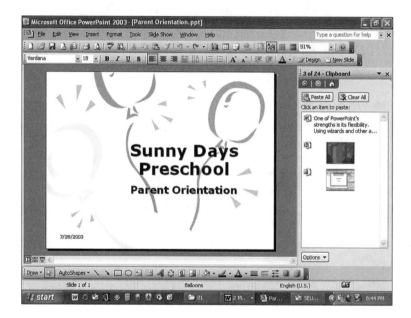

Click an item on the Clipboard task pane to paste it on the current slide (where the cursor is active). On this task pane, you also can

- Click the Paste All button to paste all collected objects into the open presentation or document.
- Click the Clear All button to delete all collected items from the Clipboard.
- Right-click on a selected item and choose Delete from the menu that appears to delete only that item.
- Click the Options button for five more options:
  - **Show Office Clipboard Automatically**—Automatically displays the Clipboard when you copy or cut an object.
  - **Show Office Clipboard When Ctrl+C Pressed Twice**—Shows the Clipboard when you press Ctrl+C twice in a row.

- **Collect Without Showing Office Clipboard**—Lets you copy and cut text and objects without displaying the Clipboard.
- **Show Office Clipboard Icon on Taskbar**—Displays a Clipboard icon on the taskbar in the lower-right corner of your screen when the Clipboard task pane is open.
- **Show Status Near Taskbar When Copying**—Displays the Clipboard's status (such as 6 of 24 collected) next to the Clipboard icon in the taskbar when you copy text or an object.

SEARCHING FOR FILES

Sometimes you won't immediately be able to find a presentation you want to open. You might have so many saved presentations that you've forgotten their names, making it very difficult to find one you want. Or you might have saved the file you're looking for in another folder and can't find it. Using the Basic File Search task pane, you can conduct sophisticated searches based on text in a particular presentation, as well as on specific presentation properties, to help you find the file you need. Basic Search is the default PowerPoint task pane, but you can click the Advanced File Search hyperlink on this task pane to open the Advanced File Search pane, where you can do more detailed searches based on file properties.

PERFORMING A BASIC FILE SEARCH

To open the Basic File Search task pane, choose File, File Search from the menu bar. Figure 1.11 shows this task pane.

Figure 1.11
To search for specific text in a presentation, use the Basic Search task pane.

To perform a basic search, follow these steps:

1. Enter the text you want to search for in the Search text field. This can be any text included in the presentation you want to find.

2. In the Search in field, select the folder or folders you want to search from the drop-down list. These can be folders on your computer, on a connected network drive, on the Web, or in Microsoft Outlook. To expand a folder, click the plus (+) sign; to collapse it, click the minus (-) sign. When you find the folder you want, place a check mark in the box that precedes it.

TIP

> If you have no idea where the file is located, choose Everywhere to search in all locations. Be aware, however, that it takes longer to search all folders rather than to focus on specific folders.

3. Select the type of files to look for in the Results Should Be drop-down list. Options include a variety of Office file types (PowerPoint, Word, or Excel files, for example) or Web pages.

TIP

> If you want to enable PowerPoint's Indexing Service, click the Search options hyperlink to open the Indexing Service Settings dialog box (see Figure 1.12). Enabling Indexing Service directs Office to index your files when your computer is idle so that searches are faster and more accurate. If Fast Search isn't installed, you'll first need to click the Install hyperlink to install it before you can see the Search Options hyperlink.

Figure 1.12
Indexing speeds up searching a large collection of files.

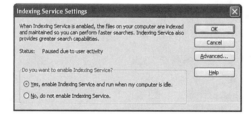

4. Click the Search button to begin the search process. PowerPoint finds matching presentations and displays them in the task pane, which is renamed Search Results (see Figure 1.13).

5. Double-click the file you want to open.

NOTE

> For more options, click the down arrow next to the selected file. From the menu that appears, you can edit the file, create a new file from this file, copy the link to the Clipboard, or view the file's properties.

Figure 1.13
PowerPoint displays the results of your search.

Click the Stop button to stop a search in progress. Click Modify to return to the Basic Search task pane.

PERFORMING AN ADVANCED FILE SEARCH

If you want to search on specific file properties, use the Advanced File Search task pane. These properties align to the information you see in the Properties dialog box. To open the Advanced File Search task pane, click the Advanced Search hyperlink at the bottom of the Basic File Search task pane. Figure 1.14 shows the Advanced File Search task pane.

Figure 1.14
You can search on the properties in the Advanced File Search task pane.

→ If you want to know the exact definition of each file property, **see** "Setting Presentation Properties" in Chapter 21, **p. 463**.

1

Table 1.2 lists all the properties you can search on the Advanced Search task pane as well as the conditions available for each, which fall into three main categories: text, numbers, and dates.

TABLE 1.2   ADVANCED SEARCH PROPERTIES AND CONDITIONS

Property	Available Conditions
Address	Is (exactly), includes
All day event	Is yes, is no
Application name	Is (exactly), includes
Attendees	Is (exactly), includes
Author	Is (exactly), includes
Category	Is (exactly), includes
CC	Is (exactly), includes
Comments	Is (exactly), includes
Company	Is (exactly), includes
Contents	Is (exactly), includes
Creation date	On, on or after, on or before, today, tomorrow, yesterday, this week, next week, last week, this month, next month, last month
Date completed	On, on or after, on or before, today, tomorrow, yesterday, this week, next week, last week, this month, next month, last month
Date due	On, on or after, on or before, today, tomorrow, yesterday, this week, next week, last week, this month, next month, last month
Description	Is (exactly), includes
Email	Is (exactly), includes
End	On, on or after, on or before, today, tomorrow, yesterday, this week, next week, last week, this month, next month, last month
Fax	Is (exactly), includes
File Name	Is (exactly), includes
Format	Is (exactly), includes
From	Is (exactly), includes
Importance	Equals Low, equals Normal, equals High, not equal to Low, not equal to Normal, not equal to High
Job title	Is (exactly), includes
Keywords	Is (exactly), includes
Last modified	On, on or after, on or before, today, tomorrow, yesterday, this week, next week, last week, this month, next month, last month

Property	Available Conditions
Last printed	On, on or after, on or before, today, tomorrow, yesterday, this week, next week, last week, this month, next month, last month
Last saved by	Is (exactly), includes
Location	Is (exactly), includes
Manager	Is (exactly), includes
Name	Is (exactly), includes
Number of characters	Equals, not equal to, more than, less than, at least, at most
Number of characters + spaces	Equals, not equal to, more than, less than, at least, at most
Number of hidden slides	Equals, not equal to, more than, less than, at least, at most
Number of lines	Equals, not equal to, more than, less than, at least, at most
Number of multimedia clips	Equals, not equal to, more than, less than, at least, at most
Number of notes	Equals, not equal to, more than, less than, at least, at most
Number of pages	Equals, not equal to, more than, less than, at least, at most
Number of paragraphs	Equals, not equal to, more than, less than, at least, at most
Number of slides	Equals, not equal to, more than, less than, at least, at most
Number of words	Equals, not equal to, more than, less than, at least, at most
Owner	Is (exactly), includes
Phone	Is (exactly), includes
Priority	Equals Low, equals Normal, equals High, not equal to Low, not equal to Normal, not equal to High
Received	On, on or after, on or before, today, tomorrow, yesterday, this week, next week, last week, this month, next month, last month
Resources	Is (exactly), includes
Revision	Is (exactly), includes
Sent	On, on or after, on or before, today, tomorrow, yesterday, this week, next week, last week, this month, next month, last month
Size	Equals, not equal to, more than, less than, at least, at most
Start	On, on or after, on or before, today, tomorrow, yesterday, this week, next week, last week, this month, next month, last month
Status	Equals Not Started, equals In Progress, equals Completed, equals Waiting for someone else, equals Deferred, not equal to Not Started, not equal to In Progress, not equal to Completed, not equal to Waiting for someone else, not equal to Deferred
Subject	Is (exactly), includes

continues

TABLE 1.2   CONTINUED

Property	Available Conditions
Template	Is (exactly), includes
Text or property	Includes
Title	Is (exactly), includes
To	Is (exactly), includes
Total editing time	Equals, not equal to, more than, less than, at least, at most
Web page	Is (exactly), includes

Depending on your selection in the Condition field, the Value field might activate. For example, if you search the Last printed property and choose Yesterday as your condition, no further value is required. However, if you search the Title property and select Includes Words as the condition, you have to enter a value to indicate the exact words to include.

As another example, let's say that you want to find a specific presentation whose filename you've forgotten. You do remember, however, that you created the presentation sometime last week. To find this file, you could search the Creation date property for the last week condition. Based on this information, you can locate all presentations created within the past week, which should narrow your search considerably.

To use the Advanced Search task pane, follow these steps:

1. Select a property from the drop-down list.
2. Select a condition from the available choices for the chosen property.
3. If required, enter a value for the criterion for which you're searching.
4. Click the Add button to add this criterion to the search list.
5. Continue adding search criteria as needed. As you add criteria, choose either the And or Or option button to specify whether the search should look for this criterion *and* other specified criteria or whether it should look for this criterion *or* other specified criteria.

NOTE

> To remove a search, select it in the list and click Remove. To remove all searches, click Remove All.

6. Continue with steps 2 through 5 described in "Performing a Basic Search," earlier in this chapter.

WORKING WITH THE RESEARCH TASK PANE

The Research task pane gives you access to reference information on your computer and online from within PowerPoint. It offers these services:

- Reference books built into Office, including dictionaries and thesauruses in various languages and a word and phrase translator.

- Research Web sites, including searches of the Web, major news services, and the Encarta encyclopedia in various languages. Some of these services require that you register, pay a small fee, or have a Microsoft Passport.

- Business and financial Web sites, where you can get company information and stock quotes. To access some of this information, you might have to register or pay a small fee.

To open the Research task pane, click the Research button or choose Tools, Research. Figure 1.15 shows the Research task pane.

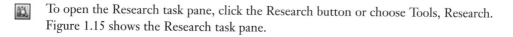

Figure 1.15
Use the Research task pane to look up definitions, synonyms, news stories, company information, and more.

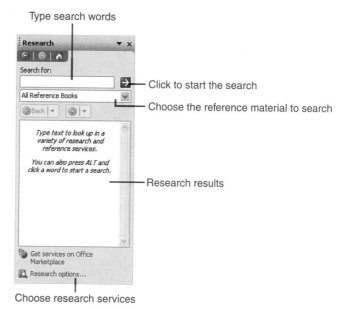

Type search words
Click to start the search
Choose the reference material to search
Research results
Choose research services

DOING RESEARCH

To research a word or phrase, type it in the Search For field. Then, in the field right below the Search For field, click the arrow and choose the reference source to search. Choose a specific reference source, or choose

- All Reference Books to search the dictionaries and thesauruses you have installed and translate the word or phrase into another language.

- All Research Sites to use all news and Web search sites you've enabled and to search the Encarta encyclopedia.

- All Business and Financial Sites to search all business and financial sites you've enabled.

Now click the Start searching button (the green button with the white arrow next to the Search For field). The Research task pane shows you its results. Figure 1.16 shows you an example.

Figure 1.16
Searching all research sites for Engineering returns these results.

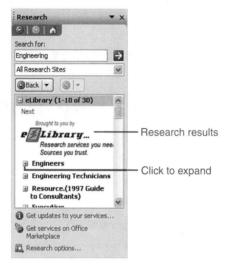

Research results

Click to expand

Not getting any results? See the "Troubleshooting" section near the end of the chapter.

When you see a small plus-sign button next to anything returned, click it to see more information. You'll usually see a couple sentences that describe the research information and a hyperlink to the information itself. Figure 1.17 shows an example.

Figure 1.17
An expanded item, showing a link to the actual research information.

Click to see the research information

1

Click the hyperlink to see the research information. When the information is on the Web, your browser opens to the Web page that contains it. If you use Internet Explorer, the Research task pane appears in the browser, as Figure 1.18 shows. You can continue your research in Internet Explorer, avoiding your having to switch back and forth from PowerPoint.

Figure 1.18
Research information appears in Internet Explorer. The Research task pane appears, too.

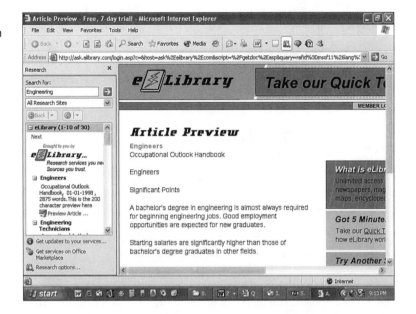

If the word you want to research is already in your presentation, it might be faster to do it on-the-fly. To look up a word, right-click it in the presentation and choose Look Up from the menu that appears. The Research task pane opens with whatever settings it last used. If necessary, choose the reference tools to use and click the Start Searching button.

CHOOSING RESEARCH SERVICES

The Research task pane comes with a lot of reference materials in many languages, but only a few of them are enabled after you install PowerPoint. You can enable others, or disable services you don't want, in the Research Options dialog box (Figure 1.19). To open this dialog box, in the Research task pane, click the Research Options hyperlink.

In the Services list, to enable a service, click its box so that it contains a check mark. To disable a service, click its box so that it's empty.

Microsoft might add research services, or you might learn of a service you want to use. To add a service to your Services list, click the Add Services button. The Add Services dialog box appears (see Figure 1.20). Either choose an advertised service from the list, or type the Web address of the service you want to use in the Address box, and click Add.

Figure 1.19
Choose the research services to enable in the Research Options dialog box.

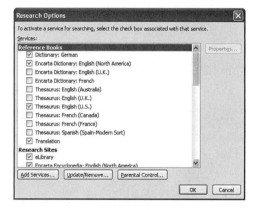

Figure 1.20
Choose the research services to add a research service.

To remove a service that you don't want to use anymore, click the Update/Remove button and follow the instructions. If you want to filter research results to remove questionable or offensive content, click the Parental Control button and follow the instructions.

UNDERSTANDING THE SHARED WORKSPACE TASK PANE

 A shared workspace is an area where you can work with others on a presentation. To use a shared workspace, you need access to a SharePoint server site. This is something you're unlikely to have unless you use PowerPoint at work and your corporation has embraced SharePoint technology. Check with your system administrator to find out whether a SharePoint server is available to you.

The Shared Workspace task pane, shown in Figure 1.21, opens whenever you open a document from a SharePoint document library.

This task pane has these tabs:

- **Status**—This tab tells you whether the open presentation is in sync with other members' copies and whether you "checked it out" to work on it. It also tells you the document's Information Rights Management settings, which control access to the document.

- **Members**—This tab lists the users who are part of this shared workspace. You can also use this tab to invite others to join you.

Figure 1.21
The Shared
Workspace task pane.

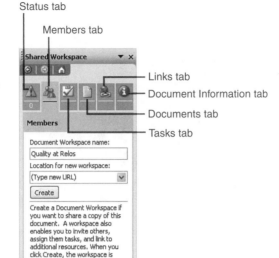

Status tab

Members tab

Links tab

Document Information tab

Documents tab

Tasks tab

- **Tasks**—This tab lists any to-dos that you share with other members of this shared workspace. You can also assign tasks to other members.
- **Documents**—This tab lists any documents you share with other members that relate to this presentation.
- **Links**—This tab lists references, either files or Web sites, helpful to the presentation.
- **Document Information**—This tab lists document properties.

UNDERSTANDING POWERPOINT VIEWS

PowerPoint includes three different *views*, which are arrangements of slides and tools on the screen that you use to work with and view your presentation. Which view you use depends on what you're doing. To display a particular view, click its View button in the lower-left portion of the PowerPoint window.

PowerPoint's three views are

- **Normal view**—This is the default view. It displays three panes: the Normal View pane, which includes the Outline and Slides tabs, the Slide pane in the center, and the Notes pane beneath it. Figure 1.22 illustrates Normal view.

    Note that your screen might also display a task pane. This is a separate pane and isn't connected to your choice of view. If you have a task pane open, it appears in both Normal view and Slide Sorter view, but it won't appear if you present a slide show.

    The three Normal view panes are

Normal View pane
Outline tab
Slides tab
Slide pane

Figure 1.22
Normal view is
PowerPoint's default
viewing option.

Slide Show View button
Slide Sorter View button
Normal View button

Notes pane

- The Slide pane, which is the largest of the three panes. You can add text, graphics, tables, charts, and other objects to your presentation on the slide pane.

NOTE

> You can use the scrollbar on the right side of the slide pane to navigate between presentation slides. You can also use the Page Up and Page Down keys to move among slides.

- The Normal View pane, on the left side of the screen. This pane offers an Outline tab, which displays an outline of your presentation, including the initial text of each slide. It also offers a Slides tab, which displays thumbnails of your slides. You can use this pane to rearrange and organize slides or to display a particular slide in the Slide pane. You can also enter content on the Outline tab. Note that when you click the Outline tab, PowerPoint uses text in the tab labels, but when you click the Slides tab, PowerPoint uses icons as the tab labels.
- The Notes pane includes space for you to write speaker's notes or notes to yourself about your presentation.

→ For suggestions on creating effective speaker's notes, **see** "Creating Notes and Handouts" in Chapter 10, "Creating and Printing Presentation Materials," **p. 200**.

> You can resize the panes in Normal view. To do so, drag the border between panes to a new location. If you want to hide the Normal View pane, click its Close button. You can always reopen it later by choosing View, Normal (Restore Panes).

■ **Slide Sorter view**—This view, shown in Figure 1.23, displays miniature previews of all the slides in your presentation, making it easier for you to organize them.

Figure 1.23
Seeing miniature versions of your slides can help you rearrange them.

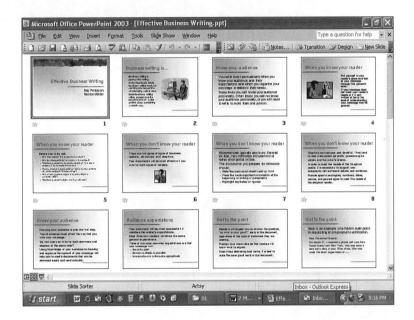

→ To learn how to use this view, **see** "Using the Slide Sorter View" in Chapter 6, "Formatting Slides and Presentations," **p. 115**.

■ **Slide Show view**—Slide Show view displays your slides as they would appear in a slide show, full-screen, without any menus, toolbars, or other features. Figure 1.24 shows this view.

→ For details on viewing slide shows, **see** Chapter 9, "Presenting a Slide Show," **p. 175**.

> PowerPoint's default view is Normal view with the Outline tab selected. If you want to change this, choose Tools, Options and go to the View tab on the Options dialog box, as shown in Figure 1.25.

> On this tab, you can specify your default view from the Open All Documents Using This View drop-down list.

Figure 1.24
Slide Show view demonstrates how your presentation will look when you present it.

Figure 1.25
You can change PowerPoint's defaults in the Options dialog box.

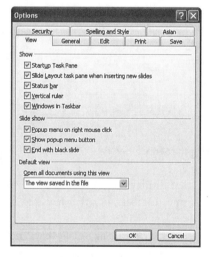

GETTING HELP

PowerPoint includes several ways to get help, one of which should suit your needs and the way you use information. Options include the Ask a Question box, the Office Assistant, a full-search Help window, and help on the Web.

NOTE

At times, PowerPoint might not behave as expected, or it might deliver an error message when none is needed. To find and repair these problems automatically, choose Help, Detect and Repair.

USING THE ASK A QUESTION BOX

The Ask a Question box (see Figure 1.26) puts help at your fingertips, always available on the menu bar.

Ask a Question box

Figure 1.26
Use the Ask a Question box for fast and easy help.

Type a question or keyword in the box and press Enter. The Search Results task pane opens, listing help topics. Click the one that best matches what you need to know. The Microsoft PowerPoint Help window opens with specific information on the topic you chose, shown in Figure 1.27.

Figure 1.27
The Help window displays detailed help on your selected topic.

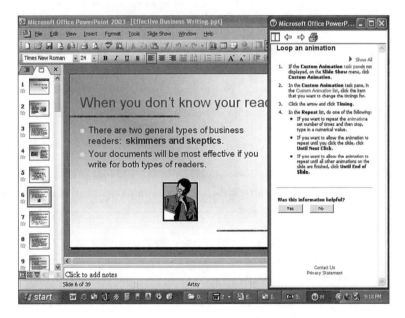

➔ To learn more about the Microsoft PowerPoint Help window, **see** "Using Microsoft PowerPoint Help" in this chapter, **p. 35**.

USING THE OFFICE ASSISTANT

The *Office Assistant* lets you ask natural language questions, such as "How do I insert WordArt?" It provides help topics that answer these questions. To see the Office Assistant, choose Help, Show the Office Assistant. Click the Assistant when you need help, and a balloon appears that asks you what you want to do (see Figure 1.28).

Figure 1.28
The Office Assistant can answer your PowerPoint questions.

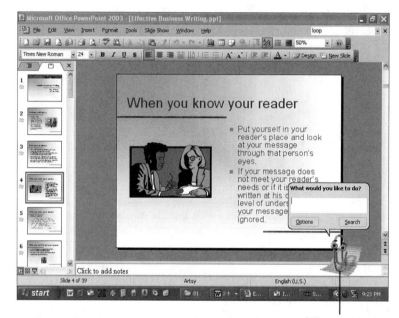

Office Assistant

Type your question—or just a word or phrase if you like—and click the Search button. The Search Results task pane opens, listing relevant Help topics. Click the most relevant topic to open the Microsoft PowerPoint Help window.

NOTE

Click See More at the bottom of the Help caption to view additional help topics.

You can change to a different Office Assistant if you don't like Clippy, the default. Click the Options button in the Assistant balloon and choose the Gallery tab on the Office Assistant dialog box, shown in Figure 1.29.

The Gallery offers a few other Assistant images, including Rocky, Mother Nature, and the Dot.

Turn off the Office Assistant by choosing Help, Hide the Office Assistant or by right-clicking on the Assistant and choosing Hide.

Figure 1.29
Make Rocky your
Office Assistant, if
you like.

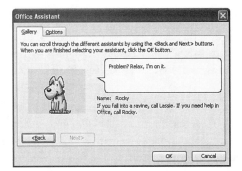

NOTE

The Office Assistant settings you make in PowerPoint, or another application such as
Word or Excel, are used in all Office applications.

USING MICROSOFT POWERPOINT HELP

You can access the Microsoft PowerPoint Help task pane through the Ask a Question box,
through the Office Assistant, or directly by pressing F1 or clicking the Microsoft
PowerPoint Help button. Figure 1.30 shows this task pane.

Figure 1.30
The Help task pane is
the portal to all the
ways Microsoft helps
you learn PowerPoint
and use it more
effectively.

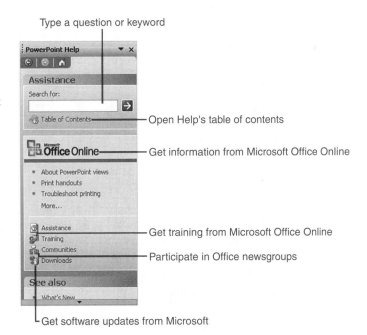

The Help task pane offers you these ways to get help:

- Type a question or keyword in the Search box to find answers. Press Enter to launch the search. PowerPoint opens the Search Results task pane and lists the matching Help topics, training modules, and other content at Microsoft Office Online. Click an item to open it.

- Click the Table of Contents hyperlink to see an organized list of all PowerPoint Help topics. Click a purple book to see its contents. Click document icons to see Help topics, or click globe/question-mark icons to see information at Microsoft Office Online. Figure 1.31 shows the table of contents, a portion of it expanded.

Figure 1.31
The table of contents organizes PowerPoint Help by subject.

Click to collapse this section
Click to expand this section

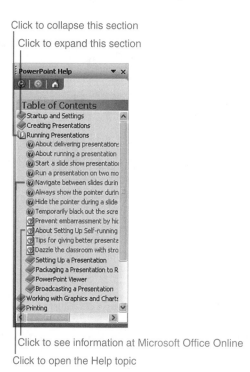

Click to see information at Microsoft Office Online
Click to open the Help topic

- Click the Office Online graphic to open Microsoft Office Online in your browser. There you can get help and training as well as download templates, clip art, media, and software updates. To go straight to help, training, or software downloads, click the hyperlinks at the bottom of the Office Online area. There's also a Communities hyperlink that takes you to Office discussion groups where you can post questions for others, including PowerPoint experts, to answer.

NOTE

> Another way to open the Microsoft Office Online Web site is to choose Help, Office on Microsoft.com.

TROUBLESHOOTING

DISPLAYING SCREENTIPS

A ScreenTip doesn't appear when I pause the mouse over a toolbar button.

Verify that the Show ScreenTips on Toolbars check box is checked on the Options tab of the Customize dialog box. Access this dialog box by selecting Tools, Customize.

DISPLAYING HIDDEN TOOLBAR BUTTONS

I can't find a button I need on the toolbar.

If you've moved your toolbars or placed two toolbars on the same row, all buttons might not be visible. Click the Toolbar Options button (it looks like a small down arrow) at the far right of the toolbar to display additional buttons.

GETTING RESULTS IN THE RESEARCH TASK PANE

I'm not getting any worthwhile results when I use the Research task pane.

The more specialized your search phrase or the more specific you are in choosing a reference source, the less likely the Research task pane will return results. Instead of choosing to search just a dictionary or just a particular news search service, choose to search an entire category of services (such as All Reference Books or All Research Sites). If that fails, try searching a different category of services.

For example, if you try to find a synonym for *cyclometer*, which is a small electronic device you can put on a bicycle to measure speed and distance, you'll get no results, even if you search All Reference Books. But if you search All Research Sites, MSN Search returns a Web site from a cyclometer manufacturer, which also refers to the devices as *cyclocomputers*. There's your synonym!

DESIGN CORNER: REARRANGING TOOLBARS

One of the nice things about PowerPoint is its flexibility. Even if you don't yet have strong knowledge of how to customize PowerPoint, you can still rearrange your basic work tools to better suit your needs—in just a few seconds. For example, you can easily arrange toolbars to make working with PowerPoint easier. Let's say that the Standard and Formatting toolbars currently appear on two separate lines at the top of your screen and the Drawing toolbar appears at the bottom. You would like to have more screen space and make the drawing tools accessible in another location on the screen. To accomplish this quickly, follow these steps:

1. Choose Tools, Customize and select the Options tab.
2. Remove the check mark from the Show Standard and Formatting Toolbars on Two Rows check box.
3. Click the Close button.

4. Drag the move handle on the left side of the Drawing toolbar to place it in a new location on the screen; it becomes a floating toolbar.

5. To resize the toolbar to appear as a square or rectangle, pause the mouse pointer over the left or right edge of the toolbar and drag the toolbar edge when the pointer becomes a two-headed arrow.

BEFORE

Figure 1.32

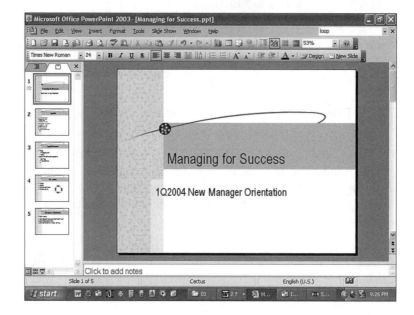

AFTER

Figure 1.33

Standard and Formatting toolbars on the same row

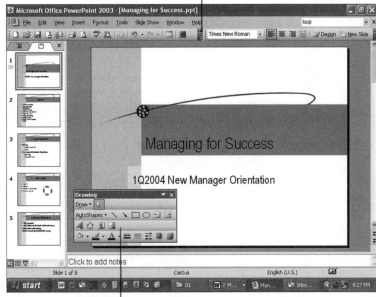

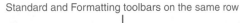

Floating toolbar for easy access

CHAPTER 2

CREATING A BASIC PRESENTATION

In this chapter *by Patrice-Anne Rutledge and Jim Grey*

UNDERSTANDING POWERPOINT PRESENTATIONS

After you learn—or refresh your memory of—how to navigate PowerPoint, you can create a basic presentation. This chapter gets you up and running on presentation basics so that you can quickly move forward to more advanced and sophisticated PowerPoint techniques.

Before you start, though, it helps to understand *design templates* and *slide layouts*, which are presentation building blocks.

UNDERSTANDING DESIGN TEMPLATES

A *design template* includes preformatted fonts, colors, and styles that blend together to create a consistent look and feel for your presentation. You apply design templates using the Slide Design task pane. It's usually a good idea to apply a single design template to a presentation for consistency, but you can apply multiple design templates to a single presentation if you want. Figure 2.1 illustrates a sample design template.

Figure 2.1
A casual design is good for an informal crowd, but isn't something you would use for a corporate audience.

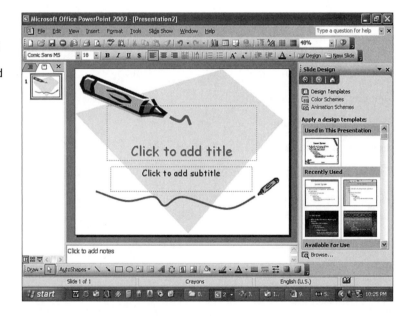

→ To learn more about the impact of choosing a design template, **see** "Working with Design Templates" in Chapter 25, "The Media—Designing Visual Support," **p. 535.**

The AutoContent Wizard selects a design template that is suited to the type of presentation you want to make. If you don't use the AutoContent Wizard and instead select your own design template, be sure that the template you select suits your audience and fits your presentation's message.

[Design] Depending on which method you use to create a new presentation, your presentation might already contain a design template. If you want to view the templates ahead of time, apply one directly to a presentation, or change to a different template, click the Design button on the Formatting toolbar to open the Slide Design task pane.

UNDERSTANDING SLIDE LAYOUTS

In addition to a design template, the other important design feature you need to consider is a *slide layout*. A slide layout helps you add specific types of content to your slides, such as text, tables, charts, and pictures.

Even though PowerPoint provides a lot of layout combinations, these layouts contain only seven different elements. They are

- **Text**—A placeholder on a slide into which you can add text, such as a title or bulleted list.

- **Tables**—A table that you can format, customize, and fill with data.

- **Charts**—A chart you can fill with information and format into various types, such as a bar, column, and pie. Charts are good at showing relative sizes or amounts, such as cost allocations and percentages of sales figures. Figure 2.2 illustrates a chart.

Figure 2.2
Charts can add visual punch to a presentation.

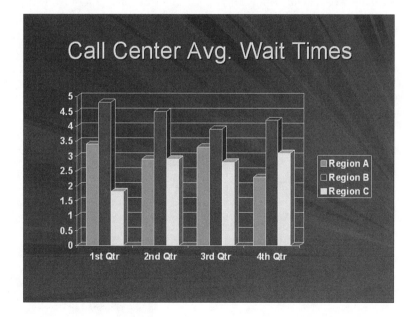

- **Diagrams**—One of several diagram types you can use to organize and display information. From the Diagram Gallery, you can create organization charts and cycle, radial, pyramid, Venn, and target diagrams. Figure 2.3 shows an organization chart.

Figure 2.3
Use an organization chart to help present your organization to new team members.

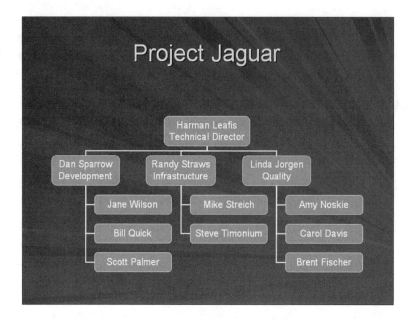

■ **Clip Art**—A clip art image from Office's vast collection of ready-made graphic images, from your own computer or network, or from the Internet. Figure 2.4 shows a slide that contains clip art.

Figure 2.4
Clip art helps you illustrate your presentation's basic concepts.

■ **Media Clips**—A sound clip or movie file you can use to add musical effects to your presentation or play a video within it.

- **Pictures**—Graphic files such as GIFs and JPEGs. A picture is similar to clip art, except that you use the Insert Picture dialog box to find graphic images instead of inserting one from the clip gallery.

You add each of these elements to a PowerPoint slide using the Slide Layout task pane. On this task pane, PowerPoint offers 27 different types of slide layouts divided into four categories:

- **Text Layout**—A text layout slide contains only text. The slide might contain one or two columns of text, with or without a title.

- **Content Layout**—Content layout slides can contain up to four pieces of content in several arrangements. Content is a graph, a photo, an organization chart, or some other visual element.

- **Text and Content Layout**—The seven text and content layouts place text and content on a slide in various arrangements.

- **Other Layout**—The other layouts don't fit the other categories. For example, you can create a slide with a single table, diagram, or organization chart. You can also create combinations with text, media clips, clip art, and charts.

N O T E

> If none of these predefined layouts is what you want, you can modify a blank slide or customize one of the existing layouts by adding, moving, or deleting objects.

Depending on which method you use to create a new presentation, it might already contain slide layouts. If you want to look at these layouts before you create a presentation, apply them directly to a slide, or change a layout, choose Format, Slide Layout to open the Slide Layout task pane.

Many of PowerPoint's slide layouts include an option for inserting content. For example, if you choose any of the layouts under Content Layout or Text and Content Layout in the Slide Layout task pane, a content palette will appear as a placeholder. This content palette includes six buttons:

- Insert Table
- Insert Chart
- Insert Clip Art
- Insert Picture
- Insert Diagram or Organization Chart
- Insert Media Clip

ou'll note that, with the exception of pictures, PowerPoint also includes separate layouts pecifically for adding the other content types. For example, you can also insert a table using the Table slide layout or a chart using the Chart, Text & Chart, or Chart & Text slide layouts. These layouts give you extra choices of content location, formatting, and content combinations. Experiment with the available slide layouts to figure out which ones work best for your presentations.

CREATING A PRESENTATION

You can create a presentation in several different ways, depending on the amount of content and design assistance you need. You can create

- **A presentation using the AutoContent Wizard**—The wizard chooses a design template that fits your presentation's purpose and creates a series of slides that contain content and slide layout suggestions. You can use the AutoContent Wizard when you're in a hurry, when you don't know what to say, or if you aren't yet design savvy.

- **A presentation using a design template**—A design template gives you a consistent design scheme—fonts, layout, colors, and so on—into which to add slides and content. You can also create a presentation using your own template on a Web server or computer, or you can download a template from Microsoft's Web site.

- **A new presentation using an existing presentation**—Using this option, you create a presentation by copying another one and then editing and modifying it. (Doing this doesn't change the original presentation.)

- **A blank presentation**—A blank presentation is, well, blank—black text on a white background with no content suggestions. Create a blank presentation only when you are very experienced with PowerPoint and want to create a custom design.

> **TIP**
>
> Even if you want to create a custom presentation, it often saves you time to start with a similar existing design and then customize it.

USING THE AUTOCONTENT WIZARD

The AutoContent Wizard guides you step-by-step through creating a PowerPoint presentation. Of all the ways to create a presentation, the AutoContent Wizard gives you the most assistance and automation. You answer a few basic questions about the presentation you need to make, and PowerPoint does the rest. The result is a complete series of slides with content suggestions based on the presentation type you chose. PowerPoint also applies a design template suitable to the kind of presentation you want and applies a slide layout to each individual slide.

→ To learn techniques for adding dynamic content to your presentations, **see** Chapter 24, "The Message—Scripting the Concept," **p. 491**.

From here, revise the content suggestions with your own information, and you'll be ready to present. As an alternative, you can modify the appearance of your presentation by applying a different design template, modifying the design, adding or removing slides, and so forth.

To start the AutoContent Wizard, follow these steps:

1. Select File, New to display the New Presentation task pane if it isn't already displayed.

2. Click From AutoContent Wizard on the New Presentation task pane. The wizard appears (see Figure 2.5).

Figure 2.5
The AutoContent Wizard offers detailed guidance on creating a presentation.

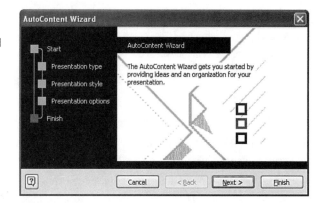

3. Click Next to continue to the next step, shown in Figure 2.6.

Figure 2.6
You can choose from several kinds of presentations.

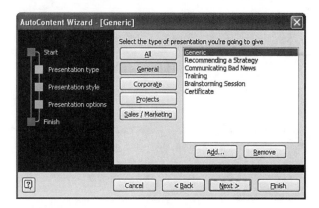

4. Click the button for the kind of presentation you want to create. The adjacent box displays the available presentations.

TIP

To add your own presentation to the AutoContent Wizard, click the Add button. To remove a presentation, click Remove.

5. Select the presentation you want to use and click Next.

 Having trouble finding a design template to fit your recurring needs? *See "Creating Your Own Template" in the "Troubleshooting" section near the end of this chapter.*

CAUTION

When you installed Office, some presentations weren't copied to your hard drive. If you choose a missing presentation type, PowerPoint asks if you want to install it. Put your Office 2003 installation CD in the CD-ROM drive to do this.

6. Select the type of output to use. Choices include the following:

- **Onscreen presentation**—The standard PowerPoint presentation format, delivered on a computer screen
- **Web presentation**—For presentations delivered via the Web
- **Black-and-white overheads**—Useful as a backup or as a cost-effective alternative to full-color transparencies
- **Color overheads**—For full-color transparencies
- **35mm slides**—Formatted for delivery to a service bureau for conversion to 35mm slides

PowerPoint chooses a background and color scheme suited to the output you select. Press Next.

TIP

To change the background after you've created your presentation, click Color Schemes on the Slide Design task pane and choose from the available options.

7. Enter a presentation title.
8. If you want to include a footer on each slide, enter it. For example, you could enter your company name or a copyright statement in the Footer field.
9. Select the Date Last Updated check box or Slide Number check box to include this information in the presentation.
10. Click Finish.

PowerPoint displays a presentation with sample content that you can replace. You can also delete images and slides that you don't need, change the design of your presentation, and otherwise modify it to your satisfaction. Figure 2.7 illustrates a sample presentation for explaining the strategy for a new project.

Figure 2.7
The AutoContent Wizard includes content suggestions for introducing a project to its stakeholders.

USING A DESIGN TEMPLATE

If you don't want or need the AutoContent Wizard to create sample slides and content, start with a design template and add your own slides and content.

To create a new presentation from a design template, follow these steps:

1. Select File, New to display the New Presentation task pane if it doesn't already appear.
2. Click From Design Template on the New Presentation task pane. The Slide Design task pane appears, displaying all available design templates in preview format (see Figure 2.8). The design template used in the current presentation (if there is one) appears at the top, followed by the most recently used templates (only if you've previously applied a template), and then all other available templates.

TIP

> If you want larger previews of the design templates, click the down arrow that appears to the right of any template preview when you hover the mouse over it. Then, choose Show Large Previews from the shortcut menu that appears. The preview templates get bigger. To go back to normal-size previews, simply select this option again to remove the check mark.

Figure 2.8
PowerPoint includes many design templates from which to choose.

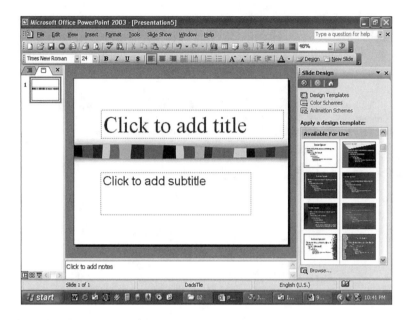

2

CAUTION

Not all design templates are already installed. If PowerPoint displays a warning that you need to install a template, be sure to have the Office CD-ROM in your CD-ROM drive and follow the installation instructions in the warning.

3. Select the template you want to use. PowerPoint applies this design to your new presentation and displays an empty slide with the Title Slide layout.

From here, you can add content to your presentation, format it, and insert additional slides.

→ To learn how to apply a new design template to a presentation you've created or use more than one design template in a single presentation, **see** "Applying a New Design Template" in Chapter 6, **p. 119**.

USING A TEMPLATE

You've already seen how you can create a PowerPoint presentation using a content template (with the AutoContent Wizard) or a design template. You can also directly attach an existing template located on your computer, a Web server, or the Office Online site:

1. Select File, New to open the New Presentation task pane.

2. From the Other templates section of the New Presentation task pane, choose one of the following options:

   • A recently used template, whose name appears at the top.

   • Click On My Computer, which opens the New Presentation dialog box (see Figure 2.9), where you can search for a template stored on your computer or network.

Figure 2.9
Choose from the templates on your computer or network.

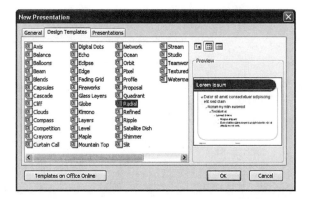

- On My Web Sites, which opens the New Presentation dialog box, where you can select a template on a Web server.

You can also use the New Presentation task pane to search for templates on Office Online. In the Templates area, type search keywords in the Search field. Office Online returns a list of templates to choose from. You can also click the Templates home page hyperlink to open the Office Online Web site and choose a template from the Template Gallery.

Using an Existing Presentation

Another way to create a new presentation is simply to copy an existing presentation whose content and format are similar to what you want to create:

1. Select File, New to display the New Presentation task pane.
2. Click From Existing Presentation. The New from Existing Presentation dialog box opens, shown in Figure 2.10.

Figure 2.10
Creating from an existing presentation can save you a lot of time.

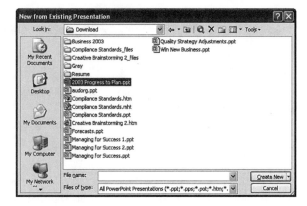

3. Select the existing presentation on which you want to base the new one.
4. Click the Create New button. PowerPoint creates a copy of the original presentation, which you can modify.

FROM SCRATCH

You can create a blank presentation by following these steps:

1. Select File, New to display the New Presentation task pane.
2. Click Blank presentation on the New Presentation task pane. A blank presentation appears, and the Slide Layout task pane opens.
3. Choose the slide layout you want to use for the first slide. PowerPoint applies it.

Figure 2.11 illustrates a sample blank presentation.

Figure 2.11
To have complete design control, you can use a blank presentation.

Next, you can add more slides and adjust formatting to suit you. You can even attach a design template if you want.

CAUTION

Be sure that none of the existing design templates suit your needs before starting with a blank presentation.

SAVING A PRESENTATION

After you create a presentation, you'll want to save it. PowerPoint lets you save a presentation in a variety of ways, including as

■ A regular presentation readable by this version of PowerPoint and several earlier versions (2002, 2000, 97, and 95)

- A Web page as a folder or a Web archive as a single file
- A design template
- A PowerPoint show, ready to run on its own
- A graphic image, enabling you to display a slide as a graphic on a Web page, for example
- An outline, which you can format later in Word or another program

To save a PowerPoint presentation you created, follow these steps:

 1. Press Ctrl+S or click the Save button on the Standard toolbar. If this is the first time you've saved the presentation, the Save As dialog box appears, as shown in Figure 2.12.

Figure 2.12
Specify Save As parameters in this dialog box.

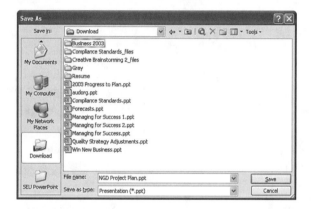

2. From the Save In drop-down list, select the folder in which to save your presentation.

> **TIP**
> The default folder in which to save your presentations is My Documents. You can customize the default folder on the Save tab in the Options dialog box (Tools, Options).

 Your presentation doesn't get saved in the right location? *See "Choosing a Save Location" in the "Troubleshooting" section near the end of this chapter.*

3. Type a name for the presentation in the File Name field.

> **CAUTION**
> The drop-down list in the File Name field includes previously saved presentations. Even if you choose one of these filenames, PowerPoint warns you so that you don't accidentally overwrite an existing presentation.

4. Choose the file format from the Save As Type drop-down list.

Presentation is the default file type, but you can also save your PowerPoint presentation as a Web page, as a design template, or in a previous PowerPoint version format such as PowerPoint 2002, 2000, or 97. Table 2.1 lists the available options for saving your presentation.

TABLE 2.1 POWERPOINT FILE TYPES

File Type	Extension	Result
Presentation	PPT	Saves as a regular PowerPoint presentation
Web Page	HTM, HTML	Saves as a Web page in a folder
Single File Web Page	MHT, MHTML	Saves as a Web page in a single file
PowerPoint 97–2003 & 95 Presentation	PPT	Saves as a presentation you can open in PowerPoint 95, 97, 2000, 2002, or 2003
Presentation for Review	PPT	Saves as a presentation with change tracking enabled
Design Template	POT	Saves as a design template that you can use for future presentations
PowerPoint Show	PPS	Lets you run the presentation directly as a slideshow
PowerPoint Add-In	PPA	Saves as a custom add-in
GIF Graphics Interchange Format	GIF	Saves as a graphic for use on the Web
JPEG File Interchange Format	JPG	Saves as a graphic for use on the Web
PNG Portable Network Graphics Format	PNG	Saves as a graphic for use on the Web
Tag Image File Format	TIF	Saves as a TIFF graphic image
Device Independent Bitmap	BMP	Saves as a bitmap graphic image
Windows Metafile	WMF	Saves as a 16-bit vector graphic image
Enhanced Windows Metafile	EMF	Saves as a 32-bit vector graphic image
Outline/RTF	RTF	Saves as an outline in Rich Text Format, which you can open in Microsoft Word

5. Click Save to save the file.

TIP

After you've saved a presentation, clicking the Save button on the toolbar once saves your changes without opening the Save As dialog box.

> **NOTE**
>
> To set and modify Save options such as fast saves and AutoRecovery, choose Tools, Options and go to the Save tab of the Options dialog box.

OPENING A PRESENTATION

You can open an existing presentation in several different ways:

- Click More in the Open section of the Home task pane. If this pane doesn't appear, select View, Task Pane.

> **TIP**
>
> You can also directly open one of the previous four PowerPoint files you used by selecting it at the top of the Open section of the Home task pane. The File menu also displays these files at the end of the list of menu options.

- Click the Open button on the Standard toolbar.
- Press Ctrl+O.
- Choose File, Open.

> **NOTE**
>
> You can also double-click a PowerPoint presentation's icon in Windows Explorer to open the presentation.

The Open dialog box appears, shown in Figure 2.13.

From the Open dialog box, follow these steps to open a file:

1. Click the arrow button at the end of the Look In drop-down list to start navigating folders to find the presentation you want.

> **TIP**
>
> You can also use the Desktop, My Recent Documents, My Documents, My Computer, and My Network Places buttons on the left side of the dialog box to navigate to the file you want to open.

Can't find a presentation you know you saved? See "Finding a Saved Presentation" in the "Troubleshooting" section near the end of this chapter.

2. If necessary, select the type of file you're looking for from the Files of Type drop-down list. This is useful if you have a large number of files on your computer.

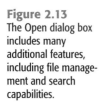

Figure 2.13
The Open dialog box includes many additional features, including file management and search capabilities.

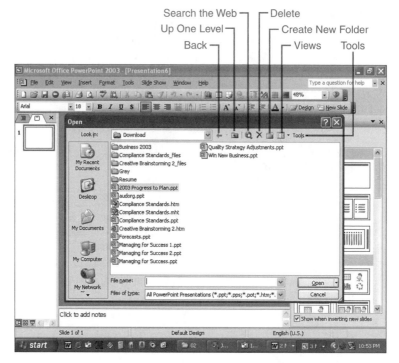

3. When you find the file, click it. Its name appears in the File Name field.

4. Click Open to open the presentation.

The down arrow to the right of the Open button provides several other options. You can also

- **Open Read-Only**—Opens the file as read-only. For example, if you've applied a password to the presentation, others may only be able to open it read-only. To change and save this file, choose File, Save As from the menu and save with another name.

- **Open as Copy**—Opens the presentation as a copy of the original. You might do this if you want to keep your original and create another presentation based on it.

- **Open in Browser**—Opens a presentation saved in a Web page format (.HTM, .HTML, .HTX, or .ASP) in your default browser.

 Can't open your Web presentation in a browser? *See "Opening a Presentation in a Browser" in the "Troubleshooting" section near the end of this chapter.*

EXPLORING THE OPEN DIALOG BOX

The top of the Open dialog box includes several buttons that help you open and manage files. These include

- **Back**—Returns you to previous folders or drives you have viewed. It lists the name of the folder as the button name. Click the down arrow to view previous folders.

- **Up One Level**—Moves up one level in the directory structure.

- **Search the Web**—Opens the MSN search page, `http://search.msn.com`.

- **Delete**—Deletes the selected file.

- **Create New Folder**—Opens the New Folder dialog box. When you type a name for a new folder and click OK, Windows adds a folder with that name in the current folder.

- **Views**—Includes several options for displaying your files and arranging icons by name, type, size, and date.

- **Tools**—Displays a menu that lets you find, rename, delete, or print files, as well as add them to your Favorites folder, map to a network drive to find a file, or display file properties.

NOTE

You can perform sophisticated searches by choosing Tools, Search, which opens the Search dialog box. The functionality in this dialog box is nearly identical to what you can do with the Search task pane.

SETTING VIEW OPTIONS

You can view files in several different ways in the Open dialog box. Click the down arrow next to the Views button and choose the view option you prefer:

- **Thumbnails**—Previews presentations as thumbnails.

- **Tiles**—Lists files and folders as large icons.

- **Icons**—Lists files and folders as medium-sized icons.

- **List**—Lists files and folders as small icons.

- **Details**—Lists files and folders with small icons and information about size, type, and date last modified.

- **Properties**—Lists files and folders as small icons, and displays a property sheet for the selected file.

- **Preview**—Lists files and folders as small icons, and if the selected file is a presentation, displays a preview.

DELETING A PRESENTATION

To delete a PowerPoint presentation you no longer want, select it in the Open dialog box and press the Delete key on the keyboard. A warning dialog box appears, verifying that you want to delete the file and send it to the Recycle Bin. Figure 2.14 shows this dialog box. Click Yes to confirm the deletion.

Figure 2.14
PowerPoint confirms
that you want to
delete a presentation.

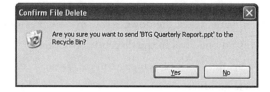

TIP

> You can also delete a PowerPoint presentation in Windows Explorer. To do so, click the
> presentation file in Explorer and press the Delete key.

RENAMING A PRESENTATION

To rename a PowerPoint presentation, select it in the Open dialog box and choose Tools,
Rename. PowerPoint converts the filename to an edit box in which you can overwrite it, as
shown in Figure 2.15.

Figure 2.15
Rename a presenta-
tion something more
meaningful.

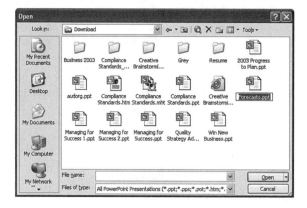

NOTE

> There are three other ways to rename a file. The first way is to right-click it and choose
> Rename from the menu that appears. The second way is to just click on the file's name
> (not its icon), wait a second, and click on it again. The third way is to click the file and
> press F2. In all ways, the next step is to type a new name for the file.

TROUBLESHOOTING

CREATING YOUR OWN TEMPLATE

I don't like any of the existing design templates. What can I do?

You can create your own design template and then save it for future use. Start by modifying
an existing template and then save it as a design template in the Save As dialog box. Chapter 6, "Formatting Slides and Presentations," covers this in more detail.

The Web is also a rich source of design templates. Many are free; some are for purchase. To get started, type "PowerPoint templates" in your favorite search engine.

CHOOSING A SAVE LOCATION

My presentation didn't save in the folder where I thought it would.

By default, your presentation is saved in the My Documents folder unless you specify another location in the Save As dialog box. To change this default, choose Tools, Options, click the Save tab, and type a different pathname in the Default file location field.

FINDING A SAVED PRESENTATION

I can't find a PowerPoint presentation I saved.

The Open dialog box might be set to a file type other than the one in which you saved your presentation. Check the Files of Type drop-down list to be sure that you chose the right file type. For example, if you're looking for a PowerPoint presentation or a Web page, be sure that you've selected that option.

Also, make sure that you're searching in the right folder. Use the navigation tools in the Open dialog box to find the folder in which you saved your presentation.

If you still can't find your presentation, in the Open dialog box choose Tools, Search to open the Find dialog box. Type words you remember being in the file's name and click Search. You can also perform similar searches using the Search task pane.

OPENING A PRESENTATION IN A BROWSER

I want to open my presentation in a browser, but the Open in Browser option isn't available from the menu next to the Open button in the Open dialog box.

You must have saved the presentation in a Web format (such as .htm, .html, .htx, or .asp) in order to open it in a browser. To save as a Web page, choose File, Save as Web Page.

DESIGN CORNER: CREATING A PRESENTATION FROM SCRATCH

Although PowerPoint offers many timesaving ways to create presentations, you sometimes get the best results if you start with a blank presentation and build from there. For example, you might be an experienced graphic designer with your own ideas of what you want to create. Or you might just want to create a basic presentation with your company logo and company colors, and none of the existing design templates really match. Even if you're not a designer, throughout this book you'll learn techniques that will enable you to design your own presentations from scratch if you want to.

Figure 2.16 shows information presented in black text on a plain white background. Figure 2.17 shows how the same information can look after just a few minutes of formatting, adding clip art, inserting a company logo, and adding a couple drawing objects. With some practice using these features, you'll be able to improve your presentation's look as well.

BEFORE

Figure 2.16

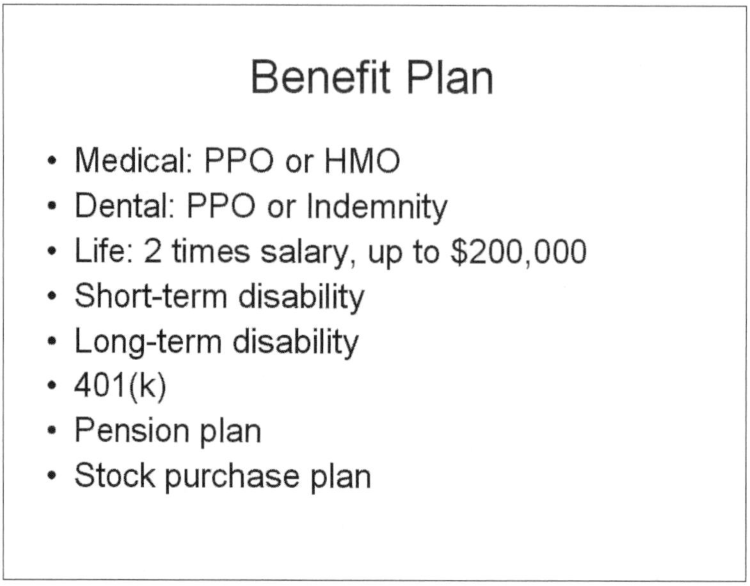

Benefit Plan
• Medical: PPO or HMO
• Dental: PPO or Indemnity
• Life: 2 times salary, up to $200,000
• Short-term disability
• Long-term disability
• 401(k)
• Pension plan
• Stock purchase plan

AFTER

Figure 2.17

Drawing objects
Clip art
Benefit Plan
• Medical: PPO or HMO
• Dental: PPO or Indemnity
• Life: 2 times salary, up to $200,000
• Short-term disability
• Long-term disability
• 401(k)
• Pension plan
• Stock purchase plan
401K
McCormick
and Associates
Custom color scheme
Logo

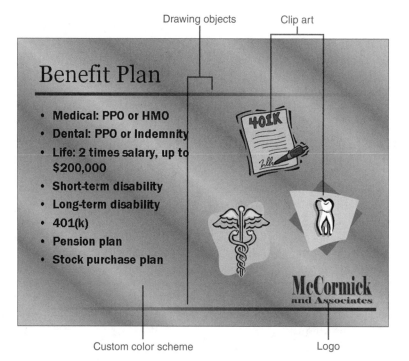

EDITING AND FORMATTING PRESENTATIONS

Working with Text

In this chapter *by Patrice-Anne Rutledge and Jim Grey*

UNDERSTANDING POWERPOINT'S TEXT CAPABILITIES

 Adding and formatting text is fairly straightforward in PowerPoint. What's usually more difficult is choosing the right fonts, colors, and effects for your presentation. PowerPoint offers sophisticated text formatting and customization, and it also automates most formatting and customization if you're in a hurry or have limited design skills. When you're done adding text to your presentation, you can verify that its spelling and style are error free with PowerPoint's spelling checker. You can also use the thesaurus to find synonyms to make your text a little livelier.

ADDING TEXT

In PowerPoint, you need to add text in a text placeholder, title placeholder, or text box. Figure 3.1 shows a text placeholder and a title placeholder, which is a text placeholder that's used just for titles.

Figure 3.1
A text placeholder is a tool PowerPoint uses for entering text.

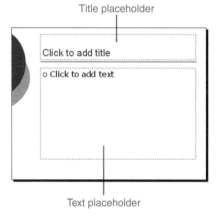

Title placeholder

Click to add title

o Click to add text

Text placeholder

If you use the AutoContent Wizard or add a slide that includes a text or title placeholder, you can immediately start creating text.

If you want to add your own text box to a blank slide, choose Insert, Text Box. You can then draw a text box on the slide using the mouse. As you add text, the box expands. Figure 3.2 shows a text box.

TIP

> You can also add a text box by clicking the Text Box button on the Drawing toolbar. If you don't see the Drawing toolbar, choose View, Toolbars, Drawing to make it appear.

Your text doesn't fit in the text box? See "Making the Text Fit" in the "Troubleshooting" section near the end of this chapter.

Figure 3.2
A text box is another tool that PowerPoint uses to enter text.

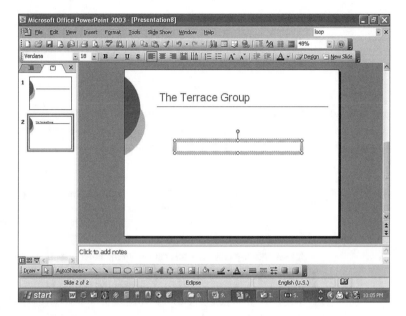

FORMATTING TEXT

PowerPoint's design templates include colors, fonts, font sizes, and other formatting parameters that are designed to work well and look good together. In this way, PowerPoint frees you to focus on your message.

→ To learn more about how typefaces and fonts affect your presentation, **see** "Choosing Typefaces and Fonts" in Chapter 25, "The Media—Designing Visual Support," **p. 535**.

You'll need to apply extensive text formatting only if you create a text box on a blank slide in a presentation without an attached design template. In most cases, you'll either use the formatting that the design template suggests or make only minor modifications to it.

→ To learn more about how to modify text and formatting on slide masters rather than on individual slides, **see** "Modifying the Slide Master" in Chapter 21, "Customizing PowerPoint," **p. 467**.

The following are some changes you might consider to enhance the presentation of your slides:

- **Enlarge or reduce font size**—If you have only a few bullet points on a slide, you can increase their font size to fill the page. You can also shrink the text in a placeholder so that it can hold more text. Be sure, however, that the font size is still appropriate for the presentation. Make sure that all text is still readable on the slide and, if you're going to do an onscreen presentation, that it isn't too small to be seen by viewers in the back of a room.

NOTE

> If you type more text into a placeholder than it can show at once, PowerPoint uses its AutoFit feature to shrink the text to fit. AutoFit only shrinks text so much, though, to prevent it from becoming hard to read.

- **Replace one font with another**—You might have a particular font you prefer to use in presentations. Be careful, however, not to be too creative with unusual fonts. You want to be sure that everyone can clearly read your presentation.

TIP

> If your presentation will end up on any computers other than yours, make sure that you choose only fonts those computers contain. If your presentation uses a font that isn't on a computer displaying it, PowerPoint substitutes a font that *is* on the computer. The results are often less than pleasing.
>
> It's safest to use only fonts that come with the other computers' version(s) of Windows. To find out which fonts Microsoft delivered with each version of Windows, go to http://www.microsoft.com/typography/fonts/default.asp. Choose the version of Windows from the drop-down list of products on this page and click Go.
>
> Fortunately, PowerPoint's design templates use fonts available in most versions of Windows. If you stick to those fonts, you'll almost always be fine.

- **Add boldface, italics, or color**—Use these to emphasize a point with a certain word or words.

You can format text in two ways:

- Use the Font dialog box to make a number of changes in one place and to set font defaults.
- Apply text formatting individually using the buttons on the Formatting toolbar.

USING THE FONT DIALOG BOX

To use the Font dialog box to format text, follow these steps:

1. Select the text you want to format and choose Format, Font. The Font dialog box appears, shown in Figure 3.3.
2. In the Font list, choose the font you want to use. Scroll down the list to see the available fonts.
3. In the Font style list, choose whether the font should be regular (neither bold nor italic), bold, italic, or bold and italic.
4. In the Size list, choose a preset size from 8 to 96 points, or type a specific point size in the box.

Figure 3.3
Make font changes quickly using the Font dialog box.

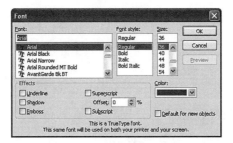

5. Apply any other effects you want by checking the check box next to any of the following:

- **Underline**—Underlines the selected text.
- **Shadow**—Applies a slight shadow to the lower right of the text.
- **Emboss**—Creates an embossed effect on the selected text.
- **Superscript**—Raises the text above the baseline and reduces the font size. Sets the Offset to 30%, which you can adjust.
- **Subscript**—Lowers the text below the baseline and reduces the font size. Sets the Offset to -25%, which you can adjust.

NOTE

Offset refers to the percentage the text displays above or below the baseline, which is the invisible line the characters sit on. For example, because subscript text is below the baseline, its offset will be a negative number.

→ To learn how to create innovative text objects with PowerPoint WordArt, **see** "Inserting WordArt" in Chapter 14, "Creating and Formatting Objects," **p. 312**.

6. Choose a color from the palette that is displayed by the Color drop-down list. For additional color choices, click More Colors from the palette to open the Colors dialog box.

→ To learn more about the Colors dialog box, **see** "Using the Colors Dialog Box" in Chapter 14, **p. 290**.

7. Click Preview to view the selected font changes on your slide.

8. If you want to use this font formatting as the default for future text, click the Default for New Objects check box.

9. Click OK to close the dialog box and apply the font formatting.

USING THE FORMATTING TOOLBAR

You can use the Formatting toolbar (see Figure 3.4) to apply common formatting elements to selected text.

Table 3.1 lists the formatting options on this toolbar.

Figure 3.4
The Formatting tool-
bar includes buttons
for commonly used
text effects.

TABLE 3.1   FORMATTING TOOLBAR BUTTONS

Button	Name	Description
Arial	Font	Applies a font to the selected text.
36	Font Size	Sets the selected text's size. Choose any common size from 8 to 96 points, or type any size in the edit box.
B	Bold	Bolds the selected text.
I	Italic	Italicizes the selected text.
U	Underline	Underlines the selected text.
S	Shadow	Applies a shadow to the selected text.
≣	Align Left	Aligns text to the object's left margin.
≣	Center	Centers text within the object.
≣	Align Right	Aligns text to the object's right margin.
≣	Numbering	Applies automatic numbering to the selected text.
≣	Bullets	Applies bullets to the selected text.
A˄	Increase Font Size	Increases the selected text's size by a few points.
A˅	Decrease Font Size	Decreases the selected text's size by a few points.
筆	Decrease Indent	Outdents the selected text.
筆	Increase Indent	Indents the selected text.
A	Font Color	Applies the color you choose from the drop-down list to selected text.
Design	Design	Opens the Slide Design task pane.
New Slide	New Slide	Creates a new slide and opens the Slide Layout task pane.

To apply one of these formatting elements, select the text you want to format and click the toolbar button. Clicking the Bold, Italic, Underline, Text Shadow, Numbering, or Bullets button a second time acts as a toggle and removes the formatting.

With the Font drop-down list, you can preview what each font actually looks like.

REPLACING FONTS

If you want to replace all occurrences of one font in your presentation with another font, follow these steps:

1. Choose Format, Replace Fonts to open the Replace Font dialog box (see Figure 3.5).

Figure 3.5
Replace fonts throughout your presentation with this dialog box.

2. In the Replace drop-down list, select the font that you want to replace. The list contains only fonts your presentation uses.

3. In the With drop-down list, select the replacement font. The list shows all fonts available to PowerPoint.

4. Click Replace. PowerPoint replaces the font.

5. Click Close to return to the presentation.

→ If you are making several text changes to all slides in a presentation, consider using the slide master. To learn how, **see** "Working with Slide Masters," in Chapter 21, **p. 466**.

CHANGING TEXT CASE

You can also change selected text's case in your presentation, such as changing from lowercase to all capitals. Do so by following these steps:

1. Select the text that you want to change.

2. Select Format, Change Case to open the Change Case dialog box, shown in Figure 3.6.

Figure 3.6
You can quickly change case if something doesn't look right.

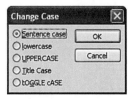

3. Choose the case to which you want to change. Options include

- **Sentence case**—Capitalizes only the first word in each sentence.
- **lowercase**—Makes all letters appear in lowercase.
- **UPPERCASE**—Makes all letters appear in uppercase.

- **Title Case**—Capitalizes the first letter of every word except for articles (*a, an, the,* and so on), conjunctions (*and, but, or,* and so on), and prepositions (*to, from, in,* and so on), which remain lowercase in titles.

- **tOGGLE cASE**—Toggles all existing cases. Lowercase becomes uppercase, and uppercase becomes lowercase.

4. Click OK to apply the case changes to the selected text.

CAUTION

Remember that an unusual use of case might be difficult to read, particularly uppercase and toggle case. With text, go for readability and clarity.

Only part of your text changes? *See "Making Your Case Work" in the "Troubleshooting" section near the end of this chapter.*

TIP

Another way to change case is to select some text and press Shift+F3 to cycle through PowerPoint's case options.

SETTING LINE SPACING

When a slide looks crowded or too sparse, the *line spacing*, or the amount of space between lines of text, might be at fault. Adjust line spacing until the text looks right. To specify line spacing, follow these steps:

1. Select the text you want to format and choose Format, Line Spacing. Figure 3.7 shows the Line Spacing dialog box that appears.

Figure 3.7
Appropriate line spacing can make a presentation easier to read.

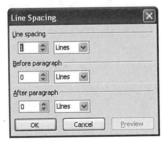

In this dialog box, you can set line spacing and space before and after paragraphs. You can set spacing in lines or points. (Points are how typographers measure type. 72 points are in an inch.)

2. Select the numeric amount from the first field and then choose either Lines or Points from the second drop-down list.

3. Click the Preview button to view the changes in your presentation before accepting them.

4. Click OK to apply the changes.

SETTING ALIGNMENT

To align paragraphs, choose Format, Alignment and then one of these options:

- **Align Left**—Aligns text to the object's left margin.
- **Center**—Centers text between the object's left and right margins.
- **Align Right**—Aligns text to the object's right margin.
- **Justify**—Spaces words and letters within words so that text touches both margins in the object.

USING BULLETS

Creating a bulleted list is a very common PowerPoint task. If you use the AutoContent Wizard, your presentation probably already contains a slide with text formatted as a bulleted list. You can add a bulleted list to any slide that contains text, as well as within a table.

 To change a numbered list or other text to a bulleted list, select the text and click the Bullets button on the Formatting toolbar. The default bullet style comes from the presentation's design template. You can change the bullet style if you want, however. To do so, select the bulleted list that you want to change and choose Format, Bullets and Numbering. Figure 3.8 shows the Bullets and Numbering dialog box that appears.

Figure 3.8
You can choose from many different bullet types.

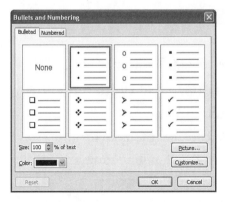

On the Bulleted tab of this dialog box, you can choose from the seven bullet styles displayed, or you can choose None to remove bullets. In the Size field, you can click the arrows to enlarge or reduce the bullet size from the default 100%.

To change a bullet's color, select a new color from the Color drop-down list. For additional color choices, click More Colors to open the Colors dialog box.

→ To learn more about the Colors dialog box, **see** "Using the Colors Dialog Box" in Chapter 14, **p. 290**.

→ To change the bullets in your entire presentation, do so on the master slide; **see** "Modifying the Slide Master" in Chapter 21, **p. 467**.

You can also create picture or character bullets if none of the seven default bullet styles suits your needs.

CREATING PICTURE BULLETS

You can use a small graphic as a bullet, giving you a wide choice of creative bullet styles. To apply a picture bullet, click the Picture button to open the Picture Bullet dialog box. Select a bullet from those that appear or enter a keyword in the text box and click Search to locate matching bullets. Click OK to apply. Figure 3.9 shows a presentation that uses picture bullets.

TIP

To import your own picture bullets (maybe a logo or something you already use on a Web site or other company literature), click the Import button to open the Add Clips to Organizer dialog box. It's best if your bullet is small—between 10 and 20 pixels square. PowerPoint shrinks larger images to fit, but the larger the image, the less desirable the result.

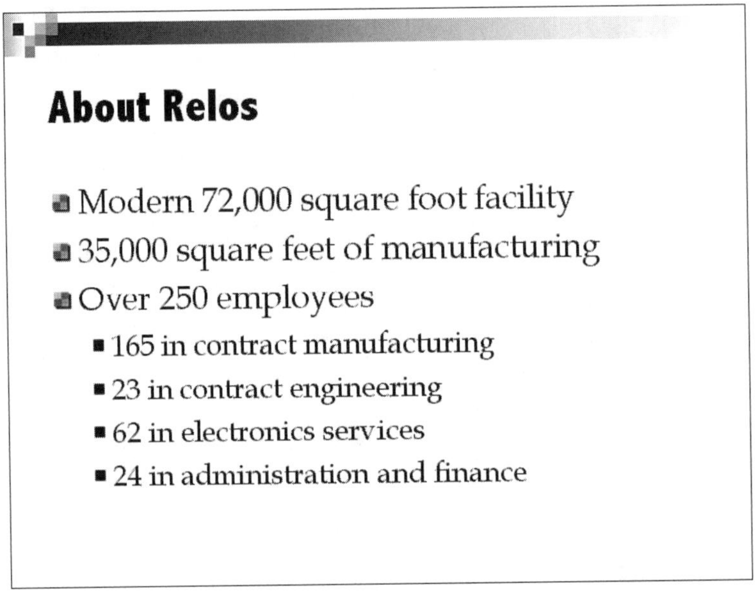

Figure 3.9
A picture bullet can enhance a creative presentation.

About Relos

- Modern 72,000 square foot facility
- 35,000 square feet of manufacturing
- Over 250 employees
  - 165 in contract manufacturing
  - 23 in contract engineering
  - 62 in electronics services
  - 24 in administration and finance

CREATING CHARACTER BULLETS

You can choose a character bullet for your bulleted list if you want something a little different. In the Symbol dialog box, you can choose from a variety of fonts. Each font displays its character set, from which you can choose a new character bullet.

To apply a character bullet, click the Customize button in the Bullets and Numbering dialog box to open the Symbol dialog box, shown in Figure 3.10.

Figure 3.10
Use a font such as Wingdings for character bullets.

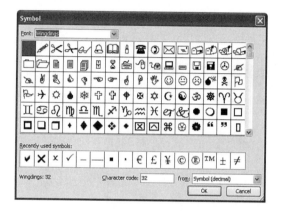

Select a font from the Font drop-down list, choose the bullet you want from the display area, and click OK. To speed up your insert process, you can view and choose from character bullets you've recently applied to a bullet list from the Recently Used Symbols section.

NOTE

You can select a color and size for your character bullet in the Bullets and Numbering dialog box.

USING NUMBERED LISTS

For a sequence of items, creating a numbered list is a good alternative to a bulleted list. For example, a series of procedural steps or a list of dollar amounts from highest to lowest would work well in a numbered list. You can create numbered lists with actual numbers, Roman numerals, or letters of the alphabet.

 To change a bulleted list or other text to a numbered list, select the text and click the Numbering button on the Formatting toolbar.

TIP

> You can also create a numbered list by pressing the Backspace key at the beginning of a bulleted list, typing the number **1** (or the letter **a** if you're using letters instead of numbers), pressing the Tab key, and entering your first list item. PowerPoint then continues numbering the series when you press Enter to move to the second line.

To change the numbering style of selected text, follow these steps:

1. Choose Format, Bullets and Numbering and go to the Numbered tab, shown in Figure 3.11.

Figure 3.11
A numbered list can put a series of items in order.

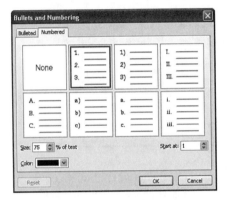

2. Select one of the seven number styles that appear. Choosing None removes the numbered list.

3. Set Size as a percentage of the text. The default depends on your design template, but is typically 75% or 100%. Lower the number to reduce the size; increase the number to enlarge the size.

4. Choose a color from the Color drop-down list. For additional color choices, click More Colors to open the Colors dialog box.

→ To learn more about the Colors dialog box, **see** "Using the Colors Dialog Box" in Chapter 14, **p. 290**.

5. If you want to start numbering at something other than 1 (or lettering at something other than a), type the starting value in the Start At field.

6. Click OK to apply the numbering.

CHECKING SPELLING AND STYLE

Creating a quality, error-free, and easy-to-read presentation is a natural objective when you use PowerPoint. PowerPoint's spelling and style checkers can help. Keep in mind that, although these automated tools can help you catch errors, they aren't foolproof and don't take the place of thorough proofreading by a real person. To set options for spelling and style checks, select Tools, Options and go to the Spelling and Style tab, shown in Figure 3.12.

Figure 3.12
You can set several spell checking options.

SETTING SPELLING OPTIONS

You can choose any of the following spelling options:

- **Check Spelling as You Type**—Places a red squiggly line under each suspected spelling error as you type it.
- **Hide All Spelling Errors**—Doesn't display red underlining for suspected spelling errors.
- **Always Suggest Corrections**—Suggests possible correct spelling options when you right-click a red-underlined word.
- **Ignore Words in UPPERCASE**—Doesn't check spelling of any word that is all uppercase.
- **Ignore Words with Numbers**—Doesn't check spelling of any word that includes a number.

SETTING STYLE OPTIONS

If you also want to check style, select the Check Style check box and click the Style Options button. This opens the Style Options dialog box, shown in Figure 3.13.

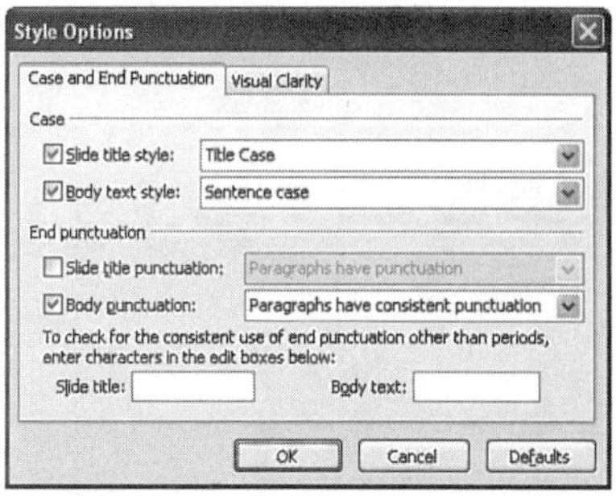

Figure 3.13
Setting default case and punctuation helps give a more consistent look to your presentation.

NOTE

The style checker uses the Office Assistant to check style. If the Office Assistant isn't enabled, PowerPoint asks you to enable it.

CAUTION

Although having PowerPoint search for potential style errors can help you find mistakes you wouldn't otherwise notice, be careful to look closely at the changes it suggests rather than just automatically accepting all style changes. Language is often too subtle and complex for automated style checkers, which often yield unusual and unwanted results.

On the Case and End Punctuation tab, you can select the default case and end punctuation styles for your presentation slide titles and body text. Options include the ability to

- Set Slide Title Style to Sentence case, lowercase, UPPERCASE, or Title Case (the default).
- Set Body Text Style to Sentence case (the default), lowercase, UPPERCASE, Title Case, or Consistent case. Sentence case is your best choice for regular body text because it's the most readable. Avoid UPPERCASE; it's the least readable.
- Set Slide Title Punctuation to either Paragraphs Have Punctuation (the default) or Paragraphs Do Not Have Punctuation.
- Set Body Punctuation to Paragraphs Have Punctuation, Paragraphs Do Not Have Punctuation, or Paragraphs Have Consistent Punctuation (the default, which ensures that your punctuation choices match). For example, a bulleted list in a well-designed presentation shouldn't have a mixture of periods and no periods at the end of the bulleted text; it should be consistent—all list items should end with a period, or none of them should.

Select the check boxes next to each option you want, and choose the style rule you want from the drop-down list.

TIP

> If you want to place a character other than a period at the end of the slide title or body text, enter the character in the Slide Title or Body Text edit box. For example, you might want to use a colon instead of a period in some cases. In that case, PowerPoint would look for the colon instead of the period.

NOTE

> If you've enabled another language, such as Japanese, additional grammar options might appear for that language.

→ To learn more about foreign language options, **see** Chapter 22, "Using PowerPoint's Foreign Language Capabilities," **p. 473**.

On the Visual Clarity tab, you can view and revise the existing defaults for font clarity and presentation legibility.

On this tab, you can set the

- Maximum number of fonts
- Minimum point size for title text
- Minimum point size for body text
- Maximum number of bullets
- Maximum number of lines per title and per bullet

The Visual Clarity tab already includes default selections for these options that are based on basic design principles, but you can change any settings in the adjacent drop-down lists. When you run PowerPoint's spelling checker, it looks for violations of these constraints.

CAUTION

> Even though you can change these defaults to suit your needs, think carefully first. Exceeding the recommended number of fonts and bullets and changing to overly small or overly large fonts can make your presentation difficult to read.

If you change the settings on the Style Options dialog box and want to return to PowerPoint's defaults, click the Defaults button.

RUNNING A SPELLING AND STYLE CHECK

After you set the spelling and style options you want, you can check your presentation.

If you set the option to have PowerPoint check spelling as you type, you know immediately when you've possibly misspelled a word. PowerPoint places a red squiggly line under all suspected misspellings, as Figure 3.14 shows. You can either fix the error yourself or right-click to see some suggested alternatives from which to choose. Figure 3.14 shows some suggestions.

Figure 3.14
When you right-click a spelling error, PowerPoint suggests some possible spellings.

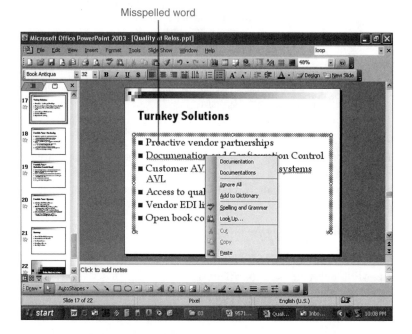

 PowerPoint missing some of your spelling or style errors? *See "Checking Spelling and Style" in the "Troubleshooting" section near the end of this chapter.*

You can also spell check your entire presentation all at once. To do so, follow these steps:

1. Click the Spelling button on the Standard toolbar, or choose Tools, Spelling and Grammar.

2. When PowerPoint encounters an error, it displays the Spelling dialog box, shown in Figure 3.15.

3. The Not in Dictionary field highlights the misspelled word, and the Change To field suggests the most likely alternative. The Suggestions box also provides additional alternatives.

Figure 3.15
The Spelling dialog box offers several options for handling potential misspellings.

4. Select the correct spelling or type it in the Change To field.

5. The Spelling dialog box also includes several buttons that provide other options:

- **Ignore**—Ignores the misspelling and continues checking spelling.

- **Ignore All**—Ignores all instances of this misspelling in the presentation and continues checking spelling.

- **Change**—Changes the individual misspelled word to the spelling offered in the Change To field.

- **Change All**—Changes all instances of this misspelled word to the spelling offered in the Change To field.

- **Add**—Adds the suspect word to the custom dictionary as a correctly spelled word.

- **Suggest**—Provides additional spelling suggestions.

- **AutoCorrect**—Adds the misspelled word and its corrected version to the AutoCorrect list.

- **Close**—Closes the dialog box.

→ To learn more about AutoCorrect, **see** "Setting AutoCorrect Options" in Chapter 21, **p. 447**.

TIP

To further change your custom dictionaries, go to Microsoft Word and choose Tools, Options from the menu bar. On the Spelling and Grammar tab of the Options dialog box, click the Custom Dictionaries button. The Custom Dictionaries dialog box opens, from which you can make additional modifications to your custom dictionaries.

You'll find custom dictionaries stored as text files in one of two locations, depending on your operating system and configuration: C:\`Windows_folder`\Profiles\ `User_name`\Application Data\Microsoft\Proof, or C:\`Windows_folder`\ Profiles\`User_name`.

NOTE

PowerPoint also targets unknown words as spelling errors, such as a person's name, a company name, or a product. Be sure to check carefully for these and add the names and words you commonly use in presentations to the dictionary.

When PowerPoint finishes checking spelling, it informs you with another dialog box.

LOOKING UP SYNONYMS WITH THE THESAURUS

If you ever have trouble coming up with just the right word, PowerPoint can help you with its thesaurus. Here's how to use it:

1. Click in the word you want to look up. (If you can't think of the exact word, type a word that's close to it.)

2. Click the Research button on the Standard toolbar. Or choose Tools, Research. Or right-click the word and choose Look Up from the menu that appears. The Research task pane opens, as Figure 3.16 shows.

Research task pane

Figure 3.16
The Research task pane offers a dictionary, a thesaurus, and more.

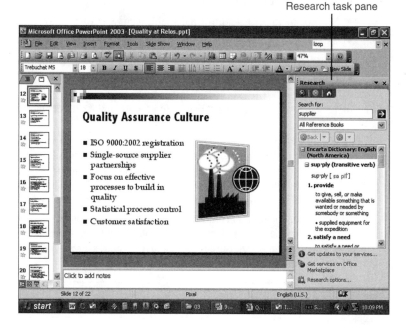

3. If the results don't show the thesaurus entries, click the arrow at the end of the field that appears below the Search For field. Choose Thesaurus from the drop-down list. Figure 3.17 shows the results.

4. To use one of the words, right-click it and choose Insert from the menu that appears.

Click to choose a reference book

Figure 3.17
The thesaurus lists synonyms of the selected word.

TROUBLESHOOTING

MAKING THE TEXT FIT

My text doesn't fit in my text placeholder.

Select the placeholder and then choose Format, Placeholder to open the Format AutoShape dialog box. Go to the Text Box tab and be sure that you've checked the Resize AutoShape to Fit Text check box.

MAKING YOUR CASE WORK

I tried to change the case of my text, but only part of it changed.

If you select only part of a sentence and change the case, the change applies only to the selected text, not to the entire sentence/paragraph. It isn't enough just to place the cursor in the specified line or paragraph. Select the entire text you want to change and then choose Format, Change Case again.

CHECKING SPELLING AND STYLE

I ran the spelling checker, and it didn't find my spelling or style errors.

PowerPoint checks the spelling only in the basic presentation; it doesn't check text in charts, WordArt objects, or embedded objects.

PowerPoint's style checker looks for only the style flaws you specified on the Spelling and Style tab on the Options dialog box (Tools, Options). It doesn't check for any other style errors.

DESIGN CORNER: DRESSING UP YOUR LIST

To make a bulleted list that's unique to your organization, consider using a logo or other internal image as a picture bullet. To import a logo for use a picture bullet, click the Import button in the Picture Bullet dialog box. In the Add Clips to Gallery dialog box, select your logo and click Add. Now you can add your logo to a bulleted list just as you would any other picture bullet, adding some additional style and personalization to your presentation.

BEFORE

Figure 3.18

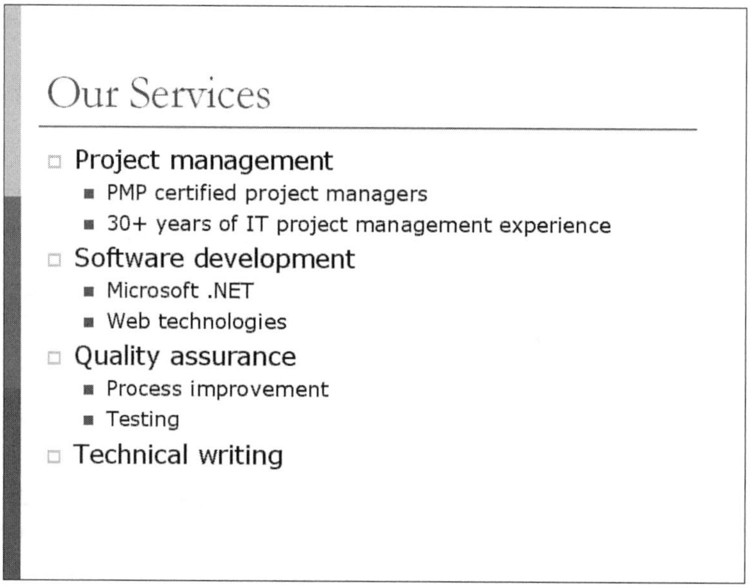

Our Services

- Project management
    - PMP certified project managers
    - 30+ years of IT project management experience
- Software development
    - Microsoft .NET
    - Web technologies
- Quality assurance
    - Process improvement
    - Testing
- Technical writing

AFTER

Matching picture bullet

Figure 3.19

Our Services

- Project management
  - PMP certified project managers
  - 30+ years of IT project management experience
- Software development
  - Microsoft .NET
  - Web technologies
- Quality assurance
  - Process improvement
  - Testing
- Technical writing

Flags Consulting

Company logo

3

CHAPTER

4

WORKING WITH TABLES

In this chapter   *by Patrice-Anne Rutledge and Jim Grey*

UNDERSTANDING TABLES

A *table* is an object that conveys related information in columns and rows. If you've created tables in other applications, such as Word, you know how valuable they are for communicating information. Tables are also efficient and flexible. For example, rather than creating three separate bullet list slides, each listing the five most important features of your three main products, you could summarize all this information in a table on a single slide. You could still present information on individual slides, and then summarize everything in a table at the end of the presentation.

You can include a table in a PowerPoint presentation in one of two ways:

- **Insert a table in PowerPoint**—PowerPoint's basic table insertion feature places a table into a slide based on the number of rows and columns you specify. You can then format, customize, and add data to the table.

- **Draw a table in PowerPoint**—When you need to create a complex table, one that the basic table feature can't make, you can draw it right on your slide. It takes longer to draw your own table, though.

NOTE

You can also integrate tables from Microsoft Word, Excel, and Access with PowerPoint. To do this, choose Insert, Object to open the Insert Object dialog box. Select the Create from File option and browse to the file that contains the table you want to import.

ADDING A TABLE

New Slide To add a new slide that contains a table, select Insert, New Slide or click the New Slide button on the Standard toolbar. In the Slide Layout task pane, choose the Title and Table slide layout. You can also choose any slide layout that includes content and click the Insert Table button on the content palette.

NOTE

If you use the AutoContent Wizard to create your presentation, it might already have a slide that contains a table.

Figure 4.1 illustrates the start of a sample table slide.

Double-click the Table object to open the Insert Table dialog box, illustrated in Figure 4.2.

NOTE

You can also insert a table into an existing slide by clicking the Insert Table button on the Standard toolbar or by selecting Insert, Table.

Figure 4.1
You can start adding a table by double-clicking the table object.

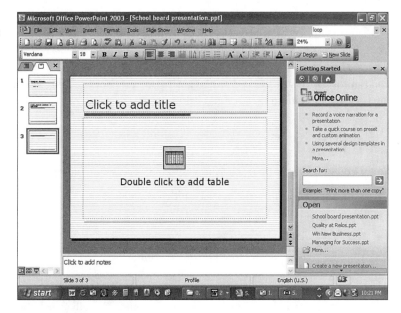

Figure 4.2
Choose the number of rows and columns you want to include.

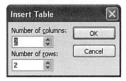

Choose the number of columns and number of rows to display and click OK.

A blank table appears in your slide, as Figure 4.3 shows.

Figure 4.3
Enter the title and table text to complete your table.

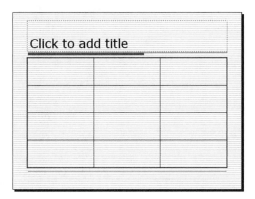

Click the title placeholder to remove the placeholder text and enter a title for the slide. Next, add the text you want in each cell of the table, clicking inside the table and then either tabbing to the cell or clicking in the cell.

NOTE

Table text doesn't appear on the Outline tab, but the slide title does.

You can format this text as you would any other text. For example, you might want to make the first row or column bold, or add other special formatting.

FORMATTING A TABLE

PowerPoint lets you format tables in a number of ways, including

- Applying different border styles, widths, and colors
- Inserting and deleting rows and columns
- Merging and splitting cells
- Aligning cell text to the top, bottom, or center

Use the Tables and Borders toolbar to format tables. If this toolbar isn't visible, open it by clicking the Tables and Borders button on the Standard toolbar or by selecting View, Toolbars, Tables and Borders. Table 4.1 explains this toolbar's buttons.

TABLE 4.1   TABLES AND BORDERS TOOLBAR BUTTONS

Button	Name	Description
	Draw Table	Draws table lines
	Eraser	Erases table lines
	Border Style	Applies the border style you choose to table lines you add or change
1 pt	Border Width	Applies the width you choose to table lines you add or change
	Border Color	Applies the color you choose to table lines you add or change
	Borders	Sets outside and inside border lines for cells you select
	Fill Color	Fills the interior of selected table cells with the color you choose
Table ▾	Table	Lists emenu options for formatting tables
	Merge Cells	Merges selected cells into one cell

Button	Name	Description
	Split Cell	Splits the selected cell into two cells
	Align Top	Aligns text to the top of the cell
	Center Vertically	Aligns text to the vertical center of the cell
	Align Bottom	Aligns text to the bottom of the cell
	Distribute Rows Evenly	Resizes the rows you select so that they're the same width
	Distribute Columns Evenly	Resize se the columns you select so that they're the same height

 If you applied multiple formatting changes and want to undo something you did a few steps back, see the "Troubleshooting" section near the end of the chapter.

MERGING AND SPLITTING CELLS

One way PowerPoint makes tables flexible is that you can *merge* and *split* table cells. For example, if you want a table to have a title centered at the top, you can merge all the cells across the top row. Or, if you need to show two separate bits of information in one location, split one cell into two.

To merge cells, select the cells you want to merge and click the Merge Cells button on the Tables and Borders toolbar. Figure 4.4 illustrates two cells that were merged into one.

Figure 4.4
Merged and split cells have a variety of applications within a table.

Merged cells

Snow Mountain Ski Shop

Q1 2003 Overview		
Skis	Accessories	Trips
Store 1 \$16,901	Store 2 \$22,167	

Split cells

CAUTION

> If you already have text in each of the cells you merge, each cell text becomes a line of text in the new single cell.

To split a cell, select the cell you want to split and click the Split Cell button on the Tables and Borders toolbar. Figure 4.4 illustrates a cell that was split into two.

CREATING A BORDER

Use borders to draw attention to your table or even to specific information in your table. New tables get a black, solid line border by default, but you can change this. To format the border, select the table and use the Tables and Borders toolbar to change the border style, width, and color, and to set where borders appear.

SETTING BORDER STYLE

To set the border style, click the Border Style drop-down list on the Tables and Borders toolbar and choose the border style you prefer. The list includes the option to apply no border, a solid line, or a variety of dashed line styles, shown in Figure 4.5.

Figure 4.5
Choose the border style that suits your table.

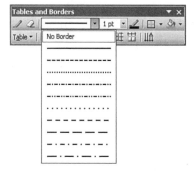

SETTING BORDER WIDTH

To set the border width, click the Border Width drop-down list on the Tables and Borders toolbar and choose the width you prefer. Options include point sizes from 1/4 point (a very thin line) to 6 points (a thick line), shown in Figure 4.6.

Figure 4.6
Use a thick border to create more emphasis, a thin border to create less.

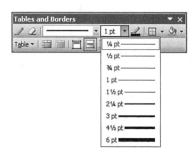

SETTING BORDER COLORS

To set the border color, click the Border Color button. The box that appears offers several possible colors based on the presentation's color scheme. For more color choices, click More Colors to open the Colors dialog box.

→ To learn more about the Colors dialog box, **see** "Using the Colors Dialog Box" in Chapter 14, "Creating and Formatting Objects," **p. 290**.

CREATING BORDERS

You can specify which parts of your table contain borders—the whole table or only specific outside or inside areas.

To set borders, click the down arrow to the right of the Borders button on the Tables and Borders toolbar. A palette appears with several border options, as Figure 4.7 shows.

Figure 4.7
You can have both inside and outside borders on your table.

SETTING TABLE FILL COLOR

You can change the color that fills one or more cells in your table.

CAUTION

> Be sure that your table text is still readable if you change a cell's fill color. For example, if your text is black, don't fill cells with dark blue.

To change fill color, select the cells that you want to change and click the down arrow next to the Fill Color button on the Tables and Borders toolbar.

You can

- Choose from the colors that appear on the palette. If you applied a design template to your presentation, these colors complement the design template and give you the best results.

- Click More Fill Colors to display the Colors dialog box. You can either choose from a large number of colors in this dialog box or create a custom color.

- Click Fill Effects to choose from a number of gradients, textures, patterns, and pictures.

→ To learn more about the Colors and Fill dialog boxes, **see** Chapter 14, **p. 281**.

To remove a fill you no longer want, click the down arrow next to the Fill Color button and choose No Fill from the palette.

Working with Columns and Rows

It never fails—as soon as you create a table and format it just so, you find that you need to add or remove information.

Inserting Rows and Columns

To insert a row into your table, click in the row above or below where you want to insert the row. Then choose Table, Insert Rows Above or Insert Rows Below, as appropriate, from the Tables and Borders toolbar. PowerPoint inserts the row, as Figure 4.8 shows.

Figure 4.8
Add rows if you didn't create enough during the initial table creation.

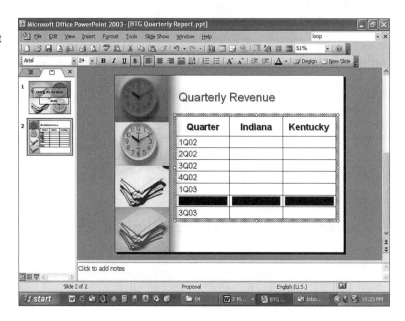

TIP

You can resize the height or width of any row or column by selecting the row or column separator and dragging it to the new location.

CAUTION

When you add or delete rows and columns, your table might no longer fit well on the slide. You then need to resize the table by dragging a corner. Be careful, however, that you don't hide existing text by making the cells too small during resizing.

 If your table no longer fits after inserting rows or columns, see the "Troubleshooting" section near the end of the chapter.

If you want to insert multiple rows, select that number of rows before selecting the Insert command. For example, if you select two rows and then choose Table, Insert Rows Above in the Tables and Borders toolbar, PowerPoint inserts two rows above the selected rows.

To add a new column to your table, click in the column to the left or right of where you want to insert the column. Then choose Table, Insert Columns to the Left or Insert Columns to the Right from the Tables and Borders toolbar. PowerPoint inserts the column, as Figure 4.9 shows.

Figure 4.9
You can add columns if your table design changes.

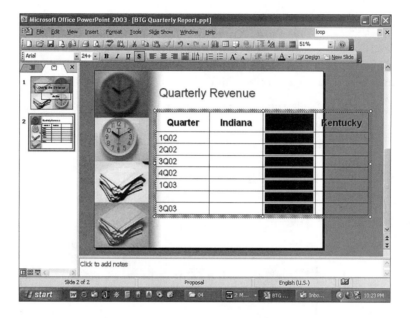

DELETING ROWS AND COLUMNS

To delete rows or columns, click in the row or column you want to delete and then choose Table, Delete Rows or Delete Columns from the Tables and Borders toolbar. PowerPoint deletes the entire column or row of the cell(s) you select.

DELETING TABLES AND TABLE CONTENTS

To delete text in a cell, select the text (not just the cell) and press the Delete key.

CAUTION

> You must select the actual text or cell—not just place the cursor in the cell—to delete the text.

To delete an entire table, choose Table, Select Table from the Tables and Borders toolbar and then press the Delete key. PowerPoint replaces the table with a Double Click to Add Table directive.

TIP

Another way to delete a table is to click the outside border of the table to select the entire table and then press the Delete key.

FORMATTING WITH THE FORMAT TABLE DIALOG BOX

The Format Table dialog box (see Figure 4.10) duplicates some of what you can do with the Tables and Borders toolbar. It also gives you some formatting options that aren't available anywhere else. You can access this dialog box in one of two ways:

- Click the Table button on the Tables and Borders toolbar and choose Borders and Fill from the menu.
- Select Format, Table from the main PowerPoint menu.

Figure 4.10
Use the Format Table dialog box to apply many formatting options.

USING THE BORDERS TAB

The Borders tab lets you set these attributes:

- **Style**—Choose a border style from the available options.
- **Color**—Choose a color from the drop-down list. For more colors, click More Colors to open the Colors dialog box.

→ To learn more about the Colors dialog box, **see** "Using the Colors Dialog Box" in Chapter 14, **p. 290**.

- **Width**—Choose a border width from the drop-down list.
- **Borders**—Click on the diagram to apply borders where you want them and remove them where you don't.

USING THE FILL TAB

Use the Fill tab, shown in Figure 4.11, to specify fill color for your table cells.

To fill selected cells with a color, click the Fill Color check box and choose a color from the drop-down list. From here, you can also access the Colors and Fill Effects dialog boxes to apply additional color and fill options.

Figure 4.11
You can apply fill colors to your tables, but be sure that the text is still readable.

→ To learn more about the Colors and Fill Effects dialog boxes, **see** "Specifying Colors" in Chapter 14, "Creating and Formatting Objects," **p. 290**.

To lighten the color so that you can read text more easily on it, click the Semitransparent check box.

USING THE TEXT BOX TAB

Use the Text Box tab, shown in Figure 4.12, to set alignment and margins in your table.

Figure 4.12
The Text Box tab lets you set a variety of alignments.

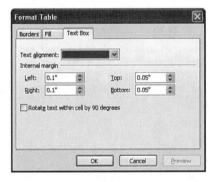

To set text alignment, click the drop-down list and choose from one of these alignment options: Top, Middle, Bottom, Top Centered, Middle Centered, or Bottom Centered.

You can also set internal margins for the left, right, top, and bottom margins within the table cells. Doing so changes how far your text is from the cell's edges.

Select the Rotate Text Within Cell by 90 Degrees check box to rotate selected text vertically.

ADDING BULLETED AND NUMBERED LISTS WITHIN TABLES

To create a bulleted list within a table cell, select the cell and click the Bullets button on the Formatting toolbar.

To create a numbered list within a table cell, select the cell and click the Numbering toolbar button.

TIP

> For more bullet and numbering options, select the text you want to format and then choose Format, Bullets and Numbering to open the Bullets and Numbering dialog box. This dialog box gives you more control over your lists by letting you choose a color for numbers and bullets, change numbering to alphabetical or outline, use picture bullets, and more.

DRAWING A TABLE

If the default table options don't give you what you need, create a custom table. Drawing your own table lets you make columns and rows of varying widths, for example. For some people, drawing a table is faster than customizing a table created using a table placeholder.

To draw a table, select the Draw Table button on the Tables and Borders toolbar. The mouse pointer becomes a pencil. Drag the mouse diagonally across the slide to create a box about the size you think the table should be. Then use the mouse to draw lines inside the box to make columns and rows.

If you make a mistake or want to imitate the Merge Cell feature, click the Eraser button on the Tables and Borders toolbar. Use this eraser to remove the lines between rows and cells as necessary.

TIP

> To make it easier to create rows and columns, display rulers and guides on your slide. Select View, Ruler to display a ruler. You can also create invisible grids and guides to help you draw and create objects (View, Grid and Guides).

TROUBLESHOOTING

MAKING ROOM FOR ADDITIONAL ROWS AND COLUMNS

I added some rows and columns to my table, and now they don't fit in the slide.

Try resizing your table to fit, but doing this might hide text from view. If that happens, try making the text smaller until it all fits. But be careful not to make it so small that it's hard to read. If you haven't already invested a lot of time in creating and formatting your table, you might be better off deleting the table and starting again.

UNDOING MULTIPLE FORMATTING CHANGES

I applied several formatting options to my table, and I don't like the results.

Click the down arrow next to the Undo button on the Standard toolbar to see a list of formatting tasks you can undo.

DESIGN CORNER: IMPROVING INFORMATION DESIGN THROUGH THE USE OF TABLES

By now, you've learned of the value of using tables to present information in PowerPoint and the ways you can customize tables to blend with your presentation's design. Obviously, including a table in every slide can be monotonous, but the judicious use of tables can enhance your presentation. For example, the bulleted lists in the "Before" example convey the information adequately but duplicate it in certain places. Using a table's column and row format, you can convey the same information without duplication and in a way that more clearly shows the data's relationships. The "After" example eliminates these redundancies, and by using fill colors and custom borders, it looks nicer, too.

BEFORE

Figure 4.13

Quality Strategy Adjustments

o Release 1
- No requirements reviews
- No design reviews
- Code reads
- Unit testing
- System testing
- Validation testing

o Release 2
- Requirements reviews instituted
- Design reviews instituted
- Code reads
- Unit testing
- System testing
- Validation testing

AFTER

Figure 4.14

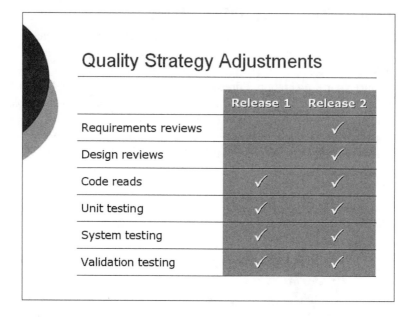

CHAPTER **5**

ORGANIZING PRESENTATIONS

In this chapter   *by Patrice-Anne Rutledge and Jim Grey*

EXPLORING POWERPOINT'S OUTLINING FEATURES

PowerPoint's outlining features make it easy to create a well-organized presentation. You can organize a presentation in several ways, depending on how you work best and whether you've already created an outline in another program. You can use the Outline tab in Normal view to easily organize and rearrange your presentation. For more options, try the Outlining toolbar. This toolbar lets you promote and demote outline points, as well as move, collapse, and expand them. You can also create a summary slide or display font formatting. If you create outlines in Word or another program, you can import them into PowerPoint.

ORGANIZING PRESENTATIONS

Before you actually create a presentation, you should determine the presentation's purpose, organize your ideas, and establish the flow of what you're going to say. You need to create an outline.

→ To learn some useful outlining techniques, **see** "Creating an Outline and Storyboard" in Chapter 24, "The Message—Scripting the Concept," **p. 506**.

PowerPoint offers four ways to create an outline. One of the easiest ways is to create your presentation using the Outline tab in Normal view. If you're more comfortable adding content directly to slides, PowerPoint displays your information on the Outline tab. Creating a presentation using the AutoContent Wizard is a good idea if you want to receive detailed content suggestions for a particular type of presentation. The wizard also creates a basic outline for you. And finally, if you already have an outline in another application such as Word 2003, you can easily import the outline into PowerPoint.

→ To learn how to import existing outlines, **see** "Working with Outlines Created in Other Programs" in this chapter, **p. 108**.

As you create your outline, keep several things in mind:

- Start nearly every presentation with a title slide that introduces your topic and its presenter.

- Think of several main points to cover and design your presentation around those points.

- Try not to cover more than one main topic or concept in an individual slide.

- Remember that a PowerPoint outline is usually designed to accompany a verbal presentation. Keep in mind what you want your audience to see versus what you want them to hear during your presentation.

- Keep bulleted lists balanced and consistent. For example, a single bullet on a slide doesn't really make sense; a list should contain at least two bullets. Too many bullets on one slide and very few on another also might not work well.

- Consider using a summary slide to summarize the points you made during your presentation and conclude it.

USING THE OUTLINE TAB

No matter which method you use to create your outline, you'll probably want to use PowerPoint's Outline tab to organize this information at some point. In Normal view, the outline appears on the left side of the window and shares the desktop with the slide itself and related notes.

NOTE

> You can change the size of any pane in PowerPoint by dragging its border to a new location. To do this, move the mouse over the border and, when the cursor changes to a double-headed arrow, click and drag.

To view the Outline tab, click the Normal View button in the lower-left corner of the PowerPoint window. The Outline tab is selected by default, and your presentation's outline will appear on the left side of the window. Figure 5.1 shows the Outline tab.

Figure 5.1
The Outline tab offers a flexible approach to creating an outline.

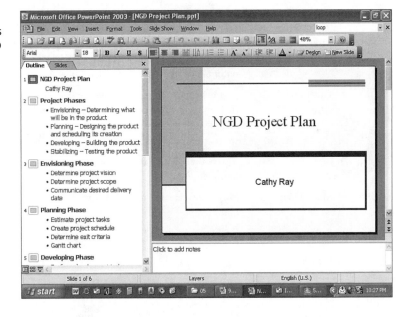

Each slide is numbered and followed by a slide icon and the title text. The body text is listed under each slide, up to five levels. This body text includes bulleted and indented lists, as well as other text information. The title text is also referred to as the *outline heading* and each individual point in the body text as a *subheading*. Clip art, tables, charts, and other objects don't appear in the outline.

NOTE

> Any text that you enter other than in the Click to Add Title or the Click to Add Text place-holder doesn't display in the outline.

Adding new outline information is simple. Enter the content and press the Enter key to move to the next point. To delete a point you no longer need, select it and press the Delete key.

USING THE OUTLINING TOOLBAR

You can use the Outlining toolbar to help organize and rearrange your slides on the Outline tab. To display the toolbar, choose View, Toolbars, Outlining. It appears vertically on the left side of the Outline tab. Table 5.1 lists the buttons on this toolbar.

TABLE 5.1   OUTLINING TOOLBAR BUTTONS

Button	Name	Description
	Promote	Changes the selected text's outline level to the previous level, applying that level's style and formatting. For example, promoting text at outline level two moves it to level one.
	Demote	Changes the selected text's outline level to the next level, applying that level's style and formatting. For example, demoting text at outline level three moves it to level four. Demoting a slide title moves the text of the selected slide to the previous slide.
	Move Up	Moves the selected text so that it appears before the previous item in the outline.
	Move Down	Moves the selected text so that it appears after the next item in the outline.
	Collapse	Hides all body text for the selected slides.
	Expand	Displays all body text for the selected slides.
	Collapse All	Hides all body text in the outline.
	Expand All	Displays all body text in the outline.
	Summary Slide	Creates a slide that summarizes the presentation by listing slide titles.
	Show Formatting	Shows the actual presentation font formatting on the Outline tab.

5

NOTE

> You can move the Outlining toolbar to another location on the screen by dragging the move handle (above the Promote button) to another location.

PROMOTING AND DEMOTING OUTLINE POINTS

You can demote outline headings and promote and demote subheadings to reorganize and rearrange your presentation. Promoting a first level subheading makes it a heading (slide title) in a new slide. Promoting a secondary-level subheading (such as indented text or lower-level bullet) moves it up to the next level. Conversely, promoting indented text out-dents it.

For example, if you select the text of a second-level bullet in the outline and click the Promote button, the bullet becomes a first-level bullet (see Figure 5.2).

Figure 5.2
Promoting the list item moves it up one level but doesn't change its location.

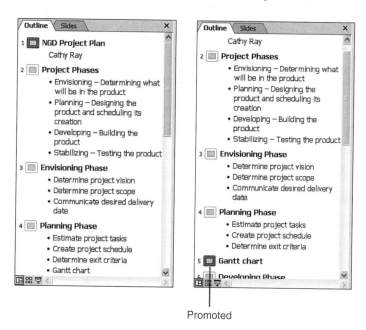

Promoted

If you promote a first-level bullet, it becomes a slide title, and PowerPoint inserts a new slide into the presentation.

The Demote button works in much the same way as the Promote button. Demoting a slide title makes it a second-level item and adds the slide's contents to the end of the previous slide. (If your slide contains notes or graphics, PowerPoint asks whether you're sure before doing this.) Demoting other text indents the text to the next outline level.

5

TIP

You can also demote an item by selecting it and pressing the Tab key.

 Do you lose notes and graphics when demoting? *See the "Troubleshooting" section near the end of the chapter.*

MOVING OUTLINE POINTS UP AND DOWN

You can also move each outline item up or down in the outline. To move an item up, select it and click the Move Up button. For example, say that you want to move an item up three slides. Figure 5.3 shows an item's original position, and then where it appears after clicking Move Up seven times.

Figure 5.3
Moving an item up the outline.

Original position

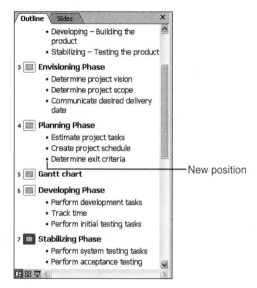

New position

If you want to move an item down the outline, as you might expect, you click the Move Down button.

TIP

Use Slide Sorter view to view your actual slides as you rearrange them.

COLLAPSING AND EXPANDING OUTLINE POINTS

To make it easier to read a long outline, you can collapse and expand slides and their body text.

To collapse the body text of an individual slide, select it and click the Collapse button. The slide number and title remain, but the related body text is hidden from view. Figure 5.4 shows a collapsed slide.

Figure 5.4
Collapsing a slide
hides its body text.

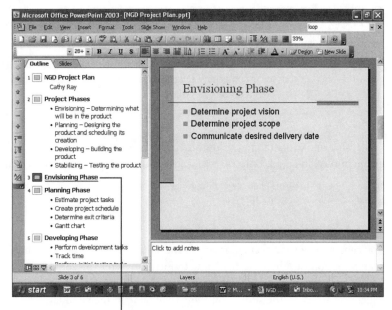

Envisioning Phase collapsed

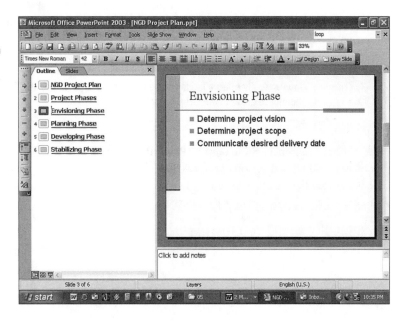

Select the slide again and click Expand to display the hidden text.

To collapse the entire outline, click the Collapse All button. Figure 5.5 illustrates an outline that is entirely collapsed.

Figure 5.5
Collapsing an entire
presentation creates a
presentation outline
summary.

5

To display the outline details again, click the Expand All button.

> **TIP**
>
> If you want to collapse and expand more than one slide, but not all slides, press Shift, choose the consecutive slides, and then click the Collapse or Expand button. The slides you select must be consecutive.

Collapsing and expanding your outline make it easier to print as well. You can print an entire outline in detail, only certain sections in detail, or only a collapsed summary outline.

→ To learn how to print outlines, **see** "Printing an Outline" in Chapter 10, "Creating and Printing Presentation Materials," **p. 209**.

CREATING A SUMMARY SLIDE

You can create a slide that summarizes the slide titles for all or selected slides in your presentation. You can then use that slide to introduce your presentation, to highlight the areas you're going to discuss, or to close your presentation by reviewing it. To create a summary slide, first select all the slides you want to include in the summary.

> **NOTE**
>
> From the Outline tab in Normal view, you must choose either all slides or a series of consecutive slides. If you want to create a summary slide from non-consecutive slides, switch to Slide Sorter view first.

Usually it's easier to select slides if you collapse all the headings by clicking the Collapse All button on the Outlining toolbar.

> **TIP**
>
> You can easily select all slides in the presentation by selecting the first slide and dragging the mouse down to the last slide or by pressing Ctrl+A.

Next, click the Summary Slide button. PowerPoint automatically creates a summary slide that contains a bulleted list of all the selected slide titles in your presentation. The summary slide is inserted before the first selected slide, but you can move it to another location if you want. Figure 5.6 shows a sample summary slide.

Figure 5.6
Create a summary slide to introduce or close your presentation.

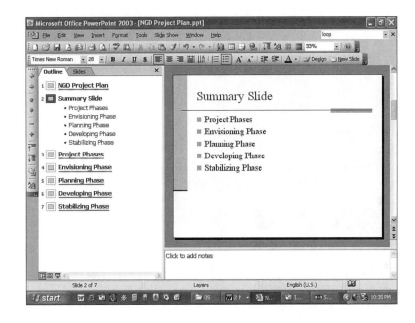

SHOWING SLIDE FORMATTING

 By default, the Outline tab displays each heading and subheading in the same font, bolding the headings for emphasis. If you want the outline to appear using the actual fonts and formatting of the presentation itself, click the Show Formatting button on the Outlining toolbar. Figure 5.7 shows a sample outline with formatting.

Figure 5.7
This outline displays text formatting.

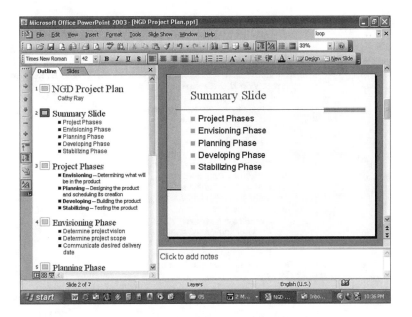

Each item's specific font and attributes—such as size, bolding, italics, underlining, and shadow—now appear in the Outline tab. The text's color is always black, though, regardless of its actual color.

WORKING WITH OUTLINES CREATED IN OTHER PROGRAMS

If you create outlines in other programs, such as Word, you can either export them from their original application into PowerPoint or save the outlines and import the files directly into PowerPoint. PowerPoint can work with outlines in many different formats, such as the following:

- Word documents (.doc)
- Rich Text Format (.rtf)
- Text files (.txt)
- Excel worksheets (.xls)
- HTML (.htm)

For example, if you create an outline in Word, you use heading 1, heading 2, and heading 3 styles to format your document. When PowerPoint imports your outline, each heading 1 becomes a slide title, each heading 2 becomes first-level text, and each heading 3 becomes second-level text. Figure 5.8 shows a Word outline and its components.

Figure 5.8
Outline in Word and then export your outline to PowerPoint.

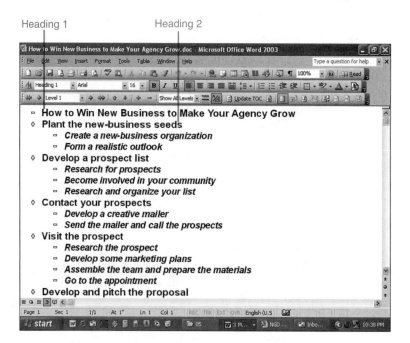

If the file you export doesn't contain these heading styles, PowerPoint uses paragraph indentations and tabs to determine the structure of the outline. PowerPoint does the best it can, but sometimes guesses an item's outline level wrong. Use the Outlining toolbar buttons to reorganize the outline.

To export an outline to PowerPoint from within Word, choose File, Send To, Microsoft PowerPoint. PowerPoint creates a presentation from this information. Apply a design template, and your presentation is complete. Figure 5.9 illustrates an example of an exported outline.

Figure 5.9
The outline now appears in a PowerPoint presentation.

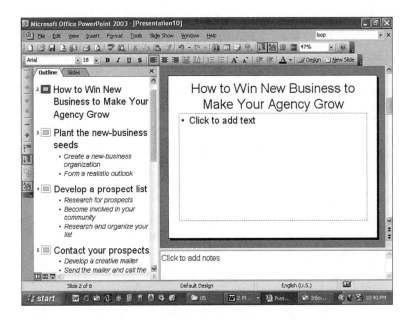

Although this is the easiest way to create a PowerPoint presentation from a Word outline, there are other ways to import different types of outlines into PowerPoint. You can

- **Import an outline from within PowerPoint**—To do this, click the Open button to display the Open dialog box, select All Outlines from the Files of Type drop-down list, choose the outline you want to import, and click Open. With this method, PowerPoint creates a new presentation. Note that you might be prompted to install a converter if one isn't already installed.

- **Import an outline into an existing presentation**—To do this, select the slide on the Outline tab after which you want to insert the new outline. Choose Insert, Slides from Outline to open the Insert Outline dialog box. Choose the outline you want to import and click Insert.

 Does your imported outline look strange? *See the "Troubleshooting" section near the end of the chapter.*

- **Copy the outline text from the source application**—Then just paste into PowerPoint and reformat to quickly create a basic presentation.

TROUBLESHOOTING

PREPARING FILES TO IMPORT

I imported an outline, and it doesn't look right.

PowerPoint imports an outline from another application "as is." Before you import the outline, be sure that the existing document makes a suitable outline. For example, a lengthy text file or a detailed spreadsheet might not make sense as an outline.

DEALING WITH DEMOTIONS

I demoted a slide, and the text moved to the previous slide, but the notes and graphics disappeared.

When you demote a slide using the Demote button on the Outlining toolbar, the text content remains and carries over to the previous slide, but any graphics or notes are deleted. To keep the notes and graphics, copy them to their destination using the Clipboard, and then demote the slide.

DESIGN CORNER: REORGANIZING A SLIDE'S CONTENTS IN THE OUTLINE TAB

Your eighth-grade English teacher was right: Before you write (or create a presentation), outline your thoughts to ensure a logical flow. Creating an outline can call attention to flow problems early, when it's easiest to fix them. PowerPoint's outlining features make it easy to correct and perfect your outline.

For example, say that your team is selecting new accounting software, and it's your job to present the selection process to them. You entered the basic points on your introductory slide, but on review you realize that the subtopics aren't indented correctly under the main topics you want to cover. You can correct this easily with the Outlining toolbar:

1. Click on the Outline tab in Normal view. If the slide's contents aren't clearly visible, drag the pane's border to resize it.

2. Select the Goals and Objectives bullet points on the Outline tab and click the Demote button on the Outlining toolbar.

3. Select the Final deadline: May 1, 2004 bullet point and click the Promote button on the Outlining toolbar.

BEFORE

Figure 5.10
Demote these two bullet points, which are part of the project introduction. Promote this bullet point, which is its own topic.

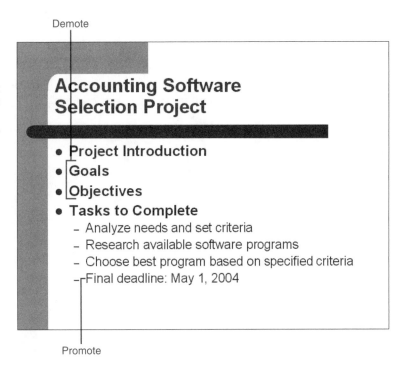

Demote

Accounting Software Selection Project

- Project Introduction
- Goals
- Objectives
- Tasks to Complete
  - Analyze needs and set criteria
  - Research available software programs
  - Choose best program based on specified criteria
  - Final deadline: May 1, 2004

Promote

AFTER

Figure 5.11
The reorganized slide.

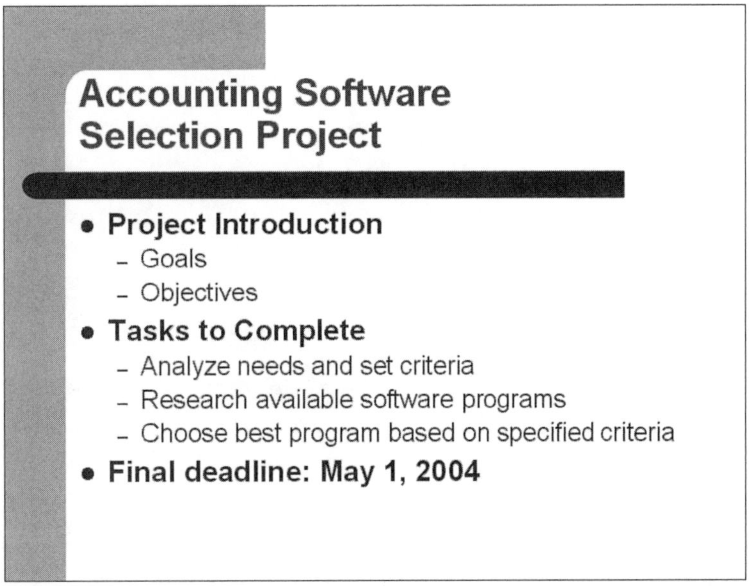

Accounting Software Selection Project

- Project Introduction
  - Goals
  - Objectives
- Tasks to Complete
  - Analyze needs and set criteria
  - Research available software programs
  - Choose best program based on specified criteria
- Final deadline: May 1, 2004

5

CHAPTER 6

FORMATTING SLIDES AND PRESENTATIONS

In this chapter   *by Patrice-Anne Rutledge and Jim Grey*

EXPLORING POWERPOINT FORMATTING OPTIONS

After you create a presentation, you might want to change it. It's easy to add, delete, rearrange, copy, and move slides in PowerPoint. You can also make more detailed changes to your presentation's format, such as applying a new design template, changing colors and color schemes, and applying a special effects background.

ADDING SLIDES

After you create a presentation, you might want to add new slides. To add a new slide to an open presentation, click the New Slide button on the Formatting toolbar or press Ctrl+M. PowerPoint adds a new slide immediately following the current slide and opens the Slide Layout task pane. Select the slide layout you want to use; PowerPoint applies that layout to the slide (see Figure 6.1).

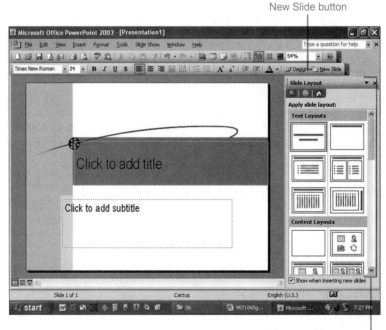

Figure 6.1
Choose from many different slide types on the Slide Layout task pane.

New Slide button

Slide Layout task pane

→ To learn more about each layout type, **see** "Understanding Slide Layouts," in Chapter 2, "Creating a Basic Presentation," **p. 43**.

DELETING SLIDES

If you no longer need a slide or make a mistake and want to start again, you can delete it. In Normal view, select the slide on either the Outline tab or the Slides tab, and press the Delete key. If these tabs don't appear, click the Normal View button in the lower-left corner of the PowerPoint window to restore them.

To delete multiple consecutive slides, press the Shift key and select the slides you want to delete before pressing the Delete key. You can delete multiple nonconsecutive slides in Slide Sorter view by holding the Ctrl key, selecting the slides you want to delete, and pressing the Delete key.

REARRANGING SLIDES

You can rearrange slides in three different locations in PowerPoint. These include the

- Outline tab in Normal view
- Slides tab in Normal view
- Slide Sorter view

Select the icon of the slide you want to move and drag it to a new location. Which method is best? The Outline tab is useful if you want to read the content of your slides as you reorganize. The Slides tab is a good choice if you know exactly what you want to move and want to do it quickly. If you have major reorganization to do on your presentation, you might want to use Slide Sorter view because it provides more flexibility as well as the capability to view the contents of your slides as you rearrange them.

TIP

> If you want to do a major reorganization of a presentation that contains numerous slides, consider printing handouts with either six or nine slides per page first so that you can more easily analyze your entire presentation before making changes.

→ To learn more about using Slide Sorter view to organize your slides, **see** "Using the Slide Sorter View," later in this chapter, **p. 115**.

→ To discover more outlining techniques, **see** "Moving Outline Points Up and Down" in Chapter 5, "Organizing Presentations," **p. 104**.

6

USING THE SLIDE SORTER VIEW

You can use the Slide Sorter view to organize and rearrange your slides. To open this view, click the Slide Sorter View button in the lower-left corner of the PowerPoint window or select View, Slide Sorter. Figure 6.2 displays this view.

Figure 6.2
Analyze and organize slides in Slide Sorter view.

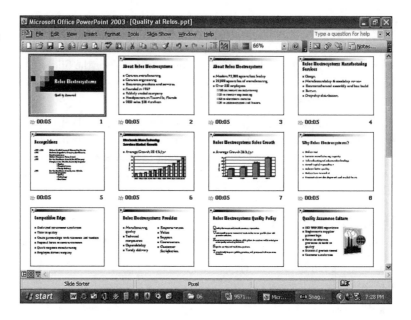

In this view, you see smaller versions of your slides in several rows and columns. By viewing the basic content of each slide, you can more easily rearrange their order.

To move a slide in the Slide Sorter, select it and drag it to a new location.

To view a particular slide in more detail, click on the desired slide and select the Normal View button at the lower-left corner of the PowerPoint window (see Figure 6.3).

To delete a slide in Slide Sorter view, select it and press the Delete key. To select multiple slides to delete, press Ctrl, select the slides, and then press the Delete key.

TIP

Occasionally, you might also want to hide slides from view during an onscreen presentation but not delete them from the presentation itself. To do that, select the slide or slides you want to hide and click the Hide Slide button on the Slide Sorter toolbar. The slides remain in the presentation, but they don't appear when you run your slideshow. This is often easier than creating a custom show, particularly if you don't plan to repeat this version of your presentation.

The Slide Sorter toolbar also includes buttons for applying optional effects, such as transitions, animation effects, and speaker's notes.

→ To learn why you might want to use speaker's notes, **see** "Creating Notes and Handouts," in Chapter 10, "Creating and Printing Presentation Materials," **p. 200**.

→ To learn how to create transitional effects, **see** "Setting Slide Transitions," in Chapter 15, **p. 321**.

Select any slide

Figure 6.3
Choose how you
want to view your
presentation.

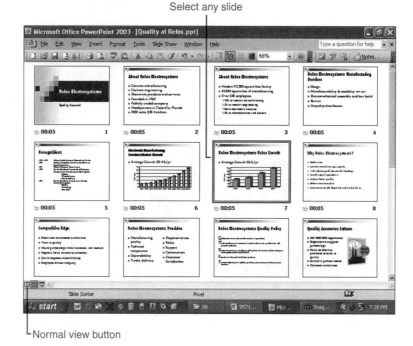

Normal view button

COPYING AND MOVING SLIDES FROM ONE PRESENTATION TO ANOTHER

Using the Slide Sorter view, you can copy or move slides from one presentation to another. To do this, open both the source and destination presentations in Slide Sorter view. Choose Window, Arrange All. PowerPoint displays both presentations in different window panes in Slide Sorter view, shown in Figure 6.4.

To copy a slide, select it and then drag it to the desired location in the other presentation. PowerPoint places the slide in the destination presentation, but it also remains in the source as shown in Figure 6.5.

To move a slide, select it, click the Cut button on the Standard toolbar, position the mouse in the new destination location, and click the Paste button. The slide is removed from the source presentation and inserted in the destination presentation. To move or copy more than one slide at a time, press Ctrl as you drag slides from the source presentation.

If each presentation uses a different design template, the slide changes to the template of the new presentation and the Paste Options button appears. If you want to retain the design template of the source presentation, click the down arrow to the right of the Paste Options button and choose Keep Source Formatting. To go back to the design template of the target presentation, choose Use Design Template Formatting.

6

Slide you want to move or copy

Figure 6.4
By splitting panes
between two presen-
tations, you can copy
or move slides
between them.

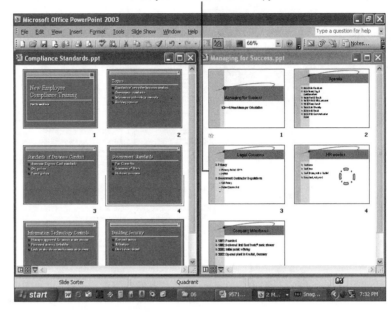

The slide is copied to the target presentation

Figure 6.5
Copying a slide is
easier than creating
it again.

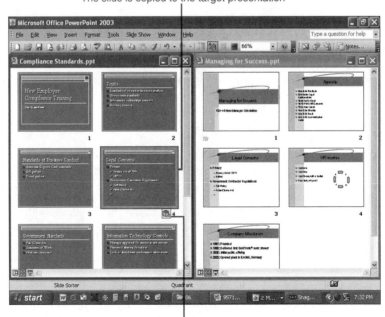

Paste Options button

6

CAUTION

Although you can combine multiple design templates in a single presentation, think carefully before doing so. Combining design templates can make your presentation confusing.

Problems with multiple design templates? *See the "Troubleshooting" section at the end of this chapter.*

To remove the dual window view, click the Close button in the upper-right corner of the presentation you no longer want to view and then the Maximize button in the upper-right corner of the presentation you want to keep active.

If arranging both presentations in one window is too distracting, you can put them in separate windows:

1. Open the presentation from which you want to copy or move slides.

2. Click the Slide Sorter View button at the lower-left side of the screen to display the presentation in this view.

3. Select the slides you want to copy or move. To select multiple noncontiguous slides, press the Ctrl key and then choose slides.

4. Press Ctrl+C to copy the slides; press Ctrl+X to cut the slides if you would rather move them.

5. Open the presentation in which you want to place the selected slides.

6. Click where you want to insert the slides and press Ctrl+V to paste them.

NOTE

If more than one presentation is open at a time and each is in a maximized window, you can press Ctrl+F6 to cycle through each one. This helps when you want the full-screen view and want to copy/move from one presentation to the next without having to use the Window menu.

Lost slides when you copied from one presentation to another? *See the "Troubleshooting" section at the end of this chapter.*

APPLYING A NEW DESIGN TEMPLATE

You can easily change the design template originally applied to your presentation. To do so, click the Design button on the Formatting toolbar. The Slide Design task pane appears, displaying all available design templates in preview format (see Figure 6.6).

The existing design template used in the current presentation appears at the top (if there is one), followed by the most recently used templates, and then all other available templates.

Select the template you want to use. PowerPoint applies this new design to your presentation.

Figure 6.6
Choose a design template that matches your presentation's mood and goals.

CAUTION

Not all design templates are already installed. If PowerPoint displays a warning that you need to install a template, be sure to have the program CD in your CD-ROM drive, and then follow the installation instructions in the warning.

→ To learn more about design templates and how to use them best, **see** "Understanding Design Templates," in Chapter 2, "Creating a Basic Presentation," **p. 42**.

→ To learn how to apply a design template to a presentation when you create it, **see** "Using a Design Template," in Chapter 2, **p. 49**.

→ To learn more about the effect of choosing a design template, **see** "Working with Design Templates," in Chapter 25, "The Media—Designing Visual Support," **p. 548**.

NOTE

To download additional design templates from the Web, go to Microsoft Office Online. Choose Help, Office on Microsoft.com or go directly to http://office.microsoft.com.

PREVIEWING DESIGN TEMPLATES

To view larger previews of the design templates, click the down arrow to the right of any template preview and choose Show Large Previews from the shortcut menu that appears. The preview templates will roughly double in size. To go back to the normal-size previews, simply select this option again to remove the check mark. Figure 6.7 shows design template in large previews.

Figure 6.7
Preview lets you see what a presentation looks like before you apply it.

APPLYING MULTIPLE DESIGN TEMPLATES TO A SINGLE PRESENTATION

PowerPoint lets you use more than one design template in a presentation. Although it's very easy to do this, you should carefully consider whether it's a good idea or not. Too many contrasting styles and designs make your presentation confusing and difficult to follow. Even if you decide to apply multiple design templates, your best bet is to keep them reasonably similar. Here are some suggestions for when multiple design templates would be appropriate:

- You want to use one design template for your title slide and another for the rest of your presentation. For example, the title slide could include a logo that the rest of the presentation doesn't have.

- Your presentation is broken into several distinct sections, and you want to use a separate design template for each. For example, let's say that you're giving a summary presentation about three divisions of a large corporation and each division uses a different default design template for its PowerPoint presentations. You might want to use the standard template for each division for that part of the presentation.

- You want to make minor design template modifications based on the content of the slide. For example, you could create two similar design templates—one with a graphic image in the lower-right corner and one without. On slides with extensive content, you might prefer to use the design template without the graphic image.

To apply a different design template to a selected slide, follow these steps:

1. Select the slide or slides to which you want to apply a separate design template.
2. Select the preview of that template on the Slide Design task pane.
3. Click the down arrow to the right of the selected template.
4. Choose Apply to Selected Slides. PowerPoint applies the design template only to the selected slides. The unselected slides still retain the original design template.

6

To return to a single design template, select that template and choose Apply to All Slides from the menu that appears when you click the down arrow.

CREATING YOUR OWN DESIGN TEMPLATES

Sometimes none of the existing design templates offers exactly what you're looking for. In that case, you can either modify an existing template or create one of your own. The following are some ideas of what you might want to do to customize or add to a blank slide:

- Change the master title or text style to a different font (View, Master, Slide Master).
- Change the background color (Format, Background).
- Change the slide color scheme (choose Color Schemes from the Slide Design task pane).
- Change the bullet styles (Format, Bullets and Numbering).
- Add objects such as a logo, picture, or WordArt image.

To save a customized design template for future use, follow these steps:

1. Choose File, Save As to open the Save As dialog box.
2. In the Save As Type drop-down list, choose Design Template. The Save In drop-down list selects the folder in which you store design templates by default.
3. Enter a name for your design template in the File Name field.
4. Click the Save button.

The saved design template is available the next time you open the Slide Design task pane.

NOTE

To delete a design template you no longer want or created by mistake, select the template in the Open dialog box and press the Delete key.

DOWNLOADING NEW TEMPLATES

Microsoft sometimes makes new templates available for download from Microsoft Office Online. To see what's new and to download templates that interest you, choose Format, Slide Design to open the Slide Design task pane and scroll to the end of the design template list. The very last item in the list is Design Templates on Microsoft Office Online. Click it. Microsoft Office Online opens in your browser to the PowerPoint Design Templates page, as Figure 6.8 shows.

To preview a template, click its hyperlink. The preview appears, as Figure 6.9 shows. If you like the template, click Download Now to download it.

Figure 6.8
Download new design templates from Microsoft Office Online.

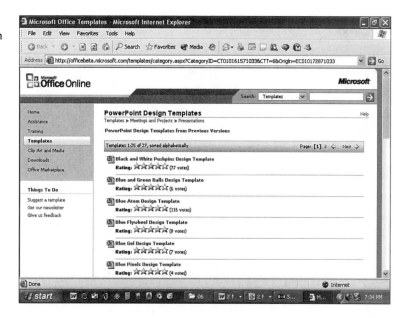

Figure 6.9
Catch a preview of the template and download it if you like it.

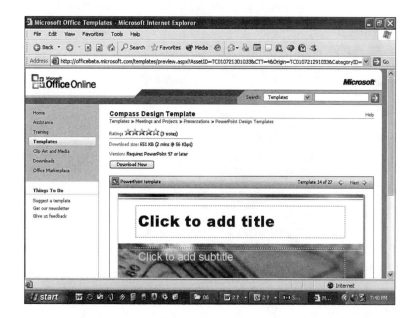

After the download finishes, PowerPoint creates a new presentation using the new template.

CHOOSING A NEW SLIDE COLOR SCHEME

Each design template includes several color schemes from which you can choose. A color scheme is a set of eight coordinated colors that applies to the following parts of your slides:

- Background
- Text and lines
- Shadows
- Title text
- Fills
- Accent
- Accent and hyperlink
- Accent and followed hyperlink

For example, you might like a basic design template but prefer to use different colors. You might want to use the same presentation for both onscreen and overhead delivery, but they require different color schemes.

APPLYING A NEW COLOR SCHEME

To apply a new color scheme to your presentation, follow these steps:

1. Click the Design button on the Formatting toolbar. The Slide Design task pane opens.
2. Click the Color Schemes link on the Slide Design task pane. The available color schemes for the design template of the current presentation appear (see Figure 6.10).

Figure 6.10
You can modify your presentation's color scheme.

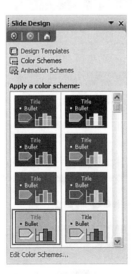

3. Select a new color scheme; PowerPoint applies it to your presentation.

→ For more information about color theory, **see** "Using Color," in Chapter 25, **p. 566**.

PREVIEWING COLOR SCHEMES

If you want to view larger previews of the available color schemes, click the down arrow to the right of any scheme and choose Show Large Previews from the shortcut menu that appears. The preview schemes roughly double in size. To go back to the normal-size previews, select this option again to remove the check mark.

APPLYING MULTIPLE COLOR SCHEMES TO A SINGLE PRESENTATION

To apply a different color scheme to selected slides, follow these steps:

1. Select the slide or slides to which you want to apply a separate color scheme.
2. Select the preview of that scheme on the Slide Design task pane.
3. Click the down arrow to the right of the selected scheme.
4. Choose Apply to Selected Slides. PowerPoint applies the color scheme only to the selected slides. The unselected slides retain the original design template.

To return to a single color scheme, select that scheme and choose Apply to All Slides from the menu that appears when you click the down arrow.

CAUTION

> Although the capability to apply multiple color schemes to your presentation adds flexibility and creativity, be sure not to overdo it. Consider carefully before applying more than one color scheme to verify that your presentation is still consistent and readable.

APPLYING A COLOR SCHEME TO NOTES AND HANDOUTS

In addition to applying a new color scheme to your actual presentation, you can also apply color schemes to notes or handouts that you create.

To apply a color scheme to notes, select View, Notes Page and then apply a color scheme from the Slide Design task pane.

To apply a color scheme to handouts, select View, Master, Handout Master and then apply a color scheme from the Slide Design task pane.

6

CREATING A CUSTOM COLOR SCHEME

Occasionally, you might want to customize the individual colors in a color scheme. For example, you might like a particular scheme but want to modify only the background color. To do this, follow these steps from the Slide Design task pane:

1. Click Edit Color Schemes to open the Edit Color Schemes dialog box with the Custom tab selected, displayed in Figure 6.11.
2. Choose the object whose color you want to change, such as the background or title text.

Figure 6.11
Change the color of certain areas of your presentation to customize it.

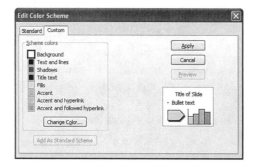

3. Click the Change Color button, which displays the dialog box in Figure 6.12. (The dialog box's name depends on the color you're changing—Background Color, Shadow Color, and so on.)

Figure 6.12
Choose a standard color or specify a custom color.

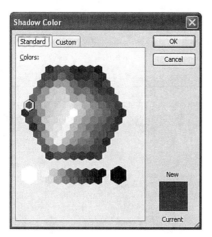

4. Choose a color from the Standard tab or formulate a custom color on the Custom tab. The New preview box compares this new color with the Current color.

→ For more details on color selection dialog boxes, **see** "Specifying Colors" in Chapter 14, "Creating and Formatting Objects," **p. 290**.

5. Click OK to return to the Edit Color Scheme dialog box.

6. Click the Preview button to preview this new color in your presentation.

7. Click Apply to apply the color scheme.

8. Click the Add As Standard Scheme button if you want to add this scheme to your selections on the Slide Design task pane (see Figure 6.13).

You can now apply this new color scheme as you would any other color scheme.

You can delete a color scheme just as easily as you created a new one. To delete a color scheme, go to the Standard tab on the Edit Color Scheme dialog box, select the scheme you no longer want, and click the Delete Scheme button.

Figure 6.13
The color scheme you created is now a standard selection.

New color scheme

APPLYING A BACKGROUND

In addition to specific color backgrounds, you can also add special background effects such as shading, patterns, textures, and pictures to your presentation. To apply a special background, choose Format, Background to open the Background dialog box, illustrated in Figure 6.14.

Figure 6.14
You can apply a special effects background to your presentation.

From the drop-down list in the Background Fill group box, you can choose

- One of the compatible colors under the Automatic color box.
- More Colors to open the Colors dialog box, in which you can select from many other colors or even specify your own custom color.

→ For more information about the Colors dialog box, **see** "Specifying Color" in Chapter 14, **p. 290**.

- Fill Effects to open the Fill Effects dialog box, where you can apply special effects such as gradients, textures, patterns, and pictures.

→ For more information about the Fill Effects dialog box, **see** "Specifying Fill Color" in Chapter 14, **p. 290**.

6

After you select the background you want, you can click the Preview button to see the effects before applying them—Apply to the current slide only or Apply to All the slides in your presentation.

USING AUTOMATIC FORMATTING

PowerPoint can perform certain formatting for you, if you like. It can format pasted items to match your design template, change the font size of some text so that it fits into its placeholder, and adjust a slide's layout to accommodate a pasted object.

In many cases, you will find these features useful. However, if you *want* a pasted item to keep its original formatting, text to keep its size, or a slide to keep its layout, you can disable these features.

USING PASTE OPTIONS

When you paste something into PowerPoint, such as text, a placeholder, or a slide, PowerPoint applies the design template's formatting to it.

Sometimes you might want a pasted item to keep its original formatting. The Paste Options button makes this possible. After you paste the item, look for the Paste Options button at the item's lower-right corner. Figure 6.15 shows a pasted item and the Paste Options button.

Figure 6.15
After you paste an item, the Paste Options button lets you control formatting.

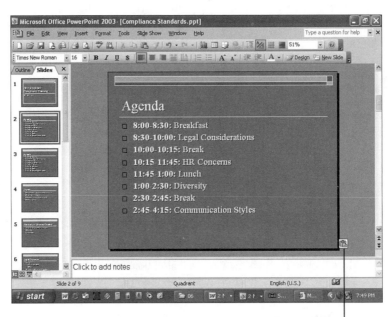

Paste Options button

Click the Paste Options button and a menu of formatting options appears (see Figure 6.16).

- **Keep Source Formatting**—Format the item as it was formatted in the place from which you copied it.

- **Use Design Template Formatting**—Apply the design template's formatting to the item (default).

- **Keep Text Only**—Removes all formatting from pasted text. Appears only when you paste text without having a text placeholder open first. PowerPoint creates a placeholder for the text as it pastes it.

Figure 6.16
Choose whether to apply the design template's formatting or keep the original formatting.

USING AUTOFIT

Sometimes, you might have slightly too much text to fit into a placeholder. AutoFit can often help by shrinking the text size until it all fits. It works as you type—as soon as your text spills outside the placeholder, AutoFit starts shrinking it. When it does, the AutoFit Options button appears next to the placeholder. Figure 6.17 shows an example.

Figure 6.17
This long agenda fits the slide nicely thanks to AutoFit.

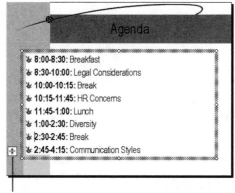

AutoFit Options button

6

TIP

AutoFit will shrink text until it's so tiny that your audience can't read it. When any text on your slide is smaller than 20 points, consider breaking the text across two slides.

NOTE

If AutoFit doesn't appear to be on, choose Tools, AutoCorrect Options and click the AutoFormat As You Type tab. If the AutoFit title text to placeholder and AutoFit body text to placeholder check boxes are empty, click them to turn AutoFit on. Then click OK.

When you click the AutoFit Options button, a menu of formatting options appears (see Figure 6.18).

Figure 6.18
The AutoFit Options menu gives you several ways to make text fit.

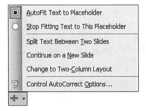

- **AutoFit Text to Placeholder**—Shrinks the text in the placeholder until it fits.

- **Stop Fitting Text to This Placeholder**—Restores the text to its original size.

- **Split Text Between Two Slides**—Creates a new slide after the current slide and moves the last half of the placeholder's text to it. Use this on a finished slide when you notice that the text is too small (less than 20 points). This item appears only in the Title and Text layout, which contains only a title placeholder and a text placeholder.

- **Continue on a New Slide**—Creates a new slide after the current slide so that you can add more text. Use this before AutoFit shrinks the text so small in the placeholder you're creating that your audience couldn't read it. This item appears only in the Title and Text layout, which contains only a title placeholder and a text placeholder.

- **Change to Two-Column Layout**—Changes the slide's layout to two columns so that you can type more text in the second column. This option is most helpful when your text is a list of short items. This item appears only in the Title and Text layout, which contains only a title placeholder and a text placeholder.

- **Control AutoCorrect Options**—Opens the AutoCorrect dialog box to the AutoFormat As You Type tab (see Figure 6.19), which you use to turn AutoFit on or off. Use the AutoFit Title Text to Placeholder check box to enable or disable AutoFit in title placeholders. Use the AutoFit Body Text to Placeholder check box to enable or disable AutoFit in text placeholders. Click OK to keep your changes.

Figure 6.19
The AutoFormat As You Type tab of the AutoCorrect dialog box lets you turn AutoFit on or off.

WORKING WITH AUTOMATIC LAYOUT

When you insert an object (a picture, a diagram, a movie clip, and so on) into a slide, PowerPoint applies a slide layout that matches the elements on your slide and makes a placeholder out of the object you inserted. When PowerPoint applies the layout, an Automatic Layout Options button appears in a lower corner of the new placeholder, as Figure 6.20 shows.

Figure 6.20
The cycle diagram is in a placeholder thanks to Automatic Layout.

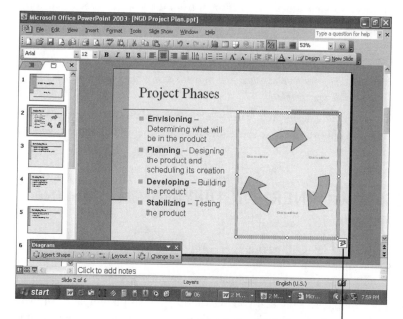

Automatic Layout Options button

When you click the Automatic Layout Options button, a short menu of options appears, as Figure 6.21 shows.

Figure 6.21
Click the Automatic Layout Options to see this menu.

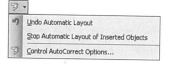

- **Undo Automatic Layout**—Removes the placeholder and places the inserted object in the center of the slide. You can then format the slide any way you want.

- **Stop Automatic Layout of Inserted Objects**—Turns off automatic layout.

- **Control AutoCorrect Options**—Opens the AutoCorrect dialog box to the AutoFormat As You Type tab (refer to Figure 6.19), which you use to turn AutoFit on or off. Use the AutoFit Title Text to Placeholder check box to enable or disable AutoFit in title placeholders. Use the AutoFit Body Text to Placeholder check box to enable or disable AutoFit in text placeholders. Click OK to keep your changes.

TROUBLESHOOTING

COPYING VERSUS CUTTING PRESENTATIONS

I thought I copied slides from one presentation to another, but now they've disappeared from my original presentation.

Be sure to use Ctrl+C (copy) rather than Ctrl+X (cut) if you want to keep the original slides in place. Moving slides removes them from their original location; copying just creates duplicates.

CONSOLIDATING DESIGN TEMPLATES

I copied slides from several other presentations to my current presentation and ended up with multiple conflicting design templates.

To use a single design template, select the template you want from the Slide Design task pane and choose Apply to All Slides from the menu that appears when you click the down arrow.

DESIGN CORNER: MODIFYING AN EXISTING DESIGN TEMPLATE

Often you'll find a design template whose basic design and concept you like, but the colors are wrong or you would like to change other design elements. In PowerPoint, it's easy to modify an existing design template to create a new one.

For example, let's say that you like the Eclipse design template, but would prefer a dark background and some other color changes and would also like to change the bullet styles. To do so, follow these steps:

1. Apply the Eclipse design template to your presentation from the Slide Design—Design Template task pane and then click the Color Schemes Hyperlink.

2. Choose a new color scheme from those that appear; PowerPoint applies it to your presentation.

3. Click the Edit Color Schemes hyperlink to open the Edit Color Schemes dialog box.

4. Choose the item whose color you want to change, such as Title Text, and click the Change Color button to open the Title Text Color dialog box.

5. Choose your new color and click OK.

6. Continue applying color changes in this manner until you're done; click Apply to close the Edit Color Scheme dialog box.

7. Select the bulleted text and choose Format, Bullets and Numbering to open the Bullets and Numbering dialog box.

8. Choose a new bullet style and click OK.

You can apply these changes only to the current presentation or save them as a new design template (choose Design Template as the file type in the Save As dialog box).

BEFORE

Figure 6.22

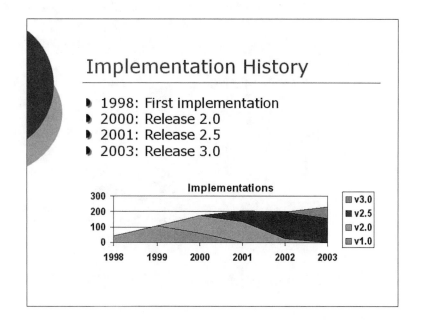

AFTER

Figure 6.23

New bullet style   Modified font colors

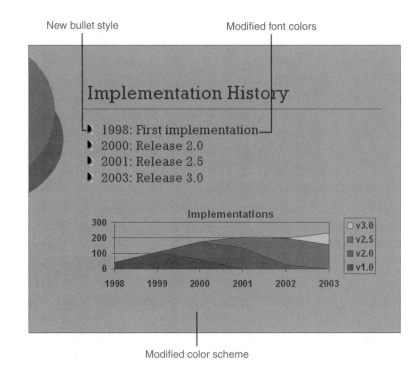

Modified color scheme

6

CHAPTER 7

COLLABORATING ON PRESENTATIONS

In this chapter   *by Patrice-Anne Rutledge and Jim Grey*

DEFINING WAYS TO COLLABORATE IN POWERPOINT

Being able to get feedback easily on a presentation you've created or work collaboratively with a group of people on a presentation is important for many organizations. PowerPoint offers features that let you collaborate electronically on creating and reviewing presentations. You can work with others on presentations in document workspaces, as well as send presentations for review and manage the feedback you receive.

WORKING ON PRESENTATIONS IN DOCUMENT WORKSPACES

A document workspace is a Microsoft Windows SharePoint Web site that contains one or more documents. This site lets a group of people work together on a presentation, share files, and hold discussions. When you collaborate on a presentation, you can work on the document workspace copy or work on your own copy (as long as you periodically save your changes to the document workspace copy).

> **NOTE**
>
> A SharePoint Web site provides access to documents throughout your organization. You can find and use documents regardless of location and format.
>
> To use document workspaces and SharePoint Web sites, you and your collaborators must be connected to a Microsoft Windows SharePoint server. You are most likely to find a SharePoint server in a corporate environment. Check with your company's network administrators to see whether a SharePoint server is available.

You interact with the document workspace using the Shared Workspace task pane, which Figure 7.1 shows. To open this task pane, choose Tools, Shared Workspace.

Figure 7.1
Use the Shared Workspace task pane to interact with document workspaces.

To create a new document workspace, type a name for it in the Document Workspace name field. Then in the Location for New Workspace field, choose the SharePoint server from the drop-down list or type its URL. Click the Create button to make the document workspace.

After you create the workspace, use this task pane's tabs to manage it:

- **Status**—This tab tells you whether the open presentation is in sync with other members' copies and whether you "checked it out" to work on it. It also tells you the document's Information Rights Management settings, which control access to the document.
- **Members**—This tab lists the users who are part of this shared workspace. You can also use this tab to invite others to join you.
- **Tasks**—This tab lists any to-dos that you share with other members of this shared workspace. You can also assign tasks to other members.
- **Documents**—This tab lists any documents you share with other members that relate to this presentation.
- **Links**—This tab lists references, either files or Web sites, helpful to the presentation.
- **Document Information**—This tab lists document properties.

REVIEWING PRESENTATIONS

There are two ways to handle sending and receiving reviews: with Microsoft Outlook and without Microsoft Outlook (by using another email program, a network server, or disks, for example). If you use Outlook, you can take advantage of special features that make collaborative reviewing easier, particularly if you want to monitor several reviewers' feedback. But you can also review without using Outlook, especially if you don't really need its added functionality.

No matter which method you use, there are four main steps to a review cycle:

1. The original author sends the presentation out for review.
2. The reviewer (or reviewers) reviews the presentation—either by making changes directly to it or by adding comments.
3. The reviewer returns the presentation to the author.
4. The original author merges the reviewed presentation(s), compares them, and finalizes the presentation.

How you use PowerPoint's reviewing features depends on both the method you choose to handle the physical review and your goals for the review process. You might only want to send your presentation to one person for review. In that case, you need to decide whether you want to use PowerPoint's advanced reviewing tools (such as the Revisions task pane) or whether you would rather just have your reviewer add comments where necessary and send the presentation back to you.

7

If, on the other hand, you want to formally track reviews or incorporate several reviewers' comments and revisions, it's helpful to use tracking tools and the Revisions task pane. In any case, PowerPoint's review features are both powerful and flexible enough to suit most requirements.

SENDING A PRESENTATION FOR REVIEW

The first step in collaborating on a PowerPoint presentation is to send the presentation out for review. Depending on the method you use to handle reviews, how you do this varies slightly.

To send a presentation for review using Outlook, follow these steps:

1. Open the presentation you want to send for review.

2. Choose File, Send To, Mail Recipient (for Review). Microsoft Outlook opens with an email ready to send (see Figure 7.2).

Figure 7.2
Your presentation is set up automatically to draw the attention of a reviewer.

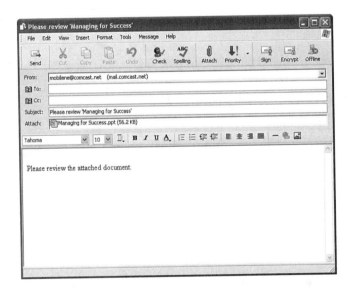

3. Enter the email address of the person to whom you want to send the presentation.

4. Type review instructions in the message area.

5. Click the Send button to send your presentation.

To create a review copy of your presentation that you can send using another email program, place on a network server, or copy to a disk, follow these steps:

1. Open the presentation you want to send out for review.

2. Choose File, Save As. The Save As dialog box opens, shown in Figure 7.3.

3. Enter a name for the review copy in the File Name field.

Figure 7.3
Save your file as a
presentation for
review.

4. Choose Presentation for Review in the Save as Type drop-down list.

5. Click Save.

From here, you can send your presentation to reviewers using your preferred method—
email, network server, or disk.

PERFORMING THE REVIEW

What happens during the actual review depends on a number of things: the methodology
the author communicated to the reviewers, the amount of change required, the kind of
review (quick glance versus detailed content analysis), and each reviewer's preferences.

In PowerPoint, reviewers can either make changes to the presentation itself or add comments about individual slides in the presentation. If a reviewer revises the actual presentation, the author will be able to use the Revisions task pane to determine what changes were
made. If the reviewer uses comments, they appear as yellow boxes on the screen. When a
reviewer changes the actual content of a presentation, PowerPoint tracks these changes.
Table 7.1 lists the kinds of changes PowerPoint tracks, in addition to the actual text itself.

TABLE 7.1   REVIEW CHANGES POWERPOINT TRACKS

Change	Description
Presentation-level changes	Slide size Content and list of named shows Headers and footers for slides, title slides, and notes
Slide-level changes	Color scheme Animation settings List of shapes Slide master IDs and locked templates Slide master list of color schemes, default text styles, background, and objects Slide transition and layout Headers and footers

7

TABLE 7.1	CONTINUED
Change	**Description**
Shape-level changes	Action settings Recolor information External objects
Paragraph-level changes	Bullet typeface, color, size, animation schemes, margins, and tabs Paragraph indent, alignment, direction, margin, and tabs East Asian word wrap and alignment settings
Text-level changes	Font typeface, color, and size Languages Hyperlinks

USING THE REVIEWING TOOLBAR

The Reviewing toolbar offers features that are useful both to reviewers and to authors reconciling reviews. Depending on the stage of the review cycle and the review activity you're performing, some of the Reviewing toolbar buttons might be unavailable or hidden.

The Reviewing toolbar displays automatically during certain reviewing activities, such as adding comments or reconciling reviews. You can also open it manually by choosing View, Toolbars, Reviewing.

Table 7.2 lists the buttons on the Reviewing toolbar and explains how they're used.

TABLE 7.2	REVIEWING TOOLBAR BUTTONS	
Button	**Name**	**Description**
	Markup	Toggles the display of comments and changes on and off
Reviewers...	Reviewers	Lets you select the reviews and comments of specific reviewers
	Previous Item	Moves to the previous comment in a presentation
	Next Item	Moves to the next comment in a presentation
	Apply	Lets you apply the current change, all changes on the current slide, or all changes in the current presentation
	Unapply	Lets you unapply the current change, all changes on the current slide, or all changes in the current presentation
	Insert Comment	Inserts a comment box on a slide

TABLE 7.2	**CONTINUED**	

Button	Name	Description
	Edit Comment	Lets you edit a selected comment
	Delete Comment	Deletes a selected comment or marker, all comments and markers on the current slide, or all comments and markers in the presentation
	Revisions task pane	Opens and closes the Revisions task pane

 Can't find buttons on the Reviewing toolbar? See the "Troubleshooting" section at the end of the chapter.

ADDING COMMENTS TO SLIDES

When you want to write a note to the author explaining changes you think should be made, use comments.

NOTE

> Comments aren't the same as notes. You add comments within a presentation to provide input on specific slides. You usually delete comments after you read them and update your presentation. Notes are information you keep with your presentation to provide additional information as you speak.

→ For details on creating notes, **see** "Creating Notes and Handouts" in Chapter 10, "Creating and Printing Presentation Materials," **p. 200**.

To add a comment to a slide, click the Insert Comment button on the Reviewing toolbar or choose Insert, Comment. If it isn't already open, the Reviewing toolbar appears when you insert a comment.

→ To learn more about the buttons on the Reviewing toolbar, **see** "Using the Reviewing Toolbar" in this chapter, **p. 140**.

A yellow box appears at the top-left corner of your slide; your name appears as the reviewer. Figure 7.4 illustrates a sample comment box.

NOTE

> You can't add a comment in Slide Sorter view.

7

Figure 7.4
Comments provide a way to get feedback on your presentation.

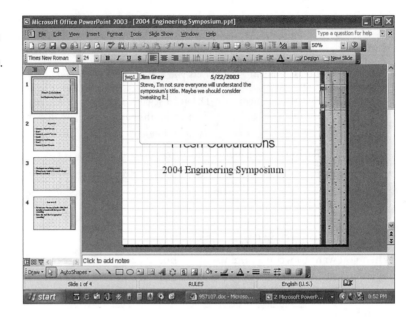

PowerPoint places all general comments in the upper-left corner of the slide. If you add more than one comment to the slide, it appears on top of the existing comment, covering most of it. You can move the comment from its default location by selecting it and dragging it with the mouse.

You can also attach a comment to a selected element on the slide. For example, you could create a comment about the overall content that appears in the top-left corner and then attach individual comments to selected text or a selected graphic object as well.

Enter your comments in the yellow box, which expands to fit the length of your comment.

To change the reviewer name, choose Tools, Options, and enter a new name in the User Information group box on the General tab.

REVIEWING COMMENTS

If you don't plan to use the Revisions task pane to review comments in a presentation, you can use the Reviewing toolbar to move from comment to comment, evaluating each comment as you progress. To review comments, click the Markup button on the Reviewing toolbar if comments don't appear.

 Don't want comments to appear in your presentation? See the "Troubleshooting" section at the end of the chapter.

In general, comments should be apparent because of their yellow color. Still, in a long presentation, it can be easier to jump to the next comment rather than look at each slide. To do this, click the Next Item button on the Reviewing toolbar.

NOTE

> To jump back to a previous comment and look at it again, click the Previous Item button.

NOTE

> When you reach the end of a presentation, clicking the Next Item button brings you back to the presentation's first comment.

After you read a comment, you might want to delete it. To do so, select it and click the Delete Comment button on the Reviewing toolbar.

SENDING BACK THE REVIEW

After entering all comments and changes, the reviewer sends the presentation back to the author for final reconciliation. A reviewer who received a presentation through Outlook can send it back by choosing File, Send To, Original Sender from within PowerPoint.

If the reviewer uses a version of PowerPoint other than PowerPoint 2003 or PowerPoint 2002 to perform the review, choose File, Send To, Mail Recipient (as Attachment) to return the presentation to the author.

Unless instructed otherwise, reviewers receiving a presentation as an email attachment, on a network, or on a disk should save the presentation and return it to the author in the same way it was received.

RECONCILING REVIEWS

If you're the author of a presentation, the final step includes merging the reviews, checking the comments and changes of all reviewers, accepting or rejecting their suggestions using the Revisions task pane or Reviewing toolbar, and saving your final presentation.

TIP

> No one right way exists to handle the review and reconciliation process. You can use a combination of features on the Revisions task pane List and Gallery tabs and on the Reviewing toolbar to complete your presentation.

COMPARING AND MERGING PRESENTATIONS

If you're using Outlook to do revisions, open the email that contains the reviewed presentation, double-click it, and click Yes in the prompt dialog box that asks whether you want to merge this presentation. PowerPoint merges this presentation with the original.

If you're using another email program, a network server, or a disk to handle reviews, follow these steps:

7

1. Open the original presentation in PowerPoint.

2. Choose Tools, Compare and Merge Presentations. The Choose Files to Merge with Current Presentation dialog box opens (see Figure 7.5).

Figure 7.5
Comparing and merging your presentation lets you see all reviewers' comments in the same place.

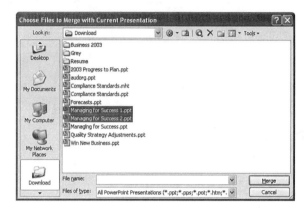

3. Select a file (or files) to merge and click the Merge button. The presentations are merged, and the Revisions task pane opens. Other buttons can be added to the Reviewing toolbar.

USING THE REVISIONS TASK PANE TO RECONCILE REVIEWS

The Revisions task pane lets you view and reconcile the comments and changes of multiple reviewers. It should appear automatically when you compare and merge presentations, but you can also open it manually by choosing View, Toolbars, Revisions Task Pane. Figure 7.6 illustrates the Revisions task pane.

The List tab displays color-coded comments and changes for each reviewer. To see those for specific reviewers, select them from the Reviewers drop-down list. The default is to display the comments of all reviewers.

On the List tab, you can click an individual comment to view it and then click the Delete Comment button on the Reviewing toolbar to remove it from your presentation. Depending on the contents of the comment, you might want to make additional changes to your presentation. If the comment is informational only ("Great presentation"), you can continue to the next review item.

On the List tab, you can also click a change marker to display its contents and click in the check boxes if you want to accept the changes. You can also hover the mouse over a change marker on your slide to view the proposed change. Then click on that change marker to display the menu with check boxes for accepting changes (or in some cases, an individual change).

To move to the next slide, click the Next button on the pane. To go back to a previous slide, click Previous.

Comment   Change marker

Figure 7.6
Use the Revisions task
pane to look at
reviewers' changes
and accept or reject
them.

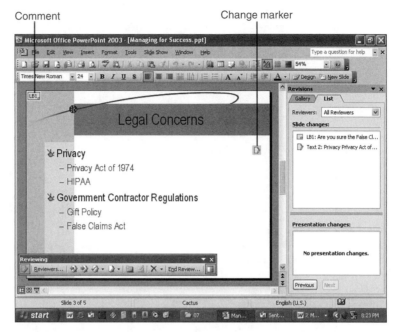

On the Gallery tab, you view thumbnails of the changed slides by reviewer.

On this tab, you can click the check box next to the name of a reviewer to apply all changes suggested by that reviewer. You can click the down arrow next to the thumbnail to view a list of other options, including the ability to apply changes, unapply changes, view only a specific reviewer's changes, preview animation, or tell PowerPoint that you're done with that reviewer.

TROUBLESHOOTING

HIDING COMMENTS

I don't want to see comments on my slides, but I don't want to delete them, either.

If you don't want to delete your comments, you can hide them so that they don't appear on a slide. To do so, click the Markup button on the Reviewing toolbar. Comments don't appear in a slideshow.

LOCATING MISSING BUTTONS

The button I need doesn't appear on the Reviewing toolbar.

Many of the buttons on the Reviewing toolbar appear as a result of an action in the review process. For example, you might need to open a presentation for review to activate some buttons or merge presentations to view others. If you can't find the button you want, be sure that you've completed the prerequisite steps to get where you want to be in the review process.

CHAPTER 8

USING SPEECH AND HANDWRITING RECOGNITION

In this chapter   *by Patrice-Anne Rutledge and Jim Grey*

UNDERSTANDING SPEECH AND HANDWRITING RECOGNITION

8

All Office applications include speech and handwriting recognition, sharing it with Internet Explorer and Outlook Express. Using speech recognition, you can dictate the content of PowerPoint slides or use voice commands to perform basic tasks such as formatting text. Speech recognition uses a speech recognition engine. Microsoft currently offers three engines: one in U.S. English, one in Japanese, and one in Simplified Chinese.

NOTE

> If you're a native speaker of English from a country other than the United States (such as the U.K. or Australia) or if English is your second language, the speech recognition engine might not work as well for you because it's trained to recognize American accents.

Using handwriting recognition, you can "write" using a handwriting input device, such as pen stylus and tablet (or even your mouse, although a tablet works much better), and have your written text transcribed into typed text in PowerPoint. Handwriting recognition needs a handwriting recognition engine. Microsoft currently offers five engines, in U.S. English, Japanese, Simplified Chinese, Traditional Chinese, and Korean.

The uses and advantages of both speech and handwriting recognition are numerous, with the most important being the ability to cut down on keyboard and mouse time while still remaining productive. These tools are an acquired taste, however, and might take some time to get used to. If you're interested in seeing how they could assist in your own productivity, it's worthwhile—and fun—to at least give them a try. Remember though, that speech and handwriting recognition can't be a complete substitute for working with a keyboard and mouse. They're most effective when working in conjunction with these traditional tools.

LOOKING AT HARDWARE AND SOFTWARE REQUIREMENTS

Office's speech and handwriting recognition tools have specific hardware and software requirements. They also have specific minimum requirements in terms of computer speed and memory.

CAUTION

> Although you might be able to activate speech and handwriting recognition tools with less than the minimum specified requirements, their performance will be problematic or unreliable.

To use speech recognition, you'll need

- A close-talk headset microphone with gain adjustment support to modify microphone amplification for appropriate sound recognition. Microsoft recommends a microphone that plugs in to a USB (universal serial bus) port on your computer.

- A 400MHz or faster computer.

- At least 128MB of memory.

- Internet Explorer 5.0 or later.

To use handwriting recognition, you'll need

- A 75MHz or faster computer

- 24MB of memory or more with Windows 98 or ME; 40MB of memory or more with Windows NT 4.0 or later

- As a writing tool, a mouse (minimum) or a handwriting input device such as a pen stylus and tablet connected through a serial or USB port (recommended)

INSTALLING SPEECH AND HANDWRITING RECOGNITION

To install speech recognition automatically, choose Tools, Speech from the menu bar and then proceed with the step-by-step setup guidance. To install handwriting recognition, you'll need to return to the Office setup CD. You can also install speech recognition from this setup CD.

→ For a more in-depth explanation to set up the speech recognition feature, **see** "Setting Up Speech Recognition" later in this chapter, **p. 150**.

To install these features from the Office CD, follow these steps:

1. Insert the Office Setup CD in your CD-ROM drive to reopen the Microsoft Office Setup dialog box (see Figure 8.1).

Figure 8.1
You can add or remove speech and handwriting recognition features.

8

2. Select the Add or Remove Features option button, and click Next to continue.

3. Click the Choose Advanced Customization of Applications check box and click Next.

4. Click the plus sign next to Office Shared Features and then the plus sign next to Alternative User Input.

5. Click the down arrow next to Microsoft Handwriting Component and choose Run from My Computer from the menu that appears. Figure 8.2 illustrates both speech and handwriting recognition installed.

Figure 8.2
Running these features from your computer means that they're installed.

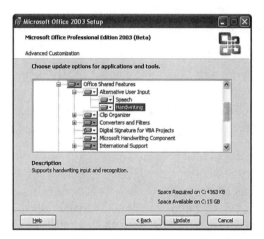

NOTE

> If you want to uninstall either of these features, choose Not Available from the menu.

6. Click the Update button to update your system with the selected changes.

After you install speech and handwriting recognition, it's available in all Office applications.

SETTING UP SPEECH RECOGNITION

Before you can set up speech recognition, you need to verify that both your microphone and speakers are connected and work properly. Because the specific hardware you're using will vary, consult the manual that came with your microphone and speakers if you have any issues regarding setting them up. After you connect your hardware, you're ready to begin. Position the microphone to the side about an inch from your mouth; close enough to hear your words, but not so close as to hear your breath.

Setting up speech recognition is essentially a two-step process: Configure your microphone, and complete a voice training session so that PowerPoint recognizes your speech when you dictate or issue voice commands. Although you can perform these steps separately or go back to make adjustments, PowerPoint walks you through the entire process step-by-step the first time you use speech recognition.

To set up speech recognition for the first time, follow these steps:

1. In the Language toolbar, which appeared when you installed speech recognition, click the Speech Tools button and choose Options. The Welcome dialog box appears. Click Next to continue.

2. From the Microsoft Wizard Welcome dialog box, click Next to continue to the first step of the Microphone Wizard, shown in Figure 8.3.

Figure 8.3
The Microphone Wizard walks you through microphone setup step by step.

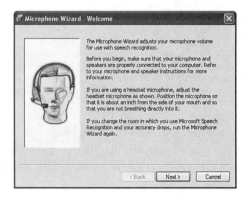

3. Follow the instructions in the wizard, shown in Figure 8.4, reading the sentence indicated to test the microphone volume. Click Next to continue.

Figure 8.4
Adjust your microphone using the Microphone Wizard.

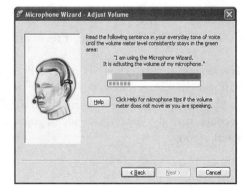

NOTE

To readjust the microphone at a later time, return to the Speech Recognition tab of the Speech Properties dialog box and click the Configure Microphone button.

8

4. If you use a headset microphone, follow the instructions in the wizard, reading the sentence indicated to test the positioning of the microphone. (If you don't have a headset microphone, you can skip this step.) Click Finish to continue to the Voice Training series of steps. Figure 8.5 illustrates the first step.

Figure 8.5
Voice training helps the speech recognition engine get used to your voice.

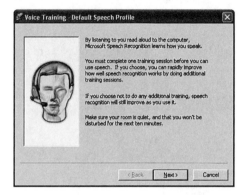

5. Continue through the voice training steps, carefully following the detailed instructions and tips on the screen as you read sample text that the speech recognition engine will record and analyze. Be sure that you're in a quiet room and the microphone is positioned correctly.

NOTE

If you want to do additional voice training, click the More Training button before you finish.

6. When you reach the final step, click Finish to close the dialog box.

Now that you've set up speech recognition, you can use it in PowerPoint or any other Office application. You can start using the speech tools right away or make further customizations based on how you plan to use this feature. But first, you should get acquainted with the Language bar, which contains all the buttons and menus you'll need to access both speech and handwriting recognition tools.

USING THE LANGUAGE BAR

After you install speech or handwriting recognition, the Language bar automatically appears. With this toolbar, shown in Figure 8.6, you can use and customize Office's speech and handwriting recognition tools.

Figure 8.6
The Language bar provides all the buttons and menus you'll need.

The Language bar is also available if you activate an *IME* (*input method editor*, used to enter Asian characters). Microsoft refers to speech and handwriting recognition, IMEs, and alternative keyboard layouts as *text services*.

The exact buttons that display can vary, according to the text services you've installed and the Office applications you have running. For example, if you have both Word and PowerPoint open and are currently using Word, the Correction button appears on the Language bar. Switch to PowerPoint, and this button disappears from the Language bar.

TIP

> Text services are very memory intensive and can hurt your computer's performance, particularly if you don't have a state-of-the-art system. If you aren't planning to use a specific text service, remove it for best system performance.

→ To learn more about removing a text service, **see** "Adding and Removing Text Services" later in this chapter, **p. 155**.

To move the floating Language bar, pause the mouse over the vertical bar on the left side of the Language bar and drag it.

SPECIFYING LANGUAGE BAR OPTIONS

You can set a variety of Language bar options from the menu that appears when you right-click the Language bar. These include

- **Minimize**—Minimizes the Language bar so that it remains open but is out of the way and appears as an icon in the taskbar. You can also click the Language bar's Minimize button (upper-right corner of the bar) to minimize in one step.

NOTE

> To restore the Language bar, click the Language bar icon in the taskbar and then choose Show the Language Bar from the menu that appears.

- **Text labels**—Serves as a toggle to add or remove text labels on the Language bar. Text labels (the default) are an advantage if you're unfamiliar with the Language bar, but they do take up additional space. Figure 8.7 illustrates the Language bar with traditional toolbar buttons rather than text labels.

8

Figure 8.7
If you're familiar with the Language bar, you might not need text labels.

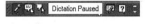

- **Vertical**—Displays the toolbar vertically, instead of horizontally.

- **Additional icons in taskbar**—Places icons for specific text services directly on the taskbar, for easy access without displaying the Language bar on the desktop. Simply click the taskbar icon to perform the specific service, such as speech and handwriting recognition.

- **Settings**—Opens the Text Services and Input Languages dialog box, from which you can add and remove services, change service properties, and change Language bar properties and set keystrokes that let you change languages on-the-fly.

- **Close the Language bar**—Closes the Language bar and removes it from the desktop. If you installed an IME, you can't close the Language bar. However, you can still minimize it to get it out of the way.

To reopen the Language bar after closing it, choose Start, Control Panel (or, if you use something other than Windows XP, choose Start, Settings, Control Panel) and then double-click the Regional and Language Options icon. In the Regional and Language Options dialog box, click the Languages tab. In the Text services and input languages area, click the Details button. In the Text Services and Input Languages dialog box, click the Language Bar button and click the Show the Language Bar on the Desktop check box.

CAUTION

> Closing the Language bar isn't the same thing as removing specific text services; these services will remain installed and continue to take up computer memory unless you remove them.

SPECIFYING TEXT SERVICES SETTINGS

Click the Settings option from the Language bar menu to open the Text Services and Input Languages dialog box, shown in Figure 8.8.

Here, you can select your default input language and access other text services options.

→ For more information on speech recognition engines in other languages, **see** "Changing to Another Speech Recognition Engine" later in this chapter, **p. 165**.

Figure 8.8
You can add and
remove text services
in this dialog box.

8

ADDING AND REMOVING TEXT SERVICES

In the Installed services group box, you can add and remove installed text services for the language you selected in the Default Input Language drop-down list. If you don't plan to use a specific text service, you should remove it here because each installed service uses valuable computer memory, which can slow down your system. To add a text service, click the Add button to open the Add Input Language dialog box, shown in Figure 8.9.

Figure 8.9
Select the specific text
service you want to
add.

Select the Input Language from the drop-down list and then click the check box for the text service you want to add (Keyboard Layout/IME, Handwriting Recognition, or Speech). Choose the specific option or component you want from the drop-down list and then click OK to close the dialog box. If certain options are grayed out, they're either installed already or aren't available.

To remove a text service, select it from the Installed Services list on the Text Services dialog box and then click the Remove button.

CAUTION

You can't remove all text services; at least one must remain.

8

SPECIFYING LANGUAGE BAR SETTINGS

Click the Language Bar button to open the Language Bar Settings dialog box, shown in Figure 8.10.

Figure 8.10
You can further customize the Language bar.

In this dialog box, you can select

- **Show the Language Bar on the Desktop**—Displays the Language bar on the desktop. Selected by default.

- **Show the Language Bar as Transparent when Inactive**—Lets you view what's behind the Language bar when it appears on the desktop.

- **Show Additional Language Bar Icons in the Taskbar**—Places icons for available text services on the taskbar.

- **Show Text Labels on the Language Bar**—Displays text labels on all Language bar buttons, making it easier to decipher the Language bar's icons, but also increasing the Language bar's size. Selected by default.

NOTE
> If you choose not to display text labels on the Language bar, pause the mouse pointer over the button to view a ScreenTip with the button's label.

VIEWING ADDITIONAL LANGUAGE BAR SETTINGS

You can view additional options from the Language Bar Options menu. To view this menu, click the Options down arrow on the Language bar. (It's the small down arrow on the lower right of the bar.) From this menu, you can add or remove Language Bar buttons (a check mark indicates that a button appears on the bar), click Settings to open the Text Services dialog box (refer to Figure 8.8), or click Restore Defaults to restore the Language bar to its default settings.

CAUTION
> Restoring defaults only restores Language Bar buttons, not any changes you made to text labels or Language bar transparency. You must change these separately.

DISPLAYING LANGUAGE BAR MESSAGES

You can display informational messages on the Language bar that provide help as you work with speech recognition tools. The messages vary, depending on the tool and mode you're using. For example, the message balloon could tell you that you're speaking too softly for Dictation mode to understand your words or let you know that you're currently dictating (see Figure 8.11).

Figure 8.11
Let Language bar messages provide helpful tips.

Language bar message

To activate these messages if they don't already appear, click the Tools button on the Language bar, choose Options, click Show Speech Messages in the Speech Input Settings dialog box, and then click OK. To hide the speech messages, repeat these steps, making sure that the Show Speech Messages check box is empty before you click OK.

USING SPEECH RECOGNITION

Before you begin using speech recognition, be sure to place your mouse pointer in a location that can accept text, such as a bulleted list or other text area on a slide. To improve accuracy, talk in a consistent, even tone. Speaking too slowly or quickly can decrease the level of recognition. Also, don't stop and start. Pauses and gaps make it harder to recognize your speech.

USING DICTATION MODE

To dictate text using the speech recognition engine, follow these steps:

1. Click the Microphone button on the Language bar to turn on the microphone.
2. Click the Dictation button on the Language bar (or say "dictation") to activate speech recognition.
3. Dictate your text into the microphone.

Of course, getting dictation to work exactly as you want it to is more complicated than 1-2-3, but the basic premise is really quite simple. When you're finished dictating, be sure to turn off the microphone; the speech recognition engine will continue to record your words until you do so.

NOTE

You can use Dictation mode with the Ask a Question box. Simply place the insertion point in the box and dictate your question.

8

 Problems getting your microphone to recognize your speech? *See the "Troubleshooting" section near the end of the chapter.*

DICTATING PUNCTUATION

During dictation, you'll probably need to add some form of punctuation or a special character to your text. You can do this easily using one of the many dictation commands the speech recognition engine recognizes. For example, if you want to place a period at the end of a bullet point, just say "period." If you want to include a Web address, the engines will know what you mean when you say "dot." Table 8.1 lists the most common dictation commands.

TABLE 8.1 SAMPLE DICTATION COMMANDS

Say	Result
Ampersand	&
Asterisk	*
At	@
Colon	:
Comma	,
Dot	.
Exclamation point	!
Period	.
Question mark	?
Semicolon	;
Backslash	\
Slash	/
Vertical bar		
Hyphen	-
Double dash	--
Equals	=
Plus	+
Pound sign	#
Percent	%
Dollar sign	$
Underscore	_
Tilde	~
Ellipsis	...

8

Say	Result
Greater than	>
Less than	<
Caret	^
New line	Enter
New paragraph	Enter twice
Left bracket	[
Right bracket	]
Left brace	{
Right brace	}
Left parenthesis	(
Right parenthesis	)
Open quote	"
Close quote	"
Open single quote	'
Close single quote	'

DICTATING NUMBERS

If you're going to dictate numbers using Dictation mode, here are a few things to keep in mind. The speech recognition engine

- Spells out numbers from one to 20
- Inserts numbers greater than 20 as digits
- Inserts fractions as digits (one-fourth becomes ¼)
- Recognizes a series of seven numbers as a telephone number and formats it as such (555-1234)
- Lets you insert all numbers as digits if you say "forcenum" before saying the numbers

SPELLING OUT UNCOMMON WORDS

At times, the speech recognition engine simply won't be able to recognize what you say. This is particularly common when you say the name of a company, product, or person or use specific industry jargon. In these circumstances, you can quickly spell out the word or words you want to dictate. To do so, say "spelling mode" and then begin spelling letter by letter. Another option is to add these common words to the speech recognition dictionary.

→ To learn how to add words to the dictionary, **see** "Adding Words to the Speech Recognition Dictionary" later in this chapter, **p. 165**.

CORRECTING SPEECH RECOGNITION ERRORS

As you know, Office's speech recognition tools might accurately recognize only 80% to 95% of your speech. To fix errors, you have two choices:

- Select the error (either a single word or section of text) and repeat your dictation.
- Manually fix the error using the keyboard.

USING VOICE COMMAND MODE

Voice command functionality has a variety of uses. You can use voice commands to say the name of

- An active toolbar button to perform its command. For example, you could say "save" to save the presentation you're currently working on or "bold" to apply a bold format to selected text. If you're not sure of the name of a toolbar button, pause the mouse over it to display its ScreenTip.
- A menu to open it. For example, say "insert" to open the Insert menu. From there, you can say the name of the menu item you want to choose or say "expand" instead of clicking on the double down arrows to view additional menu options.
- A dialog box tab to move to that tab.
- A dialog box option to select it. For check boxes, saying its name again acts as a toggle to remove the check mark.
- A hyperlink in a task pane to activate it.
- A punctuation command, such as comma, period, or colon, to enter the symbol for that command.
- The individual letters of words that the speech recognition engine would have trouble recognizing (say "spelling mode" before doing this).

NOTE

> To create a new blank presentation from the New Presentation task pane, say "new file."

→ For more information on spelling mode, **see** "Spelling Out Uncommon Words" earlier in this chapter, **p. 159**.

ISSUING VOICE COMMANDS

To activate voice commands, first verify that your microphone is on and then click the Voice Command button on the Language bar (or say "voice command"). If you were in Dictation mode, PowerPoint no longer transcribes your words as dictation, but instead understands them as commands. Try out all the suggested ways to use voice commands to determine which ones will help in your own personal productivity. You can control a great deal of PowerPoint's functionality with voice commands, but you'll probably need to experiment for a while to learn how to use this new way of working more effectively.

EXPLORING VOICE COMMANDS

You can also use voice commands to navigate within PowerPoint in addition to controlling menus, toolbars, and fields in dialog boxes and task panes. Table 8.2 lists some additional voice commands to try.

TABLE 8.2   SAMPLE VOICE COMMANDS

Say	Result
New line	Moves to the next line
New paragraph	Starts a new paragraph
Microphone off	Turns off the microphone
Tab	Tabs once
Enter	Presses the Enter key
Spelling mode	Enters spelling mode, enabling you to spell out difficult words letter by letter
Forcenum	Enters a numeral rather than spelling the actual word (for example, "three" becomes "3")
Right-click	Right-clicks the current object (to display a menu, for example)
Backspace	Deletes the previous character
Last word	Moves to the last word
Space	Inserts a space
Escape	Presses ESC
Up	Moves up one line
Down	Moves down one line
Left	Moves left one character
Right	Moves right one character
Previous Page	Moves to the previous page
Next Page	Moves to the next page
Page Down	Moves down one page
Page Up	Moves up one page

CUSTOMIZING SPEECH RECOGNITION

After you've tried using speech recognition to dictate and issue voice commands, you might decide that you want to customize it a bit. For example, you could create an additional profile for another location in which you work, customize audio settings, add words to the speech recognition dictionary, or perform additional voice training.

8

TIP

> If you're the only person using your computer, you might not think multiple profiles would be useful. But if you're mobile and work in a variety of locations—home, office, in the field, and so forth—creating a profile for each location can help increase accuracy. Even if you're working in a very temporary location such as a hotel room, it's worthwhile to create a new profile if you're planning to use speech recognition.

WORKING WITH SPEECH RECOGNITION PROFILES

A recognition profile stores the speech data—records and analyzes when you do voice training. When you set up speech recognition for the first time, PowerPoint automatically records your speech in the default user profile. If you're the only person using speech recognition on your computer and you use your computer in only one location, this might be the only recognition profile you need.

You can, however, create multiple profiles in PowerPoint. This is useful if more than one person uses your computer, but it can also be useful if you want to use speech recognition with different microphones or in different environments (for example, if you have a notebook computer and work in a variety of locations). Creating a separate profile of your speech under each of these conditions helps ensure that the speech recognition tools take these environmental changes into consideration as well.

CREATING A NEW SPEECH RECOGNITION PROFILE

If you want to create a recognition profile other than the default profile, follow these steps:

1. Click the Tools button on the Language bar, and choose Options from the submenu that appears. The Speech Input Settings dialog box opens. Click the Advanced Speech button. The Speech Properties dialog box opens, as shown in Figure 8.12.

Figure 8.12
Adding a new speech recognition profile is just one of the tasks you can perform in the Speech Properties dialog box.

2. On the Speech Recognition tab, click the New button. Figure 8.13 illustrates the Profile Wizard dialog box that opens.

Figure 8.13
Give your new profile a name.

3. Enter your name in the Profile text box. If you're creating multiple profiles of your speech in different environments, you could enter something like "Pat Smith—Office."

4. Click Next to continue to the first step of the Microphone Wizard.

5. Continue on from step 3 in the earlier section "Setting Up Speech Recognition" to complete setup, which is nearly identical to setting up your first speech recognition profile (the default user).

MODIFYING RECOGNITION PROFILE SETTINGS

To modify recognition profile settings, click the Settings button on the Speech Recognition tab of the Speech Properties dialog box. The Recognition Profile Settings dialog box will open, shown in Figure 8.14.

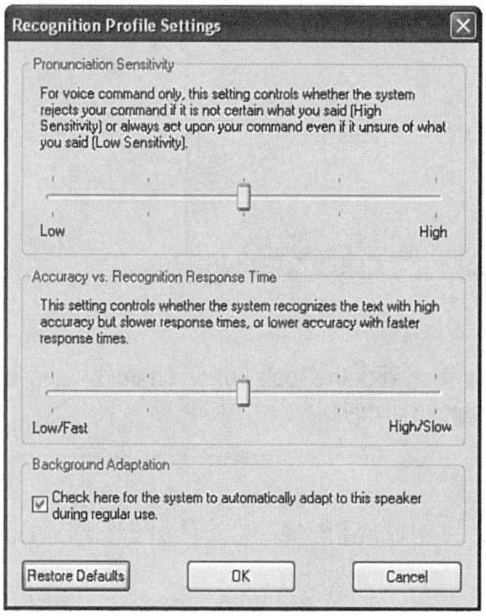

Figure 8.14
Customizing settings is another option.

8

In this dialog box, you can set specifications on pronunciation sensitivity and accuracy versus recognition response time, as well as choose to have the system automatically adapt to your voice to increase accuracy.

To restore your default settings, click the Restore Defaults button.

DELETING A SPEECH RECOGNITION PROFILE

To delete an existing recognition profile, return to the Speech Recognition tab of the Speech Properties dialog box. Select the profile you want to delete from the Recognition Profiles group box and click the Delete button.

PERFORMING ADDITIONAL VOICE TRAINING

You can perform additional voice training when you set up speech recognition by clicking the More Training button before you complete the setup process. You also can return at a later time to do additional training. The more samples Office has of your voice, the better it recognizes your speech. You don't need to do all the training at once, however. It's often a good idea to do the initial training, see how accurate your results are when you use the speech recognition tools, and then go back and do more training.

To continue with additional voice training at a later time, click the Tools button on the Language bar and choose Training from the submenu. The Voice Training dialog box shown in Figure 8.15 opens for the current user. Here you can choose from additional training sessions.

Figure 8.15
Additional voice training helps increase your accuracy.

NOTE

> To change the current user, click the Tools button on the Language bar and then choose a user from the Current User menu.

At first, your accuracy might only be around 85%–90%, but after additional training it should increase to around 95%.

ADDING WORDS TO THE SPEECH RECOGNITION DICTIONARY

You can add unusual words that might not be in Office's speech recognition dictionary. This is particularly useful if you want to add proper names, company names, or industry terms—anything unusual that might not be in the standard dictionary. To add and delete words to this dictionary, follow these steps:

1. Click the Tools button on the Language bar.
2. Click Add/Delete Word(s) to open the Add/Delete Word(s) dialog box, shown in Figure 8.16.

Figure 8.16
Add uncommon or unfamiliar words to the dictionary.

3. Enter the word you want to add to the dictionary in the Word text box.
4. Click the Record Pronunciation button and speak the word into the microphone. When the speech recognition engine recognizes the word, it adds it to the dictionary list.
5. To delete a word from the dictionary, select it in the list and click the Delete button.

NOTE

> To spell out an unfamiliar word, say "spelling mode" when you're in Dictation or Voice Command mode and then spell the word letter by letter.

CHANGING TO ANOTHER SPEECH RECOGNITION ENGINE

If you plan to use speech recognition in more than one language, you need to switch speech recognition engines. To do so, follow these steps:

1. Click the Tools button on the Language bar and choose Options from the submenu that appears. Then click the Advanced Speech button. The Speech Properties dialog box opens (refer to Figure 8.12).

8

2. On the Speech Recognition tab, choose the alternative engine from the Language drop-down list. If you're speaking U.S. English, the default engine will be Microsoft English (U.S.) v6.1 Recognizer.

3. Click OK to close the dialog box.

You'll need to restart PowerPoint for this change to take effect.

CHANGING TO ANOTHER SPEECH RECOGNITION PROFILE

If you've created multiple speech recognition profiles, you need to switch to the appropriate profile before using PowerPoint's speech recognition tools. To change profiles, click the Tools button on the Language bar, choose Current User, and then select the profile you want to use. The submenu displays all profiles you've recorded (default, those for other users, those for other environments such as office or home, and so forth).

ADJUSTING AUDIO INPUT SETTINGS

On the Speech Recognition tab of the Speech Properties dialog box, you can adjust your microphone's audio input settings by clicking the Audio Input button. Figure 8.17 shows the Audio Input Settings dialog box.

Figure 8.17
Adjust audio input
settings if you like.

On this dialog box, you can choose the preferred (default) audio input device or select an alternative device from the drop-down list.

NOTE

> To choose an audio input line, click the Properties button. To adjust the volume, click the Volume button. Unless you have advanced knowledge of audio systems or settings, you'll probably want to use the defaults.

USING HANDWRITING RECOGNITION

Using handwriting recognition, you can enter text on your PowerPoint slides and in other Office applications without using a keyboard. You'll have best success if you use a pen stylus and a tablet, although you can probably manage a few words here or there with your mouse. Either way, you can write out your content and let Office convert it to text onscreen. This is useful for people who need to limit their use of the keyboard and for those who just don't like to type.

Office's handwriting recognition engine doesn't require any training. You can start using it as soon as you install the feature. Handwriting recognition tools include several components:

- A Writing Pad, which lets you "write" text in a window with a lined note pad.

NOTE

> In Japanese and Chinese, you'll use the Boxed Input window rather than the Writing Pad.

- The Write Anywhere window, which lets you write anywhere on your screen.
- A Drawing Pad that's available only with Microsoft Word or Outlook. You'll still see the Drawing Pad option available in menus and on toolbars within PowerPoint, but you won't be able to activate the window until you switch to a program that supports it.
- Onscreen keyboards for entering text and symbols (such as foreign language characters). These keyboards are meant for touch-screen computers. You can use them with a mouse if you want, but they're not very practical that way.

You can access these components by clicking the Handwriting button on the Language bar and then choosing the appropriate component from the drop-down menu.

USING WRITING PAD

To open the Writing Pad window, click the Writing Pad button on the Language bar, or say "writing pad." If you don't see the Writing Pad button, click the Handwriting button and choose Writing Pad from the menu that appears. Figure 8.18 illustrates the Writing Pad.

Figure 8.18
The Writing Pad lets you write text on an onscreen note pad.

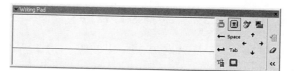

Position the insertion point where you want to insert the text on your PowerPoint slide. Using either your handwriting input device or your mouse, "write" the text you want to enter on the solid line in the Writing Pad. The handwriting recognition engine recognizes your writing and converts it to text at the insertion point.

NOTE

> The handwriting recognition engine works with any AutoCorrect options you've set. So if you have AutoCorrect set to change "js" to "John Smith," entering "js" on the Writing Pad corrects to "John Smith" as well.

8

On the right side of the Writing Pad is a palette of buttons (also available on the Write Anywhere window) that you can use for editing and navigation. Table 8.3 describes these buttons.

TABLE 8.3 WRITING PAD AND WRITE ANYWHERE BUTTONS

Button	Description	Result
	Ink	Enters the actual words you write as handwriting rather than converting them to text. This button is active only in Microsoft Word and Outlook.
	Text	Converts what you write to text.
	Backspace	Deletes the previous character.
	Space	Enters a space.
	Enter	Moves to a new paragraph line.
	Tab	Tabs once.
	Recognize Now	Enters what you've written on your slide if you haven't set Automatic Recognition on the Handwriting Options dialog box.
	Write Anywhere	Switches to the Write Anywhere window.
	Drawing Pad	Switches to the Drawing Pad in Microsoft Word and Outlook. In PowerPoint, clicking this button has no effect.
	On-Screen Standard Keyboard	Switches to the On-Screen Standard Keyboard.
	Up Cursor	Moves the cursor up.
	Left Cursor	Moves the cursor to the left.
	Right Cursor	Moves the cursor to the right.
	Down Cursor	Moves the cursor down.
	Correction	Displays correction options (not available in PowerPoint).
	Clear	Deletes what you've entered on the Writing Pad.
	Reduce	Reduces the number of buttons that appear on the Writing Pad.
	Expand	Expands the buttons that appear on the Writing Pad.

Button in the Writing Pad or Write Anywhere window not working? *See the "Troubleshooting" section near the end of the chapter.*

USING WRITE ANYWHERE

The Write Anywhere window lets you write anywhere on your screen rather than on the lined Writing Pad. To open the Write Anywhere window, click the Write Anywhere button on the Language bar, or say "write anywhere." If you don't see this button, click the Handwriting button and choose Write Anywhere from the menu. Figure 8.19 shows the Write Anywhere window, which consists of a series of buttons similar to those on the Writing Pad window. Table 8.3 describes these buttons.

Figure 8.19
You can write anywhere on your screen.

Using either a handwriting input device or your mouse, "write" your text where you want it on your screen. By default, the handwriting recognition engine immediately transcribes your text.

CORRECTING HANDWRITING RECOGNITION ERRORS

If the handwriting recognition engine doesn't interpret your handwriting correctly, you can select the incorrect text and either use your handwriting input device to rewrite the text or type the correction using the keyboard.

SETTING HANDWRITING OPTIONS

To set handwriting options, click the down arrow in the upper-left corner of the Writing Pad or Write Anywhere window and choose Options from the submenu that appears. Figure 8.20 illustrates the Handwriting Options dialog box that opens.

On the Common tab, you can customize the pen color and pen width from the choices available in the drop-down lists.

Click the Add Space After Insertion check box to add a space after every word you insert. Select the Automatic Recognition check box to recognize what you write immediately, instead of waiting for you to click the Recognize Now button on the Writing Pad or Write Anywhere window.

To speed up or slow down the rate at which the handwriting recognition engine recognizes your writing, adjust the Recognition Delay scrollbar.

Finally, you can customize the appearance of the toolbar buttons on the Writing Pad in the Toolbar Layout group box. You can move the buttons to the left or right and make the buttons smaller or larger.

Figure 8.20
Specify exactly how you want your handwriting tools to appear.

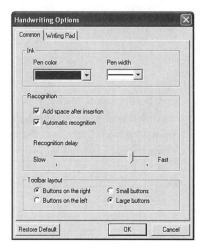

If you make customizations and want to return to the default settings, click the Restore Default button.

On the Writing Pad tab, you can customize the background color of the Writing Pad (choices include the default yellow as well as white, parchment, and system colors) and the number of lines that appear.

TROUBLESHOOTING

RESOLVING MICROPHONE PROBLEMS

I spoke into the microphone, but nothing happened.

First, make sure that you've installed and set up speech recognition, you've clicked the Microphone button on the Language bar, and clicked the appropriate speech button (either Dictation or Voice Command) on the Language bar. Also, make sure that your insertion point is in a location that accepts text. If the software doesn't seem to be the problem, take a look at your actual microphone. Be sure that you've turned it on, connected it properly, and haven't pressed a mute button. If you still have no luck, try the microphone with another program to see if it works. If it doesn't, read your microphone manual for additional troubleshooting advice.

UNDERSTANDING POWERPOINT'S SPEECH AND HANDWRITING RECOGNITION LIMITATIONS

The buttons in the Writing Pad and the Write Anywhere window don't work.

Some handwriting recognition's capabilities don't work in certain Office applications. For example, when you click the Drawing Pad, Ink, or Correction buttons in PowerPoint, nothing happens because PowerPoint doesn't support those functions. Switch to Word and the buttons become active.

DESIGN CORNER: USING OFFICE'S SPEECH AND HANDWRITING RECOGNITION TOOLS

8

Using Office's new speech and handwriting recognition tools in PowerPoint can increase your productivity, but these new features are most effective when combined with the more traditional keyboard and mouse. For example, open PowerPoint, click Voice Command on the Language bar, and then say the verbal commands "file, new" to open the New Presentation task pane. From there, say "new file" to create a new presentation. Say "design" to open the Slide design task pane and apply a design template. Switch to Dictation mode and then dictate a title and subtitle. You can add a new slide by saying "new slide" and, if you choose a bulleted list, you can dictate each bullet followed by "new line." Finally, say "save" to open the Save As dialog box and then say "save" again to save your presentation in progress.

MAKING PRESENTATIONS

CHAPTER 9

PRESENTING A SLIDESHOW

In this chapter

by Patrice-Anne Rutledge and Jim Grey

SETTING UP A SHOW

After you create all the slides in your presentation, you'll want to plan how you're going to present them in a slideshow. Fortunately, PowerPoint makes it easy to set up and rehearse your presentation, as well as configure it to work with a projector.

You can deliver a PowerPoint presentation in three different ways:

- **Present it live with a speaker**—This is the most common method of delivering a PowerPoint presentation—full screen in front of an audience.
- **Browse it individually through the PowerPoint browser**—This option lets someone view your presentation at any convenient time in a browser window with navigation elements such as a scrollbar.
- **Display it at a kiosk**—This method lets you create a self-running presentation. It appears full screen and loops continuously—that is, after the final slide, the presentation starts over. Timings you set determine how long each slide is visible. You might set up a kiosk show as part of a tradeshow demonstration. You can add voice narration if you want, but be sure that your show plays where the narration will be audible.

Before you deliver a PowerPoint presentation, think through its entire visual flow. This is the time to rehearse in your mind what you want to present and how you want to present it, as well as plan for the technical aspects of your presentation.

→ To learn more about how to prepare yourself to deliver a presentation, **see** Chapter 27, "The Mechanics of Function—Developing Internal Presentation Skills," **p. 619**.

→ To learn about staging, projectors, overheads, and using laptops, **see** Chapter 28, "Exploring Technicalities and Techniques," **p. 643**.

Next, start to set up your presentation within PowerPoint. To do this, follow these steps:

1. Choose Slide Show, Set Up Show to open the Set Up Show dialog box (shown in Figure 9.1).
2. Select a Show Type. Options include Presented by a Speaker (full screen), Browsed by an Individual (window), or Browsed at a Kiosk (full screen). Figure 9.2 illustrates a full screen presentation; Figure 9.3 shows you the navigation elements of the PowerPoint browser window.

NOTE

If you choose Browsed by an Individual, you can select the Show Scrollbar check box to display a scrollbar on the right side of the browser when viewing. Viewers can then use the scrollbar to navigate your presentation.

→ If you want to learn how to use the Slide Transition dialog box, **see** "Setting Slide Transitions" in Chapter 15, "Working with Animation," **p. 321**.

 Can't browse your presentation at a kiosk? See the "Troubleshooting" section near the end of this chapter.

Figure 9.1
Specify the type of presentation you want to make in this dialog box.

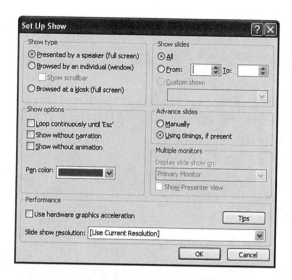

Figure 9.2
Having a speaker present a slide show is the most common way to deliver a presentation.

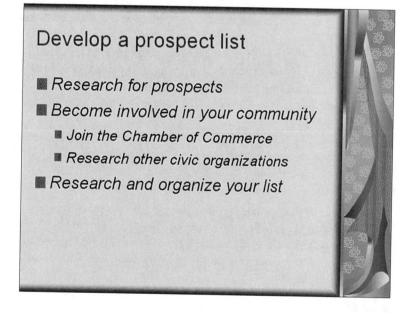

→ To learn about the advantages of rehearsing timings, **see** "Rehearsing Timings" later in this chapter, **p. 179**.

3. Specify the Show Options you want to set:

- Select the Loop Continuously Until 'Esc' check box if you want your presentation to play over and over until you press the Esc key. This check box is available only if you select the Presented by a Speaker or Browsed by an Individual option. A presentation loops continuously by default if browsed at a kiosk.

Figure 9.3
Choosing the Browsed by an Individual option lets users view your presentation on demand.

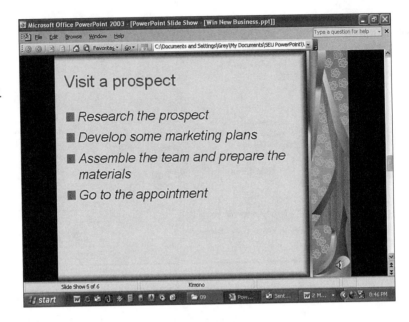

- Select the Show Without Narration check box to temporarily deactivate any accompanying narrations. For example, if you are presenting at a show, narrations might be either inaudible or distracting.

→ For more details about creating narrations, **see** "Recording a Voice Narration" later in this chapter, **p. 180**.

- Select the Show Without Animation check box to temporarily deactivate any accompanying slide animations. For example, you might want to use animations in some situations, but not all.

→ If you want to add animation to your presentation, **see** Chapter 15, **p. 319**.

- Specify a pen color if you're going to use the pen function when presenting. This option is available only when you choose Presented by a Speaker as your show type. Click the arrow to the right of this field and either choose a default color or click More Colors to open the Colors dialog box and choose from a wider variety of colors.

→ To learn more about using the pen function during your presentation, **see** "Setting Pointer Options" later in this chapter, **p. 190**.

4. Choose the slides you want to include in your presentation. Options include All, a certain range of slide indicated by the From and To boxes, and Custom Show, which you can select from the drop-down list. The Custom Show option is active only if you've created a custom show.

→ To learn how to create a custom show, **see** "Working with Custom Shows" later in this chapter, **p. 182**.

5. To advance slides, choose either Manually or Using Timings, if present. To advance the slide manually, you need to press a key or click the mouse.

N O T E

Choosing Manually in this Field overrides any timings you previously set.

→ For more information about slide transitions, **see** "Setting Slide Transitions" in Chapter 15, **p. 321**.

→ To learn more about timings, **see** "Rehearsing Timings" later in this chapter, **p. 179**.

6. If you're using more than one monitor, select the monitor on which to present your slideshow.

7. If you're concerned about performance, select the appropriate options in the Performance group box. For example, 800×600 resolution gives you higher quality but, on an older PC, perhaps slower performance. 640×480 is faster on that older PC, but the quality isn't as good. (If you're running newer hardware, resolution probably won't affect speed.)

8. Click OK to close the Set Up Show dialog box.

REHEARSING TIMINGS

PowerPoint can automate slide transitions by letting you set transition timing. PowerPoint shows a slide for the amount of time you choose, and then transitions to the next slide. You can also set timings by rehearsing your presentation—PowerPoint keeps track of how long you spend on each slide. After you rehearse a presentation, you can save those timings.

You might not always want PowerPoint to move you from slide to slide, however. For example, it can sometimes take you more or less time to discuss a slide in person, or an audience member might interrupt your presentation with a question. Even if you don't want to automate your slide transitions, rehearsing timings can be useful because it helps you adjust your presentation to fit into an allotted amount of time.

To rehearse and set timings, choose Slide Show, Rehearse Timings. The presentation appears in Slide Show view, opening the Rehearsal toolbar in the upper-left corner, shown in Figure 9.4.

Begin talking through your presentation, clicking the Next button in the toolbar (or clicking your mouse, or pressing any key) to advance to the next slide. If you need to stop temporarily, click the Pause button. If you make a mistake and want to start over, click the Repeat button.

The elapsed time of the current slide appears in the Slide Time box in the center of the toolbar. You can also manually enter a time in this box. The time field on the right side of the toolbar shows you the elapsed time of the entire presentation.

9

Figure 9.4
The Rehearsal toolbar helps you rehearse and record slide timings.

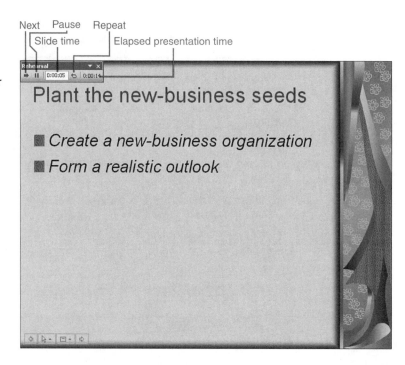

NOTE

> You can manually enter timings in the Slide Transition dialog box as well.

→ To learn more about slide transitions, **see** "Setting Slide Transitions" in Chapter 15, **p. 321**.

After you rehearse the last slide, PowerPoint asks whether you want to save the timings. If you click Yes, the presentation opens in Slide Sorter view with the timings displayed under each slide.

If you record and save timings but don't want to use them to automatically advance your presentation, you can select the Advance Slides, Manually option in the Set Up Show dialog box.

RECORDING A VOICE NARRATION

Using voice narration, you can record your own voice-over to accompany

- A Web-based presentation.
- An on-demand presentation that people can listen to at any time.
- An automated presentation, such as one you run continuously at a tradeshow booth.

■ A presentation delivered by a speaker that includes special recorded commentary by a particular individual. An example of this would be a human resources representative delivering an employee orientation that includes voice narration from the CEO.

Before recording your narration, create a script and rehearse it several times until it flows smoothly and matches your presentation.

CAUTION

> You need to have a microphone and a sound card to record a narration. And remember—the better quality equipment you use, the more professional your narration will sound.

9

 Can't hear your other sound files after recording a voice narration? See the "Troubleshooting" section near the end of this chapter.

To record a voice narration, follow these steps:

1. Choose Slide Show, Record Narration to open the Record Narration dialog box, shown in Figure 9.5.

Figure 9.5
Add voice narrations to your slideshows.

2. Before you record your narration, verify that your microphone is set up properly. To do this, click the Set Microphone Level button. The Microphone Check dialog box appears (see Figure 9.6).

Figure 9.6
Set your microphone level to record properly.

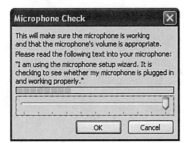

3. Read the sentence that appears into the microphone, and the Microphone Wizard automatically adjusts your microphone level. Click OK to return to the main dialog box.

4. To change the sound quality to CD, radio, or telephone quality, click the Change Quality button to open the Sound Selection dialog box. The better the sound quality, however, the larger the file size.

5. By default, PowerPoint stores your narration inside your presentation. To store the narration as a separate file, click the Link Narrations In check box. PowerPoint stores your narration in a separate WAV file in the same folder as your presentation. To store your narration in another folder, click the Browse button and choose the folder you want in the dialog box that appears. If you want to embed the narration in the presentation, be sure that the Link Narrations In check box is cleared.

> **TIP**
>
> Linking a narration is a good idea if you want to easily transport your presentation without the accompanying narration, such as on a disk or via email. Otherwise, it's easier to just embed the narration in the presentation without creating a separate WAV file.

6. Click OK to start recording. PowerPoint displays your presentation in Slide Show view.

7. Continue narrating as the slide show is displayed.

8. When you reach the end of the presentation, a message box prompts whether or not you want to save the timings with each slide. If you do, click Yes.

The presentation appears in Slide Sorter view with the slide timings below each slide if you chose to save them with the presentation.

> **TIP**
>
> To delete the narration from a slide while in Normal view, select the sound icon that appears in the lower-right corner and press the Delete key. You need to repeat this for each slide that has a corresponding narration.

WORKING WITH CUSTOM SHOWS

You might sometimes need to deliver a presentation to several audiences, but you need to adjust the presentation for each audience. Use a custom show to create one presentation, but set in advance which slides you'll show to which audience. This saves you from creating several nearly identical presentations.

For example, you might want to create a sales presentation that you can use with three different types of prospective clients. Let's say that the first seven slides of your show cover information about your company and its history, which remains the same for all three types of prospects. But you've also created individual slides for each of your three prospect groups that detail your successes in those industries. You can then design three custom shows—

each of which includes the seven main slides, plus the specific slides that pertain only to a certain prospect type. This helps save you time and effort when you need to update information in the seven main slides; this way, you need to do it only once.

To create a custom show, follow these steps:

1. Choose Slide Show, Custom Shows to open the Custom Shows dialog box, shown in Figure 9.7.

Figure 9.7
Customizing your slideshows saves time and reduces duplication.

2. Click the New button to open the Define Custom Show dialog box, shown in Figure 9.8.

Figure 9.8
Add a new custom show in this dialog box.

3. Replace the default name in the Slide Show Name text box with a title for your show.

4. From the Slides in Presentation list, choose the first slide to include in your custom show.

5. Click the Add button to copy this slide to the Slides in Custom Show list.

6. Repeat steps 4 and 5 until you've copied all the slides you want to this list. If you need to remove a slide from the Slides in Custom Show list, select it and click the Remove button.

TIP

You can reorder the slides. For each slide to reorder, select it and click the up and down buttons on the right side of the dialog box until you have it where you want it.

9

7. Click OK to save the custom show and return to the Custom Shows dialog box. From this dialog box, you can edit, remove, or copy any selected custom show.

> **TIP**
>
> Copying a custom slideshow is useful if you want to create several similar versions of a custom show and don't want to repeat the same steps.

8. To preview what the show will look like, click the Show button. The show previews in Slide Show view.

9. Click the Close button to close the Custom Shows dialog box.

To play a custom show, select it in the Custom Shows dialog box and click Show. Or select it from the Custom Show drop-down list in the Set Up Show dialog box. Then either press the F5 key or select the Slide Show, View Show menu command.

INSERTING SLIDES FROM OTHER PRESENTATIONS

As an alternative to creating a custom show, you can insert slides from another presentation into your current presentation. This helps save time and redundant effort as well.

> **NOTE**
>
> A major difference between custom shows and inserting slides is that inserting makes a copy of the slide and, if you change the original, the copy isn't affected. Custom shows "link" to the slides, so they are stored only once.

To insert slides, follow these steps:

1. Select the slide after which you want to start inserting other slides and choose Insert, Slides from Files to open the Slide Finder dialog box, shown in Figure 9.9.

Figure 9.9
The Slide Finder helps you add slides from other presentations.

2. Click the Browse button to open the Browse dialog box (see Figure 9.10). You can also type the filename and path directly in the File field in the Slide Finder.

Figure 9.10
Browse to find your source presentation.

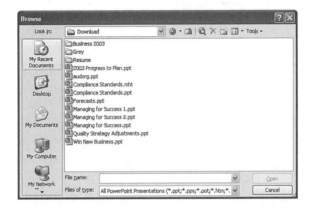

3. Select the presentation you want and click Open. The Browse dialog box closes, and the slides appear in the Select Slides section of the Slide Finder, as shown in Figure 9.11.

Figure 9.11
Display the presentation in the lower portion of the dialog box.

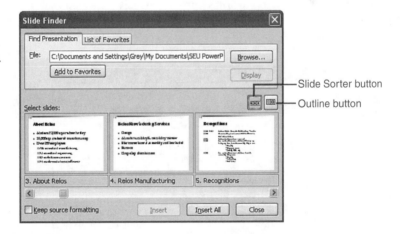

—Slide Sorter button
—Outline button

4. The Slide Sorter button is selected by default, and displays visual images of three slides across the Select Slides area. Or you can click the Outline button to display the presentation's outline with one slide at a time (see Figure 9.12).

5. Select the slide to add and click Insert. To insert all the slides from this presentation, click the Insert All button.

6. If you want the slide to assume the design template of the target presentation, make sure that the Keep Source Formatting check box is empty. If you want the slide to keep its design template, click the Keep Source Formatting check box until it contains a check mark.

9

Figure 9.12
Use an outline to find the slide you want to insert.

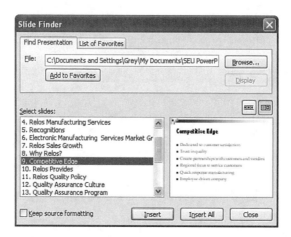

7. Continue selecting and inserting slides until you finish. The slides are inserted in the order you select them, following the active slide in the current presentation.

8. Click the Close button to exit the dialog box.

If you frequently insert slides from the same presentation, you can add them to a favorites list by clicking the Add to Favorites button. The next time you want to insert slides from this presentation, go to the List of Favorites tab in the Slide Finder dialog box (see Figure 9.13) to find them.

Figure 9.13
Using the List of Favorites tab makes it easier to find commonly used slides.

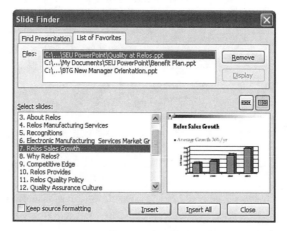

NOTE

In addition to inserting slides, you can also hide them. To hide a selected slide or slides, choose Slide Show, Hide Slide. This doesn't delete the slide; it simply prevents it from appearing in the show.

VIEWING YOUR SHOW

After you plan and set up your PowerPoint presentation, it's time to present it. To do this, select Slide Show, View Show or press F5.

NOTE

> Before presenting your show live, you should preview it to test content, flow, and narration. After you determine that your show itself is flawless, you should work on perfecting your delivery, particularly if you don't deliver live presentations very often. By simulating live conditions as much as possible in your practice sessions, you'll increase your odds of delivering a perfect presentation.

PowerPoint presents a show using the settings you enter in the Set Up Show dialog box. For example, you can view in a browser or full screen, depending on what you entered in this dialog box. Whether you need to advance each slide manually depends on your choices in this dialog box. How you navigate the presentation also depends on how you view it:

- **Full screen**—The presentation appears full screen if you choose the Presented by a Speaker or the Browsed at a Kiosk option in the Set Up Show dialog box. The major difference between the two is that when you present by a speaker, you have numerous navigation options available because a person is in control of the presentation. When you browse at a kiosk, these navigation options aren't available because the show runs itself.

- **PowerPoint browser**—The show appears in the PowerPoint browser if you choose Browsed by an Individual in the Set Up Show dialog box. This is similar to other browsers, such as Internet Explorer or Netscape Navigator. You can use the scrollbar to scroll through the presentation if it's available, or you can use the Page Up and Page Down keys to navigate manually. To switch to the full screen view, choose Browse, Full Screen from within the PowerPoint browser.

TIP

> Displaying a scrollbar can make it easier for viewers to navigate your show. Specify whether to display a scrollbar in the Set Up Show dialog box.

→ For more information about the Set Up Show dialog box, **see** "Setting Up a Show" earlier in this chapter, **p. 176**.

TIP

> To present the show starting with the current slide, click the Slide Show button in the lower-left corner of the window.

NAVIGATING A SHOW FULL SCREEN

If you choose to present your PowerPoint slideshow by a speaker, the presentation appears full screen. If you set up your show without automatic timing, you have to manually move among the slides during the show. Table 9.1 lists all the ways PowerPoint gives you to navigate a slideshow.

TABLE 9.1   SLIDESHOW ACTIONS

Slideshow Action	Method
Advance to next slide	Left-click the mouse Press the spacebar Press the letter N Press the right-arrow key Press the down-arrow key Press the Enter key Press the Page Down key
Return to previous slide	Press the Backspace key Press the letter P Press the left-arrow key Press the up-arrow key Press the Page Up key
Go to a specific slide	Enter the number of the slide and press the Enter key
Black/unblack the screen (toggle)	Press the letter B Press the period key
White/unwhite the screen (toggle)	Press the letter W Press the comma (,)
Display/hide the arrow (toggle)	Press the letter A Press the equal sign (=)
Stop/restart a timed show (toggle)	Press the letter S Press the plus sign (+)
End the show	Press the Esc key Press Ctrl+Break Press the minus (–) key
Erase screen drawing made with pen	Press the letter E
Advance to hidden slide	Press the letter H
Rehearse using new timing	Press the letter T
Rehearse using original timing	Press the letter O
Activate the pen	Press Ctrl+P
Activate the arrow pointer	Press Ctrl+A

Slideshow Action	Method
Hide pointer/button	Press Ctrl+H
Automatically show/hide pointer	Press Ctrl+U

TIP

> Right-click anywhere on the screen and choose Help from the shortcut menu to display this list of shortcuts within your slideshow.

NOTE

> The capability to toggle a black or white screen is a useful tool. For example, if you want to explain a detailed concept and want your audience to focus on what you're saying and not on the slide, you can temporarily make the screen either black or white. This is also useful during breaks for long presentations.

 You have other ways to navigate a PowerPoint show. Right-click anywhere on the screen to see a shortcut menu. You can choose any of the following options:

- **Next**—Moves to the next slide.
- **Previous**—Moves to the previous slide.
- **Last Viewed**—Moves to the slide last viewed.
- **Go to Slide**—Displays a list of the slides in the presentation (see Figure 9.14). Select the slide you want to see.

Figure 9.14
Jump directly to any slide in your presentation.

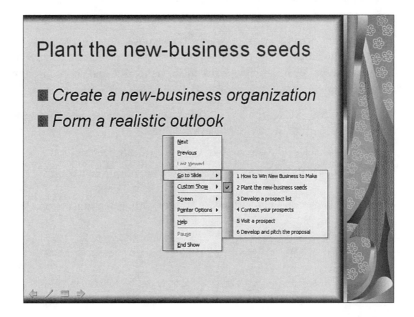

9

- **Custom Show**—Displays a menu listing available custom shows. Click the one you want to view.
- **Screen**—Lets you switch to a black or white screen, show speaker's notes, and display the Windows taskbar so that you can switch to another application.
- **Pointer Options**—Activates the pen, lets you set the pen's ink color, lets you erase pen markings, and hides and displays the mouse cursor.
- **Help**—Displays a list of the shortcut keystrokes you can use during a slideshow.
- **Pause**—Pauses a slideshow that's running automatically.
- **End Show**—Ends the show and returns to PowerPoint.

TIP

> Although the options on this menu are useful, you'll probably want to avoid using these features during an actual presentation because a break in your flow can be distracting. One case in which you might want to do so during a presentation would be when you have to go back to previous slides to answer questions or clarify a point and don't want to page through numerous slides to do so.

SETTING POINTER OPTIONS

You can use or hide an arrow pointer during a PowerPoint presentation. The arrow pointer can help you draw the audience's attention to objects on your slides.

To turn on the arrow, move the mouse. You can also right-click and choose Arrow. The arrow appears as a standard mouse pointer arrow on your screen, which you can use to point to specific areas.

By default, the arrow disappears after three seconds of inactivity, and reappears whenever you move the mouse. This setting is fine for most presentations, but you can choose to have the arrow always or never appear. To do so, right-click and choose Pointer Options, Arrow Options from the menu that appears. Then choose one of these three commands:

- **Automatic**—Makes the arrow appear when you move your mouse and disappear after three seconds of inactivity (default).
- **Visible**—Makes the arrow always appear in your presentation.
- **Hidden**—Makes the arrow never appear in your presentation.

Figure 9.15 shows the standard arrow pointer with which most people are familiar.

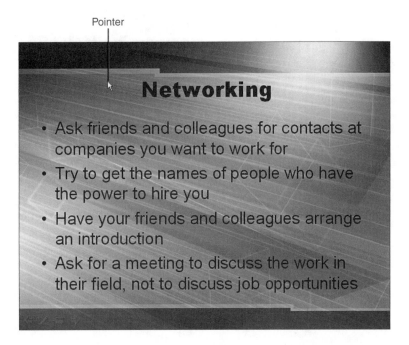

Figure 9.15
Use a pointer during your slide presentation.

Using Ink to Mark Your Presentation

Using *ink*, you canactually mark right on your slides as you deliver a presentation. This feature works smoothest if you have a pen tablet or a Tablet PC, but you'll also get good value from it if all you have is a mouse.

PowerPoint gives you three kinds of ink:

- **Ballpoint pen**—Draws a thin line.
- **Felt tip pen**—Draws a medium line.
- **Highlighter**—Draws a fat line that appears behind text and objects on the slide.

Use the pens to draw. You can draw shapes and objects to emphasize a point, circle important words, or even write text (challenging with a mouse, easy with a pen tablet or a Tablet PC). Use the highlighter to highlight text and objects on the screen.

To use ink, right-click, choose Pointer Options, and choose the kind of ink to use (Ballpoint Pen, Felt Tip Pen, or Highlighter). Your mouse cursor becomes a dot (when you choose a pen) or a colored bar (when you choose highlighter). Click and hold the mouse button, and then drag the cursor to make your mark. Figure 9.16 shows some ink markings.

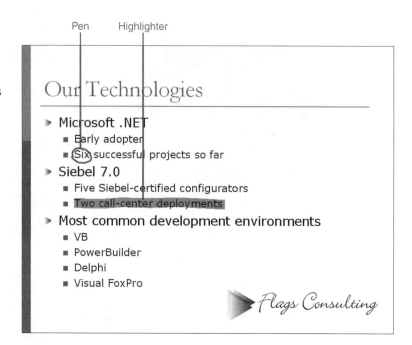

Figure 9.16
Use a pen or the highlighter to draw attention to elements in the presentation.

You can choose your ink's color. When you set the ink color for one pen, you set it for both. But the highlighter's ink color is independent of the pens. To set ink color, choose a pen or the highlighter and right-click. From the menu that appears, choose Pointer Options, Ink Color, and choose the color to use. You can also preset the pens' ink color in the Set Up Show dialog box.

→ To set up the pens' ink color in the Set Up Show dialog box, **see** "Setting Up a Show" earlier in this chapter, **p. 176**.

You can erase your markings, too. To erase a specific ink marking, right-click and choose Pointer Options, Eraser from the menu that appears. The mouse cursor looks like an eraser. Click an ink marking to erase it. To erase all of your ink markings, right-click and choose Pointer Options, Erase All Ink on Slide from the menu that appears or press the letter E.

You can choose your pen color in the Set Up Show dialog box, or you can set it by right-clicking, choosing Pointer Options, Pen Color, and selecting a color from the list that appears.

After you finish delivering your presentation, PowerPoint asks whether you want to keep your annotations. If you click Yes, the annotations become drawing objects in the presentation.

PACKAGING PRESENTATIONS ONTO A CD

Sometimes, a presentation needs to run on a computer other than the one on which it was created. For example, you might travel to a meeting without your laptop computer and need to give a presentation using a supplied computer. You can save your presentation to a floppy disk or email it ahead; but still, you worry. Are the fonts in your presentation installed on the computer? Is this version of PowerPoint installed? Is *any* version of PowerPoint installed? Did I remember all the linked files the presentation uses?

Package for CD relieves these worries. It writes your presentation, with its fonts and linked files if you want, to a CD. It also includes the PowerPoint Viewer by default so that you always have everything you need to run your presentation. You can choose whether the presentation runs automatically when you insert the CD into a computer. You can also package more than one presentation onto a CD and choose whether they should run automatically in sequence.

To package presentations onto a CD, follow these steps:

1. Open a presentation to package.

2. Choose File, Package for CD to open the Package for CD dialog box, shown in Figure 9.17.

Figure 9.17
With Package for CD, you can deliver your presentation on another computer.

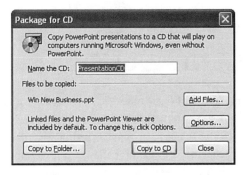

3. In the Name the CD field, type a name that describes the presentation(s) you're packaging. This becomes the name that Windows calls the CD.

4. The current presentation's filename appears in the Files to Be Copied area. To package more presentations onto this CD, click the Add Files button. The Add Files window appears (see Figure 9.18). Select the presentations to package and click Add.

5. If you are packaging more than one presentation, the Package for CD box resembles Figure 9.19. You can arrange the presentations in the order you want them to run. To move a presentation, click it and then click the arrow buttons to reposition it.

Figure 9.18
Choose the presentations you want to package.

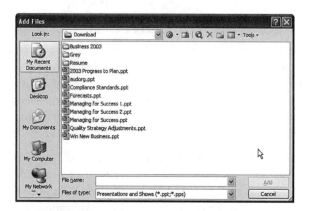

Figure 9.19
Click the arrow buttons to arrange the presentations in the order they should run.

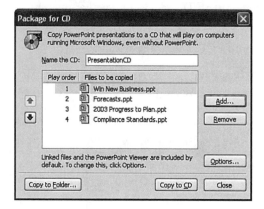

6. Click the Options button. The Options window opens (see Figure 9.20). Set these options and click OK when you're done:

- PowerPoint packages the PowerPoint Viewer by default. If you don't want to package the Viewer, click the PowerPoint Viewer box to remove the check mark.

→ To learn what this viewer is and how it works, **see** "Using the PowerPoint Viewer," the next section in this chapter, **p. 196**.

- When you package the PowerPoint Viewer with the presentations, choose how the presentations play in the viewer: play them automatically in the sequence you set, play only the first presentation automatically, let the user choose which presentation to play, or don't launch the CD automatically.

- PowerPoint packages linked files by default. If you don't want to package them, click this box to remove the check mark.

- If your presentation uses any fonts you're not positive are on the computer you'll use, click the Embedded TrueType fonts box so that it contains a check mark. PowerPoint packages the fonts so that your presentation is sure to look the way you created it.

CAUTION

You can embed other TrueType fonts that you install only if they aren't restricted by license or copyright. You'll receive an error message if you try to embed a restricted font.

- If you want to prevent others from opening or changing your presentations, type **passwords** in the Password fields.

Figure 9.20
Specify whether to package the PowerPoint Viewer, linked files, and fonts.

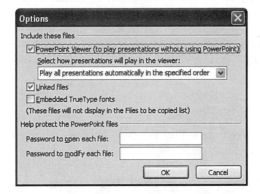

7. If you want to create a folder on your hard drive that contains everything that will be on the CD, click the Copy to Folder button. The Copy to Folder dialog box appears (see Figure 9.21). Type a name for the folder, choose where to add the folder, and click OK. PowerPoint creates the folder and copies all the files to it.

Figure 9.21
Choose where to create the folder and what to call it.

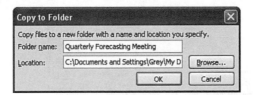

8. Place a blank writeable CD into your CD-R or CD-RW drive. If Windows asks you what to do with the CD, click Take No Action and then click OK. Go back to the Package for CD dialog box and click Copy to CD. PowerPoint writes the files to the CD.

When PowerPoint finishes creating the CD, it opens the CD drawer and asks whether you want to copy the same files to another CD. If so, place another writeable CD in the drive and click Yes. Otherwise, click No.

USING THE POWERPOINT VIEWER

The PowerPoint Viewer (`pptview.exe`) lets people view a PowerPoint presentation when they don't have PowerPoint installed on their computers. You can freely distribute the Viewer without any license fee. Using Package for CD, you have the option of including the Viewer in your presentation package.

→ To learn more about how to use Package for CD and how it works with the PowerPoint Viewer, **see** "Packaging Presentations onto a CD," the previous section in this chapter, **p. 193**.

9

CAUTION

> PowerPoint Viewer will play all PowerPoint content except linked and embedded objects and scripting.

To run the Viewer, follow these steps:

1. Double-click `pptview.exe` from within Windows Explorer. Figure 9.22 illustrates the Microsoft PowerPoint Viewer dialog box.

Figure 9.22
The PowerPoint Viewer lets you deliver slideshows on computers without PowerPoint.

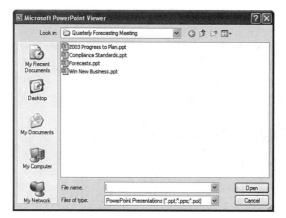

2. Navigate to the presentation you want to view or enter its name in the File Name field.
3. Click Open to start the show.
4. When the show ends, the Microsoft PowerPoint Viewer dialog box returns. Click Cancel to close it.

TIP

> PowerPoint Viewer plays PowerPoint presentations created only with versions of PowerPoint going back to PowerPoint 97. If you have a presentation created in PowerPoint 95 or earlier and want to play it in the PowerPoint Viewer, first open the presentation in this version of PowerPoint and then save it.

TROUBLESHOOTING

DISPLAYING HIDDEN SLIDES

My presentation doesn't display all the slides I created.

Be sure that you don't have any hidden slides. To verify this, open your presentation in Slide Sorter view and verify that none of the slide numbers has a strikethrough, which indicates that it's hidden. To unhide a slide, select it and choose Slide Show, Hide Slide.

ADVANCING SLIDES AT A KIOSK

I want to browse my presentation at a kiosk, but the slides don't advance.

Be sure that you set automatic timings if you want to browse at a kiosk because you can't do this manually. Also verify that you chose the Using Timings, If Present option in the Set Up Show dialog box.

LISTENING TO A VOICE NARRATION

I added a voice narration, and now I can't hear other sound files I've included.

If you insert media clips such as sounds, and then add a voice narration, the narration takes precedence over the media clips. As a result, you'll hear only the narration. To resolve this, delete the narration if the media clips are of more importance, or find a way to include the other sounds in the narration you record.

CHAPTER **10**

CREATING AND PRINTING PRESENTATION MATERIALS

In this chapter *by Patrice-Anne Rutledge and Jim Grey*

EXPLORING PRESENTATION OUTPUT OPTIONS

You can print slides, of course, in PowerPoint. You can also print notes to remind you of what you want to say while presenting, handouts to give to your audience, and outlines to help you proof your content. PowerPoint also includes numerous customization options for printing auxiliary materials. You can export these to Microsoft Word for even more flexibility.

CREATING NOTES AND HANDOUTS

In addition to slides and outlines, you can print notes and handouts. You create notes in the Notes pane, which is visible in Normal view. Figure 10.1 shows the Notes pane in which you can create detailed speaker's notes about your presentation.

Figure 10.1
Add notes for yourself or your audience in the Notes pane.

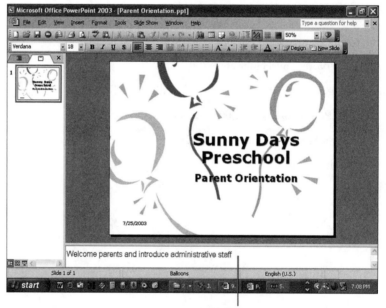

Notes pane

NOTE

Notes are not the same as comments. A comment appears in a yellow box inside a slide and provides commentary about its content. You use comments most often during the review process to get feedback from others, and you usually delete them later. Notes are designed to be kept with a presentation as a reference for the speaker or audience members.

➜ For details about the use of comments, **see** "Adding Comments to Slides" in Chapter 7, "Collaborating on Presentations," **p. 141**.

You can use notes to remind yourself of what you're going to present, to create an entire script for your presentation, or to record information you print out for audience members.

Printing handouts is similar to printing slides except that with handouts you can print up to nine slides on a page. This can greatly reduce the number of pages and amount of printer toner required to print your presentation. When you print handouts, you see only the slides, not the accompanying notes.

→ To learn more about how and when to use handouts, **see** "Creating Handout Materials" in Chapter 25, "The Media—Designing Visual Support," **p. 550**.

PREPARING TO PRINT YOUR PRESENTATION

To avoid wasting paper, first make sure that your PowerPoint presentation is truly ready to print. Set page and print options, customize headers and footers, and preview your presentation in the color scheme in which you will print it. If you're going to give handouts to your audience, you definitely need to print your presentation. But even if you plan to deliver your presentation onscreen only, it's still a good idea to print your presentation. When you proof a hard-copy version of your presentation, you'll often notice problems that you didn't catch on the screen.

10

TIP

If you're going to provide your audience with handouts, you might want to hand them out *after* you're finished presenting. If you hand them out before you start the presentation, some people will read ahead and not hear what you say. This is especially important when your slides contain only talking points and the presentation's meat is in what you say.

→ For more details on proofreading and spell-checking your presentation, **see** "Checking Spelling and Style" in Chapter 3, "Working with Text," **p. 74**.

SETTING UP THE PAGE

Before you print, set page options such as the default output and orientation. To do this, follow these steps:

1. Choose File, Page Setup to open the Page Setup dialog box, shown in Figure 10.2.

Figure 10.2
Set up page orientation and other defaults in the Page Setup dialog box.

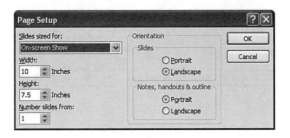

2. Select your output from the Slides Sized For drop-down list. Options include On-screen Show, Letter Paper, Ledger Paper, A3 Paper, A4 Paper (international standard), B4 (ISO) Paper, B5 (ISO) Paper, 35mm Slides, Overhead, Banner, and Custom.

> **TIP**
>
> If you want to create 35mm slides from your PowerPoint presentation, you can send them to a service bureau (often electronically) to have this done. Genigraphics (www.genigraphics.com) is one example of a bureau that specializes in PowerPoint presentations.

3. The Width and Height settings appear in inches automatically, based on your selection in step 2. You can customize these settings, if you want.

4. In the Number Slides From field, select the number to use on the first slide.

5. Choose either portrait or landscape orientation for your slides. Landscape is the default.

6. Choose either portrait or landscape orientation for your notes, handouts, and outline. Portrait is the default for these, but you can switch to landscape if your presentation doesn't fit on the page with portrait orientation.

7. Click OK to close this dialog box.

CUSTOMIZING HEADERS AND FOOTERS

You can also add headers and footers to your outline, notes, and handouts when you print them. To do this, choose View, Header and Footer and go to the Notes and Handouts tab in the Header and Footer dialog box, shown in Figure 10.3.

Figure 10.3
Indicate the headers and footers you want to print.

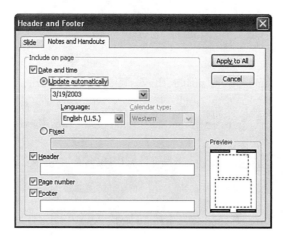

You can add any or all of the following when you print notes, handouts, or outlines:

■ **Date and Time**—Select this check box and then either enter a fixed date or choose to automatically update the date. If you choose to update automatically, pick a format from the drop-down list. Options include displaying the date only, the time only, or the date and time in up to 13 different ways. You can also choose your base language and calendar type, depending on the language you choose in the Language drop-down list. If only English is enabled, the Language list isn't active. The date and time appear on the upper-right corner of the page.

→ For details on multilingual presentations, **see** Chapter 22, "Using PowerPoint's Foreign Language Capabilities," **p. 473**.

NOTE

The date options you can choose from the Update Automatically drop-down list depend on your choice of language/country. For example, choosing English (UK) results in date options that display a dd/mm/yy format rather than the mm/dd/yy format used in the United States.

■ **Header**—Prints the header text you enter in the text box on the upper-left corner of the page.

■ **Page Number**—Prints a page number on the lower-right corner of each page.

■ **Footer**—Prints the footer text you enter on the lower-left corner of the page.

Click Apply to All to close the dialog box.

PREVIEWING A POWERPOINT PRESENTATION

Before you print your presentation, you can preview it using PowerPoint's Print Preview feature.

 To preview, click the Print Preview button on the Standard toolbar or choose File, Print Preview.

You have several formatting and output options from this view:

 ■ **Previous Page**—Goes back to the previous page.

 ■ **Next Page**—Moves to the next page.

 ■ **Print**—Opens the Print dialog box, from which you can print your presentation.

→ For more information on the Print dialog box, **see** "Printing PowerPoint Presentations," later in this chapter, **p. 207**.

■ **Print What**—Lets you select what you want to print from a drop-down list. Options include Slides, Handouts (from one to nine per page), Notes Pages, and Outline View.

■ **Zoom**—Reduces or enlarges the size of the content on your screen. Sizes range from 25% to 400%. You can also choose to fit the slide to the screen.

TIP

> Clicking the slide is another way to zoom in and out. Clicking serves as a toggle between a 100% view and fitting the slide to the page.

■ **Landscape**—Displays the presentation in Landscape mode.

■ **Portrait**—Displays the presentation in Portrait mode.

NOTE

> The Landscape and Portrait buttons aren't available when you choose Slides in the Print What field.

■ **Options**—Opens a submenu with additional options including the following:

• **Header and Footer**—Opens the Header and Footer dialog box, where you can modify headers and footers for printing.

→ For more information on the Header and Footer dialog box, **see** "Customizing Headers and Footers," earlier in this chapter, **p. 202**.

• **Color/Grayscale**—Opens a submenu from which you can preview your presentation in color, grayscale, or pure black and white.

→ For more information on color previewing, **see** "Previewing in Grayscale and Black and White," later in this chapter, **p. 205**.

• **Scale to Fit Paper**—Changes the size of slides to fit the paper, making them either larger or smaller as appropriate.

• **Frame Slides**—Includes a border around the slides.

• **Print Hidden Slides**—This option is available only if your presentation includes hidden slides.

• **Print Comments**—Prints comment pages with your presentation.

• **Printing Order**—Displays a submenu from which you can choose to print slides horizontally or vertically. This isn't the same as printing in portrait or landscape orientation, but rather refers to how multiple slides appear on a single page. Look at the preview to the right of the option buttons to see how the printing order changes depending on whether you select Horizontal or Vertical.

■ **Close**—Closes the preview and returns to the presentation.

PREVIEWING IN GRAYSCALE AND BLACK AND WHITE

If you don't have a color printer, you can print a color presentation in three different ways:

- **Color**—Your printer will do the best it can to convert your presentation's colors to shades of glorious gray. Depending on your presentation's colors, sometimes this works well and other times it doesn't. Figure 10.4 shows a color slide as it might look printed in "color" to a grayscale printer.

Figure 10.4
This slide uses the Kimono design in salmon, orange, green, and tan.

- **Grayscale**—PowerPoint converts your presentation to grayscale, as Figure 10.5 shows. It also converts all slide backgrounds to white to avoid the bad results you sometimes get with a straight grayscale conversion (which is what printing color on a grayscale printer gives you).

Figure 10.5
The same slide printed as grayscale.

- **Black and white**—PowerPoint converts your presentation to pure black and white. This option usually yields the least interesting results, as Figure 10.6 shows.

Figure 10.6
The same slide printed as black and white.

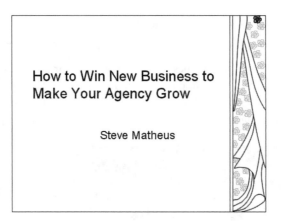

Table 10.1 illustrates how each PowerPoint object appears when printed in grayscale or black and white.

TABLE 10.1   GRAYSCALE AND BLACK-AND-WHITE OBJECTS

Object	Grayscale	Black and White
Bitmaps	Grayscale	Grayscale
Charts	Grayscale	Grayscale
Embossing	None	None
Fill	Grayscale	White
Frames	Black	Black
Lines	Black	Black
Patterns	Grayscale	White
Shadows (object)	Grayscale	Black
Shadows (text)	None	None
Slide backgrounds	White	White
Text	Black	Black

 To preview what your color presentation will look like in grayscale, click the Color/Grayscale button on the Standard toolbar and choose Grayscale from the menu.

To preview the same presentation in black and white, choose Pure Black and White from the menu. To return to viewing your presentation in color, choose Color from the Color/Grayscale submenu.

The Grayscale View floating toolbar appears when you preview in grayscale or pure black and white (it doesn't appear when you're viewing in color). You can manually change how an object prints in either grayscale or black and white with this toolbar. To do so, click Setting from the Grayscale View toolbar and choose the color option you prefer.

To close the Grayscale View toolbar, either return to viewing your presentation in color, or click the Close Grayscale View or Close Black and White View button on the Grayscale View toolbar.

PRINTING POWERPOINT PRESENTATIONS

To print an open PowerPoint presentation, follow these steps:

1. Choose File, Print to open the Print dialog box shown in Figure 10.7. You can also click the Print button on the Standard toolbar if you want to print with the defaults rather than setting options in the Print dialog box. Be sure that your default settings match the output you want, such as grayscale or black and white. You can set these defaults in the Print dialog box.

Figure 10.7
You can specify numerous print parameters in the Print dialog box.

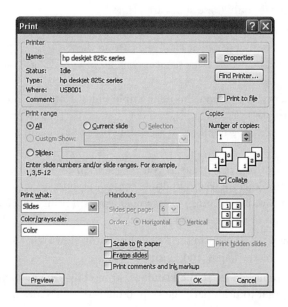

2. Select the printer to use in the Name drop-down list.

> **NOTE**
>
> Click the Properties button to change the selected printer's properties and print parameters.

> **NOTE**
>
> If you want to fax your presentation, preinstall faxing software and be sure that your computer is connected to a phone line. Then you can choose the fax from the Name drop-down list, and click OK to start the fax.

NOTE

> You can print your PowerPoint presentation to a file by selecting the Print to File check box. The Print to File dialog box then opens when you print your presentation, prompting you for a filename to save as a printer file (PRN). Printing to a file is useful if you want to print at a resolution higher than what your current printer supports. You can then use another printer that supports the same print language, such as PostScript, to print your file without having to open PowerPoint itself.

3. In the Print Range group box, select the slides you want to print. Choices include

- **All**—Prints all slides in the presentation.
- **Current Slide**—Prints only the currently selected slide.
- **Selection**—Prints the selected slides. For example, if you select specific slides on the Outline tab, only these slides are printed.
- **Custom Show**—Lets you select a custom show to print. This option isn't available if you haven't created at least one custom show.

→ For more information on custom shows, **see** "Working with Custom Shows" in Chapter 9, "Presenting a Slideshow," **p. 182**.

- **Slides**—Lets you pick and choose multiple slides. Enter the numbers of the slides you want to print. For example, you could enter 1-4, 10 to print slides 1, 2, 3, 4, and 10. Specify slide numbers in ascending order—1, 6, and 8 works, but 1, 8, and 6 doesn't.

4. Enter the number of copies to print. If you choose to print more than one copy, specify whether to collate. Collating keeps multiple copies in sequence. If you print five copies of a presentation without collating, for example, you will print five copies of page one, and then five copies of page two, and so on.

5. Specify what you want to print in the Print What drop-down list. Options include Slides, Handouts, Notes Pages, and Outline View.

6. If you choose to print handouts, the Handouts group box becomes active. Indicate how many slides you want to print per page—up to nine—in the Slides per Page field and choose either Horizontal or Vertical Order for the flow of slides on the page.

TIP

> If you choose to print three slides per handout, PowerPoint provides lined spaces to the right of each slide on which you can write notes. If you choose another number of pages, you won't have this note space.

7. From the Color/Grayscale drop-down list, choose the color options you want. Options include

- **Color**—Prints the presentation in color, optimized for a color printer. If you select this option and print to a grayscale printer such as a typical office laser printer, the presentation prints in grayscale. Slides can look muddy when the slide background's shade of gray isn't very different from the shades of gray of other slide elements.

- **Grayscale**—Prints the presentation in grayscale, but converts slide backgrounds to white so that your presentation prints cleanly.

- **Pure Black and White**—Prints the presentation in black and white only, without any gray.

8. Next, choose any of the following print options that apply:

- **Scale to Fit Paper**—Changes the size of slides to fit the paper, making them either larger or smaller as appropriate.

- **Frame Slides**—Includes a border around the slides. Not available when you print in Outline view.

- **Include Comment Pages**—Prints comment pages with your presentation.

- **Print Hidden Slides**—This option is available only if your presentation includes hidden slides.

9. Click the Preview button to see what your printed presentation will look like, based on your selected options. When you're satisfied with your print choices, close the preview and click OK to print the presentation.

Having trouble printing? See "Resolving Print Problems" in the "Troubleshooting" section near the end of the chapter.

TIP

> You can customize printing defaults for the existing presentation in the Options dialog box. To access it, choose Tools, Options and go to the Print tab.

→ For more information about printing, **see** "Changing Print Options," in Chapter 21, "Customizing PowerPoint," **p. 458**.

PRINTING AN OUTLINE

In the Print dialog box, you can choose to print a presentation's outline by selecting Outline View in the Print What drop-down list.

→ For more detailed information about printing, **see** "Printing PowerPoint Presentations" in this chapter, **p. 207**.

Before you do this, however, set up your outline for printing.

 To print the entire contents of each slide, click the Expand All button on the Outlining toolbar. If the Outlining toolbar doesn't appear, choose View, Toolbars, Outlining.

To print only the title of each slide, click the Collapse All button on the Outlining toolbar.

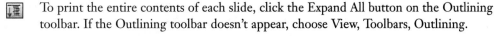

To print an outline with the same formatting as the presentation itself (font styles and sizing, line spacing, and the like), click the Show Formatting button on the Standard or Outlining toolbar.

→ To better understand outlines, **see** "Collapsing and Expanding Outline Points" in Chapter 5, "Organizing Presentations," **p. 104**.

PRINTING A POWERPOINT PRESENTATION WITH MICROSOFT WORD

If you want to make more customizations than PowerPoint provides, you can also send your presentation to Word, customize it, and print from that application. Choose File, Send To, Microsoft Word to open the Send To Microsoft Word dialog box, shown in Figure 10.8.

Figure 10.8
The Send To Microsoft Word dialog box includes several options for exporting to Word.

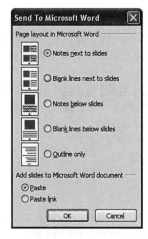

This dialog box includes several choices on how to display the PowerPoint presentation in Word.

You can either paste slides into Word, or paste a link to the slides in Word. Pasting is the equivalent of embedding. If you embed a PowerPoint presentation into Word and later change that presentation in PowerPoint, those changes won't appear in the Word document. If you paste a link to the slides into Word and later make changes in PowerPoint, these changes appear the next time you open the document in Word.

→ To learn more about linking objects, **see** "Linking Office Objects" in Chapter 19, "Integrating with Office 2003," **p. 404**.

→ For more information on embedding, **see** "Working with Embedded Office Objects" in Chapter 19, **p. 408**.

Click OK to send your presentation to Word and open it in that application. When your presentation is open in Word, you can use all of Word's features to customize your notes and handouts.

ENSURING A SMOOTH PRINT PROCESS

The following are some tips to help ensure a smooth process in printing your PowerPoint presentation:

- If you want to continue working with PowerPoint while printing a large presentation, choose Tools, Options, and select Background printing on the Print tab. With some printers, background printing can also be a setting of the printer itself. For example, if your printer lets you set up print spooling, this has the same effect as background printing.

- If your print job is moving too slowly, turn off background printing.

 Not printing fast enough? See "Speeding Up the Print Process" in the "Troubleshooting" section near the end of the chapter.

- To save time and money, proof your presentation carefully before you print it. Run the spelling and grammar checker, verify the content, look at the placement of all graphics, and ensure that the color scheme and design templates are appropriate. When you're confident about your presentation, print it.

- If the fonts in your presentation don't print properly, use other fonts. For example, if you use a non-TrueType font that your printer can't recognize, it prints a different font that might not be what you want.

 What should you do if your graphics don't print in their entirety? See "Resolving Incomplete Graphics Printing" in the "Troubleshooting" section near the end of the chapter.

- If you're going to distribute notes or handouts to your audience, carefully consider the quality and color of paper you use. Although heavier paper might make attractive handouts, not all printers are equipped to handle the heavier weight. Specialty paper is also more expensive. In terms of color, light colors other than white can work well, but be wary of paper that's too dark or bright. It can make your presentation hard to read.

TROUBLESHOOTING

RESOLVING PRINT PROBLEMS

I can't print. What should I do?

If you're having problems printing, first verify that your printer is turned on, that you selected the right printer in the Print dialog box, and that your printer doesn't have an error condition. (See the printer's status panel or the printer's queue window, which you can open by double-clicking the printer icon in the system tray.) To further isolate a printing problem, check to see whether you can print another PowerPoint presentation or a document from another application. If not, the problem is probably with the printer and not PowerPoint or your presentation.

SPEEDING UP THE PRINT PROCESS

My print job is printing too slowly. How can I speed up the print process?

Turn off background printing to speed up the print process. To do so, choose Tools, Options and remove the check mark by Background printing on the Print tab of the Options dialog box.

RESOLVING INCOMPLETE GRAPHICS PRINTING

My graphics don"t print completely. How do I fix this?

First, verify that a document without graphics prints properly. If so, your printer might not have enough memory to complete a print job with complex graphics. Refer to your printer manual for information about memory and memory upgrades.

DESIGN CORNER: CREATING CUSTOM POWERPOINT HANDOUTS

If you're just going to provide handouts for internal reference, PowerPoint's handout creation feature might easily handle all your needs. But if you need to create polished, professional handouts (for an important client presentation, for example), you might need a bit more flexibility and sophistication. This is where the integrated power of Office comes in handy—create your presentation in PowerPoint and then polish the handouts in Word. With Word's advanced formatting features, you can create a custom PowerPoint handout that meets your exact specifications. Just choose the page layout options you want in the Send To Microsoft Word dialog box (File, Send To, Microsoft Word) and then customize the output in Word.

BEFORE

Figure 10.9

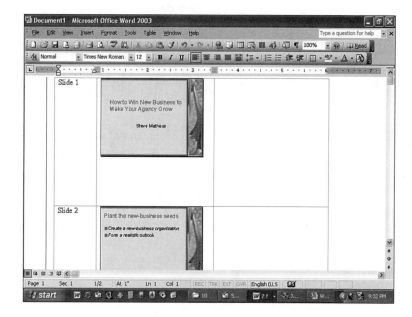

AFTER

Custom font   Header

Figure 10.10

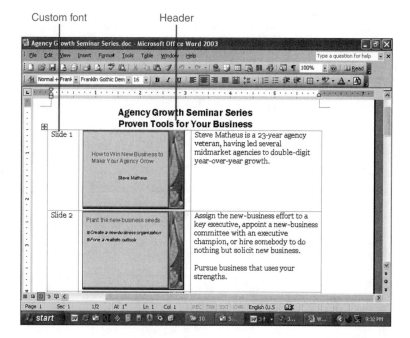

WORKING WITH GRAPHICS, CHARTS, AND MULTIMEDIA

CHAPTER **11**

WORKING WITH CHARTS

In this chapter   *by Patrice-Anne Rutledge and Jim Grey*

EXPLORING CHART POSSIBILITIES

PowerPoint charts can be as simple or as complex as you like. You can create a basic chart right inside PowerPoint using Microsoft Graph, or you can create a full-featured chart using Microsoft Excel and insert it into your presentation. You can choose from common chart types such as column, bar, line, and pie charts; try something out of the ordinary such as a doughnut or radar chart; or create a chart type of your own. PowerPoint charts are preformatted based on the attached design template, but you can also change nearly every aspect of a chart—its color, text, labels, and more.

A chart, also referred to as a *graph*, can be a useful tool for communicating numeric information in a concise format. You could create a chart illustrating sales revenue per region or the percentage of sales allocated to each of your products, for example. As you begin to work with charts, you'll discover a multitude of uses for them.

UNDERSTANDING CHARTS IN POWERPOINT

You can use Microsoft Graph to create charts in your presentation, or you can insert charts created in another application, such as Excel. Using Microsoft Graph inside PowerPoint is the easiest way to create a graph, but doesn't offer any calculation or formula capabilities for your chart data. If you've already created a chart in Excel or you need to analyze complex data, it's best to insert an Excel chart.

NOTE

> For the sake of consistency, we use the term *chart* throughout this chapter to match PowerPoint's interface—even though the application you use to create charts is called Microsoft Graph. Essentially, *chart* and *graph* are synonyms for any kind of graphical representation of numeric information.

Before you start creating a chart using Microsoft Graph from within PowerPoint, you should become familiar with chart terminology. Table 11.1 lists these terms and their definitions.

TABLE 11.1 CHART OBJECT TERMINOLOGY

Term	Definition
Axis	A line that frames one side of the plot area. The two most common axes are the value axis and the category axis.
Datasheet	A grid that resembles a spreadsheet, in which you can enter data for your chart.
Data label	Text that describes a specific data marker or series of data markers. This can be a numeric value, text, a percent, or a combination of these items.
Data marker	A value that represents a single cell or data point in a datasheet.

TABLE 11.1 CONTINUED	
Term	**Definition**
Data series	The main categories of information in a chart—usually reflected in a chart's legend and in the first cell of each datasheet row or column.
Data table	A grid in the chart that lists the exact data in the datasheet.
Gridlines	Lines that display across the category or value axes to make a chart easier to read. By default, major gridlines are in increments of 10 and minor gridlines in increments of 2.
Legend	A box that lists and color-codes all data series.
Trendline	A line that forecasts future values based on current data.

Figure 11.1 shows some of these chart objects.

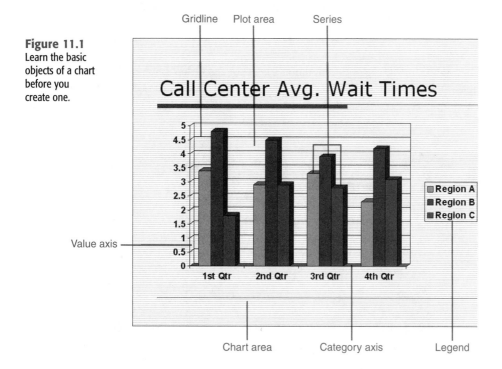

Figure 11.1
Learn the basic objects of a chart before you create one.

ADDING A CHART

The fastest way to add a chart to your presentation is to add a slide and apply a layout that contains a chart. To do so, click the New Slide button on the Formatting toolbar and then choose a layout from the Slide Layout task pane. The next step varies depending on the slide layout you choose.

If you choose any of the layouts in the Content Layouts or Text and Content Layouts sections, you need to click the Insert Chart button on the content palette that displays (see Figure 11.2) to activate the chart and Microsoft Graph.

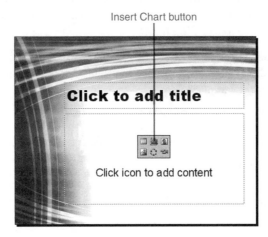

Figure 11.2
Click the Insert Chart button to start creating a chart.

If you choose one of the layouts containing a chart in the Other Layouts section, you need to double-click the chart placeholder to activate the chart and Microsoft Graph. Figure 11.3 shows a sample chart slide with a chart placeholder.

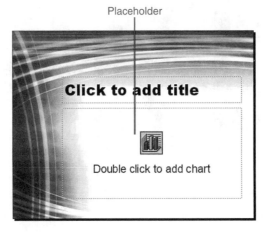

Figure 11.3
You can start adding a chart by double-clicking the placeholder.

TIP

If you want to create a slide with a single chart and no other content, choose the Title and Chart slide layout.

→ To learn more about how slide layouts affect your presentation, **see** "Understanding Slide Layouts" in Chapter 2, "Creating a Basic Presentation," **p. 43**.

NOTE

If you use the AutoContent Wizard to create your presentation, it might already have a slide that contains a chart.

You can also insert a chart into an existing slide by clicking the Insert Chart button on the Standard toolbar or by selecting Insert, Chart.

 Figure 11.4 shows what you see after you click the Insert Chart button on a content palette or double-click a chart placeholder. A sample 3D clustered column chart appears, and the related datasheet opens. The menu bar and toolbars are also customized for Microsoft Graph. The menu bar now includes Data and Chart menu items, and the Standard toolbar includes several new options, explained in Table 11.2.

Figure 11.4
PowerPoint displays a chart with sample data.

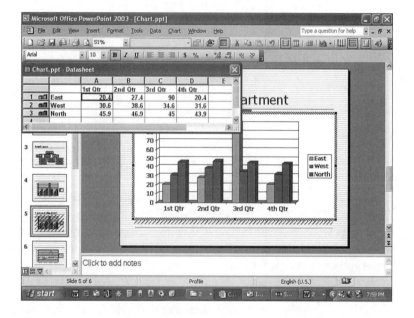

TABLE 11.2 STANDARD TOOLBAR CHART OPTIONS

Button	Name	Description
Category Axis	Chart Objects	Lets you select a chart object such as a plot area, a chart area, a legend, an axis, or a series.
	Format	Opens a Format dialog box tailored to the selected chart object.
	Import File	Opens the Import File dialog box from which you can import chart data from another file, such as an Excel worksheet, into your chart.

TABLE 11.2   CONTINUED

Button	Name	Description
	View Datasheet	Displays the chart's datasheet.
	By Row	Displays datasheet row data as the data series (the default).
	By Column	Displays datasheet column data as the data series.
	Data Table	Displays a table with all the datasheet data in your chart.
	Chart Type	Lets you apply a new chart type from a palette that appears.
	Category Axis Gridlines	Displays category axis gridlines.
	Value Axis Gridlines	Displays value axis gridlines.
	Legend	Displays a legend on your chart.
	Drawing	Displays the Drawing toolbar.
	Fill Color	Lets you apply fill color and fill effects to selected objects.

→ To learn more about object-formatting options in PowerPoint, **see** "Using the Format Dialog Box" in Chapter 14, "Creating and Formatting Objects," **p. 296**.

If you don't see these menu and toolbar options, Microsoft Graph isn't active. To activate it, double-click the chart in PowerPoint and you'll then be able to view the Data and Chart menus and chart toolbar options.

N O T E

> Many of these toolbar buttons act as a toggle. For example, clicking the View Datasheet button displays the datasheet if it's closed, but closes it if the datasheet already displays.

To determine what each object is in a chart you've created, place the mouse on that object or part of the chart and a chart tip displays its name. Figure 11.5 shows an example of a chart tip with the name and numeric value for a data series.

Figure 11.5
This chart tip lets you know the name of the chart object as well as its value.

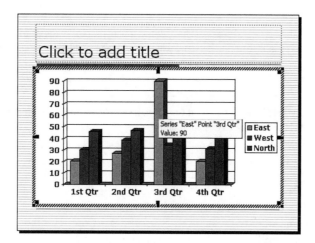

If the chart tip doesn't display, activate Microsoft Graph by double-clicking the chart, choose Tools, Options, and then verify that the Show Names and Show Values check boxes are selected on the Chart tab of the Graph Options dialog box (see Figure 11.6).

Figure 11.6
PowerPoint displays names and values in chart tips by default.

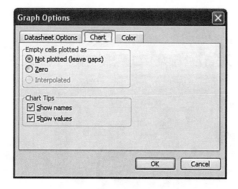

MODIFYING YOUR CHART

You can quickly create a basic chart, and you can make numerous enhancements and formatting changes. After you activate Microsoft Graph to create a chart, it's easiest to proceed in this order:

1. If you don't want a 3D column chart, change the chart type.
2. Type the text and numbers for your chart in the datasheet.
3. Type a title for the chart slide.
4. Modify and format chart objects as needed.

TIP

> Before creating an actual chart, design a paper sketch of the chart you want to create. This can help you understand which chart type is right for your specific chart.

NOTE

> For help in using Microsoft Graph, choose Help, Microsoft Graph Help. This opens the help file specific to this application.

SELECTING A CHART TYPE

PowerPoint offers plenty of chart types and sub-types for almost every kind of graphic representation you could want to create. Sub-types are variations on a basic chart type, such as 3D options. PowerPoint includes these basic chart types:

- **Column**   Creates vertical columns to compare the values of categories of data. Column, bar, and line charts work well if you want to compare values over time periods such as months or quarters. Figure 11.7 illustrates a sample column chart.

Figure 11.7
A column chart makes it easy to compare series of data.

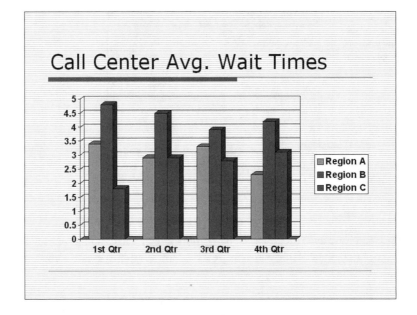

- **Bar**   Creates horizontal bars to compare the values of categories of data.
- **Line**   Creates a line with markers for each data value.
- **Pie**   Creates a pie that analyzes percentages of a total number. Use a pie chart to see how items contribute to a total. For example, you might want to compare the year's expenses for each department in your company. Figure 11.8 shows a pie chart.

Figure 11.8
Use pie charts to
show percentages of
a total amount.

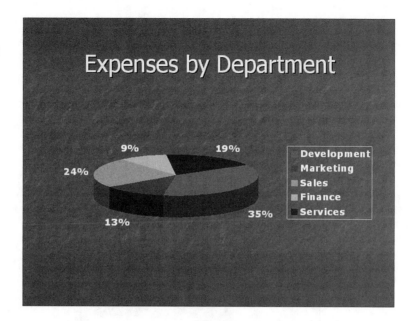

- **XY (Scatter)** Creates a chart that compares sets of values.
- **Area** Creates a chart that shows the trend of values in a single solid area.
- **Doughnut** Creates a pie chart that can contain more than one series.
- **Radar** Assigns a value axis (radiating from the center) for each category, and draws lines to connect all values in the same series. The chart compares the collected values of several data series.
- **Surface** Creates a single 3D surface that helps you finding the best combinations between two sets of data. Colors and patterns indicate areas that are in the same range of values.
- **Bubble** Compares three sets of values displayed as bubbles.
- **Stock** Shows a stock's high, low, and close figures.
- **Cylinder** Creates columns shaped like cylinders.
- **Cone** Creates columns shaped like cones.
- **Pyramid** Creates columns shaped like pyramids.

If you already know that you want to create a 3D clustered column chart, which is the PowerPoint default, you don't need to do anything to select a chart type. However, if you want to use a different chart type, you should select it before you enter any data or make any other modifications. There are two ways to change the chart type in PowerPoint. You can click the down arrow next to the Chart Type button on the Standard toolbar and select the chart type you want to apply from the palette that appears. Place the mouse over a specific chart type to view a chart tip that tells you the chart type's name. PowerPoint applies the chart type to your chart, which reformats itself in the new type. Not all chart types are available through the Chart Type button, however. If you can't find what you need on the palette that appears, try the Chart Type dialog box (Chart, Chart Type).

In either case, if you don't like the new chart type you applied, click the Undo button on the Standard toolbar to return to your original selection.

To apply a new chart type using the Chart Type dialog box, follow these steps:

1. In Microsoft Graph, choose Chart, Chart Type from the menu. The Chart Type dialog box appears, as shown in Figure 11.9.

Figure 11.9
PowerPoint offers many different chart types.

2. On the Standard Types tab, select the type of chart you want from the Chart Type list. A variety of sub-types appears in the Chart sub-type area.

3. Click the sub-type you want. The text box below provides detailed information about this sub-type.

4. To preview what an actual chart of this type looks like, click the Press and Hold to View Sample button. A sample chart temporarily replaces the Chart Sub-Type box, as shown in Figure 11.10.

5. If you want to change this to your default, select the Set as Default Chart button.

6. If none of the chart types in the Standard Types tab suits your needs, click the Custom Types tab to view more options. Figure 11.11 illustrates this tab.

Figure 11.10
You can preview
changes before
making them.

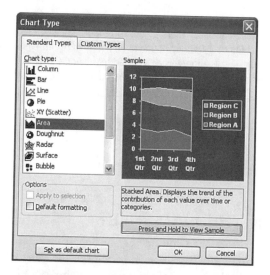

Figure 11.11
Custom charts
provide variety and
options.

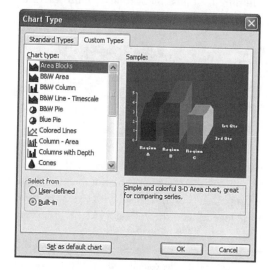

NOTE

Custom charts include detailed formatting, and some are customized specifically for a
certain kind of output, such as onscreen presentations. The text box beneath the example
indicates these details.

7. Click the Built-In option button to display PowerPoint's ready-made custom charts.

NOTE

> You can also add an active chart in your current presentation to the list of chart types. Simply select the User-Defined option button on the Custom Types tab, click the Add button, and enter details about this active chart to the Add Custom Chart Type dialog box that appears. Microsoft Graph adds this chart to its list of custom chart types.

8. Select the chart type you want to use from the Chart Type list. An example displays in the Sample box.
9. Click OK to apply the chart type and return to your presentation.

ENTERING DATA IN THE DATASHEET

The default datasheet that opens when you first create a chart includes four columns and three rows. This is a common chart format—comparing specific categories over periods of time—but only one of the hundreds of possible formats. Figure 11.12 illustrates this datasheet.

Figure 11.12
Enter chart data in a datasheet, similar to an Excel worksheet.

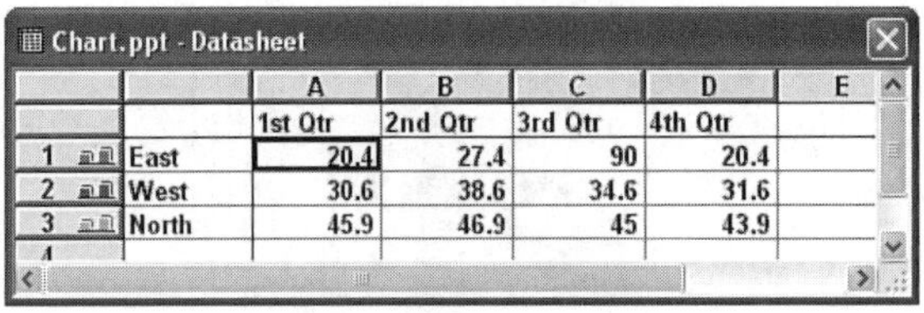

		A	B	C	D	E
		1st Qtr	2nd Qtr	3rd Qtr	4th Qtr	
1	East	20.4	27.4	90	20.4	
2	West	30.6	38.6	34.6	31.6	
3	North	45.9	46.9	45	43.9	
4						

The first row and column of a datasheet serve as headers for the information in the datasheet. Therefore, the second row begins with the number 1 and the second column with the letter A. In this example, the columns display as the category axis, the rows display as the data series listed in the legend, and the cell data (A1:D3) represents the value axis.

TIP

> To reverse the chart and use the column data as the data series instead of the row data, click the By Columns button on the Standard toolbar. Microsoft Graph redesigns the chart based on this change. For example, if you changed the default chart to display in columns, the quarters appear in the legend and the locations appear in the category axis.

To input your own data, just type over the existing information in each cell.

Does your chart have extra spaces? *See the "Troubleshooting" section near the end of this chapter.*

If the data you need is already in an Excel spreadsheet , you can import directly from Excel without reentering this information in the datasheet. Click the Import File button on the Standard toolbar to open the Import File dialog box. Choose the Excel file you want to import and click Open. The Import Data Options dialog box guides you through this process. Note that you can import from Lotus 1-2-3 and text file formats as well.

INSERTING AND DELETING DATASHEET ROWS AND COLUMNS

To delete a row or column, place the cursor within the appropriate row or column and choose Edit, Delete from the menu. To remove the contents of a cell rather than the cell itself, choose Edit, Clear, Contents. Clearing the contents is best when you want to remove existing data and replace it with new data. If you no longer need the row or column, you should delete it. You can delete a row or column by selecting its heading and pressing the Delete key.

NOTE

> You can also cut (Ctrl+X), copy (Ctrl+C), and paste (Ctrl+V) data in the datasheet by using keyboard commands or by choosing the appropriate buttons on the Standard toolbar.

To insert a new row, select the row below where you want to place the new row and choose Insert, Cells. Microsoft Graph inserts a new row directly above the selected row.

To insert a new column, select the column heading to the right of where you want to place the new column and choose Insert, Cells. Microsoft Graph inserts a new column directly to the left of the selected column.

If you want to insert a new cell, rather than a complete row or column, select the cell where you want to insert a cell; choose Insert, Cells; and choose either Shift Cells Right or Shift Cells Down in the Insert dialog box (see Figure 11.13).

Figure 11.13
Determine the direction to move the existing cells in the Insert dialog box.

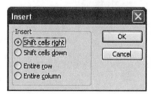

PowerPoint inserts a new cell and shifts the row to the right or shifts the column down, depending on your selection. You can undo insertions and deletions by clicking the Undo button or pressing Ctrl+Z.

FORMATTING DATASHEET COLUMN WIDTH

To format the datasheet's column width, follow these steps:

1. Select the heading of the column whose width you want to adjust.

2. Choose Format, Column Width. The Column Width dialog box appears, as shown in Figure 11.14.

Figure 11.14
You can customize
the width of a
datasheet column.

3. Type a width for the column the Column Width field. To adjust to the standard width, select the Use Standard Width check box. Or, click the Best Fit button to have the columns adjust automatically based on the existing data.

4. Click OK to return to the datasheet.

FORMATTING DATASHEET NUMBERS

You can format the text and numbers in your datasheet if you want. To format numerical data, select the cell or cells you want to format and choose Format, Number. The Format Number dialog box appears, as shown in Figure 11.15.

Figure 11.15
Customize the way
numbers appear in
this dialog box.

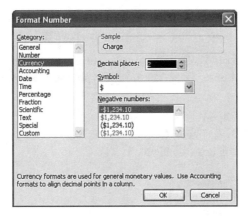

Select the type of number format you want from the Category list, such as date, time, or currency format. Based on your category selection, the right side of the dialog box offers additional formatting options related to the category.

For example, if you choose Currency, the right side of the dialog box lets you choose the currency symbol such as the dollar, pound, or yen. Several of the numeric categories also let you choose the number of decimal places you want to include.

Click OK to accept the formatting changes and to update your chart.

 Do your datasheet numbers display in an exponential format? *See the "Troubleshooting" section near the end of the chapter.*

INCLUDING AND EXCLUDING ROWS AND COLUMNS

You can include rows and columns in your datasheet, but temporarily hide them in your presentation. To do that, select the column or row that you want to hide, and choose Data, Exclude Row/Col. The row or column appears shaded in your datasheet and temporarily disappears from your presentation. Figure 11.16 shows an example of a hidden column in a datasheet.

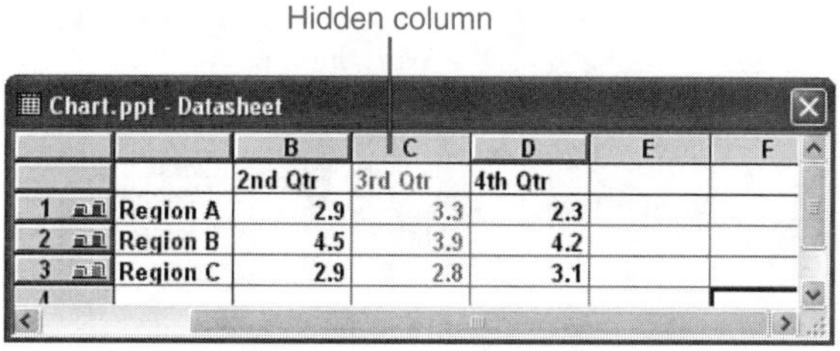

Hidden column

Figure 11.16
This hidden column will temporarily be removed from the chart.

		B	C	D	E	F
		2nd Qtr	3rd Qtr	4th Qtr		
1	Region A	2.9	3.3	2.3		
2	Region B	4.5	3.9	4.2		
3	Region C	2.9	2.8	3.1		

To include this information again, choose Data, Include Row/Col.

TIP

> You can also double-click the row or column head to include or exclude the rows or columns. In this case, the action serves as a toggle.

RETURNING TO THE PRESENTATION FROM THE DATASHEET

When you finish formatting and modifying the datasheet, you can close it by clicking the View Datasheet button on the Standard toolbar. Or you can return to working on the presentation while the datasheet remains open by clicking on any section of the presentation.

To reopen the datasheet, click the View Datasheet button again.

FORMATTING A CHART

Microsoft Graph offers detailed precision in chart creation and the opportunity to make numerous formatting changes. You can set overall chart options or format specific chart objects. Before making major changes to the chart's default settings, be sure to carefully consider your reason for customizing. Different is better only when it adds value or clarity to your chart.

NOTE

> If the chart isn't active, you won't see the chart menu and toolbar options. Double-click the chart to select it and display chart options.

SETTING OVERALL CHART OPTIONS

Use the Chart Options dialog box to set overall chart options for the chart type you selected. In Microsoft Graph, choose Chart, Chart Options to display this dialog box, shown in Figure 11.17.

Figure 11.17
Set a variety of chart-formatting options in this dialog box.

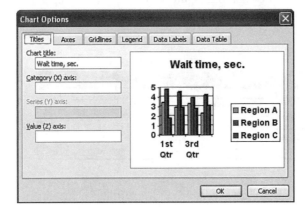

We'll use the clustered 3D column chart type as an example as we explore the tabs of this dialog box. If you select a different chart type (such as a pie), the options and tabs might differ slightly.

Make any necessary changes within the tabs of this dialog box, and then click OK to apply them to your presentation.

ENTERING CHART TITLES

On the Titles tab, you can enter titles for the overall chart and the available axes such as category, value, or series. The example to the right previews these changes in your chart.

CAUTION

The chart title isn't the same as a slide title. If you create a chart title, your chart will have two titles—one for the slide and one for the chart.

FORMATTING AXES

On the Axes tab, shown in Figure 11.18, you can choose whether to display category, series, and value axes. If a particular axis isn't available, you won't be able to choose it. In this example, the category axis displays the data you entered in the first row of cells in your datasheet. The value axis displays a numerical series based on the values you entered in the datasheet.

Figure 11.18
Specify whether to display a particular axis.

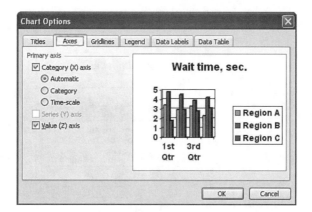

FORMATTING GRIDLINES

On the Gridlines tab (see Figure 11.19), you can choose whether to display major or minor gridlines for all available axes.

Figure 11.19
Major gridlines, selected by default, can make values easier to read.

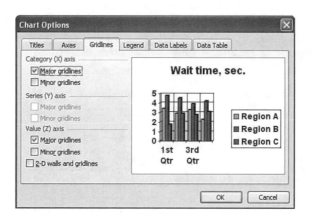

11

> **NOTE**
> Pie and doughnut charts don't have gridlines.

DISPLAYING A LEGEND

On the Legend tab, shown in Figure 11.20, you can choose to display a legend by selecting the Show Legend check box.

Placement options include placing your legend at the bottom, corner, top, right, or left of your chart.

> **NOTE**
> After you place a legend on your chart, you can select and drag it to a new location.

Figure 11.20
A legend makes
a chart easier to
understand.

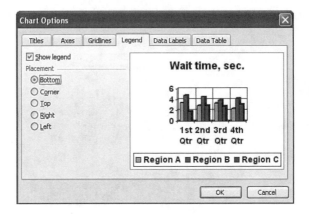

DISPLAYING DATA LABELS

A data label makes data in your chart easier to identify. You can display a value, percent, text label, text label and percent, a bubble size, or no label at all. Figure 11.21 shows the Data Labels tab.

Figure 11.21
Data labels are
optional means of
identifying chart
information.

11

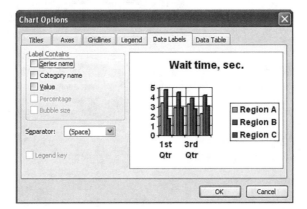

NOTE

Depending on the chart type you select, not all data label options are available.

If you do choose to display a data label, the Legend Key check box appears. Check this box if you want to display a color-coded box next to the data label to associate it with the legend.

DISPLAYING A DATA TABLE

If you want to include a table with all your datasheet data in your chart, you can choose the Show Data Table check box in the Data Table tab (see Figure 11.22).

Figure 11.22
If your chart contains complex numerical data, a data table can make this information more meaningful.

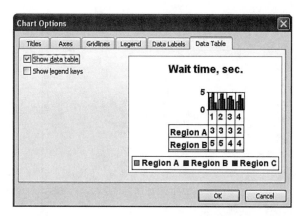

If you select this option, you also have the choice to Show Legend Keys if you want to display a color-coded box in the table columns to associate them with the legend.

FORMATTING CHART OBJECTS

You can format individual chart objects, such as the chart area, axes, series, legend, and gridlines. To format a specific chart object, select it from the Chart Objects drop-down list on the Standard toolbar, and then click the Format button to the right of the drop-down list. A Format dialog box customized for the type of object you select appears. For example, you might see the Format Axis dialog box or the Format Data Series dialog box, depending on the selected chart object. If the Format button isn't available, no formatting options exist for the selected chart object.

You can modify many formatting options from the Format dialog box, including pattern, font, placement, scale, alignment, and shape. Remember, though, that numerous changes don't always enhance a chart. Go easy.

→ To learn more about the available options in this dialog box, **see** "Using the Format Dialog Box" in Chapter 14, **p. 296**.

Some things you might want to consider changing include the following:

- Apply a different color to the data series fill areas. To do this, select the data series you want to modify from the Chart Objects drop-down list and click the Format button. Figure 11.23 illustrates the Format Data Series dialog box.

  Choose a new color from the Area group box and click OK. PowerPoint updates the color in the presentation.

- Increase or decrease font size to make text more readable or to make it fit a specific area. For example, to change the font size of the legend, select the legend in the Chart Objects drop-down list and click the Format Legend button to display the dialog box of the same name (see Figure 11.24).

  From the Font tab, you can increase or decrease the font size as needed.

11

Figure 11.23
Change fill color in
this dialog box.

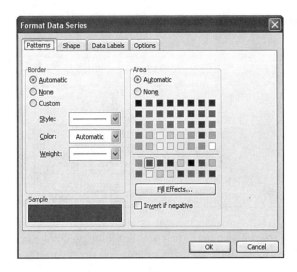

Figure 11.24
Adjusting the font size
is a common format-
ting change.

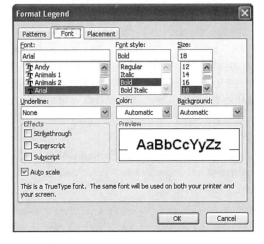

11

- Adjust the value axis scale. To do this, select the value axis from the Chart Objects drop-down list and click the Format Axis button. Figure 11.25 shows the Scale tab in the Format Axis dialog box.

You can change the minimum and maximum values or the major and minor gridline units on the Scale tab. For example, if all the values in your chart are more than 100 and you want to see the variations in the existing values more clearly, change the mini-mum value from 0 to 100. PowerPoint updates the presentation, making the differences between the three data series much more apparent.

Figure 11.25
You can adjust the axes and gridlines in the Format Axis dialog box.

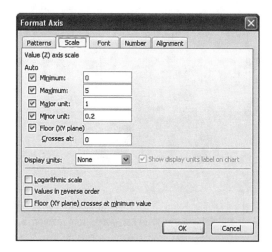

FORMATTING 3D VIEW

If you choose a 3D chart type, you can format 3D viewing options such as elevation, rotation, height, and perspective. Table 11.3 explains each of these options.

TABLE 11.3   3D VIEW OPTIONS

3D View Option	Description
Elevation	Lets you control the elevation level from which you view the chart. The range is from –90° to 90° with a default of 15°.
Rotation	Lets you control the plot area rotation around a vertical axis. The default rotation is 20° with a possible range of 0° to 360°. On 3D bar charts, the range is only up to 44°. Be careful not to overdo rotation, however. A 90° rotation on a typical column chart yields unreadable results, for example.
Height	Lets you control the value axis height as a percentage of the category axis length. A height of 150% makes the chart height one and a half times the category axis length.
Perspective	Lets you control the chart depth view in degrees. With a default of 30°, the range is from 0° to 100° and measures the ratio of the chart front to back. This option is unavailable when the Right Angle Axes check box is selected or when the chart type is a 3D bar.

To format these options, follow these steps:

1. In Microsoft Graph, choose Chart, 3-D View to open the 3-D View dialog box, as shown in Figure 11.26.

Figure 11.26
Modify the way your chart displays 3D objects in this dialog box.

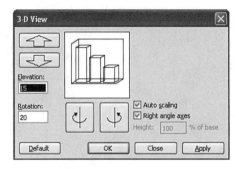

CAUTION

Again, the default settings for 3D options are designed to work with this chart. Be careful making changes! Major changes to a chart's elevation, rotation, height, or perspective can make it unreadable.

→ To learn more about 3D, **see** "Adding Shadow and 3D Effects" in Chapter 14, **p. 303**.

2. Enter a new elevation in the Elevation field or click the up and down arrow buttons above this field to adjust elevation. The box to the right displays an example of what the selected change looks like.

3. Enter a new rotation or click the left and right arrow buttons to the right of the field to change the rotation. The sample box previews this change.

4. Click the Auto Scaling check box to automatically scale the chart to fit the slide.

5. If you remove the check mark from the Auto Scaling check box, the Height field appears. In it, you can set height as a specific percentage of the base.

6. If you remove the check mark from the Right Angle Axes check box, the Perspective field and associated arrow buttons appear. Set the perspective manually or use the buttons to modify the perspective.

7. Click the Apply button to view the effects of potential changes to chart.

8. Click the Default button to set the 3D changes you've made as your new default.

TIP

If you make a mistake, click Close to exit the dialog box without saving changes.

9. Click OK to apply the changes and return to your presentation.

ADDING A TRENDLINE

A trendline creates a forecast of future trends based on existing data. For example, you can use a trendline to predict future revenues based on existing revenue data in a chart. This is also referred to as *regression analysis*.

You can use trendlines to make basic forecasts, but a solid understanding of regression analysis and statistics is necessary to make the best use of this feature.

You can display a *trendline* in unstacked area, bar, column, line, stock, XY (scatter), and bubble charts that don't have a 3D effect.

To create a trendline, follow these steps:

1. Choose Chart, Add Trendline to open the Add Trendline dialog box, shown in Figure 11.27.

Figure 11.27
Predict future values by creating a trendline.

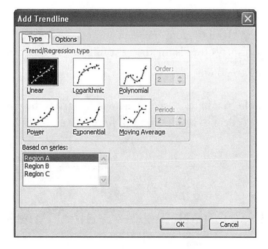

 Can't access the Add Trendline menu option? See the "Troubleshooting" section near the end of this chapter.

2. Choose the Trend/Regression Type, such as Linear or Moving Average, from the group box.
3. Select the data series on which you want to base the trend from the Based on Series list.
4. Click the Options tab for more options, shown in Figure 11.28.
5. You can enter a custom name for the trendline or accept the default. The default uses the type of trendline you selected in the Type tab, followed by the series name in parentheses.

Figure 11.28
Specify the period of
time you want to
forecast.

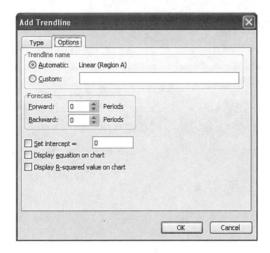

6. Indicate how many periods you want to forecast either forward or backward. For example, if your chart displays data for four quarters and you choose to forecast four periods
   forward, PowerPoint displays trends for the next full year in quarterly increments.

7. Click OK to apply the trendline.

Figure 11.29 shows a sample trendline. Based on actual data from the past year, it forecasts
for the next year how long callers to a help line will have to wait on hold before speaking to
someone.

Figure 11.29
This chart illustrates
both current
values and future
predictions.

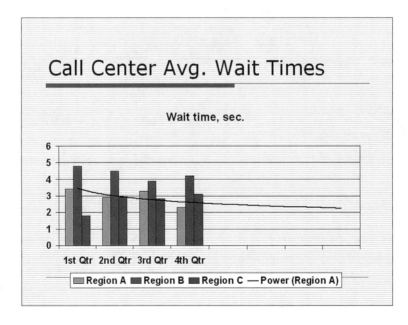

TROUBLESHOOTING

LOCATING MISSING MENUS AND TOOLBARS

I can't find the menus or toolbar buttons you mention.

Be sure that Microsoft Graph is active if the text mentions that this menu or toolbar button is part of that application. If you're in PowerPoint, the Graph options aren't on the screen. To activate Microsoft Graph, double-click your chart.

RESOLVING DATASHEET FORMAT PROBLEMS

My datasheet numbers display in exponential formatting.

You need to apply a formatting category other than the default General formatting if your numbers exceed 11 digits. To do so, choose Format, Number from within Microsoft Graph and change to a category such as Number or Currency.

FINDING THE ADD TRENDLINE MENU OPTION

I can't see the Add Trendline option from the Chart menu.

You can only create a trendline with unstacked area, bar, column, line, stock, XY (scatter), and bubble charts that don't have a 3D effect. To make this menu option available, change your chart to one of these types.

REMOVING EMPTY SPACES

My chart has empty spaces where there should be a data series.

If you don't need one of the existing datasheet rows or columns, you need to remove it entirely from the datasheet, not just the contents. Otherwise, it can display as an empty space on your chart and disrupt formatting. If a series you entered is missing, verify that none of your columns or rows is hidden. To include a hidden row/column, choose Data, Include Row/Col from within Microsoft Graph.

DESIGN CORNER: USING CHART FORMATTING OPTIONS

PowerPoint, in combination with Microsoft Graph, offers numerous chart-formatting options to help you create visually appealing charts. This example shows how even minor changes can enhance your chart.

For example, you could create a basic column chart by choosing the Title and Chart layout from the Slide Layout task pane (see the "Before" figure). To liven up the chart (see the "After" figure), follow these steps using the techniques you learned in this chapter:

1. With your chart active, choose Chart, Chart Options to open the Chart Options dialog box.

2. On the Titles tab, enter a title for your chart.

3. On the Legend tab, place your legend on the bottom.

4. Click the down arrow to the right of the Chart Type button on the Standard toolbar to display a palette of options.

5. Click the Bar Chart button to change to a bar chart format (pause the mouse pointer over the buttons to identify the right button).

6. For each chart object that has text, select it and set the font to match the font used in the slide design.

In only a couple of minutes, you enlivened your chart and made its format better suit your needs.

BEFORE

Figure 11.30

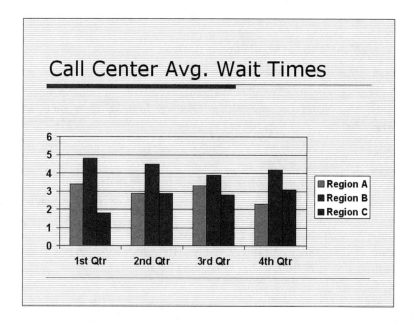

AFTER

Figure 11.31

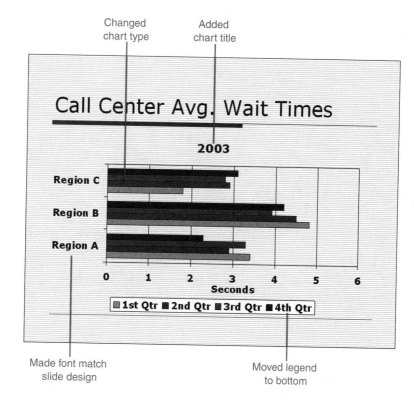

CHAPTER 12

WORKING WITH DIAGRAMS AND ORGANIZATION CHARTS

In this chapter

by Patrice-Anne Rutledge and Jim Grey

UNDERSTANDING DIAGRAMS AND ORGANIZATION CHARTS

PowerPoint's diagramming features let you add detailed diagrams and organization charts to presentations. Using diagram types such as cycle, radial, pyramid, Venn, and target, you can visually represent a variety of concepts and ideas—and make the diagrams match the color scheme and look of your presentation. PowerPoint's organization chart lets you display a hierarchical structure of your organization—and more. Although organization chart terminology—subordinate, co-worker, and so forth—is directed to a corporate environment, you can use an organization chart anywhere you need to set up a hierarchy of people. For example, an organization chart could describe a volunteer committee, school organization, club, or not-for-profit group. You can even use organization charts to show how ideas and projects are organized.

GETTING STARTED WITH DIAGRAMS AND ORGANIZATION CHARTS

The fastest way to add a diagram or organization chart to your presentation is to apply a slide layout that contains one. To do so, click the New Slide button on the Formatting toolbar and then choose an appropriate layout from the Slide Layout task pane. The next step depends on the slide layout you choose.

If you choose any of the layouts in the Content Layouts or Text and Content Layouts sections, click the Insert Diagram or Organization Chart button on the content. The Diagram Gallery opens (see Figure 12.1).

If you choose the Title and Diagram or Organization Chart layout in the Other Layouts section, double-click the placeholder to open the Diagram Gallery. Figure 12.2 shows a slide with this placeholder. If you want to create a slide with a diagram or organization chart and no other content, choose this slide layout.

→ To learn more about how slide layouts affect your presentation, **see** "Understanding Slide Layouts" in Chapter 2, "Creating a Basic Presentation," **p. 43**.

You can also insert a diagram or organization chart by clicking the Insert Diagram or Organization Chart button on the Drawing toolbar. Figure 12.3 illustrates the Diagram Gallery, which offers not only an organization chart, but also cycle, radial, pyramid, Venn, and target diagrams. If you're unsure of the best use of any of these diagram options, single-click its image on the Diagram Gallery and explanatory text appears below.

Figures 12.4 and 12.5 illustrate examples of each of these diagrams or charts.

Insert Diagram or Organization Chart button

Figure 12.1
Click the Insert
Diagram or
Organization Chart
button to get started.

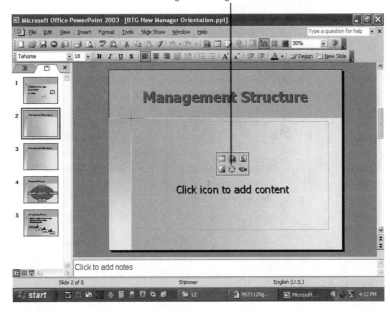

Double-click the placeholder to open the Diagram Gallery.

Figure 12.2
You can also start by
double-clicking a
placeholder.

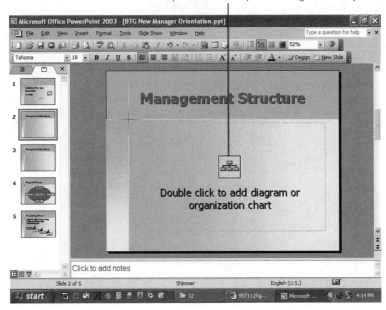

12

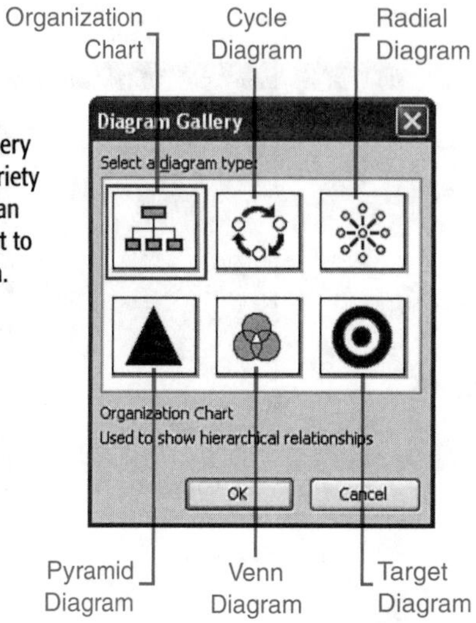

Figure 12.3
The Diagram Gallery lets you add a variety of diagrams and an organization chart to your presentation.

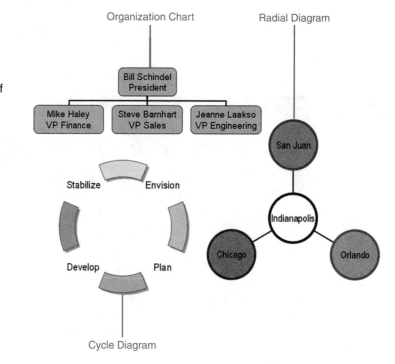

Figure 12.4
There are a variety of ways to illustrate information in PowerPoint.

Figure 12.5
Additional diagram
options are also
available.

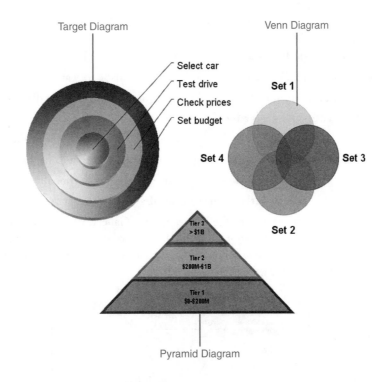

Target Diagram

Venn Diagram

Select car
Test drive
Check prices
Set budget

Set 1

Set 4

Set 3

Set 2

Tier 3
> $1B

Tier 2
$200M-$1B

Tier 1
$0-$200M

Pyramid Diagram

ADDING A DIAGRAM TO YOUR PRESENTATION

To add a diagram, choose one of the five diagram styles in the Diagram Gallery and click OK. If you find that the diagram type doesn't suit your needs, you can change it later.

 Can't find the right diagram? See the "Troubleshooting" section near the end of this chapter.

12

NOTE

> Remember that diagrams are only one way to visually present information in PowerPoint. You can also create flowcharts and other illustrations, for example, to convey similar information using PowerPoint's AutoShapes.

→ To learn how to use AutoShapes to create flowcharts or other diagrams, **see** "Adding AutoShapes" in Chapter 14, "Creating and Formatting Objects," **p. 288**.

PowerPoint inserts the diagram in your presentation and opens the Diagram and Drawing toolbars. The Diagram toolbar includes the following options:

 ■ **Insert Shape**—Inserts an additional shape in your diagram. For example, if you have a pyramid diagram with four levels, clicking Insert Shape adds a fifth level.

→ For more information on using the Drawing toolbar, **see** "Using the Drawing Toolbar to Create Objects" in Chapter 14, **p. 282**.

 ■ **Move Shape Backward**—Moves the selected shape backward.

 ■ **Move Shape Forward**—Moves the selected shape forward.

■ **Reverse Diagram**—Reverses the positioning of the selected diagram.

Layout ▾ ■ **Layout**—Displays a menu with the following options:

  • **Fit Diagram to Contents**—Resizes the diagram to fit the allotted space.

  • **Expand Diagram**—Expands a smaller diagram to fit the allotted space.

  • **Scale Diagram**—Rescales the diagram proportionally to the allotted space.

  • **AutoLayout**—Applies an AutoLayout.

Fit Text ■ **AutoFormat**—Opens the Diagram Style Gallery, where you can choose from many different styles for your diagram. The box to the right previews the style you select. Click Apply when you find the style that suits your presentation. Figure 12.6 illustrates this style gallery.

Figure 12.6
Choose from a variety of style options for your diagram.

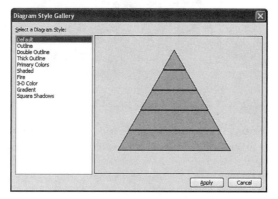

Change to ▾ ■ **Change To**—Displays a menu of other diagram styles, so you can quickly modify your diagram if your original choice (which is dimmed on the menu) wasn't quite right. Options include Cycle, Radial, Pyramid, Venn, and Target.

ADDING TEXT TO YOUR DIAGRAM

You can add text to radial, pyramid, and Venn diagrams by clicking a Click to Add Text placeholder or by right-clicking the placeholder and choosing Edit Text from the menu that appears. The temporary text disappears and a cursor appears so that you can type your text. You can format the text in this box as you would any other text, applying boldface, a new font, and so on.

Even if you chose a diagram that doesn't support adding text in this manner, you can add text in the form of a text box. To add a text box, click the Text Box button on the Drawing toolbar, click where you want the text box to appear, and type your text.

→ For more information on using the Drawing toolbar to create a text box, **see** "Using the Drawing Toolbar to Create Objects" in Chapter 14, **p. 282**.

FORMATTING YOUR DIAGRAM

You can format a diagram just as you format any other PowerPoint object. For example, you can reposition your diagram, change its colors, modify fonts, and so on. Formatting your diagram can not only make it more visually appealing, but also make it better match your presentation's design scheme. You'll primarily handle formatting tasks in the Format dialog box or by using the Drawing toolbar.

→ For more information about the Format dialog box and the Drawing toolbar, **see** Chapter 14, **p. 281**.

You can also animate a diagram to add additional emphasis during a presentation. For example, you could animate a pyramid diagram by having each level of the pyramid display one at time on your slide. Using the Custom Animation task pane, you can easily apply sophisticated animations like this to the parts of your diagrams.

→ To learn more about animating diagrams, **see** Chapter 15, "Working with Animation," **p. 319**.

DELETING A DIAGRAM

To delete a diagram, select it and press the Delete key. The content palette or placeholder appears, depending on which slide layout you chose. If you want to create another diagram, you can start over from here, accessing the Diagram Gallery by clicking the placeholder or the Insert Diagram or Organization Chart button on the palette. If you want to delete the diagram entirely, select the frame around the palette or placeholder and press the Delete key again.

NOTE

If you delete a diagram and a content palette or placeholder does *not* appear, you created the diagram by choosing Insert, Diagram.

12

ADDING AN ORGANIZATION CHART TO YOUR PRESENTATION

To add an organization chart, choose the Organization Chart option in the Diagram Gallery and click OK.

→ For a refresher on how to open this dialog box, **see** "Getting Started with Diagrams and Organization Charts" earlier in this chapter, **p. 246**.

> **TIP**
>
> It's best to design your organization chart on paper first, particularly if you're not familiar with this application. This lets you focus on creating the chart rather than on content.

PowerPoint inserts the organization chart into your presentation and opens the Organization Chart and Drawing toolbars. The button image for each option on these toolbars shows you what its layout style looks like. The Organization Chart toolbar includes the following options:

■ **Insert Shape**—Either adds a subordinate box or, if you click the arrow at the end of the button, opens a menu of types of boxes to add. Choices include Subordinate, Co-worker, and Assistant. To add a box, first click the box in the chart to which you want to add a box. Then click the arrow at the end of Insert Shape and choose the kind of box to add. The box you chose appears on the chart.

> **CAUTION**
>
> If you've selected the top-level position in the organization, you can't add a co-worker. This option appears dimmed.

■ **Layout**—Displays a menu of layout options, including
  • Standard
  • Both Hanging
  • Left Hanging
  • Right Hanging
  • Fit Organization Chart to Contents
  • Expand Organization Chart
  • Scale Organization Chart
  • AutoLayout
■ **Select** Lets you select a specific part of your organization chart so that you can format it. Options include Level, Branch, All Assistants, and All Connecting Lines.

- **AutoFormat**—Opens the Organization Chart Style Gallery (see Figure 12.7), where you can choose from several styles for your organization chart. The box to the right previews the style you choose. Click Apply when you find the style that suits your presentation.

Figure 12.7
Choose from a variety of style options for your organization chart.

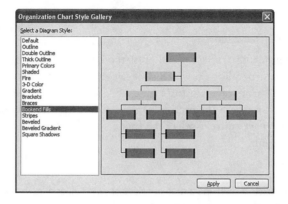

CAUTION

The Organization Chart Style Gallery gives you a lot of flexibility and creativity. But be sure that your style choice keeps your chart readable and matches your overall presentation tone. It's easy to choose a style that looks cool in the preview, but makes the chart impossible to read because of your slide's design and other style settings.

ADDING TEXT TO YOUR ORGANIZATION CHART

You can add text to your organization chart by clicking the Click to Add Text placeholder that appears in the boxes in your chart. Depending on the size of the box, you might not see this placeholder. If not, just click in the shape itself. Then type your text in the box. If the text doesn't fit, the box grows to fit it. You can format organization chart text just as you would any other text—by changing fonts, applying bold and italics, resizing it, and so on.

→ For a refresher of text formatting techniques, **see** Chapter 3, "Working with Text," **p. 63**.

FORMATTING YOUR ORGANIZATION CHART

You can format an organization chart just as you format any other PowerPoint object. For example, you can reposition it, change its colors, modify line width, and so on. You'll primarily do this in the Format dialog box (right-click and choose Format AutoShape from the menu) or using the Drawing toolbar.

→ For more information about the Format dialog box and the Drawing toolbar, **see** Chapter 14, **p. 281**.

You can also animate your organization chart for extra emphasis.

→ To learn more about animating organization charts, **see** Chapter 15, **p. 319**.

CAUTION

> Remember to consider readability and visual clarity when you modify an organization chart's defaults. Some formatting can enhance a chart's appearance, but too much formatting can make it confusing or—worse—unreadable.

DELETING AN ORGANIZATION CHART

To delete an organization chart, select it and press the Delete key. Either the content palette or placeholder appears, depending on which slide layout you chose. If you want to create another chart, you can start over again from here, accessing the Diagram Gallery by clicking the placeholder or the Insert Diagram or Organization Chart button on the palette. If you want to delete the chart entirely, select the frame around the palette or placeholder and press the Delete key again.

NOTE

> If you delete a chart and a content palette or placeholder does *not* appear, you created the diagram by choosing Insert, Diagram.

TROUBLESHOOTING

FIXING A PROBLEM ORGANIZATION CHART

I tried creating an organization chart for the first time, and it's a real mess. Do I have to delete the entire slide?

No, just delete the organization chart itself. From there, you can begin again. If you see a palette, click the Insert Diagram or Organization Chart button. If you see a placeholder, double-click the placeholder. If you see nothing, choose Insert, Diagram. In each case, the Diagram Gallery dialog box appears.

EXPANDING DIAGRAM CHOICES

I can't create the diagram I want with the Diagram Gallery choices.

Remember that you can apply style options using the Diagram Style Gallery. If those options aren't enough, you can create a diagram yourself from the Drawing toolbar by adding an AutoShape or manually designing an illustration using PowerPoint's drawing tools. As a last resort, create your diagram in another program (such as Visio or Illustrator) and then insert it.

Design Corner: Enlivening Your Organization Charts

You can use PowerPoint's organization chart to create all kinds of hierarchical charts and then use the style gallery and other formatting features to enliven your chart and make it coordinate with the rest of your presentation. For example, let's say that you created a basic organization chart for your department using the default options, showing you as the department manager with an assistant and three staffers reporting to you. It conveys the basic information you want, but lacks pizzazz (see Figure 12.8). You decide that you want to apply a different style, bold the names and titles to make them easier to read, and increase the font size in the shape that contains your name and title. (You are the boss, after all.) To quickly do this, follow these steps:

1. Click the AutoFormat button on the Organization Chart toolbar to open the Organization Chart Style Gallery.
2. Select the style you prefer (such as Bookend Fills) and click Apply.
3. Hold down the Ctrl key and click all management-level boxes.
4. Click the Bold button on the Formatting toolbar to bold the text in management boxes.
5. Select the top-level box; click the Increase Font Size button on the Formatting toolbar to increase the font size of this organization chart shape.
6. For each line manager who has reports, select the manager's box and choose Layout, Right Hanging on the Organization Chart toolbar.

Figure 12.9 illustrates the improved organization chart. If you wanted, you could make other changes as well—revising font colors, italicizing job titles, modifying the options in the Format Organization Chart dialog box (right-click and choose Format Organization Chart to open), and so forth. Just be careful not to go overboard and make your organization chart harder to read.

12

BEFORE

Figure 12.8

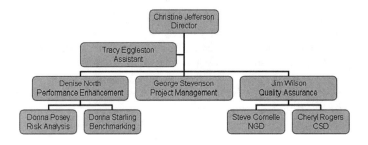

AFTER

Figure 12.9

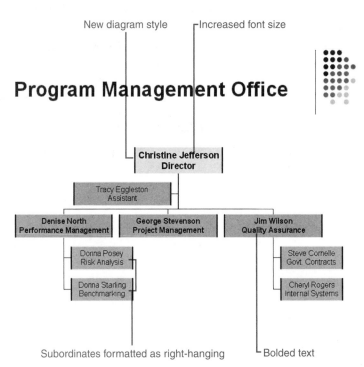

CHAPTER 13

WORKING WITH PICTURES, MOVIES, SOUNDS, AND THE CLIP ORGANIZER

In this chapter

by Patrice-Anne Rutledge and Jim Grey

EXPLORING CLIP ART, PICTURES, MOVIES, AND SOUND

Clip art, pictures, movies, and sounds can add a full multimedia effect to your presentations. You can insert picture, sound, and video clips from several sources—from the Microsoft Clip Organizer, from Microsoft Office Online, or from your own stash of pictures, sounds, and videos.

UNDERSTANDING CLIP ART

Office offers thousands of clip art images that you can use to illustrate your presentations. Microsoft's Web site includes even more images. After you insert clip art into your presentation, you can reformat, recolor, and redesign it to suit your needs.

Office includes clip art images in the following formats:

- Windows Metafile (WMF)
- Computer Graphics Metafile (CGM)
- Graphics Interchange Format (GIF)
- Joint Photographic Experts Groups (JPEG)

You can also add images in the Portable Network Graphics (PNG) and Bitmap (BMP) formats.

UNDERSTANDING PICTURES

A picture is any drawing or photograph you insert from your own files. Unlike clip art, you can't control its format or color after you insert it into a presentation. PowerPoint accepts pictures in a many formats. Table 13.1 lists the most common picture formats.

TABLE 13.1   PICTURE FORMATS

File Extension	Format
.jpg, .jpeg, .jfif, .jpe	JPEG File Interchange Format
.png	Portable Network Graphics
.bmp, .dib, .rle, .bmz	Windows Bitmap
.gif, .gfa	Graphics Interchange Format
.tif, .tiff	Tagged Image File Format
.cdr	CorelDraw
.eps	Encapsulated PostScript
.pcd	Kodak PhotoCD

File Extension	Format
.pcx	PC Paintbrush
.pct, .pict	Macintosh PICT

UNDERSTANDING SOUND AND MOVIE FILES

PowerPoint lets you insert media clips (sound and movie files) in to your presentations. To play them, you need to have a sound card and speakers installed on your computer.

Media clips work in much the same way as clip art and pictures, and are also available through the Microsoft Clip Organizer. Common media clip file formats include the following:

- **MIDI**   Musical Instrument Digital Interface.
- **WAV**   Microsoft Windows audio format.
- **MPEG**   Motion Picture Experts Group, a standard video format.
- **AVI**   Microsoft Windows video format.
- **GIF**   Graphical Interchange Format. Animated GIFs (a series of GIF images that appear animated) are stored with other video files.

Media clips can greatly enhance your presentation's multimedia effect, but remember that, as with clip art and other images, overuse of media clips can clutter a presentation.

→ To learn more about ways to include multimedia content in your presentations, **see** "Incorporating Multimedia" in Chapter 28, "Exploring Technicalities and Techniques," **p. 665**.

PowerPoint can play a clip automatically during a slideshow, or you can customize the clip to play only by a mouse action. Other multimedia options include recording your own sounds or playing a CD track as a slideshow background.

INSERTING CLIPS

There are several ways to add clips to your PowerPoint presentations. The method you choose depends on where the clip is located (in the Clip Organizer or only on your computer, for example), how you prefer to use PowerPoint, and whether you know exactly what you want to insert.

13

INSERTING CLIP ART

To insert clip art, you can do any of the following:

- From the Slide Layout task pane, choose any of the content layouts and click the Insert Clip Art button from the content palette. The Select Picture dialog box opens (see Figure 13.1), displaying clips from the Clip Organizer.

Figure 13.1
Inserting a clip from a slide layout is just one option.

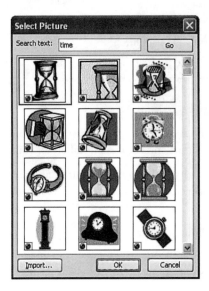

Select the picture you want to insert and click OK to insert it on your slide. If you want to search for a specific image, enter its keyword in the Search Text field and then click Search.

NOTE

If you want to import a clip, click the Import button. This opens the Add Clips to Organizer dialog box, where you can choose the clip you want to import.

- From the Slide Layout task pane, choose the Title, Clip Art, and Text; Title, Text, and Clip Art; or Title, Clip Art, and Vertical Text layout; and then double-click the clip art placeholder to open the Select Picture dialog box.
- Choose Insert, Picture, Clip Art to open the Clip Art task pane, shown in Figure 13.2. Search by keyword for the type of clip art you need, and then select it. Click the down arrow to the right of the thumbnail and then choose Insert. The clip will be inserted on your slide.

NOTE

You can also drag your selected picture from the task pane to the slide.

The first time you open the Clip Art task pane, the Add Clips to Organizer dialog box appears. Use this dialog box to have PowerPoint automatically organize your clips for you.

Figure 13.2
Search for clip art by keyword.

- Choose Insert, Picture, Clip Art to open the Clip Art task pane. Click the Organize clips link to open the Microsoft Clip Organizer from which you can view clip art collections. Figure 13.3 shows the Clip Organizer.

Figure 13.3
Browsing the collections in the Clip Organizer is another way to locate clip art.

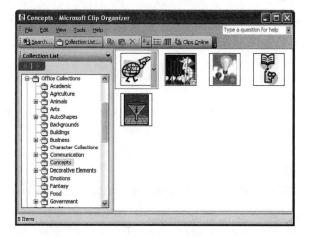

13

Within the Clip Organizer, you can either copy and paste a clip into your presentation, or drag and drop it if your windows are arranged to accommodate this.

- Click the Insert Clip Art button on the Drawing toolbar to open the Clip Art task pane. From here, you can either use the task pane's search functionality to search for clip art, or click the Organize clips link to go directly to the gallery.

INSERTING PICTURES

To insert a picture on a slide, do any of the following:

- From the Slide Layout task pane, choose any of the content layouts and click the Insert Picture button from the content palette. The Insert Picture dialog box opens (see Figure 13.4), which is similar to the Open dialog box.

Figure 13.4
Find and insert a picture from this dialog box.

→ To learn more about the advanced features of the Open dialog box that are shared with the Insert Picture dialog box, **see** "Exploring the Open Dialog Box" in Chapter 2, **p. 56**.

Select the picture you want to insert and click Insert to insert it on your slide.

- Choose Insert, Picture, From File to open the Insert Picture dialog box.
- Choose Insert, Picture, From Scanner or Camera to open the Insert Picture from Scanner or Camera dialog box.

→ To learn more about inserting pictures from scanners or cameras, **see** "Adding Clips from a Scanner or Camera" in this chapter, **p. 270**.

- Click the Insert Picture button on the Drawing toolbar to open the Insert Picture dialog box.

INSERTING SOUNDS OR MOVIES

To insert a media clip (sound or movie) to your presentation, do any one of the following:

- From the Slide Layout task pane, choose any of the content layouts and click the Insert Media Clip button from the content palette. The Select Media Clip dialog box opens, displaying available clips from the Clip Organizer. This dialog box is nearly identical to the Select Picture dialog box; simply choose the clip you want to insert and click OK.

A message box asks whether you want to play the file automatically in the slideshow. Click Yes if you do. Otherwise, you need to click the file to play it.

N O T E

> To change how the clip is played, you can choose Slide Show, Action Settings to specify mouse-click and mouse-over effects. You can set additional play options on the Custom Animation task pane. Access this task pane by choosing Slide Show, Custom Animation.

- From the Slide Layout task pane, choose either the Title, Media Clip, and Text or Title, Text, and Media Clip layout, and then double-click the media clip placeholder to open the Select Media Clip dialog box.

- Choose Insert, Movies and Sounds, Movie from Clip Organizer or Sound from Clip Organizer. The Clip Art task pane opens; select one of the options in the task pane or click the Organize clips link to open the Clip Organizer.

- Choose Insert, Movies and Sounds, Movie from File or Sound from File. Depending on your selection, either the Insert Movie or Insert Sound dialog box opens, as shown in Figure 13.5.

Figure 13.5
You can insert your own movie or sound file and have it play automatically.

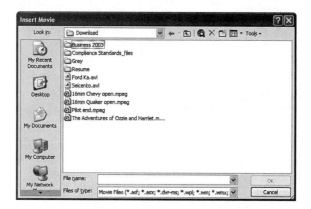

Select the sound or movie you want to insert and click OK. A dialog box asks whether you want the clip to play automatically when you display the slide. Click Yes if you want to do this. Otherwise, you need to click the clip to play it.

A sound clip appears as an icon on your slide, whereas a movie clip appears as a black box that is as tall and as wide as the movie. You can move the icon or box to another part of the slide if you want to.

- Choose Insert, Movies and Sound, Record Sound to open the Record Sound dialog box from which you can record your own sound. You need a microphone to record a sound.

→ To learn how to record your own sound file, **see** "Recording Sound Files" in this chapter, **p. 264**.

- Choose Insert, Movies and Sound, Play CD Audio Track to open the Movie and Sound Options dialog box, where you can specify a CD audio track to play during your presentation.

→ For details on inserting CD audio tracks, **see** "Playing a CD Audio Track" in this chapter, **p. 265**.

13

NOTE

> You can also insert a sound or video file by choosing Insert, Object and selecting the appropriate object from the Insert Object dialog box. In general, use this method of inserting a media clip only when PowerPoint doesn't support the clip format you want.

After you insert a sound or a movie, you can set some playback options. Right-click the icon or box and choose Edit Movie Object (or Edit Sound Object) from the menu that appears. The Movie Options (or Sound Options) dialog box appears. Figure 13.6 shows the Movie Options dialog box. You can control the clip's volume, hide the clip when it isn't playing, and show the clip at full screen if it's a movie.

Figure 13.6
Set playback options.

RECORDING SOUND FILES

You can record your own sound clips to insert into your PowerPoint presentation. You need to have a microphone and sound card to do this.

TIP

> In addition to adding a sound clip to a single slide, you can record a narration for your entire presentation by choosing Slide Show, Record Narration. Narrating your presentation is particularly effective if you're planning to publish to the Web or create a self-running slideshow (such as for a trade show).

→ To learn how to narrate your presentations, **see** "Recording a Voice Narration" in Chapter 9, **p. 180**.

To record a sound, follow these steps:

1. Choose Insert, Movies and Sound, Record Sound to open the Record Sound dialog box, which appears in Figure 13.7.

2. Enter a description for this sound in the Name field.

3. Click the Record button to begin recording your sound.

Figure 13.7
Record a sound to play with a particular slide.

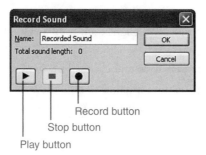

Record button

Stop button

Play button

4. Click the Stop button when you finish recording. To play back the sound, click the Play button.

5. Click OK to save the sound with the presentation; click Cancel to exit and start over.

The sound now appears as an icon in your presentation, and you can use it anywhere in that slideshow. For example, you can play the sound when you click a specific object using PowerPoint's action settings.

→ To learn how to play sounds with action settings, **see** "Using Action Settings" in Chapter 15, **p. 333**

PLAYING A CD AUDIO TRACK

You can also play a specific audio track from a CD during a PowerPoint presentation. For example, you might want to include music from a CD as a background or to introduce your presentation. To do this, follow these steps:

1. Choose Insert, Movies and Sound, Play CD Audio Track to open the Insert CD Audio dialog box, shown in Figure 13.8.

Figure 13.8
Music from a CD can serve as a background sound.

13

2. In the Clip selection group box, choose the start and end tracks to play.

3. If you want to play only part of one track, indicate the time spans in the Start At Time and End At Time fields. For example, you might want to play only the first two minutes of a track.

4. If you want, click the Sound volume button and choose how loud the audio will play.

5. In the Display options group box, choose whether to hide the CD icon when the music isn't playing. Also, choose whether to show playback controls that let you pause the audio and adjust the volume during playback.

6. Click OK to close.

PowerPoint displays a CD icon on the open slide. These steps insert the CD clip in to the slide, but you must use the Custom Animation dialog box to set up your presentation to play this file during the slideshow.

→ For details on setting up custom animation options, **see** "Creating Custom Animations" in Chapter 15, **p. 324**.

UNDERSTANDING THE MICROSOFT CLIP ORGANIZER

The Microsoft Clip Organizer, available from within Office applications, includes thousands of ready-made illustrations, photographs, sound files, and video clips to use in your presentations. You can search the Organizer by keyword or category to find the right clip, import your own clips to the Organizer, categorize clips, or download clips from the Clip Art and Media page on the Microsoft Office Online Web site.

OPENING THE CLIP ORGANIZER

You can access the Clip Organizer in these ways:

- From the Windows desktop, select Start, All Programs, Microsoft Office, Microsoft Office Tools, Microsoft Clip Organizer.

- Select Insert, Picture, Clip Art to open the Clip Art task pane. Click the Organize clips link on the task pane.

- Select Insert, Movies and Sound, Sound from Clip Organizer or Movie from Clip Organizer to open the Clip Art task pane. Click the Organize clips link on the task pane.

If you have pictures, sounds, or movies on your computer that you would like to have available when you insert a clip, choose File, Add Clips to Organizer, Automatically. The Add Clips to Organizer dialog box (see Figure 13.9) appears.

Figure 13.9
Automatically adding clips to the Clip Organizer can save time and make it easier to find your own clips when you need them.

From here, you can

- Click OK if you want the Clip Organizer to automatically categorize pictures, photos, sounds, and videos it finds on your computer.
- Click Cancel to close the dialog box and have it remind you to do this later.
- Click Options to open the Auto Import Settings dialog box, shown in Figure 13.10, which lets you place a check in all the folders you want categorized and remove the check from any folders you don't want categorized.

Figure 13.10
Specify the folders you want to import.

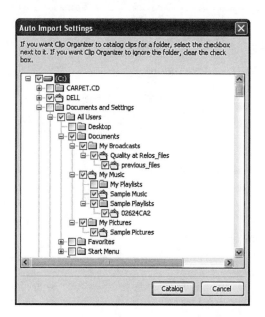

Having the Clip Organizer automatically categorize your clips doesn't move them, but rather just creates catalog entries that help you find them within the Clip Organizer.

13

EXPLORING THE CLIP ORGANIZER

If you're familiar with other Office programs, the Clip Organizer (shown in Figure 13.11) will be easy to navigate and use. You can access the most common features from the toolbar, illustrated in Table 13.2.

Figure 13.11
The Clip Organizer lets you store, categorize, and view all types of media clips.

TABLE 13.2 CLIP ORGANIZER TOOLBAR BUTTONS

Button	Name	Description
Search...	Search	Displays the Search task pane, from which you can search for an image
Collection List...	Collection List	Displays the Collection List task pane, which offers a hierarchical view of your clip collection
	Copy	Copies the selected clip
	Paste	Pastes the clip from the Clipboard
X	Delete from Clip Organizer	Removes the selected clips from the Clip Organizer
	Thumbnails	Displays the clips in the selected collection as thumbnails
	List	Displays the clips in the selected collection as a list of filenames
	Details	Displays details about the clips in the selected collection, such as filename, type, size, caption, keywords, and date created
Clips Online	Clips Online	Opens the Clip Art and Media page at Microsoft Office Online in a browser window (button active only if connected to the Internet)

NAVIGATING THE COLLECTION LIST

By default, the Clip Organizer displays the Collection List task pane on the left side of the window and thumbnails of the clips in the selected collection on the right. The Clip Organizer offers four different kinds of collection folders: My Collections, which stores your own clips that you've added to the Organizer; Office Collections, which stores clips that come with Office; Shared Collections, which stores clips on a file server set up by a network administrator; and Web Collections, which stores online clips, including clips provided by Microsoft partners.

To expand collections, click the plus (+) sign; to collapse them, click the minus (-) sign. When you find the folder you want, click it to display its contents.

In thumbnail view, you can click the down arrow to the right of the thumbnail image to view a list of options for that particular clip—most of which duplicate functions available on the toolbar. One particularly useful item on this shortcut menu is Preview/Properties. This option opens the Preview/Properties dialog box for the selected clip. Figure 13.12 shows this dialog box, which provides details such as file type, resolution, date created, and keywords.

Figure 13.12
Learn more about an individual clip in the Preview/Properties dialog box.

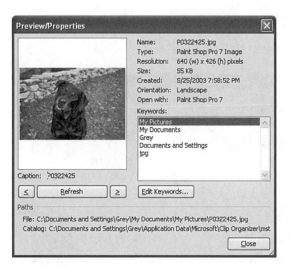

ADDING CLIPS TO THE CLIP ORGANIZER

The Clip Organizer contains clips from Office. Adding your own clips (clip art, photos, sound files, and videos) located on your hard drive or network can make this feature even more useful. You can add clips to the Clip Organizer in three ways: automatically, independently, or through a scanner or digital camera.

 Clips don't appear in the Clip Organizer? *See the "Troubleshooting" section near the end of the chapter.*

13

ADDING CLIPS AUTOMATICALLY

To have the Clip Organizer automatically add and categorize your clips, choose File, Add Clips to Organizer, Automatically. The Add Clips to Organizer dialog box opens, from which you can specify how you want the Clip Organizer to perform this task.

→ For details on how to use the Add Clips to Organizer dialog box, **see** "Opening the Clip Organizer" in this chapter, **p. 266**.

ADDING CLIPS ON YOUR OWN

To add clips to the Clip Organizer on your own, follow these steps:

1. In the Collection List task pane, select the folder in which you want to add a clip.

NOTE

To create a new collection, choose File, New Collection, and enter the new collection's name in the New Collection dialog box.

2. From within the Clip Organizer, choose File, Add Clips to Organizer, On My Own. The Add Clips to Organizer dialog box opens (see Figure 13.13). You'll notice that this version of the dialog box looks very different from the dialog box of the same name that you use to import clips automatically.

Figure 13.13
Adding clips on your own gives you total control as to how and where they're added.

3. Select the clip you want to add to the organizer and click the Add To button.
4. Click OK to return to the Add Clips to Organizer dialog box.
5. Click Add to add the clip to Clip Organizer.

ADDING CLIPS FROM A SCANNER OR CAMERA

It's also easy to use a scanner or digital camera to add clips to the Clip Organizer. To do so, follow these steps:

1. From within the Clip Organizer, choose File, Add Clips to Organizer, From Scanner or Camera. The Insert Picture from Scanner or Camera dialog box opens (see Figure 13.14).

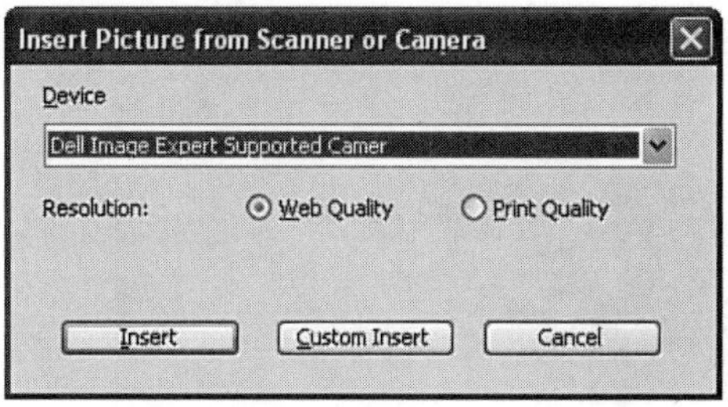

Figure 13.14
If you use a digital camera or scanner, you can easily import your photos into the Clip Organizer.

2. Select the device from which you want to transmit the clips, such as a specific scanner or digital camera connected to your computer, from the Device drop-down list.
3. Select the resolution to use—either Web Quality or Print Quality.
4. Click Insert to begin the import process. Depending on the hardware device you're connected to, any remaining steps could vary.

N O T E

Click Custom Insert to specify custom details—such as resolution, color, scanning area, and size—before importing.

ADDING OBJECTS TO THE CLIP ORGANIZER

You can also add objects created in PowerPoint or other Office applications to the Clip Organizer. Examples include pictures, WordArt, or AutoShapes you create and want to reuse. To add these objects to the Clip Organizer, follow these steps:

1. In PowerPoint, select the object you want to add, such as a picture, WordArt image, or AutoShape.
2. Click the Copy button on the Standard toolbar.
3. Choose Insert, Picture, Clip Art to open the Clip Art task pane.
4. Click the Organize clips link on the task pane.
5. In the Clip Organizer, select the collection to which you want to add the object.
6. Click the Paste button. The Clip Organizer adds the object to the specified collection.

ADDING CAPTIONS AND KEYWORDS

After you add new clips to the Clip Organizer, you'll probably want to add captions and keywords that make them easy to find in the future. To do so, follow these steps:

13

1. Select the clip to which you want to add or edit keywords.

2. Choose Edit, Keywords. The Keywords dialog box opens, with the Clip by Clip tab selected (see Figure 13.15).

Figure 13.15
Specifying keywords for your clips makes them easier to find, particularly with large collections.

3. Add or edit the caption, which is a name for the clip.

4. Enter the keyword you want to add in the Keyword field and click the Add button. The keyword is added to the Keywords for Current Clip list.

5. To delete a keyword, select it and click Delete.

6. Click OK to save your changes and exit the Keywords dialog box. The next time you search on the keywords you added, the selected clip appears with the matching results.

To save time, you can apply the same keyword to multiple clips, such as a group of photos of Carmel, California, to which you want to add the keyword Carmel. To do so, open the collection that contains the clips, press Ctrl+A to select them all, and go to the All Clips at Once tab in the Keywords dialog box to add your keywords.

SEARCHING FOR A CLIP

To search for a clip based on its location or keyword, follow these steps:

1. Click the Search button on the Clip Organizer toolbar. The Search task pane appears, shown in Figure 13.16.

NOTE

This task pane is also available from within PowerPoint itself.

2. Enter the keyword you want to search for in the Search Text field. If you know the name of the clip (its caption), you also can enter that here.

Figure 13.16
You can search for clips by collection or keyword.

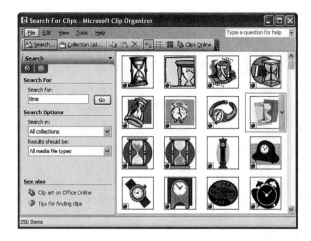

Use these tricks for better results when you search:

- Use wildcards to expand your search. A question mark (?) matches a single character, and an asterisk (*) matches multiple characters. For example, pr* matches both presentation and present. Pr? matches pro, but not presentation or present because it looks only for single characters.

- Use parentheses to search for specific phrases such as "Phil's Photos." Entering Phil's Photos without the parentheses would search for anything that included both these words, not just that specific phrase.

- Use a comma to set or criteria. Entering carmel, photos would search for clips that match either carmel or photos, whereas entering carmel photos would search for both words.

3. In the Search In field, select the collection you want to search from the drop-down list. To expand a collection, click the plus (+) sign; to collapse it, click the minus (-) sign. When you find the collection you want, place a check mark in the box that precedes it.

> **NOTE**
> If you have no idea where the clip is located, choose Everywhere to search in all locations. Be aware, however, that it takes longer to search all collections than to focus on specific collections.

13

4. Select the type of files to look for in the Results Should Be drop-down list. Options include All Media File Types, Clip Art, Photographs, Movies, or Sounds.

5. Click the Search button to begin the search process. The Clip Organizer finds matching clips and displays them in the task pane.

Can't find a clip by keyword? *See the "Troubleshooting" section near the end of the chapter.*

WORKING WITH THE CLIP ORGANIZER

One of the best things about the Clip Organizer is that it makes your clips easy to find. After you've added clips to the gallery, you might want to move, copy, or delete them:

- **Create a new collection**   Choose File, New Collection; in the New Collection dialog box, enter the name of the new collection, choose a location, and click OK.

- **Move a clip to another collection**   Select the clip you want to move; choose Edit, Move to Collection; choose the new collection in the Move to Collection dialog box; and click OK.

- **Copy a clip to another collection**   Select the clip you want to move; choose Edit, Copy to Collection; choose the new collection in the Copy to Collection dialog box; and click OK.

- **Rename a collection**   Select the collection you want to rename; choose Edit, Rename Collection. You can only rename a collection you've created, not one that comes with the Clip Organizer.

- **Delete a clip**   Select the clip you want to delete; choose Edit, Delete from Collection or Delete from Clip Organizer. A prompt confirms the deletion before proceeding. The clip is deleted from the location you specified in the Clip Organizer, but it still remains on your computer's hard disk.

- **Delete a clip collection**   Select a collection you added from the Collection List task pane, right-click, and choose Delete Collection from the shortcut menu. The Clip Organizer will delete the collection and its associated clips.

COMPACTING THE CLIP ORGANIZER CATALOG

Compacting the Clip Organizer helps repair and prevent corrupted data and can help prevent clips from disappearing. To perform the compacting process quickly, choose Tools, Compact. The Clip Organizer displays a message telling you that it's compacting the Organizer. The compacting process doesn't remove any files from the Organizer.

USING THE CLIP ORGANIZER'S ONLINE FEATURES

Click the Clips Online hyperlink or button in either the Clip Organizer or PowerPoint's Clip Art task pane to open the Clip Art and Media page at Microsoft Office Online. Click the Accept button to accept the end user license agreement and access the site, shown in Figure 13.17. From the Design Gallery Live, you can search for clip art, photos, and sound and motion files and download selected clips to your own computer.

Figure 13.17
Search for the right image from a vast collection of design options.

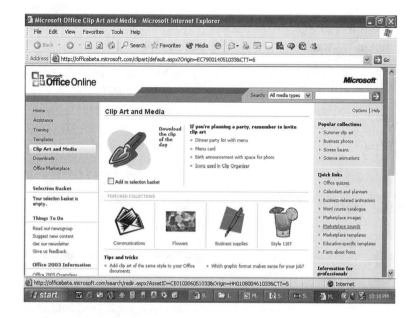

WORKING WITH PICTURES

Getting pictures into PowerPoint and having them look good can sometimes be challenging. Here are some tips to get the best results:

- Prepare your pictures *before* you use them in PowerPoint. If you have good photo-manipulation software such as Photoshop or Paint Shop Pro, touch up and size and crop your pictures there first. They will look their best that way.

- If your presentation contains a lot of pictures, the presentation's file size can get very large. Use the Compress Pictures button on the Pictures toolbar to make them smaller.

- For better control over your pictures' file sizes, save the picture using the least number of colors possible. You can tell you've saved the picture using too few colors when it starts to look blotchy or grainy.

MODIFYING CLIP ART IMAGES

After you insert a clip art image or picture into a PowerPoint presentation, you can modify it to suit your needs. Using the Picture toolbar, you can make both minor and major adjustments to an inserted clip, such as changing its color or adjusting its contrast. Table 13.3 describes each button on the Picture toolbar.

13

TABLE 13.3   PICTURE TOOLBAR BUTTONS

Button	Name	Description
	Insert Picture	Opens the Insert Picture dialog box from which you can choose another image
	Color	Lets you convert the image to a grayscale, black-and-white, or washout image
	More Contrast	Increases the contrast of the selected image
	Less Contrast	Reduces the contrast of the selected image
	More Brightness	Increases the image's brightness
	Less Brightness	Reduces the image's brightness
	Crop	Lets you crop the image to another size
	Rotate Left 90°	Rotates the image 90 degrees to the left
	Line Style	Shows a list of varying line widths and styles from which to choose
	Compress Pictures	Lets you compress the picture, reducing its file size
	Recolor Picture	Lets you change the clip art image's color
	Format Picture	Offers many options for formatting an image's lines, color, size, and position
	Set Transparent Color	Converts a single color to a transparent image
	Reset Picture	Returns the image to its original state

To open the Picture toolbar, choose View, Toolbars, Picture.

→ To get more ideas on how to format images in PowerPoint, **see** Chapter 14, "Creating and Formatting Objects," **p. 281**.

13

RECOLORING A CLIP ART IMAGE

You can recolor a Windows metafile image (WMF), such as a clip art image, after you place it in a PowerPoint presentation. This can be useful if you want the image to match the colors of your design template or perhaps of your corporate logo.

 Can't recolor your image? *See the "Troubleshooting" section near the end of the chapter.*

To recolor a WMF image, follow these steps:

1. Select the image you want to recolor and click the Recolor Picture button on the Picture toolbar. The Recolor Picture dialog box opens, as shown in Figure 13.18.

Figure 13.18
Change the color of a WMF image to match your presentation.

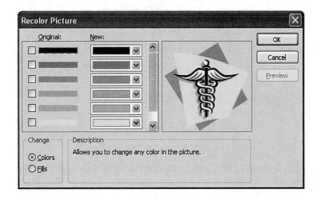

2. Select the Colors option button to change the actual image colors or the Fills option button to change background colors.

> **NOTE**
>
> Selecting Fills doesn't affect line colors.

3. Under Original, place a check mark next to the color you want to change.
4. Select a color from the New drop-down list.

> **NOTE**
>
> The New drop-down list shows the slide template's colors. Click More Colors to open the Colors dialog box and choose any color you like.

→ To learn more about applying colors to objects, **see** "Specifying Colors" in Chapter 14, **p. 290**.
→ For details on color theory, **see** "Using Color" in Chapter 25, "The Media—Designing Visual Support," **p. 566**.

13

5. Click the Preview button to view the suggested color changes before you make them.

6. Click OK to apply the changes to the presentation.

FORMATTING CLIP ART IMAGES

When you place a clip art image in your presentation, you can make changes to its lines, size, and position in the Format dialog box. You can also combine clip art with WordArt pictures to create a complete graphic image such as a logo.

→ For details on using the Format dialog box and working with WordArt, **see** "Understanding WordArt" in Chapter 14, **p. 312.**

To create this image, place both a WordArt picture and clip art on the slide and adjust their positions to create the image you want. You should also group these two images together to make them one.

→ For instructions on how to group PowerPoint objects, **see** "Grouping Objects" in Chapter 14, **p. 311.**

TROUBLESHOOTING

FINDING YOUR OWN CLIPS IN THE CLIP ORGANIZER

The Clip Organizer doesn't contain my own pictures and photos.

You need to add your clips to the Clip Organizer before the Search function of the Clip Art task pane can find them.

SEARCHING BY KEYWORD

The Search task pane can't find my clips by their keywords.

First be sure that your clips are actually in the Clip Organizer. Then verify that the keyword you used is actually associated with the clip (click the down arrow next to the clip and choose Preview/Properties to verify the list of keywords). Click Edit Keywords to make keyword modifications if necessary.

RESOLVING RECOLORING PROBLEMS

I can't recolor my clip art image.

You can't recolor BMP, JPG, GIF, or PNG images. Instead, you have to use an external program, such as Microsoft Photo Editor, to convert the color of these images.

DESIGN CORNER: ENLIVENING YOUR PRESENTATION WITH MULTIMEDIA

You can enliven any presentation by adding multimedia options such as clip art, pictures, sound, and movies. For example, you could take a simple bulleted list and make it both more interesting and more meaningful to your audience with a few simple additions.

Create this slide by choosing the Title, Text, and Clip Art layout from the Slide Layout task pane (click the New Slide button to open the task pane). Add your bullet items on the left side and then double-click the clip art placeholder. Select a picture from the Select Picture dialog box which appears (enter some search text to narrow down your choices).

From here, you can add a music clip to play in the background as an introduction; again, something that relates to your topic works best. How about music from your company's radio or TV ads, or something motivating if you want to inspire your employees? To do this, choose Insert, Movies and Sounds, Sound from Clip Organizer to view the sound files in the Clip Art task pane. When you choose the appropriate sound file, you can specify that PowerPoint play it automatically in your slideshow. Adding a movie clip would be another option (Insert, Movies and Sounds, Movie from Clip Organizer). With a quick click, you could demo your company's latest TV ad. Sound and movie files can display visually on your slides or you can hide them (as illustrated in this example).

BEFORE

Figure 13.19
There's nothing wrong with this slide, but it isn't very exciting either.

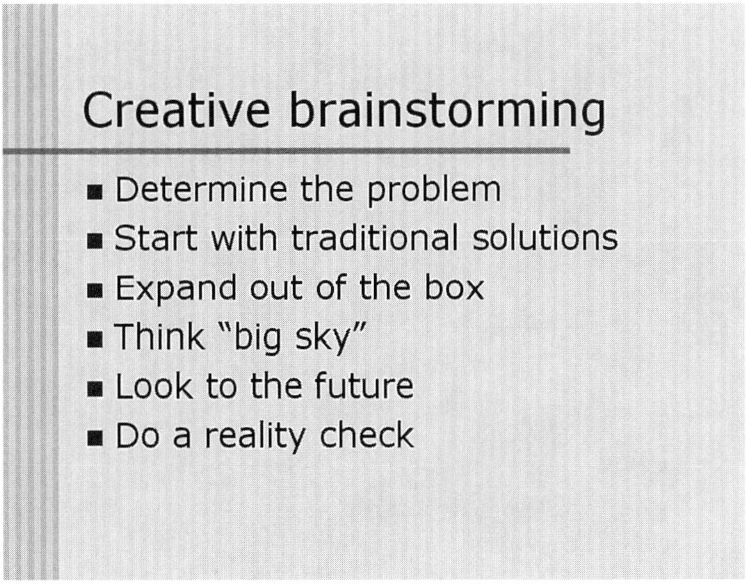

Creative brainstorming

- Determine the problem
- Start with traditional solutions
- Expand out of the box
- Think "big sky"
- Look to the future
- Do a reality check

13

AFTER

Figure 13.20
Add clip art and other multimedia effects to enliven your presentation.

CHAPTER 14

CREATING AND FORMATTING OBJECTS

In this chapter   *by Patrice-Anne Rutledge and Jim Grey*

EXPLORING OBJECT CREATION AND FORMATTING

An *object* is anything you can place on a slide, such as a text placeholder, a picture, a movie, an AutoShape, a diagram, and clip art. After you use PowerPoint for a little while, you'll probably want to *reformat* it—that is, change the way it looks.

PowerPoint includes so many drawing and object formatting options that you might not have the opportunity to use them all! These features are simple enough to meet the needs of the casual user, yet powerful enough that a sophisticated PowerPoint designer can heavily customize them. The Drawing toolbar is the centerpiece of PowerPoint's suite of drawing tools and includes buttons that let you insert images, shapes, WordArt, and clip art. This toolbar also lets you color, position, format, and manipulate objects you create or insert.

With practice, you can use PowerPoint's object formatting options to make your presentations communicate your message more effectively.

USING THE DRAWING TOOLBAR TO CREATE OBJECTS

You can use the Drawing toolbar to add visual objects such as rectangles, ovals, AutoShapes, WordArt, and clip art to your presentation. You can also use the Drawing toolbar to apply shading, 3D, color, and other effects to existing objects.

To open this toolbar, choose View, Toolbars, Drawing. Table 14.1 lists all the buttons on this toolbar.

TABLE 14.1   DRAWING TOOLBAR BUTTONS

Button	Name	Description
Draw ▾	Draw	Displays a menu with a variety of drawing options such as placement and formatting
⬚	Select Objects	Activates a pointer that lets you select drawing objects
AutoShapes ▾	AutoShapes	Displays a menu of AutoShape types from which to choose
╲	Line	Lets you draw a line
↘	Arrow	Lets you draw an arrow
▭	Rectangle	Lets you draw a rectangle
◯	Oval	Lets you draw an oval

14

Button	Name	Description
	Text Box	Lets you place a text box on your slide
	Insert WordArt	Opens the WordArt Gallery
	Insert Diagram or Organization Chart	Opens the Diagram Gallery from which you can insert a diagram or organization chart
	Insert Clip Art	Opens the Insert Clip Art task pane
	Insert Picture	Opens the Insert Picture dialog box from which you can add a picture, such as a GIF or JPEG, to your slide
	Fill Color	Opens the Fill Color palette from which you can choose a fill color or pattern
	Line Color	Opens the Line Color palette from which you can choose a line color or pattern
	Font Color	Opens the Font Color palette from which you can choose a font color
	Line Style	Lets you apply several different line styles to a selected line
	Dash Style	Lets you apply several different dash styles to a selected line
	Arrow Style	Lets you apply several different arrow styles to a selected arrow
	Shadow Style	Opens the Shadow palette from which you can choose a shadow to apply to a selected object
	3D Style	Opens the 3D palette from which you can choose a 3D effect to apply to a selected object

ADDING LINES AND ARROWS

You can add lines and arrows to your presentation to draw attention to something, show how things are connected, or show how one thing leads to another. For example, you might want to add a line beneath a word or phrase to draw attention to it. You might also use an arrow to point to text or an object of special importance. You can also draw simple graphics with the line, rectangle, and oval tools.

14

NOTE

PowerPoint's drawing tools won't work well or easily when you need more complex graphics. Use a drawing tool better suited to the job, such as Microsoft Visio or Jasc Paint Shop Pro, to create the graphic. Then insert the graphic into PowerPoint.

NOTE

If you use the drawing tools to emphasize text, remember that the drawing objects don't move even when you add or remove text. You have to move each drawing object manually.

CREATING A LINE

 To draw a line on your presentation, click the Line button on the Drawing toolbar. The mouse pointer becomes a plus sign. Click (and hold down) where you want the line to begin and drag to where you want the line to end.

If the line looks crooked or is the wrong length, you can adjust it. First, select the line. Then hover your mouse over one of the circles that appear at the end of the line. The mouse pointer becomes a line with an arrow head at both ends. Click and drag the circle to lengthen the line or adjust its angle.

If the line isn't in the right place, you can move it. First, select the line. Then hover your mouse over the line. The mouse pointer becomes a cross with arrow heads at all four ends. Click and drag the line to move it.

TIP

Press the Shift key as you drag the mouse to create straight horizontal or vertical lines. This lets you draw lines at angles evenly divisible by 15 (0, 15, 30, 45, and so forth), which makes it much easier to create a straight line. Press the Ctrl key as you drag the mouse to draw a line from a center point, lengthening the line in both directions as you drag.

 To change the line's style, select the line and click the Line Style button. The Line Style palette appears, as shown in Figure 14.1.

You can choose from several single and double lines and one triple line from 1/4 point to 6 points wide. For additional options, select More Lines, which opens the Format AutoShape dialog box where you can set additional line options. You can also open this dialog box by right-clicking on the line and choosing Format AutoShape.

Figure 14.1
Create thick or thin, single, double, or triple lines in your presentation.

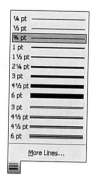

You can change your line to a dashed line by clicking the Dash Style button and choosing a dash style.

You can also use the Line Style palette to format lines associated with other objects such as arrows, rectangles, ovals, and AutoShapes.

CREATING AN ARROW

 To draw an arrow on your presentation, click the Arrow button. The mouse pointer becomes a plus sign. Click (and hold down) where you want the line to begin and drag to where you want the line to end. You can adjust and move the arrow in the same way you adjust and move a line.

 To choose an arrow style, select the arrow and click the Arrow Style button on the Drawing toolbar. The Arrow Style palette appears, as shown in Figure 14.2.

Figure 14.2
You can choose to place arrows at either or both ends and select from several different arrow styles.

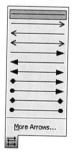

For more arrow options, choose More Arrows, which opens the Format AutoShape dialog box.

Figure 14.3 shows several lines and arrows you can create in PowerPoint.

Figure 14.3
You can create many styles of lines and arrows.

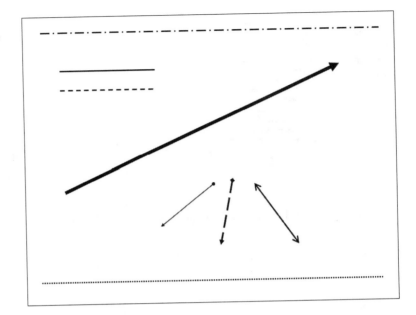

ADDING RECTANGLES AND OVALS

You can draw rectangular and oval shapes directly on your presentation. Using shapes lets you emphasize important information (contained in your shape) or group information or illustrate other ideas or concepts.

To draw a rectangle, click the Rectangle button on the Drawing toolbar. The mouse pointer becomes a plus sign. Click where you want the rectangle to appear, and drag to draw the rectangle.

> **TIP**
> To draw a square, press the Shift key while you draw the shape.

To draw an oval, click the Oval button on the Drawing toolbar. The mouse pointer becomes a plus sign. Click where you want the oval to appear, and drag to draw the oval.

> **TIP**
> To draw a perfect circle, press the Shift key while you draw the shape.

Figure 14.4 shows how you can use rectangles and ovals in a slide.

14

Figure 14.4
Rectangles and ovals can illustrate a process, group like items, and more.

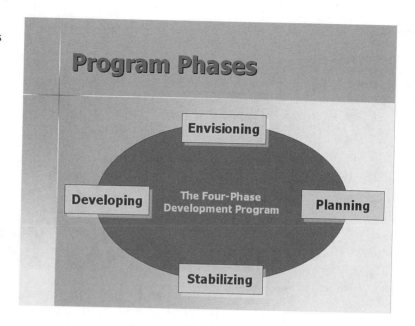

You can then reshape and resize these images or apply other formatting to them.

 You can add text to a rectangular or oval shape. If you only want to add a word or two, select the object and type in the text you want to enter. Or click the Text Box button on the Drawing toolbar and create a text box inside the original object. Be sure, however, that the text box fits into the object without overlapping its borders.

ADDING TEXT BOXES

 Use a text box when you need to add text to a slide outside its original text placeholders or when you need to frame special text. To create a text box, click the Text Box button on the Drawing toolbar, click where you want to place the text box on the slide, and start typing. Figure 14.5 shows a text box.

You format text in a text box as you would any other text, including formatting the font, font size, color, and style.

TIP

> Some people prefer using text boxes over text placeholders for entering text into their slides. Text boxes give you greater control over text placement—create as many text boxes as you need and arrange them on the slide any way you want. To use text boxes instead of text placeholders, choose a slide layout that doesn't contain any text placeholders.

14

Figure 14.5
A text box calls attention to something you want to say and lets you place the text exactly where you want it.

Text box

ADDING AUTOSHAPES

An *AutoShape* is any shape you can draw in a presentation. Rectangles and ovals are AutoShapes—so common that they get their own toolbar buttons. Other AutoShapes, such as a hexagons, triangles, and stars, are available on the AutoShape menu on the Drawing toolbar.

AutoShapes let you easily highlight, diagram, and illustrate using callouts, flowcharts, block arrows, and other special objects.

 To insert an AutoShape, click the AutoShapes button on the Drawing toolbar and choose the type of AutoShape you want from the menu. Options include the following:

- **Lines**—Includes straight lines and arrows, as well as special line forms such as curves, scribbles, and freeform.
- **Connectors**—Draws lines between objects, but when you move an object, the connector stays attached and moves with it. You can choose from three different kinds of connectors to connect objects—straight, elbow, and curved.

TIP

To force a connection between two objects to be the shortest distance, reroute the connector. To do this, click the Draw button on the Drawing toolbar and choose Reroute Connectors.

- **Basic Shapes**—Includes common shapes such as
  - Polygons such as a hexagon, a triangle, a parallelogram, and so on
  - 3D shapes such as a box and a cylinder
  - Fun shapes such as a crescent moon, a smiley face, and a lighting bolt
  - Grouping and connecting shapes such as brackets and braces
- **Block Arrows**—Offers large block arrows, curved and bent arrows, and callouts with arrows.
- **Flowchart**—Offers flowchart images such as process, decision, document, input, and terminator.
- **Stars and Banners**—Offers waves, scrolls, ribbons, explosions, and pointed stars.
- **Callouts**—Includes several kinds of callouts. A *callout* is a line with a text box connected to one end. You put the line's free end on something you want to highlight, place the text box to the side, and type descriptive text in it.
- **Action Buttons**—Includes several action buttons. Action buttons make your presentation interactive, performing actions such as navigating among slides, running programs, and playing sounds.

To place an AutoShape on a slide, click AutoShapes on the Drawing toolbar. Then click the menu for the kind of AutoShape you want (Lines, Basic Shapes, and so on), and click the AutoShape from the palette that appears. Click on your slide where you want the AutoShape to appear, and drag until the AutoShape is the right size. You can then format the AutoShape as you would any other object. Figure 14.6 shows some sample AutoShapes.

Figure 14.6
You can illustrate, highlight, and diagram with AutoShapes.

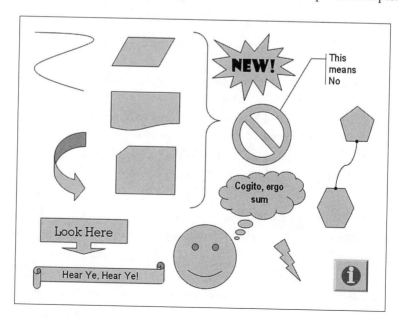

14

TIP

Choose More AutoShapes from the AutoShapes menu to open the Insert Clip Art task pane, which offers even more AutoShapes.

SPECIFYING COLORS

You can apply color to objects, text, and lines using three different Drawing toolbar buttons. The Fill Color, Font Color, and Line Color buttons all work in basically the same way, with slight differences based on the selected object. To apply the default color, click the button directly. To apply a different color, click the arrow next to the button and choose a color from the palette that appears. You can also specify color in the Format dialog box.

SPECIFYING FILL COLOR

 To set an object's fill color, select it, and click the arrow next to the Fill Color button. The Fill Color palette displays, as shown in Figure 14.7.

Figure 14.7
You can add colors or patterns to fill an object.

You can do one of the following in this palette:

- Click No Fill to make the object transparent. You'll see the slide background through the object.
- Choose one of the colors that appears under the Automatic color box option. These colors are compatible with your slide's color scheme.
- Click More Fill Colors to open the Colors dialog box—from which you can choose from many other colors or create a custom color.
- Click Fill Effects to open the Fill Effects dialog box in which you can fill the object with a gradient, a texture, a pattern, or a picture.

USING THE COLORS DIALOG BOX

Click More Fill Colors on the palette to open the Colors dialog box, illustrated in Figure 14.8.

To choose a new color, click it in the palette on the Standard tab. The color appears in the New section of the preview box to contrast with the Current color.

14

Figure 14.8
Choose from many common colors in the Colors dialog box.

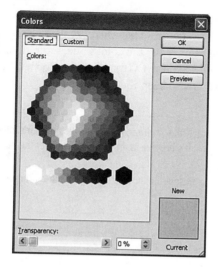

NOTE

> You can set transparency (making the color appear transparent) by dragging the Transparency scrollbar or by entering a specific transparency percentage. The higher the percentage, the more transparent the color, allowing things behind the object to show through.

Click the Preview button to preview what the color will look like in your presentation. Click OK to keep the color or Cancel to return to the original color.

USING A CUSTOM COLOR

To add a custom color, click the Custom tab on the Colors dialog box, shown in Figure 14.9.

Figure 14.9
Create a custom color to suit your exact needs.

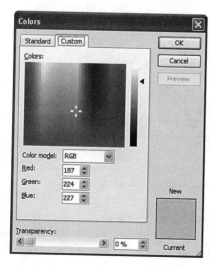

14

You can create a custom color in two ways. One way is to click and drag the crosshair in the Colors area until you find the color you want. The other way is to choose either RGB or HSL in the Color model field, and then adjust the color's hue, saturation, and luminance (for HSL) or level of red, green, and blue (for RGB). Click the Preview button to see how the color looks on your slide. Click OK to keep the color or Cancel to discard it.

NOTE

Hue represents the actual color, *saturation* represents the color's intensity, and *luminance* represents the color's brightness. In general, the lower the number, the lighter or less intense the color.

Red, green, and *blue* represent the amount of each of these primary colors in the color you're creating.

→ For more information about color theory, **see** "Using Color" in Chapter 25, "The Media—Designing Visual Support" **p. 566**.

SPECIFYING FILL EFFECTS

To set fill effects, select the object to format, click the arrow next to the Fill Color button, and choose Fill Effects from the palette that appears. The Fill Effects dialog box, shown in Figure 14.10, opens, giving you several kinds of fill effects: gradients, textures, patterns, and pictures.

Figure 14.10
Choose from gradient, texture, pattern, and picture effects.

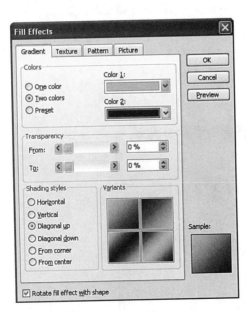

APPLYING A GRADIENT FILL A gradient creates a smooth transition from one color to another using gentle blending. To apply a gradient, click the Gradient tab on the Fill Effects dialog box. In the Colors group box, choose one of the following:

- **One Color**—Lets you choose one color for the gradient. Choose the color from the Color 1 drop-down list. You then choose how much to darken or lighten this color by adjusting the scrollbar that appears below the Color 1 field. PowerPoint creates a gradient between the color you choose and its darkened or lightened counterpart.

- **Two Colors**—Lets you choose the two colors you want to use from the Color 1 and Color 2 drop-down lists.

- **Preset**—Displays a drop-down list of preset color combination options such as Daybreak, Peacock, and Rainbow.

Next, set the transparency by dragging the Transparency scrollbars or by entering specific transparency percentages.

Finally, use the Shading Styles area to choose how to apply the gradient. Options include Horizontal, Vertical, Diagonal Up, Diagonal Down, From Corner, and From Center. Click an option in the Variants group box; it displays in the Sample box. Click Preview to see the gradient in your presentation. Click OK to keep the gradient or Cancel to discard it.

APPLYING A TEXTURED FILL   To apply a texture, click the Texture tab on the Fill Effects dialog box and scroll down the available textures until you find one you like. Click it and click OK. Figure 14.11 shows the Texture tab.

Figure 14.11
Textures can add visual depth to an object.

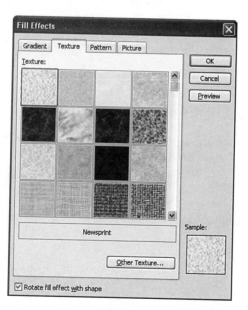

If you have a graphic file on your computer that you'd like to use as a texture, click the Other Texture button to open the Select Texture dialog box. Navigate to where you keep the graphic file, click the file, and click the Insert button. The graphic appears among the textures in the Fill Effects dialog box. Click the graphic and click Preview to see what it

14

looks like in your slide. Click OK to use the graphic as a texture, or click OK to discard the change.

APPLYING A PATTERNED FILL   To apply a pattern, select the Pattern tab on the Fill Effects dialog box (see Figure 14.12).

Figure 14.12
PowerPoint provides many different pattern effects.

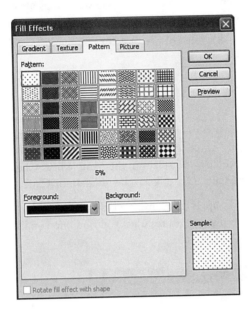

Choose foreground and background colors and then select from the many available patterns.

CAUTION

If you plan to print your presentation, be sure to verify how your chosen pattern looks when printed. Certain patterns are too dense to print well on some printers.

NOTE

The default foreground and background colors coordinate with your object's color.

Click Preview to preview the fill effect. Click OK to keep the fill or Cancel to discard it.

APPLYING A PICTURE FILL   You can even fill an object with a picture. Click the Picture tab on the Fill Effects dialog box, which Figure 14.13 shows.

Click the Select Picture button to open the Select Picture dialog box, shown in Figure 14.14.

Find and select your graphic image and click Insert to return to the Fill Effects dialog box. Click OK to apply the fill or Cancel to discard it.

Figure 14.13
Use your own image, such as a logo, as a fill.

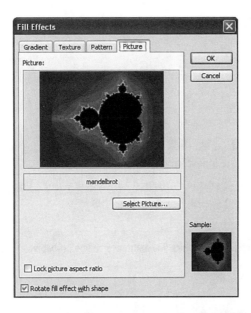

Figure 14.14
Choose a picture of your own to apply as a fill.

CAUTION

Some pictures just don't look good as fills. Look at yours carefully. If it doesn't look good, press Ctrl+Z to undo it, and then apply some other fill.

SPECIFYING LINE COLOR

 To add color to a selected line, click the arrow to the right of the Line Color button on the Drawing toolbar. The Line Color palette appears, as shown in Figure 14.15.

Choose from the following options:

- Click No Line to hide the existing line.
- Choose one color under the Automatic color box. These colors are compatible with your slide's color scheme.

14

Figure 14.15
Format or remove
lines in the Line Color
palette.

- Click More Line Colors to open the Colors dialog box in which you can select from many other colors or create a custom color.
- Click Patterned Lines to open the Patterned Lines dialog box. This dialog box is almost identical to the Pattern tab on the Fill Effects dialog box.

> **NOTE**
>
> Unless you create a very thick line, patterns in a line probably won't be visible.

SPECIFYING FONT COLOR

 To add color to selected text, click the arrow to the right of the Font Color button on the Drawing toolbar. The Font Color palette appears, as shown in Figure 14.16.

Figure 14.16
Specify the color of
your text here.

You can choose a color in two ways:

- Select one of the colors under the Automatic color box. These colors are compatible with your slide's color scheme.
- Click More Colors to open the Colors dialog box in which you can choose from many other colors or create a custom color.

If you don't want to use one of the compatible colors, be sure that the color you choose is clear and readable on your slide.

USING THE FORMAT DIALOG BOX

14

You can use the Format dialog box to apply numerous object formatting changes all in one place. The Format dialog box duplicates some of the functions of the Drawing toolbar, but also has some special features of its own. Depending on the object you're formatting, the full name of the Format dialog box might vary (Format AutoShape, Format Text Box, and so forth).

To open the Format dialog box for an object, double-click the object, or right-click it and choose Format from the menu that appears. Figure 14.17 shows a sample Format dialog box—Format AutoShape.

Figure 14.17
The Format AutoShape dialog box lets you make many changes in one place.

Only the tabs and fields relevant to the selected object are available for you to use.

FORMATTING COLORS AND LINES

On the Colors and Lines tab, you can set colors and styles for fill, lines, and arrows. Most of these options duplicate the Line Color, Line Style, Dash Style, and Arrow Style buttons on the Drawing toolbar. The drop-down lists provide palettes that are very similar to the ones you access from those buttons. The effect is the same whichever method you use to apply a specific color or line format.

Click the Preview button to preview the changes in your presentation. If you want these changes to be the default for future objects in your presentation, click the Default for New Objects check box.

FORMATTING SIZE

On the Size tab (see Figure 14.18), you can manually set size, rotation, and scaling options.

You can specify the exact height and width of an object, rather than resizing it with the mouse, if you want. This is useful if you want to create several objects of the same size and need greater precision than you can achieve by resizing with the mouse. You can also specify an exact rotation percentage, rather than rotate using menu options.

14

Figure 14.18
Specify the object's
exact size on this tab.

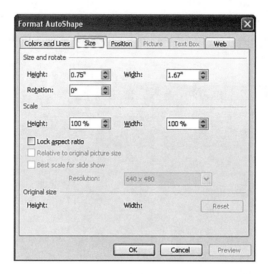

TIP

> Another quick way to create multiple objects of the same size is to copy and paste from
> the same master object.

To resize the selected object by scale, you can adjust the percentages in the Scale Height
and Width fields. For example, you might want to reduce an object to 50% of its
original size.

 Is your rescaled object distorted? *See the "Troubleshooting" section near the end of this
chapter.*

If you want to size the object diagonally so that it keeps its shape, click the Lock Aspect
Ratio check box.

You can also set the object's size as Relative to Original Picture Size or as Best Scale for
Slide Show to automatically set the proper proportions.

FORMATTING POSITION

On the Position tab, shown in Figure 14.19, you can specify the exact position of the object
on the slide.

Enter the exact horizontal and vertical positions for the object. For example, to place an
object so that its upper-left corner is exactly one inch left of the slide's center, type -1 in the
Horizontal field and 0 in the Vertical field and choose Center in both of the From fields. Or
to move an object that's 2.75 inches from the slide's left edge one inch to the left, type 1.75
in the Horizontal field and make sure that the From field contains Top Left Corner.

14

Figure 14.19
Put an object exactly where you want it using this dialog box.

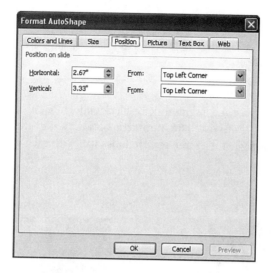

FORMATTING A PICTURE

If the selected object is a picture, the Picture tab (see Figure 14.20) offers several formatting options.

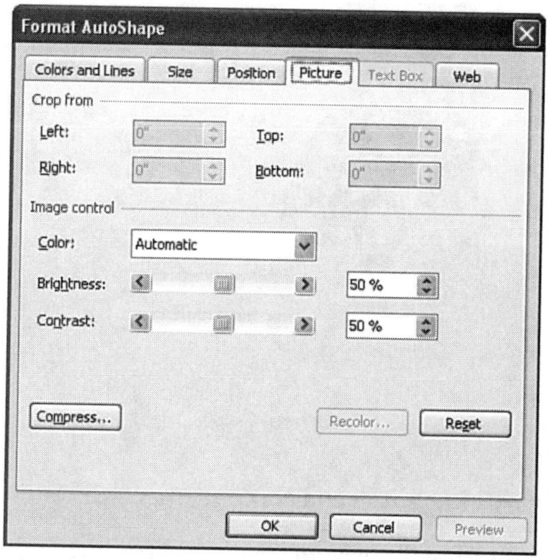

Figure 14.20
Set options for a picture, such as a clip art image, on the Picture tab.

You can *crop* a picture if it contains things you don't need to show in your presentation. For example, you can crop a portrait to show just the person's face. Cropping involves a bit of guesswork. In the Left, Right, Top, and Bottom fields, type how much, in inches, to remove from each edge of the figure. Click Preview to see what it looks like. If you cut too much or too little from an edge, change the amount to remove and click Preview again. Keep doing this until the image looks right. Click OK to keep the cropping or Cancel to discard it.

14

NOTE

Most people find it easier to crop a picture using the mouse. Click the Crop button on the Picture toolbar. Drag the cropping handles to crop the image. Click outside the image when you're done.

If you want to show a color image in grayscale or black and white or wash out (lighten) an image, use the Color drop-down list. The Automatic option returns the image to its original colors. Figure 14.21 shows what the same picture looks like with each option applied.

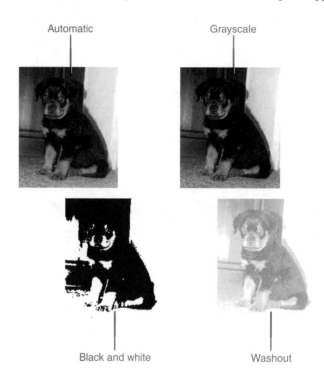

Figure 14.21
Adjust an image's color format if necessary for your presentation.

→ For interesting information about color theory, **see** "Using Color" in Chapter 25, "The Media—Designing Visual Support" **p. 566**.

You can also specify a picture's brightness and contrast.

To change the color of a PowerPoint object or a WMF clip art image, click Recolor. The Recolor Picture dialog box appears.

Click Preview to see what the changes would look like in your presentation before you save them. Click Reset to restore everything to its original setting.

14

TIP

Pictures can make your presentation use a lot of hard disk space. Click the Compress button to open the Compress Picture dialog box where you can reduce the size of the pictures in your presentation, thereby reducing the size of the presentation itself. You can also use this dialog box to delete cropped parts of images—PowerPoint keeps them, but hides them unless you use this dialog box to delete them.

→ To learn more about all these picture formatting options, **see** Chapter 13 **p. 257**.

Formatting a Text Box

If the selected object contains text, you can format the text's placement and behavior in the Text Box tab, shown in Figure 14.22.

Figure 14.22
You can make several text box customizations.

You can set a text anchor point to align your text in the text box. Options include Top, Middle, Bottom, Top Centered, Middle Centered, and Bottom Centered. The Centered options move the text to the horizontal center of the text box, whereas the other options do not. This is different from justification—a right-justified block of text moves to the center when you choose a Centered option, but the text remains right-justified.

The Internal Margin section lets you determine how much open space—or internal margin—to display in the text box. You can select fractions of inches in the Left, Right, Top, and Bottom fields.

Other options include the following:

■ **Word wrap text in AutoShape**—Choose this option when you place text in an AutoShape object. If you don't, the text displays straight across the shape, rather than neatly inside it.

14

■ **Resize AutoShape to fit text**—Resizes the AutoShape object to fit the text exactly. For example, if you have one word inside an AutoShape, it reduces the shape to a size that precisely surrounds that word.

■ **Rotate text within AutoShape by 90°**—Rotates text 90 degrees clockwise.

Formatting Web Information

When you'll deliver your presentation over the Web, use the Web tab (see Figure 14.23) to enter the text to display while the image loads. If you're conversant in HTML, this text appears in the IMG tag's ALT attribute. This text also appears as a ScreenTip when you pause the mouse cursor over the image.

Figure 14.23
In this dialog box, type what you want people to see while the Web graphic loads.

Manipulating Objects

You can easily cut, copy, paste, move, and resize PowerPoint objects.

 To cut a selected object, click the Cut button on the Standard toolbar or press Ctrl+X. To cut more than one object, hold down the Shift key while selecting objects or drag a selection box around all the objects with the mouse.

NOTE

If you cut something by mistake, click the Undo button to retrieve it.

 To copy a selected object, click the Copy button or press Ctrl+C.

14

TIP

> To copy the attributes of one object and apply them to another object, use the Format Painter button on the Standard toolbar. For example, if you select an object with 3D effects, click the Format Painter button, and then select another object, that new object gets the same 3D effects.

To paste a cut or copied object, click the Paste button or press Ctrl+V.

NOTE

> PowerPoint's clipboard can store 24 different items. To see what the Clipboard contains, choose Edit, Office Clipboard to open the Clipboard task pane.

To move an object, click and drag it to a new location.

Resizing an object is easy. When you select an object, resizing handles display around its edges. Figure 14.24 illustrates these handles.

Figure 14.24
Resizing handles make it easier to adjust the size and shape of your object.

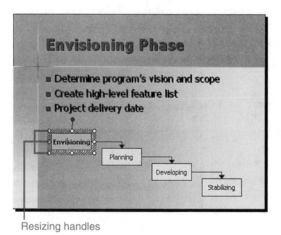

Resizing handles

Drag the handles with the mouse to make the object smaller, larger, or a different shape. Notice that depending on which sizing handle you select—a corner or interior handle—you can either enlarge the entire object or change its shape. To resize the object proportionately so that it keeps its shape, press the Shift key and drag a corner handle.

ADDING SHADOW AND 3D EFFECTS

You can add shadow and 3D effects to objects, including AutoShapes, WordArt, and clip art.

Select an object and click the Shadow Style button on the Drawing toolbar. The Shadow palette appears, as Figure 14.25 shows.

Figure 14.25
Shadows can dramatically emphasize a presentation.

Choose a shadow style from the available palette options.

TIP

> To remove a shadow immediately, click the Undo button. To remove a shadow later, select the shadowed object, click the Shadow button on the Drawing toolbar, and choose No Shadow.

You can also customize the shadow by specifying its exact position and color. To do this, select Shadow Settings from the Shadow palette. The Shadow Settings toolbar displays, as described in Table 14.2. Figure 14.26 shows an object with a shadow.

Figure 14.26
Get dramatic with shadows.

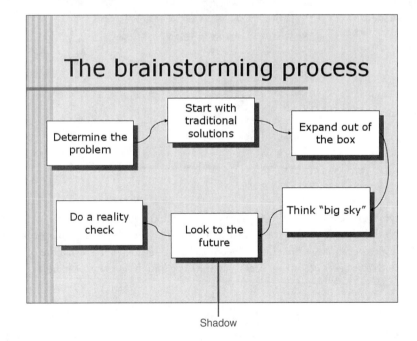

Shadow

TABLE 14.2   SHADOW SETTINGS TOOLBAR BUTTONS

Button	Name	Description
	Shadow On/Off	Adds or removes the shadow
	Nudge Shadow Up	Moves the shadow up slightly
	Nudge Shadow Down	Moves the shadow down slightly
	Nudge Shadow Left	Moves the shadow slightly to the left
	Nudge Shadow Right	Moves the shadow slightly to the right
	Shadow Color	Lets you change the shadow's color to a complementary color, a semitransparent color, or (via the Colors dialog box) any color you want

To add 3D effects, select the object you want to modify and click the 3-D button on the Drawing toolbar. The 3-D palette displays, as illustrated in Figure 14.27.

Figure 14.27
Get creative with 3D, but be sure that your object doesn't become too distorted.

Choose the 3D style you want to apply from the available palette options.

 Can't apply 3D effects? See the "Troubleshooting" section near the end of the chapter.

TIP

> To immediately remove a 3D effect, click the Undo button. To remove 3D later, select the object, click the 3-D button on the Drawing toolbar, and choose No 3-D.

You can also customize the 3D effect by specifying its tilt, depth, direction, lighting, surface, and color. To do this, select 3-D Settings from the 3-D palette. The 3-D Settings toolbar appears, described in Table 14.3.

TABLE 14.3   3-D SETTINGS TOOLBAR BUTTONS

Button	Name	Description
	3-D On/Off	Adds and removes 3D
	Tilt Down	Turns the object slightly downward
	Tilt Up	Turns the object slightly upward
	Tilt Left	Turns the object slightly to the left
	Tilt Right	Turns the object slightly to the right
	Depth	Lets you adjust the 3D effect's depth from 0 points to infinity (12 points = 1 inch)
	Direction	Lets you set the 3D effect's direction, viewing it either in perspective or in parallel
	Lighting	Lets you set the direction and intensity of the lighting
	Surface	Lets you change the object's surface to matte, plastic, or metal, or lets you remove the surface so that you see only a wireframe
	3-D Color	Lets you change the 3D effect's color to a complementary color, a semitransparent color, or (via the Colors dialog box) any color you want

Figure 14.28 shows an object with 3D effects.

Figure 14.28
Properly used, 3D effects can enhance a presentation.

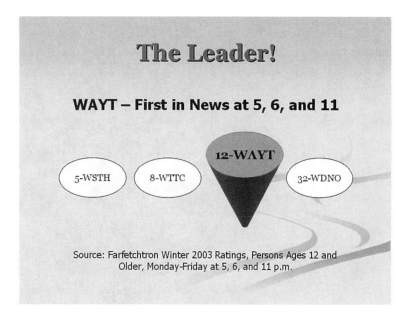

Setting Object Order

When you place two objects on a slide, you might want part of one to appear on top of part of the other. This is called *layering* the objects. You can do this for pure visual effect or to indicate that the overlapping objects have a relationship to each other. PowerPoint lets you control each object's layering, so if two objects are layered and you want the one below to appear on top, you can change it. To rearrange an object's layer order, choose it, select the Draw button on the Drawing toolbar, and choose Order from the menu. You can also right-click and choose Order from the shortcut menu. Either way, a menu appears with four layering options:

- **Bring to Front**—Brings the selected object to the front layer of the stack, placing all other objects behind it.
- **Send to Back**—Sends the selected object to the back layer of the stack so that all other objects appear above it.
- **Bring Forward**—Brings the selected object one layer closer to the front. This is most useful when more than two objects are layered.
- **Send Backward**—Sends the selected object one layer to the back. This is also most useful when more than two objects are layered.

Figure 14.29 shows several layered objects.

14

Figure 14.29
You can layer objects for a special effect.

TIP

> If the object you want to select is hidden from view, press the Tab key to cycle through all objects to find the one you want.

ALIGNING OBJECTS

You can align and distribute objects relative to each other or to the slide. Select the objects you want to align, click the Draw button on the Drawing toolbar, and choose Align or Distribute from the menu. A submenu appears. If you want to align or distribute relative to the slide, select Relative to Slide. If you want to align or distribute relative to the objects, make sure that Relative to Slide is not selected. Then choose from these options:

Option	Relative to Objects	Relative to Slide
Align Left	Moves the selected objects horizontally until their leftmost points are as far left as the leftmost point of the leftmost object.	Moves the selected objects horizontally until their leftmost points touch the left edge of the slide.
Align Center	Moves the selected objects horizontally until their vertical centers are along the vertical centerline of the rectangular area created when you selected the objects.	Moves the selected objects horizontally until their vertical centers are on the vertical center of the slide.

Option	Relative to Objects	Relative to Slide
Align Right	Moves the selected objects horizontally until their rightmost points are as far right as the rightmost point of the rightmost object.	Moves the selected objects horizontally until their rightmost points touch the right edge of the slide.
Align Top	Moves the selected objects vertically until their topmost points are as far up as the topmost point of the topmost object.	Moves the selected objects vertically until their topmost points touch the top of the slide.
Align Middle	Moves the selected objects vertically until their horizontal centers are along the horizontal centerline of the rectangular area created when you selected the objects.	Moves the selected objects vertically until their horizontal centers are on the the horizontal center of the slide.
Align Bottom	Moves the selected objects vertically until their bottommost points are as far down as the bottommost point of the bottommost object.	Moves the selected objects vertically until their bottommost points touch the bottom of the slide.
Distribute Horizontally	Moves the objects horizontally so that the objects are spaced evenly between the leftmost point on the leftmost object and the rightmost point on the rightmost object.	Moves the objects horizontally so that the objects are spaced evenly between the left and right edges of the slide.
Distribute Vertically	Moves the objects vertically so that the objects are spaced evenly between the topmost point on the topmost object and the bottommost point on the bottommost object.	Moves the objects vertically so that the objects are spaced evenly between the top and right edges of the slide.

NUDGING OBJECTS

It can be hard to precisely position an object using the mouse. When you experience that frustration, give up the mouse for a minute and try *nudging* the object. To do this, select the object, click the Draw button on the Drawing toolbar, choose Nudge, and then select a direction: Up, Down, Left, or Right. The object moves a few pixels in the direction you choose. You might need to nudge an object several times to put it exactly where you want it.

14

The advantage to nudging is that you can control very small movements, which is difficult to do if you move an object with the mouse.

TIP

Alternatively, you can also select an object and use the arrow keys to nudge the object in the direction of the arrow.

SNAPPING TO A GRID OR SHAPE

When you align or move objects, they snap to an invisible grid that guides their positioning. This helps you more precisely align and position objects, creating a more polished and professional look. If you want to use other objects as a positioning guide, you can snap to shapes. To choose these options, click the Draw button on the Drawing toolbar and choose Grid and Guides to open the Grid and Guides dialog box (see Figure 14.30).

Figure 14.30
Snap objects to a grid or another object.

In this dialog box, you can choose to snap objects to either a grid or other objects. You can also indicate the spacing of your grid in inches (from 1/24th of an inch to two inches).

Select the Display Grid on Screen check box to activate the grid. You'll see horizontal and vertical dotted lines on your screen in the spacing width you specified, which helps you position your objects. Although the grid appears on the screen, it doesn't appear in print or during a slideshow.

Another option is to use adjustable drawing guides by selecting the Display Drawing Guides on Screen check box. This places one adjustable vertical line and one adjustable horizontal line on your screen, which you can drag to position where you want them. These, too, are invisible in print or during a slideshow.

To set these options as your default, click the Set as Default button. Click OK to close the Grid and Guides dialog box.

14

GROUPING OBJECTS

If you need to move a few objects on your slide after carefully positioning them, it can be hard to keep them positioned correctly. Fortunately, you can *group* two or more objects so that PowerPoint treats them as one object. For example, if you combine WordArt with a clip art image to create a logo, you can group these objects so that they stay together when you move them. A grouped set of objects moves in unison, always remaining in the same relative positions. When you format grouped objects, the formatting applies to all the objects. For example, let's say you have two grouped objects that were originally different colors. If you now recolor them, the new color applies to both objects, not just one. To make individual changes, you have to ungroup the objects.

To group selected objects, click the Draw button on the Drawing toolbar and choose Group. The object handles now treat the objects as one, shown in Figure 14.31.

Figure 14.31
Group objects to treat them as one.

You can ungroup a selected grouped object by clicking the Draw button again and choosing Ungroup.

> **NOTE**
>
> Choose Regroup from the Draw menu to regroup items you just ungrouped.

ROTATING AND FLIPPING OBJECTS

Many times when you add an AutoShape or clip art image, it ends up facing the wrong direction. For example, you might add a callout to draw attention to specific text, but the callout is pointing the wrong way.

> **NOTE**
>
> To rotate or flip a single object in a group, you need to ungroup it first and regroup the objects when you're done.

14

To quickly rotate an object, select it, and place the mouse pointer over the green rotate handle that appears at the top of the object (attached by a line to the top-most resizing handle). Drag this handle to rotate the object.

You can also use rotation options from the Drawing toolbar. To rotate or flip a selected object, click the Draw button on the Drawing toolbar, choose Rotate or Flip, and then select one of the following menu options:

- **Free Rotate**—Lets you openly rotate the object.
- **Rotate Left**—Moves the object counterclockwise.
- **Rotate Right**—Moves the object clockwise.
- **Flip Horizontal**—Turns the object horizontally.
- **Flip Vertical**—Turns the object vertically.

UNDERSTANDING WORDART

WordArt lets you create special text effects such as shadowed, rotated, stretched, or multicolored text. PowerPoint treats WordArt pictures as drawing objects, not text, so the properties that apply to other drawing objects, such as formatting, the use of 3D, and the like, also apply to WordArt.

CAUTION

Spell check doesn't work with WordArt because it's a drawing object, not text. You must check spelling the old-fashioned way in WordArt pictures.

Figure 14.32 provides some samples of the type of text formatting you can do with WordArt.

CAUTION

Be careful not to overuse WordArt in your presentation or it can become cluttered and confusing. Use WordArt only for emphasis.

INSERTING WORDART

To insert a WordArt image in your slide, follow these steps:

1. Select Insert, Picture, WordArt to open the WordArt Gallery dialog box shown in Figure 14.33.

Figure 14.32
WordArt provides numerous options for creating words with special graphic effects.

Figure 14.33
Preview WordArt styles before you choose one.

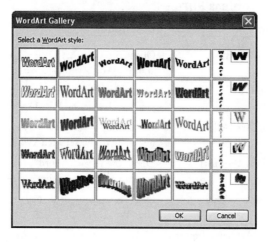

You can also open the WordArt Gallery dialog box by clicking the WordArt button on the Drawing toolbar.

2. Select the WordArt style you want and click OK. The Edit WordArt Text dialog box appears, as shown in Figure 14.34.

3. Type the text that you want to format using WordArt.

4. Choose the font and size you want. If you want to make the text bold or italic, click the Bold and Italic buttons.

5. Click OK to placei the WordArt on your slide.

14

Figure 14.34
Enter the word or
words you want to
format in this dialog
box.

FORMATTING WORDART

After you insert a iWordArt image, the WordArt toolbar appears. You can use this toolbar to apply additional formatting options. Table 14.4 describes the WordArt toolbar buttons.

TABLE 14.4 WORDART TOOLBAR BUTTONS

Button	Name	Description
	Insert WordArt	Opens the WordArt Gallery so that you can add another WordArt image
Edit Text...	Edit Text	Opens the Edit WordArt Text dialog box so that you can change the WordArt's text
	WordArt Gallery	Opens the WordArt Gallery so that you can apply a new style to the selected WordArt
	Format WordArt	Opens the Format WordArt dialog box in which you can format color, lines, size, and position
	WordArt Shape	Displays a palette of shapes that you can apply to your WordArt
	WordArt Same Letter Heights	Makes all letters in a WordArt picture the same height
	WordArt Vertical Text	Rotates your WordArt to make it vertical
	WordArt Alignment	Lets you set WordArt alignment, including left, right, center, and justified alignments
	WordArt Character Spacing	Lets you make character spacing looser or tighter than normal

14

FORMATTING WORDART CHARACTERS

You can customize several aspects of character spacing and orientation using WordArt.

Click the WordArt Character Spacing button on the WordArt toolbar to choose spacing options from a menu that appears.

You can also set a custom percentage for character spacing. The default is 100%. A higher percentage loosens the text, and a lower percentage tightens the text. Select the Kern Character Pairs option if you want to adjust sets of characters together.

Click the WordArt Same Letter Heights button to make all the letters in your WordArt the same height as the tallest character.

Click the WordArt Vertical Text button to make your WordArt from horizontal to vertical orientation and back again. You might have to resize the picture to make it fit properly by dragging the bottom side with the mouse.

Figure 14.35 illustrates examples of text spacing modifications.

Figure 14.35
Spacing and orientation make WordArt adjust to your presentation needs.

Original WordArt

Same letter heights

Vertical text

Very loose character spacing

Very tight character spacing

14

NOTE

> Click the Undo button to undo any WordArt formatting option that you apply.

MODIFYING WORDART

To modify WordArt, select it to display the WordArt toolbar. Use the toolbar buttons to change or further customize the WordArt picture.

TROUBLESHOOTING

UNDERSTANDING 3D LIMITS

I want to add 3D effects to a selected object, but the effects on the 3-D palette are dimmed and unavailable.

If you can't apply 3D effects to the selected object, the 3-D palette won't be active. For example, you can't apply 3D effects to pictures or text boxes because it wouldn't make sense to do so.

RESCALING OBJECTS

I tried to rescale an object in the Format dialog box, but it became distorted.

To preserve the ratio of height to width in an object that you're rescaling, be sure to check the Lock Aspect Ratio check box. Otherwise, the object might become distorted.

DESIGN CORNER: ENHANCING PRESENTATIONS WITH FORMATTING EFFECTS

By adding special formatting effects such as AutoShapes, shadows, and line styles, you can greatly enhance your presentation. For example, you can enliven an existing presentation in just a few minutes. Or you can design a presentation from scratch with a goal of using special formatting to create something unique and effective. To understand what works and what doesn't, experiment. Take a sample presentation and try some formatting techniques to find your favorites. One word of caution, though. It's easy to get carried away with special formats and effects. If you're creating a basic business presentation, you'll want to use these effects to *enhance* your presentation, not overwhelm it. Even if you're creating something other than a business presentation, remember to add formatting effects sparingly. The rule is to *use restraint*.

In this example, a set of steps for achieving a goal was made more visually appealing by drawing it out and highlighting the goal, as discussed in this chapter.

BEFORE

Figure 14.36

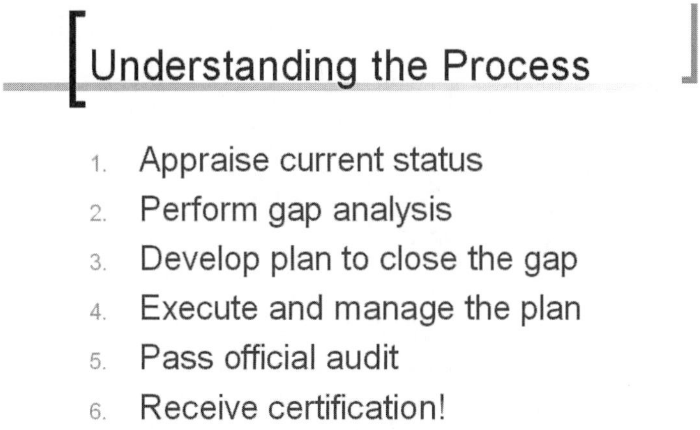

Understanding the Process
1. Appraise current status
2. Perform gap analysis
3. Develop plan to close the gap
4. Execute and manage the plan
5. Pass official audit
6. Receive certification!

AFTER

Figure 14.37

Understanding the Process
1
Appraise Status
2
Perform Gap Analysis
3
Develop Plan to Close Gap
4
Execute and Manage Plan
5
Pass Official Audit
6
Receive Certification!

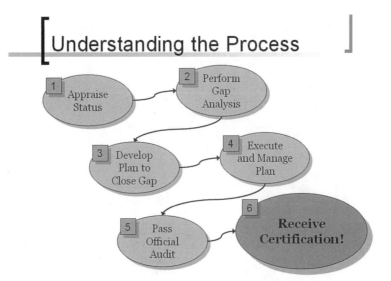

CHAPTER **15**

WORKING WITH ANIMATION

In this chapter   *by Patrice-Anne Rutledge and Jim Grey*

UNDERSTANDING ANIMATION

PowerPoint includes a number of ways to animate your slides. You can animate the transition from one slide to another or animate how objects and text appear on a slide. You can also customize these basic animations in a variety of ways. You can have action buttons or other objects perform a specific action in your presentation, such as opening a Web page on the Internet.

Like most of PowerPoint's capabilities, animation can be either very simple or detailed and complex. It all depends on how creative and sophisticated you want to make your presentation. Animation can definitely enliven any presentation, but as with any special effect, be careful not to overdo. Too much animation can actually detract from your presentation. Animation also increases a file's size.

→ To learn more about animation and visual design, **see** Chapter 25, "The Media—Designing Visual Support," **p. 535**.

Depending on what you want to animate (slide, text, drawing object, chart, media clip, and so forth) and what kind of animation you want to use (a direction or an action), you have several ways to create an animation effect in PowerPoint. Your basic choices include the following:

- **Slide transitions**—Let you determine how to change from one slide to the next in your presentation. By default, when you move from one slide to another, the next slide immediately appears. With animation, you can make the old slide fade away to reveal the new slide or make the new slide move down from the top of the screen to cover the old slide.

- **Animation schemes**—Let you animate PowerPoint objects, such as text or drawing objects, using directional effects similar to slide transitions. For example, you can use an animation scheme to dissolve or wipe title text into your presentation.

- **Custom animation**—Lets you set more sophisticated animation options, such as the order and timing of multiple animation objects in one slide. You can also use custom animation on charts and media clips such as sound and movie files.

- **Action settings**—Let you attach an action to a PowerPoint object. For example, you can open a Web page, go to another slide, or start an external program by clicking the mouse on—or even by just passing the mouse pointer over—the object. An action setting differs from the previous kinds of animation in that it performs an action rather than defines how to introduce an object or slide.

- **Action buttons**—Let you attach an action to a specific button. An action button is a predefined object that includes an action setting. You can attach an action setting to an object you create, or you can use an action button instead.

SETTING SLIDE TRANSITIONS

Setting slide transitions is one of the most common animation effects. You can apply a slide transition to the entire presentation or just to the current slide. PowerPoint offers a variety of transition options, including the capability to fade, dissolve, wipe, or even display items as a newsflash. Within each of these main categories, you can choose a direction. For example, you can wipe up, down, left, or right.

As with so many PowerPoint features, use restraint with slide transitions. For the most professional results, choose one transition to use for every slide in a presentation. Or, if you want to highlight one or two particular slides, you can apply just the right transition to those, but apply no transition to the rest. Too many different transitions can make your presentation confusing and inconsistent, detracting from your message.

You can set slide transitions in either Normal view or Slide Sorter view. Follow these steps:

1. Choose Slide Show, Slide Transition. The Slide Transition task pane appears, as shown in Figure 15.1.

Figure 15.1
You can specify how you want to move from one slide to another slide during a presentation.

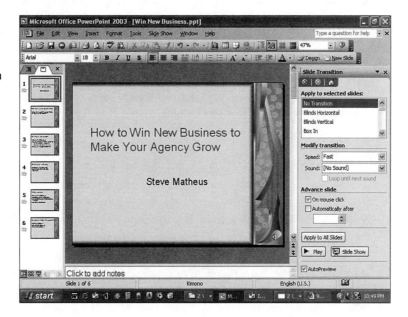

> **TIP**
> If you already have a task pane open, you can click the down arrow at the top of the pane and select Slide Transition from the menu that appears.

2. Select the slide or slides to which you want to apply the transition in either Slide Sorter view or in the Slides tab of Normal view. To select all slides, press Ctrl+A.

3. From the Apply to Selected Slides list, select the transition you want to apply.

15

TIP

Make sure that the AutoPreview check box is selected so that you can preview transitions as you choose them in the Apply to Selected Slides list. Depending on your screen resolution and whether your PowerPoint window is maximized, this check box might be hidden. If it is, pause your mouse over the small arrow at the bottom of the task pane, and the pane will scroll up so that you can see the hidden fields.

4. Choose a transition speed of Slow, Medium, or Fast, depending on how quickly you want the transition to occur in a slideshow.

CAUTION

If your presentation is to be fast paced, choose a fast or medium transition. A slow transition might be too slow for you, especially if your computer is a few years old or more.

5. To add a sound effect to your transition, select a sound from the Sound drop-down list. If you want to use a sound elsewhere on your computer, choose Other Sound from the drop-down list to open the Add Sound dialog box, navigate to the sound to use, select it, and click OK. If you want the sound to continue playing until the presentation encounters another sound file, click the Loop Until Next Sound check box.

CAUTION

Use sounds sparingly on slide transitions. They can unintentionally generate laughter or even annoyance in your audience.

 Can't hear your sound files? See the "Troubleshooting" section near the end of this chapter.

→ To learn how to add WAV and other sound files, **see** "Inserting Sounds or Movies" in Chapter 13, "Working with Pictures, Movies, Sounds, and the Clip Organizer," **p. 262**.

6. Select the On Mouse Click check box to advance to the next slide when you click the mouse or press a key such as the spacebar, Enter, Page Up, or Page Down. This is selected by default.

7. If you would rather have PowerPoint automatically change to the next slide after a specified amount of time, select the Automatically After check box and enter a specific time, in minutes and seconds, in the field beside it. Any timings you've already added to your slideshow appear in this box.

8. Click the Apply to All Slides button to apply the transitions to all slides in your presentation.

9. To preview your transitions, either click the Play button to preview within your current view (or preview it again if you selected the AutoPreview check box), or click the Slide Show button to start a slideshow.

→ To learn more about running slideshows, **see** Chapter 9, "Presenting a Slideshow," **p. 175**.

USING ANIMATION SCHEMES

You can apply preset animation to slide text using animation schemes that provide options ranging from subtle to highly creative animations. Pinwheel, Neutron, and Boomerang and Exit are just a few examples of PowerPoint animation schemes. To preview their effects, try out a few to find the one that's right for your presentation.

To apply an animation scheme to one or more selected slides, follow these steps:

1. Choose Slide Show, Animation Schemes. The Slide Design task pane, shown in Figure 15.2, opens with the Animation Schemes option selected.

Animation Schemes option

Figure 15.2
Animation Schemes offers a fast and simple way to animate your slides.

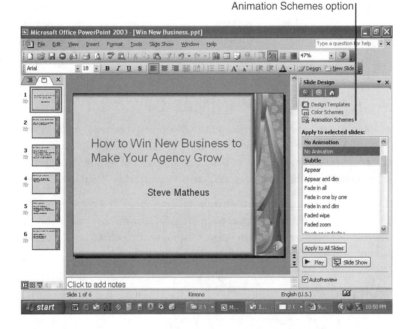

TIP

If you already have a task pane open, you can click the down arrow at the top of the pane and choose Slide Design—Animation Schemes from the menu that appears.

2. Choose the animation you want from the Apply to Selected Slides list. The list displays the Recently Used animation schemes first and then divides the remaining schemes into the Subtle, Moderate, and Exciting categories.

TIP

Make sure that the AutoPreview check box is selected so that you can preview your animations as you apply them.

3. To preview what this animation effect looks like within the current view (or preview it again if you selected the AutoPreview check box), click the Play button. To start a slideshow, click the Slide Show button.

→ To learn more about running slideshows, **see** Chapter 9, **p. 175**.

4. To apply the animation scheme to the entire presentation, click the Apply to All Slides button.

If you later decide you don't want a particular animation scheme, choose the No Animation option in the Apply to Selected Slides list in the Slide Design—Animation Schemes task pane.

NOTE

> When you run a slideshow of your presentation, only the title appears at first when a slide appears. To make each bullet point appear, click the mouse.

CREATING CUSTOM ANIMATIONS

If animation schemes don't provide the flexibility you need, try custom animation. The Custom Animation task pane offers more advanced animation options, such as the ability to set order and timings and to animate certain parts of a slide. You also use this task pane to set animation effects for charts, diagrams, organization charts, and media clips.

If you've already applied an animation scheme to a slide, these animation events appear in the Custom Animation list on the Custom Animation task pane. You can either delete these animations and start over with custom animation by clicking the Remove button on the task pane or add more enhancements to your animation schemes.

→ To learn more about animation schemes, **see** "Setting Special Animation Effects" later in this chapter, **p. 327**.

NOTE

> Applying a custom animation is far more complicated than applying an animation scheme. Be sure that you really need the power offered by custom animations before you spend the time to set them up.

To apply a custom animation to text or an object, follow these steps:

1. Choose Slide Show, Custom Animation to open the Custom Animation task pane, as shown in Figure 15.3.

TIP

> If you already have a task pane open, you can click the down arrow at the top of the pane and select the Custom Animation task pane from the menu that appears.

Figure 15.3
Custom Animation offers more complex options.

2. Select the text or object to animate.

3. Click the Add Effect button to display a menu of additional options:

   - **Entrance**—Determines how the text or object enters the slide. Options include Blinds, Box, Checkerboard, Diamonds, and Fly In.

   - **Emphasis**—Adds emphasis to the text or object. Options include Change Font, Change Font Size, Change Font Style, Grow/Shrink, and Spin.

   - **Exit**—Determines how the text or object exits the slide. Options include Blinds, Box, Checkerboard, Diamonds, Fly Out, and Whip.

   - **Motion Paths**—Sets a path that the selected text or object follows. Options include Diagonal Down Right, Diagonal Up Right, Down, Left, Right, and Up. You can also draw a custom path based on a line, curve, freeform, or scribble shape.

NOTE

Not all options are always available, depending on what you select to animate. For example, text-based animation options such as Change Font or Change Font Size are only available if you select text.

4. Click the type of effect you want and choose from the submenu of additional options. It appears in the Custom Animation list.

15

TIP

Verify that the AutoPreview check box is selected so that you can preview your transitions as you apply them.

5. To see a complete list of effects, choose the More Effects menu option, which opens a dialog box of related effects, such as the Add Entrance Effect or Add Emphasis Effect dialog box (see Figure 15.4).

Figure 15.4
Additional custom effects are available, ranging from subtle to extravagant.

The effects in these dialog boxes are grouped by style—basic, subtle, moderate, or exciting, for example. If the Preview Effect check box is selected, you can see the effect on your slide when you click it in the dialog box. If you want to use one of these effects, select it and click OK to close the dialog box.

6. From the Start drop-down list in the Custom Animation task pane, choose when you want the animation to start. Some choices might not appear in the drop-down list, depending on the sequence of the animation.

7. Depending on which custom animation you choose, additional drop-down lists might appear, such as Direction, Speed, Font Style, Duration, and so forth. Select the options you prefer.

8. Click the Play button to see the animations in your current view, or click the Slide Show button to see the animations in a slideshow.

→ To learn more about running slideshows, **see** Chapter 9, **p. 175**.

Each animation event you add appears in the Custom Animation list in the order you enter it. The icon that precedes it tells you what kind of animation it is and corresponds to the icons that precede the choices on the Add Effect menu (Entrance, Emphasis, and so forth). Hover the mouse over the animation in the list to display more information, such as the start option and effect type. If you have multiple animations in this list, the list is numbered and the numbers also appear on your slide to show where the animations are located. These numbers don't appear in print or during a slideshow, however. Figure 15.5 shows a list of animation options.

Figure 15.5
PowerPoint lists your custom animations in sequence.

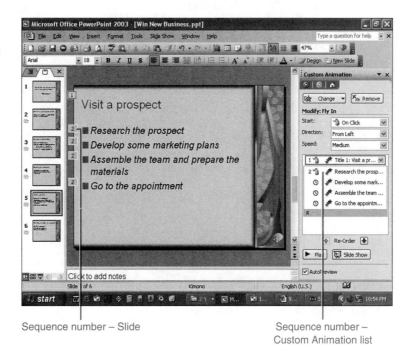

Sequence number – Slide

Sequence number – Custom Animation list

SETTING SPECIAL ANIMATION EFFECTS

The Custom Animation task pane also offers the option to add more animation effects, set timings, reorder animation events, and animate parts of diagrams, organization charts, media clips, or other charts you've added to your slides.

SETTING ADDITIONAL EFFECTS

To add effects to an animation event in the Custom Animation list—such as directional, sound, text, and color enhancements—click the down arrow to the right of an animation in the list and choose Effect Options from the menu that appears. A dialog box opens with the Effect tab selected (see Figure 15.6).

The dialog box's name and content depend on the kind of animation event you're customizing. For example, if you choose the Box entrance effect, the Box dialog box appears. We will use the Box dialog box to explore the range of customizations you can make, but remember that depending on the effect you choose, this dialog box would have different fields or tabs.

Figure 15.6
Continue to customize your custom animation with the options in this dialog box.

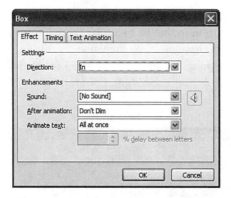

The Effect tab on the Box dialog box has the following options:

- **Direction**—Specify a direction for the selected animation, such as In, Out, Horizontal, or Vertical.

> **NOTE**
>
> Only those directions that apply to the selected animation event will appear in this drop-down list.

- **Sound**—If you want a sound effect to accompany the effect, select a sound from the drop-down list. If you don't want to include a sound, choose No Sound, which is the default option. For even more sounds, choose Other Sound to open the Add Sound dialog box.

> **CAUTION**
>
> Use sounds sparingly—they can quickly annoy your audience.

→ To learn how to add sound files, **see** "Inserting Sounds or Movies" in Chapter 13, "Working with Pictures, Movies, Sounds, and the Clip Organizer," **p. 262**.

- **Volume**—Click the Volume button to raise or lower the sound effect's volume level. You can also choose to mute the effect here.
- **After Animation**—Specify how to end your animation in this drop-down list, such as displaying the object in a new color or hiding it after animation. Options include
  - **Standard Colors**—Let you apply a color from the default palette, which changes the object's color after the animation finishes.
  - **More Colors**—Displays the Colors dialog box from which you can choose any color. The object changes to this color after the animation finishes.

→ To learn more about the Colors dialog box, **see** "Specifying Colors" in Chapter 14, "Creating and Formatting Objects," **p. 290**

- **Don't Dim**—Continues to display a static image of the object after animation.
- **Hide After Animation**—Hides the object after animation.
- **Hide on Next Mouse Click**—Hides the object when you click the mouse.

■ **Animate Text**—From the drop-down list, choose a method for introducing text: All at Once (the default), By Word, or By Letter.

■ **% Delay Between**—If you choose the By Word or By Letter option, you can set how long PowerPoint waits after starting to display one word or letter before starting to display the next word or letter. 50% means that the previous word is 50% displayed when the next word begins to display.

SETTING TIMINGS

To set exact timing effects for your custom animations, click the down arrow next to an animation in the Custom Animation list and choose Timing from the menu that appears. A dialog box opens with the Timing tab selected, as shown in Figure 15.7.

Figure 15.7
Make additional timing modifications on the Timing tab.

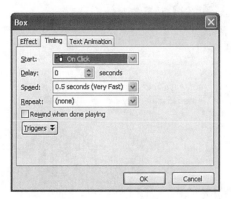

Remember that the name of this dialog box reflects the type of animation effect whose timing you want to customize. On the Timing tab, you can set the following options:

■ **Start**—Specify when to start the animation:
- **On Click**—When you click the mouse
- **With Previous**—As soon as the previous animation in the list starts
- **After Previous**—After the previous animation in the list finishes

■ **Delay**—Enter the delay in seconds.

■ **Speed**—Choose a speed level—from very slow to very fast.

■ **Repeat**—Indicate how many times you want the animation to repeat. Options include none (which means that it plays once); two, three, four, five, or ten times; until the next mouse click; or until the next slide.

15

- **Rewind when Done Playing**—Click this check box if you want to return the animation to its original position when it finishes playing.

- **Triggers**—Click the Triggers button to display two more fields on this tab that let you determine what triggers this animation to start:

  - **Animate as Part of Click Sequence**—Click this radio button to animate as part of the click sequence in the Custom Animation list.

  - **Start Effect on Click Of**—Click this radio button and then choose a specific animation from the drop-down list on which to trigger this animation.

You can also display the Advanced Timeline, which lets you further customize timings by dragging the timeline's scrollbar. To open this timeline, right-click the Custom Animation list and choose Show Advanced Timeline. Figure 15.8 illustrates this timeline.

Figure 15.8
Define specific timings to give your presentation a professional polish.

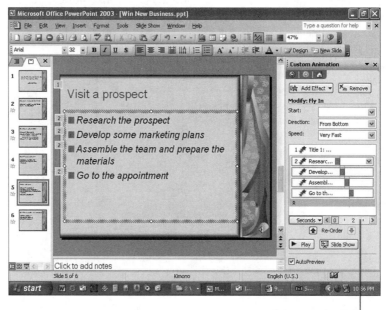

Advanced timeline

To close the timeline, right-click again and choose Hide Advanced Timeline.

ANIMATING CHARTS

You can add more effects to a chart to which you've applied a custom animation. To do so, click the down arrow next to the chart in the Custom Animation list and choose Effect Options from the menu. Figure 15.9 shows the dialog box that appears. (Remember that the dialog box name reflects the type of effect you've applied, such as Box or Spin.)

Click the Chart Animation tab and, from the Group chart drop-down list, indicate how you want to introduce the chart elements. Options include As One Object, By Series, By Category, By Element in Series, and By Element in Category.

Figure 15.9
Animating a chart is another possibility.

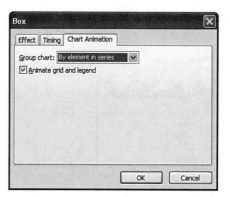

TIP

> If you choose any option other than As One Object, the Animate Grid and Legend check box activates, letting you include the chart grid and legend in the animation.

→ To learn how to create a chart, **see** Chapter 11, "Working with Charts," **p. 217**.

ANIMATING DIAGRAMS

Animating parts of diagrams or organization charts is another animation customization you can apply. To do so, click the down arrow next to the diagram in the Custom Animation list, choose Effect Options from the menu, and click the Diagram Animation tab, shown in Figure 15.10.

Figure 15.10
Animating parts of a diagram is another custom animation option.

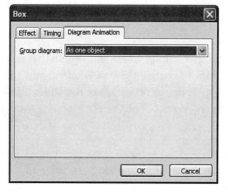

From the Group Diagram drop-down list, choose the way you want to introduce the diagram onto the slide. The choices depend on the kind of diagram.

ANIMATING MEDIA CLIPS

You can also customize animations to media clips such as a sound or video file. For example, to customize a sound clip animation, click the down arrow next to the clip in the Custom

Animation list and choose Effect Options from the menu. Figure 15.11 shows the Effect tab of the Play Sound dialog box that appears. This tab includes choices for starting and stopping the media clip.

Figure 15.11
The Effect tab adds fields for animating media clips.

REORDERING ANIMATIONS

The animations in the Custom Animation list appear in the order you enter them, but you can change this order if you prefer. To specify the order in which to animate multiple objects on a single slide, select the object you want to reorder and click either the up or down Re-Order button. Or you can drag an animation to another location in the list.

MODIFYING ANIMATIONS

After you apply custom animations to a slide, you might decide that you want to modify them. For example, you might want to change the type of effect you applied from Box to Diamond or from Grow/Shrink to Spin. To do so, select the animation in the Custom Animation list and click the Change button. Then select a new custom animation to apply.

NOTE

The Change button is the same as the Add Effect button. Its name changes when you modify an existing animation rather than add a new one.

DELETING ANIMATIONS

To delete a custom animation, select it in the Custom Animation list and click the Remove button. To delete all animations, select the first animation in the list, press the Shift key, select the last animation in the list, and then click the Remove button.

If you make a mistake and want to restore your deletions, click the Undo button on the Standard toolbar.

USING ACTION SETTINGS

Use the Action Settings dialog box to start an action by clicking an object with the mouse or simply by passing the mouse pointer over it.

For example, you can place an object, such as a rectangle, in your presentation and have it connect to the Web, play a sound, run a macro, or open another program when you click it or pass the mouse over it. This can be useful when you want to demonstrate other applications during your presentation, but don't want to take the time to try to locate and open them in the middle of a slideshow.

To add an action to a PowerPoint object, follow these steps:

1. Select the object to which you want to add an action.
2. Choose Slide Show, Action Settings to open the Action Settings dialog box, shown in Figure 15.12.

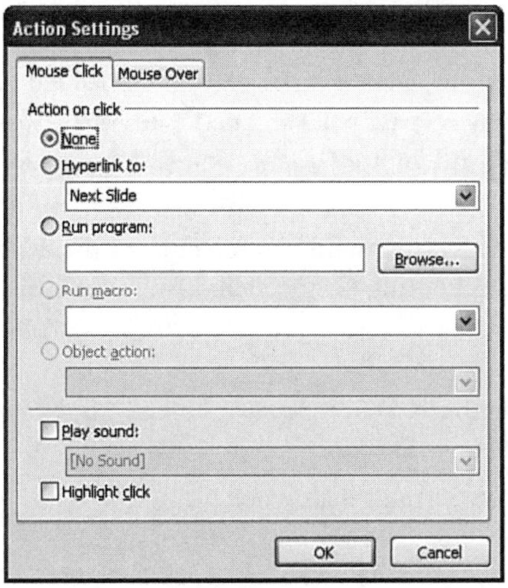

Figure 15.12
Use a mouse click or mouse over to perform actions in your presentation.

Action Settings
Mouse Click | Mouse Over
Action on click
● None
○ Hyperlink to:
Next Slide
○ Run program:
[   ] Browse...
○ Run macro:
[   ]
○ Object action:
[   ]
☐ Play sound:
[No Sound]
☐ Highlight click
OK   Cancel

3. Choose the Mouse Click tab if you want to start the action with a mouse click; choose the Mouse Over tab to start the action by passing the mouse over the object. The Mouse Click and Mouse Over tabs are nearly identical. The only real difference is the method by which you start the action.

CAUTION

Passing the mouse over an object to start an action is the easier method, but be careful not to get too close to the object too soon or you might start the action before you intend to.

4. Choose the action to take when you click or hover over the object:

- **None**—No action occurs. Choose this option to remove a previously placed action.

- **Hyperlink To**—Creates a hyperlink to a selected slide within your presentation, another PowerPoint presentation, another file on your computer, or a Web page.

→ For further explanation about using hyperlinks in PowerPoint, **see** "Adding Hyperlinks" in Chapter 16, "Using PowerPoint's Web Features," **p. 342**.

- **Run Program**—Runs the program whose path you specify in the text box. Click the Browse button to open the Select a Program to Run dialog box, where you can search for the program.

> **TIP**
>
> You can also use this field to open a file in another program. For example, entering `c:\download\budget.xls` opens Excel and the Budget worksheet that's in the Download folder.

- **Run Macro**—Lets you choose from a list of PowerPoint macros you've created.

→ To learn how to create macros, **see** "Running a Macro from the Toolbar" in Chapter 20, "Working with Macros," **p. 425**.

- **Object Action**—Lets you open, edit, or play an embedded object. This option is available only for objects that you can open, edit, or play, such as a media clip or something created with another application and embedded into your presentation.

- **Play Sound**—Lets you play a sound you select from the drop-down list. You can select other sounds by choosing Other Sound from the drop-down list.

→ To learn about sound files, **see** "Inserting Sounds or Movies" in Chapter 13, "Working with Pictures, Movies, Sounds, and the Clip Organizer," **p. 262**.

- **Highlight Click/Highlight When Mouse Over**—Highlights the selected object when you perform the mouse action.

5. Click OK to close the Action Settings dialog box.

 Are your animation effects not working when using PowerPoint? *See the "Troubleshooting" section near the end of the chapter.*

USING ACTION BUTTONS

Action buttons are another way to use objects to perform certain actions. PowerPoint includes 12 different action buttons.

These buttons function in much the same way as applying an action setting to an existing object. In fact, when you place an action button on a slide, the Action Settings dialog box appears. You can then specify mouse actions for the action button. Many action buttons perform common tasks such as moving to a previous slide, so this action is defined by default in the Action Settings dialog box.

To place an action button on a PowerPoint slide, choose Slide Show, Action Buttons. The Action Buttons palette appears, as shown in Figure 15.13.

Figure 15.13
This palette includes several ready-made action buttons.

TIP

> You can also create an action button from the Drawing toolbar by choosing AutoShapes, Action Buttons.

To place an action button on a slide, click a button on the palette and then click and drag on the slide to create the button. As soon as you finish, the Action Settings dialog box opens—in which you can accept the default action setting or specify the action to attach to this button. Enter the required information and click OK. The action button now appears on your PowerPoint slide, as illustrated in Figure 15.14.

Figure 15.14
Use action buttons in your presentation for added flexibility and convenience in changing to other slides or applications.

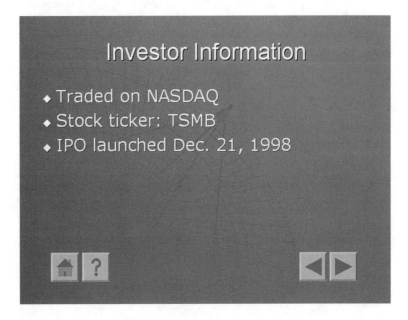

Investor Information

◆ Traded on NASDAQ
◆ Stock ticker: TSMB
◆ IPO launched Dec. 21, 1998

You will probably want to resize and move the button on the slide.

→ To learn how to move, resize, copy, delete, and format an object, such as an action button, **see** Chapter 14, **p. 281**.

TROUBLESHOOTING

RESOLVING SOUND FILE PROBLEMS

I can't hear sound files I embedded in my presentation.

You must have a sound card and speakers to hear sounds that you add to your presentation. Also, verify that your volume is turned up sufficiently to hear the sounds.

WORKING WITH PREVIOUS VERSIONS

I opened my presentation in an older version of PowerPoint, and the animations don't work.

The features and functionality of PowerPoint aren't always available in previous versions of the software. With animations, PowerPoint either converts animations to effects supported by the software version you used to open the presentation or eliminates the animation effect entirely, depending on the animation you applied.

DESIGN CORNER: SPICING UP YOUR PRESENTATION

With PowerPoint's animation features, you can enliven presentations using transitions, action buttons, or preset animation. But before you apply animation to your presentation, have a plan. First, be sure that you understand PowerPoint's animation options and how best to use them. If you're not sure, experiment a little. Trial and error can often be the best teacher in learning what works and what doesn't. Second, figure out how you will be integrating animation into your presentation—where, how much, what kind, and so forth. A little animation goes a long way; over-animating can clutter your presentation, detract from your message, and make the file size too large. Finally, implement your plan by adding the actual animations. (This is the easy part.) When you're done, be sure to preview the entire presentation to verify that what you've planned is truly effective.

In the example shown here, an informative slide is made more eye- and ear-catching by adding animation and sound effects.

BEFORE

Figure 15.15

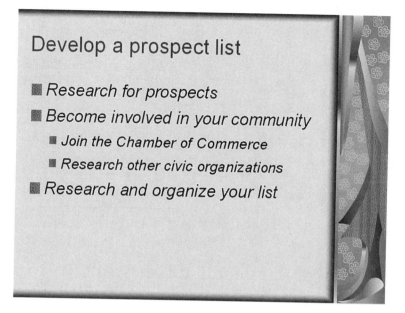

AFTER

Figure 15.16

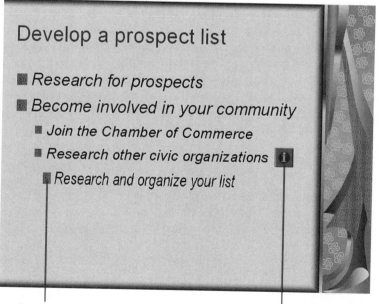

Present each bullet separately using an entry animation such as Swivel

Include an action button to perform an action such as linking to a Web page from your presentation

PART V

WORKING WITH POWERPOINT ON THE WEB

CHAPTER **16**

Using PowerPoint's Web Features

In this chapter

by Patrice-Anne Rutledge and Jim Grey

WORKING WITH HYPERLINKS

If you've ever surfed the World Wide Web, you're already familiar with *hyperlinks*. PowerPoint offers hyperlinks, too. By clicking your mouse on a linked object, you can jump to another location in your presentation, to another program, or even to a location on the Web.

Unlike a book or a typical slideshow in which you must proceed sequentially through the material, a hyperlinked presentation can let you move through a presentation in whatever order makes sense for the audience or let you hide information that you can show only if your audience needs or asks for it. Suppose that, for example, you are making a presentation to the board of directors of your entertainment company. You suspect some board members will want to know more about current promotions by a rival company. You can create a hyperlink in your slideshow that opens up your Web browser, connects to the Internet, and displays your competitor's Web site. Of course, if no one asks or if time is running short, you don't even need to use the link. But you know it's there, just in case.

ADDING HYPERLINKS

The first step in creating a hyperlink is to identify the object to link. You can link any object, including text, clip art, WordArt, charts, AutoShapes, and more. To create a link, follow these steps:

1. While in Normal view, select the text or object you want to link (see Figure 16.1).

Selected text

Figure 16.1
Select text or any other object to which you want to add a hyperlink.

Quality Assurance Culture

- ISO 9002 registration
- Single-source supplier partnerships
- Focus on effective processes to build in quality
- Statistical process control
- Customer satisfaction

2. Click the Insert Hyperlink button. Or choose Insert, Hyperlink or press Ctrl+K. The Insert Hyperlink dialog box appears (see Figure 16.2).

Figure 16.2
Use the Insert Hyperlink dialog box to specify the location you want to link to the selected text or object.

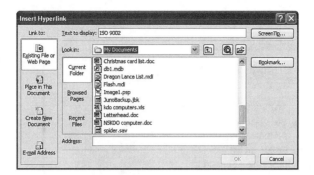

NOTE

When you create a hyperlink for the first time, use the Insert Hyperlink dialog box. If you change the hyperlink, use the Edit Hyperlink dialog box. These dialog boxes are identical except for the Remove Link button found in the Edit Hyperlink dialog box.

3. Type the URL in the Address field.

CAUTION

Be sure to type the URL exactly as it appears, including uppercase and lowercase letters and all special characters (such as the tilde ~). If you can, go to the site, cut the URL from the Address field in your browser, and paste it in this field.

4. Click OK.

If you added a link to text, that text now appears underlined and in a different color (see Figure 16.3). The actual color you see depends on the PowerPoint design template you are using. If you added the link to any other object, the object's appearance doesn't change, but the object is linked nonetheless.

When you open the Insert Hyperlink dialog box, PowerPoint displays the Link to Existing File or Web Page view by default. This view lets you find the URL you want in several ways:

- If you know the URL, type it in the Address field.
- If the link is to a location that you have visited recently, you can select it from the list of displayed URLs in the Address field.
- If you don't remember the location's URL but have recently visited there, click the Browsed Pages button and choose the location from a list of places you've recently visited on the Web.
 - You can click the Browse the Web button to go to your browser, enabling you to browse for the Internet location you want. When you find the location, switch back to PowerPoint (use the Windows taskbar or press Alt+Tab), and the URL from your browser appears in the dialog box.

16

Figure 16.3
Linked text appears
underlined and in a
different color.

Linked text

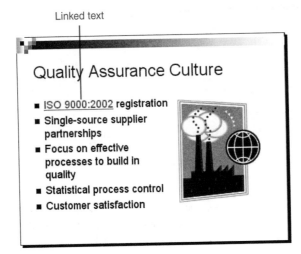

NOTE

Don't forget that you must be connected to the Internet if you want to browse for a URL.
Generally, those connected directly to a network need not be concerned; those using
dial-up connections must first make sure that they are connected.

■ If you want to jump to a specific location within a Web page after inserting the URL,
click the Bookmark button. If the Web page contains bookmarks, PowerPoint lists
them (see Figure 16.4). Select a bookmark and choose OK. PowerPoint adds the pound
sign (#) and the bookmark name to your URL.

Figure 16.4
If you need to link to
a bookmark,
PowerPoint can con-
nect to the Web site
and return a list of
bookmarks in the tar-
get Web page.

CREATING INVISIBLE HYPERLINKS FOR TEXT

Linked text looks different from the nonlinked text around it—it's underlined. You might not want the text to look different, but you still want to be able to click that text and jump to the linked page or document. The solution is simple: Cover the text with an AutoShape, link the AutoShape, and then make it invisible.

→ For more information about creating AutoShapes, **see** "Adding AutoShapes" in Chapter 14, "Creating and Formatting Objects," **p. 288**.

To create an invisible hyperlinked object, follow these steps:

1. Use the Drawing toolbar to draw a rectangular box that covers the text you want to link (see Figure 16.5).

Figure 16.5
To create the effect of linked text without making it look linked, use an AutoShape to create the link, and then make the image invisible.

2. With the AutoShape selected, click the Insert Hyperlink button (or choose Insert, Hyperlink or press Ctrl+K).

3. Type the URL in the Address field.

4. Click OK. This creates the link to the AutoShape image.

5. Right-click the AutoShape, and choose Format AutoShape; or choose Format, AutoShape from the menu bar. PowerPoint displays the Format AutoShape dialog box (see Figure 16.6).

6. Click the Fill Color drop-down list and choose No Fill.

7. Click the Line Color drop-down list and choose No Line.

8. Click OK.

An invisible linked object now appears over the text you want linked (see Figure 16.7). When you play your slideshow, move the mouse pointer to that text area and click when the mouse pointer changes to a hand. To the audience, it appears that you are clicking on text, although you are really clicking a linked invisible graphic shape.

Figure 16.6
Use the Format
AutoShape dialog box
to remove fill color
and line color, thus
making the
AutoShape invisible.

Figure 16.7
An invisible
AutoShape can be
linked, making it
appear that the text
beneath it is linked.

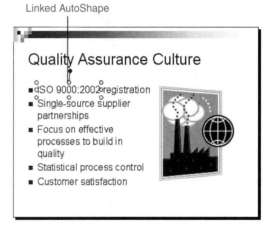

An additional benefit to using an invisible link is that no one but you has to know the link is there. If you don't use it, no one will ever know. Text linked in the normal manner, on the other hand, begs to be clicked because the text looks so obviously different.

JUMPING TO OTHER SLIDES

In addition to Web sites—and perhaps of more practical use—you can link to other slides in your presentation and even to a slide in another presentation.

Creating links to other slides helps you customize your slideshow so that you can go quickly to those slides you need. For example, after your opening title slide, you might want to include a table of contents slide, with hyperlinks from each topic to a specific location in the slideshow. On the last slide for each topic, you could include a link back to the table of contents slide. To create an internal link, follow these steps:

1. Select the object to be linked and click the Insert Hyperlink button to open the Insert Hyperlink dialog box.

2. Click the Place in This Document button. PowerPoint displays a list of slides in the current slideshow (see Figure 16.8).

Figure 16.8
To link to a slide in your current presentation, click Place in This Document and select the slide you want.

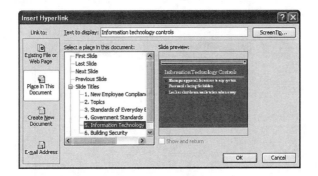

3. Select the slide to which you want to jump.

4. Click OK.

To create a link to another presentation, do the following:

1. Select the object to be linked and access the Insert Hyperlink dialog box.

2. Click the Existing File or Web Page button.

 3. Choose the presentation to which you want to jump. Use the Browse for File button if necessary.

4. Click the Bookmark button. PowerPoint displays the Select Place in Document dialog box (refer to Figure 16.4).

5. Select the slide to which you want to jump.

6. Click OK twice to return to the PowerPoint editing screen.

JUMPING TO ANOTHER FILE

PowerPoint also lets you create a hyperlink to another document either on your own computer or on the network, if you are connected to one. When you jump from your presentation to another file, the application displaying that file starts. Other PowerPoint files open in PowerPoint, Word documents open in Word, HTML files open in your browser, and so on.

To link to a file from the Insert Hyperlink dialog box, do one of these things:

- Type the name of the file, including its full pathname (for example, `c:\my documents\sales.xls`).

- Click the Recent Files button to display a list of recently accessed files.

- Click the Browse for File button and browse your computer or network for the file you want.

CREATING OTHER TYPES OF LINKS

Finally, you can insert links to files you haven't even created, as well as links to send electronic mail. Creating a link to a new file (by clicking the Create New Document button) is a handy way to create a hyperlink and create a new PowerPoint presentation at the same time. And adding a link to an email address can be useful if you publish to the Web and want your audience to be able to contact you after viewing your presentation (see Figure 16.9).

Figure 16.9
You can even link to a yet-to-be-created document.

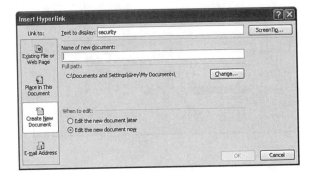

To create a link to an email address, click the E-mail Address button in the Insert Hyperlink dialog box. Type the address in the E-mail Address field and enter a subject. You can even select the email address from a list of recently used email addresses (see Figure 16.10).

Figure 16.10
Create a link to an email address, enabling a viewer to send a message.

TIP

As a shortcut, just type your email address directly on your slide (jsmith@work.com). PowerPoint recognizes common email formats and automatically creates a link for you.

NOTE

Traditionally, PowerPoint presentations were designed to be presented to an audience by a speaker. PowerPoint is now designed so that viewers can also be allowed to run the presentation by themselves. PowerPoint presentations placed on a company network or on a Web site can be designed so that viewers can navigate and even interact with the presentation at their own pace.

CUSTOMIZING A HYPERLINK'S SCREENTIP

When you point your mouse at a linked object during a presentation, a ScreenTip appears, detailing the location of the link. You can customize the ScreenTip to make it easier for you (or the audience) to know just where you will go if you click the linked object.

To change the ScreenTip, follow these steps:

1. Select the object to be linked and access the Edit Hyperlink dialog box.
2. Click the ScreenTip button. PowerPoint displays the Set Hyperlink ScreenTip dialog box (see Figure 16.11).

Figure 16.11
Customize the ScreenTip that appears when you move the mouse pointer to a linked object.

3. Type the text you want to appear in the ScreenTip in the ScreenTip Text field. The note about ScreenTips in Internet Explorer refers to slideshows viewed in the browser, not to slideshows presented normally.
4. Click OK twice to keep the ScreenTip.

MODIFYING HYPERLINKS

The Edit Hyperlink dialog box is a powerful tool for quickly and efficiently modifying your hyperlinks. To change the URL for a hyperlink you created, follow these simple steps:

1. Click or select the linked object.
2. Right-click the object and choose Edit Hyperlink; or choose Insert, Hyperlink; or press Ctrl+K. PowerPoint displays the Edit Hyperlink dialog box (see Figure 16.12).

Figure 16.12
The Edit Hyperlink dialog box lets you update or change an existing hyperlink.

3. Type the new URL or use one of the dialog box tools to select what you want to link to.

4. Choose OK to update the hyperlink.

REMOVING HYPERLINKS

After inserting a hyperlink, you might decide that you don't want it or that you need to link a different object instead. To remove a hyperlink, select the object, access the Edit Hyperlink dialog box, and click the Remove Link button.

CHANGING A HYPERLINKED OBJECT'S ACTION SETTINGS

The most important action for a linked object is to jump to a desired location. However, using PowerPoint's action settings feature, you can control how you activate the hyperlink and also add some style to the linked object.

→ To learn more about action settings, **see** "Using Action Settings" in Chapter 15, "Working with Animation," **p. 333**.

To access the Action Settings dialog box

1. Select the linked object.

2. Right-click and choose Action Settings or choose Slide Show, Action Settings. PowerPoint displays the Action Settings dialog box.

If you've created a hyperlink, Hyperlink To is already selected, and the location of the link is listed. Note that the action appears on the Mouse Click tab, which means that you have to click the linked object to activate the hyperlink. The Mouse Over tab offers the same options, but actions are activated merely by passing the mouse pointer over the linked object without clicking.

NOTE

You might be able to save some time by both selecting an object and using the Action Settings dialog box to create the hyperlink and to set any actions you want.

CAUTION

You don't want surprises during your slide presentation. Unfortunately, the Mouse Over option for activating hyperlinks can take you places before you're really ready to go. Generally, you should activate hyperlinks only by clicking the mouse.

You can add some style to your presentation by creating actions that produce sound effects or that highlight linked objects. For example, you can require a mouse click to activate a hyperlink, but you can highlight the object (graphic objects only) or add a sound effect when the mouse pointer is passed over the object.

To add Mouse Over sound and highlighting effects, follow these steps:

1. Select the object to which you want to add the effects.

2. Right-click and choose Action Settings or choose Slide Show, Action Settings. The Action Settings dialog box appears.

3. Click the Mouse Over tab (see Figure 16.13).

Figure 16.13
Add action settings to a link that are activated when you pass the mouse pointer over the linked object.

4. Click the Highlight When Mouse Over check box. (You cannot select this option if the object you have selected is text.)

5. Click the Play Sound check box.

6. Click the Play Sound drop-down list, and select the sound effect you want to use.

> **NOTE**
> You can associate any WAV sound file with the object. Choose Other Sound from the drop-down list and browse until you find the sound you want.

> **NOTE**
> If you add action settings to an object, the Action Settings dialog box opens when you click the Insert Hyperlink button (rather than the Insert Hyperlink or Edit Hyperlink dialog box). You can still edit the URL, but you have to remove any action settings if you want to access the Edit Hyperlink dialog box.

TESTING HYPERLINKS

Before you present to an audience, test all your hyperlinks to make sure that you set them up correctly. The last thing you want during your presentation is a surprise when you click a hyperlink.

NOTE

Don't forget that you must be connected to the Internet, either via a network or through a dial-up connection, if you want to test links to the Web.

To test a hyperlink, follow these steps:

1. Go to the slide you want to test.
2. Click the Slide Show view to start the presentation from the selected slide. Choosing Slide Show, View Show (or pressing F5) starts the show at the beginning of your presentation.
3. Move the mouse pointer to the linked object.
4. Check that the ScreenTip appears properly.
5. Note whether action settings work properly (such as the sound effect on mouse over).
6. Click the linked object and verify that you are taken to the appropriate Web location, slide, or file.
7. Return to your slideshow by closing the linked location. Usually, this involves closing the application, although you can also just minimize the application if you want it to start more quickly the next time you use it.

Test all the links in the presentation. This means starting the slideshow at the beginning and trying out each hyperlink. (We'll talk about how to do that in the next section.) Stop and fix any hyperlink that doesn't work the way you expect it to.

TIP

If you're presenting at a remote location and want to use hyperlinks to the Internet, be sure to arrive early to test your Internet connection and hyperlinks again. Even if you tested your hyperlinks at home and they worked fine, you need to verify your network connectivity at an unfamiliar location and have enough time to resolve problems before you present.

NAVIGATING A HYPERLINKED PRESENTATION

You would probably never get lost in a sequential slide presentation, but in a hyperlinked presentation it's easy to lose track of what slides, URLs, or files you've viewed.

You can minimize the likelihood of getting lost by rehearsing your presentation many times, trying out various links, and learning what will happen and how to get back on track.

Some typical techniques for returning to the right place in your presentation include the following:

- If you go to a browser, use the browser's Back button to return to PowerPoint. Generally, this doesn't close the browser, but keeps it open in case you need to use it again during the presentation.

- If you jump to another PowerPoint presentation, you can right-click the slide in the new presentation and choose Last Viewed to return to the original presentation. If your browser was open prior to opening a second slideshow, the browser might be closed.

- If you link to another document that opens another program, such as Word, press Alt+Tab to return to PowerPoint without closing the other application.

- If you are linking primarily to other slides within your presentation, you can also add navigational links, such as action buttons, that help you stay on course.

16

LINKING TO THE WEB DURING A PRESENTATION

The more elements you add to your presentation, the more complex it becomes, thus increasing the chances that something will go wrong. This can be particularly true when you link to the Internet during a presentation. Try to determine what parts of your presentation are most critical, and have a backup plan in case things don't work the way you hope they will. Make allowances that minimize your risk, and consider the following:

- Test links thoroughly. Remove broken links and update incorrect ones.

- Test your links for speed relative to other sites. If the linked URL contains a lot of graphics, uses Java, or is served by a slower Web server, you might not want to wait during your presentation for the site to appear.

- Always evaluate and reevaluate just how important the link is. If you don't need it, don't use it. What takes a few seconds to load in your office will seem like an eternity when you're standing in front of your audience.

- Have a backup plan in case your hyperlinks don't work. One method is to copy the files from the URL to your local computer (or network) and display them from there. However, the complexity of some sites, as well as copyright considerations, might make this impractical.

- Consider creating other slides that convey the same information as the Web site you wanted to connect to. They might not measure up to the actual Web site, but then again, you won't have to stand there waiting for the URL to come up, only to find that network congestion prevents it from doing so.

- If you're using a slower dial-up connection to the Internet during your presentation, be sure to consider page download times. Even a short delay while a page loads can distract an audience.

- If you can't get around these challenges, consider taking screenshots of the Web pages you want the audience to see and paste them in to your presentation. You won't be able to navigate the site, but at least you will get to show the key pages.

PUBLISHING TO THE INTERNET

The World Wide Web has become a fixture in our lives. Everyone wants either to receive or to publish information via the Web. PowerPoint makes it easy to convert your presentation into a format that Web browsers can view.

Before doing so, however, consider the following:

- A Web version of your presentation can be viewed by anyone who has access to your Web server. Unless your server is limited to your company (such as a corporate intranet), anyone from anywhere in the world can look in.

- A Web version lets your viewers see the presentation at their convenience. This can be particularly important for global audiences in vastly different time zones.

- You have less control over a Web version of your presentation. No longer can you dictate the sequence of the slides, nor can you add clarifying comments if they are needed.

- In the case of classroom presentations, a Web version could encourage students to skip class, knowing that they can get the presentation off the Web at another time.

- Some people in your audience might have older computers that might not let them view your presentation the way you intend it to appear.

After you determine that you really want to publish your presentation to the Web, you next need to be sure that the slideshow is well designed for Web use. Consider the following:

- Use good presentation design principles. If the slideshow works for an audience that sits before you, it will probably work well on the Web.

- Because the presentation will be viewed unattended, be sure that you have abundant navigational aids so that viewers don't get lost. Include a table of contents or Home, Back, and Forward buttons to assist the viewer.

- Be more judicious in your use of graphics, animations, and other multimedia effects. What works well from a hard disk or over a local area network might be deadly slow over a modem connection. Keep such elements small or eliminate them altogether if they don't really add to the presentation.

- Be aware of issues related to accessibility for disabled users. For example, consider whether you need an alternative text-based page for the visually impaired who use special voice readers.

 Do you have the right folders in the right place on your Web server, but some of your files are not appearing in the Web slideshow? *See "Restoring Missing Files" in the "Troubleshooting" section near the end of this chapter.*

CAUTION

> Be careful to understand and follow copyright laws and guidelines when publishing your slideshow to the Web. If any of your material, including images and sounds, is copyrighted by someone else, you might be required to limit access to the material or not use it at all if you don't first get permission.

SAVING A PRESENTATION AS A WEB PAGE

PowerPoint not only lets you save your work directly in HTML format, but also lets you open your HTML slideshows directly into PowerPoint, edit them, and save them again in HTML. As you will see, this is not only easy, but it also saves a lot of time and space because you don't have to keep an original PowerPoint show and convert it each time.

Publishing your show to the Internet involves two steps: saving the presentation in HTML format and transferring the resulting files to a Web server. If you're lucky enough to be connected directly to your Web server over a company network, you don't even have to worry about transferring files because you can save the show directly at the Web site.

To save a slideshow as a Web page, follow these steps:

1. Choose File, Save as Web Page, and PowerPoint displays a somewhat modified Save As dialog box (see Figure 16.14).

Figure 16.14
Saving a PowerPoint presentation as a Web page can be quite simple, or you can customize the Web page.

2. Browse to the location where you want to save your presentation, displayed in the Save In field.

3. Edit the filename if you want. Note that the filename ends in .htm, a standard extension for HTML files.

4. In the Save As Type field, choose to save the presentation as a single-file Web page (with an .mht file extension) or as a standard Web page (with an .htm extension).

NOTE

> If you save your presentation as a standard Web page, you get an HTML file plus a folder that contains a bunch of files your presentation needs to run in your browser. If you save your presentation as a single-file Web page, you get a single file that contains everything you need. If you need to move your presentation to other computers, it's better to save it as a single-file Web page because there's less risk that you'll accidentally forget to copy all the needed files.

5. Click the Change Title button to change the page title in the Set Page Title dialog box. This title appears in the browser's title bar.

6. Click Save to save your presentation as a Web page.

NOTE

> If you know that PowerPoint's Web options are set the way you want them, you can save time by choosing Save. By default, this gives you a frame-based Web page that includes an outline, navigation buttons, and other tools, along with the slide. The file is also optimized for use with Internet Explorer 4.0 or later.

If you want to customize the way you present your slideshow as a Web page, follow these steps:

1. Choose File, Save as Web Page.

2. In the Save As dialog box (refer to Figure 16.14), click Publish to customize the Web page display. PowerPoint displays the Publish as Web Page dialog box (see Figure 16.15).

Figure 16.15
Publishing a presentation as a Web page lets you customize how the page will appear on the Web.

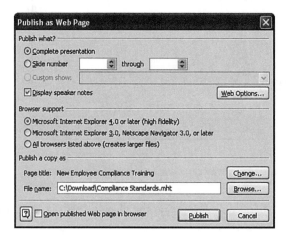

3. Choose the options you want (see the next section).

4. Click Publish to save your presentation as a series of HTML files that work together to display your slides on the Web.

CUSTOMIZING A WEB PRESENTATION

The many options for saving your presentation as a Web page let you tailor your Web page to match the needs of your viewers. For example, some browsers won't be able to view animations, whereas others can.

To customize a Web presentation, first decide exactly what you want to publish to the Web: the entire presentation, selected slides, a custom show, or speaker's notes (refer to Figure 16.15).

You can also optimize the Web presentation for browsers that audience members are likely to use by selecting the following options under Browser Support:

- To attain the highest fidelity to your original presentation, publish the presentation for use by selecting Microsoft Internet Explorer 4.0 or Later (High Fidelity). This option lets viewers with the latest browsers see animations and experience other multimedia features.

16

> **TIP**
>
> You must decide whether to ignore users with older browsers or force them to upgrade to view your Web page. If you're pretty sure that most of your audience's browsers are up-to-date, optimize for the highest quality. Otherwise, you might want to choose an option that allows all browsers to view the Web page.

- To enable users of older Web browsers to view your Web page content, choose Microsoft Internet Explorer 3.0, Netscape Navigator 3.0, or Later. Some features in your presentation might be lost with this conversion.
- All Browsers Listed Above is a special dual-HTML feature that lets viewers see the best presentation they can, based on the browser they use. This option creates larger files, which means slower downloads, but it helps you avoid having to guess which browsers your audience members are going to use.

The Web Options button opens the Web Options dialog box (shown in Figure 16.16), where you have many other options.

Figure 16.16
General Web options determine how the Web page is to be laid out and whether animations will be active.

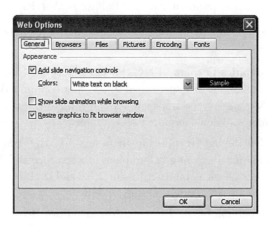

16

On the General tab, you can set several appearance options, including the ability to add slide navigation controls, show slide animation while browsing, or resize graphics to fit the browser window.

NOTE

> The options on the General tab affect only slideshows prepared for and viewed by Internet Explorer 4.0 or later. However, navigation control color options, even when turned off, do affect the navigational outline in Web pages targeted for Internet Explorer 3.0 and Netscape Navigator 3.0 or later.

On the Browsers tab (see Figure 16.17), you can choose the browser your viewers will use.

Figure 16.17
Set the optimal browser viewing options on this tab.

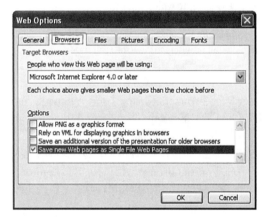

The earlier the browser version you choose, the smaller your Web pages will be. However, an earlier browser version might not support all PowerPoint's functionality, such as animations. You can also set a browser preference in the Publish as Web Page dialog box.

Based on your browser selection, the Options check boxes have the following default options selected:

- **Allow PNG as a Graphics Format**   PNG (Portable Network Graphics) is a Web graphics format that takes less disk space than some other common Web graphics formats and can have better color and transparency control. However, older browsers (pre–Internet Explorer 4.0) don't support PNG graphics.

- **Rely on VML for Displaying Graphics in Browsers**   VML (Vector Markup Language) is a method for describing 2D graphics in a text format. VML works only with the newer browsers, such as Internet Explorer 5.0 and later. If your audience might be using older browsers, do not use this option.

- **Save an Additional Version of the Presentation for Older Browsers**   This option ensures that the maximum number of viewers can view your presentation clearly, but it increases the disk space required for your presentation.

- **Save New Web Pages as Single File Web Pages**   Saves as a single-file Web page, which lets you store all parts of your Web site into a single file (text, graphics, other content, and so on). This option uses the MHTML (MIME encapsulated aggregate HTML) file format, which is supported by Internet Explorer 4.0 and later.

Click the Files tab in the Web Options dialog box to access file-naming and location options. Here you can specify to organize supporting files in a folder, use long filenames, and update links on save (see Figure 16.18):

Figure 16.18
File options let you specify how files will be named, how they'll be organized, and whether you can edit the resulting HTML files in PowerPoint.

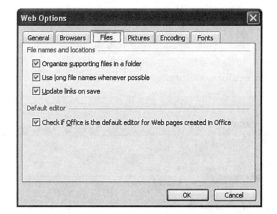

The Pictures tab lets you target monitor screen size. If you have chosen the Internet Explorer 4.0 Browser Support and the Resize Graphics to Fit Browser Window options, changing this setting has no effect. However, if you publish your presentation for use on older browsers, this option lets you specify how large the slides should be.

TIP

> Using a screen size that matches the target browser screen setting usually results in a slide that is too small for the available screen. If you want to fill up the browser window with a larger slide, select the next-highest resolution (for example, select 1024×768 if the target screen is 800×600).

Finally, the Encoding and Fonts tabs let you modify the output for use in browsers that support other languages.

→ For more information on the use of other languages in your presentations, **see** Chapter 22, "Using PowerPoint's Foreign Language Capabilities," **p. 473**.

TRANSFERRING YOUR WEB PAGE TO A WEB SERVER

Typically, you create your presentation and save it as a Web page on your local hard disk. Working offline saves time and, in some cases, dial-up connection charges. When you're finally ready to make your presentation available to the rest of the world, you must transfer your files from your own computer to the Web server that will host your Web page.

16

If you are connected to a company intranet, you might be able to publish your Web page directly to the Web server. Check with your network specialist to find out whether this is possible and how to do it.

If you aren't connected directly to your Web server, you have to transfer files to it following the instructions provided by your Internet service provider (ISP) just as you would any other Web site or pages.

TESTING YOUR WEB PAGE

More likely than not, you will test your Web page as you go. At the bottom of the Publish as Web Page dialog box, you can check the Open Published Web Page in Browser option so that each time you publish your presentation, your default browser starts and displays the page using files saved on your local computer (see Figure 16.19). If you find something wrong or want to try other options, simply return to PowerPoint and publish the presentation again.

Figure 16.19
A Web page published for Internet Explorer 4.0 or later includes an outline, the slide, and several navigation buttons.

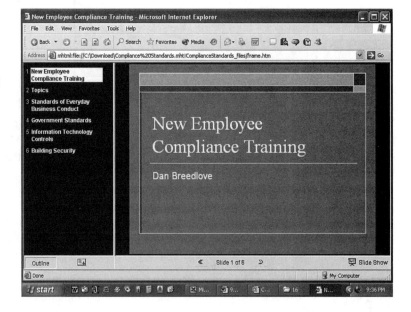

After you transfer your files to your Web server, you should again test your presentation in your browser over the Internet. Some things you should check for are the following:

- All files should be in their proper place. If you find missing pages or graphics, be sure that you have transferred files to folders and locations that correspond *exactly* to the folders on your hard disk.

- Test links individually to be sure that they work as you expect. Test using a computer other than the one on which you created the presentation to make sure that you haven't accidentally linked to something on your computer.

CAUTION

> The World Wide Web is a dynamic, constantly changing medium. Links that work today might not work tomorrow. If your Web page contains links, you should check periodically to be sure that they're still active.

- If some of your audience use dial-up connections, test how long it takes to download your presentation using a modem. You might discover that certain slides simply take too long to download because of large graphics, sound, or even video elements. You have to determine just how important those elements are and consider eliminating them to speed up the presentation.

- Not all browsers are created equal! You should test your Web page using both Internet Explorer and Netscape Navigator, including new and older versions of those programs. If you want, you can download older versions of browsers from the Microsoft and Netscape Web sites. (Yes, all this is quite time-consuming.)

- Not all computers and screen settings are the same, either. Test your pages on screens at 640×480, 800×600, and 1024×768 resolutions.

- Test your Web page on the Macintosh and any other operating system you anticipate your audience might use. Screen resolution and colors sometimes are maddeningly different on the Macintosh.

NOTE

> If everyone in your audience uses the same browser and has the same type of computers (for example, in a corporate intranet setting), you might not need to perform such extensive testing. If you have a wider audience and you want to look good on a wide variety of computer screens (for example, in a university setting), you can't assume that everyone uses the same computer and browser that you do. Ultimately, because you have only so much time, you might have to decide to test only certain combinations of browsers, screen resolutions, operating systems, and so on. If you do, tell your audience before they try to view the presentation.

MODIFYING OR UPDATING YOUR WEB PAGE

If you find during testing that you need to change your Web page, or if at a later date you want to update the information in your presentation, you can still use PowerPoint to edit the presentation.

The easiest way to edit a PowerPoint Web page is to open the main HTML page directly into PowerPoint. Because it uses XML and other advanced processes, the HTML page retains all PowerPoint's special features, including animations and other multimedia objects.

TIP

> You don't need to keep both a PowerPoint (PPT) and an HTML version of your presentation on your local computer. Keep only the HTML copy, which you can open, edit, and play just as you do any regular PowerPoint presentation.

After you make the changes you want, save the presentation again as a Web page and transfer the resulting files to your Web server, if necessary.

TROUBLESHOOTING

RESTORING MISSING IMAGES

Why aren't some of the image files from my presentation appearing in the HTML slideshow?

If you place your supporting files (such as images) in a subfolder, you must create the same folder structure on your Web server and transfer your files to their correct locations. If you transfer all your files to the same location, without subfolders, your slideshow will not work properly.

RESTORING MISSING FILES

I have the right folders in the right place on my Web server, but some of my files still aren't appearing in the Web slideshow. What else can I do?

You must create filenames and folder names *exactly* as you created them when you published your Web page locally, including uppercase and lowercase characters. Using the wrong case in even one character of a filename or folder name can prevent your Web page from working properly.

DESIGN CORNER: CREATING INVISIBLE LINKS

Linked text in your slideshow can make it easy to jump from one place to another, but because the links themselves look markedly different from the text around them, they can also distract from the overall design of your slide (see Figure 16.20). To remedy this, follow these steps:

1. Enter the text to which you want to add a hyperlink.
2. Select the Rectangle button on the Drawing toolbar and create an AutoShape that covers your text.
3. Select the AutoShape and click the Insert Hyperlink button on the Standard toolbar.
4. Enter your hyperlink in the Insert Hyperlink dialog box and click OK.
5. Right-click the AutoShape; set the fill color to No Fill and the line color to No Line in the Format AutoShape dialog box and click OK.

An invisible linked object now appears over the text you want linked, whereas the text itself has not changed in appearance from the text around it. When you present your slideshow, you simply move the mouse pointer to that text area and click when the mouse pointer changes to a hand (see Figure 16.21). To the audience, it appears that you are clicking on text, although you are really clicking a linked invisible graphic shape.

BEFORE

Figure 16.20

AFTER

Figure 16.21

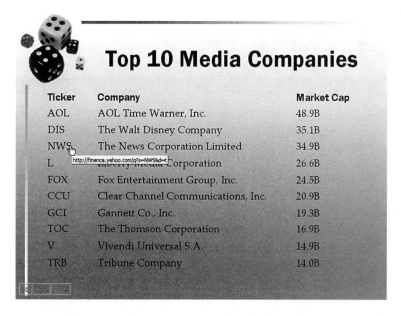

WORKING WITH WEB SCRIPTS

UNDERSTANDING WEB SCRIPTS

With PowerPoint's Web functionality, you can save presentations as HTML documents and edit them in the Microsoft Script Editor. If you know HTML, you can edit HTML tags in this editor. If you know a scripting language such as VBScript or JScript, you can create powerful scripts to augment and automate your Web-based presentations.

Microsoft Internet Explorer has embedded inside it the general-purpose core of the lightweight, object-oriented programming language called JScript. This embedded code lets browsers read and execute JScript code contained in HTML documents.

NOTE

> Internet Explorer also recognizes the VBScript scripting language. If you've ever used Visual Basic or Visual Basic for Applications, VBScript will seem familiar.

When the browser executes the code, it's called *client-side* scripting. There's also something called *server-side* scripting. Understanding the client-side/server-side distinction can be tricky. In Web scripting, the *server* is the computer (called the *Web server*) that contains Web pages and "serves" them to computers that request them over the Internet, and the *client* is the PC of a user viewing the Web pages over the Internet.

Whether a script is called client side or server side depends on where it runs. A server-side script executes on the Web server, which sends the results to the client's browser. A client-side script executes in the client's browser after the Web server sends the script to it.

CREATING AND EDITING WEB SCRIPTS

The Microsoft Script Editor is a powerful tool for editing HTML and Web scripts that provides a high level of functionality and ease of use for both the experienced and novice developer. This chapter doesn't teach you VBScript or JScript, and assumes that you already know something about scripting and HTML.

→ To learn more about VBScript or JScript, **see** "Expanding Your Knowledge of Web Scripts" later in this chapter, **p. 375**.

The Microsoft Script Editor lets you view and edit the HTML files you generate when saving your presentation as a Web page. From here you can add scripts, whether they are VBScript or JScript.

Thanks to the comprehensive Document Object Model (DOM) that Microsoft products support, Microsoft Script Editor lets you create event handlers for virtually any element in a PowerPoint presentation. *Event handlers* are scripts that run in response to user actions, such as mouse clicks, or browser actions, such as loading the document.

Editing features aren't limited to event handlers. You can also use the Microsoft Script Editor to create independent blocks of script to contain any script you choose.

CAUTION

Use the Microsoft Script Editor to edit only `.htm` and `.asp` files. If you edit other files (such as `.doc` files) when you save or refresh the file, ID parameters, `<SPAN>` and `<DIV>` tags, and some `VALUE` parameters might be changed.

From within PowerPoint, you can open a presentation in the Microsoft Script Editor by following these steps:

1. Save your presentation as a Web page (`.htm` format) by choosing File, Save as Web Page.

2. Name your file and select a folder in which to save it.

3. Click Save.

4. With your presentation onscreen, choose Tools, Macro, Microsoft Script Editor. This opens the Microsoft Script Editor, as shown in Figure 17.1. (This tool might not be installed the first time you try to use it. The system will ask whether you want to install it.)

Document Outline pane   Project Explorer

Figure 17.1
You can also open the
Microsoft Script Editor
by pressing
Alt+Shift+F11.

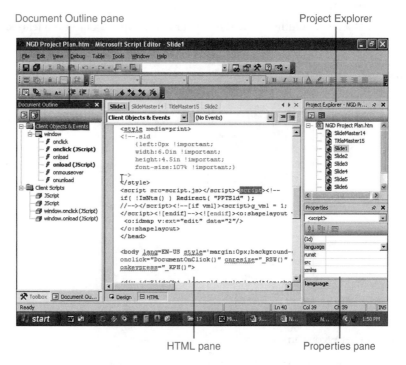

HTML pane   Properties pane

The Web page you view in the Microsoft Script Editor is actually a copy of your presentation. If you change this copy of the Web page in the Microsoft Script Editor, the copy in PowerPoint doesn't contain the changes. Conversely, if you change the presentation in PowerPoint, the copy in the Microsoft Script Editor doesn't contain the changes. When you change the Web page in one of the applications, a Refresh toolbar appears in the other. To incorporate the changes, click the Refresh button on that toolbar.

NOTE

> If you change the Web page in the Microsoft Script Editor and save the changes, PowerPoint refreshes for you.

Scripting in the Microsoft Script Editor

The Microsoft Script Editor consists of four primary panes for working with Web scripts: the Document Outline, HTML, Project Explorer, and Properties panes.

To represent a document's scripts, the Document Outline pane uses a hierarchy tree similar to that seen in Windows Explorer. The HTML pane shows the presentation's hard code. The Project Explorer pane uses a hierarchy tree to show the files in a presentation. You set certain HTML and scripting attributes in the Properties pane.

Looking at the Document Outline Pane

The Document Outline pane shows your presentation's object model (see Figure 17.2).

Figure 17.2
The Document Outline pane is divided into folders, or nodes, representing the file's object model.

From here, you can

- Display a tree view of all elements in your presentation that have already had their ID or NAME attributes set
- Display the events for each element
- Quickly navigate to any script in the page
- Generate new event handlers for any element in the presentation

Table 17.1 describes each node in the Document Outline pane. Depending on what you're doing in the Microsoft Script Editor, some of these nodes might not appear.

TABLE 17.1   THE DOCUMENT OUTLINE PANE'S NODES

Document Outline Pane's Nodes	Function/Use
Client Objects & Events	A hierarchy of the elements that support client scripts or have client scripts attached. Under the node for each element is a list of the events for which you can write handlers.
Client Scripts	A set of nodes for each client script on the page. There is a node for each script block on the page and a separate node for each function or subroutine defined within a script block. There is also a node for inline scripts defined as part of a control definition, as in this example: `<INPUT TYPE="button" NAME="button1" ONCLICK="alert('Clicked!')">`.
Server Objects & Events	A list of nodes for each element that supports server scripts or that has server scripts attached. Under each node is a list of the events for which you can write handlers. The Server Objects & Events node also displays the Microsoft Internet Information Server object model, including the Session object, Application object, and so on. In the Document Outline pane, these objects do not display events.
Server Scripts	A set of nodes for each server script on the page. Functions and subroutines are identified by name. Inline server scripts appear in a tree, but are not identified by name.

NOTE

> The Document Outline pane doesn't include elements that are added to a page using an INCLUDE file.

LOOKING AT THE HTML PANE

The HTML pane (see Figure 17.3) lets you view and edit scripts and HTML.

This window was designed for working with the raw code of a Web document's code, giving you more precise control over a page's attributes. It lets you switch between visual and text representation of all controls on the page using the Design and HTML tabs.

Figure 17.3
Edit and view code in
the HTML pane.

17

CAUTION

> Design view is not available for pages created in PowerPoint or any other Office applica-
> tion. You can use Source view to modify the script, but you have to make design changes
> in PowerPoint. Design view is available only for pages that are opened from within the
> Microsoft Script Editor.

If you accessed Microsoft Script Editor through PowerPoint and want to take advantage of
Design view's capabilities, close the HTML pane and select File, Open, File. From here you
can navigate to the folder containing the associated files for your presentation in the Open
File dialog box. By enabling Design view in this manner, you are able to extend the WYSI-
WYG attributes of the editing environment.

NOTE

> To preview your presentation in a browser, choose File, View in Browser.

LOOKING AT THE PROJECT EXPLORER PANE

The Project Explorer pane displays the file in the folder created when you saved your presentation. From here, double-click a file's icon to open its source code in the HTML pane.
You can add the individual .htm files of the presentation you generated by saving each file as
a Web page and simply repeating the steps outlined previously to enable Design view for
your presentation.

LOOKING AT THE PROPERTIES PANE

The Properties pane (see Figure 17.4) displays the various HTML and scripting properties
within the Web page.

Alphabetic sort

Figure 17.4
Use the sort buttons
to view your
attributes.

Click here to open the Property Pages dialog box.

Categorized sort

From this window, you can change default settings such as client and server script types. This window provides three buttons for viewing and editing page attributes: Sort Properties Alphabetically, Sort Properties by Category, and Property Pages.

The Property Pages button opens the Property Pages dialog box shown in Figure 17.5, in which you can define specific document properties.

17

Figure 17.5
Select HTML and
scripting attributes in
the Property Pages
dialog box.

You can also click in the far-right column of the Properties pane, which displays individual properties, and make your selection there.

NAVIGATING TO SCRIPTS

You can use the Document Outline pane to move between scripts by first clicking the appropriate node to expand the Document Outline tree until you see the script you want to view, and then clicking the script's name. The insertion point in the HTML pane moves to the script's location in the file. If you are working on a script in the HTML pane, you can match up your location in the Document Outline pane to see where you are in the context of the overall page.

To synchronize your position with the Document Outline pane, right-click and choose Synchronize Document Outline.

ADDING WEB SCRIPT COMMANDS TO YOUR TOOLS MENU

To facilitate scripting in PowerPoint, Microsoft gives you three commands you can add to your Tools menu:

- Insert Script
- Remove All Scripts
- Show All Scripts

To insert these items, follow these steps:

1. In PowerPoint, choose Tools, Customize. This opens the Customize dialog box, as shown in Figure 17.6.

Figure 17.6
From the Customize dialog box, you can drag new tools to your menus.

2. In the Categories box, click Tools.
3. Scroll down in the Commands box until the scripting commands become visible.
4. Drag Insert Script from the Commands box to the Tools menu on the main PowerPoint menu bar. From here, drag down to the Macro submenu. When the Macro submenu opens, drag to where you want the Insert Script command to appear and then release the mouse button.
5. Repeat steps 3 and 4 for the Show All Scripts and Remove All Scripts commands.
6. Click Close.

The Insert Script command invokes the Microsoft Script Editor, which brings up the page that was open in PowerPoint when you executed the command. The Show All Scripts command places a *glyph*, or a tiny icon, at every spot where a script appears in the presentation. As the name suggests, Remove All Scripts removes the scripts from a presentation.

If at any time you want to remove a command from the Tools menu, simply select Customize and reverse the process by dragging the undesired command off the Macro submenu.

CREATING EVENT HANDLERS

The Document Outline pane shows you all scriptable elements in your page, and for each element, the events for which you can write handlers. This window divides the elements and scripts into those that will run on the client and those that will run on the server.

When you expand an object node in the Document Outline pane (as shown in Figure 17.7), a list of potential event handlers for that object appears. If the event name is bold, a handler already exists for that event.

Event
Handlers

Figure 17.7
Click the plus sign
next to the node to
see the available
event handlers.

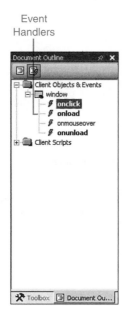

To create a new event handler, expand the appropriate object node until you see the event name for which you want to create a script. Then double-click the name of the event. The editor performs the following actions:

- Creates or moves to one of the following script blocks at the top of the document, depending on where the script will run and what language it will be in:
  - `clientEventHandlersJS`
  - `clientEventHandlersVBS`
  - `serverEventHandlersJS`
  - `serverEventHandlersVBS`
- If the script will be in JScript, adds an event attribute (for example, `onclick=`) to the element.

Finally, the editor inserts a new script block for the event you selected with a bare handler function that you then must flesh out to suit your needs.

The handler is created in the default language for the current context. For example, if you are creating a server script, the handler is in the default language for the server, as set in the Property Pages dialog box for the current document.

For VBScript functions, the format is

```
Sub elementID_event
{insert code here}
End Sub
```

For JScript functions, the format is

```
function elementID_event(){
{insert code here}
}
```

When creating JScript event handlers, the editor also adds the following attributes to the HTML element itself:

```
event="return elementID_event()"
```

SETTING THE DEFAULT SCRIPT LANGUAGE

In the Properties pane, scroll down until the `defaultClientScript` or `defaultServerScript` category is visible in the bottom-left column, as shown in Figure 17.8. To change the default settings, select the category in the left column and then click on the facing cells of the far-right column to display a drop arrow. Clicking this arrow displays the options JavaScript (or JScript) and VBScript.

Figure 17.8
VBScript has been chosen instead of the default language, JavaScript.

CREATING STANDALONE SCRIPTS

In addition to creating event handlers, you can create standalone script blocks. This is useful if you want to create procedures (subroutines or functions) called by other scripts, or if you want to create a global script that runs as soon as the browser loads the page.

To create a new standalone script block, follow these steps:

1. Select the HTML pane.
2. Position the cursor where you want the new script to appear.
3. Right-click and choose Insert Script Block, Client, or Server.

The Script Editor then generates a new <SCRIPT> block. If you choose Server, the script tag contains the attribute RUNAT=SERVER. The script block's LANGUAGE attribute is set to the default language for the client or server.

 Can't get your scripts to work? Not sure where to place them? See the "Troubleshooting" section at the end of this chapter.

EXPANDING YOUR KNOWLEDGE OF WEB SCRIPTS

If you don't have a background in creating scripts with JScript or VBScript, but this initial exploration of the Microsoft Script Editor has piqued your interest, take a look at the Microsoft Script Editor Help window. From within the Microsoft Script Editor, choose Help, Microsoft Script Editor Help. Here you'll find reference guides and tutorials for both JScript and VBScript as well as an HTML reference.

You don't need to become a programming expert to learn enough of one of these scripting languages to make some worthwhile enhancements to your Web-based PowerPoint presentations, but if you would like to delve further into these topics, consider *Special Edition Using JScript* and *Special Edition Using VBScript*, also by Que.

TROUBLESHOOTING

GETTING SCRIPTS TO WORK

Why won't my simplest scripts work?

Proper syntax is always a concern in programming. Consequently, it is important to pay strict attention to detail when writing scripts. If you mean for a particular parameter to be a string, for example, you will run into trouble if you forget to enclose it in quotation marks when you type it.

PROPERLY PLACING YOUR SCRIPTS

Is there a difference in where I put my scripts on the HTML page?

The scripts you write are interpreted as part of your Web browser's HTML parsing process. This means that if the script you create is located inside the <HEAD> tag in a document, it will be interpreted before any of the <BODY> tag is looked at. If you have objects that are created in the <BODY> tag, they don't exist at the instant the <HEAD> is being parsed and, therefore, can't be manipulated by the script.

CHAPTER 18

USING ONLINE BROADCASTS AND MEETINGS

In this chapter   *by Patrice-Anne Rutledge and Jim Grey*

UNDERSTANDING ONLINE BROADCASTS AND MEETINGS

You've thoroughly polished your presentation. It's clear, organized, and to the point. Your visuals are coordinated, your script is down pat, and maybe you've even added background sound to make the presentation really move. Now it's time to deliver—online. This chapter shows you how to use PowerPoint's presentation broadcast and online meeting tools to do exactly that.

PowerPoint can run a live, simultaneous broadcast of your presentation from your PC to tens, hundreds, or even thousands of other PCs tuned in to hear what you have to say. You can also add live audio or video content to the presentation as you make it. Using PowerPoint to do a presentation broadcast is much more convenient than physically gathering your audience into one room and getting the necessary facilities, large-screen computer projectors, and sound equipment organized.

By itself, PowerPoint can transmit a presentation broadcast to as many as 10 other people. Your audience needs Internet Explorer 5.1 or later to view this broadcast. For broadcasts to 11 or more people, you need to have access to a Microsoft Windows Media Server. This is a digital media platform that supports streaming media in your presentation (such as audio and video). If you don't have access to a Windows Media Server, you can sign up for an account with a third-party service provider to handle these technicalities. If your company or organization has an IS department, contact its staff for advice on using Windows Media Server in your network environment.

NOTE

> Broadcasting to a large audience and using Windows Media Server can be complex. To learn more about broadcasting PowerPoint presentations to large audiences, refer to the Microsoft Office Resource Kit (http://www.microsoft.com/office/ork/).

PowerPoint also offers online meetings, which are a nice complement to presentation broadcasts. A *broadcast* is a one-way connection between you and your audience, whereas an *online meeting* is a two-way channel. In an online meeting, everyone can communicate with everyone else to brainstorm, hash out a tough decision, or even create a presentation together.

CHOOSING A BROADCAST OR MEETING

To use online meetings, you need Microsoft's NetMeeting group collaboration software installed on your computer, and so will everyone else who takes part in the meeting. NetMeeting comes with the versions of Windows required to run Office 2003.

Here are some guidelines to help you decide which online presentation approach is right for you.

Choose a presentation broadcast when

- You want to reach a large number of people at once.
- You want to save your presentation broadcast so that people can watch it later.
- You want your presentation to be one way.
- Your audience doesn't have very powerful computers or fast network connections. (All they need is Internet Explorer 5.1 or later to see your broadcast.)

Presentation broadcasts can be used in corporate training sessions, general company announcements, and online presentations to business partners or clients.

Choose an online meeting when

- You want to interact with the people to whom you are presenting.
- You don't need to reach many people (say, 10 or fewer).
- Your audience has powerful enough computers with fast enough network connections to handle Microsoft NetMeeting (and the computers have the NetMeeting software installed). You shouldn't try this unless your computer runs on a Pentium III processor, has at least 128 MB of RAM, and has a broadband Internet connection.

Online meetings can be used for group brainstorming sessions (especially those now done with videoconferencing equipment), online staff meetings, and one-on-one planning meetings with a colleague.

Later, we'll cover a third online collaboration tool—Web discussions.

RECORDING AND SAVING A BROADCAST

Because running a live presentation broadcast can be complicated, it's usually better to practice recording and saving a broadcast before presenting it live. Even if your ultimate goal is to conduct a live broadcast, doing several "practice runs" in which you record, save, and replay your broadcast can help you perfect your presentation and delivery—and make you more confident when it's time to go live.

To get started, choose Slide Show, Online Broadcast, Record and Save a Broadcast. If this is the first time you've tried to create a presentation broadcast, a message appears telling you that PowerPoint needs to install some extra software to enable this feature (see Figure 18.1). Choose Yes to install the software.

Figure 18.1
The first time you try
to set up a presenta-
tion broadcast,
PowerPoint needs to
install its presentation
broadcast feature.

A message box appears, showing you the installation progress. You can click the Cancel button if you want to stop the install for any reason. After the online broadcasting feature is
installed, the Record Presentation Broadcast dialog box opens (see Figure 18.2).

Figure 18.2
Enter a title and
description for your
recorded presentation
broadcast.

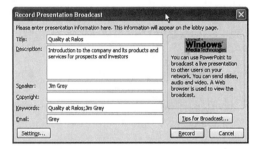

The Record Presentation Broadcast dialog box sets up the basic information your audience
will see in the presentation lobby page and lets you configure more advanced broadcast
options. Enter a title and description for your broadcast, as well as the speaker's name and,
if you want, the email address of the person organizing the broadcast. You can also add
copyright and keyword information. You should provide sufficient detail here so that potential audience members will know what the presentation will be about and for whom it was
designed. Specifying the length of the presentation is also a good idea. Click the Tips for
Broadcast button to display related content in the PowerPoint Help window.

CONFIGURING BROADCAST SETTINGS

After you've entered information on the Record Presentation Broadcast dialog box, you'll
need to specify a few more technical broadcast settings. Click the Settings button on the
Record Presentation Broadcast dialog box to open the Broadcast Settings dialog box (see
Figure 18.3).

The first group of options on the Presenter tab (Audio/Video) lets you specify whether you
want to broadcast live audio or video (or both) with your presentation. Regardless of what
you choose here, audio in the presentation itself (such as a saved narration or slide transition sounds) doesn't get broadcast.

Figure 18.3
The Broadcast Settings dialog box lets you set various presentation options.

If you want to broadcast audio, you need to have a sound card and a microphone set up at your computer. If you want to provide video (usually a picture of you talking along with the presentation), you'll need to have a video camera and video capture card installed at the broadcast station. Remember that the people tuning into your broadcast need to have audio-capable computer hardware to hear any sound.

You can also choose whether to let audience members see your speaker notes by selecting the Display speaker notes with the presentation check box.

In the Save broadcast files in edit box, type or browse for the location where you want to save your broadcast. Because you're recording and saving this broadcast, rather than presenting it live, you can save either on your C:\ drive or in a shared network location. For your audience to view your final broadcast, however, you need to move the main broadcast Web page and its associated folder to a shared network location at some point. Type network location names using the format \\servername\sharename.

From the Slide show mode drop-down list, specify whether to display a full screen or a resizable screen. If you plan to access other programs during your broadcast (for example, to demonstrate other software), use a resizable screen.

The Advanced tab of the Broadcast Settings dialog box (see Figure 18.10) includes options you'll primarily use for live broadcasts.

→ To learn more about the options available on the Advanced tab of the Broadcast Settings dialog box, **see** "Scheduling a Live Broadcast" later in this chapter, **p. 385**.

NOTE

> You can also directly access the Broadcast Settings dialog box by choosing Slide Show, Online Broadcast, Settings from the menu bar.

RECORDING YOUR BROADCAST

Click the Record button on the Record Presentation Broadcast dialog box to open the Broadcast Presentation dialog box, shown in Figure 18.4.

Figure 18.4
In the Broadcast Presentation dialog box, you'll prepare to record your broadcast.

NOTE

If you're rerecording your broadcast, PowerPoint displays a dialog box verifying that you want to overwrite the existing broadcast.

PowerPoint verifies that the network locations you typed earlier are valid; then it checks that your audio and video inputs are working correctly (if you enabled those options in the Broadcast Settings dialog box when you set up the presentation broadcast).

If you selected real-time audio, PowerPoint displays a Microphone Check dialog box (see Figure 18.5) to verify that your audio levels are set correctly.

18

Figure 18.5
Read this window's text into your microphone to check your audio levels.

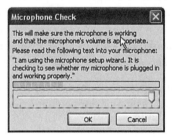

After you've read the text out loud (and you've seen the horizontal volume bar move), click OK to continue. If you want to check the microphone level again, click the Recheck Microphone button.

If you selected real-time video, PowerPoint displays a Camera Check dialog box in which you can preview the video you'll transmit to your audience. Click the Recheck Camera button to check the video again.

When the Broadcast Presentation dialog box flashes Press Start when ready, click the Start button to begin. Your presentation appears in Slide Show view (see Figure 18.6); record your broadcast, speaking into your microphone (and looking into the camera, if you're including video).

Figure 18.6
Record the broadcast you want to save and replay.

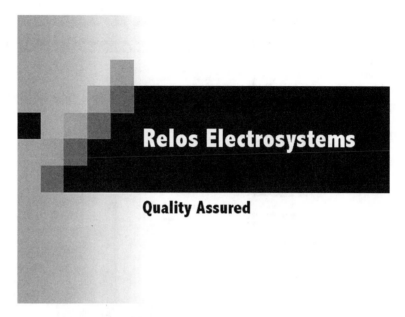

In many ways, this process is similar to presenting a live, in-person slide show. When you finish recording, a message box appears telling you where PowerPoint has saved your broadcast (in an HTML format).

→ To learn more about presenting a live, in-person slide show, **see** "Setting Up a Show" in Chapter 9, "Presenting a Slide Show," **p. 176**.

Click Replay Broadcast to immediately replay the broadcast and preview what your audience will see. Click Continue to return to PowerPoint.

REPLAYING YOUR BROADCAST

If you clicked the Replay Broadcast button when you finished recording, your broadcast launches in Internet Explorer (see Figure 18.7).

In the upper-left corner of the browser, if your broadcast includes video, it appears in the Windows Media Player window. If your broadcast is audio only, this window is empty.

Immediately below it, you'll see basic information about the broadcast (title and presenter's name) that remains throughout the broadcast.

The upper-right corner of the browser window offers links to View Previous Slides, Email Feedback, and Help.

The lobby page appears in the slide area, providing additional presentation information and the Replay Broadcast button. Click this button to start the actual broadcast, which appears in the slide area. Figure 18.8 illustrates an example of a broadcast.

Video displays here   Your presentation appears in the slide area.

Figure 18.7
The lobby page
of your recorded
broadcast appears.

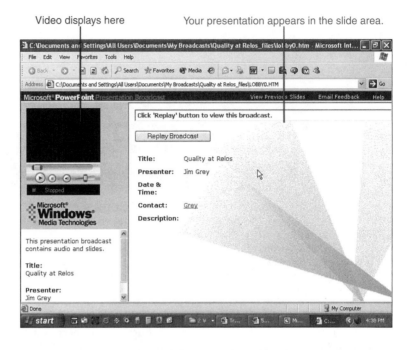

Presentation appears in the slide area

Figure 18.8
View your PowerPoint
presentation in the
slide area of the
browser.

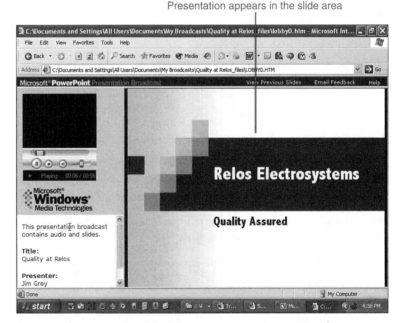

If you saved your   broadcast to your C:\ drive, you
must move it (the HTML file in the My Broadcasts folder as well as the associated folder of
the same name) to a shared network location before others can view it. Send an email with a

link to the HTML lobby page to people you want to view the broadcast. When viewers load this Web page, instruct them to click the Replay Broadcast button to start.

 Get an error message about VML when you try to replay? *See the "Troubleshooting" section near the end of the chapter.*

SCHEDULING A LIVE BROADCAST

The first step in presenting a live online broadcast is to schedule it. This step prepares PowerPoint to broadcast your presentation and sets up a special Web page (called a *lobby page*) that your audience will use as an online gathering place before the presentation starts.

TIP

> You can schedule your broadcast on a machine different from the one you actually use to make the broadcast. As long as your PowerPoint file is with you (which contains your broadcast settings inside it), you can use any computer you want to do the broadcast. Remember, the broadcast computer needs sound and video capabilities if you want to include those features. It must also have PowerPoint installed and a fast network connection.

As part of setting up a schedule, you can also send electronic mail to people whom you'd like to view the presentation, inviting them to the show and telling them how to view it.

To start the scheduling process, open the presentation you want to broadcast and choose Slide Show, Online Broadcast, Schedule a Live Broadcast. The Schedule Presentation Broadcast dialog box opens (see Figure 18.9), which is similar to the Record Presentation Broadcast dialog box (refer to Figure 18.2).

Figure 18.9
Enter a title and description for your upcoming presentation broadcast.

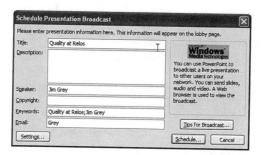

Refer to the earlier section, "Recording and Saving a Broadcast," for instructions on how to specify broadcast options and settings in this dialog box. In the Broadcast Settings dialog box (open it by clicking the Settings button), you'll note several options on the Advanced tab for live broadcasts (see Figure 18.10).

To use a remote Windows media encoder, enter the name of its computer in the edit box.

18

Figure 18.10
Using a Windows
Media Server lets you
broadcast to a large
audience.

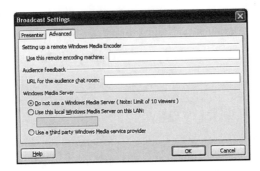

To enable participants to have real-time chats during your broadcast, enter a valid URL in the URL for the audience chat room field. You must already have a chat room (not part of PowerPoint) set up to use this feature. Check with your network administrator to find out what's available at your company if you aren't sure.

Finally, you can specify Windows Media Server settings. Remember that you'll need to use Windows Media Server if you're broadcasting to more than 10 participants. Your choices include

- **Do not use a Windows Media Server**—Select this option if you have 10 or fewer participants.
- **Use this local Windows Media Server on this LAN**—Type the name of the server or computer that has the Windows Media Server you'll use for your presentation.
- **Use a third party Windows Media service provider**—Lets you search for a third-party service provider for a live presentation only.

> **NOTE**
>
> You can still change your presentation after you've scheduled a broadcast; nothing's set in stone. You can even switch to presenting a completely different file if you want to, without redoing your broadcast schedule setup.

→ To learn more about how to reschedule a broadcast, **see** "Rescheduling a Broadcast" later in this chapter, **p. 387**.

After you've finished entering your broadcast description, broadcast settings, and server options, you're ready to actually schedule the broadcast. Click the Schedule button on the Schedule Presentation Broadcast dialog box to continue.

PowerPoint starts your email client to send an announcement to the people you'd like to invite to your presentation. If you're using Microsoft Outlook as your email client, you'll be able to schedule the presentation using Outlook's group meeting facilities.

You've finished scheduling your presentation. PowerPoint displays a confirmation message to let you know that your presentation broadcast settings have been saved. Press OK to close the message.

RESCHEDULING A BROADCAST

If you decide you want to change the broadcast time or other settings before the show actually starts, you can easily modify your settings. To do so, open the presentation you want to reschedule and choose Slide Show, Online Broadcast, Reschedule a Live Presentation to open the Reschedule Presentation Broadcast dialog box (see Figure 18.11).

Figure 18.11
Even though you've already scheduled your broadcast, you can change your mind later.

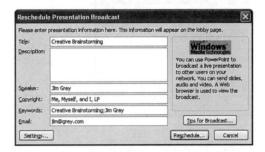

This dialog box is nearly identical to both the Record Presentation Broadcast and Schedule Presentation Broadcast dialog boxes. Note that you must have a previously scheduled presentation open to see the Reschedule a Live Presentation option from the Slide Show menu. Otherwise, you'll see the Schedule a Live Presentation option.

→ To learn more about modifying the settings of the Record Presentation Broadcast and Schedule Presentation Broadcast dialog boxes, **see** "Recording and Saving a Broadcast" earlier in this chapter, **p. 379**.

To notify audience members that you're rescheduling your broadcast, click the Reschedule button. Your email client will open, and you can send an email to your participants. You can also cancel a scheduled broadcast this way as well.

STARTING THE BROADCAST

You can broadcast a presentation that you've already scheduled or broadcast a new, unscheduled presentation. If you want to start a broadcast you haven't previously scheduled, you still need to specify which options and settings you want to use. You should start a broadcast about 30 minutes before you actually want to present to allow time for your presentation to be uploaded to the server. This also gives you time to send messages to waiting viewers before the presentation starts.

→ To learn more about how to schedule a broadcast presentation, **see** "Scheduling a Live Broadcast" in this chapter, **p. 385**.

NOTE

You can tweak your presentation until the moment you click the Start button. After that, your presentation files are copied to the server for broadcast. If you still want to change the presentation, you can close the Broadcast Presentation window by clicking Close; making your changes; and then choosing Slide Show, Online Broadcast, Start Live Broadcast Now.

To start an actual broadcast, follow these steps:

1. Open the PowerPoint presentation you're going to broadcast and then choose Slide Show, Online Broadcast, and Start Live Broadcast Now. The Live Presentation Broadcast dialog box appears (see Figure 18.12).

Figure 18.12
Choose the event, either scheduled or unscheduled, to broadcast.

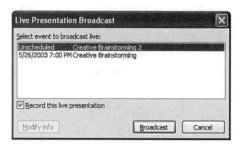

2. Select the broadcast you want to present from this list, which includes both scheduled and unscheduled broadcasts for the open presentation.

3. Select the Record this live presentation check box if you want to record your live broadcast and save it for later viewing.

NOTE

> If you want to make additional changes to the settings of a previously scheduled broadcast, click the Modify Info button to open another version of the Live Presentation Broadcast dialog box (see Figure 18.14). This is nearly identical to the other presentation broadcast dialog boxes you've seen in this chapter.

4. Click the Broadcast button to continue. If you selected a scheduled broadcast, the Broadcast Presentation dialog box opens (shown in Figure 18.13), and you can skip to step 8. If you selected an unscheduled broadcast, the Live Presentation Broadcast dialog box opens (see Figure 18.14), from which you can establish broadcast settings and invite participants.

Figure 18.13
Do your last-minute checks from this dialog box.

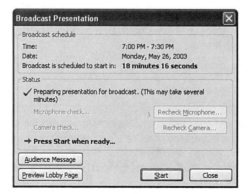

Figure 18.14
If you haven't previously scheduled your broadcast, enter information about it here.

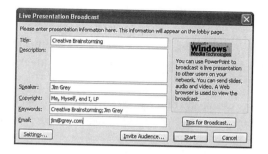

5. Click the Settings button to open the Broadcast Settings dialog box (refer to Figure 18.3). In this dialog box, you can specify the exact broadcast settings you need for this presentation.

   → To learn more about the settings in the Broadcast Settings dialog box, **see** "Configuring Broadcast Settings" earlier in this chapter, **p. 380**.

6. Click the Invite Audience button to open your email client (such as Microsoft Outlook) and send an email to your audience.

7. Click the Start button to open the Broadcast Presentation dialog box (refer to Figure 18.13).

8. PowerPoint verifies that the network locations you typed in earlier are valid; then it checks that your audio and video inputs are working correctly (if you enabled those options in the Broadcast Settings dialog box when you set up the presentation broadcast).

9. If you selected real-time audio, PowerPoint displays the Microphone Check dialog box (refer to Figure 18.5) to verify that your audio levels are set correctly. After you've read the text out loud (and you've seen the horizontal volume bar move), choose OK to continue. If you want to check the microphone level again, click the Recheck Microphone button.

10. If you selected real-time video, PowerPoint displays a Camera Check dialog box in which you can preview the video you'll transmit to your audience. Click the Recheck Camera button to check the video again.

11. To send a message to all waiting audience members, click the Audience Message button (handy if you want to announce a brief delay), enter a message in the Audience Message dialog box, and click Update.

12. To preview the presentation's lobby page, click the Preview Lobby Page button, and a browser window will open (refer to Figure 18.7). When your audience is ready to view the presentation, they will use their Web browsers to go to this lobby page, which is specific to your presentation broadcast. There they will find out how long it is before the presentation actually starts, as well as the presentation title and description you typed in.

13. When the Broadcast Presentation dialog box flashes Press Start When Ready, click the Start button to begin.

CONDUCTING THE BROADCAST

Now that you've accessed your broadcast, audience members need to arrive as well. This is a simple process—they just need to click the URL to the broadcast lobby page that you provided them in your broadcast invitation email.

A broadcast presentation won't look any different to you (the presenter) than if you were running a slide show on your computer. Just move through your presentation as you normally would, but remember to not go too quickly. It takes 10–15 seconds for your clients to download each new page.

TIP

> You might want to set up a nearby computer and log in as a participant so that you can see what your audience is actually seeing. Connect as your participants will connect—either on a LAN or on the Internet. Based on tests, the time it takes for each slide to reach client systems varies from slow to really slow. Take your time and double-check to be sure that you aren't getting ahead of your audience.

→ To learn how to hold your audience's attention when you're not physically in front of them, **see** Chapter 29, "Presenting in a Variety of Settings," **p. 673**.

What audiences see in a Web broadcast slide area (refer to Figure 18.7) is close to what they would see if they were actually looking at your screen in person. PowerPoint's pen and pointer features don't work over presentation broadcasts. However, if you want to use them, consider switching to an online meeting, which does support them. It's best to just go with a simple design and format when using presentation broadcasts. You can go back and forth through the slides in your presentation using your Page Up and Page Down (or Space and Backspace) keys as you normally would.

 Can't connect to the broadcast? *See the "Troubleshooting" section near the end of the chapter.*

ENDING THE BROADCAST

When you've finished your broadcast, just press Esc to end it. (If any questions have been emailed during your presentation, you might want to answer them verbally before you wrap things up.) You'll be asked to confirm your decision to end the broadcast. Your audience will be sent back to the presentation lobby page, which will tell them that the presentation has ended.

USING INTERACTIVE ONLINE MEETINGS

In addition to presentation broadcasts, PowerPoint also provides *online meetings*, which are a much more interactive way of sharing your ideas with others. Online meetings take interactive presentations online, where you can bring together people from anywhere, present your ideas to them, and then discuss your ideas with them.

Just as with presentation broadcasts, online meetings let you show your live presentation to others, and include real-time audio and video commentary. However, online meetings also let your audience in on the action. Instead of passively watching your presentation, participants in a PowerPoint online meeting can jot down ideas on a shared whiteboard; send messages back to you and the group; and even take control of the presentation in midstream, make some changes to the presentation, and then give control back to you. Online meetings are suited for roundtable discussions and for immediate decision making.

STARTING AN ONLINE MEETING

The first step in starting an online meeting is to open the presentation you want to present in the meeting. Then choose Tools, Online Collaboration, Meet Now to start the program PowerPoint uses for online meetings. This group collaboration tool, called Microsoft NetMeeting, is installed as part of Microsoft Office.

NOTE

If for some reason you don't have NetMeeting installed on your computer, you can download it from the Microsoft Web site (http://www.microsoft.com/windows/netmeeting). This site also includes detailed information and resources about NetMeeting. If you've never used NetMeeting before, familiarize yourself with its basic functionality before you start an online meeting in PowerPoint.

If you've run NetMeeting before, the Find Someone dialog box opens (see Figure 18.15).

Figure 18.15
Conference someone into your meeting by typing his name and then choosing Call.

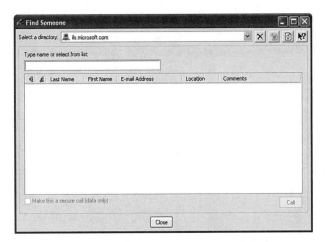

If you haven't used NetMeeting before, the NetMeeting dialog box asks for your name, your email address, and a NetMeeting directory server. Choose any server you want from the list, or type your company's private NetMeeting directory server. (Ask your network administrator for its name.) All the people who will join this meeting must log in to the same NetMeeting server, however, so be sure to let your audience know which server to use ahead of time.

18

Setting up an online meeting in NetMeeting is different from running a broadcast presentation. Instead of letting your audience come to you, you need to bring in people one by one, just as in a telephone conference call.

The Find Someone dialog box gradually displays a long list of logged-in users as NetMeeting downloads the server user list.

CAUTION

The most common problem at this point is that your selected server might become too busy to handle numerous login requests, for both your meeting and other parties' meetings. If this happens, participants should just try to log in again by selecting that server's name from the Directory box.

Type in the name of the person you want to conference into your online meeting to quickly jump to his name in the list. When you've found the person you want to call, select that name and then click the Call button.

NetMeeting tries to make the connection. If the other person accepts the call, the Find Someone dialog box disappears, and the Online Meeting toolbar appears (see Figure 18.16).

Figure 18.16
The Online Meeting toolbar provides all the tools for conducting your online meeting.

 Can't get online meetings to work? See the "Troubleshooting" section near the end of the chapter.

JOINING AN ONLINE MEETING

 If you want more than two people in the meeting, call more people by clicking the Call Participant button on the Online Meeting toolbar, and repeat the process. Your guests can also call in on their own using NetMeeting. If they do, they will be told that you're in a meeting, but they can ask to join the meeting. NetMeeting then notifies you, as the meeting host, of the incoming call and asks whether you'd like to accept it.

PRESENTING YOUR IDEAS

After all the right people are connected at the same time (which can take some effort, depending on how busy the NetMeeting servers are), you're ready to start presenting.

Each of the people in your meeting now sees on his screen an exact duplicate of what's on your PowerPoint screen. This is a live view, so whatever you do appears on all the meeting attendees' screens—all your menu choices, mouse movements, and typing: everything.

Sound is the one exception, however. Any transition sounds you have in your presentation won't be sent over the broadcast because the NetMeeting software is already using your sound hardware for itself.

TIP

Consider using your phone to do an audio conference call along with the online meeting to get around the sound limitations.

Right now, with the exception of sound, you've got close to the same result as you would have had using a broadcast presentation. What's really different about the NetMeeting approach is that it enables other meeting attendees to interact with each other.

USING ONLINE CHAT AND WHITEBOARDS

The easiest way for online meeting participants to interact is through NetMeeting's chat window. Click the Display chat window button of the Online Meeting toolbar to open the chat window (see Figure 18.17). You can send a text message to everyone in the meeting by typing whatever you want in to the Message box and then clicking the Send button.

Figure 18.17
A chat window makes it easy to communicate with everyone at the same time in an online meeting.

18

You can also open a graphical whiteboard by clicking the Display Whiteboard button; the whiteboard works just like the chat window (except you can draw on it). Figure 18.18 illustrates the whiteboard.

Figure 18.18
A whiteboard is another online collaboration tool.

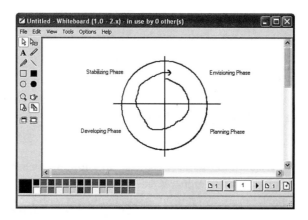

ENABLING ONLINE GROUP EDITING

The ultimate form of interaction in online meetings goes even further than chat and whiteboard windows, however. With your permission, meeting participants can take direct control of your PowerPoint window and work with it as if they were sitting at your desk. This is a great way of creating a presentation together—if someone is having a hard time getting across what he'd really like to see, he can take control and drive for a while.

To enable application sharing, you, as meeting host, have to tell PowerPoint it's okay for others to take control. Click the Allow Others to Edit button on the Online Meeting toolbar to do so.

The other people in the meeting can now double-click the image of your screen (displayed in their monitors) and take control. They can type right in to the presentation open on your computer, add new slides, change slide order, and anything else you could do by yourself.

To take back control, just click anywhere in your PowerPoint window. You might want to turn off the Allow Others to Edit button just so people don't accidentally take control. It can be tricky to know who's in control sometimes.

NOTE

> Application sharing doesn't require that anyone but the meeting host have PowerPoint installed on his computer. The only software other people need to have is NetMeeting.

TIP

> You can tell who's in control when using application sharing by looking for that person's initials in tiny letters at the bottom right of the mouse pointer.

ENDING AN ONLINE MEETING

 To end an online conference, click the End Meeting button on the Online Meeting toolbar. During the meeting, individual attendees (except for you, the meeting host) can join and leave as they like. When you end the meeting, everyone gets disconnected.

SCHEDULING AN ONLINE MEETING

Although the method we've covered here lets you start an online meeting whenever you want, PowerPoint also has hooks into Outlook that make it easy to schedule an online meeting.

Choose Tools, Online Collaboration, Schedule Meeting. PowerPoint starts an Outlook meeting request, which includes a specified online meeting directory server location and your email address (see Figure 18.19). You can even have Outlook automatically start NetMeeting when the meeting begins.

Figure 18.19
Schedule a future online meeting using Outlook.

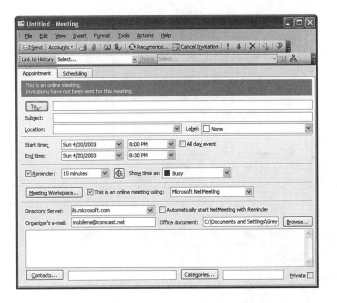

PARTICIPATING IN WEB DISCUSSIONS

PowerPoint's online collaboration capabilities don't stop with presentation broadcasts and online meetings. You can also access Office's Web-based discussion forums from PowerPoint as you can with all the other Office applications.

These forums work like a newsgroup or message forum and let you carry on a discussion with others without all of you having to be present at the same time. Web forums are there whenever you have a chance to check in to see what's new. It's handy to have the choice between the two approaches.

STARTING A WEB DISCUSSION

To start a new Web discussion (or access a previously created one), choose Tools, Online Collaboration, Web Discussions. The Web Discussions toolbar appears (see Figure 18.20).

Figure 18.20
The Web Discussions toolbar provides all the functionality you'll need to conduct a Web discussion.

To start a discussion about your presentation, click the Insert Discussion About the Presentation button. PowerPoint asks you to specify a discussion server. Click Yes, and you'll see the Discussion Options dialog box (see Figure 18.21).

Figure 18.21
You can add new discussion servers here as well as configure what kind of information appears on them.

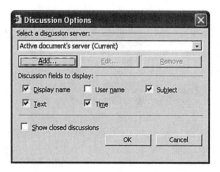

If you haven't set any discussion servers before, click the Add button to specify your first one. The Add or Edit Discussion Servers dialog box (see Figure 18.22) opens.

Figure 18.22
You need to type in the server name of your Office discussion server to access a Web discussion.

Your network administrator must set up a discussion server ahead of time. A discussion server is a Web server with special software, called the Office Server Extensions, installed on it.

Type the server name that your network administrator has provided in to the top box of this window and, if you want, type an easy-to-remember name in to the bottom box of the window. This name will be your identity during the discussion. Then choose OK to finish this step.

PowerPoint returns you to the Discussion Options dialog box, where you can add, edit, or remove Office discussion servers, as well as decide which fields you'd like to see displayed on the discussion server. The default settings are usually adequate, so you can just click OK.

When you close the Discussion Options dialog box, you're ready to use the Web Discussions toolbar to control your discussion. Table 18.1 describes the buttons on this toolbar.

TABLE 18.1 WEB DISCUSSIONS TOOLBAR BUTTONS

Button	Name	Description
Discussions ▾	Discussions	Displays a drop-down list of options enabling you to insert a discussion about the presentation; filters, refreshes, or prints the discussion; or redisplays the Discussion Options dialog box.
	Insert Discussion About the Presentation	Displays the Enter Discussion Text dialog box, which lets you enter a comment about the presentation. Comments appear at the bottom of the screen.
Subscribe...	Subscribe	Displays the Document Subscription dialog box, where you can tell the Office Discussion Server that you'd like to be notified by email when this document changes or when someone else adds a comment to the discussion database.
	Stop Communication with Discussion Server	Stops communication with the discussion server.
	Show/Hide Discussion Pane	Serves as a toggle to display or hide the discussion pane.
Close	Close	Closes the Web discussion.

18

TROUBLESHOOTING

RESOLVING BROADCAST CONNECTION PROBLEMS

People trying to watch the presentation broadcast get a message saying that their computers can't connect to the broadcast.

Be sure that the network location you specified for the location of the presentation broadcast files is accessible by everyone you want to see the broadcast. (People outside your company won't normally be able to access your presentation broadcast location, for example.)

DISPLAYING THE LOBBY PAGE

When audience members open the broadcast lobby page, the Web page is nearly empty.

Be sure that all your viewers are using Microsoft Internet Explorer 5.1 or later as their Web browser. Netscape Navigator won't display the presentation broadcast correctly.

CALLING ONLINE MEETING PARTICIPANTS

When I try to call someone using PowerPoint's Online Meeting tools, I get a message saying, "The person you called is not able to accept Microsoft NetMeeting calls."

The person you are calling either doesn't have Microsoft NetMeeting started or hasn't logged in to the same NetMeeting directory server you have. You have to let meeting participants know ahead of time that they should have NetMeeting open and be logged in to your chosen directory server so that they can get your call. (They can also configure their systems to always have NetMeeting run unobtrusively in the Windows taskbar so that their computers are always "listening" for incoming NetMeeting calls.)

CONNECTING TO THE DIRECTORY SERVER

When I try to log into a NetMeeting directory server, I get a message saying that there was a problem connecting to the directory server.

Any network problem between you and the NetMeeting directory server (or an overloaded server) will cause these kinds of problems. Just reselect the name of the server from the Directory box to connect to the directory server again. If the problem persists, try switching to a different directory server or use the Advanced button to call people using their Internet hostname or IP address.

DESIGN CORNER: REHEARSING FOR A LIVE BROADCAST

Conducting your first live presentation broadcast can be both exciting and unnerving. To ensure that everything goes well, you should first record, save, and replay your broadcast several times, perfecting both your technical understanding of the process and your actual delivery. This also gives you a chance to hear or see yourself present, as well as let others critique your recorded broadcast. To record and play back your presentation, follow the steps outlined in the section "Recording and Saving a Broadcast" in this chapter. When you replay it, first verify that everything is working correctly—you can access the broadcast and see it clearly, the sound is audible, and the video quality is crisp. Then take a second look for content, aesthetics, and pacing. Does your presentation still look good as a broadcast? Do your words adequately convey your message? Are you speaking too quickly or too slowly? Do you look professional and at ease in the video window? Undoubtedly, you'll find things you want to change. Go ahead and make improvements, recording and replaying your presentation again…and again if you need to.

18

ADVANCED POWERPOINT

CHAPTER 19

INTEGRATING WITH ·OFFICE 2003

In this chapter *by Patrice-Anne Rutledge and Jim Grey*

UNDERSTANDING OFFICE INTEGRATION

The big benefit to using a suite of programs such as Office is that the applications work together. You can use all the applications together to build more effective documents. PowerPoint probably makes the greatest use of the other Office applications. By its nature as a presentation tool, PowerPoint can work with all your other applications, tools, and documents to create a single powerful and effective slide presentation.

LINKING OFFICE OBJECTS

By now, you've probably used the Clipboard to cut or copy content between and within Office applications. The Clipboard is one of the most significant tools that Windows offers, and Office makes it even more powerful by letting you cut, copy, and paste several objects as a group or one at a time.

Despite all that power and convenience, the pasting process is limited. For example, after you paste an Excel chart into your PowerPoint slide, the pasted chart doesn't reflect any changes you make to the original Excel chart or its data. Simple pasting establishes no connection between the copied chart and its source. To establish such a connection, you must *link* the source and the target so that the target can be kept in sync with the source.

USING PASTE SPECIAL TO CREATE A LINK

The Paste Special command lets you control the format of what you paste. You can establish a link between two applications using the Edit, Paste Special command, as these steps explain:

1. In the source document, select the content to be copied to your PowerPoint slide (the target). Figure 19.1 shows a section of an Excel worksheet, selected for copying.
2. Choose Edit, Copy or click the Copy button.
3. Switch to or open your PowerPoint presentation, and go to the target slide.
4. Choose Edit, Paste Special. The Paste Special dialog box opens (see Figure 19.2).
5. Click the Paste Link option. If more than one type of object is in the As box, select the one that most closely matches the source of your content.
6. If you want your linked object to appear as an icon, select the Display as Icon check box. The content of the object will be visible only if you (or a person viewing your presentation) want to see it. To view a link icon, double-click it.
7. Click OK to insert the linked content.

After you insert the linked object, test the link—go back to the source application and make a change to the content. Switch back to the target slide, and view the updated content. It now reflects the change made to the source.

Figure 19.1
When selecting content from another application, imagine it in your slide—will it fit? Does its content effectively communicate your information or message?

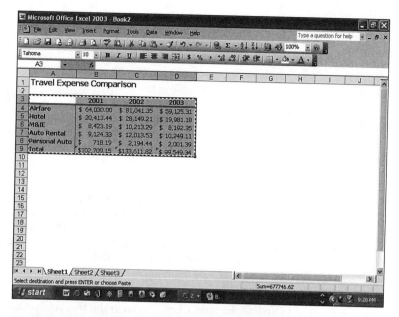

Figure 19.2
When pasting Excel worksheet content, PowerPoint displays that object type in the As box.

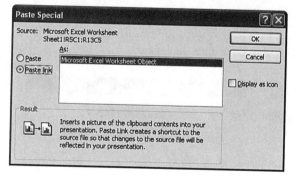

NOTE

You can resize the linked object by dragging diagonally from the object's corner handles. Drag inward to shrink the object, outward to increase its size.

CAUTION

Excel doesn't work properly unless you make sure that you save the workbook file before creating the link the first time.

 Your pasted Excel content lost its formatting? See the "Troubleshooting" section near the end of this chapter.

UPDATING LINKS

After a link is established, PowerPoint asks you whether you want to update that link each time you open the target presentation (see Figure 19.3).

Figure 19.3
You can update the target file with any changes that have been made to the source content.

This lets you choose whether to allow any changes that have occurred in the source document to update the linked content in your PowerPoint presentation. To update, click the Update Links button.

> **TIP**
>
> Why would you choose not to update your target file? Maybe you need to print the presentation with the older data or save it before changes are made. Or perhaps your presentation pertains to second quarter sales, and the source content has been updated with third quarter data, which you're not ready to use. If for any reason you want to maintain the target data in its current form, click Cancel.

If you choose not to update the links when you open the file, you can always update them later by following these steps:

1. Choose Edit, Links. The Links dialog box opens (see Figure 19.4), displaying a list of files that are linked to your open document.

Figure 19.4
Click the Open Source button to view the linked data before updating it.

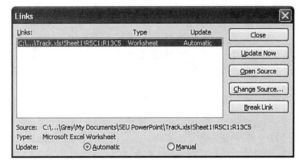

2. Choose the link you want to update, and click the Update Now button.
3. Click Close to update the target with any changes to the source.

MAINTAINING LINKS

For the most part, links you establish between files with Paste Special require little or no active maintenance on your part. To be sure that your links remain intact, simply follow these basic rules:

- Don't rename the source or the target file.

- Don't move or delete the source file.

- Don't move or delete the target file.

If you must move or rename either the source or target file, you will have to reestablish the link through the Links dialog box while in the target file. Click the Change Source button and navigate to the source file's new location, as shown in Figure 19.5.

Figure 19.5
The Change Source dialog box lets you find, select, and reestablish a link between a source and target if one of the files has been moved or renamed.

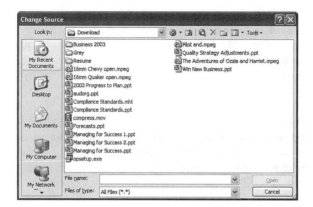

When you change your source document, remember that it is linked to a target file. Whether you're editing content or applying formats, make sure that these changes are useful in the target document. If you need to make changes to the source that won't be appropriate in the target, consider breaking the link. You'll have to update the former target manually (to make content changes), but you won't risk unwanted changes to the target file.

CAUTION

If you aren't the only person using the source or target file, be sure to alert other users to changes you make to the source that might not be appropriate in the target file. If another user chooses to update a link, he might be unhappy with the resulting changes.

REMOVING THE LINK BETWEEN SOURCE AND TARGET FILES

After you establish a link, it remains in force (even if updates between the source and target are rarely or never performed) unless one or both of the files are moved or renamed. Moving or renaming either the source or target file breaks the link between the files because the files can't find each other anymore.

Although this method technically breaks the link, it doesn't do a very clean job. The target document continues to store a record of a link to a moved or renamed file. To make a clean break, severing all ties and any record between your source and target files, follow these steps:

19

1. In the target file, choose Edit, Links.
2. In the Links dialog box (refer to Figure 19.4), select the link you want to break.
3. Click the Break Link button.

After you break the link, the pasted content remains in the target document, but it retains no connection to the source data. Changes you make to the source don't appear in the target, and when you open the target file, PowerPoint doesn't ask you to update your link.

NOTE

> A linked paragraph or table from Word or a worksheet section from Excel is seen as an object. After a link is broken, the pasted content is seen as a picture, a simple graphic component of your slide.

TIP

> One benefit of breaking a link by moving or renaming the source or target file is that the link can be reestablished easily by putting the file back where it was or renaming it to the original filename. Many users use this technique to make a temporary break, allowing changes to the source without the risk of updating the target until it becomes appropriate.

WORKING WITH EMBEDDED OFFICE OBJECTS

Whereas linking connects two applications through a pasted file or a portion of a file, embedding places an entire document and the tools of its native application in another application file. You choose to embed, rather than link, based on what you want to do with the object and, in some cases, who will be using the application in which the embedded object resides. Here are two typical situations in which it's best to embed an object:

- **Limited system resources**   Rather than have two applications open at once, embed one in another by embedding an object. While the object is active, the object's application is also active (and its tools appear in the target application window). Close the source application after you edit the object, leaving the object in the target file and freeing system resources for the target application.

- **Simplicity**   Instead of linking (and having to decide when and if to update links), embed an application object and build the content you need, using the embedded application's tools. There is no need to restrict your moving and renaming of the file because no other files are linked to it.

EMBEDDING NEW AND EXISTING FILES

Embedded objects can be blank, meaning that you have to build the content within the object after it's embedded, or they can be derived from a file with existing content. The latter approach can save you some work because the content is already there. Consider some of these examples of embedded objects in a PowerPoint presentation:

- **Excel worksheets**   Whether you need a block of cells on your slide or tools for formatting and performing calculations, embed an existing Excel worksheet (if the content of the worksheet will fit on the slide) or start with a blank worksheet and build it within the object.

- **Excel charts**   Build a chart in your PowerPoint presentation, using Excel's formidable charting tools. The object consists of a worksheet with a Chart tab and a Sheet tab, letting you enter data and then watch it turn into any sort of chart you need. This is an excellent approach for a user who spends more time in PowerPoint than Excel, but who needs Excel's superior charting and spreadsheet tools to create an effective chart for a presentation.

- **Word text**   If your content is intended only for use in your PowerPoint presentation, you needn't create it in Word first and then copy it to PowerPoint. Instead, create it in PowerPoint through an embedded Word object. Without switching between applications, you're able to take advantage of Word's extensive text formatting tools. You can use this technique to embed an existing Word document, too.

> **TIP**
>
> You can also embed a PowerPoint presentation in a Word document or an Excel worksheet. This can be especially useful when sending a presentation and its supporting data to someone for review.

Embedding a New Object

A new object is one that has no content and is not based on an existing file. You will build all content within the embedded object, and the object and its content will exist nowhere except the slide in which you embed it.

To embed an object in your PowerPoint presentation, follow these steps:

1. Go to the slide that will contain the object.
2. Choose Insert, Object.
3. In the Insert Object dialog box (see Figure 19.6), choose Create New.

Figure 19.6
Scroll through the list of object types to find the Microsoft Word or Microsoft Excel object that you need.

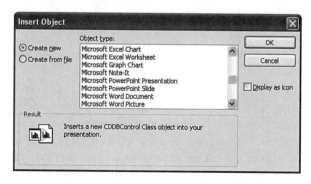

4. Select the object type.

5. If desired, click Display as Icon. This option is useful when you want to save visual space. The object will open up only for entry and editing (or for simply viewing the content) when you double-click the icon.

6. Click OK to insert the object.

When inserted, the object can be edited in terms of content or formatting, using the tools of the object's native application. Figure 19.7 shows an embedded Excel chart and the Excel toolbar in a PowerPoint presentation window.

Figure 19.7
An inserted object can be selected for movement or resizing or activated for editing.

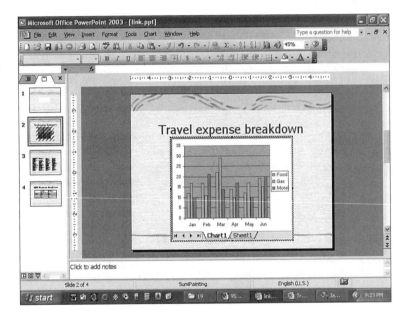

TIP

When the embedded object's application tools appear, they appear in the arrangement you set in the source application. For example, if you turned off the option to have the Standard and Formatting toolbars share one row, they appear on two rows in the embedded application as well.

EMBEDDING AN OBJECT FROM AN EXISTING FILE

Embedding an existing file gives you much of the same power as a linked object. Your content need only be updated in one place—and offers all the convenience of an object that lives within the target presentation. Because the file and its content already exist, you only need to edit and reformat the embedded version of the file if or when it's required. When changes are necessary, you have the source application tools at your disposal without having to open a separate application—the object's application tools appear in the target application window as soon as the object is activated by a double-click.

To embed an existing file in your PowerPoint presentation, follow these steps:

1. In your open PowerPoint application, go to the slide on which you want to embed the file.

2. Choose Insert, Object.

3. In the Insert Object dialog box, click the Create from File option (see Figure 19.8).

Figure 19.8
Save yourself the time and effort of entering your object's content by embedding an existing file.

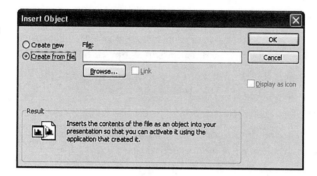

4. Type the pathname and filename of the file you want to embed, or click the Browse button to find it.

5. If you want to be able to change the original document either in its native application or from within PowerPoint, click the Link check box.

CAUTION

If you choose to establish a link between the source file and the embedded object, be sure to update the link only when you're sure that changes to the source won't conflict with editing that might have been applied to the embedded object. This is especially true when more than one person will be accessing and editing one or both files.

6. When the correct pathname and filename appear in the File box, click OK to insert the object and close the dialog box.

USING WORD TABLES

Just as tables are a powerful feature in Word, they are equally powerful and effective in a PowerPoint presentation. For this reason, PowerPoint's Slide Layout task pane offers several options for inserting tables, and the Insert Table button appears on the Standard toolbar in your PowerPoint application window. However, if you're more comfortable using Word's table tools (and the complete Table menu found in Word) or you already have an existing Word table and don't want to duplicate efforts, you can build your table there and paste it into your PowerPoint presentation.

19

INSERTING A WORD TABLE

A Word table is simple to insert, and with a little forethought (how many columns and rows you need), you can add one to any slide in a matter of seconds. You'll use Word's tools to create and then bring the table into your PowerPoint presentation with the following steps:

1. Build your table in Word, using your familiar Word tools (found in the Table menu or using the Insert Table button).

2. You can enter your content after building the table, or you can wait until the table is in your PowerPoint slide.

3. Copy the table to the Clipboard using Edit, Copy or by pressing Ctrl+C.

4. Switch to or open your PowerPoint presentation, and go to the slide (in Slide view) into which you want to paste the Word table.

5. Choose Edit, Paste, or press Ctrl+V to insert the copied table.

6. Edit the content and dimensions of the table using the Tables and Borders toolbar, which appears whenever the table is active (see Figure 19.9).

Figure 19.9
Use the Tables and Borders toolbar to format the table.

→ For more info on using PowerPoint's own table creation tools, **see** Chapter 4, "Working with Tables," **p.85**.

TIP

> If your Word table already exists and you want to use it in a PowerPoint slide, you can link it to your slide so that future updates to the table's content appear in the PowerPoint version as well.

NOTE

> Like any slide component (regardless of its source), you can easily delete a table. Click the table to select it, and then click its border to disable the cursor in the table's cells. To remove the table from your slide, press the Delete key.

USING POWERPOINT PRESENTATIONS IN OTHER APPLICATIONS

If you're like most people, most of the time you'll bring Word and Excel content or tools into your PowerPoint slides. But there might be times when you'll want to use PowerPoint content and slides in Word and Excel as well. Fortunately, you can do that.

You can add any PowerPoint slide content—graphics, organization charts, text boxes—to a Word document or Excel worksheet by copying and pasting it into the Word or Excel file. You can also link the pasted content, as discussed earlier in this chapter, so that changes to the PowerPoint content are reflected in the Word or Excel target.

Another way to use PowerPoint content in other applications is to use entire slides. You can save an individual slide in several common graphic file formats, including GIF, TIF, JPG, PNG, and BMP. You can then insert it as a graphic in any Word or Excel document.

To save a PowerPoint slide as a graphic file, follow these steps:

1. Select the slide you want to save as a graphic.
2. Choose File, Save As to open the Save As dialog box (see Figure 19.10).

Figure 19.10
Before saving the file, it pays to check which formats are acceptable to your target application. Choose the most commonly used formats for greatest usability.

3. In the Save as Type list, scroll through the formats and select a graphic file format such as JPG, TIF, GIF, or BMP.

TIP

It's a good idea to experiment with the graphic format you choose because the quality and results can vary. For example, high-color presentations don't look good when saved as GIFs because they are reduced to 256 colors. And JPG compression could make your presentation look grainy. Saving as a BMP or TIF creates the best quality output, at the expense of large file size.

TIP

If you will be using the graphic on a Web site, save it in GIF format. This format is acceptable to most Web design programs and creates small files, which is desirable for creating fast-loading Web pages.

4. Type a name for your file in the File Name box.

5. Click Save. PowerPoint asks whether you want to export every slide in the presentation or just the selected slide.

6. Click Current Slide Only, which exports (saves) only the selected slide.

When you save a slide as a graphic, use the Insert, Picture command in Word or Excel to insert the graphic. You can size and format the graphic using the Picture toolbar.

TROUBLESHOOTING

RETAINING EXCEL FORMATTING

When I paste Excel content into another file, I lose my formatting.

Excel formatting should be retained when worksheet cells or charts are pasted into your PowerPoint slides. If the pasted content looks different from the source content, however, consider these solutions:

- Delete the pasted content and repeat the Copy and Paste procedure.
- If you're using Paste Special to link the content to the PowerPoint slide, be sure that you choose the correct object type.

If neither of these options solves the problem, consider embedding an Excel object in the slide and pasting the content there. You'll be able to edit and format the content in its own application, negating the possibility of lost formatting.

FIXING A BROKEN LINK

I broke the link on something, but now I want it back. How do I unbreak the link?

You can't restore a link after it's broken. You can, however, create the link over again. Open the file, find the information to which to link, copy it, choose Edit, Paste Special in PowerPoint, click the Paste Link button, and choose to paste it as a document object.

You will also have to redo any formatting you performed on the linked object.

DESIGN CORNER: PRESENTING WITH EMBEDDED OBJECTS

PowerPoint becomes a natural place to combine the best results of your efforts in Word and Excel to create an effective presentation. You can use the Clipboard and linking and embedding to reuse existing Word and Excel content as well as to create new slide elements through embedded Word and Excel objects. This saves both time and effort and assures consistency throughout your Office documents.

For example, using the techniques described in "Working with Embedded Office Objects," you can embed an Excel chart in your PowerPoint presentation. To the presentation audience, the tools used to build the chart are invisible, but to the presenter, having an entire Excel worksheet available through a simple double-click is a significant convenience, despite the costs of larger files and increased use of system resources during editing.

BEFORE

Figure 19.11

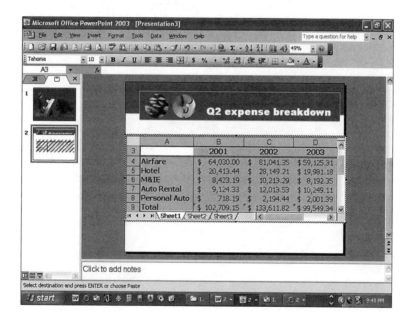

AFTER

Figure 19.12

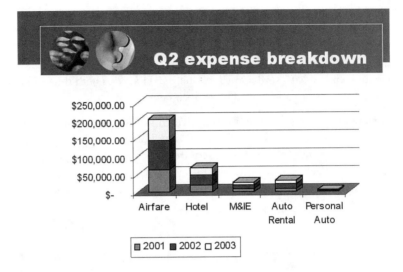

19

CHAPTER 20

WORKING WITH POWERPOINT MACROS

In this chapter

by Patrice-Anne Rutledge and Jim Grey

UNDERSTANDING MACROS

After you've created several PowerPoint presentations, you might find some tasks to be repetitive. Or if you work in an office, you might find that there's little consistency in how presentations are formatted, even within a small workgroup.

Fortunately, there's a way to automate tedious and common tasks. *Macros* are programs that execute a series of functions in PowerPoint to achieve a particular goal. Macros are simple to create and easy to run. You can easily create a macro by recording a series of tasks that you would otherwise perform yourself. You can record any number of steps in a task, from applying a format to running a slideshow, and choose from a variety of ways to run the macro in the future.

You can also create a macro by writing a Visual Basic for Applications (VBA) program.

NOTE

> Don't worry—recording, editing, and using macros require little or no knowledge of VBA. You can improve your ability to edit and troubleshoot your macros by becoming acquainted with VBA, but many (if not most) users don't interact directly with VBA to create, change, or run their macros.

Perhaps you can't imagine how you could use macros to speed up or simplify your use of PowerPoint. Check the following list for some ideas:

- **Getting started**—Your macros can be run as soon as your toolbars appear and the first slide is onscreen. Create a macro to apply a design template and create a series of standard slides for your presentation. After that, all you have to do is add any extra slides that aren't part of your standard presentation, and enter your content. Much of your content entry also can be done with macros.

- **Building an outline**—If you create the same sales or productivity presentations every quarter, don't reinvent the wheel each time, and don't reuse your old presentations and risk overwriting them or leaving old data behind. Create a macro that builds the basic presentation, from choosing slide layouts to entering slide titles. Then, all you have to do is enter the new data and your presentation is complete.

- **Making changes to the master**—Create a series of macros that insert a logo on your slide master, add a slogan to your title master, or change the font of your text on all masters. Any changes that you find yourself making on all or most of your presentations can be automated with macros.

- **Setting up a slide**—If your slide layout needs are not met by any of the installed layouts, simply create a macro that inserts chart objects, tables, text objects, and graphics. The macro can include your placement and sizing of these objects so that when the macro is run, all you need to do is fill in the blanks—double-click and insert the chart data, edit the organization chart, or type your text—and the layout is done for you.

20

- **Inserting hyperlinks**—Do all your presentations have links to your company Web site or an internal database? Create a macro that inserts the hyperlink. This includes choosing the linked site or file and entering the text or graphic that serves as the link.

- **Building an organization chart**—With the exception of the names of new or relocated people, the organization charts of most companies don't vary from presentation to presentation. Rather than having to manually copy and paste a chart from a previous presentation, you can record a macro that inserts your company's completed organization chart. After running the macro, all you have to do is edit the names and titles to reflect changes in the roster since you recorded the macro. If, over time, the changes are significant, you can simply edit the source chart so that when the macro inserts it, the majority of the needed changes have already been made.

- **Running a slideshow**—Rather than make your audience sit through the process of opening the presentation and starting the show, record a macro that can be run as soon as you open PowerPoint. You will have rehearsed your show and set any automatic slide timings before recording the macro so that all the macro needs to do is start the show.

CREATING A MACRO

When you record a macro, it's as though you've turned on a video camera that watches your keystrokes, mouse movements, and command selections—the macro recorder notes every move you make and converts your actions to programming code. After you name your macro and perform all the steps you want to automate, stop the recorder, and by using the name you've given the macro, you can run it at any time. A macro enables you to perform a virtually unlimited series of steps in just seconds.

> **NOTE**
>
> In earlier versions of Office, the Word, Excel, and PowerPoint programs didn't have features such as AutoCorrect and AutoText. Before these features existed, users created macros to correct common misspellings and turn abbreviations into words, phrases, and paragraphs. As Office evolves, the number of common tasks you'll need to automate by yourself will continue to decrease.

RECORDING A MACRO

Before you begin to record a macro, you need to do some planning. Think about where you are in the process of developing or running a presentation when the macro you're about to create is invoked. What situation must exist for the macro to be successful? If the macro formats existing slide content, the content must be displayed and selected before the macro is run. If the macro runs a slideshow, the presentation must be placed in the same folder where the macro was recorded. In short, set the stage for your macro to begin, and record it only when the scenario is appropriate.

After you set the stage, record your macro by following these steps:

1. Choose Tools, Macro, Record New Macro.

2. In the Record Macro dialog box (see Figure 20.1), enter a macro name to replace the default name. Your macro's name cannot contain any spaces. If your macro name is more than one word, use an underscore to separate the words.

Figure 20.1
Give your macro a short yet descriptive name.

Use an underscore to give the appearance of a space in the macro name.

3. As needed, type a description of the macro in the Description box. It's a good idea to leave the name and date text that is already in the box and add your description at the end of that text.

4. Click OK.

5. Perform the steps you want to record, using the mouse or keyboard to issue commands.

6. When your steps are complete and you reach the end of the procedure you want to automate, choose Tools, Macro, Stop Recording.

CAUTION

Try to test your macros immediately, especially if you've developed them for others to use. This will prevent any unpleasant surprises when you or another user attempts to use the macro, and enables you to edit it as needed while the procedures are fresh in your mind. The process of running a macro is discussed later in this chapter.

 Can't get your macro to run the way you want? *See the "Troubleshooting" section near the end of this chapter.*

CREATING A MACRO IN THE VISUAL BASIC EDITOR

If you're familiar with VBA, you can build a macro without recording your steps as described in the previous section of this chapter. Instead, you can type the macro programming code directly in to an editing window provided by Office XP's Visual Basic Editor (see Figure 20.2).

To enter the editor, select Tools, Macro, Visual Basic Editor, and then choose the macro you want to edit from the Declarations drop-down list (on the upper-right corner of the large module window). The editor consists of three separate windows—each designed to assist you in the creation and editing of a macro:

Project window   Declarations list

Figure 20.2
Even a novice VBA
user can learn a lot
from building and
editing macro code in
this window.

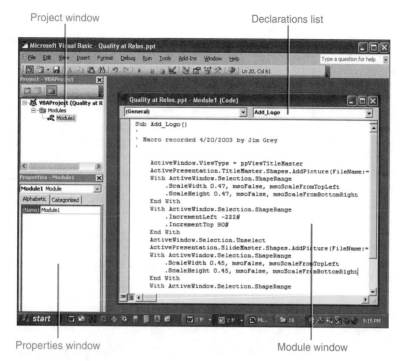

Properties window   Module window

- **Project**—The Project window shows a hierarchical tree, displaying your macro's modules or sections of code. A simple macro will probably have only one module.

- **Properties**—This window also lists the project's modules, but this time either alphabetically or by category.

- **Module**—The macro code appears in this window. Type new or edit existing VBA code in this window.

Figure 20.3 shows the Module window with the parts of a simple formatting macro identified.

To create a macro in the Visual Basic Editor, follow these steps:

1. Choose Tools, Macro, Visual Basic Editor.
2. Click inside the Module window to make it active.
3. As needed, choose Insert, Module. This creates a blank module for you to begin writing your code.
4. Type **Sub** followed by the name of your macro and press Enter. Your End Sub statement is added automatically (see Figure 20.4).
5. Type your lines of code for the steps your macro should perform.
6. Choose File, Close and Return to Microsoft PowerPoint.

20

Figure 20.3
A knowledge of VBA is required for building a macro from scratch in the Visual Basic Editor.

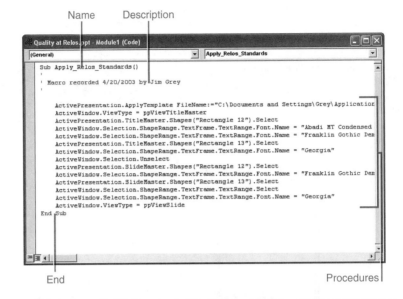

Name   Description

End   Procedures

Figure 20.4
If the name of your macro includes spaces, use the underscore character to represent them, as in Format_title.

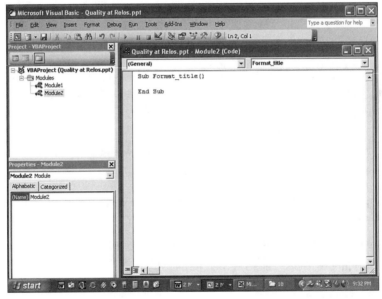

EDITING A MACRO

You can use the Visual Basic Editor again whenever you want to edit a macro. Unless you're familiar with creating macro code in this editor, however, it's probably a good idea to delete and rerecord a macro if it's not working or requires significant changes to work properly. But for simple changes, even a user unfamiliar with VBA can use the editor to make minor modifications. You can change text entries that the macro inserts. The macro adds any text in quotes to your presentation (see Figure 20.5). Edit or retype this text as needed.

Figure 20.5
Misspell something while recording your macro? Fix the text in the Visual Basic Editor window.

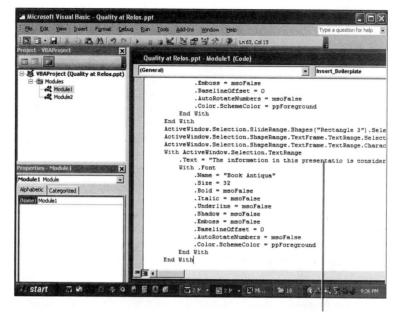

Misspelled word in macro

You can choose different formats and fonts, depending on your needs. Figure 20.6 shows how you can change Book Antiqua to Georgia.

Figure 20.6
Change your font by editing the programming code.

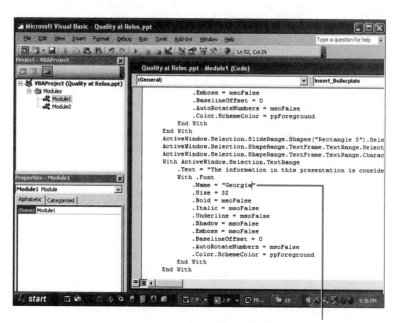

Font changed to Georgia

You can also select a different element. For example, if your macro currently types text in to a title box and you want the macro to type it in to a subtitle box, change the code and redirect the entered text.

TIP

> Interested in learning more about VBA or want to decipher what a snippet code really means? Choose Help, Microsoft Visual Basic Help from within the Microsoft Visual Basic window. Here, you can view detailed reference materials or search on a specific topic. The first time you try this, Office might ask you to install the feature, so have your Office CD-ROM handy.

DELETING A MACRO

Perhaps your macro is obsolete, or has so many problems that you find it easier to delete it and start over than to edit it. In any case, deleting a macro is simple if you follow these steps:

1. In the presentation that contains the macro, choose Tools, Macro, Macros. The Macro dialog box opens (see Figure 20.7).

Figure 20.7
See a list of your current macros, created for the open presentation.

2. Select the macro you want to delete.

3. Click the Delete button. PowerPoint asks you to confirm your intention to delete the selected macro. Click Yes.

CAUTION

> After you delete a macro, you can't retrieve it. Be careful to read the description box for each macro before you delete it, especially if you have several similarly named macros or if your macro names are not terribly illustrative.

Creating a Macro Template

If you want to build a series of macros to use in all your new presentations, create a blank presentation template that includes all your macros. Whenever you want to build a presentation that utilizes your macros, start the presentation based on that template by choosing File, New and selecting the appropriate template.

RUNNING A MACRO FROM THE TOOLBAR

When you want to run a macro fast, it's annoying to use two levels of menus and a dialog box. You can make it much easier to run a macro by assigning it to a toolbar button. Here's how:

1. In the presentation that contains the macro(s) you want to assign to the toolbar, choose Tools, Customize to open the Customize dialog box.

2. Click the Commands tab (see Figure 20.8).

Figure 20.8
Select Macros in the Categories list to view all the macros available in the open presentation.

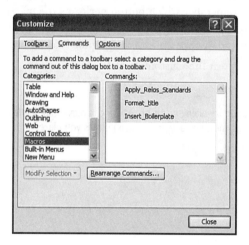

3. Scroll through Categories and select Macros.

4. A list of your macro names appears in the Commands box. Click and drag a macro name (one macro at a time) up to the toolbar.

5. When your mouse pointer is on the spot where you want to add the macro button, release the mouse.

6. Right-click the new button (which appears with the macro name on it, as shown in Figure 20.9), and choose Change Button Image from the shortcut menu.

7. Click to select one of the graphic images from the palette.

Figure 20.9
If your macro name is long, it might be better to have a picture represent the macro rather than to take up a lot of space on the toolbar.

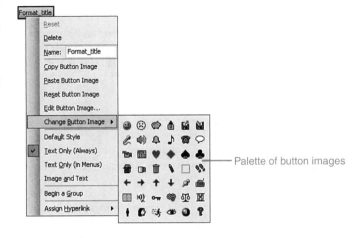

Palette of button images

8. Whether your macro name is long (and is wasting toolbar space) or you feel you don't need to see the name to remember which button performs the macro, remove the text portion of the button image. Right-click the button and choose Text Only (in Menus). The text name of the macro disappears, and the graphic image remains.

9. Click the Close button to exit the Customize dialog box.

TIP

> While the Customize dialog box is open, you can move and delete any of the existing toolbar buttons, including any new macro buttons you place.

→ For more information on customizing PowerPoint toolbars, **see** Chapter 21, "Customizing PowerPoint," **p. 429**.

TROUBLESHOOTING

RESOLVING MACRO PROBLEMS

The macro I created doesn't work properly, and I'm not sure why.

PowerPoint macros (and macros in any Office application, for that matter) might not work as expected when the following situations exist:

■ Items required by the macro (slides from another presentation, fonts, graphics, sound files) are not available. After you create a macro that inserts something into your chart, be sure not to rename or delete that item.

■ The stage isn't set for the macro to run. If your macro was designed to move from slide 4 to slide 8, it might not work as expected if you invoke it while on slide 5. If your macro is to run during an important slideshow, be sure to test it ahead of time and note the circumstances that must be in place for the macro to do its job.

- You've run out of system resources. PowerPoint presentations contain so much graphical content that a machine with marginal resources (memory, speed) might crash or begin to work poorly if your macro opens a presentation or inserts or runs a memory-intensive file. In this situation, it's the hardware, and not the macro, that is at fault. Be sure to close all unnecessary programs before running your slideshow so that PowerPoint and the necessary files are all that are open during your show.

- A macro just doesn't record some things you do in PowerPoint, including the Find and Replace commands, the Increase Font Size and Decrease Font Size commands, and several options in the Links dialog box (choose Edit, Links).

DESIGN CORNER: USING A MACRO TO INSERT A TITLE

As you've seen from this chapter, macro automation can simplify repetitive tasks and help you become more productive and efficient. To find good macro targets for your presentations, think of the tasks you repeat again and again. For example, if you create a variety of presentations that include your company logo, you could create a macro that automatically enters this logo in the location you specify. In this example, Figure 20.10 shows a blank slide with the Insert Title toolbar macro available, and Figure 20.11 shows the results of running this macro. If you create a number of macros to help you automate your presentation creation, you could create a Macros menu (or toolbar) and place all your macros in one easy-to-access location.

To create the macro that inserts a company logo and the text "Client List" in a slide title and makes the macro available from the toolbar, follow these steps:

1. Position the cursor in the title text box of a slide in your presentation.
2. Choose Tools, Macro, Record New Macro to open the Record New Macro dialog box.
3. Enter the name and other details about your macro and click OK to start the recording process.
4. Choose Insert, Picture, From File and choose the logo. Place it over the title placeholder, and size it to fit if needed.
5. Type **Client List** in the title placeholder and size the placeholder so that it starts where the logo ends.
6. Choose Tools, Macro, Stop Recording.
7. Choose Tools, Customize to open the Customize dialog box; select the Commands tab.
8. Scroll down the Categories list, choose Macros, and then select the macro you want to place on the toolbar from the Commands list.
9. Drag the macro name from the Customize dialog box to the specific location on the toolbar where you want to place its associated toolbar button.
10. Click Close to exit the Customize dialog box.

BEFORE

Insert Title toolbar macro

Figure 20.10

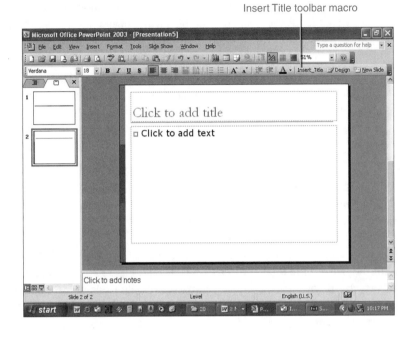

AFTER

Title text is added automatically
and with the desired formatting

Figure 20.11

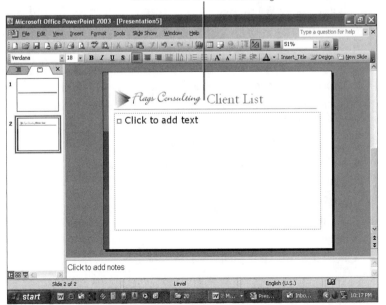

CUSTOMIZING POWERPOINT

CUSTOMIZING TOOLBARS

Toolbars help make PowerPoint and other Windows programs easy to use. A quick click on a button and you avoid having to search through endless menus to get to the command you want. PowerPoint has several predefined toolbars and displays a few of them each time it starts. For example, the Standard and Formatting toolbars appear by default at the top of the screen, and the Drawing toolbar appears at the bottom, above the application bar (see Figure 21.1).

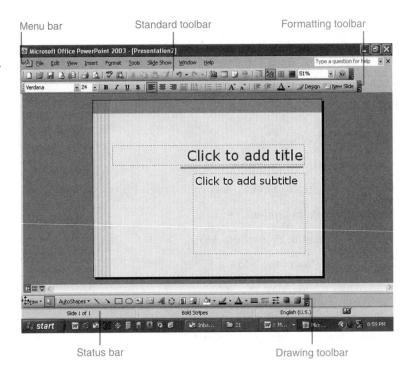

Figure 21.1
PowerPoint uses tool-bars to help you access commands easily and quickly.

You can customize toolbars so that PowerPoint will work more how you want it to. The rest of this section tells you how.

DISPLAYING OR HIDING TOOLBARS

The Standard and Formatting toolbars contain buttons for the most commonly used PowerPoint commands, such as saving, printing, editing, and formatting. If you need other features easily at hand, you can choose additional toolbars for specific tasks. To display tool-bars, choose View, Toolbars, and scroll through the list that appears to choose the toolbar you need. The choice of toolbars includes

- **Control Toolbox**—This toolbox is handy for building dialog boxes using Visual Basic. Most PowerPoint users will probably never need it.
- **Drawing**—This toolbar lets you draw and enhance objects in your presentation.

- **Outlining**—If you click the Outline tab in Normal view, the Outlining toolbar appears along the left side, ready to help you create or edit the slideshow outline.

> **NOTE**
> Some toolbars appear automatically when you select a feature or command related to that toolbar. For example, the Picture toolbar appears when you select a picture.

- **Picture**—When you click a picture object, the Picture toolbar appears to help you modify the picture's colors, brightness, contrast, lines, and so on.
- **Reviewing**—This toolbar helps you collaboratively edit a slideshow. Reviewers can add comments or review comments by others, create Outlook tasks, or send the show as an attachment via email.
- **Revisions**—Displays the Revisions pane, in which you can see what changes reviewers have suggested.

> **NOTE**
> The Revisions task pane replaces a Revisions toolbar that was in older versions of PowerPoint. Microsoft kept the Revisions command on the Toolbars menu so that long-time PowerPoint users wouldn't think the Revisions toolbar's features had gone away.

- **Tables and Borders**—With this toolbar, you can quickly and easily draw or edit free-hand tables and borders.
- **Task Pane**—Opens the task pane.
- **Visual Basic**—For advanced users, this toolbar helps you create Visual Basic scripts.
- **Web**—This toolbar helps you add hyperlinks and search for and link useful information from the Internet.
- **WordArt**—Use this toolbar to add or modify WordArt objects quickly and easily.

When you don't need a toolbar on the screen anymore, you simply hide it from view. If the Web toolbar is on the screen but you don't need it, choose View, Toolbars, and click Web to deselect that toolbar.

> **NOTE**
> You can also right-click any toolbar to display the Toolbar menu. You then select or deselect the toolbar from that menu.

To close a floating toolbar, click the Close button at the right side of the title bar.

NOTE

> When you close a toolbar that opened automatically, that toolbar no longer automatically opens when needed. You must open the toolbar from the menu to display it and also to make it appear automatically in the future.

REPOSITIONING TOOLBARS

Typically, you expect a toolbar to appear at the top of the screen. However, you've already noted that the Drawing toolbar is located at the bottom. When you select other toolbars, they might appear vertically along the side of the screen. Toolbars that appear on any side of the screen are said to be docked, whereas floating toolbars can be found in the middle of the screen.

You can reposition a toolbar simply by dragging it to the desired location. For example, to move the Standard toolbar to the left side of the screen, follow these steps:

1. Place the mouse pointer on the Move handle on the toolbar. A four-way arrow appears (see Figure 21.2).

Figure 21.2
Drag a toolbar by clicking and dragging the toolbar's Move handle.

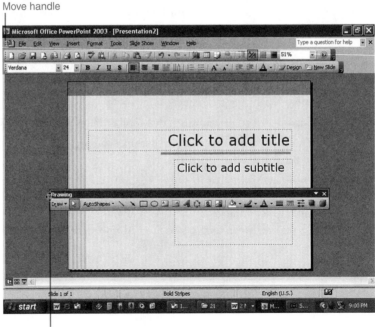

Move handle

Move pointer

2. Click and, while holding the left mouse button down, drag the toolbar away from the edge. PowerPoint displays the toolbar along with a title bar (see Figure 21.3). If you release the mouse button at this stage, the toolbar appears as a floating toolbar.

Figure 21.3
A floating toolbar also displays a title bar and can be placed anywhere on the screen.

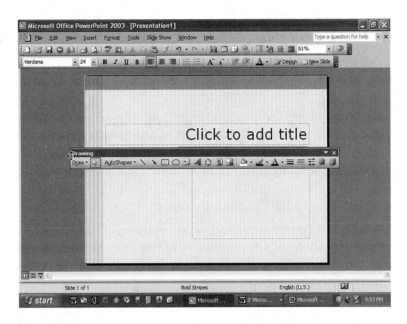

3. Continue dragging the toolbar to the desired location—for example, along the left edge.

4. When the toolbar's title bar disappears and the Move handle reappears, release the mouse button to dock the toolbar along the edge of the screen (see Figure 21.4).

Drawing toolbar   Standard toolbar   Formatting toolbar

Figure 21.4
Docked toolbars can appear at any side of the screen.

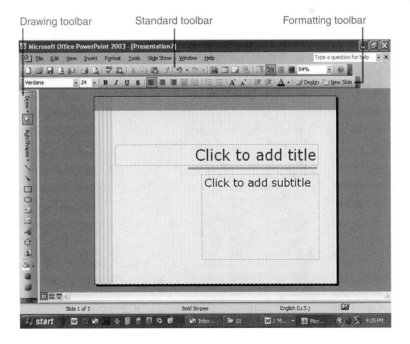

21

NOTE

It's easy to lose toolbars as you drag and drop them. For example, if you accidentally drop a toolbar on top of another one, you might not notice that they've been combined. Use the Move handle to drag one toolbar from on top of another one.

NOTE

If you drag a toolbar to a new location, it remains there until you move it again, even if you close PowerPoint.

ADDING AND REMOVING TOOLBAR BUTTONS

Everyone uses PowerPoint differently. You use some of the buttons on the PowerPoint toolbars on a regular basis, whereas you rarely or never use others. PowerPoint makes it easy to add or remove buttons so that you can have just the buttons you want on any toolbar.

ADDING AND REMOVING BUTTONS FROM THE TOOLBAR

To add or remove toolbar buttons directly from the toolbar, follow these steps:

1. Click the Toolbar Options down arrow at the right end of the toolbar.
2. Choose Add or Remove Buttons from the menu.
3. Choose the name of the toolbar you want to customize from the menu, such as Standard or Formatting. A complete list of currently selected and commonly used buttons associated with that toolbar appears (see Figure 21.5).

Figure 21.5
Select or deselect commands to add or remove buttons from this list.

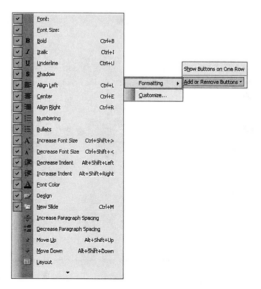

4. Click a button to add or remove it from the toolbar. A check mark appears next to active toolbar buttons. PowerPoint removes buttons you deselect and adds buttons you select to the end of the toolbar.

5. Click anywhere on the screen to close all menus.

If you want to go back to the original toolbar but forget which buttons it contains, scroll to the bottom of the Add or Remove Buttons menu and click Reset Toolbar.

ADDING AND REMOVING BUTTONS IN THE CUSTOMIZE DIALOG BOX

You can also add or remove toolbar buttons using the Customize dialog box, which offers additional options. To add buttons using this method, follow these steps:

1. Select View, Toolbars, Customize to open the Customize dialog box, as shown in Figure 21.6.

Figure 21.6
The Customize dialog box offers several options for customizing your toolbars.

2. On the Toolbars tab, select the toolbar you want to modify if it doesn't already appear on the screen. A toolbar is active if a check mark appears in its check box on this list.

3. Click the Commands tab to see a comprehensive list of standard PowerPoint buttons by category (see Figure 21.7).

4. Find the command you want to add. For example, if you want to add a button to insert an Equation Editor object so that you can make a mathematical equation, first click Insert in the Categories list, and then scroll through the Commands list until you find Equation Editor.

5. Click and drag the button to the target toolbar.

6. Position the button using the I-beam mouse pointer as a guide (see Figure 21.8).

21

Figure 21.7
The Commands tab shows all the commands you can add to a toolbar.

Figure 21.8
Drag a command button to the target toolbar and use the I-beam pointer to position it.

Drag the toolbar button

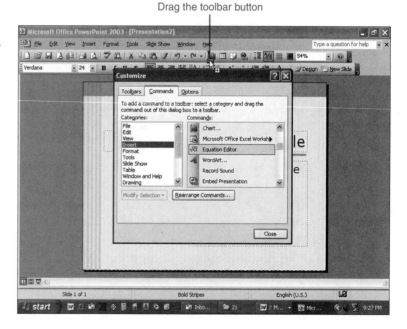

7. Release the mouse button to add the button to the toolbar.

8. To save changes to the toolbar, click the Close button to close the Customize dialog box.

To remove a button from the toolbar, open the Customize dialog box, select the button you want to remove, and drag it from the toolbar.

You can also reposition buttons on the toolbar by dragging them to their new locations. Note that you can't drag and drop toolbar buttons if the Customize dialog box isn't open.

 Customized your toolbar too much and want to start over? See the "Troubleshooting" section near the end of this chapter.

ADDING COMMANDS TO MENU BUTTONS

Some toolbar buttons also function as menus. For example, the Font Color button on the Formatting toolbar displays a menu of color options (also referred to as a palette). Figure 21.9 illustrates this menu.

Figure 21.9
The Font Color toolbar button also displays a menu of options.

You can customize menu buttons by adding and removing commands. To add a new command to an existing menu button, follow these steps:

1. Open the Customize dialog box by choosing View, Toolbars, Customize and clicking the Commands tab.

2. Locate the first command you want to add to the toolbar button's menu (for example, Insert, Duplicate Slide).

3. Drag the command from the Customize dialog box to the desired toolbar button and wait until the menu drops down.

4. Position the new command where you want on the menu, using the I-beam as an insertion guide (see Figure 21.10).

5. Drop the command where you want to place it on the drop-down menu.

6. Repeat steps 2–5 until you have added all the menu commands you want.

7. Click Close to close the Customize dialog box and to save changes to your toolbar menu.

To remove a command from a toolbar button's menu, open the Customize dialog box, and then select the command and drag it off the toolbar.

21

Figure 21.10
An I-beam shows where to position a command you want to add to a drop-down menu from a toolbar button.

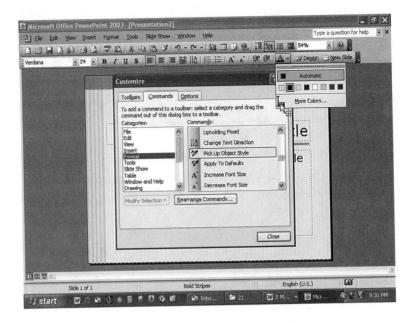

MODIFYING TOOLBAR BUTTONS

How much power and ease of use you get from using toolbars instead of menus depends largely on how readily you identify a button and its function just by looking at it. If you find that one of PowerPoint's standard toolbar buttons doesn't convey to you the visual informa-tion you need to quickly identify its function, you can modify the button or even create an entirely new one. Also, some commands you might add to a toolbar don't have an icon. You can create icons for such buttons.

To modify a toolbar button, follow these steps:

1. Open the Customize dialog box by choosing View, Toolbars, Customize.
2. Select the button on the toolbar that you want to modify. A black border surrounds it.
3. Right-click the selected button to display the Modify Selection menu (see Figure 21.11).

> **NOTE**
>
> You can also access this menu by selecting the Commands tab and clicking the Modify Selection button. Note that this button is only available if you've already selected a tool-bar button to modify.

4. Select one of the following modifications:
   - **Reset**—Restores the button to its original PowerPoint default. Removes any changes you made to the button.
   - **Delete**—Removes the button from the toolbar.

Figure 21.11
The Modify Selection menu lets you customize a toolbar button.

- **Name**—Sets the button's name. The name appears if you choose to display text along with or instead of the button, or if the command appears in a toolbar menu. Also, if you point the mouse at the button, a text prompt appears to remind you what the button does. If you add the ampersand (&) before a letter in the name, that letter appears underlined in menus so that you can select the command using the keyboard. For example, you can execute File, Open by pressing Alt+F, and then O.

NOTE

> The name you choose can be important in making it easy to identify a button's function. Be descriptive but brief because the name might appear in menus too.

- **Copy Button Image**—Copies the selected button image to the Clipboard.
- **Paste Button Image**—Pastes a copied button image to the selected toolbar button.

NOTE

> Avoid having two identical icons on the same toolbar. Also avoid using icons that are commonly used for other functions (such as Save, Print, and so on).

- **Reset Button Image**—Resets the button image to its original state.
- **Edit Button Image**—Opens the Button Editor dialog box, shown in Figure 21.12. Use it to move the direction of your button's image, change its color, or even design a new image by adding colors pixel by pixel. Click the Preview button to preview your changes before accepting them.

21

Figure 21.12
Let your creative side take over as you create or edit new button images.

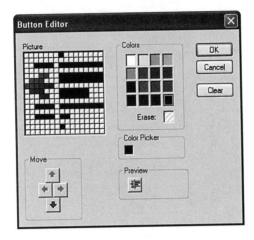

TIP

> Even if you plan to create your own image, you can get a head start by first changing the image to something that closely resembles what you want to create. You then simply edit that image instead of completely starting from scratch.

- **Change Button Image**—Displays a palette of optional button images (see Figure 21.13) you can apply to your toolbar button. If you don't like your selection, you can choose Reset Button Image to restore the original image.

Figure 21.13
If you don't like the current button image, you can choose from a palette of alternative images.

- **Default Style**—Displays the button as an image when it appears as a button or as image and text when it is located in menus.
- **Text Only (Always)**—Ignores the image and displays only text.
- **Text Only (in Menus)**—Displays an image when the command is a button, but ignores the image when the command is located in menus.
- **Image and Text**—Displays both image and text, even when the command is a button.
- **Begin a Group**—Adds a vertical line to the left of the selected button, establishing the beginning of a group of buttons.

NOTE

As you add, move, or delete buttons, you might find that you want to group your buttons so that they're more easily distinguished by function. You can do this by adding a vertical line between buttons on the toolbar. You might not notice these vertical lines right away, but if you look to the left of the Bold button and to the right of the Underline button on the Formatting toolbar, you can see existing group lines.

- **Assign Hyperlink**—Lets you add a link to the button which, when clicked, takes you to the Web or to another document or program.

    → For details on adding links to PowerPoint objects, **see** Chapter 16, "Using PowerPoint's Web Features," **p. 341**.

TIP

Don't be afraid to experiment with changing toolbar buttons. You want to create buttons that work for you, and you can always reset the images if things go awry.

5. Click the Close button to close the Customize dialog box.

CREATING A NEW TOOLBAR

If you're like many of us, it seems that the buttons we use on a regular basis are scattered about on different toolbars. Perhaps you'd like to create your own toolbar with all those buttons you use the most. Creating your own toolbar also means that you won't have to modify PowerPoint's original toolbars.

To create your own toolbar, follow these steps:

1. Choose View, Toolbars, Customize to access the Customize dialog box.
2. Click the Toolbars tab.
3. Click the New button. PowerPoint displays the New Toolbar dialog box (see Figure 21.14).

Figure 21.14
Create a new toolbar using the New Toolbar dialog box.

4. Create the name of the toolbar (for example, "My Tools") in the Toolbar Name text box.
5. Click OK and PowerPoint displays a new floating toolbar (see Figure 21.15).

21

Figure 21.15
A new toolbar also needs command buttons to make it complete.

 — Add buttons to your toolbar to make it complete

6. Click the Commands tab to add and arrange buttons and groups.

→ To learn more about accessing the Commands tab, **see** "Adding and Removing Buttons in the Customize Dialog Box" earlier in this chapter, **p. 435**.

7. Dock the toolbar along one of the sides of the screen, or position the floating toolbar where you want it to appear when you access it.

8. Click the Close button to close the Customize dialog box.

RESETTING THE TOOLBAR

If you make many changes to a toolbar, you will find that it's nearly impossible to remember which buttons were original to the toolbar and which ones you added. If you decide you want to restore your original toolbar, you can do this in one of two ways.

Click the Toolbars tab in the Customize dialog box, select the toolbar you want to restore, and click Reset. PowerPoint asks if you're sure you want to do this, and if you're sure, just click OK.

You can also click the Toolbar Options down arrow at the right end of the toolbar, choose Add or Remove Buttons from the menu, choose the name of the toolbar you want to customize from the menu, and click Reset Toolbar.

CUSTOMIZING MENU COMMANDS

By default, PowerPoint menus tailor themselves to the way you work. Initially, only the most commonly used commands appear on the menus (see Figure 21.16). If you click the double arrows at the bottom of the menu or wait a few seconds, the menu expands to include other commands you have used rarely or not at all (see Figure 21.17). If you begin to use a command regularly, PowerPoint then adds that command as a regular menu item.

Figure 21.16
By default, PowerPoint shows only the most common menu commands along with recently used commands.

Click here to expand the menu

Figure 21.17
Clicking the arrows at the bottom of a menu reveals all of its commands.

You can further customize how menus work by changing menu options, adding or deleting menu commands, and even adding entirely new menu categories.

CHANGING MENU OPTIONS

You customize menu options using the same dialog box you use for customizing toolbars. Open the Customize dialog box by right-clicking the menu bar and choosing Customize. Then click the Options tab, which has the following options (see Figure 21.18):

- **Show Standard and Formatting Toolbars on Two Rows**—Select this option to display these two frequently used toolbars on separate rows; to save screen space, deselect this option to display both toolbars on one row. On high-resolution screens, you might be able to see all the buttons from both toolbars. On other screens, however, the toolbars are collapsed and you must click the More Buttons button to see and use the entire list of buttons.

- **Always Show Full Menus**—Select this check box to always show the full menu.

- **Show Full Menus After a Short Delay**—This option enables the full menu to appear after a few seconds. Otherwise, you must click the Expand button (the double arrows) at the bottom of the menu to see the entire menu.

- **Reset Menu and Toolbar Usage Data**—Suppose that you use a command quite often for a specific project, but don't otherwise use it very much. You can click this button to reset the history of your use of PowerPoint's commands so that only the default menu commands appear. You then begin establishing once again a history of commands as you use them.

21

Figure 21.18
Set menu options on the Options tab.

■ **Large Icons**—This option displays the buttons about four times larger than usual. You probably won't use this option unless you are visually impaired or you have a very high-resolution screen and have the room required for large buttons.

> **TIP**
>
> Although the Large Icons option takes up a lot of space, you can create a custom toolbar with a minimal set of buttons that fit on a single row. (See "Creating a New Toolbar" earlier in this chapter.)

■ **List Font Names in Their Font**—PowerPoint displays font names in the toolbar font list using the actual fonts (see Figure 21.19). This might cause the list to appear slowly, especially on older, slower computers. To list them in a standard Windows font, deselect this option.

Figure 21.19
Display font lists using the fonts themselves or a standard Windows font.

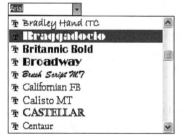

■ **Show ScreenTips on Toolbars**—When you point at a toolbar button, PowerPoint displays the button's name in a small colored box. This helps you identify the button if its icon doesn't give you enough of a clue. If you want to turn off this option, deselect this check box.

- **Show Shortcut Keys in ScreenTips**—If you prefer to use the keyboard whenever possible, but don't always know what keystroke to press for a particular function, select this check box. Then, whenever a toolbar button has an equivalent keystroke, the keystroke appears in the ScreenTip.

> **TIP**
>
> Although using the mouse might make it easier to find features and commands you don't often use, you can usually access commands more quickly by using keyboard equivalents. For example, if you're already typing, pressing Ctrl+S to save the presentation is faster than moving your hand to the mouse, and then finding and clicking the Save button on the toolbar. Use toolbar button ScreenTips to learn keystrokes that can save you time.

- **Menu Animations**—Use this drop-down list to control how menus appear. Choose Unfold to make menus slide out from the top left, Slide to make them slide out from the top, Fade to make them quickly fade in, or Random to randomly use any of these animations. You can also choose System Default to apply the default Windows setting for how menus appear.

> **NOTE**
>
> All Microsoft Office programs share the settings in this dialog box. When you change a setting, you change it for all Office programs.

CREATING A NEW MENU ON THE MENU BAR

If you find using menus easier than using toolbars, you can create and add your own menus to the menu bar. Suppose, for example, that you want your own Quick Stuff menu, using the letter *Q* as the hotkey. On that menu, you intend to add items from the Formatting toolbar because you plan not to display that toolbar.

> **NOTE**
>
> The menu bar functions and is modified in exactly the same way as toolbars. That is, not only can you add menu items to toolbars, but you can add commands to the menu bar as well. Information in preceding sections about modifying toolbars also applies to customizing menu bars.

To create a new menu and to add items to that menu, follow these steps:

1. Open the Customize dialog box by right-clicking the menu and choosing Customize.
2. Click the Commands tab in the Customize dialog box.
3. Scroll to the bottom of the Categories list and click New Menu.
4. Drag the New Menu button from the Commands list (see Figure 21.20) to the menu bar. You can place the button anywhere on the menu bar.

Figure 21.20
Create new menu items and place them anywhere on a menu or toolbar.

5. Click the Modify Selection button. PowerPoint displays the Modify Selection menu (see Figure 21.21).

Figure 21.21
The Modify Selection menu lets you customize new menus.

6. Choose Name and edit the text to change the name from "New Menu" to something more descriptive of the menu's purpose (for example, "My Menu"). If you want to make M the hotkey, place an ampersand (&) before the letter M. Press Enter or click anywhere outside the menu to close it.

7. Next, locate the first button you want to add to the custom menu (for example, Format, Bold).

8. Drag the command button to the new menu (for example, My Menu) and wait until a menu drops down. The first time you do this, the menu consists of nothing more than a blank gray square (see Figure 21.22).

Figure 21.22
Drag and drop commands to the blank square beneath a new menu entry.

— Blank square

9. Drop the command on the drop-down menu (or blank square). As you drag the button up and down the menu, a horizontal line indicates where you will drop the button.

10. Repeat steps 7–9 until you have added the menu commands you want.

To remove a new menu or menu command, drag it off the menu bar when the Customize dialog box is open.

SETTING AUTOCORRECT OPTIONS

AutoCorrect is a useful feature that can help save you time and automatically correct mistakes you frequently make. If you need to frequently enter a long term or name, it can save you time and effort if you enter a shorter term and have PowerPoint fill in the longer term. For example, say that the name of your latest product is "All Natural, Fat-Free Chilly Cherry Sorbet." You're tired of typing that phrase over and over, so you set up an AutoCorrect entry named "CCS" and have PowerPoint automatically enter "All Natural, Fat-Free Chilly Cherry Sorbet" any time you type the letters "CCS."

In addition, if you know that you always misspell a particular word, you can enter the word as you normally misspell it in the Replace field and the correct spelling in the With field.

To see, add, change, and delete AutoCorrect options, select Tools, AutoCorrect Options. The AutoCorrect dialog box for your installed language opens, shown in Figure 21.23.

Basic AutoCorrect options include

■ **Show AutoCorrect Options Buttons**—Displays the AutoCorrect Options button after an automatic correction occurs. Place the mouse over the small blue box beneath the correction and click the down arrow to view a menu of options (see Figure 21.24). From here, you can revert back to your original entry, stop automatically correcting this type of entry, or open the AutoCorrect dialog box.

■ **Correct TWo INitial CApitals**—Corrects instances in which you accidentally type two initial capital letters in a row. You can enter exceptions to this rule if you like (such as ID).

■ **Capitalize First Letter of Sentences**—Capitalizes the first letter of all sentences.

■ **Capitalize First Letter of Table Cells**—Capitalizes the first letter of text in a table cell.

■ **Capitalize Names of Days**—Capitalizes days of the week such as Monday, Tuesday, and so forth.

21

Figure 21.23
You can view and modify automatic correction options in this dialog box.

Figure 21.24
Choose from several options when you automatically correct text entries in PowerPoint.

AutoCorrect changed "teh" to "the"

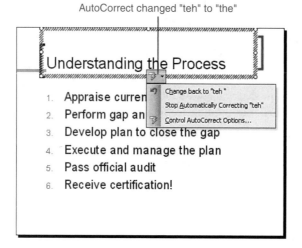

- **Correct Accidental Use of cAPS LOCK Key**—When caps lock is on and you type regular sentences, AutoCorrect turns caps lock off and fixes the capitalization of whatever you've typed.

- **Replace Text As You Type**—Replaces AutoCorrect entries as you type them.

CUSTOMIZING AUTOCORRECT ENTRIES

You can customize AutoCorrect entries. The lower portion of the dialog box includes a list of existing automatic corrections.

To delete an existing entry, select it and click the Delete button.

To change an existing entry, select it and enter the new data in the Replace and/or With fields as needed. Then click Replace.

To add an entry, enter the term to replace in the Replace field and the term to replace it with in the With field. Then click Add.

SPECIFYING AUTOCORRECT EXCEPTIONS

To specify exceptions to these rules, click the Exceptions button. Figure 21.25 illustrates the AutoCorrect Exceptions dialog box.

Figure 21.25
If you want to make exceptions to AutoCorrect functionality, you can do it here.

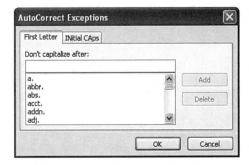

On the First Letter tab, you can specify abbreviations that end with a period that you don't want to treat as the end of a sentence. PowerPoint ignores standard rules of capitalization here and doesn't capitalize the next letter after the period. Terms such as etc. and abbr. are already included here, but you can also add your own or delete any existing entries.

On the INitial CAps tab, shown in Figure 21.26, you can enter any capitalized terms that you don't want PowerPoint to covert to lowercase.

Figure 21.26
Automatically resolve capitalization problems on this tab.

For example, to avoid having the word ID converted to Id based on the normal rules of capitalization, add it to this list.

AUTOFORMATTING AS YOU TYPE

The AutoFormat As You Type tab of the AutoCorrect dialog box lets you replace and apply a number of formatting options as you type. You save time because you don't need to manually format. Figure 21.27 shows this tab.

Figure 21.27
You can see and change automatic correction options in this dialog box.

Options include

- **"Straight Quotes" with "Smart Quotes"**—Inserts a "curly" quotation mark when you type a quotation mark. If this check box is not selected, you get "straight" quotation marks, a throwback to typewriter days.

- **Fractions (1/2) with Fraction Character (½)**—Replaces 1/4, 1/2, and 3/4 with built fractions ¼, ½, and ¾.

- **Ordinals (1st) with Superscript**—Replaces manually entered ordinals with superscript ordinals.

- **Hyphens (--) with Dash (—)**—Replaces manually entered hyphens with an em dash. Using two hyphens is a holdover from typewriter days when there was no way to type a proper dash.

- **Smiley Faces :-) and Arrows ==> with Special Symbols**—Replaces typed representations of faces and arrows with face and arrow characters, as the following shows:

Replaces This	With This
:-) or :)	☺
:-(or :(	☹
:-| or :|	☺
==>	⇒
<==	⇐
—>	→
<—	←

- **Internet and Network Paths with Hyperlinks**—Applies a hyperlink to an Internet address so that it opens a browser when you click it. For example, AutoCorrect converts www.microsoft.com to www.microsoft.com.

- **Automatic Bulleted and Numbered Lists**—Applies automatic bulleting or numbering when PowerPoint detects that you're creating a list (when you use an asterisk for a bullet, for example).

- **AutoFit Title Text to Placeholder**—Resizes text if it won't fit in a title placeholder. For example, title text is 44 points by default, but the font size can be reduced if your title is too long to fit. When PowerPoint fits title text to the placeholder, the AutoFit Options button appears (see Figure 21.28). Click the down arrow on the right side of the button to display a menu from which you can accept or reject automatic fitting and open the AutoCorrect dialog box.

Figure 21.28
Use the AutoFit Options button to change PowerPoint's automatic formatting.

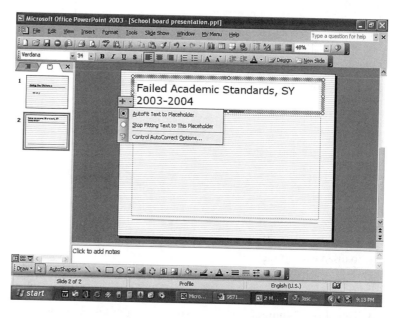

- **AutoFit Body Text to Placeholder**—Resizes text if it won't fit in a body text placeholder. This option works in much the same way as the AutoFit Title Text to Placeholder option.

- **Automatic Layout for Inserted Objects**—Automatically sets the layout for objects you insert.

These options are all selected by default, but you can remove the check mark if you want to deactivate them for any reason.

21

SETTING UP SMART TAGS

Smart tags let you do things in PowerPoint that you'd normally use other programs or Internet services to do. For example, smart tags can link a date in a presentation to Microsoft Outlook, letting you see your calendar or schedule a meeting for that date. They can also link a stock ticker symbol to financial information at MSN Money.

Use the Smart Tags tab of the AutoCorrect dialog box (see Figure 21.29) to enable smart tags and choose which recognizers (that is, kinds of smart tags) to use.

Figure 21.29
Use the Smart Tags tab to enable smart tags and choose which kinds of smart tags to use.

You can set the following options:

- **Label Text with Smart Tags**—Select this check box to enable smart tags. Deselect it to disable smart tags.

- **Date**—Makes smart tags out of dates. Date smart tags link to Microsoft Outlook to schedule meetings and open your calendar.

- **Telephone Number**—Makes smart tags out of telephone numbers. These smart tags let you make a contact in Outlook for the number.

- **Financial Symbol**—Makes smart tags out of stock ticker symbols. These smart tags link to MSN Money on the Internet, where you can bring up current financial information about the company.

- **Time**—Makes smart tags out of time, such as 3:15. These smart tags link to your Outlook calendar.

- **Person Name**—Makes smart tags from names that appear in your Outlook contacts list. When a name is in your Outlook contact list, you can send email or open the contact record. When a name isn't in your Outlook contact list, you can add it from the smart tag.

- **Properties**—Opens a page at the Microsoft Office Web site where you can set properties for certain recognizers.

- **Check Presentation**—Scans the presentation for text that matches the selected recognizers, and makes smart tags from them. PowerPoint makes smart tags as you type, but if you paste text from another application or create a presentation with smart tags disabled, you need to click this button.

- **More Smart Tags**—Opens the Microsoft Office eServices Web site—from which you can download more smart tags that let you track packages, get information about baseball teams, and news from any city.

- **Embed Smart Tags in This Presentation**—Saves smart tags with the presentation. When this check box is deselected, PowerPoint discards all smart tags when you close the presentation.

TIP

> If the Embed Smart Tags in This Presentation check box is deselected when you close a presentation, you can get the smart tags back when you reopen it. Just open the AutoCorrect dialog box to the Smart Tags tab and click Check Presentation.

SETTING POWERPOINT OPTIONS

PowerPoint lets you change many basic options, such as how you edit, save, or print your presentations, as well as how you view PowerPoint screens.

NOTE

> Changes you make in the Options dialog box become your new default settings until you change them again.

TIP

> Whenever you use a new program or an update to a program, your first inclination is to try to make the program do things the old way or the way you're used to doing them. Although it can be tempting to jump right in and make changes to PowerPoint's default settings, you probably should use PowerPoint as is at least until you decide whether those default settings might actually be better.

To access the Options dialog box, choose Tools, Options (see Figure 21.30).

21

Figure 21.30
The Options dialog box is used to change many of PowerPoint's default settings.

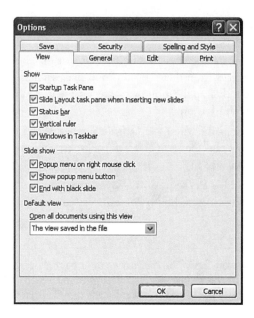

SETTING VIEW OPTIONS

Click the View tab to display options that affect what you see as you create and edit a slideshow, as well as what you see when you play the slideshow.

Show options include the following:

- **Startup Task Pane**—Displays the task pane when PowerPoint starts.
- **Slide Layout Task Pane When Inserting New Slides**—Displays the Slide Layout task pane when you insert a new slide in to your presentation.
- **Status Bar**—Displays the status bar at the bottom of the PowerPoint window. Although the status bar takes up a bit of territory, it shows you which slide you're editing and the design you're using. Also, the spelling icon appears with a red x if anything on the current slide is misspelled.

NOTE

> If you double-click the design name on the status bar, PowerPoint displays the Slide Design task pane, letting you quickly change the design template. Double-clicking the spelling button runs the spell checker.

- **Vertical Ruler**—Displays a vertical ruler along with the horizontal ruler if you choose to display rulers (View, Ruler).
- **Windows in Taskbar**—Displays a separate Taskbar icon for each open Office window. If you deselect this check box, only a single icon appears.

Slide Show options include the following:

- **Popup Menu on Right Mouse Click**—When presenting a slideshow, you sometimes need an easy way to access navigation and other options. When this check box is selected, you can right-click on the slide to display a menu of options.

- **Show Popup Menu Button**—By default, when you play a PowerPoint slideshow, PowerPoint displays a small button at the lower-left corner of the slide. Clicking this button gives you the same menu as the one you get when you right-click the slide. If you don't want this button on the screen, deselect this option.

- **End with Black Slide**—If you deselect this option, PowerPoint returns to the PowerPoint editing screen when you conclude your slideshow. Leaving this option active makes for a cleaner ending.

You can also specify your default view from the Open All Documents Using This View drop-down list. Options include the following:

- The View Saved in the File
- Normal—Outline, Notes, and Slide
- Normal—Thumbnails, Notes, and Slide
- Normal—Outline and Slide
- Normal—Thumbnails and Slide
- Normal—Notes and Slide
- Normal—Slide Only
- Outline Only
- Slide Sorter
- Notes

SETTING GENERAL OPTIONS

Click the General tab to change information about yourself and other items not easily grouped into a specific category (see Figure 21.31). General options include the following:

- **Provide Feedback with Sound to Screen Elements**—Select this option to add sound effects for menus, buttons, and other screen elements.

NOTE

> Changing this option in PowerPoint changes it for all Office applications. However, you might have to restart Windows for this option to take effect. Also, you might find that other sound schemes take precedence over these sound effects.

21

Figure 21.31
The General tab of the Options dialog box offers miscellaneous PowerPoint settings.

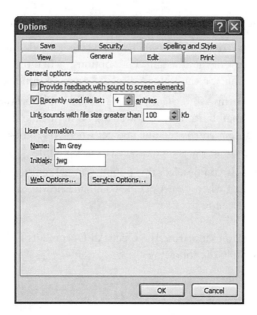

- **Recently Used File List: *N* Entries**—By default, PowerPoint displays the four most recently opened files at the bottom of the File menu. You can increase this number up to nine or reduce it to none.

- **Link Sounds with File Size Greater than *NN* Kb**—PowerPoint normally saves sound files as part of the presentation itself. However, large sound files can make a presentation unwieldy. Selecting this option means that files larger than the size specified are *not* included with the slideshow, but instead are linked from their current file location.

- **Name**—Whenever you use options that require your name, such as in the Properties Summary (File, Properties), PowerPoint uses the name found here.

- **Initials**—Whenever user initials are required—for example, during a NetMeeting—PowerPoint uses the initials found here.

- **Web Options**—Opens the Web Options dialog box where you can set various Web output options, including formatting, graphic formats, and the like.
  → For more information on Web options, **see** Chapter 16, **p. 341**.

- **Service Options**—Opens the Service Options dialog box, which lets you set preferences for showing content and links from the Office Online Web site, for working in shared workspaces, and for joining Microsoft's Customer Experience Improvement Program.

SETTING EDIT OPTIONS

Click the Edit tab to change options for editing text and charts (see Figure 21.32). These options include the following:

- **Show Paste Options Buttons**—Displays a Paste Options button that lets you make choices about how you want to paste a copied object or text, such as whether to keep source or target design template formatting.

Figure 21.32
The Edit tab of the Options dialog box offers options for text and chart editing.

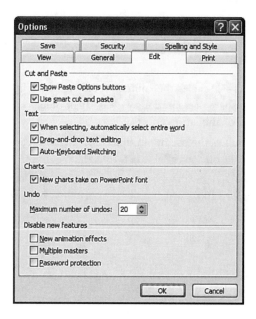

- **Use Smart Cut and Paste**—When you paste text, PowerPoint makes sure that there's one space before and after the text and that there are no spaces before the end punctuation if you paste the text at the end of a sentence. If you don't want this, deselect this check box.

- **When Selecting, Automatically Select Entire Word**—If you want to select only portions of words when using a mouse, deselect this check box.

- **Drag-and-Drop Text Editing**—Clicking selected text and dragging it to a new location is the same as cutting and pasting. If you find that this happens accidentally too often, deselect this check box.

- **New Charts Take on PowerPoint Font**—If you clear this check box, charts use a generic default font such as Arial instead of the slide's font and style.

TIP

> Although it might seem like a good idea to use the default PowerPoint fonts when creating a new chart, more generic fonts may actually look better. You might want to create test charts using both font methods before actually developing the data or making other modifications.

21

- **Maximum Number of Undos: NN**—By default, you can undo the last 20 actions. You can decrease the number of undos to as few as 3 or increase it to as many as 150.

CAUTION

> Increasing the number of undos increases the size of your document and also increases the risk of corrupting your document. Unless you really need more, stay with the default number, or fewer.

 Taking too long to save or perform other tasks? See the "Troubleshooting" section near the end of this chapter.

- **New Animation Effects**—Disables the animation effects added in PowerPoint. This is useful if you're going to share presentations with users of older versions of PowerPoint who use a different kind of animation effects.

- **Multiple Masters**—Disables the use of multiple slide masters that can cause problems when opened with versions of PowerPoint before 2002.

- **Password Protection**—Disables the use of password protection so that users of PowerPoint versions before 2002, which don't support password protection, can still open your presentations.

CHANGING PRINT OPTIONS

To change general printing defaults or to change settings for the current document only, click the Print tab (see Figure 21.33).

Figure 21.33
The Print tab of the Options dialog box offers several printing options.

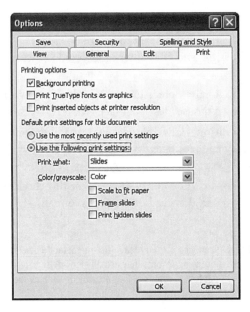

21

→ For details on printing PowerPoint presentations, **see** Chapter 10, "Creating and Printing Presentation Materials," **p. 199**.

General printing options include the following:

- **Background Printing**—If your printer doesn't have its own background-printing feature, this option lets you continue working on your slide presentation while PowerPoint prints slides in the background. If your printer has a background-printing feature and it's turned on, your printer prints in the background regardless of your selection here.

- **Print TrueType Fonts As Graphics**—If your printer has trouble printing the fonts used in your presentation, it could be that your printer can't recognize them or you are using too many fonts for your printer to keep track of. Choosing this option sends text to the printer as graphics, which avoids the problem. However, this option generally slows printing.

- **Print Inserted Objects at Printer Resolution**—This helps match graphic resolutions to the printer that's printing them. For example, your graphic image might have been created at only 72 dots per inch (dpi), but your printer can print at a much crisper 600 dpi. Selecting this option might slow printing.

When you print your current document using the Print button on the Standard toolbar, by default you use the most recently used PowerPoint print settings. You can also choose to use the following print settings:

- **Print What**—Lets you choose exactly what you want to print and its format. Options include
  - **Slides**—This is the default printing format.
  - **Handouts**—You can print two, three, or six slides per page.
  - **Notes Pages**—This prints a small version of the slide, along with any speaker notes you might have created.
  - **Outline View**—This printout appears exactly as it does in PowerPoint's Outline view.

- **Color/grayscale**—Lets you choose the color option for print. Choices include Color, Grayscale, or Pure Black and White.

> **NOTE**
>
> To preview your printout in another color format, click the Color/Grayscale button on the Standard toolbar and choose Color, Grayscale, or Pure Black and White from the menu.

- **Scale to Fit Paper**—If you're using paper other than the standard size, this option scales the slides to fit that size paper.

- **Frame Slides**—This option places a single, thin-line border around the entire printed slide.

- **Print Hidden Slides**—If you have hidden slides in your presentation, you can choose to include them in the printed version.

21

NOTE

Don't forget that print options selected from the Options menu apply only when you click the Print button on the Standard toolbar. Choosing File, Print still lets you choose print options before printing.

→ For details on printing PowerPoint presentations, **see** Chapter 10, **p. 199**.

SETTING SAVE OPTIONS

Click the Save tab to view and change Save options (see Figure 21.34).

Figure 21.34
The Save tab of the Options dialog box helps change default file saving options.

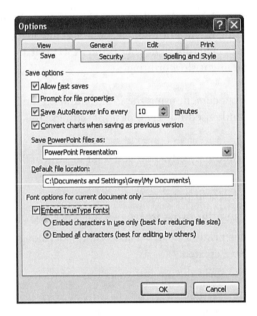

These include

- **Allow Fast Saves**—By default, when you save a presentation, PowerPoint saves only the changes you made since you last saved it. This takes less time than saving the full presentation. However, this also requires more disk space, so if your computer is already fast enough, you might want to consider deselecting this option.

- **Prompt for File Properties**—Summary, Found in File, Properties helps document the authorship and revision history of your slide presentation. If this is important to you, select this option, which automatically brings up the Properties screen the first time you save the presentation or whenever you save it with a different name.

- **Save AutoRecover Info Every *NN* Minutes**—This automatic backup provision saves a temporary copy of your presentation (typically in the \Windows\Temp folder) as frequently as you specify with this option. If you exit your document properly, the automatic backup file is erased. If you don't exit properly (for example, because of a power failure), PowerPoint opens this file the next time you use PowerPoint so that you can determine whether it contains changes you didn't save.

- **Convert Charts When Saving As Previous Version**—When saving the presentation to an earlier version of PowerPoint, use this option to convert charts to a format that version recognizes.

- **Save PowerPoint Files As**—By default, PowerPoint saves its files in the PowerPoint presentation format, which can't be opened in versions of PowerPoint earlier than PowerPoint 97.

  If you work in an environment in which some people use old versions of PowerPoint, you might need to agree on a common format for everyone to use. Then, change this option to one of the following formats:

  - PowerPoint Presentation, which can be opened and edited in PowerPoint 2003, 2002, 2000, or 97.
  - PowerPoint 97–2003 & 95 Presentation
  - PowerPoint 95 Presentation
  - Single File Web Page
  - Web Page

CAUTION

> Saving a PowerPoint presentation in an earlier format might result in the loss of certain features available only in more recent versions.

- **Default File Location**—PowerPoint saves your presentations in the folder you specify. Initially this is usually your My Documents folder (`C:\Documents and Settings\your-username\My Documents`), but that can vary depending on how PowerPoint was installed.

- **Embed TrueType Fonts**—Select this option if you want to embed TrueType fonts in the current document. Options include embedding only characters in use to reduce file size or embedding all characters so that others can edit the presentation.

SETTING SECURITY OPTIONS

The Security tab (see Figure 21.35) lets you set a variety of security options for PowerPoint, which can be useful if you share your presentations with other users or place them on a network, an intranet, or the Internet.

Options include the following:

- **Password to Open**—Protect your file by typing a password. You, or anyone else, need to enter this password to open the file again. To set encryption options, click the Advanced button.

21

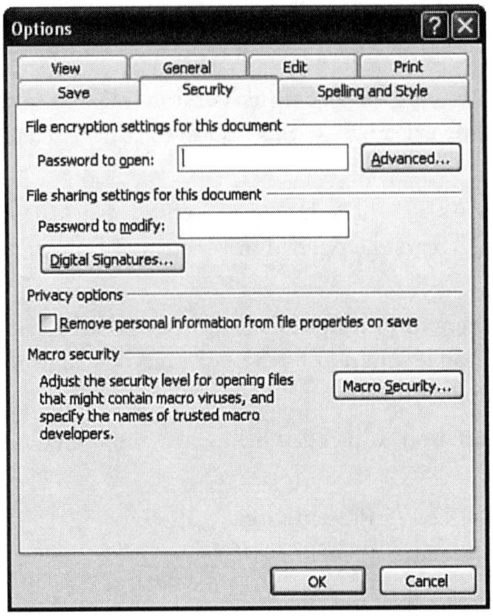

Figure 21.35
Protect your presentations using the Security tab.

- **Password to Modify**—If you want anyone to be able to open the presentation but prevent them from changing it, type a password in this field.

CAUTION

> If you forget your password, you will no longer be able to open or modify your presentation, so choose a password that's easy for you to remember or write it down in a secure location.

- **Digital Signatures**—If you plan to use digital signatures with your presentations, click this button. PowerPoint enables digital signatures using a digital certificate. A *digital signature* is an electronic, encrypted signature stamp that's attached in a certificate to vouch for its authenticity. The average PowerPoint user won't normally set up digital certificates; this is the domain of an organization's IT department.

- **Remove Personal Information from File Properties on Save**—If you're very concerned about privacy, check this box for PowerPoint to remove any personal information (such as your name) when you save the file. Note that this option doesn't remove personal information you add to your presentation yourself (for example, entering your name and address on a slide), but information PowerPoint stores by default.

- **Macro Security**—If you regularly receive presentations that include macros, you might want to set special security options to protect yourself from macro viruses. You can choose whether to accept only signed macros from sources you specify, to accept files with macros, or to disable macro protection. Macros aren't as commonly used with PowerPoint as they are with other Office programs, but you should still set at least some form of macro protection if you're going to share files with others.

SETTING SPELLING AND STYLE OPTIONS

Click the Spelling and Style tab to change default spelling and style options.

→ For detailed information on checking spelling and style, **see** "Checking Spelling and Style" in Chapter 3, "Working with Text," **p. 74**.

SETTING PRESENTATION PROPERTIES

As you create and modify your presentation, you automatically change many of the presentation's properties. You can view these properties and also change or add other properties to the document by choosing File, Properties. PowerPoint displays a dialog box with the name of your presentation. This dialog box includes the following tabs:

- **General**—Specifies the type, size, and location of the file; the dates it was created, last modified, and last accessed; as well as any attributes it carries.

- **Summary**—Lets you enter custom information about your presentation (see Figure 21.36).

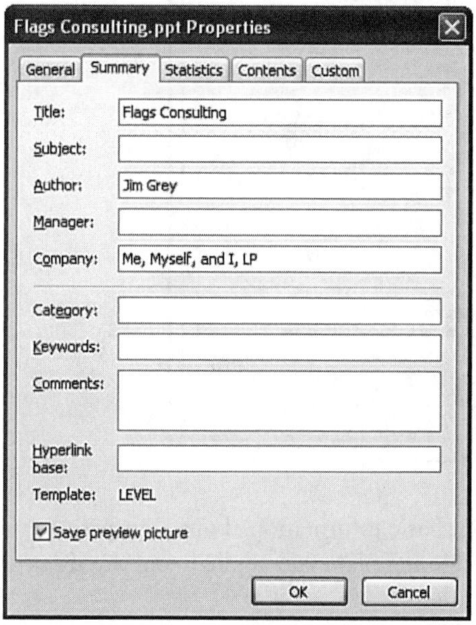

Figure 21.36
Presentation properties add information to your file that can be used for finding and organizing your presentations.

This information is useful when you have to find the file because you can use keywords, for example, even if you can't remember the name of the file.

To customize the presentation's summary, fill in the information you think is important. Assuming that you created the document and that you supplied your name when you installed PowerPoint, your name appears as the author. The title is taken from the presentation's first slide, but you can change that if you want.

21

The Save Preview Picture option lets you see a preview of the first slide when you browse the file in the Open dialog box. If you deselect this option, you can't preview the file.

NOTE

> Using the Save Preview Picture option also increases the size of the saved file. To decrease the size of the file, deselect this option.

■ **Statistics**—Displays detailed statistics about the presentation, including the number of words it contains, how many times it has been revised, total editing time, and more. Figure 21.37 illustrates this tab.

Figure 21.37
Go to the Statistics tab to learn how much time you've spent working on your presentation.

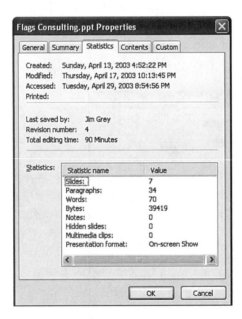

■ **Contents**—Displays other basic information about your presentation, including which fonts you've used, the design template you applied, and the titles of the presentation's slides.

■ **Custom**—Lets you create a series of customized properties that further categorize your document (see Figure 21.38). Unless you have a great number of presentations that need a high degree of organization, you will probably never use this option. If you do, see PowerPoint's online help for information about creating a custom property.

21

Figure 21.38
Custom properties help you find presentations by searching for unique characteristics you define.

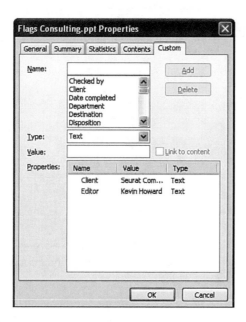

USING ADD-IN PROGRAMS

Add-ins are special supplemental programs, usually provided by third-party sources, that extend and enhance PowerPoint's capabilities. Add-ins range from programs that add multimedia capabilities to those that simply enhance PowerPoint's default menus or toolbars.

Some add-ins are free; others have to be purchased. You can even write your own custom add-in programs by using PowerPoint's Visual Basic Editor. Also, you can find many add-ins on the Web. Look at the Microsoft Web site for those provided by Microsoft or do a Web search for "addins" and "PowerPoint" to find possible PowerPoint enhancements elsewhere on the Web.

Suppose you find an add-in that enhances the shadow control toolbar. Although not an earthshaking add-in, it does add some helpful controls for dealing with object shadows. To add this, or any other add-in, follow these steps:

1. Choose Tools, Add-Ins. PowerPoint displays the Add-Ins dialog box that lists add-ins that have already been installed (see Figure 21.39).

2. Choose Add New. PowerPoint opens the Add New PowerPoint Add-In dialog box. By default, PowerPoint looks in the AddIns folder (for example, `C:\Documents and Settings\your-username\Application Data\Microsoft\AddIns`) to find add-in programs that have a `.ppa` filename extension. If the add-in you're looking for isn't in the default folder, browse to its location.

3. Select the add-in you want to install, and then choose OK.

21

Figure 21.39
Add-ins add powerful
functionality to
PowerPoint.

4. If the add-in contains macros, as virtually all add-ins do, a warning message appears that lets you disable the macros. However, if you want the full functionality of the add-in, you'll need to enable the macros.

CAUTION

> Macros can contain viruses that in turn can wreak havoc on your computer. You should always exercise caution when enabling macros from unknown sources. Knowing the source of the add-in can help protect you from such viruses. If you've installed an antivirus program on your computer and have updated it with the latest virus definitions, you should be reasonably safe.

5. After the add-in is installed, its name appears in the Available Add-Ins list with an x to the left of it. This means that the add-in is also loaded and ready to use.

6. Choose Close to return to PowerPoint.

You now can use the add-in as you work with your PowerPoint presentation.

TIP

> Add-ins do use some memory and can slow PowerPoint's performance. When you're not using an add-in, unload it by choosing Tools, Add-Ins, and then choosing Unload after selecting the add-in. The add-in remains installed but inactive, and you simply load it again when you need it.

WORKING WITH SLIDE MASTERS

PowerPoint helps you achieve a consistent look in your slide presentations. You want your audience to focus on the message and not be distracted by poor and inconsistent design from one slide to the next.

You achieve this consistency by using *design templates*, or predesigned slide presentations that coordinate background colors and designs, font styles and placement, and other graphic design elements.

When you apply a design template to your presentation, PowerPoint also applies a related slide master. If you apply a new design template, PowerPoint applies a new slide master as well. The slide master contains details about the fonts, placeholders, background, and color scheme of the related design template. If you want, you can customize the slide master to suit your needs. For example, you could change the default fonts, placeholders, background design, color scheme, or bullets; reposition placeholders; or add a logo.

→ For information on using design templates or how to change slide backgrounds and color schemes, **see** Chapter 6, "Formatting Slides and Presentations," **p. 99**.

MODIFYING THE SLIDE MASTER

To modify your slide master, choose View, Master, Slide Master. PowerPoint displays the Slide Master layout and editing screen (see Figure 21.40).

Slide Master thumbnail

Title Master thumbnail   Title area

Figure 21.40
The Slide Master editing screen helps you change the overall look and layout of your custom design templates.

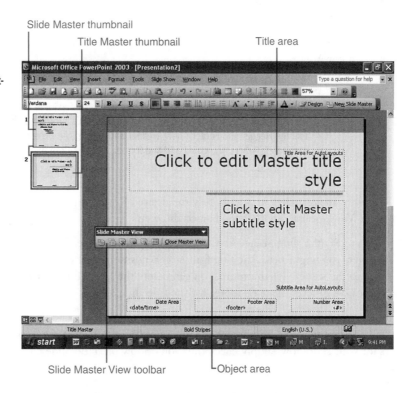

Slide Master View toolbar   └Object area

You can modify either the slide master itself, which affects the entire presentation's design, or the title master, which affects only the title slide's design.

NOTE

> All changes you make to the title or other text while in the slide master editing screen apply to all slides in your slide presentation except those based on the title master, thus helping you achieve consistency from slide to slide.

Place the mouse pointer over the thumbnails to the left side of the screen to display which thumbnail is for the overall slide master and which is for the title master. If the thumbnails don't display, close the slide master, choose View, Normal (Restore Panes) from the main menu, and then choose View, Master, Slide Master. Select the thumbnail to make formatting changes to the desired master.

The master includes several areas you can modify:

- Title Area
- Subtitle Area
- Object Area
- Date Area
- Footer Area
- Number Area

NOTE

> In the Date, Footer, and Number areas, you normally don't add text, but instead format the <date/time>, <footer>, and <#> placeholders. This information is added when you edit the Header and Footer (View, Header and Footer). An exception might be the page numbering, where you could add and format "Page" before the <#> placeholder.

To modify an area, click in it and apply the desired formatting changes either from the Slide Master View toolbar, another toolbar, or the menu.

If you modify the slide master first, perhaps little needs to be changed for the title slide. However, you might make the title font larger, position it differently, or add a graphic object to the screen. Furthermore, you can delete the Date, Footer, or Number area boxes and create a different date or footer for the title slide.

You don't need to delete the date, footer, or page number placeholders if you don't want them on the title slide. Instead, when you choose View, Header and Footer to display footers for your slideshow, simply check the Don't Show on Title Slide check box.

NOTE

> Be sure that you have modified the Slide Master before changing the Title Master. Initially the Title Master uses the same fonts and other attributes as the Slide Master.

21

Table 21.1 lists all the buttons on the Slide Master View toolbar.

TABLE 21.1   SLIDE MASTER VIEW TOOLBAR BUTTONS

Button	Name	Description
	Insert New Slide Master	Inserts a new slide master.
	Insert New Title Master	Inserts a new title master.
	Delete Master	Deletes the selected master.
	Preserve Master	Prevents a slide master from being deleted if you apply a new template.
	Rename Master	Opens the Rename Master dialog box in which you can enter a new name for your slide master.
	Master Layout	Displays the Master Layout dialog box in which you can choose to add a specific placeholder. If all placeholders display on your master, the fields won't be active.
Close Master View	Close Master View	Closes the slide master view and returns to the current presentation.

MODIFYING THE HANDOUT AND NOTES MASTERS

In addition to the presentation itself, PowerPoint lets you modify the handout and notes masters.

To modify the handout master, choose View, Master, Handout Master. PowerPoint displays the Handout Master editing screen and Handout Master View toolbar (see Figure 21.41).

On the handout master, you can

- Choose the number of slides you intend to include on each handout page by clicking a slide-positioning button (such as the Show Positioning of 6-per-Page Handouts button) on the Handout Master View toolbar. Choices include one, two, three, four, six, or nine handouts per page.

- Show the positioning of the outline by clicking the Show Positioning of the Outline button on the Handout Master View toolbar.

- Modify, reposition, or delete the Header, Footer, Date, and Page Area text boxes.

21

Figure 21.41
The handout master defines the default layout for your template's printed handouts.

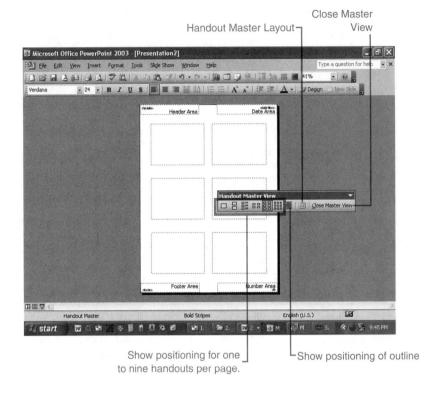

Close Master View

Handout Master Layout

Show positioning for one to nine handouts per page.

Show positioning of outline

NOTE

You can easily change the number of slides to be included in the handouts in the Print dialog box when you actually print the handouts.

To modify the notes master, choose View, Master, Notes Master. PowerPoint displays the Notes Master editing screen (see Figure 21.42).

On the notes master, you can

- Reposition or resize the slide area, depending on how much area you want for the text (notes).
- Reposition or resize the notes area.
- Modify, reposition, or delete the Header, Footer, Date, and Page Area text boxes.

NOTE

Although you can change the background colors and color schemes for the handout and notes masters, you probably won't want to do so. Handouts and notes are usually printed, and background colors aren't necessary or desired. You can, however, add a graphic element, such as a company logo, which then appears on each printed page.

Figure 21.42
The Notes Master defines the default layout for your template's printed notes.

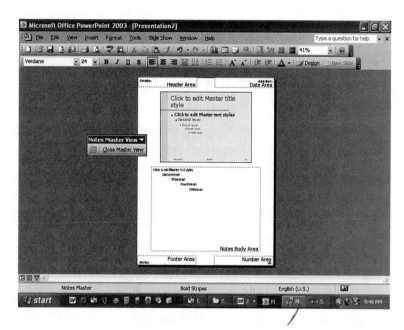

TROUBLESHOOTING

RESETTING A TOOLBAR

After experimenting with customizing my toolbar, I can't remember which buttons should be on the toolbar and which ones shouldn't. How do I reset a toolbar?

PowerPoint makes it easy to return to the original default toolbar settings. Just access the Customize dialog box (View, Toolbars, Customize), click the Toolbars tab, and click Reset. Be careful, however, because you lose all customizing you might have added to the toolbar.

SPEEDING UP PRESENTATION PERFORMANCE

After working with a presentation for some time, I notice that it takes longer to save or to perform certain tasks that were faster before. How can I make a leaner, faster presentation?

Several things can make your presentation grow unnecessarily, which in turn can slow it down. Try some of the following to reduce your file size or to otherwise speed up your work with PowerPoint:

- Reduce the number of undos (Tools, Options, Edit). By default, PowerPoint saves the last 20 changes, but you probably don't need more than 10.

- Turn off the option to save a preview picture with the file (File, Properties, Summary, Save Preview Picture).

- Unload any add-ins you might have loaded (Tools, Add-Ins, Remove).

DESIGN CORNER: MODIFYING MENUS AND TOOLBARS

Modifying menus and toolbars is often one of the most useful customizations you can make, particularly if you use certain commands frequently. Including a special menu with your most common menu tasks or placing frequently used buttons on your toolbar can be big timesavers.

For example, if you insert many Excel charts into your PowerPoint presentations, having the Insert Microsoft Excel Worksheet button on either the Standard or Formatting toolbar can save you a lot of time. To do this, follow these steps:

1. Choose Tools, Customize to open the Customize dialog box; click the Commands tab.
2. Choose Insert from the Categories list and Microsoft Excel Worksheet from the Commands list.
3. Drag the Microsoft Excel Worksheet command to the location where you want to place it on a toolbar (most likely, either the Standard or Formatting toolbar) and release the mouse button.
4. Click Close to close the Customize dialog box. The Insert Microsoft Excel Worksheet button appears on the toolbar, ready for use.

As another example, say that you want to add a "My Stuff" menu command on the menu bar so that you will have easy access to menu items you use frequently. This is a more involved process, but you should be able to create a custom My Stuff menu in about five to ten minutes by following the steps in "Creating a New Menu on the Menu Bar" in this chapter.

When you're done customizing, all of your most commonly used features and functions will be at your fingertips.

BEFORE

Figure 21.43

AFTER

My Stuff menu

Figure 21.44

Insert Microsoft Excel Worksheet button

CHAPTER **22**

USING POWERPOINT'S FOREIGN LANGUAGE CAPABILITIES

In this chapter   *by Patrice-Anne Rutledge and Jim Grey*

UNDERSTANDING POWERPOINT'S MULTIPLE LANGUAGE FEATURES

22

Microsoft Office, including PowerPoint, includes many features that simplify creating multilingual documents and presentations. In whatever languages you enable, Office can check spelling and grammar and apply formatting that's particular to those languages.

These features also make it easy to set up Office's user interface to be in a different language. In the past, if you wanted Office with a Spanish user interface, you had to buy the Spanish version of Office. No more. If your office has native Spanish speakers, you can set up Office to work in Spanish for them.

Some examples of these features are

- **A single worldwide executable**—This enables you to use one version of the application in multiple languages, including most European and Asian languages, as well as Arabic and Hebrew.

- **Independent language setup**—The MultiLanguage Pack offers independent setup for each language you want to enable, even though you can choose more than one language at a time during setup. This means that each language is treated as a separate product, letting you individually remove installed languages from the Control Panel.

- **Unicode support**—Unicode enables you to create documents in all languages installed on your operating system. This makes it easier to use an English-language version of PowerPoint, for example, to create presentations in multiple languages.

- **Language AutoDetect**—PowerPoint automatically detects the language you're using based on the keyboard and applies the appropriate proofing tools.

- **Multiple language editing**—PowerPoint enables the use of multiple languages in a single document, including the capability to check spelling and apply special formatting in the languages you enable.

- **Text editing in right-to-left languages**—If your system supports right-to-left languages, such as Arabic or Hebrew, PowerPoint displays these languages correctly and enables editing.

UNDERSTANDING THE MULTILANGUAGE PACK

The MultiLanguage Pack comes on separate CDs, not the one you use to install Microsoft Office. Install one of the Language Pack CDs if you want to use multiple languages in PowerPoint.

NOTE

Even if you install the MultiLanguage Pack to enable multilingual features in Microsoft Office, you still need to verify that your system supports the language you want to use. This varies depending on the language you want to use and the version of Windows you're using; check your operating system documentation for details on language support.

To do so, follow these steps:

1. Insert the MultiLanguage CD that contains your chosen language into your CD-ROM drive. The Microsoft Office MultiLanguage Pack Setup dialog box opens.

2. Check to accept the terms in the license agreement and click Next.

3. Select the language or languages you want to install (see Figure 22.1) and click Next.

Figure 22.1
Choose the language you want to install from a wide variety of choices.

4. Choose the language in which you want to display menus, dialog boxes, and help, as well as the default language of Office, shown in Figure 22.2. Choices include one of your installed languages or automatic setup based on your system settings. When you're done with your selections, click Next.

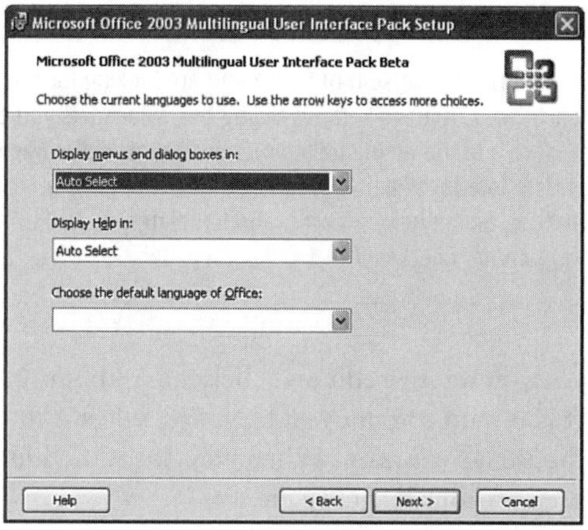

Figure 22.2
Another option is to have PowerPoint set your defaults based on system settings.

5. Choose Install Now to begin installation in the folder specified and click the Install button.

Office installs your selected languages; new features can be added to PowerPoint and other Office applications based on your language choice.

ENABLING MULTIPLE LANGUAGE EDITING

On the Enabled Languages tab of the Microsoft Office Language Settings dialog box, you can enable PowerPoint (and other Office applications) to edit additional languages. From the Start menu, choose All Programs, Microsoft Office, Microsoft Office Tools, Microsoft Office 2003 Language Settings to open this dialog box. Then click the Enabled Languages tab (see Figure 22.3).

Figure 22.3
Enabling a language activates special menus and dialog boxes related to it.

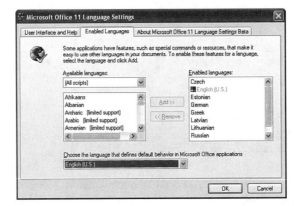

Can't find the Microsoft Office Language Settings dialog box? *See the "Troubleshooting" section at the end of the chapter.*

NOTE

If you've used a previous version of Office and are looking for the User Interface tab on the Microsoft Office Language Settings dialog box, which lets you change the language of the user interface and the online help, you need to install the Microsoft Office Multilingual User Interface Pack to view the tab. The MUI Pack includes translations for the user interface, online help, wizards, and templates, as well as proofing tools for spelling and grammar checks.

Select the language in which you want to edit and click the Add button to add it to the Enabled Languages box. If you want to remove a language, select it in the Enabled Languages box and click the Remove button. When you click OK, additional features and commands are installed based on your language choices.

For example, if you enable editing in Japanese, new menu commands appear in PowerPoint such as Format, Line Break, which opens the Asian Line Break dialog box, shown in Figure 22.4.

Figure 22.4
You can specify how to set up line breaks in Asian languages.

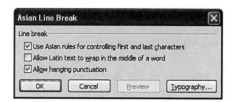

 Can't find the menu options you need? *See the "Troubleshooting" section at the end of the chapter.*

This dialog box enables you to set line break rules for Asian languages.

NOTE

> Office doesn't automatically enable all languages for editing, in order to avoid adding unnecessary options. You must manually enable editing in any language in which you create a PowerPoint presentation.

Even if you enable editing in certain languages—such as many Asian, right-to-left, and Central European languages—you must also meet certain system requirements before you can truly edit in those languages.

In other cases, you can simply install the appropriate keyboard layout to edit in a certain language. To do this, choose Settings, Control Panel from the Windows Start menu and double-click the Text Services icon in the Control Panel window. Figure 22.5 shows the Text Input Settings dialog box, where you can set keyboard and other language-related input preferences.

Figure 22.5
Adding keyboard layouts makes it easier to work in another language.

22

NOTE

If you don't see a Text Services icon in the Control Panel, your Control Panel is probably set to Category View. Click the Switch to Classic View link to see the Text Input Settings icon.

If you *still* don't see a Text Services icon, double-click the Regional and Language Options icon and click the Details button in the Text services and input languages area.

CHECKING SPELLING IN ANOTHER LANGUAGE

To check spelling in another language, follow these steps:

1. Select the text you want to spell check.
2. Choose Tools, Language to open the Language dialog box, shown in Figure 22.6.

Figure 22.6
You can spell check in multiple languages in PowerPoint.

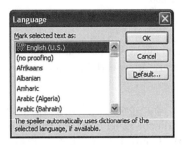

3. In the scroll box under Mark Selected Text As, choose the language whose dictionary you want the spelling checker to use.
4. Click OK to close the dialog box.
5. Click the Spelling button on the Standard toolbar to check the spelling in the language.

NOTE

You can change the default dictionary's language by clicking the Default button in the Language dialog box. PowerPoint asks whether you want to change the default language for this and future presentations to the language you select.

REMOVING A LANGUAGE PACK

If you no longer want to work in another language and want to remove it (and its related menu options and dialog boxes) from Office, choose Start, Settings, Control Panel. Double-click the Add/Remove Programs icon and choose the Microsoft Office Language Pack you want to remove.

TROUBLESHOOTING

ADDING NEW MENU OPTIONS

I can't find the menu options to edit in a certain language.

You must enable a language for editing before you can view related menu options. To do so, open the Start menu and choose Programs, Microsoft Office, Microsoft Office Tools, Microsoft Office 2003 Language Settings. Go to the Enabled Languages tab in the Microsoft Office Language Settings dialog box to enable the language you want to use.

FINDING THE LANGUAGE SETTINGS DIALOG BOX

I can't find the Microsoft Office Language Settings dialog box, or I can find it, but certain tabs don't appear.

You must install the Microsoft MultiLanguage Pack to see this dialog box.

CHAPTER 23

TROUBLESHOOTING POWERPOINT

In this chapter   *by Patrice-Anne Rutledge and Jim Grey*

23

DEALING WITH ERROR MESSAGES AND PROMPTS

Problems might arise with a presentation while you develop, edit, print, or save it. This chapter gives you some ideas of what to expect and how to handle these problems if and when they occur.

Many PowerPoint problems announce themselves in the form of an error message that appears when you try to issue a command or perform some task. Others are more subtle: The command you want to use is dimmed, or the graphic you want to rotate won't. Although it is frustrating when an error message appears, it does give you information about the nature and cause of the problem. Take advantage of this information and react to it logically and cautiously. Read the error message carefully and write down when it happened and what you were doing.

Your first choice when dealing with any technical problem should be to consult this book's index to see whether you can find a resolution. You should also consult PowerPoint's online help (press F1 to open the Help task pane). If you can't find an answer, or the suggested solution doesn't work, here are some other ideas:

- **Try again**—As best as you can, repeat the steps that resulted in the error message. If the process works with no problem, you might be out of the woods and can continue working. If the error appears again, try the other ideas listed here.

- **Get technical support**—If you work for a company that provides technical support, this is your best source of information after you've unsuccessfully tried to resolve the problem yourself. If you don't have access to an internal support staff, see what's available for online or phone support from Microsoft Product Support Services.

- **Research Microsoft's support site**—You will find Microsoft Product Support Services at http://support.microsoft.com/directory/. This site offers a knowledge base, FAQs, and other options for telephone and online support.

NOTE

> If you need to show someone exactly what displays on your screen, use Print Screen. This key, located above your Insert key on a standard keyboard, might appear as PrtScn or Print Screen. Pressing this key takes a snapshot of your screen and places the image on your Clipboard. You can then paste the image into an email message (to send to your company's technical staff) or Word document for printing. The image contains the exact message that appeared. Because the image shows what was going on in the background, the technical staff sees the error message in context.

RESOLVING PROBLEMS

You can solve some problems yourself by determining their causes and eliminating any contributing factors. Most problems you encounter in PowerPoint will probably be memory related, even if you have a lot of memory (RAM) on your computer. PowerPoint is a graphical application, and graphics use a lot of memory. Printing and display can also be problem areas if your printer doesn't have enough memory or your video card isn't powerful enough.

When you consider solving a problem, be honest—do you feel confident changing your computer's configuration? Are you comfortable with the Control Panel? If you begin tinkering in one dialog box or another, do you completely understand the nature and ramifications of all the changes and settings with which you're working? If the answers to these questions are not Yes on all counts, don't try to solve the problem on your own—call for help.

NOTE

> If you want to try a possible solution on your own, try to exit without saving or choose File, Save As and save the file under a new name and restart PowerPoint. You might lose any work (in your original file) done since you last saved it, but if the last batch of changes was what caused your problem, you've also lost them!

DISPLAY PROBLEMS

Most display problems, if they occur suddenly, are memory related. Typical complaints include the following:

- Ghosts of previous slides or dialog boxes appear behind your current slide, or even on top of it.

- Text on your slides changes to a choppy, sans serif font.

- Graphics look incomplete, grainy or choppy, or as though a pattern is placed on top of them.

- Ornate graphics or background elements take a long time to refresh as you move from slide to slide.

If any of these problems occur, save your work and exit PowerPoint. If you have other programs running, shut them down, too. You should even consider restarting your computer to empty your memory and start with a clean slate. Most of the time, however, simply restarting PowerPoint solves the problem.

If the problem is chronic, your video drivers might need updating. Visit the Web site of your video card's manufacturer (or, if you don't know that, of your computer's manufacturer) to download the latest drivers for the version of Windows you're running. The Web site should give you instructions for installing the drivers.

CAUTION

> Many workplaces don't take kindly to employees who try to fix their computers. Have your company's technical support group troubleshoot this problem and install drivers as needed.

If that doesn't work, you probably face upgrading your video card to one with more memory that can display and handle more complex graphic and multimedia content. Unfortunately, this costs money.

NOTE

If your slide's background or object-fill colors appear in stripes or just don't look as smooth as you think they should, check your zoom level. Choosing 100% should smooth out the display, removing any distortion. You can also try viewing the offending slide in Slide Show view, which lets you see the entire slide.

PRINTING PROBLEMS

Printing problems are generally related to your printer and are usually transient. Don't rush your computer in for repairs just because a print job doesn't come out as expected. Some common printing problems include the following:

- The whole page doesn't print; about a third or half-way through the page, the image appears to be chopped off.
- Text objects are missing.
- Nothing prints, or only a few pages of random characters and symbols print.

Most of the problems you will encounter when printing will be due to the printer not having enough memory. Sometimes you can limp along by printing your presentation a page at a time—that is, send page 1 to the printer, and then page 2, and so on. This might prevent the printer's memory from being overloaded. This will become very tedious by about page 4, however, and you'll probably be ready to lay out the cash for more memory in your printer.

If you print on a networked printer and the network is set up very poorly, the printer can become "confused" with too much input from too many people. If the same presentation printed fine before on the same printer, the current environment—other printer traffic—is probably the culprit. To limp along, try printing the presentation when others aren't using the printer, such as before or after hours. You can also just save the presentation to a disk and print it at a printing and photocopying store—most of them rent time on their computers and printers. But the better solution is for your company's network administrators to redesign the network to be more robust.

To reduce the amount of information that your printer must handle for your presentation, try printing in black and white (use the Print dialog box setting).

If all quick-fix or workaround options fail or are inappropriate for your immediate needs, you can take a more direct approach and check your printer's settings. Each printer's settings are different because they are based on the printer's specific capabilities, its connection to your printer or a network, and your system configuration. To access your printer's settings, open the Start menu and choose Control Panel, Printers and Other Hardware,

Printers and Faxes (or in Windows 2000, open the Start menu and choose Settings, Printers). Then right-click the icon for the printer and choose Properties from the menu that appears. The dialog box that opens shows you the current settings for your printer's connection to the computer, speed, resolution, and other options, again, depending on your printer. If you're working with someone else's computer (the computer on your desk at work, for example), it's a good idea to ask for help from a technical resource before making any changes.

A common fix for printer problems is to reinstall the printer's driver on your computer. Sometimes, printer drivers fall out of date, especially if your computer's operating system has been upgraded. Check the manufacturer's Web site for the latest driver and download it. Install it by double-clicking the Add Printer icon in the Printers and Faxes window. When asked, direct the installation program to the folder where you have stored the driver, and a new printer icon will appear, based on that driver file. Try your print job again. If it succeeds, the old driver was the culprit.

CAUTION

Many workplaces don't take kindly to employees who try to fix their computers. Have your company's technical support group reinstall your printer's driver instead.

TROUBLESHOOTING PROBLEMS WITH POWERPOINT FEATURES

PowerPoint is loaded with effective and normally efficient tools to enhance your presentations, and these features work perfectly most of the time. When they don't, however, they can truly be more trouble than they're worth. Before starting your next presentation, familiarize yourself with these situations and their resolutions:

- **AutoCorrect isn't correcting**—Be sure that it's on. Choose Tools, AutoCorrect Options, and check to see that a check mark is next to Replace Text as You Type as well as any other AutoCorrect options that you want to use.

- **AutoCorrect is working when you don't want it to**—In your presentation for the law firm of Tidwell, Evans, and Havilland, you need to type teh and not have it converted to the. You don't want to remove the AutoCorrect entry from the list, and you don't want to turn off AutoCorrect altogether. What to do? Click the down arrow to the right of the AutoCorrect Options button (it's just beneath the corrected word) and choose Stop Automatically Correcting "teh."

- **Your hyperlinks don't work**—The most common cause of this problem is that the target file or Web location is no longer valid or has been moved. It's a good idea to maintain your links by checking them periodically, especially an intranet or Web pages on the Internet. If the hyperlink fails, right-click it and choose Edit Hyperlink from the shortcut menu. In the Edit Hyperlink dialog box that appears, you can enter a new hyperlink.

- **The speech and handwriting recognition tools won't work properly**—Remember that you need at least 128MB of memory for these powerful features to work (even though you might be able to access them with less).

- **Drag-and-drop editing doesn't work**—If you've ruled out that your mouse skills are the cause of the problem—not having text properly selected can often be the culprit— be sure that the drag-and-drop feature is turned on. Choose Tools, Options and, in the Edit tab, look for a check mark in the Drag-and-Drop Text Editing option. If it's not checked, click the option box.

NOTE

If your hyperlink works but takes a long time to get to the target Web site, the server on which the target resides might be busy. Try to reach the site later, or try during times of the day that are less likely to be busy, such as early in the morning or very late at night.

SLIDESHOW PROBLEMS

If you're having a problem with your slideshow, the problem is likely that the show is too slow or your animations don't work as expected. In the case of speed, your computer's memory might be the problem; or if you're using graphic files that were scanned at a high resolution (600 or 1200 dpi), this might slow down your show as well. To see if memory is the problem, close any other programs that aren't essential and restart PowerPoint. If the show is still too slow, and you are using graphic files in your presentation, consider rescanning the graphics at a lower resolution (if you have access to the original artwork) or opening the file in a program, such as Irfanview (which is free at www.irfanview.com), Paint Shop Pro, or Photoshop, that lets you edit and resave the image at a lower resolution.

TIP

The lower the resolution, the smaller the graphic file. An 800×600 pixel bitmap (BMP) image at 16 million colors uses 1.37MB of memory. The same image at 256 colors needs only 470KB, and at 16 colors it needs only 235KB. Reducing resolution often damages the image's quality, however. If an image truly has thousands of colors and you reduce it to 256 colors, the image loses a lot of detail and might look blotchy.

If your animations aren't working as expected, try the obvious first. Go back to the slides and make sure that your settings are correct. If they are, try deleting the offending object (a piece of clip art that doesn't fly in as desired or a title that doesn't appear at all during the show) and reinserting it. Then, reapply the animation effects. Years of using PowerPoint and helping hundreds of students create presentations has proven this method; although not technically elegant, it is the most effective and expeditious way to solve such problems.

NOTE

When any PowerPoint problem occurs in printing, running a slideshow, or editing your slides, try the Ask a Question box on the menu bar. Enter your question (or a keyword if you're in a hurry) and press Enter. If you type "Printing," for example, the topics that the Ask a Question box will find for you include "Troubleshoot printing."

RUNNING DETECT AND REPAIR

PowerPoint offers a feature called Detect and Repair that finds and fixes common system problems such as missing files and Registry settings (but not individual PowerPoint presentations). Select Help, Detect and Repair from the menu bar to open the Detect and Repair dialog box, shown in Figure 23.1.

Figure 23.1
Try Detect and Repair to resolve PowerPoint system problems.

You can restore your shortcuts while repairing or discard customized settings if you want. Click Start to run the process. PowerPoint might ask for your installation CD during this process, so it's a good idea to have it handy before you start. If Detect and Repair doesn't work, the next step is to uninstall Office and then reinstall it.

PART **VII**

FROM CONCEPT TO DELIVERY

CHAPTER 24

THE MESSAGE—SCRIPTING THE CONCEPT

In this chapter

by Tom Mucciolo

EXPERIENCING IDEAS

You know what I like? I like other books. You know, the other books out there that deal with presenting, public speaking, communication—I like them. I figure, anyone who has a plan that works and puts it in writing is probably giving good advice. Of course, that statement may not apply to the pamphlet *Six Easy Steps to Safe-Cracking*, but you get the idea. While most advice is mainly subjective, when rooted in something believable, it can be of great value. So I encourage you to investigate the topic of "business presentations" through the eyes of many experts and gather their viewpoints. You can learn a lot from those who have found success.

UNDERSTANDING THE PROCESS

Guess what? There are only three things you have to think about when putting together a presentation.

The first is development of the concept; the second involves the design of the visuals; and the third concentrates on the delivery of the message to the audience. You may be involved in one or more of these stages.

In order to see the big picture, here, you have to understand where you are in the process of presenting. This is a good time to touch on how this chapter relates to the ones that follow as the process is unveiled.

The chapters ahead are separated to cover each part of the process. This chapter examines the *message* and teaches you how to script the concept into a workable presentation. Chapter 25, "The Media—Designing Visual Support," concentrates on the *media* and offers you advice on designing the visuals. This will help you make the visual expression of the message the best it can be. Chapter 26, "The Mechanics of Form—Developing External Presentation Skills," and Chapter 27, "The Mechanics of Function—Developing Internal Presentation Skills," both deal with the *mechanics* of presenting. The presentation skill is separated into two chapters, one covering external form and the other concentrating on internal *function*. I arranged these chapters in the order of theory to practice to personal skill. If I were reading this book, I'd skip the theory and practice, jump right to the personal skill, adapt to it, and ask for that raise! But, logic and order must rule our world, so the theory comes first!

Chapter 28, "Techniques and Technicalities," is dedicated to the *environmental* issues concerning a presentation, such as the room, the equipment, the seating arrangements, and other elements that may affect the *performance* of the message.

Chapter 29, "Presenting in a Variety of Settings," applies elements of the presentation process to many different situations including conference rooms, small group meetings, the outdoors, as well as interactive videoconferencing sessions.

PUTTING PEOPLE FIRST

One thing all the experts can agree on is that the success of communication is dependent on the presenter. That would be the person in the front of the room trying to keep the audience awake. The visuals are secondary to the concept, which is subject to the delivery skills of the person. All three elements are important, but without the person, you really can't call it a *presentation*.

If you think the content and the visuals are most important, try this at your next presentation. Get there early and place a chair in the front of the room, right about where you are expected to stand. For added effect, place your jacket over the back of the chair. Now, with a cassette player running a voice recording of your presentation, let the PowerPoint visuals advance automatically for the "audience." Then, using an egg timer, see how long the group remains in the room!

Communication is about people. Competition is so strong that products or services in the same category are starting to look the same. From household goods to cars to electronics—everything seems on par with everything else. The offerings of a company don't make the difference; instead, the people skills used to express those offerings are often what causes us to make a decision. The role of the presenter has taken on new meaning for companies who expect to compete in the next century.

BECOMING A VISUAL PRESENTER

Most people, especially those under the age of 40, are visual creatures. They get their information and stimulation from television, movies, computers, and video games. All of these forms are driven by action. Visual creatures demand action. In fact, they crave it! Think about it! Where do you get most of your news information? TV, right? That's because you like all the little pictures. Who doesn't? We're visual creatures! To be successful, presenters need to match the needs of an audience of visual creatures by becoming visual presenters. A visual presenter embodies a message and delivers it with action, creating a lasting impression on the audience.

My development of the concept, the design, and the delivery follows a consistent set of principles based on over 15 years of experience. The MediaNet approach focuses on messages, media, and mechanics in order to blend concepts and visual support with a person's individual delivery style.

This method has proven to be a practical, easy-to-understand, and extremely potent technique for changing ordinary business presentations into very memorable events. The techniques and tactics discussed in this book are designed for a visual presenter. This process advances a personal skill allowing an individual to reach his or her own potential as an expert communicator. The results are immediate and easily applied to new situations. Okay, what if I said you can lose 12 pounds with this method? I thought that would perk you up!

Although this book discusses one method of presenting unlike any other you are likely to encounter, it is not the only way of developing and delivering better presentations; it's just one way. But I really believe if you apply these techniques, you will enhance your proficiency, increase your effectiveness, and develop your own style. Hopefully, your style will incorporate some or all of the skills of a visual presenter, from concept to delivery.

MAKING A LASTING IMPRESSION

People remember people, not data. Very few people will come up to you at the end of your presentation and say, "You know. The third pie chart? The fourth slice? Loved it! The other slices, nahhhh, but the FOURTH slice, wow!"

No way! But a person might say, "You know. The story you told about the young woman and the two kids? I'll never forget that!"

How long after the presentation is your message still memorable? Remember: "Quality" content stimulates thinking and makes a lasting impression.

When you develop content for a presentation, the messages you place in the script should stay with an audience long after the event takes place. It's not about the messages alone; rather, it's about the way those messages are conveyed. People communicate ideas to people. Quality content is only quality content if presented that way. Obviously, if an actor plays Hamlet poorly, the quality of the content is lost.

Now don't over-analyze when you read this chapter; just let the stuff sink in slowly. The messaging issues are broken down to the smallest components so that you can see how to build lasting impressions. The good news is that you probably instinctively know most of this already without even reading it.

People and ideas need to be brought together for content to flourish and for messages to be remembered. To create a lasting impression, you'll need to pay attention to the way messages are created for both the presenter to deliver and for the audience to grasp. The trick is to get this process to the point where you are constantly saying the right things to the right people at the right times! Having said that, the three areas we need to address when scripting a message are

- Constructing the argument
- Qualifying the participants
- Assuring consistency

NOTE

> I chose the development of the message as the starting point. Many believe that the first step in creating content is to analyze the needs of the audience. Then, after meeting those needs, the message is developed. Although I agree these two issues are closely related, the process of creativity dictates that the message needs to be developed before the audience is targeted. You really have to have a reason to say something and have something to say before you can ask someone to listen. Religion, politics, and theatre are everyday examples of how messages need to exist before audiences can be reached.

CONSTRUCTING THE ARGUMENT

Whenever you take on the task of conceptualizing and creating a presentation, you probably have more information at your fingertips than you really need. Sometimes, the sheer quantity of data forces you to try to use every piece of the puzzle at any opportune moment. The problem with that process is the entire presentation becomes a "data dump" on the audience. The visuals become cluttered and the presenter stands there reading the information on each visual to a gradually dozing crowd. Sound familiar? Who has the time to be bored with more stuff than can be remembered?

My favorite test for anyone creating a presentation is to ask, "Would you go to this thing if you didn't have to?"

The good news is that this clutter problem can easily be avoided. You just need to understand that developing quality content is a process, and the more you are involved in this process, the more you will recognize similar patterns and familiar sequences of ideas, intentions, and information. Don't be concerned with details when you begin, just concentrate and focus on the larger issues. In order to collect all the details you need to understand the whole concept.

Zero Out Your Brain
A painter starts with a fresh canvas. You need to clear your mind, relax your brain, and let your inner creative state begin to work. To do this, say the following out loud, "What do I want to talk about?" In fact, sit back in a chair and look up at the ceiling when you say it. You will be amazed at how quickly you'll "zero out" most of the rubble in your head and focus on the development of the message. Of course, there's more to this than a one-sentence exercise, but I want you to understand that the initial creative process is based on very simple actions that take place in a very relaxed atmosphere.

If you just take a step back, look at the bigger picture, relax your mind, and think clearly, you can easily find the simple pattern to a successful presentation. The logical and practical steps to developing a clear message include the following:

- Establishing a purpose
- Capturing ideas
- Creating an outline and storyboard
- Structuring ideas into a flowing script
- Using an opening "hook"
- Allowing for timely grabs
- Understanding non-linear issues

ESTABLISHING A PURPOSE

From an organizational perspective, you really need to start with a reason for creating the presentation in the first place. If you know why you are creating a presentation, you can learn how to convey it most effectively. The key to all communication is action and this is most important to visual creatures who demand constant action to understand information.

Although the word purpose answers the question "why," the word objective adds "to what extent." If you think about your purpose in the form of an objective, you'll get the impression of some action or some intention associated with the word objective.

This action in your message stems from your purpose or objective, and the resulting reaction is what you expect from the audience.

Your expectation is also known as your call to action. If you know what you want the audience to do at the end of the presentation (call to action), you can set an objective (course of action) that will get you to the result.

So, let's say you want your friends to go with you to a comedy club rather than to the museum, as originally planned. Okay, so your call to action (what you want your friends to do) is to get them to choose the comedy club. Your course of action (objective) is to convince them that the comedy club is the only choice. If your argument is convincing, they will see only one choice—comedy club!

ACTION DRIVES CONTENT

In keeping with the approach of developing content for a visual presenter, action-driven concepts are the way to go.

Therefore, your objective must always be stated in terms of action, and you must express your objective actively in the form of "to do something." Whether it is to sell, to motivate, to persuade, or any other action, the entire script must adhere to the chosen objective.

After you state the "To Do" objective using an active verb, it becomes easier to shape the story to fit the objective. For example, if the purpose or objective is "to persuade," then every item in the presentation must, in some way, directly persuade the audience.

If there are components in the presentation that do not directly match the objective, you should remove them. If not, these extraneous bits of information, although indirectly supporting your topic, will become a waste of time for your live audience. This will transform them into a dead audience. It is better to place such additional information and any extensive details in the handout materials.

TIP

> Avoid redundancy and don't be redundant! If you have several ways of displaying similar information, such as a pie chart and a bar chart, don't use both. The test for such wordiness is to examine the sequence of support items and see if you can interchange their order.
>
> If, for example, you can switch the order of a pie chart and bar chart, then one of them is probably "extra" and can be dropped from the story line.
>
> Think theatre! Can you simply switch scene one with scene two without messing up the chronology of the play?

When your purpose or objective is clear, it's easier to capture ideas and gather only the relevant supporting information needed to advance the objective.

A well thought-out objective reduces information overload because it takes less data to support a single objective than it takes to support a number of different objectives.

FINE-TUNING THE OBJECTIVE

Sometimes the definition of the objective needs to be stronger. To make the objective stronger, you need to let action act on something or someone. An action verb (to do) needs to act on a noun (to do what) for a more specific result to occur. (You didn't realize how important those fourth grade language classes were, did you?)

For example, the objective "to sell," may not be as emphatic as "to excite and stir emotions." Notice how your approach to the script feels different by adding the noun "emotions." The noun gives you a target. The type of information you'd gather to support the stronger objective would be more extreme or more crucial than otherwise might have been used. Nouns help fine-tune the expression of the objective so you can narrow down the choices of support material.

Consider the expression "to paint detailed pictures." The type of information needed for this objective would contain precise elements that accurately depict the story so that there would be no question in the minds of the audience as to how to interpret the data. Now you know to look for data elements that show detail, such as segmented vertical bar charts showing individual comparisons at specific points in time, rather than line charts which show general comparisons to a trend over time. But that is not all to consider. You might begin to gather stories and examples from real life to continue to support your objective. These may or not be depicted visually but they could be described vividly to help "paint a picture" for the audience.

Here's a good one. The strong or powerful expression "to force a single choice" makes it easier for the audience to agree to your point of view. You could have used this objective for the comedy club mentioned earlier, for instance. This fine-tuned objective tends to make you gather information that is mostly one-sided and not subject to much interpretation or argument. Data elements might include comparative tables or listings, pie charts showing percentages of the whole, and horizontal bar charts which are always used to show items at a single point in time. Stories and analogies will be clearly biased to your point of view to enhance this objective. It is not important right now to know the exact information and statistics buried in your support data. You just have to have an idea of the effort you will need to gather the level of support information you think you might use in your visuals.

The whole point of fine-tuning the objective is to stimulate your brain and get your juices flowing. Compare "to convince" with "to burn an indelible mark on the soul." Which one pushes your creative buttons more?

OBJECTIVE CHARACTERISTICS

The characteristics of the objective may further define the kinds of information required for support of the message. You use an active verb (to do) to express the objective and you may add a noun (to do what) to fine-tune the objective. If you also apply an adjective (by when or for what reason) to the objective itself, you give it character and depth.

Think of being stuck in an airport. Your objective is to get to your destination, right? What if you apply a characteristic of time to that objective? Let's say it's the beginning of your business trip rather than the end. Your objective will not only be more urgent, but the means to your destination might suddenly include a car, train, or boat in order to get there.

The following are examples of characteristics:

- Specific
- Measurable
- Time-based
- Achievable (but not already achieved)
- Relevant

For example, if the objective is to force a single choice, a measurable characteristic such as comparing features and benefits of products will match the objective because forced-choice is a result of measuring comparisons. Later, when you select support information for the presentation, you will know to look for more comparative items that measure differences.

Or, if the objective is to motivate the creative team, a time-based characteristic such as establishing a deadline for a given project will match well with the objective because the motivation for the team is to meet the deadline in order to avoid a consequence. When you select support information, you can narrow your choices to those items that relate to motivating the creative team by a certain date.

When the purpose or objective of the presentation is clearly defined and carefully fine-tuned, the number of required supporting elements will be fewer. This is because a well thought-out objective lets you get to the point quickly without displaying data that doesn't directly support the theme. You are able to focus on gathering the right information to put into the presentation. Less information means less distraction!

NOTE

Although you must have an objective, you don't have to fine-tune the objective or even find a characteristic to help shape that objective. But you should consider it as an exercise in reducing data clutter. I've spent the last 15 years showing organizations how the weaknesses in their messages ultimately limit the effectiveness of their presenters. Fine-tuning and identifying characteristics of an objective help to avoid this data overload trap!

When you think about the whole purpose behind the message, you need to come up with a compelling reason to get that message into the minds and hearts of the audience. That's why working with your objective makes sense and why you have to understand the importance of this early phase of the process. After you get your brain thinking in these terms, every script you create will follow a similar pattern, even though the content itself will keep changing.

How Do You Select an Objective?

We covered that an objective must be action-driven and contain an active verb. You've also seen how it helps to fine-tune the objective into a more descriptive expression and even more beneficial to understand certain characteristics of the objective. But how do you make the choice from the start?

Is the objective chosen at random? Is it based on any secret formula? Is it an educated guess? In reality, you can be very accurate in your choice of objective by simply knowing what you plan to say at the very END of the presentation. Your conclusion is critical to your strategy and contains key points that you want to cover.

Think about it. If you tell a joke, you must know the punch line. If you get in a car, you need to know the destination. You prove to yourself all the time that you need to know the END before you know where to START.

Do Your Conclusion First

The key to selecting your objective is to create your last impression first. This doesn't mean you should present the last visual at the beginning of your presentation; rather, do your conclusion first in order to set the pattern or direction for all of the supporting elements to be presented.

Your last impression, or conclusion, is the verbal description of your overall objective. Think of your conclusion as a dartboard and each of the concepts as a dart. Each concept and support item must be directed at the dartboard in order to be effective. All components of the script MUST point to the "bull's-eye" or the overall objective. You may not always hit the bull's-eye, but if you don't even hit the dartboard—Blllllaaaannnnppp! Thanks for playing!

Remember that call to action we talked about earlier? Well here it is again.

The call to action that you expect from your audience is directly related to the expression of your objective. For example, if you plan on concluding your presentation with the phrase, "Thank you very much and I hope you will each buy one of our products," then you must have been trying to sell. Each component of your script would then support the objective of SELLING something to the audience, whether it is a product, a concept, or an idea.

If the last thing you plan to say is, "Thank you very much and I hope you learned everything about PowerPoint," then you must have been trying to educate. Every part of your script would have to support the objective of educating the audience, in some direct way, on the features, benefits, processes, or procedures of PowerPoint. Your closing remark summarized your expectation of the group ("I hope you learned") and it was originally expressed as the objective to educate.

Naturally, you can always fine-tune the objective and match a characteristic to the objective to help narrow down your choices of support material. But the original selection process comes from knowing what you want to have happen when the presentation is over.

As Stephen R. Covey, author of *The Seven Habits of Highly Effective People*, says, "Start with the end in mind."

CAPTURING IDEAS

Despite what you may have heard, great ideas are not found on supermarket shelves, they are not a dime a dozen, and they certainly aren't driven by genius. Coming up with truly great ideas usually involves brainstorming, a process that allows the mind to spontaneously bring forth ideas. At times, the development of the message is left strictly to one person; other times that brainstorming process is shared.

The good news is that in both cases the methods by which we capture ideas vary and there is no exact science as to what will produce the perfect script for a presentation. However, several techniques will help you selectively choose related concepts from the available "pool" of ideas. These tools help narrow your choices so that the next part of the process, the outline and storyboard, can be easier.

The following are four different tools that are used to capture ideas for a presentation:

- Fish-Bone Diagram
- Flow Chart
- Affinity Diagram
- Mind Map

FISH-BONE DIAGRAM

The *fish-bone diagram* links supporting visuals to a consistent theme (objective). Supporting visuals are linked by like causes while supporting the root cause. Confused yet? A good analogy might be to imagine a highway and the exit ramps off the highway. Then, think of the roads that connect to the exit ramps. That's the picture I'm painting here. Be careful how far you stray from the main highway with supporting information or else the audience may not be able to follow the map to your final destination.

Take a look at Figure 24.1. The end result (call to action) is supported by three categories for grouping your ideas. The most important category is placed closest to the end result because it represents ideas nearest the purpose (objective) of the message. Categories father from the end result represent more supportive ideas for the argument.

TIP

> A good rule is to structure about three groups that support the main message and then have no more than three supporting messages beneath each group. If you branch out too far, the audience might not be able to get back on track.

Figure 24.1
This is the layout you can use for a fishbone diagram. Notice how supporting ideas (sub-category, elements) branch from main (category) ideas.

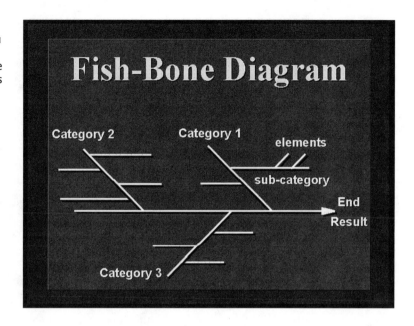

When capturing ideas to a fish-bone diagram, fill in the blank lines where needed with ideas that support the closest or most immediate concept and look for data elements (support information) that match those ideas.

FLOW CHART

A *flow chart* forces you to think in "stages" of action and tends to show that one step leads to another. Similar to the fish-bone diagram, flow charts, however, are mostly used when showing decision-based branching or interactivity. For example, non-linear electronic presentations may allow a particular subject or issue to be explored further only if the presenter prefers it that way, usually based on some cues or questions from the audience.

If you take a look at Figure 24.2, you'll see how the flow chart helps you place your ideas in sequence, noting any areas where choices might be made to further the message to its conclusion. Maybe after making your first point you check for agreement in the crowd. If they agree, you move on; if not, you bring in more evidence to support your argument. In an electronic presentation, this might mean selecting an object on the visual which contains an action to display another visual, not necessarily in sequence, which hold more information.

→ For more information on how to create interactive elements within an electronic presentation, **see** "Using Action Buttons," in Chapter 15, "Working with Animation," **p. 334**.

The key to a flow chart is in the logical flow of continuous action. Remove an element and the flow is broken. You can create a flow chart out of a simple day in your life.

If you think about your commute to work, your morning activity, your lunch hour, your afternoon, and your commute home, you have a flow chart. Now, imagine that as a giant flow chart across the wall of your bedroom. But don't lose any sleep over it. The process is a simple one.

Figure 24.2
Here's how you "flow chart" your ideas. This shows how back-up or supplemental data can be used by the presenter only if needed to force a decision at that point.

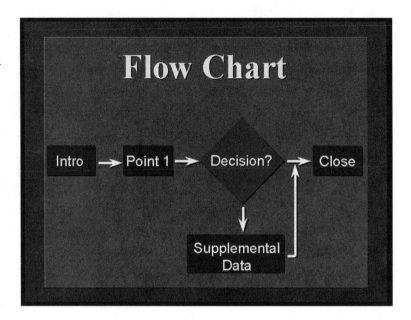

The point is to keep it simple, logical and flowing. If you have a process-driven presentation, consider using the flow chart as a tool to capture ideas into the process. You will easily see how some ideas, although seemingly important on their own, actually do not fit the flow chart's process-oriented structure. This will reduce the number of ideas you can squeeze into one continuous flow of information.

AFFINITY DIAGRAM

An *affinity diagram* helps you sort out your ideas into categories. Think about dropping your ideas into a bunch of different buckets all of which relate to the main theme. If you look at Figure 24.3, you'll see how the categories are decided in advance, before brainstorming the ideas needed to support each of the categories.

By grouping closely related activities, you outline ideas based on agreed-upon categories—or "buckets"—of information. By tossing ideas into these specific buckets, you fill each category with the main points that you know you have to make in order to satisfy the category. The key to this method of capturing ideas is to agree on the categories in the first place.

For example, Figure 24.4 shows the agreed-upon information buckets to drop ideas into for this presentation. Perhaps this is how the meeting went that day. Someone said, "We have to talk about pricing," and the idea about pricing was placed in the financial category. Someone else mentioned "memory" and the idea of memory was placed under features. But another person said, "We should discuss the service policies of the company." Even though service is an important part of the company, the idea didn't fit any of the categories originally defined. Unless we stretch the meaning of what can be included in a specific category, there won't be any service-talk in this presentation.

Figure 24.3
The affinity diagram limits your ideas to predefined categories, or "buckets." This helps you focus on the exact message and prevents you from including non-essential information.

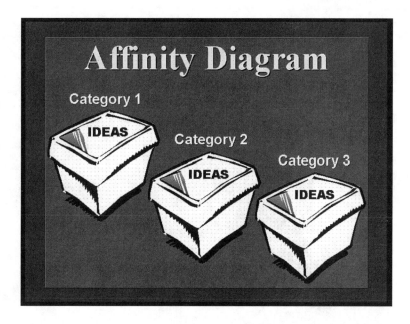

Although the service policies are important, it is not the right information to be brought up during this particular presentation. Think of it this way: Ford makes cars and trucks, but they are not shown in the same commercial.

TIP

> Limit your categories to three or four, and limit your ideas per category to about the same number. You'll need at least one item of visual support for each idea. If you have too many categories or ideas within categories, the presentation may drag on too long.

MIND MAP

If Felix Unger is the affinity diagram, then Oscar Madison is the *mind map*! But don't assume chaos is a bad thing. In fact, when it comes to brainstorming, it's quite the opposite.

Mind mapping is a technique that starts with a major theme or concept and then looks for immediate supporting issues. After the main issues are defined, additional support can be considered. Each idea you write down may spawn another related idea and so on. The underlying support for each of the main issues ultimately supports the overall theme.

However, as you place ideas farther from the center of the map, you attach a lower importance to the idea, and, as a result, you need less support information for that idea. A mind map template, shown in Figure 24.5, illustrates the placement of ideas in relation to a central theme or core concept.

Figure 24.4
A filled-in affinity diagram showing how the "tossed-in" ideas or discussion points are grouped according to four different predefined categories.

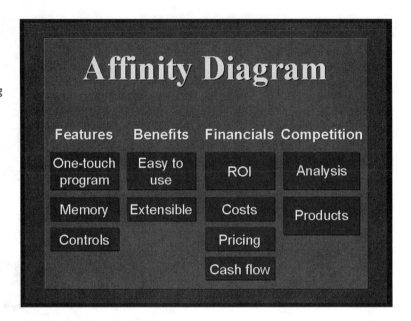

Although this appears similar to the affinity diagram, the mind map adds a different dimension to gathering ideas. It allows many ideas to make it to the table, and then tries to categorize each idea into a particular mainstream concept. The added dimension is distance. Once an idea is placed on the mind map, you are able to see how close to the center of the map it is and therefore determine its importance in the presentation.

TIP

> Think of the center of the mind map as the core of an apple. To reach the core, you have to bite deeper into the apple. Ideas (items) closer to the core need stronger support or deeper explanation. Knowing the proximity of an idea to the central theme helps you decide how in-depth a concept should be covered when presented.

Because mind maps are usually associated with concepts and concepts are abstract, one supporting idea may be usable in more than one area of the mind map. Where you decide to place the idea will determine the amount of support you'll need for that idea. If, however, you use an idea more than once on the map, then you may need to use different levels of support for the same idea at different points in the script. Is your brain hurting yet?

For example, in Figure 24.6, the idea *Recognize* appears in two areas of the map. It is part of the *Fun Workplace* concept under *Recruiting*, which is one of the issues of *Management Control*. *Recognize* also appears as part of *Motivate*, a subset of *Ownership*, which stems from *Authority*, which relates to *Accounting* (yet another issue of *Management Control*). The two ideas are at different distances from the center of the map. So when you look at each idea called "Recognize," you can count the levels each sits from the core. In one area there are two levels to pass through to reach the core; in another area there are four levels to pass through.

Figure 24.5
A sample mind map, showing how ideas are placed in relation to the core concept. A "second idea" is one that supports an original idea, which supports the core concept.

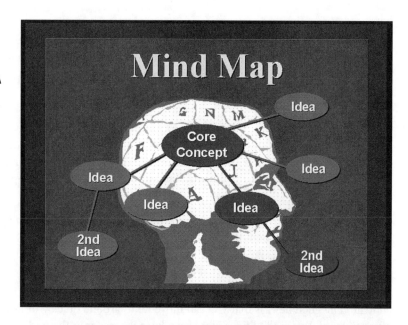

Figure 24.6
A mind map shows levels of the thought process.

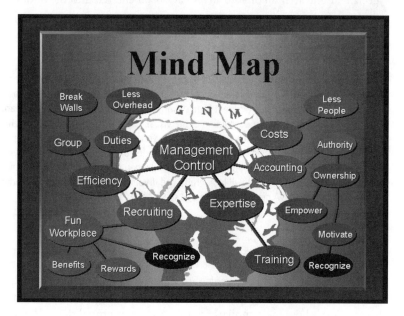

In the first instance, the idea of recognition is closer to the core or central theme of management control (count the levels). Knowing this, you should use more support and explanation during the discussion of "recognition" at this point in the presentation than during the other reference. So after seeing where in the map the idea appears and how close to ground zero it really is, then you can gather your support information accordingly.

The other advantage of the mind map is that at a glance you can decide if the ideas are straying too far from the core, causing the presentation to become more drawn out. I suggest you keep the levels to no more than three: main theme (core), supporting issues, and supporting data for those issues. This makes for a shorter, more concise presentation. Remember, a mind map is a terrible thing to waste!

CREATING AN OUTLINE AND STORYBOARD

After you have gathered the main ideas and concepts that support your overall objective, you can create an outline and storyboard. The outline is simply a list of headings with some degree of detail attached to a few items. The storyboard is a visual example of the items in the outline.

You don't really have to create both an outline and a storyboard, but it helps to see a list of items categorized in sections as well as a visual sketch of those items.

ELECTRONICALLY CREATING AN OUTLINE AND STORYBOARD

PowerPoint simultaneously updates your outline and your storyboard (visuals) as you add content. The good news is that you can move items around quickly in PowerPoint, which is especially useful after all of your ideas have been entered into the outline.

→ For more information about outline and storyboards, **see** "Understanding PowerPoint Views," in Chapter 1, "Introducing PowerPoint 2003," **p. 29**.

TIP

> As you enter each idea or concept into the outline, PowerPoint uses a default "slide layout," typically a bullet chart. If you have support information that you know will be displayed in a different format, such as a data-driven chart, simply change the layout and enter a text description of the visual, plus the type of chart you prefer (pie, bar, line, and so forth). Later, when you create your visuals, you'll know what type of chart you were considering when you entered the idea or concept. Of course, any notes you typed into the layout will have to be removed when you actually begin designing the chart. Otherwise, it will look pretty bad if your final presentation has headings that say things like "A pie chart goes in this space" and "Try a bar chart here."

When you create an outline or storyboard in PowerPoint, some serious visual design is already happening. The very nature of the software is designed to "multitask" and to do two things at once for you. Let the software do the work and don't worry. Rather than be concerned about the design issues at this point, just try to get your ideas into the outline and then organize those ideas similarly to the way you captured them. Remember, you're not designing the visuals yet, only sketching ideas into a rough visible format.

MANUALLY CREATING AN OUTLINE AND STORYBOARD

If you are creating a storyboard on paper for later input into PowerPoint, then simply make a rough sketch of how you see each idea visualized. For example, at my company

(MediaNet, Inc.), we have created over 1,000 PowerPoint presentations from handwritten notes and sketches sent to us by clients. This is probably a familiar process in your company as well. Lots of people scribble out some rough-looking visuals just to help them visualize the information. Although it is much easier to use PowerPoint for the task of organizing content, you can also tackle the process manually on paper.

On paper, you can create the outline in a hierarchical (first to last) structure. Just remember a few of the outlining rules from school, such as "every A needs a B,"—meaning that you can't have only one supporting point for a major idea—you need at least two. Still wishing you showed up for the fourth grade, huh?

The outline is easy, but the storyboard is a bit more difficult when created manually. The design of the visuals is usually taken from the original sketches in the storyboard. All the information chosen to support the story needs to be presented in a clearly readable format.

Most people belong to the "8 1/2×11 crowd." That is, those who use an entire sheet of paper, squeeze as much information as possible onto it, and then expect to later convert the clutter into a presentation visual. It's true. You take a standard sheet of paper, a magic marker (no one thinks of using a pencil with an eraser!) and you write on both sides of the sheet—and you call it—a visual. The days of the full-page of typewritten text with the little letter "o" for the bullet are gone.

CAUTION

> If you do create a cluttered storyboard with each concept represented by a massive amount of needless information, do not—I repeat—do not invite me to your next presentation! Or, invite me, but allow me to bring a pillow.

A storyboard sketch of each visual should not take up a full, 66-line typewritten sheet of paper. When projected, the final image from that original sketch needs to be clearly seen from a distance. This means the text and any other elements should be large and the only way to insure that is to limit the amount of data placed on the visual in the first place.

The best way to limit what can be placed on a single visual is to take a piece of standard paper and fold it in half before you design anything. Of course this doesn't mean you should write twice as small! But it does force you into a smaller workspace and help you avoid cluttering the image with extensive information that may not be readable for the audience when projected.

Another option is to use 5"×7" index cards to storyboard your ideas. The advantage of index cards is that they can be spread on a flat surface, like a table, and can be moved around as needed to organize your storyboard images into a proper flow. This is the manual version of the slide sorter in PowerPoint. You can probably now see how valuable the software is to the planning process when you consider the alternative of doing this manually.

The goal is to limit the information so the audience can spend more time listening and watching. Studies have shown that people retain only 10% of what they read but 70% of what they see and hear. Use this as hint to stop the data, spare us the details, and save the presentation! Can I make this any clearer! Less words on the screen means more words in your mouth. Remember the KISS principle—Keep It Simple, Stupid!

STRUCTURING IDEAS INTO A FLOWING SCRIPT

An outline and a storyboard help organize captured ideas into a format ready for design. But another issue must be addressed and that is making the presentation presentable. To support the notion of a visual presenter in terms of the script, the strategy is to link ideas so that a person can convey them. The script itself, the story line, must be structured so that the ideas flow easily from paper to people.

Earlier I asked you to think about the big picture when examining the purpose; now you should start thinking about the finer details. When you structure your ideas into some cohesive format, you may think it's easiest to give the audience the big picture and then back that up with the smaller details. That may work in some instances, but you should really consider the opposite strategy, as well.

Our world is complex and we seek simplicity. You will be more effective if you first get right to the immediate issue of the presentation and then offer the larger-than-life view.

One way to look at it is to think of a presentation as a big dinner. The menu is the view of the meal, but the selection is the anticipation of the taste. Then consider how the chosen meal is served: one course at a time. Each course needs to be segmented or cut into bite-size pieces in order to be consumed.

If the courses are the big picture items and the bite-size pieces are the details, from the server's (presenter's) point of view, the order of information should be from bigger to smaller. But, if you look at it from a taster's (audience's) point of view, the food on the fork is more important than the rest of the stuff on the table.

Maybe I've only succeeded in making you hungry, but I want you to begin to see how the details of the argument actually stimulate the anticipation of the audience more than the big picture.

Micro-to-Macro Strategy

Regardless of the method used to construct an argument, each script usually has a mixture of the "small details" and the "big picture." The terms micro and macro can be used to describe these views of the world. Typically, in a presentation, you separate the macro items (market data, trends, company information, and competition) from the micro items (stories, analogies, specific examples, features, and benefits).

Although the big picture is usually chosen as the starting point for a script, the small details are the qualifiers of the argument. Because time is an issue to a listener, getting to the details is more critical than hearing about the general trends. For example, you would obviously prefer to know whether the route you take to work is clear before you care to know that your city is the eighth most traffic-congested in the country.

When a script is constructed in a micro-to-macro fashion, the unique issues you bring to the table are discussed first and the broad-based marketing data is secondary. The good news is that if you accidentally run out of time in the presentation, the audience only misses the general information. Chances are, they can find that data if and when they choose.

No matter which way you choose to present the information, you still have to develop a pattern or a structure to the script so the information can be absorbed properly.

Think of the structure as the type of script that is used to convey the message. Most presentations follow a linear pattern, which moves from an opening through the body and, finally, into the closing. This open-body-close process is very common and usually expected as the metaphor for receiving information. The good news is that you have a choice of about five types of scripts you can use to convey a message in a linear presentation:

- Matching Ideals
- Main Points
- Question and Answer
- Meeting Needs
- Problem-Solution

Seven "F" Words

From the great works of literature to the trashiest novels, in theatre, movies, or television, you'll find basically seven scripts. No matter what the plot, it fits into one of the seven scripts. Those scripts all begin with the letter F: Fact, Failure, Fantasy, Fear, Fidelity, Freedom, and Fortune. From these scripts all plots are hatched.

The lesson here is that variety stems from simplicity. Consider that only 26 letters make up our alphabet; look at how many words we have, not to mention books! There are only 12 notes on a musical scale (including sharps and the start of the next octave), and yet look at how many songs and musical scores we have!

The writer must master the alphabet first. The singer must master the notes first. Having mastered the subtleties of action within the seven scripts, an actor is able to play many different roles.

Whether it's messages, media, or mechanics, the entire process of creativity is predicated on the notion that simplicity yields variety. When applied to the message, the simplicity in script structure yields a variety of presentations.

MATCHING IDEALS

This structure is really a "set-up" for the audience. The plan is that you describe the ideal product or service, which, of course, you know will closely resemble your product or service. Since the audience accepts your description as the "premise" of the argument, it is quite easy to match your argument to the premise you set up in the first place. This structure is usually used more for products than for services since attributes of a product are more tangible (visible) than qualities of a service.

For example, you selectively mention the ideal attributes of a good car. You say, "The ideal car has front-wheel drive, dual air bags, a rear defrost, and a trunk release." You naturally get the audience's agreement that these are the ideal attributes of a good car. Then you describe your car in terms of the ideal, making sure you only compare to about 90% of the ideal. You say, "Our car has front-wheel drive, dual air bags, a rear defrost, and we're still working on the trunk release." You see, you never want to compare to 100% because that would mean you have the "perfect" product (which no one does), and it would leave you no room for improvement (how do you improve on perfection?).

Nothing is perfect. Ever buy a pair of jeans? Wait, let me rephrase that. Ever buy a pair of jeans that fit? I rest my case. The matching ideals script is designed to lead the audience to an understanding that the product (or service) is the best one for the job, but it may not do the whole job. Sounds like a politician to me!

MAIN POINTS

Typically, this structure is used with information-based presentations such as those dealing with financial results and other historical data. The process follows the familiar pattern of:

> Tell 'em what you're gonna tell 'em
>
> Tell 'em
>
> Tell 'em what you told 'em

One way to identify this structure is the appearance of an agenda early in the presentation and a corresponding summary at the end. This lets the audience know what to expect and then anticipate what to remember.

The summary at the end is critical because main points can be hard to remember especially when a large number of supporting points are discussed. The audience may get lost unless they are constantly made aware of how the supporting information relates to the main points.

QUESTION AND ANSWER

Question and answer scripting is similar to educational activities of "pre-test" and "post-test." This is useful in training sessions with a lot of unrelated, yet comprehensive, information.

First you pre-test the audience's knowledge of a subject using easy-to-answer questions (true/false, multiple choice). The questions cover all the major points you expect to convey during the session. Then, during the session, you reveal the correct answers using supporting visual elements to explain each answer as you elaborate. Finally, you ask the audience as a group to answer the original questions (post-test).

A question and answer scripting structure can be used in a variety of situations including surveys, polls, and research studies. The important point to remember is that the objective should address how the information is used by the audience toward some result. One way to ensure that the information is more than just a data dump is to repeat key points and summarize conclusions at several stages of the presentation. Repetition will aid in retention of concepts and ideas. Repetition will aid in retention of concepts and ideas. Repetition will aid in retention of concepts and ideas. Any questions?

MEETING NEEDS

Sometimes called the "helping hand" script, this structure starts with the needs of the audience in mind. This is often used in sales presentations where you put the needs of the customer up front and then show how you can address those needs.

But, for business, a first glance at this meeting needs script may seem an easy task. But more often than not, presentations using this format tend to treat all needs on an equal basis. This becomes a problem because if all needs are truly equal, then priorities cannot be set and decisions take longer to reach. If, however, you attach importance to specific needs, you create a sense of gratification by meeting those needs in the order of their importance. This builds value for you in the eyes of the audience.

For example, suppose you are a computer consulting firm specializing in solving computer virus problems. You are giving a "new business" pitch to a potential client who has the following "needs":

- 24-hour on-site support
- High-level data security
- Detailed reporting
- Expert advice
- Budget constraints

Initially, you might flag "budget constraints" as critical (to you) since it represents your paycheck, so to speak. After all, you do want to get paid for your work. But the meeting needs script structure is meant to place the client's needs up front. In that case, data security and expert advice are more important to the client. But, if you address each of the needs equally, you create equal impact on the last item (the one critical to you). This makes meeting your needs equal to meeting the client needs and makes the client consider budget contraints as strongly as the other issues.

But, if you prioritize the needs and give more weight to the data security and the expert advice issues, you may create an opportunity to build value for your services as the client realizes how well you can meet his primary needs. Less importance will be shifted to the limitations of the budget. This ultimately serves your purpose.

Once you know the priority of the customer needs, you can address those important issues first. Then, you can summarize how you can help with other issues that may not have been verbalized as a "top priority," but may be important to the scope of the project or activity. The point is that many issues are brought into a presentation, some of which can have a negative impact on your objective. By concentrating on primary needs you limit the attention placed on less important and perhaps frivolous needs that could have otherwise stalled the process.

PROBLEM-SOLUTION

Also known as the "divide and conquer" script, the problem-solution structure is one of the most effective scripts you can use, especially for high-level, decision-based presentations. Whereas the meeting needs structure focuses on the goals ahead, the problem-solution structure concentrates on the mistakes of the past. That's why I love this script. It concentrates on failure, it thrives on fear, it accentuates the negative—and it leaves the door open for a hero to save the day! It's like Superman!

The process follows a simple pattern. First, the overall problem is described and presented in a manner that makes it look bleak or negative. Then, you dissect the problem into smaller sections that can be addressed individually. Finally, the solutions to the smaller areas will solve the big problem, as well, and the result will always look positive.

Politicians use the problem-solution scenario frequently. The political candidate announces, "The country is going downhill, crime and inflation are out of control, your children have no future." Immediately you feel depressed hearing the problems at hand. Seconds later, the candidate continues, "…but our party has the solution!" Suddenly you feel better, as if the day has been saved. Okay, it really isn't exactly that way, but you get the idea.

From a business presentation perspective, the problem-solution script can be highly effective because it plays on a very powerful human emotion: Fear. If problems can't be solved, then the consequences may be harmful. This can cause fear and anxiety.

In fact with so many companies touting solutions these days, I keep thinking we're going to run out of problems! Now that is a problem we need to solve. The solution to running out of problems would be to have fewer solutions. Then, we would end up having more problems than solutions. I feel better already, how about you?

The problem-solution script positions the presenter as a solution provider for existing problems. Try saying that five times fast! Since most people are cautious and conservative, this kind of script appeals to a sense of urgency.

Of all the structures available, I most prefer the problem-solution type. Any scripts that involve a sense of urgency will always be the most effective because urgency relates to the limits of time, and time, once lost, can never be retrieved.

Problem-Solution Scenario

Many times I find that presentations are poorly constructed using the problem-solution approach. I usually suggest this pattern. The opening of the presentation should state the case in this order: problem, consequence of inaction, sense of urgency, and solution.

For example, let's say your company markets a software program that keeps track of Internet access. The following italicized text is an example of the conceptual script that might be used.

First, you quickly tell the audience the problem. You state how *employees spend a growing percentage of the workday accessing the Internet for non-business related information*.

Next, examine the consequence of inaction. In other words, what happens if nobody does anything about the problem? You indicate that without action, the *consequence will be a reduction of productivity in the workplace*.

Okay, here's the clincher! Attach a timeframe to action in order to establish a sense of urgency. After all, without urgency there is less need to solve the problem today. In other words, if they do see the problem, how long can they wait to do something about it? You mention that *less productivity from lost time reduces the ability to adapt quickly to constant changes in the industry.*

Finally, you must address the problem with your specific solution. Without a link to your special way of solving the problem, you will only end up educating the audience by increasing general awareness of the problem. Therefore you show that your software *limits Internet access to non-business information using a unique process, thereby allowing a company to maximize productivity into a competitive advantage.*

This entire scenario—problem-consequence-urgency-solution—should be shared up front with the audience in less than one minute to set the stage for the rest of the presentation.

USING AN OPENING HOOK

We spent a lot of time covering objectives, ideas, and structures, and by now, you should have some grasp on how to construct the argument in order to move an audience to some call to action. But now we have to think about jump-starting the presentation with an opening hook.

Every time I consult on a client presentation, I ask, "What's the hook?" and the response is usually, "What's a hook?" That's when I say, "How long have you worked at the company, not counting tomorrow?" The hook is the very reason the audience wishes to remain in the room for the rest of the presentation.

A hook is used for the purpose of changing something about the way an audience thinks. A hook can be any credible or even doubtful piece of information, which, when presented, causes the audience to immediately react. Whether it be a bit of research, a little known but interesting fact, a revelation, a controversial opinion, a current event, or simply a smile in the face of defeat, the opening hook sets the stage for the rest of the presentation.

I find a statistic can make for a great opening hook. For example, an opening hook I use for my "Electrifying Presentations" seminars is a series of statistics which position the physical "presentation skill," the actual art of delivery, as contributing to over 90% of the communication message. It doesn't mean that content is unimportant; rather, that content needs to be clear and concise since we process more of what we see than anything else.

That hook is important because it forces the audience to make a choice—do they agree or disagree? For those who agree, they spend the rest of the presentation nodding their heads as the evidence to support the hook is presented. For those who disagree, they spend the rest of the presentation tilting their heads looking for more evidence as to why they should change sides. Both groups are forced to change the way they think in order to keep sitting through the presentation.

What happens is this: An audience arrives at the presentation in neutral. Their emotions and thoughts have yet to be swayed. Your goal is to get them in gear—forward or reverse—it doesn't matter, but you must create a sense of action. Just like the objective is positioned to do something, the audience needs to be pushed to do something, too. Think of them as sitting on a fence and trying to push them to one side or the other. If I'm still on the fence

24

at the end of your presentation, I haven't accomplished anything and neither have you. We both lose. You have to influence the group in some way.

Rarely is this done visually onscreen, as in a before/after comparision. The hook is more of a fact or statement that challenges the status quo or belief system. Even if you displayed a visual of something powerful, such as natural disaster or a victory celebration, you would still have to verbally interpret the hook for the audience. A visual which supports your hook needs to be placed in context and described. Usually, you don't need the visual at all since the description is likely to stand on its own.

The value of the hook is in the timing. When the presentation starts, how long does it take before the group is being influenced by your objective (to sell, to motivate, to convince, or whatever)? How long do you let them sit on the fence in neutral?

The longer it takes you to employ your objective, the harder it gets to arrive at the call to action. However, using an opening hook can instantly affect the audience and get them to make choices about your message.

For example, if you started a presentation by saying, "By the end of the day you will lose all excess weight, look 10 years younger, and add one million dollars to your income!" I'd say that's a pretty good hook. Sign me up!

NOTE

> Don't use a fact for no reason. For example, mentioning that over 83% of all Paul Newman movies have the letter H somewhere in the title may be factual, but is really just trivial, especially because the audience can't control the likelihood that future Paul Newman movies won't have an H somewhere in the title!

The hook can even tap into an audience's sense of urgency for the presentation to be over. One of the best opening hooks I heard a presenter give was to a group of time-starved executives at the beginning of a sales presentation. The presenter said, "This can take five minutes or five hours, but you're going to buy something!" Each person in that room glanced at the clock and was instantly swayed from thinking "Do I want to buy?" to wondering "Do I want buy now or five hours from now? "

ALLOWING FOR TIMELY GRABS

Although an opening hook creates action in the minds of the audience, timely grabs are used to hold the attention of the audience across sections of the script. These grabbers pepper the script at specific points with interesting information, personal experiences, or other stimulating items that relate to or help further the message.

Grabbers include:

- Stories
- Examples

- Analogies
- Statistics
- Interaction
- Questions
- Repetition
- Shock
- Suspense
- Special Effects (animation, sound, video)

TIP

> When using analogies, try to make them as real-world as possible. The advantage of drawing a likeness between something in your content and an everyday activity is that the audience transfers the benefits of the very real experience to your information.
>
> For example, a simple analogy for a maker of digital video cameras might be to specify that a particular model is the Cadillac of the industry. The public impression of Cadillac is one of quality and a transfer is made by the audience to the digital camera as having a high quality.
>
> Typical real-world analogies include references to transportation, household appliances, food, travel, and entertainment. The more the reference applies to everyday experience, the faster the connection is made by the audience.

Grabbers should directly relate to the topic, but can come from nowhere and be completely unrelated to anything you're discussing. It depends on what you want to do with the audience. Unrelated grabbers are used typically to inject life into the crowd. Let's say it's one hour after lunch. You might notice the audience is losing focus, appearing glassy-eyed, getting a bit drowsy. Although it's possible you are boring them to sleep, the head-bobbing is more from the blood leaving the head to travel to the stomach to digest food.

You might have to do something unrelated. I have a full-day seminar/workshop, which has a topic called "Multimedia vs. Multimania." It's one of the eight topics for the day, but it is strategically placed about one hour after the lunch break. In the middle of the lecture is a 10-minute game show on the order of a "Name That Tune" contest. It has less to do with the guidelines for using multimedia than it does to wake the audience up from a low energy point. Plus, it's fun! And you know something, you can have fun and learn at the same time!

UNDERSTANDING NON-LINEAR ISSUES

Non-linear presentations offer the greatest flexibility for a repetitive presentation with a changing audience. With experience, presenters learn where the questions arise and to what extent "back-up," or supporting information, is needed.

The technique employed in these presentations relates to features within PowerPoint, specifically Action buttons and hyperlinks. See Chapters 15, "Working with Animation," and 16, "Using PowerPoint's Web Features," for more information on the use of these features.

Using a non-linear structure, you can

- Answer expected or unexpected questions with back-up support information
- Analyze "what if" scenarios by linking to spreadsheets and other data
- Show "generic" presentations to different audiences and use back-up data only where necessary

If you decide to display back-up information based on audience responses, make sure the information is "general" enough to warrant display.

If you decide to do "what-if" scenarios in front of an audience where a software application needs to be used, make sure you know the software well and don't get caught up in details or small changes.

The following situations are some in which a non-linear approach may be effective:

- Show only the "overview" to busy executives and more detailed levels to subordinates
- Adapt to an audience's knowledge level by giving details only where needed
- Respond to different audiences' priorities by showing most important information to that particular audience first

The same way you tell a story based on limited time is the way to think about non-linear access to information. If you have the time, show it. But show limited amounts of information—enough to make the point.

You may have to pre-plan a lot of this "branching" information and you may not be asked to show it all. Usually, a presentation done several times to different audiences tells a presenter where the supporting information belongs.

Make sure you incorporate a "go back" button! Don't leave someone in la-la land wondering how to get back to the original story! Non-linear navigation can be confusing if you don't have a way to get back on track after you've branched off to a supporting item. This is why non-linear presentations are usually meant for an audience of one (like at a kiosk); or, they are thought-out so far in advance to cover every interactive possibility that they end up falling into the pattern of a typical linear presentation. The key thing to remember is not to lose control of the event.

QUALIFYING THE PARTICIPANTS

So what do you really know about the speaker and the listeners? The ability to understand attributes of both the presenter and the audience is critical to the message. The objective and the target audience for that objective are so closely intertwined that you should consider them as coexisting. It's like the Sinatra song "Love and Marriage," where he sings, "you can't have one, you can't have none, you can't have one without the uhhhhhhhh-uh-uhhh-ther!" (You're trying to sing that right now, aren't you? I thought so.)

The message is buried between the speaker and the listener. In fact, all presentations follow a standard communication model (Sender—Message—Receiver). For visual presenters the model can be described more theatrically as Actor—Action—Audience. Regardless of the terms, the human elements of the process—the sender (presenter) and the receiver (audience)—are key to the presentation process and crucial to message development.

You need to know the following in order to create messages that tap into specific aspects of both the sender and receiver in the communication model:

- Learning the traits of the presenter
- Knowing the particulars of the audience
- Targeting motivators and filters

LEARNING THE TRAITS OF THE PRESENTER

If you are the presenter of your own message, then you already know your own likes, dislikes, habits, and so forth. But if you have to prepare a message or even the visual support for the message for another person to deliver, then the following section can offer you some helpful information.

In order to construct a believable message, it helps if you know certain characteristics or traits of the presenter. The more the presenter is involved in the message, the better the delivery. Of course, I've seen presentations where I've questioned whether the presenter was actually alive during the event. You're not laughing because some of these people work at your company! Okay, so you have to be prepared and you have to get to know your presenters.

Some points to consider for knowing the traits of the speaker:

- Personal attributes
- Delivery style
- Expertise level
- Media preferences

In the real world, you may never have the time to really gather this information. In fact, many of those who create content do so for others to present. In a number of situations, the content providers never even see the presenters. Some actually may feel that's a good thing, but, collaboration is the key to effective messaging. So, you have to find ways of working together with a presenter who may be delivering your content. The goal is to get a dialog going. When a presenter has input, the script becomes more personal and will be delivered more emphatically.

24

TIP

> Send only the outline of the presentation to one or more presenters and ask for suggestions on the order of topics to be covered (not the content, just the order). Wherever a person makes comments, marks, or notes is where the script is more personal and appeals to the presenter.

PERSONAL ATTRIBUTES

One of the things I like to do immediately when working with a presenter is to ask one of three "favorites": I want to know his or her favorite type of movie (action, mystery, romance); favorite type of music (rock, jazz, classical); and favorite type of sport to watch or play (football, golf, tennis). (Sometimes I can even get bank account numbers if I push hard enough!)

For example, let's say I'm coaching you. You tell me that you prefer action movies. I would look for some obvious characteristics about action movies, such as "split-second decision-making, sense of urgency, attention to detail, even a hero who saves the day." Perhaps you have some or all of those traits or at least admire those traits in others.

I then look for parts of the script that relate (or could relate) to decision-making, especially the split-second kind. I would search for other parts that involve sense of urgency or attention to detail. There may even be a part in the script where a problem is solved and the "hero saves the day." At those specific points in the presentation, I would ask you, the presenter, to recount personal experiences (stories), cite specific examples, or use some other informative grabbers for the audience. Your energy and enthusiasm will be greater during any moment that is closer to some attribute of your personality. If you have a greater stake in the details, you will deliver the information with more confidence.

NOTE

> The more personal a message is to you, the more you will express it with conviction. It's not about what the topic means—it's about what the topic means to you.

DELIVERY STYLE

Whenever I am working with someone, I look for special elements in the person's delivery style. Style is an interesting word that can mean so many things. If you need to find out more about a presenter, ask some questions.

For example, is she outgoing? Does she like to interact with the audience? Is she comfortable in front of her superiors? The answers to questions such as these will help you frame the message from a presenter point-of-view.

A presenter who likes to interact and "get in close" with the audience, for example, might be more at ease sharing personal experiences rather than displaying numerous statistics. Someone who loves details and trivia may prefer to point out the hidden meanings by reading between the lines or going inside the numbers.

When you know more about the personality of the presenter, it can make your job easier as a content-provider for a speaker who needs less support data than you may have expected. As you shape the message with a presenter in mind, you may find additional opportunities for unique grabbers, such as humor, simply based on the delivery style of the presenter.

EXPERTISE LEVEL

Knowing how in-depth a presenter understands the topic and the key concepts associated with the message is extremely helpful in your efforts to shaping the quantity of content.

For example, if a presenter has a great deal of expertise, the content can be more visual than verbal, more conceptual than concrete. Ah, but keep in mind that we favor the visual presenter. The script should contain broad concepts and limited data so that the audience spends more time listening, watching, and interacting with the presenter and less time reading the screen.

However, there are times when the expertise leads to wordiness, and the audience is bombarded with too many long-winded explanations. What I've noticed is the greater your vocabulary, the harder it is for you to get to the point. It's true. For some reason, when a presenter has more command of language, the longer it takes for him or her to get to the heart of the matter.

That's why a lot of times when I'm coaching someone I'll say, "You probably write well, don't you?" People who write well tend to speak like they write. They keep adding additional phrases and lengthier descriptions as they deliver the message. They'll say "What's important here, what you really need to understand, what is truly critical to note, in this instance." *Ahhhhhhhhh* just get to the point!

I'm not saying that poor language skills make for better presenters; instead, full command of the language needs to be regulated in order to entice an audience to want to know more. If you have presenters that drone on and on, make them move through the script more quickly. Teach them three little words to say as quickly as possible: "You may leave."

MEDIA PREFERENCES

One other trait of the presenter has to do with media preference. You may have to develop the message differently based on a particular media type such as 35mm slides, overhead transparencies, or electronic images. If you know the media preference of a presenter, you can develop support for the message accordingly.

For example, for a 20-minute presentation, a person familiar with using PowerPoint to electronically deliver content will need about 35 electronic images. A person preferring overheads needs about 10 transparencies to cover the topic during the same 20 minutes (see the following note). That's because you can't scale overheads like Frisbees to try to change visuals as rapidly as you might advance an electronic show.

As the creator of the message, you may have to make some adjustments. For the person with the electronic show, you might include several builds as part of the 35 impressions—leaving the presenter some room for stories, analogies, and other grabbers. For the person with the overheads, you may have to fill each transparency with more data—leaving less time for grabbers. Or, you may make the transparencies with limited data, forcing the presenter to have more in-depth knowledge of the topic since fewer visual cues are available during the presentation.

NOTE

> MediaNet has a software utility called ShowSTARTER®, which uses artificial intelligence to help a person plan a presentation. By answering ten simple questions, a ten-page report is available that outlines the visual design, text attributes, proper colors, lead-time, and number of visuals all tied to a selected objective. You can use a free, online mini-version, ShowSTARTER® Express, by visiting MediaNet's Web site at this address: www.medianet-ny.com.

KNOWING THE PARTICULARS OF THE AUDIENCE

Knowing the audience is the most difficult task imaginable. This is why marketing professionals lose sleep at night! Just when they think they can predict the market, the market changes! Although we want to avoid turning analysis into paralysis on this issue, understanding your target audience is very important to the development of the message.

Here's my take on "audiences." I think people are basically the same. I'm not discounting diversity in any way, but I use the philosophy that whatever is true for me in my own heart is probably true for everyone else on a very basic level. Our similarities allow us to share entertainment, sports, and all types of social activities. Our differences are what business presentations try to isolate and somehow address.

Knowing how to target differences in people is important in building effective messages. We can learn more about an audience in several ways including:

■ Direct Contact

■ Demographics

■ Motivators

DIRECT CONTACT

The difference between learning the traits of the presenter and knowing particulars of the audience is direct contact. You have greater access to the presenters. They work with you! You can call them, email them, fax them, see them. This interaction helps you understand them.

You may have little contact and interaction with your audience until the presentation is starting. This is not uncommon. It happens a lot, especially to those pitching a new business. However, you may have other presentations in which the same group convenes on a regular basis. This might happen with internal presentations or briefings such as those on a monthly, quarterly, or annual basis.

The more direct contact (experience) you have with a particular audience, the easier it is to design a targeted message. Think about your family, friends, or even coworkers. You know how to handle these groups because you see them more often. Of course, in some situations you may prefer not to see them!

DEMOGRAPHICS

Experience through direct contact is getting harder to gain in the real world. Our lives are getting so busy that many of us just don't have the time to get to know a consistent audience. Be honest, aren't you amazed when you actually reach someone on the phone? You might quickly say, "What? No voice message? You're probably not that busy today, are you?" Direct contact is becoming a rare commodity.

When you can't have direct contact with the audience, you still have to try to define them or categorize them in order to look for differences. This analysis will help you design the right message for the right group. You can use demographics to gather certain information including age, gender, expertise, and culture. Note how these measurements are general and not job-specific.

For example, if your audience is primarily individuals who speak English as a second language, your message may have to be designed in very general and conceptual terms, using fewer details and wordy descriptions.

24

Nostalgia Theory

Knowing the average age of the audience is a significant piece of information that can be used effectively. The nostalgia theory works like this: Experiences and events that occurred during the mid-teen years (near puberty) are memorable for life. In other words, you can remember more things from when you were about 15 years old than almost any other time in your life. You recall specific songs, political issues, sporting events, and even the first person you fell in love with—remember?

So, if the average age of the audience is 49 and it's the year 2004, you know they were 15 in the year 1970. References to events from the late '60s and early '70s will be quickly recognized. The end of the Vietnam war, the last songs of the Beatles, Armstrong on the moon, Nixon resigns, and so on. You can reflect on history to develop examples and analogies to support your message.

MOTIVATORS

Motivators are the emotional elements that induce action. Now we're talking about the juicy stuff! Some of the more basic motivators are pride, profit, love, fear, and need.

NOTE

> Although the basic motivators are general, the type of motivator can be more specific. Need may be refined to necessity, obligation, urgency, requirement, or even compulsion. You can fine-tune the motivator, just as you can fine-tune the objective.

Decide which will best motivate your audience and fine-tune your original objective in order to help achieve the emotional response. Stop! You don't change your objective; you only fine-tune it.

How a Motivator Affects the Objective

Let's say your topic is a discussion about sales quotas. The talk is given to different groups such as marketing, senior management, and sales. Initially, you choose the objective "to inform."

You notice your next presentation of this material is at the annual sales conference. You decide that pride is the motivator for this particular audience, the sales force. You fine-tune the original objective, "to inform," and it becomes "to inspire to great heights."

You inspire by reinforcing the group's accomplishments and encourage them to achieve more. You add individual success stories. You use support information including comparisons to last year, growth in market share, perhaps even a testimonial from the president of the company.

Do you see how influential a motivator can be in the development of the message? Your original objective didn't change. It only became more specific.

You might find that more than one motivator moves an audience at different points in the presentation. You just have to match supporting elements in your script to the motivator that targets the type of response you seek. For example, if the best motivator is profit, a less obvious motivator may be fear. Thus, a chart showing the consequences of overspending may tap fear, while still supporting the underlying motive for profit.

UNDERSTANDING FILTERS

People react to information in many ways. What you say and what you show may be quite different from what the audience sees and hears. This happens every day. I say one thing; you hear something different. It's not a matter of who's right—it's a matter of agreement. Since you can't change this about people, don't even try. Just figure a way to deal with it.

Demographics and motivators affect the way an audience filters or classifies information. Each audience member puts his or her own spin on information based on how data is filtered to the brain.

A filter is the slant you apply to a message to make it your own. When someone says, "The way I see it..." you can be sure the person is applying a filter to the information in order to understand it.

The goal is to create a clear message that minimizes the distortion the audience tends to place on information. As we distort messages, we develop barriers because we make personal judgments. For example, when you see a stop sign, you know the message is the same for everyone. When you see a sign that says "Authorized Vehicles Only," you instantly become a member of a distinct group. You then form an opinion about the other group. You begin to question their right to even be authorized! Who are these people and why?

Avoid Clichés

Stereotyping is just one expression of how we filter information. This is a problem in itself because it leads to misconceptions, misunderstanding, and prejudice. Clichés also exist in business, especially when considering organizational duties.

Don't fall into the trap of shaping the message to a job function cliché. A group of accountants do not prefer only numbers. Engineers are not limited to processes. Sales and marketing people can handle details.

If the clichés for business were applied to art or entertainment, then there would have to be separate versions for everyone. Can you imagine *Gone with the Wind* for computer programmers and a different version for financial planners? How about a version of baseball only for doctors called *Medicine Ball*?

The job doesn't make the person. The person makes the job. If you changed your profession or industry tomorrow, would you really be a different person than you are today?

Avoid the job title cliché. If members of the executive team are expected to be in the audience, the message must be still created for the entire audience. If the entire audience is only the executive team, then the message is still tailored to the needs of that specific group, based on generalities, not specifics. It wouldn't matter if the CEO likes fishing. If you make every reference about fishing, the remainder of the group is likely to miss the boat! Job titles may cause anxiety for the messenger, not the message.

I avoid clichés like the plague. They're old hat. They end up making a mountain out of a molehill.

Since filters exist, a good script finds ways of overcoming those filters. Table 24.1 shows some examples of where filters are used by the audience and the method used to break through the filter.

TABLE 24.1	HANDLING DEMOGRAPHIC FILTERS
Demographic	**Method for Breaking Through Filter**
Language	Simplify the words
Age	Appeal to generation styles
Gender	Avoid stereotypes
Expertise	Adjust conceptual complexity

For example, in the preceding table, the filters associated with the demographic of age may be addressed by using analogies, references, and other data that earmark a cross section of the audience by generation. You would have less reason to make a comparison of events from the 1950s if the audience is composed of recent college graduates.

Audiences apply their own filters to motivators, too. People put unique slants on emotional responses. After all, who can truly agree on how fear or pride affects any individual? The abstract concepts associated with any motivator leads to very subjective viewpoints for each person experiencing that motivator at any given time. Thus, each person applies a filter to a motivational element based on given circumstances and conditions prevailing at the time. Table 24.2 shows how to handle motivational filters.

TABLE 24.2 HANDLING MOTIVATIONAL FILTERS

Motivator	Method for Breaking Through Filter
Pride	Show comparisons and achievement
Fear	Use reassurance and historical data
Profit	Offer reachable goals
Love	Demonstrate teamwork
Need	Meet with urgency

For example, when a company is faced with a crisis situation and the employees are motivated by fear, the initial effort should be to reassure by pointing to how such situations were dealt with in the past, as opposed to immediately suggesting alternatives for the future. Stop the bleeding before you recommend a new brand of bandages.

Assuring Consistency

Until now, we've looked at the micro view of the presentation message. The effort has been to examine all the intricacies and nuances of purpose and people to arrive at a finely tuned message.

Now we have readjust again and take a macro view of the message and examine it according to a much bigger picture. The ultimate objective and the basic philosophy of an organization play a role in the development of the message used for the presentation. We must move beyond words and begin to apply the notion of a visual presenter to the entire organization and its global expression.

The growth of the World Wide Web is enabling any organization, regardless of size, to have a presence. As technology advances, the visibility and reach of an organization becomes more global. We won't be typing to one another to converse; instead, we'll be seeing one another though the eyes of a display device. Electronic communication will be more visual allowing the diversity of our organizations to become the portal to our profits. The heavens will open up as we transgress the universe—sorry I got carried away!

To assure consistency, you must create presentations that can be delivered by a number of people in your organization to diverse audiences in a variety of settings.

This portability across presenters is easier when you design presentations that are high on conceptual ideas and low on technical information. When designed, the message will need to be scripted for the presenter, either conceptually or literally.

Maintaining the Corporate Image

Companies create and protect their corporate identities by spending millions of dollars on logos, signage, packaging, stationery, and public relations. Likewise, each employee's ability to consistently tell the company story helps establish a verbal corporate image.

Anyone who publicly delivers a message represents his or her company. In fact, the higher you are in the company, the more "you are the company." If you see the president of General Motors presenting poorly, you might instantly have a negative impression about the cars GM produces. These are not related, but in your mind they are. There is no logic to this, but it happens. The leaders are the company. In fact, the higher your level of responsibility, the tougher my coaching sessions. My logic is that if you make the big bucks, then you should present like you deserve the big bucks.

Concepts, visuals, and presenters are each part of the corporate identity. One of the goals of the presentation must be to match the consistency of your company image as demonstrated in other marketing venues. Start taking advantage of those TV ads!

For example, let's take a car company like Volvo. For years the marketing messages for Volvo have consistently stressed safety. Their TV commercials, advertisements, and brochures have always put safety first, as a way to differentiate their product. This doesn't mean Volvo's competitor's cars are not safe; rather, it simply means Volvo has made safety a primary issue. They are spending big advertising dollars to make this point.

Okay, so let's say you are developing the concepts for a new sales presentation for Volvo. One way to assure consistency in theme across other public image venues is to build references to safety into the script. Safety is related to security, protection, and even confidence. If you find stories, analogies, and other grabbers that relate to security or confidence, you will match the existing image portrayed in other marketing endeavors. In other words, you will be supporting the investment the company is already making through its advertising.

The presentation message represents the verbal corporate image, and it should try to support an image that the company is already vested in through other marketing efforts.

One of the ways a company displays its image is through a mission statement. You know, that highly sophisicated document you read through, pause, look up, and say, "We do this? Really? When?" A mission statement is not for the audience. They expect your company to do everything in that statement anyway. They don't count on anything less. The mission statement is really for the employees of the company. If your own presenters don't believe in it, how can you expect the public to buy into it?

TIP

> Examine the company mission statement or the corporate vision. These expressions are designed to set a baseline or tone for all messages. This doesn't mean that every presentation must mention the mission statement. But when the core principles of your company relate to both your objective and your call to action, the impact of your message will be greater.

USING PORTABLE CONCEPTS

Just as the corporate image is expressed in different venues such as advertising and public relations, the same image is also expressed through multiple presenters. When your message is thought all the way through the corporate philosophy, those in the company who've embraced that philosophy will have an easier time delivering the message.

This "through-line of action" takes the traits of the presenter and matches them as closely as possible to the elements within the script as well as to the components of the corporate philosophy. When all three areas—personality, message, and philosophy—are in a direct line, the audience receives the highest communication.

If your personality trait is an appreciation for truthful analysis and the message contains elements about accurate reporting and your company philosophy is built around showing specific details, then a through-line of action exists. It is at these points in the presentation that your energy level and your commitment to the argument will be at its peak.

TIP

> See if your presenters understand the company philosophy in the same way. Ask your presenters to list the three most important things the company does or provides. Then look at the mission statement and see how many of those things match. Two out of three is good. Anything less means the presenter doesn't "get it." Now if you find that a lot of presenters in your company don't get it, well maybe the executives need to communicate better to those embracing the wrong message!

Concepts need to be portable in the sense that more than one person in the company is able to express those concepts in a variety of circumstances. Naturally, a growing company is likely to have multiple presenters. However, the complexities of the supporting elements for your message may be more difficult for some presenters than others.

Your letterhead may look the same across office locations, but your presenters are all different, even if they all work in the same building. Even though you expect each to deliver your message in basically the same way, it is the individual style that shapes your message for that particular audience.

For example, if you are creating a presentation for a remote sales force and the supporting elements to your objective include several detailed charts and graphs, some of your presenters may be more confident with such details than others. Those who have a better grasp of the material will handle the delivery of the concepts with little problem. Those less certain of their knowledge of the details will present the message with difficulty. Because each presenter places his or her personal spin on the information being conveyed, individual style will breed inconsistency.

To assure a consistency among multiple presenters, consider developing support items with limited details. When faced with less information, a presenter defers to actual experience, personal philosophy, and general concepts to express the verbal corporate message. In essence, they express themselves throughout the presentation, and the result is a more believable statement of knowledge for the audience.

So now I'll add another little twist to the plot! You need to script information conceptually and develop yourself as a visual thinker in order to provide information suitable for a visual presenter. The more conceptual the message, the easier for individual presenters to personalize the message.

Developing Portable Concepts

To enhance your skill as a visual thinker and learn to develop portable concepts, try this exercise. You will need three blank sheets of paper and a candy bar. Place the candy bar away from the paper, but within reach. Now place the sheets of paper in front of you.

On the first sheet, write a one-sentence description of what your company does or what your specific department is responsible for within the company. Imagine this sentence will be part of a press release or be announced on the local news. Be descriptive, but limit your narration to one complete sentence. This is the way you naturally think about the message.

On the second sheet, create three bullet points which cover the one sentence description you wrote on the first sheet. Imagine you are creating a PowerPoint visual using a bulleted list format. This is the way you currently think about designing the visuals.

On the third sheet, reduce the three bullet points to one word for each bullet and, if possible, make each word begin with the same letter of the alphabet. In addition, make sure the structure is the same. If the first one is a verb, they should all be verbs to maintain a parallel structure. This is the way you visually think about developing portable concepts.

If you did this right, your third sheet of paper has three words on it, possibly each beginning with the same letter of the alphabet. Okay, you can have the candy bar now!

Portable concepts offer less experienced presenters an opportunity to appear knowledgeable without sacrificing the consistencies already made public by more experienced personnel. That's a polite, sophisticated way of saying that even the new people can deliver the message when the message is simple.

The disparity between newcomers and seasoned veterans is less obvious when specific details are left to the speaker and not to the speaker support. Save the details for the handouts and spare the clutter on the visuals. Both your presenters and their audiences will be more appreciative!

PROVIDING "DO" AND "SAY" SCRIPTS

One of the last stages of the scripting process is the actual process of providing the script. At times you may simply provide an outline or you may wait until the visuals are created and provide the presenter a copy of the presentation in print form. In either case you haven't assured a consistency in delivering the essence of the message you've created. You need to provide a script.

There are basically two kinds of scripts, those that do and those that say. Both are designed for the presenter and they normally show the description of each visual (or the actual visuals) and the related message for each visual. The message can be conceptual (driven by actions) or concrete (driven by words).

A Do script is conceptual and a Say script is concrete. The Do script contains suggested actions to convey each element in the presentation. A Say script contains the actual words to use during the presentation. A Say script is basically a written speech linked to the support material.

For example, you created the message and supporting data for a sales presentation and you expect each of the sales people to deliver the presentation in a local market. You need to provide each person with a script that matches each visual with a related suggestion as to how to deliver the information.

One way to guide the sales force through your message is to provide a Do script which suggests actions for each concept or supporting idea. Figure 24.7 is one visual taken from a sample do script. Table 24.3 highlights a segment of the storyboard including the reference to the visuals. The left column shows the sequence, name, and type of visual while the right column describes the action a presenter might take to deliver the information.

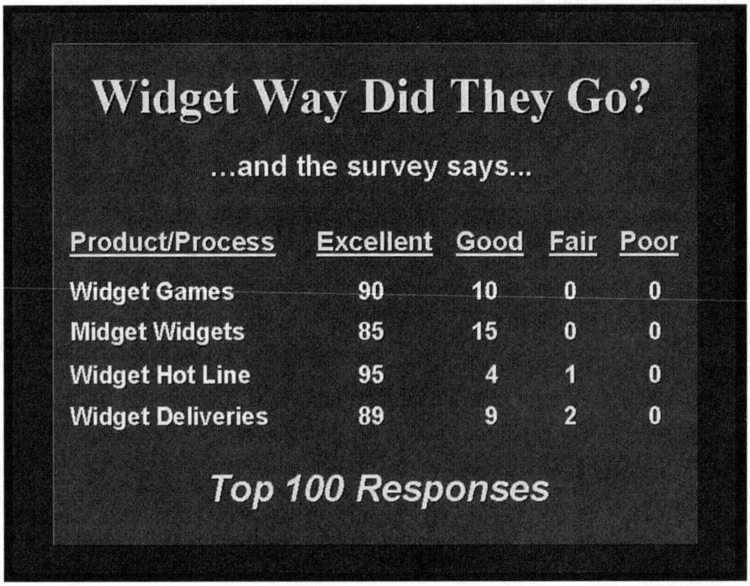

Figure 24.7
A customer survey showing "out of one hundred" satisfaction ratings for a series of products and services. This visual appears as #18 in the storyboard script.

Widget Way Did They Go?

...and the survey says...

Product/Process	Excellent	Good	Fair	Poor
Widget Games	90	10	0	0
Midget Widgets	85	15	0	0
Widget Hot Line	95	4	1	0
Widget Deliveries	89	9	2	0

Top 100 Responses

TABLE 24.3   A SEGMENT OF A DO SCRIPT

Storyboard Visual & Type	Supporting Script
#18—Customer Satisfaction (Survey shown as a table)	Tell a story that describes a personal experience in which you helped solve a customer's problem that resulted in extreme satisfaction and repeat business.
#19—Domestic Locations (U.S. map with dots country showing office sites)	Describe your relationship with other sales people around the country and give examples of how you share information and collaborate to achieve sales goals.

Do scripts enhance the authenticity of the delivery and help each presenter develop a unique delivery style. This method requires very little memorization, which reduces the chances for error and inconsistency. Simple visuals that don't lead or confine the presenter are the key to effective conceptual presentations.

Another way to guide the same sales force through your message is to provide a Say script that offers the exact wording (speech) for each concept or supporting idea. Figure 24.8 is one visual taken from a sample Say script, basically the same example as the Do script used earlier. Table 24.4 highlights a segment of the storyboard including the reference to the visuals. The left column shows the sequence, name, and type of visual while the right column gives the actual words a presenter should say when delivering the information.

Figure 24.8
A U.S. map showing office locations and demonstrating the concept that the offices are connected by a communications network. This visual appears as #19 in the storyboard script.

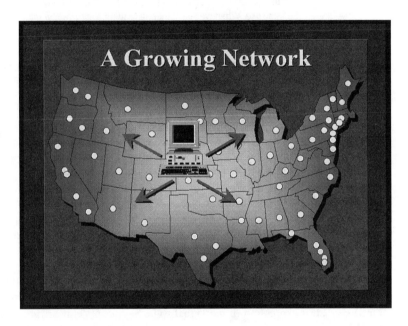

TABLE 24.4   A SEGMENT OF A SAY SCRIPT

Storyboard Visual & Type	Supporting Script
#18—Customer Satisfaction	"As a world class provider of widgets, this survey shows our (Survey shown as a table) leadership in building customer satisfaction into every product and process we deliver."
#19—Domestic Locations	"We have sales and service offices in 40 cities in the U.S. (U.S. map with dots alone. Each office is networked through a sophisticated showing office sites) computer system that allows our sales force to expedite orders and share data."

Say scripts seem to offer more consistency than Do scripts because all the correct words to support the message have been decided. Sometimes exact wording is necessary, either because someone prefers to work that way and is good at memorization (very rare) or because the person is presenting in a situation where precise timing and complete accuracy are crucial. Examples of these are presentations or speeches prepared for the media, such as TV or videotape.

Say scripts tell a presenter exactly what to say and require that the presenter memorize or read the script word-for-word. Since very few people can memorize a scripted speech, Say scripts are usually more effective when using a teleprompter. The prompter gives the appearance that eye contact is being maintained as the presenter conveys the message.

NOTE

> Because the average person can't memorize a speech, he or she will usually read it to the audience. When we see someone reading, we have less faith in that person's knowledge of the subject. In fact, we may even doubt the person's sincerity if the message is emotional.
>
> One way to help someone with a written speech is to have them go through the presentation without the words. The more someone understands the basic flow of information and can them express the ideas and main points in his or her own words, the easier it is to later substitute the words of another.
>
> In the theatre, the actors hear the first reading of the play, then play each scene in their own words (improvisation) to get familiar with actions and intentions. Later, when they learn the lines they are able to make the playwright's words more personal since those words are tied to actions and intentions already experienced.

Otherwise, Say scripts become cards or notes delivered from a lectern by a presenter who spends most of the time looking down to catch the next sentence in the script rather than looking up to catch the next response from the audience.

To support the notion of a visual presenter you need to provide the kind of script that offers the best opportunity for the message to be received by the audience. Although Do scripts offer the greatest expression of individual style, Say scripts conform to a higher expression of consistency.

As you construct the argument and qualify the participants, both presenter and audience, you will seek a consistent expression of the intended message. That message, converted into visual support, must be delivered in an effective manner in order to move an audience to action. Such are the qualities of a successful presentation.

I know we covered a lot of information in this chapter and I don't want you to feel overwhelmed. You can't apply everything I mentioned to a presentation you expect to give two hours from now. But, you can start to think more clearly about the message itself.

Maybe you'll be involved in twenty PowerPoint presentations this year at some level. If some of those scripts are in your control at the message stage, then revisit this chapter and find the elements that help you most in designing a clear, concise, and captivating message!

TROUBLESHOOTING

Is there any quick, easy, one-two-three method for scripting a presentation?

Actually there is. It's called a timeline layout. There are three segments in the timeline, based on chronology, following the pattern of past, present and future. Some people use the metaphor of "where we were, where we are, where we're going." You can probably use this process with almost any type of script or situation and it certainly makes it easier to remember your key points when you use the timeline approach.

For example, let's say you have to give a short talk on the progress of a particular project. First, you determine the outcome of the talk (the call to action). You decide you want the group to continue to support the project. Nothing major, just "continued support." People give continued support to things that have a track record of satisfaction. So the objective is to demonstrate satisfactory results. You have an objective and a call to action. Now you need a script. Of the noted types found in this chapter, you select "problem-solution."

Using the timeline layout you apply the problem-solution scenario to the past, present and future using no more than three issues for each segment of the time line. Thus, for the past you mention three specific problems which led to the need for the project and you identify at least one solution that came about to address one of those problems. This begins your journey to providing satisfactory results (remember the objective?).

Next, you focus on current issues (present) and how several initiatives are being used to address the remaining problems from the past. In addition, you show how the solution to some of the problems has opened new concerns, which may develop into problems if left unchecked. For example, you might show that the implementation of a new procedure while streamlining communication has created the need for advanced technology and additional expertise. This is your first indication to the group that you will require their continued support for the increasing scope of the project (remember the call to action?).

Then, you discuss the strategy or plan for the future and the results you expect based on the already demonstrated and satisfactory past performance. You show how the investment in already proven, additional resources will continually improve the specific business function that the project was originally intended to address. You close by showing that without continued support for the project the original problems that created the need for the project will return but the effect of those problems will be magnified based on the current economic and competitive conditions.

Your ability to remember and discuss information is based on your understanding as to where that data fits along the timeline of past, present and future. Just make sure that everything you present matches the objective (satisfactory results) and leads to the call to action (continued support).

How can I maintain consistency in all my messages yet keep them unique?

The easiest way to create and deliver messages with consistency and impact is to find yourself in the message. The closer the message is to your heart and your belief system, the easier it is to be consistent.

But don't confuse consistency with conformity. When you try to conform to the message you make sacrifices and trade-offs in order to fit yourself into the message. This cannot be done with any sincerity because your heart and soul will not allow it. When you are consistent with the message, you make the message conform to you and the message is expressed naturally, through your actions.

If I coached you to higher levels of this presentation skill, I would force you to find where in a given message you have the strongest tie. In other words, what part of the message is closest to your heart? Once you match a core principle (belief) of your life to a particular element in the message, a link is established between you and the message. That is the starting point for developing a consistency. You may have to modify the message by slanting it to your way of thinking. But that's the beauty of shaping a message to your personal and natural style.

For every message thereafter you will use the same process to find the elements in the message which match at least one of your core principles. Messages will change, but you must remain true to your own beliefs. This is why I am able to work with so many different people from such diverse groups. The consistency in the coaching is to simply create the link between the message and the messenger.

And don't think you can't match the message. A message and a corporate philosophy are created by individuals who are part of the the same race—the human race. For all the diversity that exists, we still share basic instincts and characteristics simply by the fact that we are human. So, start from the premise that you are able to find elements of a message or a philosophy that fit you. The consistency in your own heart must be the watermark for all ideas and concepts you expect to support.

In my company, the messages are top-down and the training is bottom-up. This causes a big gap between employees and executives. Who should change?

Change is inevitable for everyone. From a presentation perspective, change is more difficult for those at the top. Technology is a factor. As computers and communication systems evolve, the skills required to deliver information become more visual. Companies that recognize the need to provide presentation skills training usually start from the bottom-up. This approach is incorrect because the newest employees are already visually driven and will adapt naturally to visual communications. The top-level executives need the skills training the most because they are probably not visual presenters. Having coached for more than 15 years I see these problems affecting the bigger companies more than the smaller companies.

For example, I once dealt with the Director of Communications for a major fast food service company—we're talking major with a capital *M*—the leader in the industry. Although many of the mid-level managers had experienced the initial stages of my company's coaching, the director felt that I was not the right fit to coach the top-level executives. When I asked why, the director told me that my personality and my approach would adversely influence the top executives in a way that might affect the corporate message. He was afraid to expose the leaders to the exact skills that others in the company were experiencing and using. This indicated the director's lack of confidence in the executive team's ability to change. In an effort to protect the top-level executives, the director created a gap between management levels. This gap will eventually widen until the mid-level managers move up or until they move on (usually to a competitor).

As a company develops a visual presentation strategy, those nearest the top need the training first. Why? Because they usually deliver the core messages of the company in the most public forums to extremely diverse groups. If the leaders can't change, then the followers will change the leaders!

CHAPTER 25

THE MEDIA—DESIGNING VISUAL SUPPORT

by Tom Mucciolo

In this chapter

BRINGING YOUR STORY TO LIFE

"Image is everything," "Seeing is believing," "You oughtta be in pictures"—you've heard it all before. Well, the look and feel of your visuals will certainly make a difference in your business presentations; you just want to make sure the difference is positive.

For instance, I can look at any presentation and within the first three visuals, I can tell how bad or good the presentation will be, just from a media viewpoint. Want the truth? In most cases, the visuals are pretty bad. Is it that people just don't get it? Is it that they are just not concerned? The trouble with this world is there's too much apathy, but then again, who cares? The point is that some simple techniques can help even a first-time presenter avoid making the most common mistakes.

Face it! A well-conceived script containing a clearly defined objective should be enhanced with good visual support. The features and functions of PowerPoint help bring your outline and storyboard to life, giving you the opportunity to create visuals with impact! This chapter focuses on the effective design of the support elements used to direct your message.

NOTE

> Real-world experience is the best teacher. Since 1985, MediaNet has designed over 3,500 business presentations and conducted over 1,000 seminars on effective presentations. As a presentation skills company, we are involved in all stages of a client's event, from concept to delivery.
>
> Many of the principles, guidelines suggestions, and visual concepts discussed in this chapter are also referenced in MediaNet's original publication *Purpose, Movement, Color* by Tom and Rich Mucciolo (©1994, 1999, MediaNet, Inc., New York, NY).

A lot of people take for granted the importance of having well-designed visual support for the presentation. The components of the event, especially those that are most visible, can make or break the moment. If you keep following our notion of a visual presenter, then you can begin to see how the support for your message must be highly visual. The issues concerning the design of the images include

- Choosing a medium for your message
- Controlling eye movement
- Using color

CHOOSING A MEDIUM FOR YOUR MESSAGE

When Marshall McLuhan said, "The medium is the message," he was referring to the power of television and its influence on how we interpret information. Television is one type of media used to express information. Canvas is one type of media for a painter's artistic expression. The medium of expression is basically the link between the message and the mind.

> Media is plural and medium is singular, but sometimes media is used as a collective noun to describe a larger set (the newspaper media, for example). Okay, okay. Rather than asking you to consider semantics and form, from here on out, I will refer to everything as simply media, including flip charts, slides, overheads, electronic images, and other related items associated with the visual support used in a presentation.

The media choice represents the physical form of the message. It definitely affects the manner in which the presentation is delivered. For example, using overheads requires a different approach in delivery than an electronic presentation simply because the transparencies need to be handled (touched). Having "one more thing to do" affects the way in which the presenter delivers the message.

Although your delivery style is affected by the media choice, your objective should remain independent of the media. The very definition of visuals as "speaker-support" implies that you should be able to present your message without supporting media. I'm not trying to burst the PowerPoint bubble and suggest not using visuals at all. On the contrary, presentations with no visual support force the presenter to have the most exceptional delivery skills. Think about music. Without the orchestra, a singer is required to have perfect pitch to be a success. Unless you want to be the *acappella* presenter, I suggest you stick with visual support.

With that in mind, choosing how you expect to support your message involves the following:

- Understanding media types
- Working with design templates
- Creating handout materials

UNDERSTANDING MEDIA TYPES

Presentations involve a number of support options including transparencies, 35mm slides, and electronic visuals. I place them in the order from most to least hands-on for the presenter. Overheads will require changing, slides may involve changing carousels, and electronic presentations are mostly hands-free. *Multimedia* is just an extension of the electronic presentation, although a degree of interactivity does occur when using elements triggered by the keyboard or mouse.

Flip charts and videotapes are omitted to limit this discussion to the most likely media types you would consider when using PowerPoint to design your presentation.

> PowerPoint calls the visuals you create "slides." However, in their electronic form (on your PC), they are really "visuals" or "images." If they are produced as 35mm chromes, only then do they become slides. If they are printed to transparency film, they become overheads. In fact, I always describe an electronic presentation as a screen show, not a slide show.
>
> I am not trying to change the software, but throughout this part of the book, I will continue to use the words "visual" and "image" when referencing the media.

Overheads and slides are tangible and require an output device (printer or slide camera) to produce. Electronic visuals, although seemingly intangible, still require an output device (display) to be viewed. In all cases, the support is part of an overall production.

Okay, by now, you're probably aware that I think overheads and slides come in second in the media race. Electronic presentations work best. They offer so much more in the way of variety, interactivity, portability, and flexibility—just to name a few reasons. In fact, as you develop presentations for a visual presenter to deliver to an audience of visual creatures additional components such as sound, animation and video will become considerations in the design of the visuals. The real "power" in PowerPoint is seen in the design of effective electronic events. The electronic presentation is currently the most effective media choice for delivering business presentations.

There, I said it. Right now, the people who make color printers, overhead projectors, and slide imaging devices all hate me. But I'll probably be a keynote speaker at the LCD Projector Convention!

I'm not saying never use slides or overheads, but I am saying that an audience of visual creatures has come to expect more. It used to be that presenting electronically had to be justified in some way. Today, you'll have a hard time explaining why you chose not to present with a computer.

You may even have to explain it environmentally. Electronic presentations are "green"—that is, nothing has to be discarded at a later point that would affect the environment. Slides and overheads are not biodegradable. This is just one of many of the arguments for using electronic presentations.

In keeping with the notion of a visual presenter, you cannot ignore the growing acceptance of electronic presentations over slides and overheads. In fact, black-and-white overhead presentations are the most difficult for an audience to observe and still remain attentive to the message.

The Case for Color

When you watch a black-and-white overhead presentation, it doesn't take long before you start shifting in your seat, updating your daily planner, and checking the stack to see how many overheads are left.

Black text on a white background is called print, and print is meant for an audience of one. That's why you can work at your computer with its paper-white display. You can look away whenever you want and examine information for as long as you prefer.

A presentation is meant for an audience of more than one. An audience of more than one demands color. Color is what real life is made of; black and white is simulated and, therefore, less than real life. When people are faced with less than real visuals, they become distracted. When you present, you want the least amount of distraction possible. Present in color. Enough said.

If you evaluate types of media based on overall impact, color always supersedes black and white. In fact, if you're not using color, then you shouldn't even be thinking about 35mm slides or electronic presentations. Instead, you should stick with overheads. With color, however, the impact is greater, depending on the media type. The more flexibility you have with the media, the better the presentation.

Currently, electronic images offer the greatest flexibility when compared with slides and overheads. If you have several media choices available to you, choose the one with the most flexibility, which I find in most cases is electronic.

If you are already convinced of the benefits of presenting electronically, then you can skip the rest of this section on media types. But, if you need to justify a media choice, take a look at the following comparisons.

Flexibility in media can be examined based on the CCC Model, or Cost, Convenience, and Continuity. These three major considerations can help you decide which media choice to use for your color presentation. To better understand media types, we can apply the CCC Model to overheads, slides, and electronic images.

COST OF OVERHEADS

Sometimes referred to as transparencies, foils, or acetates, *overheads* are one of the most commonly used, yet least flexible, media types in business.

Often a company will try to use existing audiovisual equipment before investing in new technology, and the overhead projector is the most common in business. This makes sense. Moreover, for black-and-white presentations, the simplicity of inserting transparency material into a printer makes this choice an easy one with minimal cost.

NOTE

> The easier it is for you to prepare the presentation, the harder it is for the audience to stay attentive to your message. If you quickly create a few transparencies with lots of lengthy phrases, you create a presentation meant to be read and not viewed. Easy for you, tough for us. But, if you take the time to design effective visuals, the audience will find it easier to watch the presentation.

But, when overhead presentations involve color, the cost issues change. After you prepare your presentation in PowerPoint, you can outsource the production of color overheads to a creative services company, or you can use in-house equipment.

The cost of outsourcing the production of the overheads may appear to be higher because the price is reflective of the original investment in equipment, the supplies used, and the time required to monitor the process. In addition, profit is built into the price, as well. However, in-house production has similar "costs" associated with the output.

In-house production of color overheads involves a cost of acquiring a color printer and a recurring cost of supplies. In addition, the cost of time associated with the output process itself is a factor as well.

25

NOTE

The factor of time is associated with equipment-related issues and not the time it takes to create the visuals in PowerPoint. That effort is generally the same regardless of the final form of the output. Your investment of five minutes to create a bar chart in PowerPoint doesn't change if you use slides, overheads, or electronic images as the final output.

Let's use the same type of example for the comparisons to slides and electronic images. Say, for example, that a company makes only one 20-minute presentation each week. That's our reference point: one 20-minute presentation per week.

For 20 minutes of presenting, you'll create about 10 color overheads. Over one year, that's 500 overheads. The supplies aren't free. You have to buy them. You can be more exact on supplies cost if you know the actual cost of the transparency material (film) and color cartridge (toner, ribbon, or ink). On average, each color overhead costs about $1.00. If you also factor in the cost of the equipment, even a $500 color printer adds another $1.00 to the supplies cost, if you spread the cost of the printer over a single year.

Ah, but we have one other cost factor. In addition to supplies, you need to consider the cost of time to manage the process of producing the color output. Someone has to do this, whether it is you or some other member of the company. The process includes setup of the printer, maintaining supplies, fixing jams, and waiting for each transparency to print. I've seen people on a Saturday afternoon waiting for stuff to print. What's sad is they actually started the printing on Thursday!

If you count changes, mistakes, setup, and other interruptions, about 30 minutes each week is required for the 10-overhead presentation we've been discussing. Although the hourly wage of whoever is managing the process makes a difference, even a $10 per hour wage adds another $0.50 per overhead to the cost.

So, the cost of producing 10 color overheads, in-house, might be as much as $2.50 each, when you factor in supplies and time. That's $25 a week. And this is assuming you only have one presentation per week.

If you outsource the color overheads by sending a PowerPoint presentation to a service bureau, you'll probably pay twice that or higher, depending on turnaround time. This is something to consider when weighing color overheads against slides or electronic presentations.

COST OF 35MM SLIDES

For *35mm slides*, the cost of production also includes investment in equipment, plus the actual cost of developing and mounting the slides. Some companies have in-house equipment to complete the entire process, but many own a slide-imaging device (film camera) from which the 35mm film is sent to a local development lab for processing.

Although the time to maintain the equipment and manage the process is far less than for color overheads, the number of slides needed to make the same points is much higher. If you have 10 overheads in your 20-minute presentation, the same 20-minute presentation using 35mm slides would require you to use about 30 slides. The reason is simple. You use media types differently. Slides in a carousel advance more rapidly than overheads changed manually.

NOTE

> MediaNet designed ShowSTARTER® as a planning tool for a presentation. One of the calculations made by this software utility is to estimate the number of visuals you should have based on the length of the presentation. That's how I know you'll need about 30 slides or 10 overheads for the same 20-minute presentation. The actual quantities, when calculated by the software, are 31 slides and 11 overheads. But it's easier to use more rounded numbers for the example.
>
> You might ask how these calculations are derived. We studied over 1,500 presentations over three years to gather most of the information built into ShowSTARTER. One issue was time. A person usually changes overheads every two minutes or so, because they can't be scaled onto the projector like Frisbees. We noticed that when overheads are printed in portrait style, instead of landscape, there is tendency to add even more text and thus leave each overhead up for a longer time. Slides stay up for less time because the aspect ratio is different (22/35) and less space is available for data. So, to cover the same information, you usually need more slides which means you spend less time on each slide (they change faster).
>
> In addition, builds are used in many slide presentations, which increases the number of slides even though the number of full impressions is the same. A slide with four bullet points, when done as a build, will expand to five separate slides (heading plus four points). Yet those five slides still only deliver one visual impression.
>
> With electronic images the choice of using builds and overlays to reveal information in stages increases the number of visuals beyond that of slides simply because there is no limitation as there is with a slide carousel tray.
>
> This is why the number of visuals is dependent on the media choice, even though the length of the presentation is the same, regardless of the media choice.

25

Even though film cameras cost more than color printers, the cost per slide is similar to color overheads because you will use more slides per presentation. So, if you produce 30 slides per week for a year, and you invested in a $3,000 slide camera, your cost per slide is about $2.00. Add to that the actual cost of the roll of film and the developing charge, and it's about another $0.50 per slide. So, for about $2.50 per slide you could do it yourself.

If you sent a PowerPoint file to an imaging bureau, the cost of production will be somewhere between $5 and $10 or higher per slide, depending on turnaround time. Obviously, because you are using their camera equipment, their personnel, and their profit margin to image the slides, you will pay a higher cost.

COST OF ELECTRONIC IMAGES

One important advantage with electronic images is that they require no additional production output, as with slides or overheads. This is important if you're like me—time-starved!

It's true. I know I wait until the last minute to do stuff because there's always too much stuff to do. If I can work on my presentation and fine-tune the images on the plane, that's a better use of my time than sitting around waiting for film to develop!

The good news is that after you complete your PowerPoint presentation, you can use your PC to launch the screen show (slide show) using a *display device*. Nothing is free, however, and you need to consider the cost factor of the device used to project or display the image. Typically LCD projectors are used with notebook computers to present electronic PowerPoint presentations.

For cost analysis, you should only use the cost of the projection device. Don't add the cost of the PC because the computer has many more business uses beyond presentations. Also, you can't really assign a cost to each image because there is no extra charge to make 10 more electronic visuals in a presentation.

Using ShowSTARTER® to calculate the number of visuals, our 20-minute presentation will require 35 images as compared to 10 overheads and 30 slides. This is because the change from one electronic image to another is a little faster than with slides. Hence, more visual impressions are possible when the duration stays the same (20 minutes).

Looking at cost per presentation, the equipment needed to project the image can be in-house (owned) or outsourced (rented). An LCD projector varies in price depending on feature/function issues, but if we assume owning one requires an investment of about $4,000, your weekly electronic presentation will cost about $80 ($4,000 divided by 50 weeks). Compared to 10 color overheads ($25) or 30 slides ($75), this appears to be the least cost-effective choice, on paper. In fact, if you went out and rented the LCD projector, your costs for that one presentation will be even higher ($200 or more). However, the outsourced costs are always higher.

TIP

One way to know if you should buy or rent the display device is to estimate the minimum number of electronic presentations you expect to give in one year. Divide that number into the cost of a projector. If the answer is lower than a typical rental charge for that type of projector, then you might want to consider a purchase.

For example, you plan on giving 50 presentations this year. You set your sights on a shiny new projector that costs $8,000 to buy. $8,000 divided by 50 is $160. If it costs more than $160 to rent the same kind of projector, then it makes sense to buy the unit.

Use a one year scenario even though your equipment will naturally last longer. To remain current with technology you would have to upgrade every year, so the rent or buy comparison is done against a one-year time frame to take the most conservative view. A five-year comparision would surely make you choose to buy everytime. In fact, most rental prices are based on the equipment paying for itself within one year.

One big issue is that electronic images have no incremental costs per additional visual. Thus, your hard disk can store hundreds of visuals, any of which can be accessed as backup or support information. Electronic presentations offer the flexibility to make changes, updates, create builds and overlays, and even allow for more advanced activity using multi-media and hyperlinks.

From a cost standpoint, that kind of flexibility makes the electronic visuals the better choice.

CONVENIENCE OF OVERHEADS

Convenience is about portability and relevancy. I mention portability because overheads are tangible. You have to carry them around and handle them. The handling factor makes over-heads a less attractive media choice.

A three-ring binder of 50 color overheads in vinyl protective sleeves weighs about five pounds. Some presenters carry two or three times this much for certain presentations, which can amount to about 15 pounds of plastic! In addition, overheads can accidentally fall from the "stack," and many a presenter has experienced the "transparency crawl" in an attempt to quickly get everything back into the original sequence.

Another issue of convenience is relevancy, or keeping things current. Many presentations, especially financial ones, rely on the most up-to-date facts to drive home the message. Color overheads limit this timeliness of information to availability of the nearest color printer. In fact, the more specialized the printer you used, the less likely you can find a similar type when you are offsite at a presentation and you want to make changes or updates to several of your color overheads. This media is device-dependent and usually only reproduces consistently when using the same device that made it.

25

Foiled Again

I was consulting with a group of engineers from IBM several years ago (early 1990s, in case you just picked this book up at yard sale in the year 2015!). At the time, I suggested they present electronically, using an LCD panel and overhead projector. They wanted to present electronically, but hadn't budgeted for the equipment and were headed to six different cities, so renting LCD panels was not an option either. They already owned a color thermal wax-transfer printer, so they went with color overheads.

Now stay with me on this. Tektronix (big company) made the printer and that particular model had 6MB of RAM memory with PostScript features. Think of PostScript as "special fonts." (Yes, this information is important!) IBM's visuals were very "graphic" intensive, with lots of schematics, diagrams and drawings, and, every so often, text on an angle. Thank goodness for PostScript! The visuals took a while to print so the RAM memory was important.

Once prepared, the engineers embarked on the six-city tour with their binder of about 70 color overheads. First stop, Los Angeles. All goes well. But on the afternoon flight to San Francisco, somehow 12 overheads become plastic prunes from a cup of hot coffee! Yep, you guessed it—the *important* 12 overheads.

Guess what? There was no hotel or public location with a Tektronix color printer. (No surprise there.) Now it's past 5:00 p.m. and the hotel business center is closed. But, after some begging, pleading, and the usual threat of physical harm, they manage to get the hotel manager to open the business center. YES! A color printer! What luck! Oh wait, it's an ink jet, not a thermal. It's a Xerox, not a Tektronix. RAM memory? Don't even go there! PostScript? I don't think so.

They printed the overheads anyway (just to have something), and, of course, they didn't look anything like the other overheads. The audience spent more time distracted than interested, and the presentation pretty much bombed.

Moral of the story: You can't rely on off-site locations to provide consistency with color printed material since that media is device dependent.

One other issue involves the lack of convenience in printing color overheads. After your visuals are created in PowerPoint, you typically have to leave your desk and go to the location of the color printer. In larger settings, this type of printer is not the office printer located a few steps from your desk. Instead, it usually resides in a more central location and may end up being shared by a larger number of users. More people waiting to use the same device will result in longer lines!

CONVENIENCE OF 35MM SLIDES

Here's one for you: There are eight different ways to load 35mm slides into a carousel and only one way is correct. This can pose a problem if you are running out of time.

TIP

> The fast way to load 35mm slides into a carousel is to face the carousel so the first slot (number one) is to your left. This would be the same as if you were standing in front of the lens looking down at the tray. Take a slide and hold it up to the light so it appears correctly oriented as you look at it. Now simply flip it backward (which will turn it upside-down) and drop it into the slot. This look, flip, and drop process can be done fairly quickly.

Remember that convenience is about portability and relevancy. For slides, the portability issue is not so much that they are heavy (like carrying 100 overheads). Instead, you have some limitations concerning how many you can use.

For instance, the number of slots in a carousel limits slides. When glass-mounted, slides are limited to 80 per carousel tray. With cardboard or plastic mounts, you can use a carousel that holds 140 slides, but the risk of the slides getting jammed increases with the thinner and lighter mounts. Of course you can bring several carousels, but the convenience of portability is affected.

As far as relevancy goes, you actually have less flexibility for making changes when using 35mm slides. It's not that you'll have trouble finding a development lab to process 35mm film; rather, how will you get the slides shot in the first place? The good news is that you can electronically send your PowerPoint file to 24-hour services for processing. But, turnaround time is at least a day if you are out of driving range. The bottom line is that it is not likely you'll be able to make changes to the slides conveniently.

Okay, it's not all negative with slides. (No pun intended.) For certain presentations, the slide's emulsion, a maximum of 5,200 horizontal lines (resolution), offers the best contrast for color and image definition. If you are giving a medical presentation and the audience needs to see the changes in skin tissue to determine a medical condition, the subtle shades and color variations will be most accurate with 35mm slides. Electronic LCD projectors and color printers do not have the resolution (yet) to match slides, so you need to consider the importance of color definition in your support visuals.

High-color definition requirements, such as images rendered in computer-aided design and manufacturing (CAD-CAM) applications, would be another instance where I would recommend 35mm slides over electronic images.

CONVENIENCE OF ELECTRONIC IMAGES

When your images are stored on your notebook computer, you are ready to present! Now that is convenience. When you look at portability and relevancy, electronic images pass those two tests with flying colors.

Portability regarding storage issues for visuals is virtually non-existent. Your notebook computer doesn't weigh more each time you add more images. That would be like saying every time you learn something new, your brain gets heavier and you gain weight. That means the smartest people in the world would be HUGE! Einstein would have weighed about 11,000 pounds!

As far as limitations go, you can store as many visuals as your hard disk can hold. There is no slide carousel to limit you.

But electronic images address portability in a different way. It has to do with transfer. The ability to transfer or disseminate information through other electronic methods makes the electronic presentation more useful. Check out Part V, "Working with PowerPoint on the Web," if you want to stimulate your thinking about information sharing.

25

Welcome to the Machine

Electronic presentations made today can be delivered in similar form, before and after the actual event. You can reinforce your message to create lasting impact.

For example, you can send a self-running "overview" of your presentation to people in advance. Nothing prevents you from emailing your PowerPoint show to expected attendees, which contains information that helps support your message. This may even prompt better attendance.

After the event, you might have a more detailed version of the presentation available on your Web site, for example, for people to download and reference. The idea of electronic color hard copy takes on a whole new meaning in terms of cost and convenience!

Clearly you don't have the same flexibility with slides and overheads as you do with the electronic form.

I think relevancy is the best quality of this media type. Instant updates, timely changes, and custom versions allow a presenter to tailor current content to more specific audiences. You might have a product presentation for both end-users of your product and your resellers (distribution channel). Many of the visuals are the same, but the end-users aren't going to see the visuals about the "wholesale-pricing model" and the "channel-promotion program." You can either have multiple versions of this presentation on your computer, or simply go to PowerPoint's Slide Sorter view and "hide" the images you don't wish displayed to certain groups.

The electronic presentation format also offers the convenience of instant access. Action buttons and hyperlinks allow easy navigation to back up and support information, including links to other applications on the computer. The capability to do "what-if" scenarios suggests a dimension in presenting that you cannot even consider with more traditional media like slides and overheads.

So, from a convenience perspective, electronic images have too many advantages to ignore.

CONTINUITY OF OVERHEADS

The real clincher when deciding on a media type for the presentation is continuity, which is really about keeping the attention of the audience. If there is any break in the action—any interruption of the flow, any distraction at all—the continuity of the presentation will erode. This reduces the impact of the message.

From a continuity viewpoint, color overheads carry a limitation during the actual presentation process itself.

For one thing, the audience is subjected to the "blast of white light" each time there is a change to the next color overhead.

To overcome the "white light" issue, some presenters may choose to shut off the projector between changes, but that still doesn't eliminate the problem of guessing if the next visual placed on the projector will be straight when the light pops on. If the image is slanted or skewed in any way, the audience is distracted. You have to touch these things and manually place them on the projector, and you don't always get it right.

Even if the transparency is perfectly straight, the presenter, trying to make fast changes, eventually drifts closer to the projector. Soon, the presenter ends up blocking the view of the screen of some of the audience, prompting comments like "I know you're a pain but I still can't see though you!"

Finally, continuity is broken if a presenter has to search for support information. I've seen so many instances where an audience member brings up a specific issue, and the presenter spends a few minutes searching the stack of overheads for the "visual proof" of the point. During all that time, the rest of the crowd is generally distracted and they begin thinking more about dinner than discussion.

CONTINUITY OF 35MM SLIDES

You have fewer continuity problems with 35mm slides simply because there are no handling issues. Yes, slides can get jammed occasionally in a projector, but for the most part, this media type addresses the continuity issue nearly as well as electronic images.

One difference is quantity of images. The carousel is limited (80 to 140) and changing carousels during the presentation breaks the continuity. Of course, you don't want to keep an audience without a break for more than an hour, so 80 slides in a carousel should be more than enough to make it to each break.

The only minor continuity problem that 35mm slides pose is the on/off transition to the next slide. But, audiences get used to the pattern after a while, and it's not really a big deal.

In fact, many slide presentations incorporate more than one projector and cross-fade between projected images, which simulates an electronic presentation.

But if you go to that extent, why not use the computer?

CONTINUITY OF ELECTRONIC IMAGES

Certain continuity issues demand the use of electronic images. They include builds and overlays, action buttons and hyperlinks, live applications, and multimedia options.

Builds and overlays, which reveal segments of information (text or graphics), help an audience understand more complex information. These techniques are most effective when done electronically. You can use slides for these effects, but you are limited in the number per carousel. You can attempt a text build with overheads. You know, the magic piece of paper that reveals yet another bullet! Ever notice how the paper always falls off the projector somewhere past the half-way point? Well, as Socrates once said, "Give it up, Crito!" Or, as I used to say, using my old Bronx accent, "Fuh-geddda-bowd-it."

Naturally, action buttons and hyperlinks allow non-linear navigation using the computer. This, by definition, requires electronic presentations. However, the instant access is what maintains the continuity of support information to the central theme.

Live software demonstrations, real-time computer applications, and multimedia presentations can only be done electronically; otherwise, the continuity of the event is completely missing. Imagine showing up to a lecture on using PowerPoint, and the presenter is displaying only screen shots of the software on overheads! Wait—that's this book! Yeah, but a book is not a presentation; it's a book. The media must match the message.

The issues of cost, convenience, and continuity seem to point in the direction of electronic images as being the most effective media choice for business presentations. Selecting the proper media should be your first consideration, before you start designing any visuals.

25

Let's Back Up!

So, you think we should put an end to slides and overheads? Not so fast! Let me tell you a little story about the need for back-up.

There was this sales event, see, sort of like a tradeshow, see, where makers of "new products" were presenting to potential distributors. It cost $1,000 per minute to present to about 15 potential buyers. But, landing just one deal could be worth millions.

I was brought in to coach the presenters before each would make "the big pitch." I worked with this one guy named Jerry. His product was quite visual. Jerry made some changes to the presentation here and there, and left feeling much more confident.

Thirty minutes before his presentation, he arrived at the conference center, set up his laptop and LCD projector, launched his PowerPoint presentation, and made sure everything was working. As he waited for the audience to arrive, he stepped into the restroom next door for a few minutes. When he returned, his PC and projector had disappeared! No, not disappeared as in "Look, magic!"; disappeared as in "Look, stolen!"

Luckily, he still had his briefcase in which he had about seven 35mm slides from an older presentation on the same topic. Those few visuals along with several of his handwritten sketches using a flip chart helped him secure an order. Sure, they might have "felt sorry" for him for losing his equipment, but he couldn't know that in advance, even if it were true. The back-up media saved him.

Computers can be stolen, but no one wants your slides or overheads! You won't find some guy on the corner opening his jacket while you pass by, saying "Pssst! Check it out—corporate slides!" It just doesn't happen.

So, having a set of back-up materials, whether it be slides or overheads, makes those media types a very viable and important part of the presentation process. They might come in handy someday!

WORKING WITH DESIGN TEMPLATES

You already learned about templates in Chapter 2, "Creating a Basic Presentation," but I want to make a point about the relationship of the template to the readability and to the simplicity of the message.

READABILITY FROM A DISTANCE

A clearly defined purpose needs the support of clearly readable visuals. Will everyone in the room be able to see everything on the screen? Whether you use overheads, 35mm slides, or electronic images, the audience must be able to read your support information or why show it to them? You can use several ways to test whether your images are going to be readable from a distance, even before you consider templates.

For overheads, place a transparency on the floor and stand over it. If you have no problem reading the text, then the audience member in the back of the room will not have a problem reading the information when projected.

For 35mm slides, hold a slide up to the light at arm's length. If you can read all the information clearly, chances are people sitting in the back will be able to read the slide when it is projected.

For electronic images, we use the "8 to 1 rule." The rule states that eight times the height of the image is the maximum viewing distance for the audience to read small-sized text. When I say small, I mean 24 points in size.

So, if your image is 6 feet high, people sitting 48 feet away can read text with a font size of 24 points. If the font sizes are smaller, people will have to sit closer to the screen.

NOTE

> The height is based on the image, not the screen the image is projected on. You may have a 9-foot-high projection screen, but, depending on where you place your projection device, your image may not always fill the screen. In an art gallery, the size of the wall doesn't make the painting any bigger!

You can't control where people sit if you haven't planned the seating in advance. Sometimes you get to an event and the audience looks like they are sitting on another planet! You need to consider the sizes of the elements on your visuals.

TIP

> Run your slide show in PowerPoint and stand back about eight feet from your computer, assuming your screen is about one foot high. Can you read all the text on every visual? Wherever you have trouble, go back and check the font size. You may have to make some adjustments.

Knowing the importance of visibility and readability from a distance, you can examine the use of templates in PowerPoint.

The templates are very helpful because they make choices for you and let you do your real job rather than the job of a graphic artist. But, you may need to make modifications in order for the templates to be effective.

In general, I find the templates in PowerPoint are designed more closely to the media of print than they are truly designed for presentation. I'll tell you why. It has to do with point size. That's the measurement term for a typeface, or font.

NOTE

> PowerPoint calls typefaces "fonts." Actually, a typeface is a family of letter styles (Times Roman, Arial, Courier) and a font is what you do to a typeface, such as bold, italic, underline. But let's not worry about terminology for now.

25

The slide layouts that accompany nearly every template in PowerPoint tend to use the same font sizes, from 44 points in the title to as small as 20 points in the body of the layout. From an electronic visual design standpoint, you don't want to have font sizes less than 24 points on any image. This should already tell you that any text below the template's third level is probably unacceptable for your screen show.

But why dangle over the threshold of 24 points? Why push it? Set your sights on 36 points or higher. Adjust the template before you get started and make the titles 60 points and the first level 40 points. This will force you to use fewer words, making the visuals more conceptual and therefore easier for the audience to grasp and the presenter to deliver.

SIMPLICITY IN DESIGN

The templates offer a variety of graphic elements, geometric shapes, and other interesting components to carry a design theme throughout the presentation.

When you work with templates, see if the design is generic or specific. Generic templates contain very simple geometric shapes. Specific templates contain more complex and noticeable designs. Complexity forces the brain to interpret and think. You don't want the background design in your visuals to get more attention than your message. If you're marveling at the costumes, you can't be listening to the lines!

Over the years, I've learned to simplify themes. For example, at MediaNet, our *Electrifying Templates™ for PowerPoint* is a collection of very simple geometric PowerPoint presentation designs that fit the generic model of almost any topic. When designing so many presentations for so many different companies, it's easier to start with a very simple template and then add the complexity only to the visuals that require it. You can create your own templates using the same logic—simplicity!

Overall, templates should not hinder readability from a distance nor contain specific design elements that cause the audience to be distracted from the message. The presenter delivers the message; the visuals only support it.

CREATING HANDOUT MATERIALS

Almost every presentation has some form of handouts. The nature and the timing of these materials are two very important issues. When you decide to give people information to walk away with, you have to think about exactly what they will be given and when they will receive it.

NATURE OF HANDOUTS

The handouts should always be different from the presentation. I know this breaks your heart to think that you now have extra work to do, but you really need to consider this point. Let's think about the relationship between the handouts and the presentation. Typically, you might fall into the trap of printing out a hard copy of your visuals for the audience to take away with them. You can look at this in two ways—conceptually or specifically.

If your presentation is designed for a visual presenter, it is conceptual in nature. The images are clear, readable, easy to understand, and very supportive of the stories and analogies used by the presenter. A copy of these visuals will be useless after a short time. When the event is over, people will not have the presenter available to explain the concepts. Someone will find a copy of the handout about three weeks later under a pile of desk rubble. The person will see a visual with an arrow, a circle, and a big number 11 and have absolutely no clue as to what it means. That is a useless handout.

Same scenario, except the handout reads like a book. Lots of text on each image, very wordy phrases, full sentences, extremely detailed charts, and complex tables of numbers. The handout is designed specifically. Nice handout and useful for a long time, but I pity the person who attended that presentation! It was probably a data dump on the audience with a presenter who simply read from the visuals most of the time. I have seen so many of these that one look at the handouts, and I can pretty much know how the presentation went.

Do you see how you can't win if you try to do two things at once? Handouts must be different from the presentation in the same way a book is different from the movie. How would you feel if you went to a movie and the book was on the big screen? That's right, the entire book—huge pages turning slowly while you gaze in amazement, then turn to a friend, and say, "Wow, look at the size of those fonts!"

TIP

> Use the notes feature (see Chapter 10, "Creating and Printing Presentation Materials") to enter the concept or actual script for each visual. If you print a set of these for the audience, then they can review the comments long after the presentation is ended. This makes the handout more useful.

If you plan on having the audience take notes, then you can consider note-taking handouts. You can make these handouts in PowerPoint (see Chapter 10). They should include a combination of your visuals and an area for note-taking so that the audience can create personal references for later review.

To leave people with supporting documents is better than to bombard them with tons of data on every visual. Specification sheets, detailed charts, advertisements, articles, even free samples are just some of the support items that you can provide to tout your message long after you're gone.

A Pattern to Remember

Hand out more than you say—say more than you show—show it simply!

To hand out more than you say is to provide more material for later review than you verbally cover during the presentation.

To say more than you show means more words are always coming out of your mouth than people are reading on the screen. Remember that the visuals are speaker support, not the speaker. Do not read the visuals to the audience unless you plan to use a white bouncing ball over the text to help people follow along!

To show it simply is self-explanatory. No one ever complains about a business presentation that is clear and easy to understand. Simple visuals force the audience to listen to the presenter's explanation of the intended message.

TIMING OF HANDOUTS

A lot of people ask me, "When is the best time to distribute handouts—before or after the presentation?" I pause, look away for a second, and answer, "Yes." That's not an answer because there is no definite answer, one way or the other. It depends on your objective and your ability to keep the attention span of the group.

I start with a very simple question. Do you think the handouts will distract the audience from your presentation? If the answer is yes, distribute handouts at the end. If the answer is no, you can give them out at the beginning or the end.

For example, one of my seminars, "Presenting Made Easy," is a full-day workshop covering eight different topics. The audience receives a "kit" containing a book, a CD-ROM, additional handouts, and other information about technology discussed during the seminar. Although the handouts are not required to follow along through the topics, the information is provided at the beginning so that the audience can have a reference available during the workshop day. In addition, the scope of the material helps the audience decide how much note-taking is necessary. The more depth to the handouts, the less notes to take. Yes, there

25

is a risk of distraction, but that makes the presenter (in this case, me) work that much harder to keep attention focused on the issue at hand.

Check out the opposite scenario: If I give a two-hour lecture as a keynote speaker, I only provide handouts after the session. I prefer to limit the distraction of people reading ahead and maintain the highest attention for the event. Because my handouts are not copies of each visual, the audience would not be able to "follow along" anyway, so why give them out ahead of time?

You have to examine the handout materials and judge how critical a role they play in the presentation. Can the audience respond to your "call to action" without the handouts in front of them?

Regardless of when you distribute handouts, always announce them at the beginning of the presentation. Let people know what you have, what it covers, and when they can expect to receive it.

CONTROLLING EYE MOVEMENT

We know that eight seconds is the average attention span on any visual. You can leave the visual up as long as you want, but the first eight seconds set the tone for how long someone reads and how quickly that person can begin to listen. Face it, you can't read and listen at the same time. Want to test this? Hand a newspaper article to a loved one. Begin speaking right away. You'll hear, in an angry tone, "How can I read this if you keep talking?" Try it (once).

Given the need to direct the eye quickly, ask yourself some questions. When a visual is displayed, where does a person look first? At what point on the image is the concentration of attention? Where does a person look next? If you can control a physical element of the audience, you will command more attention per visual. You can do this by controlling eye movement. The part of the body most used by an audience member is the eyes. A presentation is mostly watched. You need to find effective ways to direct the eye to the most important element in the visual.

NOTE

> For this discussion, I'll use the word "eye" to mean both eyes. Another way to think about the word "eye" is as a focal point.

When designing the visuals, you need to think about several things to control eye movement. These include

- Establishing anchors
- Choosing typefaces and fonts
- Using builds and overlays
- Creating emphasis

ESTABLISHING ANCHORS

An *anchor* in a visual is really just the solid footing for the brain. It's where we dock our attention to a focal point to begin processing the information. Usually, the starting point is the upper-left corner of the visual because our reading pattern is left-to-right in the English language. But all visuals are not the same. Text changes size, charts are used, artwork appears, lines are drawn, and shapes are placed in varying spots. It can get very confusing.

Figure 25.1 is a simple text chart. The typical way your eye moves on the visual is first you read the word "agenda" in the title. Then you begin reading the numbers on the left side of the visual. Because they look the same, you scan them in a downward fashion. At about the third line (12:00), you say, "Wait, I should be reading this left to right. Let me go back." In the few moments it takes to readjust and start again, you have not been listening to the presenter.

Figure 25.1
Without an anchor, the eye initially scans the text as if it were two separate columns.

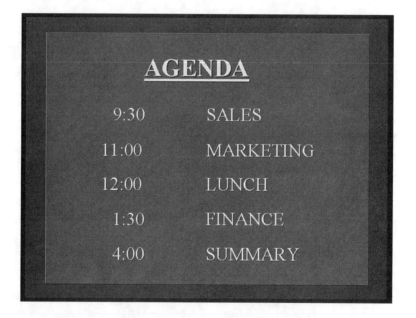

AGENDA	
9:30	SALES
11:00	MARKETING
12:00	LUNCH
1:30	FINANCE
4:00	SUMMARY

In Figure 25.2, the geometric shape in the background helps guide the eye across instead of down. Text alone cannot guide the eye. Geometric shapes guide the eye.

Geometric shapes are universal. They are not subject to cultural limitations in the way languages are. A square is the same shape in Toronto as it is in Tokyo. We process universal shapes first, and then the language next. So think global!

In Figure 25.3, the list of items covers the basic steps necessary for launching hot air balloons. It is a text chart with no geometric shapes.

Figure 25.2
The geometric shape provides an anchor to guide the eye horizontally, allowing a faster scan of the information.

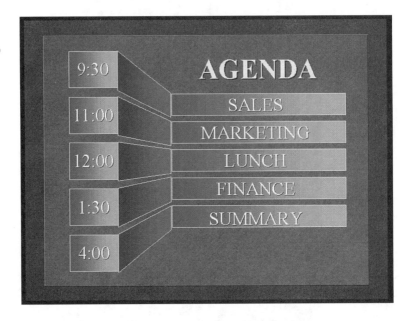

In Figure 25.4, your eye stops after the question mark in the heading and jumps to the tip of the arrowhead. But once you start checking out a geometric shape, you have to finish it to form the image in your mind. So, your eye travels to the end of the arrow at the bottom left corner of the visual to complete the shape. But, you then process the next shape (the bottom balloon) and after that, the text element near it ("Assemble Balloon"). Without thinking, you'll read the steps from bottom to top (backward, technically).

Figure 25.3
While looking at this visual, your eye will move from top to bottom, as in reading a list.

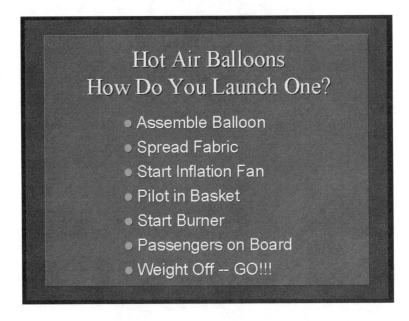

25

The whole image is designed to redirect your eye. Even the thin diagonal lines on the right side of the visual continue to help your eye move upward. In fact, as the visual forces your eye upward from the bottom, it matches the concept of launching a balloon from the ground.

Figure 25.4
The arrow is an anchor in the background. It forces you to find its origin (lower-left corner) and then you end up reading the text in an upward pattern.

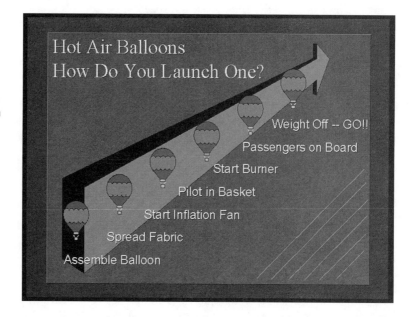

Parallel Anchors

Another method for anchoring the eye is to keep text parallel, especially in bulleted lists. If you examine only the first word in a list of bulleted items, see if they follow the same pattern. For example, if one word is a gerund (ends with "ing") and another word is a plural noun and another word is a verb, it is not parallel.

If the first word is "Teaches," then each bullet should answer a "What else does this do?" question. Other bullets might begin with "Helps," "Gives," "Makes," "Offers," and the like."

If the first word is "Teaching," then each bullet should answer a "What else is this doing?" question. Other bullets might begin with "Helping," "Giving," "Making," "Offering," and so forth.

Keeping things parallel lets the audience anchor to the pattern and allows them to scan the visual more quickly. A faster visual scan gives the audience more time to listen to the message.

CHOOSING TYPEFACES AND FONTS

The eye moves from the simplest shapes to the more complex. Geometric shapes are easiest and text gets more difficult. I mean, when you think about it, the letters of the alphabet are shapes, but because you need to interpret text (language), you can understand why the eye scans text last. That means the design of the letters (the typefaces and fonts) affects the eye movement of the audience.

Basically there are only two kinds of typefaces, serif (fancy) and sans serif (plain). You can be sure that all the fonts you have on your computer fall into one of those two categories. Fancy typefaces have little curls (or serifs) at the ends of the letters, plain (sans serif) typefaces don't.

The eye slows down on the fancy fonts and speeds up on the plain ones. Think of the font as a road. The more hooks and turns, the longer it takes to travel that road. Fancy fonts have more contours (hooks and turns), so we read them more slowly.

TIP

> If you choose to use two different fonts (please—no more than two!), use a serif typeface for the heading (title) and a sans serif typeface for the body of the chart.
>
> When you make a presentation, you want the eye to slow down while reading the heading (which has the key words), and speed up when reading the body of the chart (where there tends to be more text).
>
> Once the audience locks in on the title, they are more likely to get the rest of the text that follows. The heading is where the emphasis belongs because it's usually the first place the person looks.

25

The use of fonts and typefaces are the opposite of that in a newspaper. When you see a newspaper, the headlines are usually bold, Helvetica (sans serif), so that you can quickly scan them as you walk past the newsstand. But the body of the paper, Times Roman (serif), takes longer to read and therefore increases comprehension. That's why I keep my email messages in a plain font (Arial). I can't be bothered with comprehension. It might lead to responsibility, and who wants that?

If you look at Figure 25.5, you can see that the contours of the letters themselves cause distraction because the patterns keep changing. Don't you hate it when that happens? The eye travels along the contours of each letter and gets distracted as the different text shapes keep appearing. There should be a law against this!

CAUTION

> If you have the entire True Type Font library and feel compelled to use every font on every visual, you may be suffering from CTD, Compulsive Typeface Disorder. Seek help immediately!

Capitalization also affects eye movement. Take a look at Figure 25.6. Did you read it again? It's true. A series of all capital letters makes the text look the same. Our language thrives on ascends and descends as seen in letters like "b" and "g." These extenders give letters character. ALL CAPS leave no room for emphasis or inflection. This causes the eye to read the information again. If the words in all caps were read out loud, the sound would be monotone.

Figure 25.5
The heading "NEW PRODUCTS," is a Times Roman font. In contrast, the word "Radios" in the first bullet is Helvetica, which is a sans serif, or plain, font.

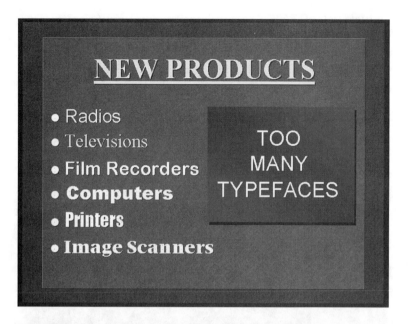

Figure 25.6
When all the words have equal weight, it makes it harder to know what's important.

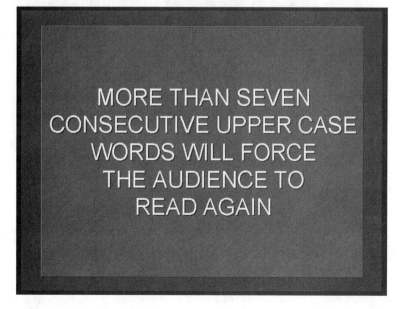

By structuring text phrases similarly to the way we read (uppercase and lowercase), you can then use capitalization to place emphasis at a particular point on the visual. Figure 25.7 shows the verbal inflection. If you read the text out loud in this example, the capitalized words would sound louder than the rest.

One other capitalization issue involves the use of "initial caps" or "first caps," as some refer to it. This is the choice to capitalize the first letter of every "major" word in a given text line to create emphasis. The problem is that there is a lack of consistency on which words to initial cap. After all, what is a "major" word? Is it one with more than four letters? Is it one that is not a preposition? How do you decide? If you are not consistent, the audience begins to get distracted since reading initial caps is not the norm, especially if the pattern in not consistent.

Stick to the natural way we read by initial capping only the first word of a text line, rather than using inconsistent or distracting capitalization methods.

Figure 25.7
The proper use of upper- and lowercase allows the visual to "speak" for itself by indicating the intended inflection.

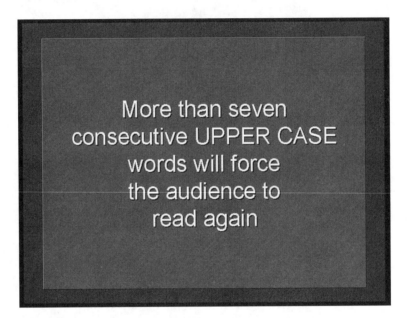

USING BUILDS AND OVERLAYS

Eye movement can be affected by the sheer amount of information the audience is allowed to see on a given visual. Sometimes I look at a visual and think the heading should start with, "It was the best of times, it was the worst of times." You don't want *A Tale of Two Cities* showing up on your visuals!

Obviously, it's easy for me to tell you to reduce the clutter. But the real world doesn't always work that way. The visuals get wordy for one reason or another and maybe you can't be the one to say stop. So what can you do?

One way to soften the blow for the audience is to use the build sequence. This simple technique is used to reveal elements of a visual in stages in order to maintain a steady focus for the audience.

Examine Figures 25.8, 25.9, and 25.10. They are shown as three visual impressions, even though only one visual would appear if you look in the Slide Sorter. That's because the build is a transition effect in PowerPoint.

→ For more information about slide effects, **see** "Setting Slide Transitions" in Chapter 15, "Working with Animation," **p. 321**.

Figure 25.8 shows the beginning of a build sequence with the first line revealed and the remaining information hidden. The presenter is able to concentrate on this element of the visual until the next item is needed.

Figure 25.8
The first in a series using builds. One line appears and limits the distraction from additional items to maintain focus.

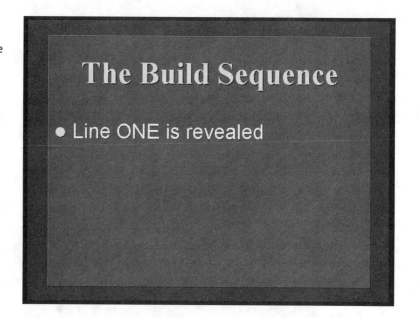

When ready, the presenter reveals the next bulleted item, as shown in Figure 25.9. I prefer using the dim-down—or gray-down—approach for a more effective text build sequence. Dimming the color of the prior item—usually to a shade of gray—then revealing the next item allows the eye to focus on the brighter and most current element and still maintains some visibility for what has already been covered. I do this to help all those people who are waking up and want to know exactly what bullet point I'm discussing before they doze off again! I'm kidding, they aren't sleeping—they are usually on their way home by that point!

Figure 25.10 shows the next bulleted item, which is revealed at whatever pace the presenter chooses, allowing direct manipulation of eye movement in a downward pattern throughout the entire visual.

Another sequencing method that helps with data clutter is when you reveal a section of information at a time. Text, data, and graphic elements—each of which contain complete thoughts—are revealed in segments called overlays.

Figure 25.9
The next item in the build sequence is revealed while using the dim-down approach to darken or dim the color of the prior item.

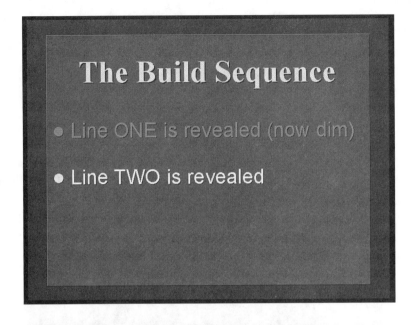

Figure 25.10
The last bulleted point in the build sequence is revealed, and you can still see the dimmed text as a reference to what has been covered.

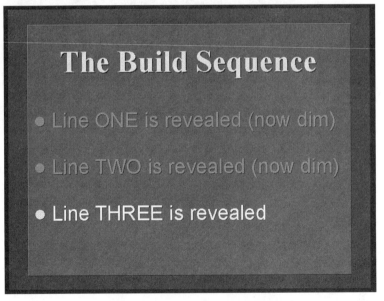

If you show the audience the completed image, too many elements would distract the eye and reduce the effectiveness of the visual. When the eye is bombarded with multiple activities or thoughts, it doesn't know where to look first. If it takes time to design the visual, you have to give the audience time to digest it.

If, however, the audience clearly sees the creative thought process that went into the complete visual, they will not be confused. So, imagine a busy puzzle. If you watch the pieces of the puzzle fall into place, you can appreciate the whole picture. Have you ever put together a model or a toy with a lot of pieces? There's always that diagram in the instruction pamphlet that shows the "exploded" view of how all the pieces come together to form the object. Have kids and you'll experience these diagrams constantly! The point is that the exploded view diagram lets you see the pieces spread apart and helps you understand how they fit together.

Figures 25.11, 25.12, 25.13, and 25.14 show the base image and the three subsequent overlays used to show a communications network linking certain office locations in the United States and connected to a central hub. Yet the image can be separated into several little stories or thoughts which, when combined, create the final impression. Consider the amount of information on each of your visuals. Ask yourself if it would be more effective to reveal some of the elements in stages by using overlays.

Figure 25.11
The base image for an overlay sequence. The map of the U.S. appears with only a title above it.

Figure 25.12
The first overlay or "layer" appears showing the office locations (dots) that the communications network will link together.

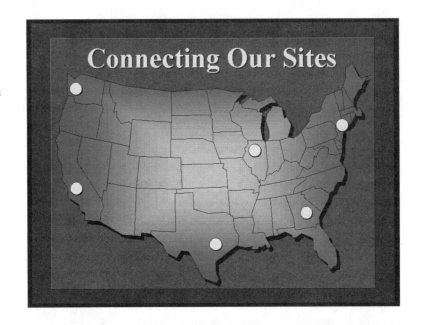

Figure 25.13
The next piece of the overlay "puzzle" shows the communications network connecting the locations.

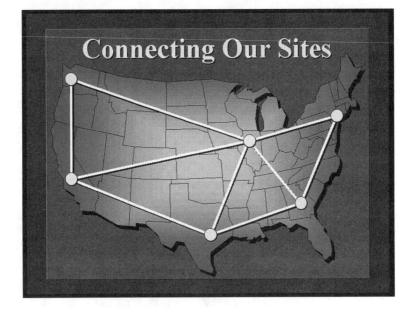

Figure 25.14
The last overlay in the sequence shows the hub or central communication area noted by the "star" in the center of the map (Chicago).

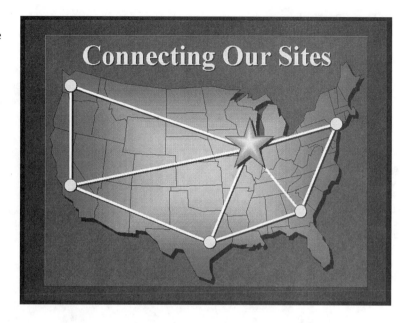

CREATING EMPHASIS

You can control eye movement by designing ways for the audience to immediately know where to look when the visual is displayed. If people are searching around, looking for something on the screen that remotely matches your words, then you have a problem. When people don't "get it," the attention span drops and boredom sets in very quickly. You can guide the eye using words or pictures. Headlines and arrows are both effective when designing guidance into visual content.

HEADLINES

How would you feel if every time you picked up the morning paper the headline read "News"? That's it, just News. Every day the same thing, News. You wouldn't be as interested. I know I wouldn't. Headlines, baby, headlines! That sells newspapers.

So, the best way to direct the eye to the important area of a visual using words is to start with *emphatic headlines*. Too many visuals have flat titles these days. Quarterly Sales—1st Quarter, Quarterly Sales—2nd Quarter, Quarterly Sales—stop already!

Death from a Pull-Down Menu?
See—a little bit of drama in the headline and you went for it! Face it, we are addicted to headlines. Why do you think the National Enquirer is so popular? That publication thrives on headlines. Actually, it's amazing how Enquirer editors pick their headlines. They have these three cardboard boxes—one with a bunch of famous names, another box full of verbs, and a third box with lots of nouns. Then, each time they need a new headline, they reach into the boxes and pull out one word from each and end up with: Donny and Marie are Aliens! And off to the presses they go!

In Figure 25.15, the two charts contain the same data. In the one to the left, I have a 25% chance that the audience will be looking at the exact part of the line chart I will refer to, even before I begin speaking. The heading is flat. However, in the same figure, the chart to the right includes the emphatic headline "Fourth Quarter Sales Post Record Highs!" which directs the eye quickly to the part of the line chart I want attention brought to—the fourth quarter as opposed to the other quarters. In fact, the headline even tells the audience how I feel about the information.

Figure 25.15
The headline tells a story. On the left, a flat heading doesn't help guide the eye. On the right, the headline quickly gets you to the exact part of the visual to be discussed.

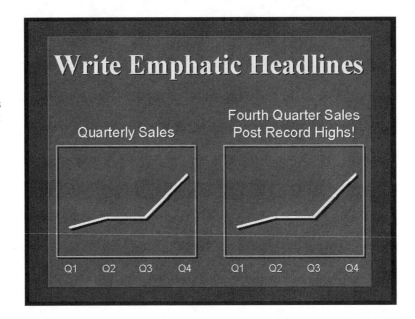

Don't waste the valuable real estate in the heading. If something is important, try to emphasize it in the title of the visual. Okay, you can't do this on every visual, but you can at least review all your headings and see where emphasis can be placed. Used wisely, emphasis in the right areas of a visual can affect both the physical and emotional reactions of the audience.

The Laser Pointer and You

You're watching a movie. The killer is lurking in the bushes. Suddenly, a big hand floats over the screen with a finger pointing to a spot near a tree. You'd shout, "Get that thing off the screen!" That's because the visual (camera) has to do the work to guide the eye of the audience.

You should never have to use a laser pointer or any pointing device during a presentation. To use one means you couldn't figure out how to guide the eye with the visual. You needed a prop. Okay, now the laser pointer people hate me.

Face it. You instantly have problems when using a laser pointer. First, no one can hold it steady. And, if you forget to shut it off, you must apologize for searing the eyes out of the people in row three. But mostly you have to spend time directing the pointer to a spot on the screen, which causes you to look away from the audience and interact with the screen. Visual creatures (the audience) demand eye contact. If you're looking at the screen and we're looking at the screen, then who's presenting? You can't interact with things that don't breathe, like the visual.

The only time a pointer makes sense is when the visual is moving, like a video clip. Because the image is in motion, the pointer helps steady the eye to a specific area within the motion. But for still images in presentations, the eye can be directed by creating emphasis.

Don't get me wrong, sometimes pointing to the screen is required in the presentation. You should always do this from a distance and never touch the screen. Touching the screen causes the visual to move or vibrate, and it forces you to step in front of the image. Never block the light source because the visual is designed for a flat surface, and not your backside!

But you can use your voice to target specific areas. You can say, "If you look at the center of the visual…" or "The object in the upper-right corner represents…". You can verbally help guide the eye quickly through very complex information.

ARROWS

The simplest graphic element for controlling eye movement is the arrow. In many instances, using arrows as part of the visual can create the emphasis you need. Arrows not only show direction, but they can also indicate conflict, options, choices, and trends.

But be careful with arrows. Eye movement can easily be distracted when arrows point in too many directions on the same visual. Take a look at Figure 25.16. The eye scans the visual elements and eventually wanders or gets lost. The colors, text sizes, inconsistent capitalization methods, and the variety of geometric shapes add to the confusion. Try to limit the number of arrows used for emphasis on a single visual.

Figure 25.16
This chart uses too many arrows! Your eye movement is actually disrupted rather than enhanced. When this happens it takes longer to scan the image, which reduces attention to the message being delivered.

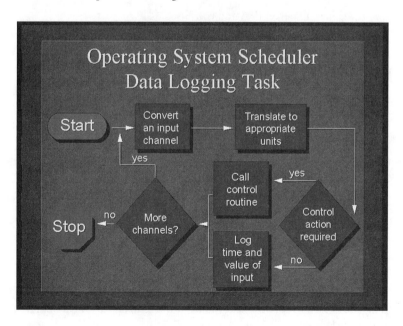

USING COLOR

I have always been fascinated with color. In 1985, my wife, Joan, worked as a fashion designer for a large sportswear company. She had to do all this research on color theory and the effect of certain colors on the emotions. I waded through several of the library reference books she gathered and said, "This stuff is great! Now when we prepare presentations at MediaNet, we can apply these color theory principles to help shape the story!" She said, "Yes, but think about the cost factor." I said, "What cost factor?" She smiled and said, "Well, it's going to take you a few days to look at all these books and they are already two weeks overdue!"

Of course, the big problem with those reference books was that the information related only to fabric and dyes, which made it difficult to relate to presentations. That's why, through experience, our company had to rely on its own research to draw conclusions as to the way colors influenced business presentations.

Over the years I've learned that correct color choices can have a tremendous impact on the success of the presentation. At the beginning of this chapter I pointed out that presentations delivered in black and white are less effective than those in color. We live in world of color and that, in itself, is an anchor to our understanding of information. Consider the following areas when using color:

- Incorporating symbols
- Investigating perception and contrast
- Understanding background colors and emotions

INCORPORATING SYMBOLS

Although geometric shapes are more universal, often you'll find that you need to use actual objects to describe something or make a point. You've heard the saying, "A picture is worth a thousand words." Of course today the saying has changed to, "A videotape is worth a million dollars," but that's another issue. Anyway, the use of imagery in a visual can be very helpful.

Symbols, to me, represent ideas. Clip art is basically a collection of symbols depicted as artistic renderings and available in PowerPoint or from other sources. Let's concentrate on how these elements can be used effectively or, for that matter, ineffectively.

I look for flexibility with symbols. Can I use them in the background of the visual? Can I make them into a silhouette for more utility? Can I avoid the distraction of details?

DEPTH

There is a whole area in the background of each visual just waiting to be used. Sometimes a template is used to fill the background. If the template already contains a lot of elements, you have less chance to use symbols as part of the background. That's why I like simple templates.

Figure 25.17 is a text chart showing how employees spend their time. It's clear, readable, and to the point. The background template is pretty simple. This allows you the option of adding a symbol to support the message.

Figure 25.17
This is a simple text chart. A series of percentages, arranged from highest to lowest, shows how employees spend their time during the workday.

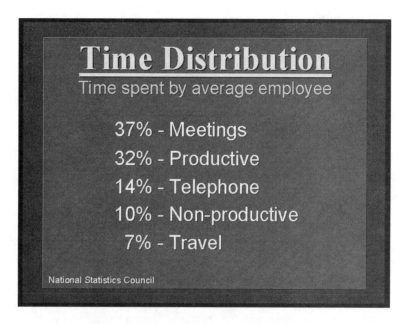

Okay, so you see the word "time" in the heading and you search the clip art library for a descriptive symbol and you find the stopwatch. As shown in Figure 25.18, if you just use a two-dimensional approach, you'll shift the text to one side and pop the clip art on the other side. This is fine, but the clip art is still pretty small and less obvious from a distance.

Figure 25.18
The hand with the stopwatch (clip art) is added and the text is moved to one side to make room for the artwork. This is a two-dimensional approach.

25

But if you think deep into the visual, there is another interpretation available. The percentages could be displayed as a pie chart. A pie chart is round, the stopwatch is round. Instead of making the graphic part of the chart, you can make a chart part of the graphic! Figure 25.19 shows a three-dimensional view of the information. The symbol is now in the background but still retains its meaning. You know it's a hand, even though text covers some of the fingers. You know it's a stopwatch, even though there's a pie in its face! The symbol and the text occupy similar space on the visual, only in layers, and create the illusion of depth.

Figure 25.19
The clip art is sized to fill the background. This three-dimensional approach creates depth while allowing the data to take a more graphical form, a pie chart.

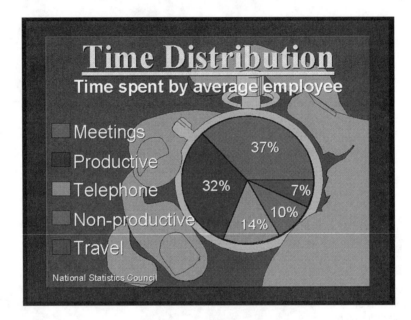

One of the best uses of the background is to incorporate photographs or natural images. A photo is the real-life symbol of an idea. Figure 25.20 is one example of how a photograph of people in a situation adds to the message in a way that clip art just can't. In keeping with our recurring theme of a visual presenter, it makes a lot of sense to use real people in real situations, not only in the message but in the media as well.

Keep in mind that photos usually contain hundreds of thousands of colors in various degrees of brightness. If you add text or other elements on top of a photo, be aware of light and dark spots. Sometimes the foreground information may blend right into the photo and not be as visible. This usually happens with text. You may have to adjust the brightness and contrast of the entire photo in order for lighter text to be readable.

All the Lonely People
Ever notice how many solutions are discussed in presentations but no people are shown using them? I think photographs are really helpful when you are trying to get an audience excited about a product or a process. If you have a "solution" message, odds are the solution is going to help people somewhere along the way. By using photographs of people in the background, you can add the human touch which might be missing among all the charts and tables in your presentations.

I'm not saying you need photos everywhere, but look at your visuals and see where pictures might enhance the story. For example, if you are describing a new project to add facilities for a growing company, photographs or even renderings may be used. But think about using photos of people working in offices, gathering around a water cooler, sharing a cup of coffee, walking through a parking lot, taking the sun with a sandwich, or just burning the midnight oil.

Scenes like these help the message appear closer to reality. Visual presenters and visual creatures are first and always people. The foundation of all communication is people.

Figure 25.20
The photograph in the background is blurred, yet still representative of the "team" concept noted in the title.

25

SILHOUETTES

I like symbols that translate well across media. Sometimes you have to think about the utility of symbols in a variety of venues. One of the things I look for is the ability to make the symbol into a silhouette. If you fill the symbol completely with black, does it still translate its meaning? Since a silhouette is only two-dimensional, the loss of depth may cause the original object to lose its meaning. For example, a stack of quarters when silhouetted would look like a cylinder. The link to money is gone. But a coffee cup would only lose depth, yet still maintain its shape as a cup.

I find this important when printing in pure black and white. Sometimes, objects in the background end up printing like big blobs and no one knows what they are. Printers today are sophisticated enough to print grayscale images, but what if you have to fax a copy of the printouts to someone? Forget about that grayscale definition you got from your laser jet!

Not every element can or needs to be a silhouette. But if the symbol translates well to a purely solid shape, you can use the shape in a lot of situations. Think about it!

DISTRACTIONS AND DISTORTIONS

Clip art images, if filled with many details, can actually become a distraction when the visual stays in view too long. The audience can get caught up in the artwork and begin to forget about the message. This can happen from the use of graphics that have a cartoonish or silly appearance. It can also happen from very sophisticated renderings that resemble a Rembrandt. The look of something is really up to you. If you don't like it, don't use it, if you don't have to.

But a more obvious distraction is a distortion. This happens when you do something to the symbol to alter its natural appearance. The alteration forces the audience to concentrate on what the symbol looked like before the distortion.

In Figure 25.21, the original bars in the chart are replaced with clip art in the form of pencils, to match the subheading of office supplies. You should always try to match a symbol closely to a concept to help clarify the message.

Figure 25.21
The pencil symbols (clip art) are sized to match the height of the original bars.

In this case, the pencils are the proper shapes to substitute for the vertically positioned bars.

But wait a minute. It doesn't always work out so conveniently. Figure 25.22 shows what happens if the height of the first pencil is not 42. Would you give someone a pencil this little? That deformed, stubby little pencil looks ridiculous. You do stuff like that to your visuals and people will wonder how you make money! Just because you have access to a clip art library doesn't mean you have to incorporate colorful symbols on every chart.

Also, be aware of the geometric shape you replace with a symbol. The bars in the previous examples were all vertical. The choice of pencils made sense. What if you decided to use a stapler as the symbol? Although a stapler is an office supply, it is meant to be viewed horizontally, not vertically. This means you would have to rotate the stapler and stand it on end to fit the vertical form of the chart.

If you have to rotate a piece of clip art, you probably picked the wrong clip art! Why? Because the audience is going to have to re-orient the clip art in their minds just to place it in context. It's even worse when you rotate text. The only people who can quickly read text at any angle are librarians. The rest of us have to tilt our heads!

Avoid distractions and distortions when incorporating symbols into your visuals.

Figure 25.22
Symbols can get distorted! To match the value for the actual data, the first "pencil" is crushed down to the point of being a distraction.

INVESTIGATING PERCEPTION AND CONTRAST

Although numerous studies have shown the beneficial results of using color in presentations, the most important reaction from color is more of a reflex. Perception is a reflex you cannot change. It happens so quickly that you barely notice it.

Try this audio perception test. As fast as you can, spell the following three words out loud and then answer the question. The key is to spell the words out loud. Come on now, you have to spell the words out loud or it doesn't count. Ready?

Spell the word MOST.

Now spell POST.

Now spell HOST.

What do you put in a toaster?

Blaaammmmmp. Wrong, if you said toast! You put bread in a toaster. It comes out as toast, but goes in as bread. If you said toast, it's because you followed the natural reflex of perception to spell the three O-S-T words and then blurt out "toast" instead of "bread." You'll try this on the next person you see. You will. I know you too well, now!

Figure 25.23 is a test in content perception. Read each of the phrases in the triangles out loud. Yes, you have to say this out loud, too. Did you read the words in both triangles? Okay, now read the phrase in each triangle, backward, one word at a time. Notice anything different on the way back? In both phrases you'll see a duplicate word.

Figure 25.23
Are you reading too much into these phrases, or not enough?

TIP

Always proofread your visuals backward, one word at a time. Reading phrases backward lets you spot not only typos, but other mistakes, as well.

If you scanned the visual and didn't notice the duplicate words, it's because you've probably heard the phrases so many times that you perceived your version to be correct. The anticipation happens because the mind moves faster than the mouth! Drink—and you can attest to this!

Color perception works much in the same way. Depending on contrast, some elements may appear closer to the eye, which may or may not enhance the message.

NOTE

The remainder of this chapter discusses color in a number of situations. Although this book is not in color, the examples I'll use should still translate well using black and white as well as contrasting shades of gray. So, when I mention a color on a visual, you'll be able to tell what I'm talking about from the shading or from the object itself.

Figure 25.24 shows how color can change perception, but it also explains why black-and-white presentations are a problem. The two red squares (the inside dark-color squares) are compared against contrasting backgrounds. The shapes appear to be different sizes but are really the same size.

Figure 25.24
The inside (red) squares are set against contrasting outer squares of white and black. Can you see a difference?

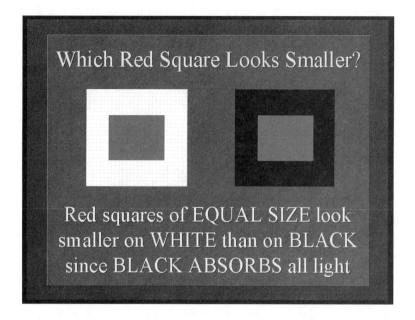

A MATTER OF CONTRAST

If you want to talk about contrast, remember that black absorbs all light. The darker the color, the more light it absorbs and therefore it seems to push the object away from the eye. White, on the contrary, reflects all light. The lighter the color, the closer the object appears to the eye. In presentations, contrast between background and foreground is critical. The objects in the background should be darker and the ones in the front should be lighter.

This is the major reason why black-and-white overhead presentations are less effective. The contrast is opposite from the norm. The data on a black-and-white overhead is black. It pulls the eye into the visual because the information seems more distant. But, the clear (white) background is reflecting white light into the audience. The problem is that the body cannot handle white light reflected into the eye for very long. It's too distracting. When you use your computer, you can look away whenever you want. But when you watch a presentation, you are being asked to keep your attention fixed for a longer period. Proper contrast is needed to keep attention.

Because too much white light is a distraction, after a while, the eye tries to avoid the conflict and with it, the content of the presentation. Try staring at a fluorescent light for a while or glancing at the sun for a few moments. Your body simply rejects massive quantities of white light.

So the rule of contrast for presentations is to use darker-color backgrounds and lighter-color foregrounds.

This is why I can never understand why anyone using an electronic presentation would choose a bright background and a dark foreground. The only time I can see this option is if you will be in a room with so much ambient light that your visuals are washed out. In that case, the backgrounds would be less visible and wouldn't matter anyway. That's the only time I would recommend dark foregrounds.

Of course, the software is partly to blame. For many years I have been critical of all software programs, not just PowerPoint, for having only about half the templates following the dark background/bright foreground model. Perhaps this is one of the reasons why so often someone presenting electronically ignores effective contrast—they picked the wrong template!

No Room for Black and White?

The white light problem does not mean that black/white overhead presentations are totally useless. (Hey, even poison ivy is useful, to the makers of calamine lotion.) The point is that you may find times when you have to present without color. You just need to be aware of the distraction caused by the amount of white light and consider ways to reduce the impact of the problem.

This may mean designing the visuals more conceptually rather than more technically. Fewer words on each visual would let the audience scan the image faster and concentrate more on the presenter than on the screen.

Reducing the number of black-and-white visuals to be presented may be more effective, as well. To compensate for using fewer visuals, more detailed handouts could be given for later reference. You do have ways you can limit the impact of white light distraction. Awareness of the problem is the first step toward solving it.

Of course, that doesn't change my personal belief that presentations should be in color to be most effective.

RED/GREEN DEFICIENCY

Certain color combinations may pose a problem for some people, particularly men. We just can't do anything right, can we? Yeah, but we still have control of the remote and that will never change. Never! HA ha hahhh! Sorry...where was I?

Some studies show that nearly 15% of men have a red/green deficiency; MediaNet's research has shown that close to 22% of men have some form of this deficiency. Women do not suffer from this problem (in significant numbers), but they should be aware of this fact when selecting colors for visuals.

If you have this deficiency, you might see purple more as blue, or you may mix up brown and green. The effect is not as noticeable with large areas of color as it is with small areas. For example, if a line chart has three lines with one line beige, one line tan, and one line orange, it's possible that someone with a red/green deficiency will not be able to tell the difference between the three lines. The result will be confusion and a loss of attention. Try to avoid red-green color combinations, especially in small areas.

EARTH-TO-SKY COLOR THEORY

When you have related elements in the foreground, arrange them in a darker-to-lighter pattern from the bottom of the chart, upward. This "Earth-to-Sky" pattern is the way we view color naturally, from the earth to the sky. The earth is darker than the trees, which are darker than the sky, which is darker than the clouds. It's the same way a room generally appears as you look from floor to ceiling. It's even a pattern in the way we dress, with darker colors usually toward the bottom.

So, when you have related foreground items that might have different colors, you can choose an order of those colors from darker to lighter.

For example, in Figure 25.25, the segmented vertical bar chart shows the darker-to-lighter Earth-to-Sky pattern used effectively. If the top segment had been the darkest color, the chart would appear top-heavy. The arrangement of colors, done naturally, allows the eye to scan the visual more quickly. A faster scan gives the audience more time to listen to the message. Since the order of the colors can make a difference, why not use it to your advantage?

Figure 25.25
The Earth-to-Sky color theory applied to a segmented vertical bar chart. Note the arrangement of colors in a dark-to-light pattern from the bottom upward.

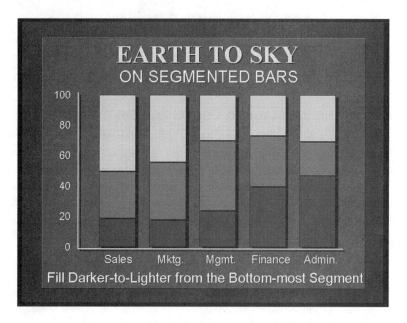

When displaying clusters of bars, as in Figure 25.26, choose a darker-to-lighter pattern starting from the left-most bar in each cluster. Don't use the "piano-key" approach by putting the lightest color between surrounding darker colors. When looking from left to right, the eye scans colors more easily when the arrangement is a dark-to-light pattern, similar to the Earth-to-Sky pattern.

Remember that the Earth-to-Sky theory is for the foreground elements in the visual, not the background color. So, if you choose gradient shading in the background of the visual, it doesn't matter if it's darker at the top, bottom, left, right, or fans out in both directions from the center. Specifically, the theory is most useful in data-driven charts, which usually shows a series of related items distinguished by color.

Figure 25.26
For related elements such as clusters of bars, keep the darker-to-lighter pattern beginning with the left-most bar in each cluster.

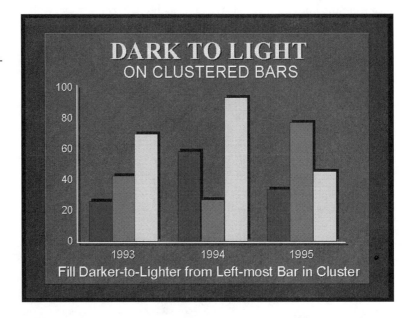

UNDERSTANDING BACKGROUND COLORS AND EMOTIONS

Color affects the central nervous system and the longer you see a particular color, the more it stimulates your emotions. During a presentation, it's best to stay consistent with your backgrounds, so the audience ends up seeing the background more often than each different foreground. The colors in the foreground keep changing and do not really affect the general feeling that the audience gets from the entire event. It's the background color choice that determines the emotional response from the audience.

TIP

> I always suggest you maintain a consistent background color and template for the entire presentation. But, if you have several different topics to cover, you can switch background colors and even design templates. I have a number of different seminar topics I deliver and the backgrounds are different in all of them, although throughout any one of the topics, the visual template is the same.

Keep in mind that a society makes psychological associations with colors based on appearances or cultural habits. Figure 25.27 shows some of these associations shared in the United States. Green is associated with money, for example. True, it is the color of money in the United States, but does green actually mean money? That would have to be true for all people everywhere. Is green the color of money all over the world? Then it can't mean money. Or else, over one hundred years ago in the United States the color gold would have meant money.

Figure 25.27
The cultural associations made with certain colors are not universal. But it's interesting to see what some colors have grown to signify in our American society.

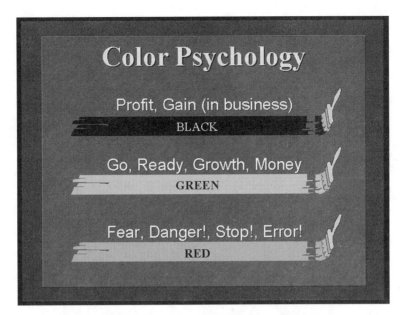

We all live under the same light of the sun. Blue looks the same in Borneo as it does in Bolivia. The effect of color on our emotions is from nature, not heritage. All people, regardless of culture, share a universal range of emotions, such as happiness, sadness, excitement, anxiety, desire, passion, and so forth. The ability to tap into these emotions using correct color choices can increase the effectiveness of the presentation.

NOTE

Be careful with colors. Don't make the presentation look like a circus. The use of too many foreground colors with a poorly selected background will become a distraction for the eye and result in an ineffective presentation.

Studies have shown that the background color of the visual produces an emotional response from the audience. Although there may be a number of different cultural interpretations of colors, the physical effect of the color is always the same. For example, red is the warmest color in the spectrum and is seen that way, regardless of any cultural associations we make such as negativity or loss (as in, "the company is in the red").

Lots of books and articles are available about color, but the following may help you in choosing a possible background color for your presentation. These recommendations are based on MediaNet's experience in developing over 3,500 presentations.

GRAY

- Neutrality
- Border between directions

- Uncommitted and uninvolved
- Concealment from other emotions
- Escape from anxiety and discontent

Gray represents a neutrality and lack of commitment. Depending on how persuasive you need to be, use of gray backgrounds may be a help or a hindrance. I would avoid using gray backgrounds when displaying any critical business information where you need to sway the audience. However, in situations where the information is left for the audience to make a decision, gray frees the presenter from influencing the audience to respond to the issue.

For best readability, we recommend charcoal or dark gray. Anything brighter than medium gray will ultimately cause glare from the visual, and any brightly colored items in the foreground will be harder to see.

BLUE

- Complete calm
- Increased sensitivity
- Loyalty, security, contentment
- Tied to tradition and lasting values
- Reduces blood pressure and pulse-rate

Blue represents a conservative, secure, yet more vulnerable approach to information. Deep, dark blue is the color of the night sky. At night, when you sleep, you're at peace with the world and most trustful in that vulnerable state.

Blue has a calming effect on the emotions and is useful for situations where you want to create an impression that appears conservative or traditional. You can definitely put critical information on blue backgrounds. The blue helps to develop credibility with the audience, especially when you introduce data based on tested facts and figures rather than speculation.

A blue background also tends to make the statement "This is the worst case scenario." It takes the "hype" out of the information and seeks to elicit an emotion of trust for the argument being presented.

TIP

> When in doubt about colors, choose dark blue backgrounds with yellow and white shadowed text. This combination is the easiest to read from any distance.

GREEN

- Operation of the will
- Resistance to change
- Analytical, precise, accurate

- Opinionated and self-assertive
- Need to impress and exercise control

Green stimulates interaction because it represents the operation of the will. If you want to involve your audience in a discussion of the topic, you should consider using green backgrounds. Green brings out the opinions in people.

In fact, presentations requiring feedback such as management issues or policy decisions may be more effective when green is introduced in the background.

I would choose deep forest green or olive green, or even a teal (blue-green) background in these situations. Avoid very bright green because foreground colors such as yellow or white will not contrast enough to be seen.

RED

- Impact of the will
- Impulse, desire, passion
- Vitality and intensity of experience
- Urge to achieve results and succeed
- Increases blood pressure and pulse-rate

A red background is stimulating. Why? Red is a warm color and warmer colors are linked to an arousal of emotion. In presentations that seek to heighten the emotions of the audience, such as sales or marketing events, or for any situations that strive to motivate the audience to action, you might choose a red background.

Since red is the warmest color of the spectrum, the tendency is for the eye to move toward red more quickly than other colors. This eye movement is most evident with foreground elements, such as a red slice in a pie chart.

From a background perspective, when you look at the color red, your heart and pulse rate increase. You can keep looking at red and keep liking it! You see this in advertising all the time. What color is the fast car, the woman's dress, the uniform of the guy shooting the basket? Typically, it's red. Face it, red backgrounds tend to be stimulating for the audience and can lead to a heightened sense of realism about the topic, even to the point of increasing enthusiasm. Want to pump up that sales meeting? Go red!

The intensity of the red you choose is important. I suggest you stick to the darker shades such as maroon or crimson as opposed to fire engine red or bright cherry red. It's better to tone down the intensity of the red and use a dark contrast for readability.

BLACK

- Negation of emotions
- Extinction and nothingness

- Surrender and relinquishment
- Powerful, strong, uncontrollable
- Stubborn protest against current state

Black is the absence of all light. This contrast is what makes black such a powerful color (or should I say non-color?) Because black absorbs all light, anything on a black background will appear closer to the eye than the background itself. An object reflecting more light appears closer to the eye than an object reflecting less light.

Because black reflects no light, it offers no emotional stimulus. When the emotional response to a color is removed, the reaction is one of surrender or relinquishment, as in having "no other choice." This can be a very effective tool.

Information on a black background leaves the audience with "no choice" on how to react to the data. It exists, as is, and the audience can do nothing about it. Thus, black is usually associated with things that have already occurred and will not change. Financial presentations, especially those filled with a lot of accounting data, are usually best represented on a black background since the data cannot be changed; it has already happened.

VIOLET

- Mystical union
- Magical and enchanting
- Unimportant and unrealistic
- Irresponsible and immature
- Attempts to charm or delight others

Also called purple or magenta, violet is a color that represents something magical or mystical. Violet is the mixture of red and blue, and the result is fantasy. Why? Because red and blue are opposites in emotional appeal and for those two colors to get along—that has to be fantasy!

Because purple is more charming, it is also adolescent and somewhat childlike. This is a tough background color to use for critical business information. For one thing, the data might be viewed as unimportant or unrealistic and, second, those who suffer from a red/green deficiency would see the violet background color as a washed-out shade of blue— a color that cannot be easily recognized, named, or judged.

If someone can't understand the color, the information carries less importance.

If your objective is to entertain or to amuse, a violet background is great for less critical information such as humor, special effects, or even for the awards dinner presentation at the annual company meeting.

BROWN

- Reduced sense of vitality
- Passive, receptive, sensory
- Establishment of a foundation
- Increased need for physical ease
- Desire for family, a home, solid roots

Pure brown is the search for something permanent to plant your feet on. Brown suggests a need to build a solid foundation that currently doesn't exist. Brown is the mix of red and green, and it actually creates an uneasy physical condition by toning down the sense of energy that red usually gives.

This reduced intensity makes brown seem more passive. For that reason, I would avoid using pure brown as a business background, especially for critical business information. The data on a brown background may be interpreted as "not standing on solid ground," hence, less credible and somewhat unstable. Not the best choice for gaining the support of your audience! So, brown is out as a background!

Now the people at UPS hate me.

KEEPING IT IN PERSPECTIVE

The support of your message with well-designed media provides the springboard to the delivery skills you'll use to inspire the crowd.

A visual presenter constantly strives to stimulate the audience in as many different ways possible. Whether it be background colors, eye movement, or a well-placed graphic, the presenter works with the message through the media in order to get the audience to react.

Although the information in this chapter may appear comprehensive, the good news is that if you simply maintain a consistency in layout and design, you'll end up with clear, concise visuals that do what they are supposed to do—support the speaker, nothing more, nothing less!

TROUBLESHOOTING

How important is it to have the company logo on each visual?

In the past, when presentation visuals were mainly prepared by outside services, some slides and transparencies would get "mixed up" among clients. Sometimes this happened during the mounting of slides or during the printing and collating of the transparencies. Putting the company logo on each individual slide or transparency decreased the likelihood of this production process mistake. However, for electronic images there is no need to identify each image with the company for the purpose of keeping the presentation visuals intact. Basically, a filename and a storage location are all you need to know in order to identify the owner of the visuals. So one approach to this is to decide if your visual content is "hard" (slides, over-heads, print materials, flip charts) or "soft" (electronic images, videotapes, Web sites, soft-ware applications). If it's hard, put the logo on each component that can be separated from another component, such as each page of a multi-page handout. If the content is "soft," then the logo makes sense on the first visual or at the very beginning of the electronic event.

Some argue that the company logo on every visual acts as a reminder to the audience. Put it this way: If your audience doesn't know what company you're with by the fourth visual, the logo isn't going to save you! The rule is that anything on a visual that doesn't add to its value is a distraction. Some say that after a while the audience doesn't notice the logo. Then that proves it's not necessary. Think about watching TV. How do you feel when the little transparent logo of the TV station stays on the screen, down in the right corner? Annoying? Enough said.

I know PowerPoint comes with so many presentation designs and templates, so why would I ever create my own?

Hey, I'm the first to tell you that you don't have to reinvent the wheel. Many of the designs and templates shipped with PowerPoint can serve your purposes for multiple presentations. In fact, you may decide to use an existing template and then modify it slightly to suit your needs. There is no reason to always start from scratch.

But for many organizations, the desire to create a unique look and feel to each presentation usually requires a "from-the-ground-up" process. Some organizations will not invest in off-the-shelf clip art because the same artwork might be used by a competitor which would reduce the chance of presenting a one-of-kind image. In fact, some companies create "standard" templates and designs for use within the company and they sometimes specify a group of images to be associated with certain presentations. For example, a sales presentation may require a certain template plus five or six visuals containing company information.

Because electronic presentations can be reproduced in other forms such as print or even publishing to a Web site, companies need to maintain a consistency across different media. So the use of predesigned templates may or may not be the choice of every company, depending on how unique they want their presentations to look.

CHAPTER 26

THE MECHANICS OF FORM—DEVELOPING EXTERNAL PRESENTATION SKILLS

In this chapter

by Tom Mucciolo

UNDERSTANDING THE OUTSIDE

"It's not what you say, it's how you say it!" We've all heard that before. And it's especially true when making a presentation.

A study of intimate relationships found that 55% of everything you say is what you look like when you say it. Another 38% is how you actually deliver the information. And only 7% is what you say. Only 7%! You might say this is a measurement derived from personal relationships and not business ones. I say our personal and business lives are so interrelated that it's hard to separate them. To me, this says that the biggest part of communication is nonverbal.

NOTE

> The referenced study is from work done by Albert Mehrabian, PhD, and Professor Emeritus of Psychology, UCLA. Dr. Mehrabian is known for his work in the field of nonverbal communication, particularly body language. His findings on communication are described in his book, *Silent Messages*, which deals with all facets of nonverbal communication and with combinations of verbal and nonverbal messages. The book contains reviews of Dr. Mehrabian's own and others' research findings on important elements of subtle or implicit communication. Communicators, leadership trainers, and political campaign managers often make use of these findings.
>
> Dr. Mehrabian specifically notes, "The equations regarding differential importance of verbal and nonverbal messages were derived from experiments dealing with communications about feelings. Unless a communicator is talking about (his) feelings or attitudes, these equations are not applicable."
>
> In our discussions, feeling is definitely an issue. From a visual presenter's perspective, the *emotional* link to an audience is critical for an effective delivery of nearly every message and makes this study especially relevant to what is covered in this section of the book. Thank you, Dr. Mehrabian!

26

Here's more proof: You can speak up to 150 words per minute, but you can listen to over 700 words per minute. Do the math and you'll find that more than 75% of the time you are processing nonverbal cues. These cues are important.

Regardless of the exact percentages, the bottom line is that delivery skills make or break the moment. This is not to say that content needs to be ignored, of course. We just spent two chapters on content! That would be like saying a playwright's words are meaningless. Not at all. But it is true that the success of the spoken lines depends on the actors. And yes, bad Shakespeare does exist—I've seen it. (Unfortunately, I've even been part of it.) Poetry can easily be ruined by a poor performance. The actions of the presenter, from a physical and vocal standpoint, can add value to the visuals and make the entire event more effective. During a presentation, the brain must process a large amount of content. Therefore, the presentation needs to be as streamlined and effective as possible; that is, clear, concise, and to the point.

Okay, now you know that the greatest percent of your communication effort is physical. It is a combination of your visual and vocal delivery. So, you need to develop the related skills to become a more visual presenter. But visual and vocal skills are directly linked to the way you think and feel. Your mind and heart play a significant role in your delivery style, just as your body and your voice do.

A Delicate Balance?

I work on a theatre principle called "off-balance" perspective. I apply this view to the message, the media, and most often to the mechanics of a presentation. The off-balance approach is a one-sided push for consistency. If I can shift your position to one side (off-balance), then I've made some change in you.

Your "position" might be your stance on a message. It might be your way of looking at visual content on the screen. It might be your view of the presenter in the room.

It actually matches the rule of thirds in photography. If you look at a framed image in three vertical sections, you should use the outer sections for the subject. In other words, when you take pictures, try not to center your subject. The image is more interesting because a bigger picture emerges for the viewer's eye to complete. This is not always done, but if you glance through magazine photos, you'll notice that most shots of people have them positioned more to one side than the other.

This off-balance approach is very effective. I use it often in developing, designing, and delivering presentations.

Through all of this, don't forget to smile. If you're not having a good time presenting, how can anyone have a good time watching? This doesn't mean that you have to tell jokes all the time, but the presenter has more impact with an inside smile. It's called energy. Without this energy, your speaking will be flat, uninteresting, and definitely less effective. It only takes two muscles to smile. Try it.

The mechanics of delivery are partly external (form) and partly internal (function). That's why two chapters are dedicated to these mechanical skills.

NOTE

> MediaNet's CD-ROM, "Mechanics-Basic Skills" (©2002, MediaNet, Inc., New York, NY), provides an interactive view of the mechanics of form discussed in this chapter, including video, audio, and other animated examples of the external delivery skills.

Let's start with the external skills, the mechanics of form, because your form is the first impression processed by the audience. The skills covering external form involve

- Conquering fear
- Using your body
- Using your voice

26

CONQUERING FEAR

According to the *Book of Lists*, the number one fear is the fear of public speaking. This eclipses even the fear of death! Wait a minute—if the number one fear is public speaking and not death, it means you'd rather be in the coffin than give the eulogy!

Call it nervousness, call it stage fright, call it whatever you want. If you can't speak in front of a group, you won't get very far in the business world. I'm probably not the first to tell you that. Now, if you have no problem speaking in front of people, then skip this section. But, if you have some anxiety when it comes to presenting to groups, pay close attention. Some powerful techniques can help you deal with being scared speechless.

So what gives? Does your fear increase as the next person enters the room? Why does the anxiety level rise in proportion to the number of people in the audience? What really causes this fear? You might think it's a simple lack of confidence. That, however, is just a symptom of a disease for which we need a cure! The fear is actually rooted in your physical presence in the situation. Think about it! If you didn't have to be there, you wouldn't have any fear!

Suppose you split communication into three types: written, spoken, and face-to-face. Match those with the way you work. You create documents such as letters, faxes, and emails for the written word. You use telephones and voice mail for conversational correspondence. You have meetings and presentations for the face-to-face method of communicating. Only one of these (face-to-face) requires your complete presence. The other two physically hide you from the receiver of the information.

When you write, you have time to edit and restate your words until you are ready to send them out for response. When you speak on the phone, you have less time to edit, but you are free to sit comfortably, and it doesn't matter how you may be dressed or how you appear. In fact, the telephone demands very little effort, especially now that you can screen calls, invent interruptions and use the ever-handy hold button. Even voice mail gives you a chance to plan your response in advance. So these two methods of communicating are less stressful simply because we can't be seen for who we really are at the moment and we get more time to collect our thoughts. When we are less visible, we have less fear. It's that simple. This protection from people helps you get through the communication effort with ease.

So let's take a look at the major problems associated with your physical presence in a situation. You can conquer the fear of presenting in two ways:

- Attacking the causes
- Learning to relax

ATTACKING THE CAUSES

Over the years I have found four main reasons why people fear public speaking. Looking foolish, being judged, appearing boring, and wasting the listener's time. Possibly hundreds of other reasons exist, but these four usually cover most people's fears.

When you examine these reasons, do you see what they have in common? Each is a result of being self-conscious. It becomes a question of "What will they think of me?" The focus of the problem is internal. It is self-directed.

So here is a good rule to remember: When the problem is internal, the solution is external. You need to concentrate on things outside of yourself in order to remove the doubt. This concentration always involves some type of action. Let's examine the four problems I mentioned earlier and see what solutions—or actions—can be used to combat the dreaded fear of presenting in public.

FOOLS RUSH IN

"I'm afraid that people will think I'm stupid!" I hear this one a lot when people discuss their anxiety concerning public speaking. Well, first I ask, "Are you stupid?" And only the really stupid people take a moment to think about that one. Hey, everyone is stupid, at times. Look at me. I'm one of the stupidest people I know. There are hundreds of people who will testify to that. But, then again, I hang around with a lot of stupid people who can't tell the difference. Then, when I'm with the really smart people, all ten of them, I use the skills in this section of the book to mask my ignorance!

Forrest Gump said that "Stupid is as stupid does"—whatever that means. Actually, it's a brilliant statement about actions speaking louder than words. If you do something crazy, others might think you really are crazy!

For many people, the typical uneasiness of speaking in public comes from this fear of looking foolish. What would cause that? Are you poorly dressed? Have you prepared your information? Are you speaking from a script you honestly believe has merit? Looking foolish is a feeling you get when you don't have control of the content as well as you hoped.

It's no different from the feeling you had in school when the teacher called on you and you didn't give the correct response. You were embarrassed. You didn't have the answer and you looked stupid! But if you knew the content—and, hence, the answer—you felt exactly the opposite. So, your first action is to get control of content. If you do this, your fear will begin to disappear.

Although you might think that content is controlled though memorization, that is not the case at all. The best way to get control of content is to first conceptualize your information, then visualize the manner in which that information will be delivered.

→ To learn about conceptualizing and visualizing information, **see** "Providing Do and Say Scripts" in Chapter 24, "The Message—Scripting the Concept," **p. 527**.

You need to script your message using concepts which link together to form the discussion or the argument. Normally, written scripts, or Say scripts, force you to simply read back the content without really knowing it. Conceptual scripts, or Do scripts, are those that segment the topic into main ideas, each of which has some associated action. The action helps you remember the concepts and allows you to present without any notes.

How Actors Learn Lines

I know you've heard the phrase "Places everyone!" Ever wonder how the actors know exactly where to be on any given line? In the theatre it's called blocking. It's the director's job to make sure everyone who paid for a seat can see all the action. Line of sight is very important, especially to folks who shelled out 80 bucks to watch the show! Blocking also helps the actors learn lines.

Here's the way it works. At the first rehearsal, the actors sit around a big table and read the script—once. At the second rehearsal, the actors are up on the stage with scripts in hand learning the blocking. The director might say to an actor, "Okay, now cross to the middle of the stage and pick up the letter from the second drawer in the desk." The actor moves to center stage, with script in hand, and stops at the yet-to-be-built set piece (the desk) and says the line, "I have the proof right here!"(or whatever). The point is that the actor remembers the line because it is linked to an action, the act of finding the letter in the desk drawer.

Obviously not every line has physical movement attached to it. But the lines become associated very quickly with the surrounding action, making it easier to memorize the words. You can learn a lot from this theatrical process.

When you link action to your words, you visualize the concept for the audience. The typical responses are, "It looks like she really knows her stuff," or "He appears to have a handle on that." Once you have obvious control of content, you won't be singing the "I'm feeling foolish" theme anymore.

JUDGMENT DAY

Another reason you might dread public speaking is the belief that the audience is judging you in some horrible, vindictive way. Let's look at that. What could possibly motivate a group of people to dislike you the moment you step in front of them? Why would such a group suddenly unite in the hopes of squashing you like a bug? What would they gain? Always remember that the audience is made up of people, people like you. The key to that statement can be found by changing the emphasis. People like you. They do. Ask Sally Field.

When you meet someone for the first time, don't you hope the meeting is positive? You're basically the same as everyone else in the world, and everyone wants to make a positive impression with each new person he or she meets. Before you open your mouth, the audience starts off by liking you.

Of course, some preexisting situations can cause the audience to not like you. If the circumstances are hostile, negative, or life threatening, then the audience is preconditioned to feel a certain way before seeing you. But barring any preexisting negative conditions, the audience is on your side. They want you to be effective.

TIP

> Here's a test you can use to see if the way you judge others has merit: Every time you make a subjective statement using the word "they" or "people," simply substitute the word "I" and see if the statement is still true. Try it.

> Say the phrase, "People just don't understand this business." Now substitute "I" for "People" and say it again. Notice a difference? Try the phrase, "They don't care about anything," then change "They" to "I." Using "I" changes your perception and, hence, the acceptance of the statement as being true. You can't separate yourself from the world. You are an integral part of it, just as I am.
>
> Think of yourself as a mirror and you will get back what you project to others. In theatre, acting is reacting. The same is true in life. If you offer a positive, nonjudgmental attitude, it truly does come back to you.

So, to reduce the fear that people are judging you, just believe in people as you do yourself. Approach an audience with the belief that they are just like you and that they just like you. This will begin to reduce the anxiety of feeling that you are being judged in a bad way.

Okay, time for a reality check. Unfortunately, it is very difficult to completely remove the fear of being judged by simply believing the audience likes you. This may work during the 15 minutes prior to your stepping onto the platform, but what happens when you look out into the room and see all of those expectant faces?

To overcome the inner feeling of being judged, you'll have to concentrate on something outside of yourself, some action or activity, to get your mind off the anxiety. To avoid being judged you need to become a judge. You can do this by focusing on the anchors in the audience.

Simply select a few people in the room to focus your attention on while speaking. These friendly faces, or anchors, are points of concentration that you must continually seek. This removes the feeling of being judged and puts the judgmental responsibility on you as you present. You are forced to judge whether those anchors are staying attentive, still interested, and still maintaining eye contact with you. In other words, your action is to judge others as to their attentiveness to the message. This will push you to make the effort to keep them awake! If you're doing the judging, then the fear of being judged is transferred to the audience.

THE BORED-ROOM

"The stuff I have to talk about is so boring." I get this a lot, especially from accountants. Well, I used be a public accountant. I found it to be the best training for a life of crime. That's a lie. Political science is the best training for a life of crime. Accounting is the best training for a life of full employment! But that's another story.

The fear is that the talk will be boring, because the topic is boring. Stop for a moment. That might be true depending on your topic. After all, not every topic needs to be delivered. However, the topic is usually not the problem when it comes to lulling the audience into a false sense of excitement. When you finish the talk, if the audience responds with a nice round of indifference, chances are you were the problem, not the content.

26

To combat a boring topic, you need to find significance. The action, for you, is to convey the importance of the topic. Look for the sense of urgency. The more you identify the critical components of your script, the more determined you get to discuss those components and get reactions from your audience. Reactions reduce boredom. Reactions give the audience something to do.

I'll use the accounting example. A budget report given monthly may seem a bit mundane. Yeah, it probably is. But let's say you linked some budget information to ways that money will be allocated to make some specific task easier for everyone. Maybe the budget for computer networking has been increased. No big deal, unless you make it a big deal. What if you pointed out that faster file transfers will reduce lag time and waiting time and give everyone more free time. In one sentence, you went from lowly accountant to giver of free time! You can't do this all the time, but if you can connect parts of your message to the needs or desires of the audience, boredom will not be your problem.

TIME FLIES

"I think I'm just wasting everyone's time when I'm up there!" This is another anxiety producer.

The feeling of wasting time may come over you more often during the presentation rather than before it. Suddenly, you have this instant loss of confidence and you can't find a compelling enough reason to ask a group of people to continue taking the time to watch you present.

Do you see the problem here? Wasting time can only happen if there is time to waste. Get it? It's the opposite problem of being boring. People get bored by monotony and hearing too much of the same thing. Wasting time is when you don't have enough relevant stuff to say!

Believe it or not, the structure of your script might cause you to try to fill up the time. Just because you have an extra 15 minutes doesn't mean you must fill it with poor content. You have to make the best use of time in order to reduce the fear of having wasted it. In some cases, that may even mean letting people leave early. Perish the thought!

The easiest way to make the best use of time is to use a form of action known as *interaction*. You can manage your time better by involving the audience throughout the presentation. This requires you to plan ahead, think quickly on your feet, ask questions, stir discussion, and even create controversy. Naturally, this shifts the concentration from yourself to your audience because you have to monitor their involvement. Activities that help audiences experience new things are seen as positive and not perceived as wasted time.

Now, instead of just planning time for the audience to ask questions, plan the time for you to ask your audience questions. Be proactive. Come up with thought-provoking ideas to stimulate discussion. Not only do you involve people in the topic, you learn from the experience, too. This type of involvement helps reduce the fear that you are wasting the listener's time.

If you can't fill the time with enough information of your own, then maybe the audience can help you. Again, you need to redirect the fear inside of you by placing the problem outside of yourself. Hand the task of not wasting time over to the audience. Believe me, they'll perk up.

LEARNING TO RELAX

Some say the nervousness before a performance is both natural and necessary. I say it might be natural, but it is certainly not necessary. If you can reduce a case of the jitters before a presentation, you will be able to deliver your message more effectively. One way to do this is to learn to relax physically. Of course, a limber body is always more relaxed under any pressure. Stretching exercises and other aerobic activities will, among many other benefits, definitely help you relax when giving a presentation.

How It All Falls Apart

Fear affects you physically. Your body "talks" to you right before the big moment. It works something like this:

Your heart starts pounding, pumping precious blood from your belly to your brain. Your stomach gets queasy as the knot tightens and the butterflies begin to bounce. Your nervous system sounds the alarm and chemistry gets the call.

Helloooo, Adrenaline! On the street they call it speed.

The slick little stimulant marinates your muscles, weakens your knees, and races to your extremities. The friction of its fury lights a fire under your flesh.

You call it nervous energy. On the street they call it sweat.

Your heart beats faster and you take deeper breaths to assault the adrenaline rush. Oh no! Too much oxygen! You picked the wrong time to fill those lungs, pal!

Wham! The aerated blood in your brain begins to pulse as the rich, red river rolls through your head, suddenly giving you the power to think quickly. Your thoughts are progressing faster than your mind can contain them. What's coming out of your mouth is making no sense at all as you stand there slobbering in your shallow shell.

You've been reduced to a hyperventilating, babbling blob of Jell-O, shivering in your own skin, as you pathetically preach to the people who pay you!

You call it presenting. On the street they call it shame!

Kinda makes the point, doesn't it?

As I mentioned, one way you can help yourself prepare for those opening moments is with some kind of physical exercise such as stretching or even something more strenuous beforehand. Another way to reduce the adrenaline rush and rapid heartbeat is create other activity (action) for yourself. For example, you can slowly take a few deep breaths before you begin. Yes, this increases the amount of oxygen in the system, but it reduces the heart rate before the adrenaline kicks in. More important, the taking of a few deep breaths gives you something to do (action), which takes the focus away from thinking about your presentation.

Once you start speaking, you may still experience some jitters. You can still create an external action—something to do to reduce the nerves—without the audience being aware of it. You might try wiggling your toes in your shoes. No one sees this and your concentration again becomes focused on some physical action. Maybe your mouth becomes dry. No you can't take a drink of water, but you can slightly bite down on the outer edges of your tongue or on the insides of your cheeks to create saliva and keep your mouth moist.

Again, you simply need to do something physical to reduce the internal nervousness, anxiety, and fear by using external means. When the problem is inside, the solution is outside. The goal is to redirect your attention away from the internal workings of the mind onto things that are external to you.

The more you concentrate on actions, the less chance you have of being self-conscious, which ultimately creates nervousness. So take a few deep breaths, wiggle your toes, and start talking!

USING YOUR BODY

Keep in mind that eliminating the fear doesn't mean you automatically will present well. That's the same as being unafraid to sing, but not knowing how to hit the right notes. (At that point, the fear is with the audience, who wonders if you will ever stop!)

Face it! You can't present well because you haven't learned the rules. You don't know how to play the game because no one taught you how. This is completely understandable. I was the same way. Then I learned to play the game.

The skills I want to share with you are based on the theatre. I was lucky enough to get exceptional acting training that very few others have ever experienced. I now apply those skills to presentations and guess what? They work! If I can make 1,500 people react to a playwright's intention, I can easily teach you a method that makes you a better communicator no matter what the topic, where the opportunity, or how big the audience. After reading this section, you'll be able to start using these skills tomorrow!

The only way to develop a method or systematic approach to any skill is to agree on the parameters that make that skill achievable. In this section, you learn to build a concrete foundation from which to work. With a core set of guidelines, you remain consistent from one presentation to the next, regardless of the content. I want you to concentrate on the basics—on things external to you. The things external to you always involve some type of action or activity and include

- Positioning and moving
- Making eye contact
- Using gestures
- Mastering the lectern
- Avoiding problems

POSITIONING AND MOVING

The first thing you have to learn is your relationship to the room. The physical space you occupy must be subject to your control. Like the home-field advantage in sports, if you know the space and feel comfortable within it, you can achieve your goal and deliver a more effective message.

For presentations, understanding the layout of the room, especially the size, distance from the group, and placement of the screen (visuals) is very important. All that stuff will change from place to place, and you may have to make certain adjustments to get the room situated comfortably for you and your audience.

But you want to develop a consistent behavior, regardless of the physical attributes of the room. These universal concepts will help you in every presentation situation because you can control all of them, at any time.

ESTABLISH AN ANCHOR

When presenting with visual support, you need to set an anchor for the audience to watch and read. Anchor your body to the same side as the starting point to read the language (that is, left-to-right or right-to-left).

For presentations in English (and many other languages), you must stand on the left side of the room; that is, the left side from the audience's point of view. In the English language, we read words from left to right. The eye is less distracted if it sees the presenter speaking from the left (in the anchored position), then glances slightly to the right to read the visual (left-to-right). The eye then naturally returns to view the speaker again as in the act of reading.

If you stand on the opposite side of the room (the audience's right), the audience has to look at your face, then navigate backward and across the visual just to find the reading anchor and then "read" just to get back to you again. This extra step is a distraction. It is a waste of time. Listening is delayed and effectiveness is reduced.

Now if you were in Israel, you could be on the other side; in Greece, stand in the middle; in China, on your head—I don't know. But in the United States, we read words from left to right, so stand on the audience's left when presenting. This is the way to establish an anchor for the audience, because it matches the reading pattern (anchor) they've grown accustomed to for some time.

26

NOTE

> If you have no visuals for the audience to view, it doesn't matter which side of the room you present from, as long as people can see and hear you. However, it is always better to choose a side and remain in that area.
>
> Off-center is always a good choice because a centered presenter ends up having to work twice as hard by shifting and moving to both sides of the room. The one-sided approach sets a positioning anchor for the audience, which, if constant and unchanging, is less distracting.

You want to present from the side of the room that matches the reading pattern of the language. But, don't worry if you get stuck on the opposite side of the room. Of course, you never know what you might be faced with when you haven't set things up yourself. If you have to present from the wrong side, just make fewer references to your visuals during the presentation to limit the distraction for the audience. Naturally you won't be the most effective you could be, but you won't necessarily walk away a failure, either.

BUILD A TRIANGLE

You want to know the biggest problem for most presenters? Moving! That's right, moving. They have no idea where they are going! They never really think about it!

Can you imagine if the actors had no idea where to go? The actor playing Hamlet would say, "To be or not to be...whoops...oh...sorry, Dave...didn't see your foot!" as he pulled himself from the floor.

The only way to know how or when to move is to know where to move first. An easy way to learn this is to design an area in front of the audience in which you can move. It's called the *Presenter's Triangle*™. It's imaginary because you must create it!

Figure 26.1 shows the triangle. Here's how you build it. While standing at a fixed distance from your display equipment, construct an imaginary line from the eyes of the person sitting on your far right, to the left edge of the screen. This line becomes the long end of the triangle, an angled wall. From each end of this angled wall, draw two lines meeting at a 90-degree angle to complete the shape behind you. Now you are standing inside an imaginary triangle.

Figure 26.1
A top-down view of the Presenter's Triangle. You create this imaginary space in which to present so that you don't block the view of anyone in the audience.

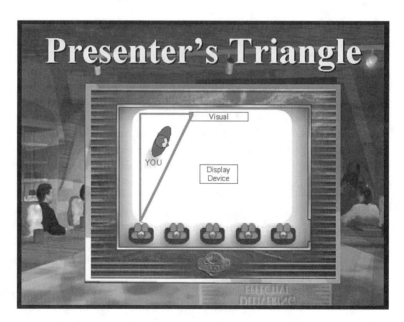

The most important point to remember is that the angled wall is a boundary you cannot penetrate. If you step through the wall, people on your right will not be able to see the screen.

NOTE

Naturally, the illustration suggests you position yourself at a fixed distance from any display equipment. If you are using transparencies or seated at a keyboard, the triangle option is limited to those times when you take a position that does not block the view of anyone. This is another reason why presenting with overheads is so difficult. The line of sight from the audience to the visual is broken for some people.

Okay, here's the good news. There are only three positions of the triangle that your body ever has to occupy. That's it —only three spots—the front, the middle, and the back!

Figure 26.2 shows a close-up view of the triangle with the three positions noted. The front is closer to the audience; the middle is where you should be most of the time; and the back is much closer to the screen. Now you will never use the full area of the triangle, unless you feel like hiding in the far corner (the shaded area) for some reason. Actually, you are really presenting inside a corridor within the triangle. You simply move along this little hallway, which follows the path of the angled wall.

Figure 26.2
A close-up view of the triangle. You can use any of the three positions along the angled wall, but you want to avoid using the far corner (the shaded portion) when you move.

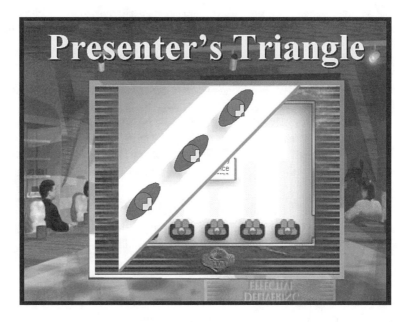

So why are there three positions? Because you have to move! You need to change the position of your body every so often or people won't watch you. If your body is not adding value for the audience, then they have less reason to watch you present the information. If you don't move, then it's talk radio. The audience will spend less time looking at you and more time updating their daily planners!

All forms of communication require some type of change to be effective. The change takes place in writing, in speaking, and in delivering. When you write, you skip lines and start new paragraphs. That's form in writing. When you speak, you pause between thoughts. That's rhythm in speech. When you're face-to-face, you create action in a defined space. That's movement in delivery.

All you have to do is treat the three positions of the triangle like peg holes or stopping points. You move to these points periodically, but with authority, remembering to stop and remain in a particular position for a while as you speak. You don't want to appear to be running back and forth, meandering aimlessly, drifting from place to place for no apparent reason. Just as you don't add paragraphs after every sentence or pauses after each word, you don't want to overdo and have constant movement while you present.

You might be wondering when to use the front, middle, and back of the triangle. Here's a guide. Choose the back of the triangle when the visual is complex. A busy visual forces the audience to keep looking at it. If your body is closer to the screen (the back of the triangle), then there is less distance for the audience to look between your visual and your voice. You don't want people moving their heads back and forth like they're at a tennis match!

Does Size Matter?

You rushed to read this one! We know each other too well! It's the size of the triangle I'm referring to!

The dimension of your space is based on the distance from the screen to the first row of chairs. At times you may have a 25-foot area to move around in. Other times, you may have only a few feet between the first seat and the screen.

For example, in a conference room you may only have a few steps between both ends of your triangle. But there is always a triangle, even if the only way to change between positions is to shift your weight. Your body must make visible changes based on the available space in order for the audience to pay attention.

So size doesn't matter for the triangle to exist. However, the more area available to you, the longer it will take to get to different spots. This will have some effect on your delivery. You'll want to make your key points when standing still for more impact. Thus, a larger triangle will force you to create additional words or phrases between those key points to naturally fill the moments needed to move to a new position.

From that perspective, when it comes to using different positions, size really does matter! Hmmm—where have I heard that before?

Choose the middle of the triangle for the majority of the talk. Think of the middle as the launching pad to move in either direction. The middle is like the…well…it's the middle! It's the midpoint between two extremes.

Use the front of the triangle when your visuals are less busy and you want to be closer to the audience. A simple visual allows the audience to reference it fewer times. This means you can be a farther distance from the screen.

Here's one more point to consider about position. If you want to convince an audience with a key point, which do you think would be most effective—to be in the front, middle, or back of the triangle? Obviously, the front, where you're closer to people. Well now you have learned one of the most valuable lessons of all—choreography drives content! It's not the

· other way around. Decide where you want to be at certain points in the presentation and then look at the visual. Does it allow you to be in that spot based on its format? If not, then change the visual.

If you know you want to emphasize an important point when you move to the front of the triangle, your visual content needs to be simple enough to allow your body to navigate to the front of the triangle. Or is the image so cluttered that half the audience is still reading while you're addressing the major issue? Change the visual to suit your movement.

Don't let content be your guide! Simply decide where you want to be on a given visual and adjust the complexity of the image according to your position in the triangle.

The triangle is important because it represents part of your physical plan of action. Without some definite planned movement, you end up wandering aimlessly, giving the audience no reason or logic for the direction. (Don't forget that the audience is processing your body language more than your visuals or your voice.)

PLAY THE ANGLES

While there are only three places to move in the triangle, there are only two body positions you have to worry about! See? It's getting easier!

You're going to find that all the power in your presentation rests in your shoulders! The angles of your body enhance communication. Figure 26.3 shows the two body positions or angles used in presenting, rest and power. For most of your talk, you should be at a 45-degree angle to the room. To create the angle, point your shoulders to the opposite corner of the room. This is a rest position. It's a nonthreatening stance, which opens your body to both the audience and the screen when you need to gesture or move.

Figure 26.3
You should only be concerned about two positions (angles) of the body: rest and power. The 45-degree angle is a rest position and the squared-off move puts you in a power position.

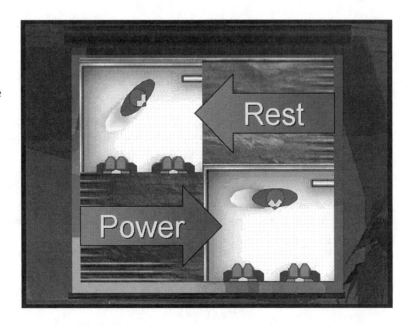

26

After you establish the rest position, you can use the power of your left shoulder. The shoulder farthest from the audience is always your power shoulder. Because you are on the left side of the room, the power comes from what you do with your left shoulder.

To get power, simply square your shoulders to the back wall of the room. Each time you turn your left shoulder toward the audience, you move into a power position. This signals that the information being communicated is of greater importance. But don't stay in that stance too long or the effectiveness of your words and actions will diminish. Constantly staying in the power position is the body's way of yelling. That's why the rest position is so important.

So, if you plan it right, you can choose the exact moments to add impact to the presentation by switching to the power position from any of the three places in the triangle.

For example, let's say you have 20 minutes to present. You start off in the middle of the triangle in a rest position. On a particularly busy visual, you navigate to the back of the triangle, closer to the screen, but still in a rest position. From that same spot, you square off to a power position just long enough to make a key point, and then you revert back to the rest position as you continue. Maybe later in your presentation you navigate to the front of the triangle to get a little closer to the crowd. You're telling an experience related to the topic and at a high point in the story, you square off for impact.

Wait; relax; calm down. You don't have to plan a move for every spoken word! But, if you practice, just like an athlete, the "moves" of your body will develop automatically. If you can get used to being a visual presenter, using the positions of the triangle and angles of the body will add enormous value to your presentation.

MAKING EYE CONTACT

So how do you please the crowd? You look at them! Yes, you look at them. It is so easy to do. Effective presenters look at people and make eye contact. This is critical to the communication process, especially to a group of visual creatures—the audience. The less time you spend looking at people, the less effective you are going to be.

The Eyes Have It!

When you watch TV, you are constantly exposed to eye contact. Think about it. The newscasters are looking right at you, with the help of a TelePrompTer®, of course. I don't understand why they have to use a TelePrompTer®. Why can't they just memorize the news the day before?

Anyway, they make constant eye contact. Characters on TV shows (sitcoms, dramas, or whatever) don't look at you, but they look at each other. Here again you are watching eye contact, only not directed at you.

Let's face it. We all watch a lot of movies and TV and are used to the idea of continual eye contact. As a visual presenter, you must not fight the expectation that a group is mostly made up of eye-contact hounds.

So, throw 'em a bone and look at 'em!

Direct Eye Contact

Direct eye contact is easier in a smaller group, simply because you have less faces to find. In a conference room with 10 people, for example, it will be easy to look at every person in the room at one time or another during your presentation. In a large audience, say 50 or more people, you can make direct eye contact with several people, but probably not everyone.

Now suppose you're afraid to make direct eye contact. You just don't like looking right into someone's eyes. Here's a trick for you: You don't have to look directly into a person's eyes. Instead, you can look between the eyes and, from a distance, it looks like you're making eye contact. Just look at the spot on a person where the bridge of the nose meets the eyebrows, and it will seem as if you are looking directly into that person's eyes. It works with everyone, every time—but it doesn't seem to work with a spouse—hmmmm.

Anchored Eye Contact

Let me ask you: What's your limit? You know, the highest number of people you feel comfortable presenting to? Is it like 5? Or 15? Or 50? Maybe 100 or more? Usually there's a number. Suppose your number is 25. Then let's say that one more person walks in the room. Do you suddenly stop, throw your hands in the air, and shout, "Hey, hey you—out. Yeah, you, out! 25 is my limit, pal!" (I don't think so.)

The point is that although the limit is in your imagination, it still doesn't change the fact that a larger group may intimidate you. The reason your "crowd-alarm" goes off is because you haven't established anchors in the audience with whom to make eye contact.

Here's what can happen: During a presentation, your eyes occasionally leave the audience, perhaps for a quick glance to your visual. When your eyes look away and then return to the audience, you suddenly see thousands of eyes staring back at you and—zap!—you lose your trend of thought. You forget the next phrase because the group—not any individual, the group—temporarily distracted you.

But, if you have identified specific people in the crowd, say a few friendly faces in separate areas of the audience, then you have a better chance of staying focused. If you look away for a moment, on your return trip to look at the crowd, you will be able to seek out those individuals and make anchored eye contact with any one of those friendly faces.

The anchors you select in the audience should be far enough apart so that it looks as if you are speaking to whole sections, even though your eyes are fixed on one person within that section. So split the audience up into a few big areas, maybe two on one side, two on the other, one down the middle—and pick out a single face inside each area as your anchor. Then, when your head turns away, the next look back to the crowd will have you finding an anchor instead of having the entire group overwhelm you. (Think of it as presenting to a just few people who happen to have lots of other people sitting around them.) This way, you maintain your concentration and you don't feel intimidated.

After you have found your anchors, any direct eye contact with other selected individuals is even more effective. If you've been looking into sections of the audience, and then suddenly lock your eyes onto one particular person (not one of your anchors), it will be extremely powerful, especially for that person. It's as if you made personal contact with that individual; in other words, you singled out someone in the audience, making that person feel special.

You may have experienced this yourself if you've ever gone to a play or a concert and the performer, while entertaining the crowd, suddenly makes direct eye contact with you, it's something you never forget. So, the more eye contact you make with people, the more involved in the presentation they become.

USING GESTURES

What do dance, ballet, mime, and most every sport have in common? With the exception of bobbing for apples, they all require the use of the hands. Presenting is no different because the hands control the eyes of the audience. What you do or don't do with your hands when you present makes a huge difference. Unfortunately, most presenters simply don't know what to do with those things at the ends of their wrists.

At times during your presentation, you'll have to guide the eyes of your audience toward your visual. Letting the audience look where they want is one thing—it's more effective if they look where you want.

Never hide your hands behind your back or inside your pockets. Avoid putting your hands together in front of you for more than three seconds. When your hands stay together for even those few moments of time, the audience tends to look at them and not at your face. Always remember, the eyes travel wherever the hands go. Keep your hands apart, yet always visible.

NOTE

> When you're nervous, your hands tend to join together or marry. In others words, they end up folded in front of you, doing nothing. Because you're a mammal, you have no skeleton in the center of your body, so you tend to protect that area by letting your hands rest together in front of you. You never see anyone with his hands on top of his shoulders saying, "Boy, am I nervous!" No way! Hands clasped in front or even locked behind your back, indicate nervousness and reduce your effectiveness.

If you aren't making any gestures, then return to a simple position with your hands at your sides. Or if your hands are up, waist high, then just avoid bringing them together.

If you are not elevated on a stage or standing on platforms (risers) when you speak, gestures are harder to see for everyone except the people in the front seats. For those viewing you from the waist up, keep your wrists higher than your elbows so that the gestures are visible. Always be aware of those sitting behind others and the view they might have of you while you speak. Gestures with your wrists lower than your elbows will generally go unnoticed and create little impact or meaning.

If used properly, the hands can orchestrate the eyes of the audience. Casual or emphatic gestures made to the screen or to the audience can create visual inflection. This helps the group recognize what is important. You can use a number of gestures with your hands and with your body that can help make your message more meaningful.

REACHING OUT

The best gesture you can make as a presenter is reaching out. The palm of your hand faces up as your arm extends out to the audience. This is a very friendly move and can be done with one or both hands. When you reach out to the audience, you appear as if you want the group involved in the event. The palm-up and the arm-out gesture is generally pleasing to the eye and indicates a warmth of expression for the presenter.

Think about your everyday actions in business. When you greet a person in business you shake hands by extending your arm out with your hand open (an exposed palm). You are reaching out to that person. You might shake hands as a greeting, a parting, or as a result of an agreement.

You can shake hands with the audience by reaching out to them. You reach out to the group as a way of greeting them, parting with them, or bringing them into agreement with you. Just because there's more than one person in the room doesn't mean your personal interactive skills suddenly disappear. When you reach out to the audience, you become more approachable and ultimately more effective.

The reaching out gesture also works best when you interact with the audience, especially in a question-answer situation. If someone asks a question, reach out to acknowledge that person. But don't stop there! You must keep your arm outstretched with your palm up until the person begins to speak, and then you can casually pull your arm back, almost as if catching the first syllable in your hand.

If you don't leave your arm extended until you get the beginning of a response, you may end up with the opposite effect, a gesture that suggests insincerity or indifference. It's called the "Like I Care" gesture. You've seen it. The presenter flings a hand at a person while asking a question, as if to say, "Yeah right, like I care about your answer!" Don't start tossing your limbs at people and then expect interaction.

26

> **TIP**
>
> The reaching out technique works best for the first question asked. After you set the stage for a nice way of interacting, the audience will be more inclined to ask additional questions.

THE LEFT HAND FOR GUIDANCE

Your left hand does the majority of the guidance for the audience. If you recall, the screen is always to the presenter's left for languages that read left to right. So, if you want to guide the eye to the screen, simply lift your left arm and use your left hand to motion slowly in the general direction of the visual. This indicates that the image should be glanced at by the group, but they should remain more focused on you. However, if you raise your left arm and dart your left hand quickly toward the screen, the more emphatic movement tells the audience that the content has more importance.

In both examples the key is to make your movements with authority. Do not make half-hearted gestures or the impact diminishes. Would you have a few images appear which were not bright enough to be seen? Would you casually whisper a few phrases that few could hear? You wouldn't make less of an effort with your visuals or your words, so don't use half-hearted moves when delivering the story.

> **TIP**
>
> Use your head! If you gesture to the screen and keep looking at the audience, the group has a choice to either stay focused on the screen or return their focus to you. This is because you are facing them and, technically, so is your visual. But if you turn your head to look at the screen as you gesture toward it, you force the audience to focus more on the visual than on you. Even if they look back at you, they see you looking at the screen and realize that's where the concentration should be. Both of these methods should be used to help shift emphasis on and off you from time to time. This variation is important.

THE LEFT HAND FOR MOVEMENT

The left hand can help you move through the triangle. That's right! You can walk toward the audience with no gestures, but you can't walk backward without an excuse. The audience needs a reason for any movement away from them. If the body retreats, it is a sign of distrust; the body language indicates that you are not telling the truth or that you are unsure of your accuracy. You appear to be "backing away" from the issue.

So you might wonder, "How will I get from the front of the triangle to the middle or back if I can't retreat?" You can retreat—with a reason—by using your left hand. If you gesture to the visual while navigating backward through the triangle, the audience accepts the movement because you are gesturing. They allow your retreat using the logic or excuse that you had to back up because you had to gesture to the screen.

> **TIP**
>
> The only way to understand this is to try it. Stand in one spot. Start describing one of your best qualities while you move backward a few steps without making any gestures. How does it feel?
>
> Okay, now pretend a screen is behind you. Stand in that spot again, use the same description and use your left hand to gesture back to the imaginary screen as you move backward. Notice the difference? It's as if some key support information exists to help make your point.

As you've just seen, only gestures can get you backward through the triangle, which is why it's so important to link your movements to your visual content. Make sure when you're directing attention to the screen (as you navigate away from the audience) that what you're saying relates to the visual to which you're gesturing. If it doesn't, you'll create even more confusion.

26

Justifying Movement

The audience needs a reason for your moving away from them. Your gesture to the screen is that reason. But only you need a reason to move toward the audience. Typically, this requires no gestures, just movement. Your reason is to get closer to them. In both cases you have justification for the movement in either direction.

But what if you had to move sideways? What if you had to break the triangle and cross to the other side of the room? The only reason to do this must be to get to a visible reference. Most likely that reference is a prop. You cross the room to get something you need to incorporate into the presentation at that exact moment.

Of course, if you don't require the item, you can gesture to it without crossing the room. However, if you know you are going to need a prop, you should place it closer to you before you begin your presentation so you don't have to cross the room to get it.

You may also want to move sideways and cross the room to interact with a person. This is not a valid reason to break the triangle; a reaching out gesture is the way to interact with anyone in the audience.

Use the rationale that a break from the triangle requires carrying something back with you from wherever you are tempted to go. You'll find few reasons, if any, to ever drift from the anchor of the triangle. But if you do, there better be a clear reason as to why.

THE LEFT HAND FOR HELP

You can only look at each visual one time! That's it, one time until it changes or something on the visual changes. If you look at the same visual more than once, the audience thinks you don't know the information. They wonder why you have to keep looking back at the visual simply to make the next point.

You might think the easy way out of that problem is to use builds. Why not? The next bullet point pops up (a visual change) allowing you an opportunity to look at the image and quickly get the next thought. Nice try, but the audience will know you're using the visual for help when you don't speak until after you read a bullet point. They'll know you're reading the stuff—maybe for the first time!

Okay, so what can you do? Yep, you guessed it—use your left hand! You already know that you can look at your visual once without a gesture. To look at the same visual again, add a gesture to the screen. It's the old "give-them-a-reason" move. The audience forgives your extra glance to the screen, silently saying to themselves, "Well, of course you had to look at the screen again. You had to gesture and be sure of the spot you were referencing."

Now suppose you have to look at the same visual a third time? With the first glance, you need no gesture. The second glance, you gesture—ahhh, but this time you leave your hand in the air. Don't drop your arm, keep it extended. Then, when you look at the visual for the third time, you only have to change the angle of your hand. Just a slight tilt of your wrist, up or down, moves your hand and creates another gesture or another excuse for the audience. You can even look for a fourth time as long as your hand changes position again. I know some presenters who haven't the slightest idea what's on each visual; but, by leaving an arm extended and glancing toward it a couple of times, the audience thinks, "What brilliance!"

TIP

> Leaving your left hand in the air can help with the pacing of the presentation. How? When you gesture toward the visual and leave your arm extended, the next time you glance back at the image, you can turn your wrist slightly until the face of your watch is visible as you look over the top of your hand. Now you'll know what time it is, and you may have to adjust your pacing, depending on how much time is left in the presentation. Of course, your watch must be on your left arm for this to work. It's also best to wear an analog watch with a contrasting face and visible hands. Digital display watches may not be as easy to read, especially if the lighting in the room is dim.

SHIFTING YOUR WEIGHT

When you are not making gestures, your hands should be at your sides and always visible. The eyes travel wherever the hands go so never hide your hands from the audience. Without gestures, your feet should be shoulder-width apart, your elbows and knees unlocked, and your weight evenly distributed. That's the position to use when you are not making gestures.

When your elbows and knees are unlocked, you have your best opportunity for movement. When you stand still, the tendency is to lock your knees and even your elbows. If your limbs are locked, you lose energy. If your limbs are unlocked, you unleash energy.

Center of Gravity

Men and women are different. I mean, in terms of the way they stand. Men have a higher center of gravity than women, located in the middle of the chest. A man tends to stand with his feet wider than his shoulders, for balance. Invariably, for some strange reason during the presentation, his feet will get farther apart, little by little. When his feet are spread too far apart, he is less likely to move and ends up in the same spot for the entire presentation. So a man should stand with his feet at the same width as his shoulders in order to make movement more likely.

Women have a lower center of gravity, closer to the hips. A woman tends to stand with her feet closer together, sometimes with the heels touching, for balance and posture. Men—don't try this stance or you'll tip over like a bowling pin! However, during a presentation a woman will often establish this posture-position and lock into that one spot for the duration of the talk. If a woman keeps her feet shoulder-width apart, she is more likely to move at some point.

So, don't mess with gravity—it's the law!

Movement is necessary and gestures are important. You know this by now. But, if you want to use your hands and make all your gestures look natural, you need to shift your weight.

You see, if your heels are both touching the floor, you can't make gestures that look natural. Instead, they appear stiff. Stand up and try it. Rest your weight evenly on each foot with both heels on the floor. Now lift your left arm to gesture. Stop! Take a look in the mirror— you look like a flagman on a highway or the person directing the plane into the gate! You look stiff. It's because your heels are touching the floor at the same time and your weight is evenly distributed on each foot.

Okay, so you have to learn to shift your weight. But first you must know the limits of your own body to do the weight-shift thing properly. Try this. Stand up and place your feet at the width of your shoulders. Both heels should be on the floor and your weight distributed evenly between both feet. Now take a half-step to your left, just far enough for the opposite heel to lift off the floor. Feel that weight shift to your left foot? Okay, now shift your weight back onto the right foot until your left heel lifts off the floor. Now you know the limits of your body to make gestures look natural. The weight must be on one foot or the other for the gesture to look smooth.

TIP

The easiest way to know if you are shifting your weight properly is to keep the base of your neck lined up with the same foot you're placing your weight on (you could also line your chin up with your knee). Now you can gesture and it will look natural.

If the nape of your neck is not lined up with one of your feet, then your weight is probably evenly distributed and you are most likely resting on both heels. If you gesture from this position, it will look unnatural.

Leaning Can Have Meaning!

Weight shifting combined with gestures can help make your message stand out. Depending on the direction you shift your weight, the effect can be quite dramatic.

For example, if you shift your weight to your left foot–toward the visual–while gesturing with your left hand, you are silently saying to the crowd, "Come with me and let's inspect this information." If you shift your weight to your right foot–away from the visual–while gesturing with your left hand, you are saying, "This information proves the point." It's like the magician who leans into the trick and then leans back to reveal the magic!

So, if you have a problem-solution script, you might want to lean toward a visual when identifying a specific problem and, later, lean away from the visual when the related solution is shown.

26

MASTERING THE LECTERN

A lectern is what you stand behind and a podium is what you stand on. However, people use both these terms to mean the same thing—a big box between you and the audience! Imagine if you wore a lectern to work each day! But you don't. It would make interpersonal communication so difficult—not to mention trying to squeeze past people in the hall!

The actors don't have lecterns. How would you feel if they did? You would think they didn't learn the lines! Why should they be forced to memorize the words of a writer? But politicians give speeches and use lecterns. Aren't they, too, actors using the words of a writer? Hmmmmm. Where do you draw the line on this one?

The problem is that visual creatures—you know, the ones under 40—expect eye contact. They get a lot of information from body language, gestures, and movement.

That's why the most difficult prop to overcome is the lectern. It covers 80% or more of your body and allows for little mobility. Although the lectern is a convenience to the speaker for reading a speech or for referring to notes, it allows for much less direct eye contact with an audience.

Lecterns are for losers! I despise lecterns! There should be a ban on them! There! I said how I really feel. I vented my anger and shouted my opinion for all the world to know! As far as I'm concerned, lecterns have no place in the life of a visual presenter.

Having said that, lecterns are still used quite a lot. So, how can you master the lectern if you get trapped behind one? You have a few options to help minimize your losses.

First, place the lectern at a 45-degree angle to the room if you can, matching the nonthreatening rest position (discussed earlier in this chapter). From that angle, both your hands can rest on or touch the lectern and you'll still be in a rest position. You can easily switch to a power position with just a turn of your upper body, leaving only your left hand resting on or touching the lectern.

If the lectern can't be angled but remains fixed and facing directly to the back wall (like a pulpit), you can still use the rest and power positions. Assume the rest position (45-degree angle) while behind the lectern. Only your right hand touches or rests on the lectern until you switch to the power position (by squaring-off to the back wall), at which point both hands can rest on or touch the lectern.

Make sure the audience sees your hands as much as possible. If you hide your hands, the interpretation is that you're hiding something. Don't let your hands disappear for too long, even if it is just to turn a page.

Even though you are stuck behind the lectern, the three positions of the triangle still exist for you to use. The middle of the triangle is when your weight is on both feet. The movement to the front or to the back happens by shifting your weight to one foot or the other. These slight changes in body position may help to keep the audience looking at you from time to time. Naturally, the lack of mobility and the fact that you are probably reading your speech or your notes limits effective communication.

Typically, the reason you use a lectern to begin with is when you are giving a speech. The lectern supports the pages of the script while you deliver (read) the speech. When you read, you make less eye contact. The following is a guide for maintaining good eye contact.

Every 20 seconds (or about 50 words) you are allowed to look away from people, but only for about one second. That means, for every one minute of speaking (or about 150 words), you're allowed just three seconds to look down and read the next group of words. In effect, you should be spending 95% of the time looking at people and only 5% of the time checking the script.

Unless you are using a see-through teleprompter, as is done on TV, the more you read from the script, the less amount of eye contact you have with the audience. Concepts are the solution. Build a conceptual script around key phrases, and you'll spend more time delivering a personal version of the topic directly to people because you won't have a lot of words to read, just concepts. Doesn't this sound like a Do script? (See Chapter 24, "The Message—Scripting the Concept.")

Don't get caught behind a lectern just reading a bunch of statistics to the audience. Think eye contact—and avoid facing the facts!

AVOIDING PROBLEMS

When the audience can't interpret your physical actions, they become preoccupied trying to figure out how the words link to the movements. The audience can't ignore these body distractions and, therefore, they need to be eliminated. If you work on removing these distractions, your message is easier to convey.

UPSTAGING

Sometimes the audience is prevented from hearing your words simply because they can't see your face or your expressions. When a part of the body passes between the speaker's face and the audience, the result is called upstaging.

Turning your back to the audience is the most obvious example of upstaging and is depicted in Figure 26.4. If you're facing the screen and the audience is facing the screen, then who's presenting? When you turn your back to the group, you can't see them and they can't see you. You lose valuable eye contact and the chance to use facial expressions. In addition, your voice is projected away from the audience and is therefore less audible, unless you have a microphone.

Figure 26.4
Don't turn your back to the audience. You lose all the face-to-face benefits of communication when no one can see your face!

If you have to turn your back to the audience, do it for as short a time as possible. At the same time, increase your volume so the group can still hear what you're saying. Avoid walking into the audience. This happens a lot when you have a U-shape seating arrangement. You might think that it's more personal to penetrate the "U" to get closer to the person you are interacting with at the moment. Not true. Your effort to get closer to one person puts your back toward everyone else you walk past as you penetrate the group. Don't alienate one person for the sake of another. You can still make eye contact and reach out to anyone in any part of the room while maintaining your position. The bottom line is that when your back is to the audience, you're least effective.

Crossing the upper body with your right hand is another example of upstaging, as shown in Figure 26.5. Whenever you gesture to the screen, use your left hand rather than your right. If your right hand goes across the front of your body, it causes a visual distraction that limits your effectiveness.

TIP

> One easy way to keep from turning your back is to make sure the person seated to your far right can always see the front of your right shoulder. This technique keeps your body facing out to everyone in the crowd as you speak.
>
> Use your left foot as a guide. To gesture to anything left of your left foot, use your left hand. Use your right hand to gesture to anything to the right of your left foot. This forces you into a more open stance when presenting and allows you to add impact to your delivery style with correct gestures and movements.

Figure 26.5
Don't cross your body with one of your arms. The gesture to the screen in this example should have been done with the left hand, not the right.

26

THE GUNFIGHTER

One stance to avoid is what I call the gunfighter position where your arms are locked at your sides as if your elbows were sewn to your rib cage! This limits the gestures you can make with your hands. So, don't press your elbows to your sides as you batter your arms about shouting "Danger, Will Robinson! Danger!"—it looks ridiculous. To avoid the gunfighter position when presenting, pretend that you must be able to touch your hands to the top of your head without bending down. This would be impossible with your elbows still attached to your sides.

THE HEAD WAITER

Be careful about folding your arms in front of you. This head waiter position not only upstages you by putting your arms across your upper body, but it also indicates that you are hiding something from the group. With your hands locked under your arms, your gestures are completely limited.

THE THIRD BASE COACH

Do not clasp your hands together behind your back. This position, the third base coach, forces you to use your shoulders and your chin to create gestures. You'll end up throwing your chin or shoulder forward to acknowledge a question and the reaction from the audience will be far from positive.

THE HAND TALKER

Avoid conversationalizing your gestures. This happens when you move your hands in the rhythm of your speech. It ends up looking like you have a gesture for every syllable. The trick with gestures is to keep them still and not have them bounce around on each word. The audience takes more time to process gestures than it does to process words. Gestures should freeze to add impact to a phrase.

Try this exercise. Say the phrase, "This is very, very, very important," and move both your hands up and down on as many words as you can. Then, say the phrase again, but this time just let your hands come down once and lock them in mid-air as you finish the rest of the phrase. Did you feel a difference? When a gesture stops moving, it is more powerful.

BLOCKING THE LIGHT

The image is meant for the screen! Sometimes you make the mistake of trying to point to something on your visual and you walk in front of the projector. Never block the light source with your hands or body unless you intend to make shadow puppets for the audience. When you block the light source, the audience finds it difficult to view the distorted image depicted on your clothes.

26

PINKIE COUNTING

Who started this habit anyway? Pinkie counting is simply counting on your fingers in front of the audience. The action occurs when you hold out your left hand, palm up, and use your right index finger to count on the left pinkie, then ring finger, and so on. The obsession plagues almost everyone from time to time. The audience has no idea when you plan to stop, although five seems to be the limit.

The reason you pinkie count is to keep track of the order of things by giving yourself tactile feedback as you count through the items you relay to the audience. This distraction can be avoided by dropping one hand to your side and simply touching your index finger to the thumb of same hand to maintain the tactile feedback. You don't need to switch to different fingers. Just touch your index finger to your thumb to click softly by your side, and you can keep track of many things. By inconspicuously using just one hand to count with, the audience is not distracted.

If, however, counting is really important to making your point, then raise your hand above your shoulder and count so that everyone can see. This will force you to limit those times that you count obsessively and it will add impact to those times that you need to count emphatically.

USING YOUR VOICE

I've been at events where some rude, inconsiderate moron in the crowd stands up, holding a chocolate donut in one hand and a buttered roll in the other and shouts "Hey—I can't hear you!" Well, at least that's one way to know if you should speak up. But—you can't always rely on me being in the audience, unless you're serving donuts and rolls!

Although I am the first to say that actions speak louder than words, your vocal delivery plays the role of interpreter for the message. If the visual media is truly the content and the body is definitely the delivery, then the voice is a combination of both. Words carry information and action. In order to develop the action in your voice, you have to consider a few issues such as:

- Breathing properly
- Phrasing and pausing
- Avoiding problems

BREATHING PROPERLY

Sometimes your choice of where to take the next breath can disrupt the flow of your words. By breathing between phrases, rather than during phrases, you get an opportunity to vocalize better. The key to this is having enough air in your lungs to sustain a longer phrase. For example, I have been known to deliver very long phrases with volume and emphasis. I believe that's from knowing how to breathe properly. Some say it's because I'm so full of hot air that the Gettysburg Address would be a cinch—but, I pay no attention to insults from family members!

When you don't have enough air, you may end up rushing through your words, and then they run together from speaking so quickly. Chances are that your emphasis and inflection will be lost. In any case, by having enough air, you can say longer phrases more slowly, which helps to make the message clear.

First, let's find out if you are breathing properly right now. Try this. Stand up and take a deep breath. Did your shoulders go up? Did your chest expand? Are you still holding the air in your lungs as you read this sentence while you turn blue? Okay, okay breathe again, please. Let the air out! Whew, that was close!

If your shoulders went up, you filled your chest with air. Unfortunately, that's not the way you naturally breathe. The air normally goes into the lower abdomen. Try this test. Lie down on the floor, face up, with a book on your stomach. No, not this book—I want you alive at the end of this exercise! Breathe normally and watch the book. Notice it moving up and down? That's your diaphragm at work. The muscles in your stomach, not your chest, control breathing. Now take a deep breath and force the book upward—it should be easy once you concentrate on the correct muscles to do the job.

Next, remove the book, stand up, and take the same deep breath, but don't expand your chest or raise your shoulders. Your stomach should expand. This is the proper way to breathe between your phrases when speaking.

TIP

> Try breathing through your nose and it will be easier to expand your stomach (diaphragm). Of course, when speaking, the tendency is to also take in air through your mouth because it is already open. It's not where the air enters but where the air reaches that makes for better vocal control.

Again, the key is having enough breath to complete long phrases or sentences without running out of air. This is important for languages such as English, in which the major points are made at the end of phrases, not at the beginning. Without enough air, your voice might trail off and the audience will not hear the key part (the end) of the sentence. The beginning of the next phrase will be less connected to the important part of the prior one. The result is confusion for the audience.

The following is an exercise for breath control. You should be able to say this entire passage in one breath.

> What a to-do, to die today, at a minute or two to two
> A thing distinctly hard to say, yet harder still to do
> For they'll beat a tattoo at twenty to two
> A rah-tah-tah-tah-tah-tah-tah-tah-tah-too
> And the dragon will come at the sound of a drum
> At a minute or two to two, today,
> At a minute or two to two.

When you develop truly excellent breath control, you will be able to say the above passage two times with one breath.

If you can't remember the above phrase, here's another breathing exercise you can try. In one breath say, "One by one, they went away." Pretty easy, right? Okay, add another to the count, like this, "One by one and two by two, they went away." Try adding another to the count and in one breath say, "One by one and two by two and three by three, they went away." Don't forget that each of these segments have to be done in one breath. You should shoot for as high as "twelve by twelve," and, with practice, fifteen or higher is possible, as you get more control of your breathing.

PHRASING AND PAUSING

Take natural pauses between your sentences. Say a phrase, pause, then say a phrase and pause, and so on. By using this technique, you can control the pacing of the presentation. Natural pauses give you a chance to make eye contact, to breathe, or even to think. You end up with smooth transitions and a more consistent delivery.

FILLERS ARE KILLERS

The funny thing about getting up in front of people is you have an altered sense of time. You think you're going too slow and you begin to pick up the pace, not so much with your speech, but more with your thoughts. You begin to think more quickly and between one phrase and another phrase the audience hears "uhhhhhh," "ummmmm," "errrrrr," "ahh-hhh," and the like—you know—the fillers. The sounds you make in between the words you say. Fillers are not language. They are grunts and groans. The audience can't process fillers. In fact, if you have a lot of them in your presentation, the audience becomes preoccupied with the distraction and they end up concentrating on your fillers, not on your phrases!

Fillers can even be whole words, such as "okay," "right," "you know," "again," and "see," to name a few. Fillers are evidence that you are thinking out loud. You're letting the audience hear you think. To counter this problem, use silence as a filler and it will appear as if you are taking natural pauses when you speak.

THE OPENING PAUSE

When I'm coaching a person, I always suggest the opening two-second pause. Right after the first phrase, such as "Good morning," you should take a two-second pause. That's right! Complete silence for two seconds. It can seem like an eternity, but it gives you the chance to establish two important things: pacing and anchors.

From a pacing perspective, the opening pause sets up the audience. They get to know right away who is in charge of the momentum. People have to know that you are in control. That's the role of the presenter—to control the flow. The role of the audience is to be controlled. If you don't appear rushed, the audience settles into the presentation at the pace you have set.

26

Those two seconds of silence help you in another way. In our earlier discussion of anchors, we talked about identifying the friendly faces to focus on. Unfortunately, you can't establish anchors in the audience until you first take the stage because that's when almost everyone is seated. You can't look out in the audience 40 minutes before the presentation, see a few people, and shout, "Hey—you three—you, you, and you—don't switch seats on me—I need you to be my anchors later!" (I don't think so.) No, you'll have to find your anchors during the opening pause. Don't worry, though, it will only take you about two seconds to scan the crowd for those friendly faces. Typically, those sitting under the most light are the easiest to spot.

WHEN IN DOUBT—PAUSE FIRST

Have you ever been asked a question during your presentation and you didn't know the answer? Well, don't blurt out the ignorance right away! Instead, pause for a moment. Here's what happens: Someone asks you a question and you don't know the answer. You stop, you pause, you look to the heavens for some revelation—you get none—you look back at the person and say, "I'll have to get back to you on that." The audience will be thinking, "Ohhhh mannn—you were sooooo close. If you only had the knowledge, you would have known!" That's a lot better than saying, "I don't know—blue?" Then the audience thinks, "Blue?—and you call yourself a doctor?" I've seen this happen plenty of times. You don't want to leap into the fire with a very quick, and likely incorrect, response. Remember that the audience is on your side. They want you to be right.

The pause maintains whatever level of credibility you had before the question was asked. By pausing for a moment, the audience actually believes that you could have answered the question, given enough time (yeah, like about a month). The point is that the group watches you search your mind for an answer, even though you never come up with one. It's politics at its best!

So, when in doubt, pause first. It buys you time and credibility. Of course, don't stop there. The words "I'll get back to you on that" indicate your intention to follow up at a later point with an answer. Make sure you do!

TARGETING PHRASES

Once you have control over your voice, you can direct your phrases for more impact. You can target your words to entire sections of the audience or simply to one person.

It's a given that everyone in the room has to be able to hear you. Sometimes a microphone will be needed for the entire audience to hear every word you say. But, because you can't count on having a microphone in every situation, you'll have to learn to project your voice.

Although proper breathing is important to voice projection, you should also target your phrases toward the back of the room to be sure everyone hears what you say. One way to do this is to play to the back third of the audience. In the theatre, it's called "playing to the cheap seats." The farthest one-third of the audience is where most of your phrases should be targeted because if they can hear you, everyone can hear you.

26

You never have to worry about the people in the front. They took those seats. They'll give you their wallets! But the people in the back—the troublemakers! Pretend that they are never sold, never convinced, never in agreement with your message. This forces you to target your phrases to them. The good news is that this causes your chin to lift slightly higher in the air, opens your throat, and makes your voice clearer. In addition, you'll find yourself facing forward more often in order to project to the back of the room. The intensity of your phrases, no matter how calm or soft-spoken, become more audible and your facial expressions more visible!

Voice projection helps when fielding responses from the audience. Sometimes an audience member speaks so softly that only you and a few other people hear the person. Make sure you repeat the question or comment so that the entire group can hear it. If you fail to do this, then your response will make sense only to those who heard the original question or comment in the first place. Also, by repeating a question, you get more time to formulate your answer.

You can also target your phrases directly to a specific person. You can do it with just a look, but you get more impact if you know the person's name. People love to hear their name. Watch a TV commercial. If it has your name in it, you love it!

A name is so important! How would you feel if you raised your hand to ask a question and the presenter knew your name but chose to identify you by your seat number instead! Names add a personal touch to the presentation.

When you reference a person by name, only the first name is needed. This makes it a little easier for you because last names can sometimes be difficult to remember or even pronounce. Of course, if you are speaking to an audience that you have never met before, it will be difficult to identify people by name. During interaction, you could ask that people identify themselves to the audience before they speak. Then, you'll know a person's name and be able to use it in your response.

Targeting your phrases to an entire section or to a specific person makes the audience more conscious of each other and more respectful of your effort to take the time to treat people as individuals.

TRANSITIONING

Transitioning is having something to say during changes in your presentation. Those changes can be as a result of movement or can be from the visuals themselves.

Movement in the triangle, from place to place, can be very obvious when your space is bigger. It may take several steps to get from the middle to the front, for example. You should not be moving on a key phrase. The words have more impact when you are still. Suppose you want to say the words "It saves money" in the front of the triangle. If you are in the middle of the triangle and a few steps away from the front, you have to add a transition or some extra words to allow you time to get to the front. Once there, and not moving, you can say the key phrase, "It saves money." Perhaps your entire phrase turns into: (said from the middle while walking to the front) "One of the most important advantages of this new product is that (now you stop at the front) it saves money." The transitional text allows you to move to the next space and deliver the key words while standing still.

Transitions are also useful whenever the visuals change, although this is less of a requirement when using slides or electronic images because they change more rapidly. But a more traditional medium, such as overheads, requires verbal transitions.

Here's what happens. The time it takes to remove one transparency from the overhead projector and replace it with the next can take several seconds. Don't let that time be filled with silence. Have a transition—something to say as you approach the equipment, as you change the visual, as you set the next visual, and as you move away from the equipment. Even in the world of state-of-the-art electronics, a pause to press a remote control is just as obvious as changing an overhead if you leave too big a gap with nothing to say.

Don't confuse silence with timed pauses. A timed pause lasts about one to three seconds and is useful to get the audience to think or to ponder a question. Dead silence lasts longer and tells the audience you can't really think of anything to say at the moment.

RULE OF THREES

People remember things in sets of threes. Our system of government is based on the number three, many religions are based on three, even the family—mother-father-child—is based around the number three. You can find this rhythm in many political or religious speeches. Key concepts or arguments are constructed around three references. For example, a politician might make the statement: "We'll be more prosperous, we'll pay less taxes, and our children will have a future." Notice the use of three references in the phrasing to make a point. Many references include a triad of some sort, such as Julius Caesar's "Veni, vidi, vici" ("I came, I saw, I conquered") and the courtroom oath of "...the truth, the whole truth, and nothing but the truth..." Even the Olympic Games grant three medals, Gold, Silver, and Bronze.

Try to incorporate the rule of threes when presenting your next topic. It's easy, it's simple and it works like a charm!

AVOIDING VOCAL PROBLEMS

Just as with the body, distractions can occur when using the voice. Most of the time, the vocal problems can be corrected, but sometimes our natural speech will sound different to diverse audiences. Accents are an example of natural speech to some, but unique speech to others.

If you have an accent, as most of us do, it means that you will sound different from what the audience may be used to hearing. My grandmother, who came from Italy, once said to me in broken English, "Don't laugh at people with accents. They speak one more language than you do!" Of course, accents from speaking a foreign language are no less noticeable than regional accents. When I delivered a seminar in Mississippi the person who introduced me

26

ended the opening remark with "at least you'll like his New York accent." Just as I began to speak, I looked at him and said "Wait a minute. I thought you had the accent."

The point is that if you have a well-rehearsed presentation and you can be understood when you speak, your accent should not reduce your effectiveness.

Some believe in eliminating regional or foreign accents, but I think they constitute diversity in voice and help make the individual stand out for an audience. If you can be understood, then don't worry about an accent. However, some other vocal issues can become major problems if not corrected.

THE MUMBLER

The mumbler is the person who does not enunciate clearly. The lips stay so close together that the audience can't even see the words forming. When the mouth stays very closed, volume decreases and the words are barely audible. Remember to loosen those lips and articulate!

> **TIP**
>
> Place a pencil across your mouth between your teeth. Push it as far back as you can, which stretches your lips. Bite down a little on the pencil and begin to talk. Say a couple of phrases for about 30 seconds up to a minute. Take the pencil away and notice how flexible your lips are and how much better you enunciate every syllable.

THE GARBLER

Another person with an enunciation problem, the garbler is the person who speaks so quickly that the audience can't hear the end of one word before the next word arrives. To correct this problem, try saying a short phrase very slowly by stretching out each and every syllable in every word. This helps to reduce the speed of speech.

> **TIP**
>
> Find a newspaper article and read the first two sentences out loud. Read them again out loud and you'll probably go even faster. Okay, now read the words in the sentences backward, one word at a time. Hear how slowly you must read and try to match that speed when you speak. Although in practice that pace is definitely too slow, your habit of speaking too quickly will offset the slow speech and the result will be a closer-to-normal speed.

THE DRONER

The droner has a constant, monotone, expressionless voice and is the closest known cure for insomnia! The problem is from little or no inflection. This is often prevalent among presenters who have limited interest in the topic or those who have been presenting the same information in the same way for too long. They are simply bored with the stuff they deliver. The voice reflects the boredom, gets lazy, and eventually becomes monotonous.

One solution to this problem is to practice placing stress on different words in a sentence. For example, the following list uses ALL CAPS to show the changing emphasis in the same phrase:

And WE offer the best service.

And we OFFER the best service.

And we offer the BEST service.

And we offer the best SERVICE.

Try saying these phrases out loud and note the difference in the stress of the capitalized words. Placing emphasis in this way forces the voice into a higher and lower pitch within a phrase by adding vocal variety to an otherwise droning tone.

THE DROPPER

The dropper is the person who starts out with a lot of volume and then gradually drops off to the point where the audience is straining to hear the disappearing words. This problem is definitely related to improper breathing. The exercises mentioned earlier can help with sustaining longer phrases. But, sometimes, the words drop off because you are not completing one thought for yourself before introducing the next. Basically, you become anxious to get to the next part of the argument. The key to avoiding this problem is to maintain volume through the end of every phrase.

TIP

In addition to breathing exercises, you can also try adding a question at the end of every sentence. Keep in mind that this is only for practice. Don't do this while presenting. For example, add the question, "Is that statement clear?" to every sentence. The question forces a slight raise in pitch and volume. Plus, the extra words make the sentence even longer, forcing you to plan for more air to get to the end. When presenting, you can still silently say the question to yourself if you feel you are dropping off in volume as you present.

When a vocal problem becomes a distraction, you need to take steps to eliminate it. When your voice becomes trained to the point where you can control it effectively, you gain another advantage in conveying the message you intend for the audience.

TROUBLESHOOTING

How do these external skills apply to small group meetings with just a few people sitting around a conference table?

Actually the skills are the same. The room is just smaller. Good presentation skills work everywhere. This is the same as writing or speaking. Would you tolerate poor grammar or poor enunciation if the crowd were only eight people in a conference room? The key difference is in how you express yourself to fit the size of the group. You are not going to make wide, sweeping gestures, but you would certainly reach out to any size group. You would still use the three positions of the triangle, even though the space is smaller. You would still use the rest and power positions to add emphasis. The point is that your "body language" is expressed all the time, regardless of the number of people observing you.

If possible, stand up when presenting. This doesn't mean you can't control a meeting while sitting; rather, you get more power when your head is higher than people. That's why kings sit high on thrones, judges sit up high, even pharmacists fall into the pattern—they're up on those platforms—it's a power thing!

If you are sitting, you can still create rest and power positions with your body by simply turning in your chair and angling your shoulders to the group. Gestures should be done with your elbows above the edge of the table and your fingertips can still be used to reach out to include one or more people in the conversation. The actions of your body are always available. All in all, small group meetings still require a physical plan in your delivery style just as large groups do.

Is there a such thing as too much eye contact?

Obviously, in large groups the chances for direct eye contact are not as great as with smaller groups. Fewer faces for you to look at means more time to look at each face. So it seems that when there are fewer people in the room, the eye contact with each one should be greater. Not exactly. Too much eye contact tends to backfire.

Let's use the smallest "group" scenario: one other person in the room with you. Let's call the other person Debbie. If you are talking with Debbie and you make constant eye contact with her as you speak, after a short time she will have to look away. She won't be able to stare into your eyes continually so the eye contact between you will be broken. That means another object is likely to catch her attention when she looks away. At that point she is no longer listening to you because her attention is diverted to something else.

However, if you break the eye contact from time to time, while you are speaking, Debbie will have no choice but to remain fixed on your eyes, even as you glance away. You will have greater control of her attention if she is busy fighting for your eyes instead of you fighting for her eyes when you speak. And you really don't look at anything specific when you break the eye contact because you are still talking and your eyes are only wandering on occasion in order to keep her more attentive.

When you are listening you should always maintain eye contact. But when you are speaking, especially to fewer people, you should break the eye contact from time to time to keep the attention of your listeners. In presentations you allow the audience to look away by giving them a chance to glance at the visual on your display screen. The object of their attention, the visual, is still part of your message. In smaller groups the visuals can be just as useful. But if the interaction is mostly one-to-one without much visual support, then allow for occasional breaks in your eye contact with your listeners when you are speaking.

CHAPTER 27

THE MECHANICS OF FUNCTION—DEVELOPING INTERNAL PRESENTATION SKILLS

In this chapter

by Tom Mucciolo

PUTTING YOURSELF FIRST

Okay, now it's time for you to get real. Read this chapter only if you are interested in developing the best presentation skills possible. If not, then avaunt, begone, cease to be! This is where we separate the presenters from the pretenders!

Okay, now I'll get real. You're going to find that this is really a fun chapter because it takes you to another level of presenting—a level that gets the audience to react to how you think and feel about your message.

Teaching about the body and the voice is somewhat easier because they are tangible and very measurable parts of the delivery skill. Hey, if you're not moving or no one can hear you, it doesn't take a rocket scientist to figure out the problem. But if you're not focused or you don't have enthusiasm—well, people notice that something is not right, but they're not sure what it is they're really missing. The audience sees external distractions, but they only sense internal ones. The external problems make them not want to look at you at the moment. The internal distractions make the audience not want to watch you again. So, the mechanics of function are what keep them coming back for more!

Perhaps sometime you've gone to a movie or a play and you left with an empty feeling, maybe unsure as to why you felt that way. This happens because you might not have the expertise to analyze the problems in the performances, but you have the experience to know what good performances should be. Well, everyone in the audience has been to a presentation before and they have the experience of both good and bad events. This is what leads people to arrive at the presentation with an expectation.

The good news is that the average audience member at a business presentation expects boredom and talking heads. You can exceed that expectation with the well-planned *mechanics of form*, the external presentation skills using the body and the voice. People are always appreciative of your having given them more than anticipated. But, if you can take the time to prepare on the outside—you know, dress the part, plan the movements, and work the voice—then you need to make the effort to prepare the inside. The inner plan is your character, shaped by thoughts and feelings.

If you truly want your message remembered and linked directly to your personal delivery of that message, you'll have to use the *mechanics of function*, the internal presentation skills. The components of these skills include

- Using your mind
- Using your heart

USING YOUR MIND

In acting, it takes someone with a lot of intelligence to play the part of ignorance. Take Carroll O'Connor and Jean Stapleton, brilliant people who played Archie and Edith Bunker on TV's *All in the Family*, a '70s sitcom. Each played ignorance in a special way. But to know all the intricacies of ignorance, a high level of knowledge is required. How would one know what is stupid unless one were smart enough to understand the difference?

The point of this is that your mind is one of your most powerful assets. As a presenter, you can think on your feet, sway the audience with reason, and persuade people with your logic. In essence, you can use your mind effectively by

- Linking intention to content
- Working with detailed data
- Selecting focal points
- Using virtual space
- Handling distractions

LINKING INTENTION TO CONTENT

This sounds more difficult than it is. The fun in this process is using your imagination to create connections between your actions and the supporting elements in your message. In other words, for every major section of information you are sharing with the audience, you need to identify the intention or sub-text that goes along with that information. The intention follows the same pattern as the objective. Based on action and described in the form of "to do" something, it isn't a feeling, although a feeling will always arise out of action. It's like a little objective.

For example, let's say it's your next presentation. The overall objective is to persuade the group to take action on a new budget item. So, at the beginning of the talk, you plan to bring up a comparison to a similar budget decision that was made in the prior year. Stop. What is your inner intention as you go through the comparison? You know you have to persuade, but use your imagination for a moment. How many ways are there to persuade? Probably a million. Pick one.

Let me pick one for you: You show the absurdity in bringing up what happened a year ago. You stress that this is like comparing apples to oranges, and the data from last year is meaningless to this issue.

Let me give you another one: You proclaim the validity of the comparison to last year. You stress the decision was made by the same management team evaluating the current project and their track record on these issues is impeccable.

Your intention is different in each case, yet the visual support looks the same. The angle of your approach is going to change depending on your inner intention.

In other words, you've got a whole bunch of little things to do inside the big thing you have to do. Just like a wedding when there are a million little details, each with an intensity, an action, an outcome. Then, you have to consider the scope of the entire event—the wedding. Details exist in so many things you do. Why would your presentation be any different? It's attention to detail that will make it successful.

27

To do this, dissect your presentation into smaller segments and see what is going on in your mind as you cover each segment. If a few charts are displayed in one part of your talk, what is your subtext, what are you really thinking? Is your intention to distract the audience with the details? Is it to drive home the point? Is it to set the stage for the next section of the presentation?

Don't chop the presentation into such tiny segments that you try to find an intention for every moment. This will result in the analysis-into-paralysis problem! Typically, your intentions cover a group of visuals. Maybe you'll have about six to eight different intentions for a 20-minute talk. You might use an intention more than once for repetitive items such as humor or storytelling. For example, the intention in each of three different stories might be to teach a lesson.

If you just concentrate on the major sections and the related intentions, the tiny moments take care of themselves. How? They happen as a result of your natural thinking pattern to accomplish tasks. Trust yourself and give yourself more credit. You wouldn't even be reading this book if you didn't have the ability to express yourself and your intentions. You've been doing this all your life. You just have to apply the process to presenting. If you understand the big segments, then the little things under every single moment will become so natural, you won't have to think about them.

Your inner intentions are buried in your brain and you have to identify them so that you can be sure that the way you offer the information is the way you expect the audience to understand it. This is what I mean by linking intention to content.

Playing the Stakes

In theatre, the actor must "play the stakes" in each scene. The actor searches for the most important moments to make clear in each scene.

The same is true in presenting. Look at any piece of information in your script and decide on its priority to the whole story. The closer it is to being essential, the higher the stakes get if you don't present it well.

You might not convince your audience if you fail to deliver the key information. So if you fear your talk will be boring, find the importance in the information and allow the audience to discover the importance with you.

You can play the stakes in a section of the presentation or even on a single visual. If you have a visual that displays several bullet points, you need to decide which of those points is most important to the story at that moment.

Although you may cover all the points anyway, you may find yourself discussing one point in much more detail. This is probably the critical element in the visual, and you should focus more of your attention on delivering that point as clearly and directly as possible. This doesn't mean the rest of the material is unimportant; instead, it helps you use the surrounding information as support for the more important item.

By playing the stakes in each visual you will add the sense of urgency to the topic that otherwise may appear to you as too boring for others to experience. In addition, the physical actions you use to play the stakes will heighten the importance of the information.

27

WORKING WITH DETAILED DATA

Sometimes your visuals contain detailed information. Typically this happens with data-driven charts (bar, pie, line, area, and so on). Most presenters display these charts for the audience and discuss the obvious items, usually the biggest slice, the tallest bar, the upward moving line—the easy stuff. Although nothing is wrong with this, it adds little value to the audience if they could have figured it out for themselves.

But a visual presenter (there's that term again!) reads between the lines and makes the detailed information come to life. It's a process of identifying the means inside the extremes.

Think of the means as internal causes for the extremes. The extremes are the external data elements that are different enough to force a comparison or a discussion.

For example, Figure 27.1 is a vertical bar chart. It contains four selected months of data showing the time (in seconds) it takes to connect to the Internet from home and from business. Wait—don't start calling your Internet service provider and complaining. I made these numbers up just for the example!

Figure 27.1
A simple bar chart showing selected months of activity. You can choose to discuss from eight different items. Look to compare the extremes; that is, any items that are different enough to warrant an explanation.

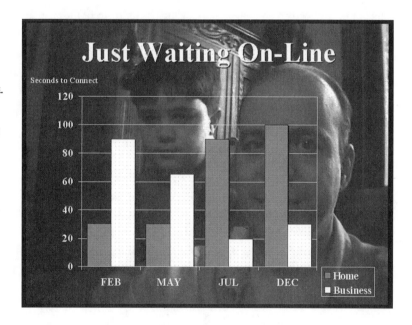

Okay, back to the example. Let's say you select one particular set of extremes related to the home group. You might point out that the connect time in February is so much faster than in December. You picked two data elements different enough to stimulate a discussion.

Now you have to stress the means of those extremes. You identify the causes of the difference. An obvious one would be a seasonal issue. The reason it takes longer to connect in December is because of the holiday season and the online calls to friends and family. Maybe you dig deeper into the means. You might bring up a recent article you read that mentioned how the home sales of digital cameras seem to peak in mid-November because people want to have holiday pictures in advance of the holiday season. The effect of more digital photos is their later transmission in December over the Internet. These photos are much larger files resulting in more traffic over the Net and, hence, slower connect times. None of this extra stuff appears on the chart—it's all in your head.

Want to try another? Let's use the same example, but pick two other extremes. Compare home to business in the month of July. What are the means inside those extremes? You could point out that more employees take vacations during the month of July than any other time during the year. Not being at the desk in the office results in fewer connections to the Internet, hence less traffic from the business group. However, vacation doesn't always mean travel away from home, and you might mention that with kids home from school, an increase in Internet activity from home results in more traffic on the Net. Maybe you dig deeper into the means. You cite a statistic from the National Education Extension Outreach Foundation (whatever) that shows a sharp increase in the number of online college-level courses being taken during the summer months when classroom sessions are fewer. The students in these electronic programs are participating from home, which is another reason for the rise of Internet activity in July and the longer connect times from the home group. Once again, the audience gets none of this from the chart on the screen.

By identifying the means inside the extremes wherever possible, you create a lasting impression on the audience. You become the critical bond for the audience between data and description. Without you as that link, anyone could have presented the topic. And a visual presenter would never allow that!

SELECTING FOCAL POINTS

We've talked about anchors a lot in the past few chapters. The audience needs anchors and so do you. Anchors don't really move during the presentation. That's why they're called anchors! The anchors are usually big—standing on the left side of the room, five friendly faces in the audience, geometric shapes to help guide the eye—these are all anchors.

But another type of anchor is called a *focal point*. It's more of a temporary anchor, but something you can use at various times during the presentation. Many of the focal points you'll use are less apparent, if at all, to the audience. But focal points are visible and fixed objects that help you target your attention as you speak.

Have you ever just stared off into space while you were thinking about something? Well, you probably weren't always looking at the night sky when you zoned out. You might have been at your desk or at home and you were looking at something, but you were not focused on the attributes of the object. You were busy thinking. The best example of this is talking on the telephone. Next time you see someone talking on the phone, watch how many places they look when talking, almost none of which are required for continuing the conversation. You do this a lot yourself. Your focal points change and vary depending on what your brain is doing.

27

As a presenter, you need to be aware of these temporary anchors and you need to use them to your advantage!

You can use two kinds of focal points: primary and secondary. Primary focal points include the screen, the display equipment, and the audience. Secondary focal points include the floor, the ceiling, the walls, the furniture, the fixtures, the exit sign, and any other decorative or noticeable objects you might glance at during the presentation.

Primary focal points are referenced a lot in the presentation and you'll find yourself gesturing to them and interacting with them constantly. The primary focal points help you concentrate your attention and they are very apparent to the audience.

Secondary focal points are less obvious to the audience. Yet, these focal points also help connect your thoughts to physical objects in order for your delivery of information to appear more natural.

You can't stare off into oblivion or space-out during the presentation, even though you do it in real life. But the very act of staring can be so effective for the audience because they can see you thinking, pondering, and struggling to make information important. Without an object to focus attention on, you can't show the audience that you're thinking. Ahhh, but focal points make thinking a reality!

For example—finally, an example! You're presenting in front of a group of 40 people. You're getting ready to start and you take note of several objects in the room that catch your attention. On the back wall is a painting of a snow-covered mountain. On the ceiling is a row of track lighting with spotlights facing the side-wall. On the other side-wall is a thermostat and, next to it, a wall telephone. All of these are usable secondary focal points.

Let's say that during the presentation you are telling of a work-related experience where you had to lead a team of people to accomplish a task. During the story you are reflecting about the experience, and your eyes glance to the painting on the back wall. It only takes a few seconds of your attention on that painting to give the impression to the audience that you are reflecting on the experience. They see you staring into space and believe you are explaining to them what you see in your mind's eye. Without an object to focus on, you might recount the story too quickly and lose some of the impact. The painting gives you a visible focal point that helps demonstrate your thoughts and makes the telling of the story look more natural.

So, you can't just look off into space; no, you need something to look at, like the painting. And, because you looked at it before (prior to the presentation), you are not distracted by the details in the painting. That's why you glance around the room before you begin the presentation. You have to know your focal points in advance. You don't want to be surprised by anything you glance at while speaking.

Sometimes the attributes of a focal point can help in your description. Okay, let's use the same example. It's later in the presentation. You're displaying a line chart and commenting on the rising costs of a current project. You glance at the thermostat briefly and you describe the skyrocketing costs as reaching the boiling point, ready to burst. The thermostat

27

as a focal point created a heat-related image in your mind, helping you build a better description for the problem.

Of course, this means you can never present unless you're in a room with a painting and a thermostat!

Focal points are extremely useful, and the more you can selectively use these temporary anchors, the easier it is to show the audience what you're thinking!

Creating Distance

Focal points have a near or far nature, similar to a camera lens. If the focal point is closer to you, the background blurs; if the focal point is more distant, the foreground blurs.

You can try this by holding your index finger up in the air at arm's length, about the height of your eyes. Look at your finger and everything behind your finger is blurry. Look past your finger at some distant point and your finger (even your hand) is blurry. In fact, you can almost see through your finger by focusing on the background. Don't close one eye or you'll lose all depth perception and your finger will become a solid mass, blocking your view of the background. Okay, okay, try it, I'll wait....

The near or far focus is helpful when describing people or things that are not visible to the audience but need to be more real for you. You might stretch your arm out and focus directly on your palm as you describe items from an invisible contract that you're holding. You could be relaying two parts of a conversation, and the face of the invisible other person is the picture frame on the far wall, making it appear that you are conversing with that person.

In both cases, creating distance requires a focal point or something to look at to help you make it appear real.

USING VIRTUAL SPACE

Virtual space is the most fun you can have in front of people with your clothes on! Okay, I just thought you needed a break from all this reading! But it doesn't take much to distract you, does it?

Just as focal points help you connect your thoughts to visible objects, virtual space helps you connect the audience to invisible objects. You use virtual space to show the audience how your mind is visualizing the concepts you're explaining.

At times during a presentation, you will mention several related concepts to the audience and not really know if the group is following along. You already see the concepts in your mind, but the audience has no idea how to distinguish among them.

For example, you mention to the group that three separate departments will be involved in a decision: marketing, sales, and finance. The instant you name the three groups, you have a visual image in your head of each of those departments. You can see where in the building the departments are, you see the faces of people who work in each area, and you are visualizing three distinctly unique departments.

Now you have to get the audience to see three different departments. You do this with virtual space. You physically place the departments in the air for the audience to reference. As you say "marketing," your right hand places the word in the air to your right. As you say "sales," your left hand places the word in the air to your left; as you say "finance," you place the word in the air in front of you, using both hands. In all three moves, your palms would open out to the audience without blocking your face.

The point is that the three departments are floating in virtual space and you can immediately reference any of the three by physically retrieving it from its floating position. If you say, "The marketing department is going to…," you can gesture to the space occupied by the word marketing, to your right, where you placed it. If instead you use the space to your left, the audience would say, "No, no—that's the sales department over there!" The audience remembers where you placed the references because they have been given focal points to reference. The concepts are floating in virtual space for the audience to see.

Use virtual space to identify concepts as separate and distinct from one another. Don't just use virtual space and then do nothing with the floating anchors you handed the audience. When you place the items in the air for the audience, immediately reference one of them to begin noting the distinction.

Other ways of using virtual space include showing timelines and distance. For example, if you are describing several events from 1990 through the present, you might use your right hand to place 1990 in the air as the beginning of the timeline. Then use your left hand to stretch an invisible thread from your right hand to a place in the air to your left to show the length of the timeline. For showing distance, you might gesture, with your left arm fully extended, to a point at the far corner of the room while you mention an office location in another state. The group would realize you are referencing a place in the distance and not somewhere nearby.

Keep in mind that the moment you change physical space, virtual space falls to the floor and disappears. For example, you're in the front of the triangle and you use virtual space to distinguish three items. You reference one item, but then you navigate to the middle of the triangle. Because you moved to another physical space on the floor, the virtual references disappear. Those little anchors or focal points for the audience can't float in space if your body is not around to support them! This means that whenever you move in the triangle, you get another opportunity to use virtual space.

Handling Distractions

When I talked about the mechanics of form in the last chapter, I mentioned some body and voice problems that the audience might find distracting. Sometimes it's the other way around, and you can get distracted while presenting. In almost every distraction, the result is a loss of concentration. Your mind loses the focus on the objective in the presentation. You usually get sidetracked because you were not prepared for the diversion. The following are some of the external forces that may challenge your attention to the message.

The Slacker

Activity in the audience is a very common distraction for a presenter, and this usually happens at the beginning of a presentation. It's called tardiness. A latecomer can cause a break in the flow for you while you speak. This is more apparent as the tardy person takes a seat closer to the front because more people have to watch the person get settled.

I think the solution for lateness is a public beheading. Now, now—relax—stay with me on this. It seems a bit cruel to do this to the person who shows up late, but I suspect the laggards will be fewer once the heads begin to roll. Actually, beheading is not a popular solution because you can't fit a guillotine in the overhead compartment of the plane, so you'll have to rent one. That just isn't cost-effective!

Okay, seriously, the best way to handle the distractions caused by someone who arrives late is by finding a way to repeat or recap as much of the story necessary for the person to catch up. What? Catch up? But the slacker was late. The actors don't recap what's happened after the play begins. True, but this is not like theatre where the ticket has already been purchased. The one who is late may be critical to your planned call to action. The tardy person may be the one making the final decision! You never know what role the latecomer plays. Don't chance alienation. Bring that lost sheep back into the fold.

In addition, the distraction of a latecomer usually messes up your current point anyway. Because you'll have to repeat what you just covered for everyone else's benefit, you can sneak in a quick sentence to recap for the slacker.

THE ATTACKER

Sometimes a hostile audience member can distract you. Hostility in the audience usually relates to the content in some way. It's simple: You counter hostility with friendliness.

Sometimes political or market forces are at work causing frustration for some people and the reactions are negative. I've seen this hostility at employee meetings right after a downsizing takes place. It happens at shareholder meetings if profits take a hit.

If you are faced with hostility, agree with your adversary as quickly as you can. Then, look at the source of the conflict and ask yourself, "Can I fix this?" Be honest. If you can address the issue, do it. If you can't, then try turning it around. Ask the person, "Do you have a suggestion?" The key to this is that your attempt to solve or ask for help in solving a problem is viewed as a friendly way of working with your adversary.

You usually can't win if you fight back in a public forum. The reason is that the audience believes you know more than you reveal and fighting back suggests you don't have an answer nor will admit to being wrong. That's why agreement helps soften the blow. I realize this approach can't cover every hostile situation, but it works in most cases.

THE KNOW-IT-ALL

Another distraction is caused by the ego of the know-it-all. Counter the conceit with fellowship. The know-it-all appears more in small group presentations because the chance to speak out is more readily available. Regardless of the venue, the know-it-all can cause you to lose your concentration.

Like the attacker, you need to side with the know-it-all right away (if possible). For example, you are discussing the tax benefits of a new copy machine for a client. In the meeting is a person from the client's accounting department. We'll call him "Zeno." Now Zeno pipes up very early in your talk and says, "Are you considering this a Section 1231 Asset for depreciation purposes?" The rest of the group rolls their eyes, having seen Zeno openly destroy others in the past! No one escapes his deadly wrath. But, for you to be discussing tax benefits, you already understand enough accounting details to easily handle Zeno. You address his concerns and respond with enough information to satisfy his hunger. Yet, you also know this is only the beginning. Zeno lives for these moments!

This is when you form the Fellowship of Accountants where you and Zeno are the charter members. Minutes after responding to Zeno, at the very next accounting issue, you look right over to Zeno and say, "And as Zeno can tell each of you, the equipment...." In other words, you make an ally. Zeno becomes your constant resident expert to support nearly every financial point that even remotely sounds confusing.

By making that person your support for complex issues, you always have a very effective way to neutralize the smart-aleck. If you fight the know-it-all, you may gain some sympathy from the rest of the group, but you'll be diverted from your topic and end up being less effective with your message.

THE TALKER

This is the person who distracts by talking during your talk. Usually, talkers travel in pairs, unless they're crazy. In that case, they are probably senior executives and we know there is no cure for them! So how do you handle people talking when you're talking?

You do nothing. That's right, nothing. Believe it or not, the audience handles them for you. Try this. Go to the movies with a friend. Start talking with your friend. It won't take long before someone (usually someone big) whirls around, stares at you, and says, "Hey, shut up!" In a play, a ballet, or an opera—anywhere people paid money—fear not, they will quiet down the talkers.

Well, people pay "good money" to attend a meeting. It's called their time. And time is good money. So trust the crowd to help you out on this one because the talkers not only disrupt the speaker, they distract the listener, too.

THE BOSS

Of all the distractions in the world, this one can stop a presenter cold. "Oh, no. My boss is watching! I'm really in trouble now!" How do you deal with a superior in the crowd? You usually freak out. The reason is that your effort to impress becomes greater, and you simply try too hard. In the theatre it's called overacting, and it usually happens when the actor knows a critic is in the audience.

You may find yourself making more eye contact and directing more of the information to your boss at the expense of the rest of the audience. This is a big mistake because you lose on two counts. First, the audience is slighted from your true attention, and second, your boss may feel singled out during every moment. This is frustrating. When a presenter pays a lot of attention to one person, that person feels obligated to listen even more attentively, almost out of courtesy. It's like being at a family function and having to sit and listen to that one relative who won't let you leave the table until the story is over. You know the type. Every family has at least one of these characters. I believe it's the law of nature!

So the solution of presenting to a superior is to treat that person as equal to all the others in the room. Don't pay any more or any less attention than you would to anyone else in the room. A boss gets dressed, eats food, travels, works, and plays just like everyone else in the audience and should not be presented to in a special way. If you deliver the talk with sincerity and you follow the objective through to the call to action, the existence of your boss will have gone unnoticed by both you and your boss. The key here is to neutralize the superiority with equality.

All in all, the distractions you might face can break your concentration if you are not prepared to handle the diversion. Typically, you don't fight fire with fire in these cases. You usually try to counter or neutralize the offender. If you stay focused, you remain in control of the presentation, and you hold the attention of your audience as you deliver the message.

USING YOUR HEART

You go to a play and the actor comes to the edge of the stage and he's crying. If you say, "Wow, look at that! Real tears!" you saw technique. But if he's crying and you're crying— you are in the moment. You are sharing the emotion, not watching it happen.

You can't limit your skill set to the physical or even the physical and mental. You have to use your heart. The reason for this is you. You're a whole person—body, voice, mind, and heart. You present with your whole being.

I once had a colleague who had the potential for complete mastery of this skill. She had so much going for her. She perfected the physical movement and developed excellent voice control; she used her head, linking intentions with content to effectively convey messages. But she failed to take the last step and use her emotions. This limited her use of humor, as well, and it restricted her growth as a consummate communicator. By not committing herself to her own feelings, a gap of emptiness will always be between her and her audiences.

The use of emotion is what separates presenting from performing. As a visual presenter you will have to create the emotional link between you and your audience. You can use your heart in your delivery by

- Understanding motivation
- Adding stories and personal opinions
- Using humor
- Developing your own style

UNDERSTANDING MOTIVATION

Think of all the means at your disposal to express your feelings to an audience. Your eyes, facial expressions, voice, and gestures—your whole body emits feeling in order to make words have meaning. But without your personal commitment, your belief and your motivation, the audience doesn't react as well as expected. Motivation requires inner energy to deliver the information with conviction.

That energy starts with you. You're the catalyst. You have to give an emotion to get an emotion. You have to be motivated before you can expect the group to be motivated. This is one of the most obvious problems I find in working with presenters. They fail to "get into it," but they expect the audience to "get it." Come on, get with it! If you can't psyche yourself up for the moment, then why should the audience be expected to do so? You have to work on yourself to get your heart into it. But before you build the desire (the motivation) to tell the story, you have to believe in your message.

SENSE OF TRUTH

The chance to stir the feelings of a group to truly believe what you believe is the essence of your skill. Your ultimate challenge is that they believe in your belief in the message. People can't have faith in the message without believing in the person representing the message. People believe in other people. The audience wants, above all, to believe what you are telling them. It is that simple. But that belief starts in your own heart because if you don't buy it, they don't buy it! You have to have a sense of truth about your message. This becomes your motivation to deliver that sense of truth with clarity and enthusiasm.

So, ask yourself, "What in the message do I really believe is true?" Everything, something, nothing? Remember that in life, truth is what you know. In presenting, truth doesn't exist until you demonstrate it. Using action, you must show your version of the truth to an audience. But if you can't justify your actions, then the truth is less obvious. Truth and belief are inseparable. So you must believe something to show its truth. It reminds me of the saying "Practice what you preach." So, in almost every coaching session I say, "Yeah…but do you believe it?"

The best way to develop a sense of truth in your message is to play the devil's advocate with the argument you constructed for the audience. Can you convincingly play both sides of the issue? Can you be the prosecution and the defense? Naturally, the side that wins has more of your sense of truth because it has more of your heart. Truth is in the heart, not the mind. So the more the message appeals to you, the more evidence you look for to support it. If you love what you do, you'll love doing it!

Your sense of truth in your topic is directly related to your belief in that topic. Whatever appeals to you most in that truth will be delivered with the most conviction.

THINKING, FEELING, WANTING

Your sense of truth in the message justifies your presenting it. Motivation makes it happen. The motivation to speak is measured by your will, your desire, and your determination.

27

Your feelings and your intellect are both supported by your will. They all work for one another and can hardly be separated. If you use your intellect (mind) to decide on some action, you must call upon your feelings (heart) and your desire (motivation) to make the action happen. You can't separate these. They all work together synergistically. Although action drives emotion, you have to "want" to create the action in the first place.

For example, let's say you must make a presentation to a group of people about a new product. You know how you will present the message because you've planned it. The planning involved a thinking process. But, it doesn't stop there. How do you feel about the plan to present the product? How do you feel about the product itself? How about the people you'll be speaking to, and even the place you'll be presenting in? And, considering those feelings, what motivates you to deliver the information at all?

You might say, "My paycheck!" Believe it or not, money can motivate only in as much as what it gives you—security, luxury, power, and so on. The point is that if the motivation is only from a need to present (to get paid), then it is not being driven by desire. It becomes one of those presentations you have to do, but would skip if you could. This, unfortunately, is the case with over 95% of all presentations.

You've heard the excuses. "I just don't have it today," or "I'm not into it right now," or, "This doesn't interest me." You've used these expressions yourself, at times.

When the motivation—the desire, the will—is missing, the feelings disappear and the mind is left alone to direct the body and the voice. When this happens, the presenter appears to be "going through the motions," and the effect of the message is usually lost.

People Make a Difference

Motivation is a key element to making presentations more effective. I have been giving the same basic skills seminar for a number of years. Often people come up to me who've seen my "show" more than once and say, "I keep getting more and more out of this seminar; what have you added?" I say, "I've changed nothing!" The response is typically, "But something is different."

True. There is one difference. Can you guess? I'll tell you in a minute.

I've had others ask, "How can you give the same seminar, over and over again, and not be totally bored with the topic?" I respond, "The same way in the theatre an actor can play the same role, six nights a week for two years, and deliver the same part with enthusiasm—because every night is different!" It's the same reason why my seminar appears "different" each time.

The answer is different people. When the people change, the event changes. That's because the event is by people, for people. It's a completely new presentation for each new audience. That's the secret behind the motivation. It's the desire and the will to share anew. Whether it's the same information for different people or even new information for the same people, the motivation is a result of change.

27

Never look to your content to stimulate your will. Look to the people who will be stimulated. It's not the joke that's funny; rather, it's the reaction. Your anticipation of the laughter motivates you to tell the joke! The inspiration you need to present the topic with conviction comes from the simple fact that people are willing to give you moments of their time. If that's not enough to get you excited about your delivery, then consider yourself one of the average communicators—one of the talking heads that people expect to see each time a presentation takes place.

Always visualize the effect of your words on the group and you will understand your motivation. Think of infecting rather than affecting the audience, and your desire to deliver the message will increase.

ADDING STORIES AND PERSONAL OPINIONS

In a world of parity products, where everything looks the same, the one difference is you. That's what being a visual presenter is all about—you! That's how companies differentiate. Not with products, but with people. So, if people make the difference, then you can bet your bottom dollar that individual experience and personal opinion count for something. And guess what? Experience means you've "been there" and have probably formed some philosophy over the years. You've learned some lessons over the course of time. So, talk about them. About the lessons. You know, the stuff you learned and about the way you see it. Talk about the way it was and you'll convince people about the way it should be. Come on, tell a story!

The best presenters tell stories. I can't stress that enough. The advantage of good stories is that they are unique. No one can copy, duplicate, reiterate, reproduce, retransmit, or recount your stories. They are personal references that allow a group of people to know something about what you have been through. Stories and personal experience are ways to share your character with an audience.

TIME, PLACE, AND CIRCUMSTANCE

The rules of storytelling are simple. The audience has to know when it happened, where it happened, and what conditions existed while it happened. If you don't establish time, place, and circumstance, you have less chance of keeping the audience attentive to your story.

For example, several years ago I was at a big conference and everything was hectic. That's the beginning of my story. But how involved are you at this point? I mean, what do you really know so far? More important, what do you visualize about the event compared to what I remember about it? Let's break it apart. "Several years ago"—whatever year you might be thinking of may not be the one I am referencing, so we are not together on that issue. I mentioned "a big conference"—but you are probably visualizing a completely different event in a much different place. Finally, I said, "everything was hectic"—to you, maybe hectic means chaotic, or confused, or frenzied, or simply wild. Adjectives are tough for everyone to agree on, you know.

27

Clearly my story doesn't put us on the same page so far. Our references are different. A story works best when we all share a common set of parameters. I need to establish time, place, and circumstance for you, very quickly, to pull you into my story.

So here it was, August 12, 1996. I'm inside the San Diego Convention Center at the Republican National Convention, escaping the 100-degree heat. But, I'm with a few thousand people crammed into this one closet-of-a-room, and suddenly—no air conditioning. Oh man, everything was hectic!

Do you see what a big difference those details made? Sure, it takes about 20 more seconds to add the description, but you are definitely with me in the story. You know the time (August 1996); you know the place (San Diego, Republican Convention); you know the circumstance (no air conditioning). We both can agree on what hectic means now!

When you specify time, place, and circumstance, you help the listener see what you are recalling in your mind. When you detail with adjectives (crammed, closet-of-a-room, and hectic), you let the listener feel what you are recreating in your heart.

Storytelling is about attributes and attitudes. Keep that in mind every time you tell a story, and you will be more descriptive of both the facts and the feelings associated with the experience.

Personal Opinions Matter

It's one thing to tell good stories, whether they happened to you or to someone else. It's also important to editorialize. You have to voice your opinion every so often so that people know you're involved in the message. The editorial is the slant on the topic that the audience expects to hear from you. It's the emotional hook that keeps them coming back for more. Just don't be afraid to say the word "I" when you speak.

For example, let's say you're giving a presentation, and you bring up a bullet chart with a list of services your company provides. You may find yourself reciting the list and maybe adding more explanation here and there. But how do you feel about any one of these services? The audience would love to know. So maybe you say, "What I really find helpful about…" or you state, "One of my favorite ways to use this…"—these are personal opinions. Your own views tell the audience so much more than your reviews. So don't be afraid to show them your take on life.

Hey, that's why we watch talk shows! We love reading those letters to the editor. We are addicted to the unsupported assertions of people we will never meet! If a schoolteacher in West Podunk, Ohio, calls in to *Larry King Live* and criticizes a comment from a state senator out of Texas, I'll sit there mesmerized while I dig deeper into my half-gallon of vanilla-fudge swirl. Why? I have no idea, other than I have to hear an opinion on anything by anybody, anywhere! Okay, so maybe you're not that bad. You have a half-gallon of Rocky Road, instead. The point is that we are fascinated by other people's opinions and stories. It's part of the intrigue of being human.

27

The bottom line is that you can be so much more effective when you break the pattern of the presentation with stories and personal opinions. It gives the audience an image of a real person who knows how to share real information in a really interesting way.

USING HUMOR

A traveling salesman walks into a local bar and orders a beer. The bar is crowded, but it's pretty quiet.

Suddenly a voice shouts out, "72!" and everyone just bursts into laughter. The salesman looks puzzled.

The crowd settles, again another voice yells, "114!" and people are just doubling over in hysterics.

The salesman leans to the bartender and says, "What's the deal with the numbers and the laughs?"

The bartender replies, "Oh, this bar has been here for years. Same crowd all the time. Well, they know all the jokes, got tired of telling them, so they numbered them all. When you want to tell a joke, you just yell the number. It's pretty simple!"

The salesman whispers, "Hey, do you mind if I try?"

The bartender says, "Give it a shot."

The salesman clears his throat, waits for a lull, and yells, "84!" Nothing! No response, not even a chuckle. He tries again, even louder, "84!" Dead silence. One more time he shouts, "84!" Blank stares. A funeral would be funnier.

Frustrated, he turns to the bartender and says, "What's up? Why don't they laugh? Is something wrong with number 84?"

The bartender shakes his head and says, "Hey, pal, face it. Some people just can't tell a joke!"

I think you get the point. If you aren't funny now, you probably won't be funny when you present. This doesn't mean you can't learn things about timing and rhythm, but humor is exactness, it's preciseness, it's accuracy! You can miss with tragedy and have some people in tears while others sniffle, but comedy is different. They either laugh or they don't. Smirks and chuckles don't count.

I don't want you to shy away from using humor; rather, I want you to realize how effective humor can be in a presentation. In a world of visual creatures, entertainment ranks high on the list of "what they want." Humor is the best entertainment you can add to an event, because it relaxes people and makes them realize that the whole world isn't coming to an end after all. The use of humor, at the right time with the right inflection, can be extremely effective.

27

OPENING LINES

"I just flew in from New York. Boy, are my arms tired!" That's fine if you are a stand-up comic. A comedian is expected to be funny. But are you expected to be funny? When someone says, "I want to start off with a joke," I ask why? What makes you think the audience expects an opening joke? For that matter, why not sing? If they expect a joke, surely they expect a song, maybe even a dance! If they've seen you present before and they know you for your humor, then yes, tell the joke. But if they don't know your style, the joke better be really funny. No, I mean really funny. If it's not, it will probably bomb.

Bombs Away!

One January, I was in Boston, coaching a group of sales executives during their annual sales conference. The CEO of the company wanted 30 minutes to work with me, early in the afternoon. He came into the room, holding a few index cards and he said, "I just want you to help me with some jokes. I was roasted at dinner last night by the senior management team and I want to get back at them. So I came up with my own jokes." I looked at him and said, "So Dan, let me get this straight, you wrote the jokes, right?" He nodded and I asked him to begin.

He told the first joke and I didn't react. I prompted him to continue and the second and third jokes were worse than the first. I helped him reword a few things. We worked a few minutes on rhythm and delivery. Still—nothing. I looked at him and said, "Forget it, Dan. These won't work. You're not funny." He looked shocked and I continued, "You're not a funny guy. You have no timing, no sense of rhythm, and the jokes stink! Other than that, you're fine!"

He insisted on using the jokes and I said, "If you do, you will bomb, big time. I am telling you the truth. Don't do it!" Sure enough, later that evening I saw him in the hotel lobby and he came right up to me, put his hand on my shoulder and said, "You were right. Not a single laugh. I stunk up the place."

I looked at Dan, glanced at his hand resting on my shoulder, smiled a little and said, "Dan, keep the day job." And we both laughed.

Dan wasn't funny because he was never funny to those people in the first place. They had no expectation or frame of reference for his humor. Dan also wasn't used to telling jokes, so his delivery style didn't fit the situation. You have to develop a skill for humor, just as you would for any other form of entertainment.

Don't just tell an opening joke for the sake of the joke. Whatever opener you choose, make it relate to the topic, the industry, the specific business, or even to a general characteristic about the group, like the fact that they are all in sales or marketing.

I was the keynote speaker at an annual meeting for a global travel agency. My opener was a Henny Youngman joke: "So, I got to the airport, walked up to the ticket counter and said, 'I have three bags here. I want one bag to go to Rome, one to Detroit, and the third one to Dallas.' The attendant said, 'We can't do that!' I said, 'Why not? You did it last week!'" For this group, the joke fit the industry.

STRETCHING THE RUBBER BAND

When I prepare my own presentations, I structure the key issues around the jokes. This is very important because it uses a theatre principle called "stretching the rubber band." Think of the emotions of the audience as a simple rubber band. One side is serious; the other side, humorous. When the rubber band is stretched, the distance between the two sides is greater. If you let go of one side, the impact from the other side is bigger. An unstretched rubber band creates less impact. (I think I read that in a fortune cookie once.)

Applying this principle to presentations, the humor offsets the serious tone of the talk. The timing is the trick. When the humor is at its peak, when you are delivering the funniest line—that's when the rubber band is stretched the most. Immediately following that moment is when you can get the greatest effect from being serious! That's right. The seriousness of the message is greater when the audience least expects it. If they are relaxed from a lighthearted comment, then they are vulnerable to the importance of an issue. The timing of your humor can effectively heighten the importance of your message.

Indicating and Apologizing

Don't indicate your humor. If you begin to laugh before the audience does, then the effect of the joke diminishes. This is because you indicated or telegraphed the result (laughter) before it could happen for the audience. If you laugh for the crowd, then they won't have to. One other way of indicating humor is by stating, "That reminds me of a joke," or "Here's a really funny story." When you say things like that, you raise the expectation of the group. In that case, it better be funny!

The best way to develop your delivery of humor is to practice telling jokes or funny stories to those closest to you. Family and friends will be the first to tell you if your jokes are funny. But make sure you find the jokes funny, as well, or you will not tell them with commitment.

Finally, if a joke falls flat, keep going. Never apologize and never comment on the failure of humor. It's done. Move on. Only a comedian has to worry about being funny all the time. If you bomb out, it only makes the audience relieved that you don't tell jokes for a living!

Developing Your Own Style

Probably the most important issue in the whole skill of delivery is the development of your own style. Think of style not as fashion, but as character.

The audience evaluates your character in relation to the message, the media, and the mechanics. All of these elements are part of the event. If you have developed your own natural way to deliver consistent messages, your style will emerge. People will remember your kind of presentation. Your style will show each time you deliver, regardless of the content.

Levels in Your Style

One way of assuring your own style is to match three levels of objectives in this order: the objectives for your life, for your role within the organization, and for your current presentation.

Start with your life. Let's say one of the objectives or goals you have in life is to attain great wealth. You want to be rich! Okay, fine. Then look at your role in your current company. Is there an objective in your job description that can possibly match your life goal of attaining

27

great wealth? Well, maybe not great wealth, but possibly a raise or a promotion—the steps to greater wealth. Finally, is there anything in the presentation that has to do with the attaining of great wealth, even if not directly for you but for the company? Look for it.

For example, perhaps part of the presentation discusses company growth. More revenue for the corporation might just increase the budget for payroll. That could mean a nice fat raise for you! The extra cash might be what you need for the mortgage payment on that piece of property you've been looking at recently. Since they're not making any more land, you know that property appreciates in value and it would be so nice to have the land as an investment for the future. The road to great wealth is paved with real estate tycoons!

The point is that during the presentation, the discussion of company growth is in direct line with your goal of attaining great wealth. Chances are you will cover this topic with more enthusiasm because it matches something that appeals to you—in your heart. That's important in the development of your own style.

Many things in your life appeal to you. If any of them exist in your work and through the presentations you give because of your work, all the better to identify them and use them! Link the little objectives of your talk through the larger objectives of your work and into the even bigger objectives of your life.

THROUGH LINE OF ACTION

Paying attention to everything that comes before, during, and following your presentation develops your character or style. It is one continuous process, which is called a through line of action. This is important in the event because it lets you link all of the elements in the presentation with the reality of the way things are.

For example, you are giving a presentation on a Monday morning to a group of people. You begin at 9:00 a.m. and plan to finish at about 11:00 a.m. There will be one 15-minute break scheduled at 10:00 a.m. Okay, pretty simple. Let's make your through line of action for this example run from the time you woke up until after lunch.

Run through the details of those moments and you'll see a range of events from the very consistent to the very unique. The wake up routine is probably the same. Depending on where the presentation takes place, locally or out of town, the commute to the event may more or less familiar. The arrival at the event will be as unique as however many times you've done this same presentation for the same people in the same space. The event itself will have some information you've mentioned many times and some new information you are presenting for the first time. You can see how just the examination of the continuous action will show you a combination of daily habits and one-of-a-kind activities.

The habits are already a part of your personal style. Don't worry about them at all. The one-of-a-kind moments are part of this through line of action, which eventually may add to your personal style, depending on how often they repeat. The more you can pinpoint and control the unique moments, the more likely they will recur the next time you present.

DON'T EVEN THINK ABOUT IT!

The examination of your through line of action—that is, the connecting points along the way—is how you develop good habits. Although habits are hard to break, the good ones last forever. You don't even need to think about them after a while because they are part of your natural way of doing things.

TIP

> Look back on all the segments in Chapters 24 through this chapter and put a check mark next to those sections you believe are already part of your style. Put a question mark next to the parts that you think you can achieve for yourself with some effort. Cross out any section that you feel is totally impossible for you to ever accomplish, regardless of how hard you try.
>
> For the check-marked items, they're already yours and you need not think about them. The question marks represent the work you have to do to make them into check marks.
>
> My guess is that you won't cross out anything because there is nothing you can't accomplish, if you try hard enough!

You know, there was a time in your life when, for a few weeks, all you did was spend every single waking moment of your day trying to accomplish a task that, today, you take for granted. It's called walking. At one time, it was a rare privilege; now, it's just part of the way you move.

When your presentation skills evolve from a rarity to a routine, your own style becomes second nature. This is the result of putting as much of yourself into the mechanics of function—the inner life of your delivery—so that no one else can copy, reproduce, or mimic your personal skill set in any way.

Your body, voice, mind, and heart combine to form the foundation of your skill as a visual presenter. Once developed, your own style will be evident in the message, the media, and the mechanics as you perform your presentation for an appreciative audience. Every move you make, every word you utter, every thought you express, and every feeling you have will be part of your natural style. You'll finally be able to trust your own skills whenever you are truly being yourself in the presentation.

So next time you present, relax, wiggle your toes and break a leg!

TROUBLESHOOTING

What's the best way to do a product demonstration for a group?

Whenever you have to focus the attention of the audience on a prop (a tangible object), you should be concerned about physical perspective. If your physical perspective of the object—your viewing angle—is different from that of the audience, the communication is lost. Many product demonstrations fail because the presenter and the audience do not share the same perspective during the demonstration.

For example, let's say the product you need to demonstrate is small enough to rest on top of a table and light enough that you can hold it up to show people. If you are standing and the audience is sitting, any reference to the object as it rests on the table will be viewed from different angles. Your angle is from above and each person in the audience, by virtue of his or her seat, has a different viewing angle to the object. That should be your first indication that you need to change the perspective. You might decide to hold the object in the air so people father back can see. But you still end up with a variety of viewing angles. What can be done to equalize the perspective?

One solution is to reproduce the demonstration for view on the screen. The display screen is the "great equalizer" of perspective. You can use a still photograph of the object or you can play a videotape of the object in use. You can even use a document camera connected to your projector to show the live demonstration on the big screen. There are many ways you can create a visual impression of the object so everyone has the same perspective. This is why movies are so entertaining. The camera is doing all the work for you.

I go to presentations as part of a team. Sometimes two or three of us present different parts of the big picture. Do you have any advice for "team" presentations?

Teams are very common in high level sales presentations, initial public offerings (IPOs), and other events where several experts are required to deliver a single message. Whatever the venue, the point is that more than one person is presenting and that fact alone changes the dynamics of the event.

The mechanics of function, as discussed in this chapter, play a very important role in the relationships established by the team for the audience. The better the team members know each other, the more cohesive the team appears. So I would first suggest you get to know the players on your team. Find out likes, dislikes, hobbies, interests, opinions, concerns, fears, aspirations, and anything else that will help you understand the characteristics of your team members.

Let's put this into perspective using a husband/wife analogy. Even if you aren't married, this can apply to any two partners who know each other very well. You and your partner are at a dinner with several friends. A suggestion is made to commit to doing something the follow-ing Saturday night. You look at your partner and you can sense, within seconds, his or her interest in the plan. This is because you understand how each of you thinks, feels, and behaves in similar situations. You share a personal history.

When I coach teams, I use exercises to build a personal history to be shared by all team members. I suggest you look for that history in your team members, as well. Have they been through this type of presentation before? Have they experienced a similar turn of events?

Another important element in team presenting is what I call "the exchange." This is the transition between presenters—you know the awkward moment when one person finishes a section and introduces the next person to continue with the presentation. It is during that moment that an audience looks for a relationship between the two individuals. Do they like each other? Are they friends? Do they get along? Most presenters will simply leave this moment blank. There are no words spoken, no dialog planned, no exchange.

You should develop a small bit of business, or banter, so the audience gets an immediate impression that the two presenters have a good, healthy relationship. Maybe you plan a humorous story where one person comments on the driving habits of the other "on the way to the presentation." Perhaps you mention a personal hobby or sport that the other person likes. The whole point is about letting the audience see that a relationship exits. If they think you work well together, they will feel more confident in the organization that supports you, as well.

Team presenting is about demonstrating relationships and relationships can only be built from sharing personal information that can be used to help the team function as a unit.

CHAPTER 28

TECHNIQUES AND TECHNICALITIES

by Tom Mucciolo

In this chapter

DEALING WITH THE CONDITIONS

Beyond the message, the media, and the mechanics, the event itself adds another dimension to the planning process. The environment plays a significant role in how the presentation is received by the audience.

For example, when you go to a movie, the lobby, the concession stand, the seats, the size of the screen, and the general conditions of the place will affect how much you enjoy the movie. These environmental elements won't really change from day to day, so they become issues you can learn about in advance of going to that particular theatre.

Now, the audience will also make a difference in how much you enjoy the event, but you can't predict the crowd, unless you already have experience with the general group that frequents that theatre. You have less control (if any) over the audience than you have over the environment.

So, you want to be ready for anything when you present and, believe me, anything can happen, even at the most well-planned events. This chapter looks at the external factors that can impact your performance. I will show you a few techniques and make you aware of some technicalities concerning the conditions of the presentation. These circumstances include

- Dressing the part
- Setting the stage
- Using technology

DRESSING THE PART

Yes, you must be dressed when you present. Even if you tried the old trick of picturing the audience naked, I doubt you really want them looking at you the same way. Come on, with that body? I don't think so!

So, the first external element to deal with involves what to wear when presenting.

When you're not presenting, anything goes based on corporate or social standards. You're all grown up so you know what you can or can't wear. But in front of a group, I suggest you stick to something *BASIC*: A Believable Appearance is Simple and the Image is Conservative.

So, try for that classically conservative look with a dash of personal style. When you dress more conservatively, the audience accepts you more quickly. You will reduce those "first impression" biases. If the costumes are very noticeable by the audience, then the actors are upstaged! Period pieces will naturally catch your eye because the context of the play is out-of-date. But a business presentation is contemporary and the clothing must not overtake the message. A few points to keep in mind to make the outfit go unnoticed are

- Focusing on the face
- Working with accessories

- Wearing business outfits
- Choosing a formality

FOCUSING ON THE FACE

Your face is looked at the most because it carries the message through your voice and your expressions. Nothing should distract the audience from seeing your face. Usually, your clothes can cause a distraction, but in some cases the items around and even on your face can lessen the impact of your expressions. Let's take a look at what it takes to keep the focus on the face.

THE SKIN

My first bit of advice is to the guys—Shave! Let me try this one more time—Shave! A clean look is an advantage because it lets all your facial expressions show, especially your smile. Now, my advice to the women—Shave! (Just seeing if you were still with me.) Actually, women have the advantage of using make-up to accent their features and make expression more visible from a distance. With make-up, be aware of lighting and how the brightness may wash out your features; if possible, apply make-up in the same type of lighting you'll be in while presenting. Cosmetics, like clothing, change style with the seasons, so avoid the make-up time warp. If you have or know of a beauty consultant, it never hurts to get advice. For both men and women, if presenting under bright lights, use pressed powder to reduce the shine, mostly caused from the heat. This is important as the lighting gets closer.

THE HAIR

Your hair must be well-trimmed, so that it enhances, not hides, your facial expressions. If you wear your hair long, try to keep it pulled back. Or else, when you turn your head, your hair might block much of your face. The audience needs to see at least one eye. With your head turned toward the visual, most people only get to see one of your eyes. If it's covered by your hair, it's like having your back to the audience.

Long hair on men is still not generally accepted in all the ranks of presenting, and depending on the audience, may generate an undesirable reaction. That's why I wear my hair in a style I call *missing*. Actually, if you are balding—I mean follically-challenged—you have a presentation advantage. You have the added expression of the brow, and of making all your facial features appear more dominant. In any case, the hair should not make a statement or the focus will not be on the face.

THE EYEWEAR

If eyewear is required, you should first opt for contact lenses because they don't hide eye expressions. If you must wear glasses, try to find ones with a non-glare finish. This will reflect less light and the audience will be able to see your eyes better. Usually, in conference rooms and most rooms with average-height ceilings, the glass-glare is most noticeable.

28

When you stand and people sit in this type of room, the angle of reflection from the overhead light breaks right at your eyes, regardless of your height. No one knows why this is so, but it is. You could try to raise the earpieces to tilt your glasses forward, but make sure they don't fall off. Otherwise you'll be crawling around on the floor, and I can guarantee the focus will not be on your face!

WORKING WITH ACCESSORIES

Collars and necklines should be kept conservative. You can add a little more expression with ties and scarves. These accessories are great because they naturally draw attention to your face. Bow ties typically get associated with a character trait, and unless the audience already knows you and your bow-tie look, they may not take you seriously. For ties, learn to make a square knot (Windsor knot) so the tie looks symmetrical at the neck. Don't wear those big cartoon ties or the ones with pictures of dead presidents. And avoid the scarves with artistic images of who-knows-what-it-is-or-cares. All these styles distract the audience.

Pins, tie clips, pocket squares, beads, cuff links, and earrings can add polish and style, but wear them sparingly and make sure they don't distract by being reflective or noisy. A watch is your most important presentation accessory because you probably need to keep track of the time. Choose a watch face that has enough size and contrast for you to easily sneak a look at the time as you gesture.

TIP

> Wear your watch on your left arm when you present, even if you normally wear it on your right. The left hand is the one that gestures to the screen and can be lifted higher than your shoulder. The glance to the face of the watch is easiest from that angle and because your face is turned away, the audience can't see you look slightly downward to see the time. If you had your watch on your right arm and then tried to look at it, your glance to your wrist would be more obvious to an audience member who is looking directly at your face.

WEARING BUSINESS OUTFITS

If the suit fits, wear it! The look, comfort, and style all depend on how well a suit fits and drapes your body. Suits that fit well make you feel better. A suit that is too baggy will look sloppy as you move, and one that's too tight will restrict your movement. Choose a suit that is well constructed and use that suit often. In fact, if you present a lot, I suggest investing in a suit that you reserve only for presentation events.

Once again, think conservative! Solid colors or subtle patterns are best. Plaids and large houndstooth patterns tend to "vibrate" and can be quite distracting. As for color, it's best to be traditional and subtle. Dark blue and dark-to-medium gray are the most conservative and traditional choices. Women have more opportunities with color choices than men, but that doesn't mean trendy selections will always work. Choosing the right clothing colors for your complexion can make you seem vibrant and energetic whereas the wrong colors can make you look tired and gloomy. Color can also complement your figure. In fact, dark colors minimize the figure; light emphasizes the figure. Based on your body type, choose accordingly.

ON THE TOP

Shirts and blouses should be fitted for movement and comfort. You don't want very tight outfits, and you should avoid short sleeves while presenting. The reason is that a short sleeve makes the arms look choppy right around the elbow because of the change from cloth to skin. Your gestures are harder to follow because they don't look smooth.

For men, the shirt should be lighter than the suit, and the tie should be darker than the shirt. When in doubt, white is never wrong. For women, the color contrast can vary a bit more, but if you plan on wearing a lavaliere microphone, make sure you wear a blouse that buttons up the front or a v-neck top so that the microphone can be clipped in the center and not to one side. Centering equalizes the sound pick-up.

Jackets and blazers, like suits, should be fitted for movement and comfort. Watch out for pairing separates of contrasting colors. Think of making a solid line of color from the floor to the neck to draw attention up to your face. A lot of people wonder whether the jacket should be buttoned or unbuttoned. Men must wear jackets unbuttoned, if they plan on moving and gesturing. This eliminates double-breasted styles because they are meant to be buttoned all the time. If a man buttons a single-breasted jacket and gestures to the screen, for example, the jacket will gape and pucker because men's jackets are cut in a boxy manner. But women have the choice to leave their jackets buttoned or unbuttoned because women's jackets are cut to fit the curves of the female frame and tend to move naturally with the figure. However, usually the jackets look better when buttoned.

TOWARD THE BOTTOM

Men will wear trousers, but women have the choice of a skirt or trousers when presenting. Trousers allow for easy movement and are generally accepted in the corporate setting when part of a suit. Avoid separates, because they tend to be less formal and more contrasting. With both skirts and trousers, pay attention to hems, making sure the length is tailored and conservative. For both women and men, socks must coordinate with trousers and be long enough to cover the calf. There may be times when you are part of a panel on a platform stage. When you sit, your pants ride up and you don't want the skin on your leg showing. Longer socks prevent this. Women should choose stockings that minimize attention to legs and create a solid look, drawing the eye from the floor to the face.

IT'S GOTTA BE THE SHOES

Footwear is a sound investment because good shoes tend to look and feel good. Of course, the funny thing is that people judge one another by their shoes. It's true. People look at your feet and decide on your grooming habits and even how much money you make! So, all things being equal, if you can't present, at least polish your shoes!

Specifically for women, heels are a symbol of authority and highly recommended for boosting your credibility (no pun intended). However, heels that are too high affect balance and breathing, so stick to one-inch or two-inch heel heights. Just remember, if you hear the word "platforms," it's probably in reference to the stage and not footwear from the '70s. Then again, add a leisure suit and a rotating mirrored ball and that might not be a bad way to present! Move over, Travolta!

Actually, platforms are a big trend in footwear right now, mostly among teens and the 20-something crowd. So when you're out shopping for shoes and hear the word "platforms," think youth, before you think presentation. Obviously, lower heels will allow for easier movement when you navigate backward in your triangle. Although the heels today that are usually worn with business suits are thicker than in the past and fairly comfortable, I have talked with some women who've worn heels for most of their careers and they say that totally flat shoes are actually uncomfortable because their calf muscles are stretching more than with heels. Well, you be the judge on this one. But like my dad always says, "When your shoes wear out, you'll be on your feet again!"

CHOOSING A FORMALITY

Just think—dress-down Fridays have caused a 20% drop in business for the pantyhose makers! Lots of companies have a business casual day at least once a week, and many offices have adapted a relaxed dress code throughout the week. In fact, with the growing number of telecommuters and people working in other non-office-like settings, casual attire is becoming more and more accepted. This definitely puts a strain on presenters who aren't sure what to wear and when. I mean, do you always wear the power suit when presenting, or do you match the corporate culture?

Here's the way to look at this issue: When in doubt, wear your suit. Otherwise, try to dress one "level" above your audience. For example, if they are wearing jeans and chambray shirts, wear khaki trousers and a sweater vest. If they're wearing khakis, wear dark wool trousers and a blazer. If they're wearing blazers, you wear the suit. Your goal is to maintain a sense of authority over your audience. A "one-level-above" in formality will help you look the part.

This whole "what-to-wear" thing is more about sincerity than anything else. Take a long look in the mirror or even ask a friend to be blatantly honest. But, it's too easy to find the flaws. Focus on what looks right and make it better. If you ever get unsolicited compliments, build on them. The problem with this world is there's too much vanity. But enough about what I think of me—what do you think of me?

Seriously, don't be afraid to consult with professionals. Lots of books cover this topic in depth, and I encourage you to read some of them. From the view of a visual presenter, the focus must be on the face, and from that point outward the gestures and movement will create the action in the presentation. The clothing should not take the attention of the audience because the outfit cannot deliver the message.

SETTING THE STAGE

You might spend a lot of your time getting prepared for the presentation, but when you arrive at the place to deliver the topic, all your difficulties may just be starting. It seems the only things that go according to plan are the problems. I know. I've been there many times.

A whole bunch of things can happen that make the audience uncomfortable, distracted, and even disinterested. Lots of these things can be dealt with in advance. Of course, experience is the best teacher. Hundreds of presentations have taught me that well thought-out logistics (the planning and coordinating) of an event make a world of difference for everyone involved, especially me.

The bottom line is that YOU are ultimately responsible for your presentation and the conditions of the event for the audience. If the group expects coffee and there is no coffee, then consider it your fault. It's certainly not the audience's fault. They did their jobs; they showed up. The rest of the event is in your hands. Even if you delegate tasks to others, the responsibilities are still yours.

If you plan ahead, you can set the stage for a great event by paying attention to some of the logistics, including

- Using risers
- Working with lighting and sound
- Choosing a display screen
- Deciding on seating arrangements

USING RISERS

Well, if you've already dressed the part, then it makes sense that everyone be able to see as much of your outfit as possible. If you use the Hollywood principle of "more face, more body, and more screen" when planning the room layout, you'll realize a good starting point is to consider risers or stage platforms. I'll use the terms interchangeably, even though a riser is typically lower than a platform.

Remember that ballrooms are designed for dinner and for dancing but not for discussion. So, the plan to make such a space "presentable" must be well thought-out. Line-of-sight is critical: If the audience can't see you or your support information, then they can't grasp the entire message.

Usually, when you stand on the same level as the chairs, most people see only the top third of your body. In larger settings, always look for the opportunity to use platforms to raise yourself one or two feet from the floor. The platforms give those sitting in the back a chance to see more of you. It is more difficult to communicate when less of your body is visible. So, when you are on the same level as the audience, I suggest that you at least keep your wrists higher than your elbows when gesturing, so that everyone has a better chance of seeing those gestures.

28

But, if given the chance to place yourself at a higher level than the floor—take it! The audience will get to see more of you, and thus get more of your physical expression of the message. Stage platforms or risers can give you that little lift you need to be seen.

Risers can range from as little as 6 inches high to large platforms that adjust from 18 to 24 inches. You can even use a fixed stage, if available, which is usually 36 inches from the floor. In some corporate auditoriums, the seating is fixed, as well, and the rows are sometimes built up on an incline (raked), similar to a playhouse or movie theatre.

Well, you won't be able to make any changes to fixed structures or stationary seating, but in most hotel situations, you can request platforms. Platforms are usually 6'×8'designs, which can be rolled into the space and locked together for stability. In some cases, the platforms are 4'×8'. In addition, most of these platforms have extension supports which can change the height from 18 inches to 24 inches.

For audiences of about 50 to 100 people, 18 inches should be the minimum. For more than 100 people, use the 24-inch height setting for maximum visibility. Of course, if the best you can get are 12-inch risers, take them. Any opportunity for the audience to see you better is worth it.

Most platforms are covered with material, like carpeting, to dull the hollow sound from your footsteps when you move. If the staging is not carpeted, you'll have to place less of your weight on your heels as you move, or simply take smaller steps to minimize any distractions.

TIP

> Check for the creaks! If possible, walk around the entire "stage" before the presentation and take note of any creaks or squeaking sounds you hear when stepping in certain areas. If you know that a part of the staging makes a noise when you walk over it, you should avoid that area as much as possible. The last thing you want is a loud squeak just as you say a key phrase. Many creaks in staging happen where the platforms meet. Some heavy-duty tape can usually eliminate the problem.

Of course, when you are up on risers, avoid leaning forward when you are in the front of the triangle. For people in the front row of the audience, this can appear intimidating. It's best to keep your weight shifted back or stand straight. Depending on platform height and proximity to the first row, the angle of your face gets distorted when you get too close to the edge of the stage.

WORKING WITH LIGHTING AND SOUND

28

If you can choose only one thing during a presentation, it should be good lighting followed closely by good sound. The whole notion of a visual presenter revolves around being seen and heard. When an audience watches your presentation, they are getting a lot from your physical delivery, and a tremendous amount of emphasis is given to your facial expressions, including your voice. Bad lighting masks your expressions and poor acoustics make the message difficult to hear. So, lighting and sound become important issues.

LIGHTING

Good lighting is the key to a good presentation. The audience should see as much of the presenter's face as possible. The goal is to create an unequal distribution of light, with most of the light on the presenter, some light over the audience for note-taking, and no light on the screen (other than from the projected image, of course).

The good news is that you need only two stage lights to cross-light the presenter effectively. Add a dimmer pack, and you can adjust the light level so that the presenter can still see the audience while speaking.

I recommend using two Leiko lights on trees. A Leiko light is a stage light of 500 to 750 watts (or more) and has four adjustable shutters for directing (cropping) the light into a specific area without spilling onto another area, specifically the screen.

The light is hung from a "tree," a big metal pole that sits in a round heavy base with a smaller metal pole across the top that holds one to four lights. When you use stage lights, it's best when the ceiling height is 15 feet or higher, and free from obstructions such as low-hanging chandeliers. The lower the ceiling, the lower the lights hang from the tree. Low-hanging lights usually spill into the first few rows of the audience, and you end up with shadows of people in your triangle. You don't want a bunch of big-headed silhouettes all over your body as you move around, which happens when the angle of the light is too low. Higher ceilings allow the light to cast down on you and not spill onto the audience. Use the shutters to crop the light from the bottom if the angles are too low.

> **TIP**
>
> In the case of low ceilings, position the light trees closer to the riser on opposite sides of the room and direct the light just a little higher (using a little bounce light from the ceiling). Be sure to keep all light from spilling onto the screen. Depending on the angle, this will be more difficult for the light positioned on the side of the room where the presenter stands. In addition, you may need to arrange a few seats differently so no one's view is blocked by light poles.

A dimmer pack can be a small switch with a round knob or it can be a complete lighting board with moving levers to reduce the intensity of the lights.

If you are not used to lighting and you stand on a stage with even one light at 100% (full intensity), you'll be seeing orange spots for about a week! If you are working with stage lights, make sure you can handle the bright light without excessive blinking or squinting. That's why a dimmer pack is important. Typically, you'll drop the level to about 60% or lower, depending on how much of the audience you need to see. The brighter the lights, the less chance of your seeing a hand raised for questions. Hmmm…maybe this could be your plan—super bright lights so you can't see anyone!

28

TIP

> One way to test how bright the lights should be is to bring them up until you see a glare off your cheeks in the lower peripheral of your eyes. The point at which your skin reflects the light into the bottoms of your eyes is the maximum brightness setting.

Two lights are needed to provide cross-lighting. Just a single light from one side creates shadows on your face on the opposite side. But cross-lighting allows light to reach you from each direction and eliminates any shadows, regardless of whether you stand in the rest or power position.

You might think it costs a lot of money to have lighting set up as I just described, but we're only talking about $250 for everything. Obviously, that's an average price and it may be higher, but it's worth checking into when planning the event.

Creative Lighting!

If lighting isn't available, you have some inexpensive options, especially if you're at a hotel or conference center. One approach is to rent two 35mm slide projectors and position them at opposite sides of the room on high stands. You can adjust the size of the projected light to fill the presenting area.

You may need a blank CLEAR slide to let the light pass through the lens, although some slide projectors will project light without a slide in the carousel. To make a blank, simply take any 35mm slide and punch out the film to make a clear opening.

Another lighting option is to rent two overhead projectors. Place them on opposite sides of you on high stands, keeping in mind that you'll have to place them much closer than slide projectors. But, you can tape sheets of paper to the overhead projector to shape the light to your exact space, similar to the way shutters work for stage lights.

In smaller venues, such as a conference room, incandescent lighting works best. These are the recessed lights that usually have a dimmer control. Avoid fluorescent lights whenever possible because they are the least flattering and least controlled, and they cast an equal amount of light around the room. When the light is equal, the audience could be distracted by wall hangings, furniture pieces, and worst of all, a clock! But, by creating an unequal distribution of light, you keep the audience's eyes focused on you and minimize other distractions in the room.

SOUND

What? Did you say sound? I couldn't hear you! Sound is especially important for groups of 50 or more. A wireless *lavaliere* microphone (one that clips to the tie or blouse) is always preferred to allow you the most mobility. The microphone, or *mic* as it is commonly called, should always be clipped in the center—not on the lapel—because most lavaliere microphones pick up sound from only one direction to eliminate background noise. So, if the microphone is on your lapel, when you turn your head away, you'll be less audible.

You have a couple of ways to select a microphone, and without getting technical, here are some things to think about.

28

The environment makes a difference. Directional mics are best when you don't want anything but the voice from one direction picked up by the mic. Typically, for presenting, this is what you will use. The microphones found on lecterns tend to be omni-directional (nondirectional), which means they pick up nearby sounds, including your voice. That's why you may hear pages turning or thumping sounds when the hands hit the lectern as you speak into the mic.

TIP

> If you are picking up sound from vibration while at a lectern, try taping another microphone to the existing microphone on the lectern. Shut the lectern mic off and use the other similar-type microphone instead. Then, any vibration caused by your hands bumping the sides of the lectern will be very muffled or completely eliminated.

Mics also fall into one of two basic types, *dynamic* or *condenser*. Dynamic mics are very durable and usually of the handheld or lectern type. They are very versatile and handle most any sound. They don't require batteries because they are directly connected to some audio power source.

Condenser mics are smaller and more sophisticated. Usually found on those wireless lavalieres, these are best for picking up the richer tones in the voice. But these mics are more breakable, especially where the cable meets the mic.

They need power, usually supplied by batteries.

TIP

> If you plan on using a wireless mic for a full-day event, change the battery at lunch time to ensure quality sound for the rest of the day.

The key to any microphone setup is to make sure the mic is far enough away from your mouth so there is no distortion. For the lavaliere microphone, keep it clipped one hand's width below your neck. What? One hand? That's right, one hand. Put your thumb at the base of your neck and lay your hand flat so it rests on the top of your chest. You'll feel your heart beating below your palm. Well, right past your hand, below your bottom knuckle, is where to clip the mic.

Finally, because the transmitter clips to your belt, place it on your left side, more toward your back, away from your hip bone. It will have less of a tendency to fall off. If you place it on your right side, a gesture you make with your left hand toward the screen is higher and usually tilts your body down to your right. This can then lift the transmitter off your right side and possibly make it fall off.

Naturally, a belt helps, but for some women's form-fitting suits, the clipping on the side may create a slight bulge through the jacket, so you can just as easily clip the transmitter behind you, near your backbone. If your suit jacket is less restrictive, you can even place the

28

transmitter in the inside or outside left pocket, depending on where it looks least distracting. The point is that if you know you are going to be wearing a mic and transmitter, plan an outfit that will accommodate the wearing of this equipment with the least problem.

CHOOSING A DISPLAY SCREEN

You have two considerations regarding the display screen. One has to do with the physical characteristics of the screen, and the other has to do with the placement of the display. Both involve visibility issues.

SCREEN TYPES

The most versatile displays are those that allow for the best viewing from all angles. For projection screens, I recommend a flat, non-glare, matte-white screen. The image will be just as bright from the sides as from the center. Conversely, glass-beaded screens tend to be very bright when viewed from the center, but gradually look dimmer when viewed from wider angles.

Rear-screen projection will be less bright than front-screen, but viewable from the same angles. This is good for situations where people may be crossing in front of the screen, as in an awards ceremony. You, as the presenter, should never cross in front of the screen, whether the image is projected from behind or from the front.

In addition, the screen should be *keystone-correcting*. An image "keystones" when the projector is positioned lower than the projection screen. The greater the angle, the more the visual appears like the letter "V," wider at the top and narrower at the bottom. Usually, a tripod screen has an extension bar at the top. When the bar is extended, the screen is able to hook onto the bar at any of several tabs or notches depending on how far forward you want the screen to lean. The more you tilt the screen toward the projector, the more the image becomes square (less like a V).

Sometimes presentations take place using a monitor or TV. The difference is that a monitor takes computer input directly, whereas a TV needs to change the computer signal using a device known as a *scan converter*. Usually, the more you pay for these converters, the closer the image looks to the original.

TIP

> Typically, converters increase the size of the computer's image, and the edges of your visual will be cut off. If you plan to present on a TV using a converter, check your images in PowerPoint's Slide Show view. Then, place your thumb up to the first knuckle on each side of any visual where you think information is close to the edge. Usually, the headings and the right side are the problem areas. Anything under your thumb may be missing when the image is sent through the scan converter. If you pretend you have this border or safety zone when creating the visual, you can be sure it will be seen through nearly any scan converter.

28

A monitor or TV has a light source from within, and therefore the lighting in the room can be quite bright and the image will still be visible. But the size of these displays is usually limited to about a 35-inch diagonal or less, which limits the number of people able to view the presentation. In addition, monitors are usually set in a wall or mounted in some other fixed position, which makes connecting another piece of equipment pretty difficult. You may have to hire a body builder to pull out one of these monster 100-pound monitors so you can get to the connectors on the back. Go for the projection screen whenever possible!

SCREEN PLACEMENT

Look at where the bottom of your visual is in relation to the floor. The bottom of your visual should be higher than your shoulder as you stand on the floor; this way, people seated behind other people will probably be able to see the entire visual. To be sure this is the case, try to get the bottom of the visual to be at least six feet from the floor.

Check this out at the next presentation you attend. Sit behind someone and you probably can see only the top two-thirds of the image, unless your view is clear. Usually, only the people in the front row have the full view of the screen. In a conference room, the views are usually fairly good for most people, but larger events are the ones with the most problems.

If only the top two-thirds of your image is viewable and you have any data-driven charts showing progress over time, chances are the comparison points are at the bottom. If the content is financial data and the audience can't see the changing dates along the bottom of the visual, how can they understand the chart? For example, Figures 28.1 and 28.2 compare the way a visual can appear, depending on your seat. Figure 28.1 shows a vertical bar chart viewed when sitting in the front row. It is completely visible.

Figure 28.1
A simple bar chart showing activity for selected months in the year. If you sit in the front row, you can see the entire image.

28

Figure 28.2 is the same visual, but note the way it appears from about row six! From this view, you can't see the lower third of the image, and the heading makes little sense because you don't know which are the best four months. Comparisons are more difficult when the people have to make an effort to see the entire image. The harder your audience works to see the full screen, the less effective you will be.

Figure 28.2
The same bar chart seen from a few rows back. When the bottom of the image is not high enough, you have to look around people to see things on the screen.

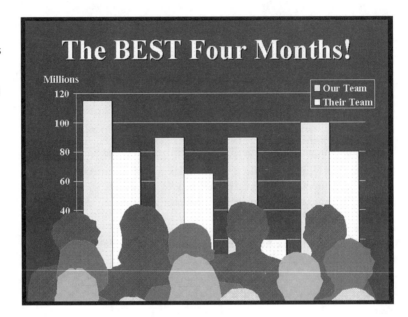

What happens when you can't raise the screen so that the bottom is at shoulder height because the ceiling is too low? As I mentioned before, look for a ceiling 15 feet or higher. In hotels, a ballroom is typical of such height. For example, if you can get a room with a ceiling height of 16 feet, you can use a nine-foot-high screen and place the bottom of the screen six feet from the floor, leaving a foot to spare!

If your ceiling height is too low, then you can try shrinking the overall size of your image so that the bottom of it is higher. If you can get the bottom to a height where anyone can see the entire image from any seat, then the only other thing you have to check is text readability from the back row. Don't shrink the image so that it is totally unreadable from a distance. That's like being able to see from a distance that a letter has a stamp on it, but not being able to see what's actually on the stamp. I'd rather lose some of the visual at the bottom in order for the rest of it to be readable.

DECIDING ON SEATING ARRANGEMENTS

You can use several different styles of seating , but they generally fall into one of two categories, theatre or classroom. The difference? Tables!

Theatre-style, no matter how you arrange the chairs, does not include tables. This style is typical for large groups, and when the seating is not fixed, flexibility improves. You will probably use theatre-style seating for groups of 50 or more, and for events of short duration (no more than a half-day). Figure 28.3 is MediaNet's suggested room layout for theatre-style seating. This diagram, along with more complete setup advice, appears on MediaNet's Web site at www.medianet-ny.com/layout.htm. You can print out these layout considerations and use them to help set up your own event.

But if the event is more than a half-day, you should provide tables for a classroom-style approach. Although this reduces the number of people the space can hold by about 60%, the comfort of your audience will be greatly enhanced.

Classroom-style seating can have all the tables facing straight to the front, as the theatre setup would be. Classroom-style can also have variations. Angling the tables toward the center of the room, called *chevron* seating, can help increase the interaction among audience members because people can see more of one another with the tables on an angle. Interaction is increased even more when you use a U-shape arrangement because almost everyone can see everyone else in the room. The *U-shape* is like a big conference table without the table.

Figure 28.3
A suggested room layout with theatre-style seating. Note the two Leiko lights, the platform staging, and the presenter's triangle. As you can see, the setup does not call for a lectern because it limits mobility of the presenter.

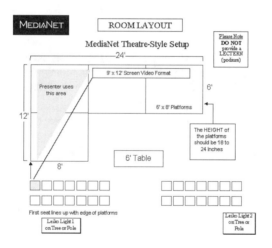

TIP

Don't make a perfect U-shape. Leave off the front-end table on the side you present from, the left side, so that you have more room for your triangle.

The smaller the group, the more likely your setting will be in a conference room or in a training room with ten-foot or lower ceilings, limited lighting options, and less area for you to move. When you are faced with a lot of limitations, arrange the seats with more people facing one another. This shifts the focus more toward discussion and allows you to play the role of both lecturer and facilitator.

28

SEATING AND DISTANCE

The size of the text displayed should relate to the distance people are seated from the viewing screen. You learned about this in Chapter 26 with the "8 to 1 rule." To recap, eight times the height of the visual (not the screen) is the maximum viewing distance to read 24-point size text. So, if your visual is 6 feet high, then people seated 48 feet away should be able to read text that is as small as 24 points in size.

Just for your reference, when you type a letter to someone, the text is usually 12-point size. The cell of a spreadsheet is about 10-point size. The pull-down menu bar on your computer screen (you know, File, Edit, View, and so forth) is about 8-point size. If you do the math, you can see that presenting software or demonstrating a Web site to an audience is going to be a lot harder than running a PowerPoint presentation. With the software program or Web page, you likely will be displaying 12-point type at best (if you're lucky). If the point size is 12 rather than 24, the "8 to 1 rule" becomes the "4 to 1 rule"! This means everyone has to sit twice as close. Using a six-foot-high image, people will have to sit no more than 24 feet from the visual (instead of 48 feet) in order to be able to read your screen. Unfortunately, when the room is set up, the hotel staff doesn't think about point size. Now you'll have to ask people in row 14 to move up to row 7. (I don't think so!)

Calculating the Distance

If you want a simple formula for calculating how far away a person can sit and still be able to read your information, use these three letters, T, V, and D. T for the type size, V for the height of the visual, and D for the maximum distance to sit. The formula is $(T/3)V=D$. (The type size T divided by 3, then multiplied by the visual height V equals the maximum seating distance D to read that type size).

Find your smallest point type size on any visual you intend to display. Divide that point size by three. Multiply that answer by the height of your image. The result is how far away people can sit and still read your visual.

Try this example. The smallest type size in your presentation is 18 point, and your visual is 4 feet high. How many feet away can a person sit and still be able to read your image easily?

Why do type size and distance make a difference? Think about the number of people attending your presentation. When you know the maximum viewing distance, you figure out if the room you plan to present in is big enough. In fact, the arrangement of the seats will make a difference as to how many people you can accommodate.

For example, using theatre-style seating (no tables, just chairs), how can you figure out the number of people that can fit in the room? First, the typical space between rows—that is, from the back of one chair to the back of the chair in the next row—should be about three feet. This leaves enough room for people to pass by. But keep in mind that to display your image, the projection equipment will take up room in the front. So, the first row of chairs is usually set up a distance away from the screen, usually about 25% of the maximum seating distance from the visual. Wait a minute—that means the audience can only occupy the space in the remaining 75% of the maximum distance.

Let's say you have an eight-foot-high image containing 24-point type, which allows a 64-foot maximum seating distance. That means the first 16 feet (one-fourth of 64) is cleared so that the projector can be set up to cast that eight-foot-high image. You end up with only 48 feet of available depth for the audience. So, because you need about three feet of space between rows, you now have room for about 16 rows of chairs.

Based on approximately 16 people across each row separated by a middle aisle, you have room for as many as 256 people (16 rows x 16 people per row).

TIP

> Set up one middle aisle and limit the width of any row on either side of the aisle to no more than 10 chairs across in any section. In this way, no one need pass in front of more than five people to exit any row into the middle or side aisle.
>
> Another way to set up the rows is to double the height of the visual. For example, if you have a 6-foot-high image, seat no more than 12 people per row. With a middle aisle, you'll have six chairs on each side.

Figure 28.4 is a section taken from the table "MediaNet Seating Calculations for Distance and Capacity." This chart is helpful in determining what changes you may have to make to your font sizes or your visual height in order to accommodate your audience. The rounded-off calculations allow for empty seats and extra rows here and there, but the general results are useful when planning your event. The entire table can be seen by visiting MediaNet's Web site at www.medianet-ny.com/seating.htm.

Figure 28.4
A section of MediaNet's seating table, showing calculations for visual heights of 6 to 8 feet and selected font sizes. If you know the height of your image and the smallest font size you used, you can get an idea as to how far back the chairs can be placed and how many people can fit in the room.

MediaNet Seating Calculations for Distance and Capacity							
Visual Height (in feet)	Smallest Font (in Pt-size)	Distance to Last Row (in feet)	Theatre-Style (Chairs only)			Classroom-Style (Tbls/Chrs)	
			Total Rows to set	Max. People in each row	Seating Capacity (full rows)	Total Rows to set	Seating Capacity (40% of theatre)
6	12	24	4	12	48	1	19
6	18	36	8	12	96	3	38
6	24	48	12	12	144	4	58
6	32	64	17	12	204	6	82
6	38	76	21	12	252	7	101
6	44	88	25	12	300	8	120
6	48	96	28	12	336	9	134
7	12	28	5	14	70	2	28
7	18	42	9	14	126	3	50
7	24	56	14	14	196	5	78
7	32	75	20	14	280	7	112
7	38	89	25	14	350	8	140
7	44	103	30	14	420	10	168
7	48	112	33	14	462	11	185
8	12	32	5	16	80	2	32
8	18	48	11	16	176	4	70
8	24	64	16	16	256	5	102
8	32	85	23	16	368	8	147
8	38	101	28	16	448	9	179
8	44	117	34	16	544	11	218
8	48	128	37	16	592	12	237

28

When seating people classroom-style, the presence of tables reduces the available seating space. Typically, fewer than half the number of people seated theatre-style can be seated classroom-style because you have about five to six feet of space between the rows of chairs to allow for the table.

For example, suppose you have an 8-foot-high image. If you use six-foot-long tables, you can seat three people per table. Put four tables across each row, separated by a middle aisle, and you will be able to seat about 12 people across (as opposed to 16 across in theatre-style seating). Not only will you have fewer rows, but you'll have fewer people per row. Based on having 48 feet of seating space, you'll end up with 8 rows of tables with chairs, instead of 16 rows of chairs only. At minumium, you should be able to fit about 96 people (8 rows x 12 people per row) in the space, give or take a few. So, when using classroom seating, estimate the capacity at about 40% of theatre-style seating, just to be on the safe side.

Visibility from a distance and the seating arrangements are important considerations when you design your support visuals. If you can't get the room set up the way you want, you may have to change the appearance of some of your visuals. Of course, the more control you have over the room conditions, the fewer changes you'll need to make to your content.

Most presenters ignore the importance of the room. They take what they get when they get there, and then wonder why the event failed. As a presenter, it is YOUR job to provide a room layout diagram to a meeting planner, a hotel A/V group, or even a major presentation service in order to get what you want.

USING TECHNOLOGY

It seems any mention of technology is obsolete before you finish reading the sentence! However, you should be aware of some generalities when you use different devices, especially from a technical perspective. As a visual presenter, you should be adept at using different pieces of equipment, although you will probably get comfortable using one particular device for most of your presentation needs. In any case, here are a few things to consider in regard to equipment:

- Handling projectors
- Working with laptop presentations
- Incorporating multimedia

HANDLING PROJECTORS

If you recall, Chapter 25 covered the "cost, convenience, and continuity" issues related to overheads, 35mm slides, and electronic images. The traditional devices—overhead and slide projectors—are not difficult to work with from an operational standpoint. Typically, the big technical question is, "How do you turn this thing on?" But for electronic presentations, you have to know a bit more than the on/off switch when you work with the current crop of LCD (Liquid Crystal Display) projectors.

→ For more information about projectors, **see** "Understanding Media Types," in Chapter 25, **p. 537**.

28

First the good news: These devices are getting easier and easier to set up, but until personal computers are a cinch to work with, these electronic projectors will carry a bit of intimidation along with them. But don't worry. If you haven't used one of these devices, chances are someone is available who has.

I don't want to get into a long list of specifications, except to tell you that the LCD projector connects directly to your PC and depending on the features of your PC, the projected image may or may not need to be adjusted.

BRIGHTNESS

The brightness of the image is a big issue when you can't control the lighting in the room. You'll probably hear the word *lumens* bandied about when people talk of a projector's brightness. Just think of lumens as a measure of brightness. The more lumens, the brighter the projector. Sure, there's more to it than that, but that's why there are professionals out there who sell these things! Audiovisual companies (A/V dealers) are excellent sources for learning more about the unique features and benefits of electronic projectors.

In a room with only fluorescent lights, go for a projector with at least 500 lumens so that your image remains visible, even with the light spilling onto the screen. Of course, if you have less light hitting the screen, the image will look even better.

RESOLUTION

Think of resolution as the quality of the image. I like to use the comparison of a chain link fence, some chicken wire, and a screen on a door. The sizes of the holes are different in each. If you took a paint brush and painted the word "resolution" on the fence, the wire, and the screen, which would be easiest to read? The screen, because the holes are closer and smaller, making the letters in the painted word appear less broken up and of higher quality. Now, if you hear "640×480 resolution," pretend that's the chain link fence. "800×600 resolution" is the chicken wire and "1,024768" is the screen door. The higher the resolution, the closer the holes, and the better the quality of the image. That's because the *pixels*, or little dots (holes), that make up the image are closer together!

PORTABILITY

Naturally, if you don't have to carry anything to the presentation but your PC, then you don't need to be concerned about the portability of the projector. Why care about weight if you're not toting it? Well, these devices are getting lighter—most are around ten pounds, but some are as light as five pounds. The convenience of bringing the device with you is that you are confident of the image you will get. If you carry the light source to the event, you have more control of the display. I have made plenty of presentations when I did not have the quality image I was used to and had to overcompensate on my delivery to make up for the poorer image. Thus, a lighter projector means more likelihood of your taking it with you to the event.

28

MULTIPLE CONNECTIONS

Having options for more than one input and output is helpful, especially if you plan on using a variety of media including video and audio. Some projectors even allow hookups for two computer sources. This can be helpful in an event with more than one presenter, each of whom has his or her own PC. The capability to connect a VCR or even a video camera or other device can add value and flexibility, as well. In my full-day "Presenting Made Easy" seminar, I use my computer and play a videotape as well, using the same projector by simply switching sources when needed. Typically, to switch between different inputs, a press of a button on the projector is all that's required.

NOTE

When a projector allows for multiple sources, it usually lets you set up each source independently. For example, when I switch from my PC to my video source, the video settings on the projector change. So, I can control volume, brightness, contrast, and so forth separately for each input because they are usually different.

Of course, not every piece of equipment works perfectly when connected to another piece of equipment, as may happen with some projector-to-computer hook-ups. Sometimes, one person's notebook PC works fine with a projector, but the next person's PC does not for a variety of reasons. And changing the settings on projectors varies among models and types, so it is best to arrive at your presentation early enough to make sure that everything works properly.

The worst moment in the world is when you start playing with menu options on the projector two minutes before the show is supposed to begin!

Many projectors have multiple outputs, as well. Outputs for video and audio can be very valuable when presenting. For example, if you plan on using sound during your presentation, having an external audio feature on the projector is very helpful. When you have a larger group of people, the tiny speakers of a projector can't disperse sound evenly to everyone in the room. It sounds louder for those who sit closer. But, in some places such as in a hotel, you can connect the projector to the sound system used for your microphone, which is typically connected through the speakers in the ceiling. *House sound*, as it is called, distributes the audio evenly to the audience.

WORKING WITH LAPTOP PRESENTATIONS

Chances are, if you use an electronic projector, you are probably connecting a laptop or notebook computer to it. You'll have some limitations with laptop systems, but I don't want to get too technical on the subject. The good news is that the laptop is a fully functioning office, complete with backup information and tons of other stuff, literally at your fingertips! You need to know a few things about computers and projectors, especially when it comes to laptop presentations.

28

REMOTE CONTROL

Okay, let me say this again. Remote Control. Wait, let me try one more time. Remote Control. Am I getting through yet? Anyone who stands in front of a group of people and advances the PowerPoint presentation with the keyboard doesn't get it! If you are one of those people—snap out of it! You're losing it! Touching the spacebar when you present with a laptop is like pushing your car to make it go. I'm sorry, but I won't even budge on this one!

Face it! A remote control offers you incredible freedom of movement and enhances your presentation skills accordingly. Please buy a remote control for the PC. I beg you. In fact, it doesn't even have to be a remote mouse because 98% of all presentations are linear (forward or backward) and do not require any interaction with a mouse pointer. Just get a two-button remote control that can advance your visuals while you stand inside your triangle and present.

Pro Presenter

Many types of remotes are available on the market right now, and, although I normally avoid endorsing products, I've got to say that I've been using the same remote control for years now. It's the perfect device for delivering linear electronic presentations. In fact, when I coach people, they are using it within seconds–that's how easy it is to control. It's called the Pro Presenter.

It's a flat, infrared wireless, handheld remote control for the PC or the Mac. The remote can be used with or without its software. It's the same size as a credit card, it fits snugly into the palm of your hand and operates from up to 35 feet away from your computer. It's a $99 wonder that frees you from ever touching the computer while you present. At the risk of sounding like I'm selling you something, visit MediaNet's Web site (www.medianet-ny.com) to learn more about this little product, which is manufactured by Varatouch Technology in California (www.varatouch.com).

Some remotes also have the capability to control the mouse pointer, as well. So, it's like having the left/right mouse buttons and the pointer all in your hand at the same time. The only thing to worry about is accidentally moving the mouse pointer while you present; and, without your knowing it, the audience sits there wondering what the heck you're pointing to on the visual!

Some remotes are RF (radio frequency) rather than infrared. This just means that you don't have to point them at the receiver while you advance the visuals. Unfortunately, these remotes tend to be larger in size. When a remote cannot fit comfortably into the palm of your hand, it becomes more obvious that you are using one.

When you think of the amount of money invested in a computer and a projector—not to mention the presentation and your time to deliver it—the cost of adding a remote control is insignificant. Think of this: A 65-cent key gets you into a Mercedes! Need I say more? Buy a remote!

SIMULTANEOUS DISPLAY

This is a very big advantage to any speaker, but particularly to a visual presenter. Think about overheads and slides for a minute. You have to turn your head back toward the screen just to glance at information. If your visuals are busy, you end up doing this even more often. But a laptop offers you a unique advantage called *simultaneous display*. The image the audience sees on the big screen appears on the display of your PC at the same time. If this feature is not already set up in your PC, you normally can send the display signal "out the back door" by pressing a combination of keys on your keyboard. Look at your notebook computer and you may see a graphic symbol that looks like a PC and a screen on one of the function keys, usually F5. This is like a toggle that can be set in three positions. One keeps the image on your notebook screen; another sends the image out the VGA (monitor) port on the back while removing it from your notebook screen; and the third setting sends the image out the back, but leaves it on the notebook screen at the same time. This is called simultaneous display.

It's like a little teleprompter, except you don't have any speech to read. In fact, if your visuals are less busy, the text displayed on your notebook screen will be larger and should be readable from however far away you are standing from the computer as you present.

In addition, if you look back to Figure 28.3, you can see how your equipment (computer and projector) are centered in the front of the room. When you glance at your notebook screen, it will appear as though you are making eye contact with the section of the audience sitting beyond the table but still in your line of sight. It takes only a slight shift of your eyes downward to catch the information on the screen. Although some may notice the movement, it certainly is not as obvious as the complete look back to the screen done constantly with overheads and slides.

Depending on your computer and the projector, the simultaneous display option may not be available, however. This is a constantly evolving issue with both the computer and projector manufacturers, but in any case, what you need to be concerned about is this: In most cases, when the resolution of the projector is lower than the resolution setting on your PC, the projector compensates for the higher signal coming from your PC and drops bits of the image. This makes smaller text appear choppy. The solution is to lower the resolution setting on your PC to match the projector. However, with some computers, that's still not enough. You may have to disable the simultaneous display feature so that the projector can project a full and clear image at the lower resolution. This is not always the case, but you'll have to try it to be sure.

On the other hand, if the projector has a higher resolution than the computer, you should have no problem, for the most part, because the projector should be able to handle the lower-resolution signal coming from your computer. But, I haven't tested every combination of notebook and projector, so you'll have to make sure for yourself. Once again, the advice of an A/V professional can be of immense help and save you a lot of headaches.

TRANSITIONS

Electronic presentations allow the use of transition effects between visuals. Rather than use transitions randomly, you should consider the way the next image will appear to the audience. The most consistent approach is to try to use a transition that matches the eye movement pattern for the upcoming visual, not the current visual. In other words, transition effects are designed for the visual yet to appear, not for the visual already displayed.

For example, let's say you're displaying a text chart with several bullet points, followed by a horizontal bar chart and then a pie chart. You could use a "horizontal blinds" transition into the text chart because the lines of text are separated by horizontal space. Then you might use a "wipe right" transition from the text chart to the bar chart because the eye will be moving from left to right when the bar chart appears. Then, from the bar to the pie chart, a "box out" transition could be used. The circle of the pie centers the eye in the visual, and the transition opens from the center matching the circle.

So, check the general geometric shapes in the next visual when planning the transition to assure a consistency in eye movement from one image to the next.

Screen Savers, Reminders, and Navigation Issues

One of the things you should do with your laptop is turn off any screen savers you may have. If you stay on one visual too long and your screen saver comes on, it may knock out the signal going to the projector. Then, suddenly, the audience is left staring at a blue screen! Check that you disable the screen saver in Windows and any time-out functions set in the computer itself. A run through your PC's diagnostics or setup screen will tell you if any system savers are enabled.

Some contact-management programs offer reminders, such as alarms, that pop up when the task is due. When you present, don't load software that has the task reminders, unless you want the audience to see just who it is you're having dinner with that night!

Finally, in PowerPoint under Tools, Options select the View tab and make sure all three check boxes in the Slide Show area are unchecked. First, you don't want the pop-up menu to display on the right mouse click. When you leave this box unchecked, then your right mouse button will do what it is supposed to do—navigate the show backward one visual. If you need to navigate to different images or you need to get other help during the presentation, you can simply go to the keyboard and press F1, and the menu of choices will pop up. Second, you don't want the pop-up menu button to show in the corner of each visual as you present. Unless you have a remote mouse, you won't be able to click this transparent icon anyway. Third, you don't want to end your presentation with a blank slide, especially if you've been using a consistent background throughout. Instead, under the Slide Show menu, choose Set Up Show, and check the box "Loop Continuously until 'Esc'," so that your show loops back to the beginning. This allows your presentation to "end" with the same image you started with, if you so choose.

Incorporating Multimedia

You know, nothing you can do with a laptop computer—using animation, sound, video, or any special effects—even comes close to what you see in the movies. We are all accustomed to seeing incredible special effects, and we have Spielberg and Lucas to thank for it. No one walks out of a business presentation and runs home saying, "Honey, you won't believe this, but at this presentation today—well, I don't know how—but the computer—well, it played

28

music and a voice came out—a real voice!" Face it! It's hard to impress people with technology these days. Your only resort is to set yourself on fire as you speak—a real attention grabber, but tough to repeat.

Although much has been said about multimedia, all I can add is this: Beware of multiMANIA. Multi*mania* is the overuse of technology to the point that the audience is enamored by your special effects, but can't remember the plot! One word—*Waterworld*—you paid how much? I think you get my drift.

The point is that you should be concerned when you think about adding elements in your presentation that go beyond your delivery. For example, playing a video clip during your presentation introduces another character to the audience, another presence—basically, another messenger. This isn't wrong, anymore than it's wrong to introduce another presenter. But elements that simulate or mimic real-life forms (speech, movement, real people in action) reach the audience in different ways than traditional visual content.

So, you just need to understand the particulars of animation, sound, and video as unique multimedia elements and their effect on the audience.

ANIMATION

This effect is simply an object in action. However, it should never be text in action. Objects can move, but text should stand still. Take this test. Move this book up and down and try to read it. I rest my case. You can't read moving text until it stops or at least slows down enough for you to anchor on it. Ever try reading the weather warning as it crosses the bottom of your TV? You can't read each word as it appears from the far right; no, you have to wait for a few words to make it to the far left of the screen so you can anchor and read left to right.

So, text should never move. All those transitions you picked with the animated bullet points—out. Just because a programmer can make it happen doesn't mean it's useful. Animated text lines can't be read until they stop. This means the only effect was the animation, the movement. If an action serves only itself, it is useless because the audience takes interest only in the action, not the information. Eventually, people will watch your text flying in from different points and begin to take bets on where the next line will enter from and when!

> **NOTE**
>
> If the text you are animating is part of a logo or is to be treated as a standalone item, then it is really more like an object and probably contains very little anchor-and-read requirement. In those cases, you can animate the text object.

Objects can be animated, but apply a sense of logic. Don't have a clip art symbol of an airplane floating from the top of the visual downward. Airplanes don't do that—at least not more than once! Yet, animated bars or moving lines showing a procedure can help the audience understand growth or flow and make the visual come alive to express an idea.

Animation is not a bad thing, as long as it is not overdone to the point that only the effect is noticed.

SOUND

The first sense you experienced was hearing. Before birth you could hear the soft echo of your mom's tender voice as she carried you from place to place. Sound is one of the most important senses throughout our lives and can dramatically affect our perceptions.

Sound can either be used or abused during a presentation. Typically, you might want to add sound at certain points to highlight a key phrase or to add value to some information.

The main thing is to be consistent with sound. The audience not only looks for anchors; they listen for them as well. Your voice becomes an anchor as people adjust to your volume, pitch, and tone. Other sounds placed in the presentation need justification and sometimes repetition to become anchored. But don't just make a noise because your software program has this great library of sounds that you feel compelled to use.

Sounds linked to elements on the visual are usually ineffective. Examples of these are the cash register sound linked to a symbol of money; the sound of applause signifying achievement; the shutter of a camera releasing each time a photo of a person appears on the visual; and, the worst of all sound effects—the typewriter sound linked to animated text and possibly to each letter on each text line!—Please, shoot me NOW—in fact, use the machine gun effect when you do! In all these cases, the sounds are one-time effects that when repeated can become phony or even obnoxious.

Don't get me wrong, sound can play a major role in the presentation if done right. Music is a good example of this. The movie *Jaws* wouldn't be the same without music. *The Omen* wouldn't be as scary. *Ishtar*? Nothing could save that one! The nice thing about music, particularly instrumental music, is that you can talk over it and the audience can blend your words with the background music. In addition, if the music track is long enough or loops continuously, the audience gets the benefit of repetition and will anchor to the music as it plays.

TIP

> Even if you don't incorporate music during the presentation, consider playing some tunes as people are coming into the room or perhaps closing off with music as people leave.

You don't even need to have the music clips stored on the computer because the files can be quite large. You can simply use your computer's CD-ROM drive (if you have one) or bring a portable CD player and connect it directly to the projector.

→ To see how to use sound effectively with the Nostalgia Theory, **see** "Knowing the Particulars of the Audience," in Chapter 24, **p. 520.**

For example, let's say you are giving a presentation in 2002 to an audience, the average age of which is 34. That means they were 15 years old in 1983. Michael Jackson's *Beat It* will be

28

a more popular sound clip for this crowd than his 1970 tune *ABC*, when the majority of this group wore diapers!

You get the idea. Continuity in sound is better than periodic or intermittent sound. You can process continual sound just like listening to the radio while driving a car. But hear a siren or horn beep (noncontinuous sound), and your attention is immediately diverted.

VIDEO

Multimedia takes on a very different flavor when you incorporate video. The multimedia issues with video come in two flavors, full-screen and full-motion. The goal is to have them both, but the technology you currently own may not allow either. Full-screen video is easy to envision. The video fills up the whole screen just like a TV. Many video clips in presentations today are half, one-third, or even one-quarter the size of the screen, depending on the computer system used to deliver the video.

Full-motion video is what you get when you watch TV—30 frames per second. That speed is fast enough for the images to appear lifelike, which is why TV is such a powerful medium. Much of the video shown through laptops is not full-motion, but about half-motion or 15 frames per second. At times, especially during longer computer or digitized video clips, you can get synchronization problems with voice and video after a while. That's when the video and voice get out of sync, and it looks like one of those foreign films with poor dubbing—you know, the ones where the character's mouth moves as if saying eleven words, but you only hear "So, Hercules."

Out of the Mouths

When my company's CD-ROM *The Art of Presenting* first came out, my son Peter was about 6 years old. I was playing one of my video clips through the PC, but outside the CD program so that only the clip appeared on the screen. My son was standing next to me as I played the little movie file on the screen of my notebook computer.

"Hey Dad! You're on TV!" he shouted. "Make it big. As big as the screen!". I laughed a bit and said, "Well, I can't make the video bigger or it will get all messed-up and won't run right. It has to be this size because of the computer."

He then asked me, "How much does that computer cost?" I replied, "About $5,000, why?" He looked at me and then into the living room and said, "Wow, then how much did the TV cost?"

I said, "Well, the TV was only $300" and then I just sat there, puzzled, wondering how to explain THAT one! I mean, here's my son looking from the PC to the TV and back to the PC, both made by the same company, wondering why the one that costs more gives you less of a picture! You can see how visual creatures expect full-motion and full-screen video, simply because of TV.

But, with most laptops, we sacrifice full-motion and full-screen for the sake of storage and speed. Naturally, the storage required for video is much greater than for still images or even clip art, for that matter. I won't go into the technical details of file sizes, but if you've ever loaded a video clip on your PC, you know that it takes up a lot of disk space. For example, a one-minute clip that plays in a window only half the size of your screen might be about 10 megabytes. Of course, one minute is a long time for a video clip when you consider that TV commercials are averaging 15 to 30 seconds. The point is that storage and speed are issues for video and you should limit the length of the clips.

So, the goal is full-screen, full-motion video. And, believe it or not, the speeds of computers are getting faster and faster so this will soon not even be an issue. But not everyone uses the most current technology, and I suspect it will be a few years before video is a breeze to watch through a PC in a presentation.

Regardless of speed, another issue with video concerns movement and direction. If your video clip is not full-screen, you may be including it as part of a visual. If the visual has text and the video clip shows something moving in one direction, make sure that direction matches the way the text reads. For example, a visual in English would have a left-to-right reading pattern. So, if your clip shows a car moving from right to left, you'll have an eye movement clash. Try to match the direction whenever possible.

IMAGE MAGNIFICATION

You may find times when your presence on stage is also reproduced on screen. This might happen if you present in a large venue where people are sitting so far back that they cannot get a good view of you or your expressions. *Image magnification* can be used to make you visible from a far distance. The way this works is that a separate screen is set up, a camera focuses on you, and the video signal is projected on the big screen. Suddenly, you're on TV! The good news is that everyone can see you as if they were in the front row. However, some problems can occur when the camera frames you for the audience. Whenever a camera is used, you should be concerned about what the framed image looks like to the audience. Figure 28.5 shows how different the perspective is when the presenter is viewed from the audience and through the eye of the camera. The banner hanging behind the presenter looks fine when viewed from the audience, but the close-up shot as framed by the camera clips some letters from the company name "Lawe Losetta, Inc." showing only the last two letters of "Lawe" and the first four letters of "Losetta"; through the camera it reads "we Lose."

Figure 28.5
To the live audience, the banner in the background presents no problem. However, when the presenter's image is magnified, the close-up view from the camera frames the presenter and the background suddenly tells a very different story.

28

In Figure 28.6, the banner is hung vertically and the framed image doesn't reveal any surprises. Always check the viewing angle when using a video camera to frame the presenter.

Figure 28.6
When image magnification is used, the framed view through the camera crops the image of the presenter and the background. A vertical banner behind the presenter remains in the framed image and allows the full company name to appear from the audience view and the camera angle.

GLITCH HAPPENS!

It goes without saying that you should practice your presentation. In fact, the more multimedia effects you have planned, the more need for a technical run-through before the event. But, let's face it. Sometimes computers cause problems and usually at the worst moments. Whether the video clip moves in a jerky motion or the sound effect doesn't play or the system just "locks up" for no apparent reason—the thing to remember is not to panic. We have all been there before, and it's not unusual for things to go wrong every so often.

If you know how to fix a problem, then fix it. At the same time, explain to your audience what you are doing. Don't just turn your back and say, "Pay no attention to that man behind the curtain!" The real issue is time. If you can fix it within three minutes, fine. But, if you think the problem will take longer to fix, then give the audience an opportunity to take a short break.

For practice, run your presentation and somewhere in the middle of it, turn off or reset the computer. Time how long it takes to reboot your PC and get it back to the exact spot where you turned it off. If it takes more than three minutes, you'll know to give the audience a short break the instant you know you may have to reboot the computer during your presentation.

Overall, if you keep calm and collected during technical difficulties, you have a better chance of keeping the attention of the audience. Of course, the more command you have of the message and the more effective your delivery skills, the easier it will be for you to overcome any technical problem.

Remember that the technology only carries the speaker support material. You are the speaker, and your delivery embodies the message. The audience will constantly look to you for guidance and direction. Never forget that YOU are in control!

TROUBLESHOOTING

Do you have any advice for the best time and place to conduct a presentation?

Usually, a "presentation" happens as part of a meeting, seminar, or some type of planned event. Regardless of the size of the group, you do have to consider the location and the calendar when planning the event. The bottom line is to develop a plan that "captures" your audience when it is most attentive. You can do this by conducting the event at the right location, on the right day of the week, and at the right time of day!

Regarding location, you should try to find a spot that contains the fewest distractions. This usually is offsite (not in your building). Most people, if close enough to their desks, will find opportunites to do a few work-related tasks and before they know it—the presentation is over! If you want the full attention of a group, keep them away from their desks by holding the event at a neutral spot (hotel or conference center) which is an easy drive, but just too far away to walk. You don't want people sneaking back to their desks at each break.

For timing, you should consider the best day of the work week for getting the most people to attend. Having conducted over 1,000 seminars, I can tell you that Tuesdays are best, followed in order by Thursdays, Wednesdays, Fridays, and, finally, Mondays. I have met other presenters who agree with the order. So, if Tuesday is open for your next meeting, chances are more people will be available than on Monday. Check it out in your own environment and see if it's true for you.

Finally, consider the time of day. Early morning, between 9 a.m. and 11 a.m., seems to be the best time of day for getting the highest attention span from a group. One hour after lunch is the worst time of day because people are digesting. When you digest food, the blood goes from your head to your stomach, your eyes get heavier and before you know it—you doze off! So, the morning is better than the afternoon. In fact, in some sales presentations when you have a choice to present first or last to a prospect, knowing your competitors are presenting on the same day to the same prospect, try to go first. Some say the last presentation is the only one remembered. In reality, it's the one the audience hopes will end most quickly. If you go first, you have the most attention from the group and you become the "tough act to follow."

If I want to use music or video in my presentations, do I need to be concerned with copyrights?

Copyrights protect intellectual properties. The rule I live by is simple: When in doubt, ask permission. However, you may already have indications as to what extent you can use certain multimedia elements without infringing on someone's rights. For example, let's say you wanted to buy a CD-ROM that contained a collection of instrumental musical selections. If the CD packaging contains a statement such as "royalty-free" or "unlimited use," it doesn't mean there is no copyright; rather, it indicates that you can probably use the selections in your presentations and you won't have to pay a fee each time you use a clip. On the other hand, it doesn't mean you can repackage the selections on a new CD and sell it.

I have been at tradeshows, for example, where the movie *Top Gun* (with Tom Cruise) is playing in someone's booth. Without permission, this would be an illegal use of the movie, especially because it is being used in a selling process. How? The movie is entertaining and the value of that entertainment brings people into the booth, at which point sales opportunities arise. Thus, the playing of the movie increases the prospects. The selling process is enhanced through the use of an intellectual property (the movie) with no payment (royalty) made to the property owner. A phone call to the copyright holder of the movie may be all that is needed to get permission to play the movie, for that one tradeshow, without infringing on the copyright.

The same applies to popular music. If you want to play some songs from a CD during your presentation, perhaps as background filler while the audience is arriving, you should get permission to use the material.

One exception I found to the copyright law involves "educational use." If you are commenting on the actual copyrighted material for educational purposes, you may not need permission. For example, Siskel and Ebert, movie critics, hosted a show called *At the Movies*. They educated the public on the quality of the films they reviewed. They did not need permission to show any of the clips they used, even though the show itself made money from advertising sponsors. If the two critics needed permission to show clips from various movies, then only the movies that got good reviews would have allowed their clips to be shown!

Surely any point of law can be argued and interpreted in different ways. This educational use issue may not always be interpreted the same way. I have a lecture called "Multimedia vs. Multimania" in which I use several popular music tracks from different CDs. To be safe, I received permission from the copyright holders and I even run "credits" at the end of the lecture to acknowledge the owners of the material. So, I insist you research any use of copyrighted material and get permission, in writing if possible, to reduce the chances of a lawsuit.

CHAPTER 29

PRESENTING IN A VARIETY OF SETTINGS

In this chapter

by Tom Mucciolo

29

ADAPTING TO EVERYDAY ENVIRONMENTS

Not every performance takes place on the big stage. The majority of business presentations are done for smaller groups, and sometimes those talks take place in unique settings. So, you have to learn to adapt to different circumstances. The good news is that the skills we've been discussing translate well to the variety of situations you may encounter when delivering your message.

I always laugh when someone tells me, "Oh, the meetings I speak at are so informal that you don't really need great presentation skills to make your point." My response is something like, "I guess you don't need to wear clean clothes on those days, either!" Don't underestimate the power of the moment. If the meeting really is unimportant, then your time is wasted. Do you really have that luxury? Yet, given that the meeting is important, you want your voice to be heard and remembered. Presentation skills are universally adaptable to almost every circumstance in which you speak and someone else listens.

The goal is to use the same skills that work in a more controlled setting and apply them to the given environment. Most of your presentations are likely to take place close to your everyday work area. Believe it or not, these environments are the ones you least prepare for and take most for granted. At other times you may find yourself in situations that challenge even the most basic of your skills. In fact, one of the biggest challenges will be in the way you use your skills in a highly visual setting, such as TV.

The good news is that the external and internal skills discussed in Chapters 26, "The Mechanics of Form—Developing External Presentation Skills," and 27, "The Mechanics of Function—Developing Internal Presentation Skills," apply to a variety of situations. In this chapter, we examine the use of these skills in various situations.

GETTING UP CLOSE AND PERSONAL

The most likely scenario you'll encounter is a presentation to a small group. I find that more than 80% of presentations are given to groups of fewer than ten people, usually in conference room settings. Typically, the fear factor is reduced when fewer people are in the room, so these up close and personal situations are easier for most presenters. Perhaps that is what makes small group presentations more common. Another reason is probably scheduling: It's easier to convene a smaller group of people in a local setting than it is to gather a crowd for a larger event.

Regardless of how these situations develop, the common fallacy among presenters is that less formality exists when the group is smaller and people know one another. Be careful! Just because everyone knows one another doesn't mean your presentation has automatic impact. Remember that it gets more and more difficult to impress a person after the first date! When presenting in those informal settings, your skills must be better, especially if you think the formality is unnecessary.

Who can really define just what "formality" means in the context of a presentation? Moreover, who can say which presentations merit formality and which do not? Use the logic that every presentation is formal in the sense that your skills must be as sharp as ever to make an impact with your message.

Your goal is to maintain consistency of style in all presentation settings. For the up-close and personal moments, you should consider the following:

- Understanding the conference room and U
- Handling one-to-one situations
- Socializing your skills

UNDERSTANDING THE CONFERENCE ROOM AND U

In Chapter 28, "Techniques and Technicalities," we discussed theatre-style and classroom-style seating in relation to the room setup. Yet, the traditional conference room offers some important seating opportunities that are a bit different from the others. This is also true of another common room setup, the U-shape. Both conference room and U-shape settings share the same seating dynamics. Because many conference room tables are longer than they are wide, most of the people at the table face one another. The same is true with the U-shape.

> **TIP**
>
> Increase the size of your triangle. You can give yourself more room to maneuver in the small group setting by moving or removing some seats. In the conference room, the first, and possibly second, seat immediately to your right can be eliminated. This makes your triangle longer (from the screen to the first available seat). When you have more space, your movements within the triangle are more distinct, and you can create more impact as you change positions during your presentation.
>
> In a U-shape, consider removing the first table on your right (the one closest to you) to create a larger space in which to move. The U-shape starts to resemble a J-shape when the first table is taken away.

If some care is taken to properly arrange the seating of your "guests," the results of your meeting may be more successful. As the presenter, you have three different audiences: There are people to your far side and your near side, as well as people seated straight ahead of you toward the middle. These three seating areas or positions are referred to as the Power, Input, and Observer seats. Depending on where people sit, an interesting dynamic may be added to the discussion.

> **NOTE**
>
> I'm assuming that you are standing to the left of the screen, from an audience perspective. Even without a screen for visual support, you should still anchor to one side, preferably to the left, to maintain the same seating dynamics throughout the talk. Moving around to different sides is not recommended, because it disrupts the original perspectives of those in the audience.

29

POWER SEATS

Those who sit diagonally opposite you as you speak are in the *power seats*. Because these seats mirror the presenter, an implied power is given to those occupying these seats. Figure 29.1 shows the location of the power seats. In a typical conference room or U-shape, these seats are grouped in the corner. Depending on the size of the table, or the U-shape, two or more people may occupy the power seats. Keep in mind that these people assume power whenever they make comments or interact in some way. Even though they are not standing when they speak, the dynamics of the room create the effect of the seating importance to the rest of the group simply because those in the power seats mirror you.

Figure 29.1
From the presenter's view, the power seats are diagonally opposite. People in these corner or near-corner seats actually "mirror" the presenter.

You can take most advantage of your rest and power positions with those occupying the power seats, because people in those seats tend to face you more than they face the other people in the room. In addition, you can stimulate more group interaction by directing your attention and targeting your gestures toward those in the power seats. Your efforts to include those opposite you will automatically spread the interest to either side, thereby including the entire group.

INPUT SEATS

As you present, the *input seats* are the ones along the far side of the conference table or U-shape. Because you normally stand to the audience's left when you have visual support, the input seats are to your left. Figure 29.2 show the location of these seats. Those sitting in the input seats have an unobstructed view of you, and they typically interact only when prompted. When they do interact, it is usually to provide input in the form of support information or to offer some type of agreement to a suggestion.

Figure 29.2
From the presenter's view, the input seats are to the far side. People in these seats have a good view and tend to interact more than those seated across from them.

Those occupying the input seats will normally interact more often with the people sitting across from them. The constant challenge of conference-room and U-shaped seating is that many people in the room are distracted because they can see and interact with one another, which diminishes their attention to your words. But the input seats still offer a direct view of you and your support visuals (if any). These factors raise the importance of the input seats.

OBSERVER SEATS

The people sitting on the near side to you as you present are in the *observer seats*. Because you normally stand to the audience's left when you have visual support, the observer seats are to your right. Figure 29.3 shows the location of the observer seats. These are the worst seats in the house. People usually have to shift their chairs on angles or lean over just to make eye contact with the presenter. More than likely the people in these seats will have to give up the convenience of the table to position their chairs to see you as you speak. This means they lose a writing surface to take notes effectively, and they just can't reach for the all-important coffee cup without making the effort obvious to the rest of the group.

One of the main reasons these seats are referred to as "observer" seats is that the people in these seats tend to spend more time observing the group than they do the presenter. When you think about it, these people have to work harder just to see you in action, and this decreases their attentiveness to your message. If you're going to lose any of your conference room crowd, it will most likely be the observers.

29

Figure 29.3
The observer seats are along the near side of the table, from the presenter's viewpoint. People in these seats have the poorest view of the presenter, and they tend to be the most distracted.

PUTTING PEOPLE IN PLACE

It would be great if you could assign seats for people based on the Power, Input, and Observer seating positions. But as a meeting comes to order, people usually take seats on a first-come, first-served basis. There are exceptions to this, of course, but for the most part the seating in any presentation is left unplanned. You can balance the scales in your favor, however, by subtly forcing people to take certain seats.

For example, let's say you want to hold one of the power seats for a key person you expect at the presentation. Of course, you have no idea when they will arrive in relation to the others in the meeting. So how can you increase the chances that the key person will occupy a power seat? You pray for luck or hope for the best. Nah! You just have to bend the rules a little.

The strategy is simple, assuming you arrive in the room before anyone else. As soon as you can, place a folder or small stack of your papers on the table, right in front of the power seat that you want to "hold" from being taken. You could also use a briefcase or jacket on the chair itself, but a chair can be moved out of place more easily.

Then, as people come into the room, be ready to greet them at the door. This helps you spot when the key person approaches. As the room fills, there is less chance anyone will take the power seat you've "held," because most people will assume the seat is already taken. People don't like to touch other people's stuff, unless of course no other place is left.

Now, as soon as you greet the key person you start a conversation as you both move into the room. If you are saying something of real value, the person will naturally follow you to keep listening. You casually meander to the open seat where your folder or papers are resting on

29

the table. Just as you get there, you break the conversation and offer the seat while apologizing for having left your "stuff" on the table. Or, you can actually have planned a moment in the discussion where you need to refer to something in the folder. Either way, the excuse to remove your things makes the seat available. As you gather your papers, you pick up the conversation right where you left off, and the person will naturally take the seat as they continue listening.

NOTE

> This is not to suggest that you will be more attentive to only one key person during your presentation. Instead, you must treat everyone the same. The difference is that the key person occupies a seat that offers the best opportunity for attention to your message. This seating strategy only plays to your advantage if you present with the same energy to everyone in the room without singling out any individual.

You'll have to practice this strategy a few times to make the transition look smooth and unnoticeable. Otherwise your intended "guest" may become wary of your intentions. Even with practice, this effort may not work every time. For that reason, your presentation skills must be at their peak under all conditions.

Seating Your Team and Their Team

Sometimes you may attend a presentation along with one or more people from your department or organization. These people are part of your "presentation team," even though some or all of them may not present information. Teams are common among many of the sales forces I coach, especially those in financial services and real estate. The "seller-buyer" relationship is very clear when representatives of two companies meet.

That same relationship exists within organizations where, in many meetings, several coworkers from one department present information to a team of workers from another department. One group is usually "selling" an idea, while the other group is asked to "buy-in." The seller-buyer relationship typically involves a persuasive argument.

I don't want to condense every possible presentation situation into a seller-buyer theme, but usually, whenever a clear separation of duties exists among the groups, some type of persuasive argument is being presented. Otherwise, what is the point of gathering members from diverse departments if not for consensus? Hey—even the holiday party meets this test. Everyone is supposed to agree that they are having fun!

Regardless of the reason members of your team are involved, you can strategize a seating plan before everyone has taken their chairs in the room. Let's separate the teams by using the simple terms *their team* and *your team*. Figure 29.4 shows how you might seat some of the attendees of the meeting.

Figure 29.4
Try to have some of your team in the observer seats and some of their team in the power/input seats. Avoid stacking everyone on your team on just one side of the room.

Obviously you want the power seats to be taken by members of their team, especially for a persuasive presentation. If you can identify key players from their team, try to get a few of them into the power seats. Following that, any of their team's subordinate decision-makers or support staff should occupy some of the input seats. Naturally, you want your team to blend in, so use the remaining input seats for members of your team, specifically those who are not presenting at the meeting.

Finally, save some of the observer seats for your team, especially for those who will be presenting during the meeting. Then, when they are ready to speak, they've had the opportunity to glance at others during your presentation to notice key reactions, interest level, and so forth. Awareness of any details about the group's reactions to information is invaluable to each presenter.

In addition, members of your team occupying the observer seats are probably familiar with your presentation. They don't need to be as attentive to your words at every moment. Come on—they've seen your act before! The target of attention for the observer seats is the rest of the group in an effort to gain insight.

Following the presentation, you should regroup with your team and discuss the behavior observed during the meeting. Someone may have noticed a perplexed look when a certain subject was covered. Another member of your team may have observed someone taking notes as soon as a specific chart was presented. Believe it or not, the observers can also notice people nodding off. Maybe the presentation is longer than it should be! In any event, the feedback from those in the observer seats can be very helpful in preparing for your next presentation.

SIT-DOWN SCENARIOS

Okay, let's scale down the setting to the times when you are just sitting down. In these meetings, typically in conference rooms, you might spend a few minutes standing and giving a presentation and then take the remaining time to sit and continue the discussion. The seating positions can still be used effectively.

Keep in mind that when seated, the position of your shoulders still controls the rest and power positions discussed in Chapter 26 (refer to Figure 26.3 for a visual example). When your shoulders match the shoulders of another person, you are in a power position in relation to that person (as they are with you). When your shoulders are at an angle to another person, you are in a rest position. Your goal is to be in a seat where the angles of your body can be used effectively with the greatest number of people in the room.

For example, avoid putting yourself in a center-seating situation at a conference-room table. Take a look at Figure 29.5. Let's say that the man in the center of the group, at the head of the table, is leading the meeting. You might think he is in a power position in relation to the others on his right and left. However, he can only take a power position with the person directly opposite, at the other end of the table (not shown in the photo).

Figure 29.5
The man at the head of the table is limited by his center-seating position. He can only create a power position with one other person at the table, namely, the one opposite him (not shown in the photo).

The seat at the head of the table is not as effective, unless you are facilitating a meeting rather than leading it. When facilitating, you represent a neutral position. This is similar to an arbitrator or mediator. If you are playing such a role, then consider a center-seating position in relation to the group.

If you want to lead and control a meeting, you have a better chance from one of the corner seats. Look at Figure 29.6. It's the same group of people shown from a different camera

29

view. The woman wearing the eyeglasses has a power seat in relation to the others at the table. She is able to square her shoulders or angle them to many different people by swiveling her chair or shifting the upper part of her body.

Figure 29.6
The woman wearing the eyeglasses occupies a power seat. She can create rest and power positions with a number of people at the table. All the corner seats are the most effective in these conference room settings.

This "off-center seating" strategy allows you to gain a wider perspective of the entire group. In addition, any props such as documents or other items will be easier to angle for view when you take one of the corner seats.

HANDLING ONE-TO-ONE SITUATIONS

Okay, what happens when you are faced with one or two people in the room with you? You can still have a seating strategy to help your message along. For one-to-one meetings, use your rest and power positions in the same way as you do in conference room settings. The smaller the group, the easier it becomes to use body angles to your advantage.

CREATE ANGLES

The most common situation to avoid is the "head-on collision" where you are directly opposite the other person and your shoulders match each other. The goal is to avoid having your shoulders parallel to the other person in what is called a "squared-off" position. Angling your body or your chair is the easiest way to avoid squaring-off to the other person. Look at Figure 29.7. In the background of the photo you see two people standing and having a conversation. Because their shoulders match, they are both in a power position in relation to each other. This is a less effective way to communicate. When two people square off like that, it's as if their bodies are yelling at one another. In the foreground of the same image, the two women are seated, but they are at angles to one another. Communication works better when your shoulders are angled to the other person.

Figure 29.7
The people standing in the background are squared-off to one another, and the two people seated are at angles. Communication is more effective when people are at angles to one another.

29

You can put yourself into an angled position in relation to another person in a number of ways. When seated, you could choose a corner of a table, or, if you are standing and someone else is sitting, you could lean on the edge of a desk (half-standing) and keep your shoulders angled to the person seated.

SHARE PERSPECTIVE

When two people look at something from completely different angles, they are not sharing a common perspective. This is not really a problem when the object in view is large enough to be seen from a distance, such as a projected image on a screen. But if the object is meant for an audience of one, then perspective becomes an issue.

The most common object for one person to look at is a document. If you are opposite a person when you hand over a document, you immediately lose a common perspective. The person is looking down at the piece of paper and you are looking upside-down at the same object. The perspective is different for each of you. It will be more difficult for you to point our specifics in the document from your perspective. You'll probably end up stretching your neck and rotating your head at some weird angle. Trust me, this looks ridiculous. Try to get the same perspective on the object as the other person.

Figure 29.8 shows a man standing next to a woman seated at a table. Both of them share a common perspective on the document in view. When people have the same point of view (literally) on something, the message is easier to convey and interpret.

Figure 29.8
By standing to the side, the man shares the same perspective on the document as the woman. A shared perspective makes communication more effective.

The photo is merely a captured moment in time. Once equal perspective is achieved regarding the document, the man can return to his original position at the other side of the table and continue the discussion, meeting, or presentation.

The same perspective can also be achieved when two people are sitting. In Figure 29.9, the two men have the same perspective looking at the papers in front of them. It will be easy for one of them to point to information on the sheets, if necessary, to facilitate the discussion. Imagine how difficult it would be if one of them was standing opposite and looking over the top of the papers to point out something specific.

Naturally, you can't always put yourself in a position to share the same perspective with another person. Yet, when an opportunity arises, you should take advantage of it, if possible.

TIP

Don't make your effort to get a common perspective so obvious that the other person wonders what you are doing. For example, if you are in a conference room with one other person and the table is long enough to hold 20 people, don't sit right next to the person. Instead, take a corner seat, if you can. Then, when you need to share a document, you can always get up and stand to the side of the person to point out information in the document.

SCAN THE EYES

A lot of information stored in your brain is in the form of pictures. It's true. These visual references are tucked away neatly in your brain waiting for retrieval. For example, if you think about your high school biology teacher, a visual image pops into your head, and you see that person in your mind's eye, so to speak. You even visualize situations that haven't happened. If I ask you to think about your own road to success, you create a little picture in your brain as you "see yourself" in some type of successful moment. The point is that everyone uses visual references. Whenever one of those references is retrieved, the eyes move in some direction to see the image in the brain.

Figure 29.9
Two people, sitting side by side, share the same perspective when looking at documents.

Therefore, in many one-to-one situations, the eyes of the other person can offer you some interesting clues as to what they might be thinking. As an observer, you can scan the eye movement of a person whenever you say something thought provoking. To interpret the other person's reaction, however, you need to learn how they personally look for the images they create.

The easiest approach is to probe for a timeline. Figure 29.10 shows how you place an imaginary timeline in front of the person's face. The timeline is always from your point of view. Start with the assumption that the person's past is to your left, and their future is to your right.

By asking a question involving reflection or something in the past, the person normally shifts their eyes in one direction to physically "look up" the visual image of the experience. You can observe which direction the eyes travel as the person recalls the experience. Not everyone glances in the same direction to look up an image, but for most people, that direction is up and to their right. Whatever the direction, it represents their past. Figure 29.11 shows how a person's eyes might move when they reflect on a past experience. You look at them through an imaginary timeline, with the past to your left and the future to your right. In this example, the direction of their eyes matches your timeline.

Figure 29.10
When scanning the eyes of another person, place an imaginary timeline in front of them. The timeline is viewed from your perspective, with the past to your left and the future to your right.

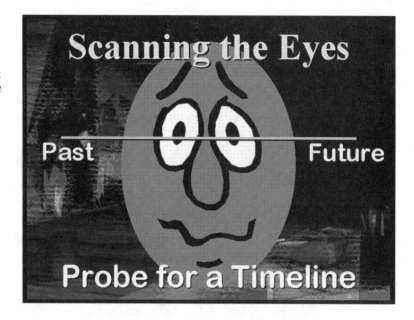

If their eyes shift the opposite way of your imaginary timeline, then reverse your timeline and realize they look up their past differently (to your right). The point is that you first have to notice how the person recalls past experiences to establish the end points of your timeline. Whatever the direction of their eyes, it represents "the past" on your timeline.

After you know the person's past, whenever you prompt a thought-provoking glance in the opposite direction, the person is likely indicating anticipation of something in the future. Figure 29.12 shows an already established timeline with a glance to the person's left indicating a vision of the future.

I have always taken the position that, whenever a person paints a picture of their future, it is always positive, unless they have some specific reasons to expect something negative to happen. Using the assumption that a person's view of the future is ultimately optimistic, a shift of a person's eyes to the "future" on the timeline you established may be the most opportune moment for you to close the deal, so to speak. After all, if the person appears to be "looking forward" to using your product or service, take that eye movement as a hint and go for it—close the deal, ask for the order, complete the call to action!

The eyes give other hints, as well. For example, if the person is staring directly at you and not shifting their eyes at all, there's a good chance that they are not listening. They are likely giving you the courtesy of direct eye contact, but they are probably drifting away in their thoughts. Break the eye contact with them and they will be attentive again. Take a look at the Troubleshooting section at the end of Chapter 26, for more comments about eye contact.

Figure 29.11
When a person reflects on the past, their eyes move in some direction. In this example, the eyes shifted up and to the person's right. In this case, the shift matches your time-line.

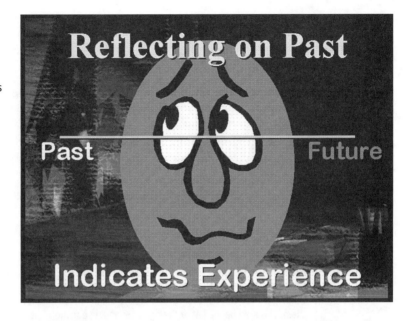

Figure 29.12
After a timeline is established and you know the person's past, a shift of their eyes in the opposite direction indicates anticipation.

SOCIALIZING YOUR SKILLS

Never underestimate the power of a coffee break! When you think about it, lots of business is conducted in a social setting such as lunch, dinner, the cocktail hour, or even a golf outing. For example, I speak at many conferences, and in many cases there is usually some type of opening reception for the attendees to walk around with little nametags and get to know one another. This is commonly called networking. The objective of the typical "cocktail hour" is to use a relaxed atmosphere to establish lasting relationships. We used to do this in college. Of course, we called it "bar-hopping." The objective was the same—to use a relaxed atmosphere to establish lasting relationships—only the effort did not require little nametags.

Anyway, these casual get-togethers are a great way to create business opportunities. During those moments, the physical positions you take can make a difference. Body angles and gestures will be your most effective communication tools. When standing and conversing, for example, you can establish a 45-degree angle to the other person and, when necessary, make important points by squaring your shoulders to face the person directly. You can use virtual space to visually explain concepts and ideas.

→ To learn more about virtual space, **see** "Using Virtual Space," in Chapter 27, **p. 626**.

TIP

> Some say to always keep a beverage in your left hand so the right hand is free to shake hands, and it won't be cold or damp from having held the glass. The truth is that in most social situations where people are mingling, there isn't a lot of hand shaking going on as introductions are made. Most people just nod their heads to greet others. So, if you are holding a glass while speaking to another person, always hold it in the hand closest to them. This may be the left or the right, depending on where the other person is standing. By keeping the glass closer to the person, your other hand is free to use a wider area for virtual space.

In all situations, hand gestures work well. Reaching out when referencing someone or hanging a gesture (keeping it still) when making a point is always effective, even during meals. These settings are also a great place to practice your gestures and get comfortable with how your hands move when you speak. For example, if you are eating dinner with a group of people and you say, "Pass the bread, please," you should take note as to how your arm extends and how your hand opens (reaches out) for the bread. The same natural flow of that gesture used at dinner should be the same as the one used on stage. Social gatherings help you with your natural delivery skills. The more you practice your one-to-one skills, the easier it will be for you to maintain those skills in more formal presentation settings.

In addition to body positions and hand gestures, one of the best communication skills for social events is storytelling. Whether the reference be fact or fiction, comedy or tragedy, the ability to use stories to augment a discussion is very useful. You can even use social settings to work on specific areas of your delivery style, such as humor. I always test new jokes or humorous comments with small groups of people, most of whom I don't really know. I work on timing, rhythm, phrase selection and I'll even try different "punchlines" with different groups to see which is most effective.

If you keep the notion that every moment with others is a presentation skill learning experience, you will increase your effectiveness each time you interact with others. You are your own best teacher (assuming you're willing to learn).

WORKING IN REMOTE LOCATIONS

Not every presentation offers you the convenience of a roof over your head. In fact, sometimes you may find yourself presenting in harsh environments or in settings that make it nearly impossible to keep an audience attentive for more than a few minutes. Many business presentations take place in remote locations much different than the typical conference room. Let's take a look at some of these situations including:

- Presenting outdoors
- Dealing with extreme conditions
- Delivering tradeshow presentations

PRESENTING OUTDOORS

When someone talks about presenting "out in the field," don't be surprised if they are referring to a stretch of land that yields wheat! A number of companies have to conduct business in outdoor environments because of the nature of what they need to discuss or show. The reasons you might conduct a presentation outdoors are for convenience or display. In some cases, you are forced to present at the location of your listeners, thus making it convenient for your audience to evaluate your message. In other cases, you ask your audience to attend your presentation so that you may display some product that would otherwise have been difficult to bring to the listeners.

For example, it is not unusual for a company that manufactures heavy construction equipment to demonstrate a large piece of machinery to a group of interested prospects outdoors. You won't find too many hotel ballrooms able to accommodate a 150-foot crane. Even if they could get one into the hotel, think of the marks on the carpet!

Naturally, there are many ways to show products in a presentation using photographs and line art. A picture of the crane or a schematic drawing of its unique functions can be inserted directly into a PowerPoint presentation. There is nothing wrong with this as a way to discuss feature and benefits.

But the most effective way for someone to grasp the entire picture is to experience the real thing, in real life. If you were considering purchasing a building, you could look at photos or renderings, but you would benefit most by going to the location and walking through the space itself. It is during these moments that presenting "outdoors" takes place.

DEMONSTRATING LARGE OBJECTS

Okay, so you're presenting outdoors, and you have a product to show or demonstrate. One of the first things to consider is the size of the "object" in relation to the group. Because you picked the outdoor venue for a reason, let's assume the object is bigger than you are. This being the case, you won't be able to pick it up and hold it. You can't pass it around for the group to examine. You won't even be able to move it, without creating an obvious effort. This is really no different than the conditions you have when you present visuals on a screen. You won't ever attempt to move the screen and the good news is you don't have to. You leave it stationary and use your own movement and gestures to reference it.

So the first thing you do with a large object is to anchor it for the audience. Leave it in the same spot for as long as you can while you present. This gives your audience a single perspective on a stationary object. If you need to change the viewing angle, decide if it is easier to reposition the object or reposition the audience by having them move in one direction or another.

For example, let's say your company manufactures cars and you want to "present" the latest model to a group of car dealers who sell your products. You decide to hold the meeting at an outdoor venue, such as a racetrack, and you gather your group in an open space to show the vehicle. To make sure everyone can see, you have the group stand on a series of raised platforms with each row higher than the row in front. The long side of the car faces the group, and you can describe features of the vehicle by moving slowly from one end of the car to the other. It doesn't matter which side you start from because there is nothing for the audience to read. Only when the visual content contains text do you have to anchor to the side of the visual where the reading normally starts.

The key to showing a large object is to create a linear path for the audience to follow. Don't move back and forth to different points. Try to plan your movements to navigate in as straight a line as possible from your starting to your ending point. This reduces distraction.

WALKING AND TALKING

Sometimes you may have to give your presentation as you lead your audience through a defined space. A number of businesses encounter these situations all the time. You can be selling real estate or conducting guided tours—the fact is that you are walking and talking with a group as you point out specific items. When the audience is moving, the dynamics of the presentation change in relation to the perspective.

Think about what happens when people are moving. They have to focus attention on where they are going, first, before they even begin to concentrate on something else. This means that attention span is shorter when the group is moving. Thus, when the group is standing still, attention is greater. As a presenter, your goal is to make your key points at times when the group has stopped moving. The more you can control the movement of your audience, the more effectively you can direct their attention.

While you are moving, especially in situations where you are walking as you guide the group through a space, you must be aware of your ability to be heard. Each time you turn your face away from the group (perhaps to see where you're going), you have to speak louder for your voice to carry. In fact, anytime you are looking away and still speaking, try directing your voice toward a hard surface rather than a wide-open space. A hard surface reflects sound. This helps your voice bounce back and return in the direction of the listeners.

To help the group focus on objects more quickly, use vocal directions prior to describing the item. For example, if you are guiding a few people through a workspace in a building and you want to point out certain objects along the way, phrases such as "to your left" or "along the floor to your immediate right" to indicate direction before a description. When what you are describing is already in view, a person can relate to your description more attentively.

When walking and talking you may also be gesturing toward things. Try to maintain a consistency with your gestures and with the direction you turn your body. Choose a repeating pattern such as using your right hand to gesture whenever your body turns to your right. The goal is to reduce distractions with a smaller variety of movements. Keep in mind the audience may be looking in three different places: at something you are pointing to, at where they are walking, or directly at you. You may be looking in three different places as well based on what you are doing at the moment. You can clearly see how a moving presenter and moving audience limit the chances to establish anchors. At least a consistent pattern of movement will not add to the confusion.

DEALING WITH EXTREME CONDITIONS

Believe it or not, circumstances occur that may make it nearly impossible to conduct the presentation in the manner that you expect. I'm not talking about a projector bulb burning out. I'm talking about extreme conditions that test the limits of your ability to deliver the message. Think of an extreme condition as one that reduces your chances of either being seen, heard, or even understood by the audience. In each of these cases the strategy is to focus your energy on the parts of the presentation that are of greater importance to your audience.

Keep in mind that the components of communication involve your body, your voice, and your visual support. The audience concentrates on each of these elements while the message is being delivered. When one of those elements is restricted, the audience places more focus on the remaining elements to get the most from the message. Knowing this helps you put more emphasis on the more obvious components of the communication. Let's take a look at some extreme conditions that can hinder your efforts to deliver a message with impact.

DARK SHADOWS

When people can't see you, that's a problem. You already know how important it is for the audience to see your body and, more specifically, your face. Expressions help a listener understand your intent behind the message. Therefore, lighting is a critical element to your being seen by everyone. Poor lighting or no lighting at all can be a major obstacle in your effort to deliver your story with impact.

We already talked about lighting in Chapter 28, including some "creative" techniques to illuminate you as you speak. But what happens when you end up presenting in the dark? Well, some people say that when there is very little light the audience falls asleep. That's a fallacy. People don't just fall asleep when the lights go down. After all, some of the most exciting moments in our lives happen in the dark. It's not the lack of light that puts people to sleep—it's lack of visible action! Come on, if lack of light induced sleep in every situation, then people would be snoring though every movie!

→ To learn more about creative lighting techniques, **see** "Working with Lighting and Sound," in Chapter 28, **p. 650**.

Because lack of visible action reduces attentiveness and interest, you need to work around poor lighting conditions as best you can. The best way to do this is to get your body in a position where it is most visible, namely, closest to any available light source. In a very darkened room, you already know that the greatest concentration of light will be on the screen displaying your visuals. The screen, then, is your closest light source. The amount of light bouncing off the screen determines how much of you the audience sees. Proximity to your screen or light source is the strategy to consider.

For example, under poor lighting conditions, you have to limit the movement in your triangle. You have to make your available space smaller and confined to those areas with the mostlight reflecting from the screen. Naturally, this forces you to play more of the action toward the back of your triangle where the light is brighter from the screen.

Another thing you can consider is reversing your color scheme. I normally suggest dark background and bright foregrounds, but poor lighting conditions are not "normal." So, you'll have to trade off some of the impact from your visuals to gain some value from your physical presence. If you use lighter backgrounds and darker foregrounds, you'll have more white (bright) light emanating from the screen. This gives you a better chance of being illuminated by the spillover of reflective light, especially as you get closer to your visual. You won't be so visible that people can see your facial expressions, but your gestures will make more sense even if the light from the screen casts you only as a silhouette for the audience to see.

From an audience perspective, when your body language and facial expressions are less visible, the concentration of attention shifts more to the two components of your content: your voice and your visual support. From a vocal standpoint, realize that the audience can't see your mouth moving when you speak. This means you'll have to speak more slowly, enunciate your words better, and use pauses more often. Pretend you are in a phone conversation with your audience where the greatest percentage of the message comes from your tone, not just from the words you say.

When referencing your visuals, use vocal directions. These are lead-in phrases such as "the second bar labeled 1999," or, "the two largest slices on the right side of this pie chart." Actually, vocal directions help guide the eye in all presentation settings, not only when you find your yourself in poor lighting conditions.

THE SOUNDS OF SILENCE

Sometimes the audience may have difficulty hearing you. Microphones are great tools for allowing people to hear your voice from a distance. But in many situations, for one reason or another, a microphone is not available. Depending on the size of the space and the distance to the last row, making yourself heard might become a real challenge.

Part of the problem may be that you aren't speaking loud enough. In Chapter 26, you learned several techniques to enhance your vocal delivery. However, even if you can raise the volume of your voice, it may create more problems than you think. For example, if you have to shout so that people in the back of the room can hear you, then imagine what effect your voice has on the people in the front! As you examine the glaring evil stares of those whose eardrums have been ruptured, you will most likely begin to lower your voice. Of course, the people in the back will strain to hear you once again. You can easily see how distance creates a sound imbalance for your audience. So what can you do?

→ For more information on vocal delivery techniques, **see** "Breathing Properly" in Chapter 26, **p. 610**.

First find a volume level that is at least audible from the back, even though it is not at the level those people prefer. Because your words have less impact, you need to show more and say less. Remember that when a component of the communication is restricted, the remaining components draw more attention from the audience. If your voice is barely audible, then your gestures, your movements, and even your visuals are more apparent.

From a physical perspective I'm not suggesting you run around flapping your arms to create more attention. But you should emphasize your words with descriptive gestures by using virtual space more often to explain things. When your words are harder to hear, your actions speak that much louder. You'll have to "act out" your thoughts. The ability to express yourself without words is important for those times when you are less audible as well as for all other times when you want to add more impact to your message above and beyond what your voice is able to do.

→ To learn more about virtual space, **see** "Using Virtual Space," in Chapter 27, **p. 626**.

TIP

> Play a visual game like *Charades* in which you have to act out a phrase without speaking. Or give directions to someone who doesn't speak your language. Or simply spend a little time entertaining an infant. In each of these situations you will have to rely more on your nonverbal skills to communicate a message completely.

Another way to compensate for your inability to be heard well is to add more visual support to your presentation. Naturally, you'll have to plan ahead for this because you can't create a whole bunch of extra visuals at the last minute. Additional content on the screen gives the audience a more visual reference for the words they may not hear. You can use builds and overlays to reveal information in stages so that the audience knows exactly where you are on a given visual. You can even create a series of additional images to support what normally might have been displayed as a single visual.

For example, suppose you have a map of the United States with three defined regions: west, central, and east. Under normal conditions you planned to cover information about all three regions without changing the visual. But because you are barely audible, you can help the audience through the topic by adding three more visuals, one for each region. On each of these subvisuals, you can add bulleted text to highlight some of the key points you are discussing. So, even if it is difficult to hear everything you are saying, the audience is "reading" more of your visual content to get a better understanding of the message.

29

Overall, whenever you find yourself "vocally challenged," realize that your audience will rely more heavily on the components of your presentation that are easiest to grasp. In situations where you can't be heard well, increase your movements in the triangle, add more emphatic gestures to the screen, use virtual space more often to describe things, and consider adding extra visual content to help tell a more complete story.

CULTURE SHOCK

In the growing world of global communication, it is not unusual to find yourself facing audience members who may have trouble understanding you, because they are less familiar with your language. Whether you present locally or abroad, you are likely to encounter language barriers with some people in your audience from time to time. In fact, you may present in another country where not only are your words difficult to understand, but your visual support is too. When an audience views cultural differences as distractions, your presentation is less effective.

In these situations, your best bet is to put the majority of your effort into the physical delivery. After all, body language is universal; spoken language is not. You can test this theory at home. Find a TV station broadcasting in a language you barely understand. If you watch for awhile, there will be enough visual clues and details for you to get some semblance of what is happening. This is because you can see the action. Now, turn your back to the TV so you can't see the screen. Because you can't understand the words, notice how little information you can get. It's obvious that observable action is a big contributor toward understanding.

Your physical actions and your visual support play the major roles in overcoming language barriers when you present. Regarding your content, consider creating images that are more graphical. Embed more photographs in the backgrounds of your visuals. Use arrows, colors, and geometric shapes to help tell your story. Avoid showing too many text charts. In fact, numbers and other data-driven charts (bar, pie, line) may be easier for the audience to understand than heavy text-based visuals.

Your physical actions are important, but presenting in a foreign country can be challenging. Gestures and movements you make may be considered distracting, rude, or even offensive without you knowing it.

TIP

> You may want to investigate this reference regarding this topic: *Cross-Cultural Communication: A Practical Guide*, by Gregory Barnard. Also, take a look at the Web site: *The Web of Culture* at www.webofculture.com.

You never know what certain actions might mean. The last thing you need is to accidentally scratch your right ear while your left elbow points at a 45-degree angle to the northwest corner of the room and, immediately, some military extremist in the middle of the crowd leaps up and declares that you've just insulted their leader! Hey, these things can happen! That's why it's always best to check with a resident about local customs and cultural issues.

And That Translates Into…

There may be times where your words have to be translated for an audience to understand. I experienced that situation recently in Sao Paulo, Brazil, where the native language is Portuguese. My visuals were in English, but my words were simultaneously translated for the audience. It was interesting to look at 300 people wearing headphones. It felt like I was at a convention of radio broadcasters!

I learned a few things that day about simultaneous translation. First of all, it's not simultaneous. There's a delay between the time your phrase ends and the time everyone else hears it translated. I noticed this after my first joke. I delivered the punchline and everyone laughed—about 10 seconds later!

I also had the chance to practice with the translator before the seminar started. Now if you've ever seen me present, you know I have a high energy level. Unfortunately, the translator had no energy level. His voice was low-key and relatively flat. So the audience was watching me deliver an action-packed presentation while a symphony of monotone phrases played through their headphones!

But perhaps the most embarrassing moment of the day happened at the very end of my three-hour session. It was time to field questions, and now I had to put the headphones on to listen to the translator convert the audience questions into English. I scan the crowd and gesture to a man sitting about ten rows back. He stands and proceeds to ask his question, in Portuguese, of course. Being the great listener that I am (just ask my wife), I stood there, attentive to every word—nay—to every syllable directed at me during this rather lengthy question. It took about 30 seconds for me to finally realize that I was listening to the man in the audience and not the translator. The bad news is that I don't speak nor understand Portuguese!

By the time I started listening to the translator, the only words I heard were from the end of the man's last phrase,"… wondering does that cause confusion?" I appeared calm, but inside my head I was in a panic. I asked myself, "Wondering does *what* cause confusion? What did this guy just say? Why am I even on this planet right now?"

I settled into my best presentation stance. I looked away, briefly, as if pondering the numerous possible answers to this important question. Realizing I was lost, I looked directly at the gentleman, still standing there clutching his tethered cap and tilting his head toward me like an innocent child waiting for permission to have a cookie. In a calm voice I broke the silence and said, "I'll tell you the real cause of confusion—headphones! That's right, headphones cause confusion!" The man, the rest of the audience, even the translator had no idea what I was talking about.

So I told the truth. I admitted that I wasn't listening to the translator during most of the man's question, and I really didn't know what he asked. That's why I related the word confusion to the headphones. Well, after everyone heard that, they all just laughed—about 10 seconds later!

DELIVERING TRADESHOW PRESENTATIONS

Many companies participate in tradeshows. Presentations at these events range from simple demonstrations to full-blown theatrical wonders! Regardless of all the hoopla and the hype, these events need to be planned and organized effectively.

The typical tradeshow involves a boatload of people from the company standing on their feet about ten hours a day for almost a week. During this time these brave souls are fielding questions, spouting out theories, running for coffee, eating junk-food, listening to arguments, shaking hands, smiling at strangers, reading badges, handing out literature, gathering business cards, and praying for the end of the show! Sound familiar?

Regardless of the excitement surrounding a tradeshow, the bottom line is that the interaction among participants is either from conversations or presentations. Conversations are the one-to-one spontaneous discussions with passersby and booth visitors. Presentations are more planned topics delivered several times a day, usually from a dedicated space inside the booth, to small groups of spectators. You can spot these setups right away. Just look for a bunch of chairs facing a screen and maybe a sign displaying something like, "The next presentation begins at…" or words to that effect.

To get the most from your tradeshow event, you should understand the underlying objective or purpose behind every moment of your "delivery," whether it is conversation or presentation. The purpose is to enlighten. The purpose is not to survey, not to brag, but to enlighten. This means that everything you say, in one form or another, must enlighten the listener with new or different information. Remember the reason people go to tradeshows—to see something new and different, something wonderful, something exciting, and something—dare I say—enlightening! So, give people what they want, and they will remember you.

TIP

One way to add value to your offerings at a tradeshow is to appeal to the most important part of an attendee's body—the feet! People walk for hours at a tradeshow, and they remember the booths with the softest carpeting! In my marketing days when I had to design our tradeshow booth, I always spent extra dollars for the thickest carpeting available. I also tried to get space nearest the restrooms. I believe these were additional reasons for people to hang around a bit longer in our booth and hear more of our enlightening stories!

INFORMAL CONVERSATIONS

Earlier in this chapter we discussed one-to-one situations and all the same rules apply to tradeshow conversations. The big difference between conference rooms and tradeshows is the underlying sense of urgency for both parties involved.

Naturally, you want to cover information quickly, and the listener wants to gather information quickly. Well, at least you each agree on the result—quick, concise data. One of the informal studies we conducted at MediaNet was a random sample of tradeshow attendees to see the average stay at any booth location. We found the average stay to be 2 minutes and 14 seconds at those booths where the attendee actually stopped to have a conversation. During that time, the attendees focused attention mostly on items directly in view while they listened to the person talking with them. If you figure on people staying only a short time, then by all means—get to the point!

That's why conversations at tradeshows should be no more than short descriptions containing key words about the product or service on display. We call these brief phrases *sound bites* (or *bytes*, if you prefer). The sound bite should be the capsule summary of a somewhat lengthier statement, which, given the extra time, you would have said. You should create a whole library of these little pieces of enlightening facts and then use them at the appropriate times during the conversation. Most people working tradeshow booths are never taught to use sound bites. That is why conversations end too quickly or drag on for too long about unimportant issues.

Sound bites are important for controlling the flow of traffic around you. Let's say you are standing in your booth and talking to one person about a new product that your company is introducing. You already know this person may walk away after a minute or two, so you use your strongest sound bites first. Your mention the top three "enlightening" features as soon you can. In the meantime, other people are passing by, eavesdropping, as they should. Before you know it, a new listener, hearing a sound bite instantly joins the small discussion. Now you have two people seeking enlightenment. Well, you can't repeat the same features for the new person because the first listener gets no added value and probably walks away. So you add a new sound bite and perhaps rephrase one of the original ones, as well. This keeps both listeners attentive a bit longer. The point is that you have to keep the enlightenment going in some small way as each new listener joins the group.

After you run out of new things to say, you will begin to lose the people who were there the longest. But if you got two minutes out of them, you made a successful contact. Even though the person received only a brief impression, it gives them the choice of either moving on or seeking even more information from you or others in the booth. Of the hundreds of people who stop and listen, many will move on, but some will stay longer, and a few of those will actually conduct some business. Just think of a tradeshow as a live version of a newspaper ad in the Sunday circular. There are lots of things to look at, only some of which you can take the time to consider buying.

One other interesting thing about conversations is the likelihood of joining one. In other words, most people would rather join an existing conversation than initiate one. Think about it. It is less work for you to approach two or more people engaged in open conversation than it is for you to approach someone and just start up a discussion from scratch. At a tradeshow, the more sound bites you have, the longer you can keep your first listener attentive. It follows that the longer a listener stays attentive, the greater the chances of another listener joining the existing conversation. As you continue to enlighten, the crowd around you grows. Even from a distance others will be attracted to see what is so interesting. Little do they know—it's just a bundle of really attractive sound bites!

PLANNED PRESENTATIONS

For many companies, the tradeshow venue includes a short presentation. Typically, these little "shows" are delivered a couple of times each day. They normally span 20 to 30 minutes, and the audience is usually seated in some theatre-style arrangement. I have trained many different groups of tradeshow presenters over the years, and the one point I make early on is that the presentation must be first and foremost entertaining. Second, the entertainment must directly relate to what your company does or sells, or else you can't make a lasting impression. This is why the magician at the tradeshow booth is a big waste of time, unless your product is truly magical! After all, if the entertainment is simply to draw a crowd, then how will you know who in the crowd is a potential customer?

I remember one company, a manufacturer of network switching equipment, insisted on using a live rock band in their booth. In addition, they decided to raffle a sports car at the end of the show. They must have gotten 10,000 leads—people that liked rock music and liked to drive sports cars—not exactly the profile of their current customers. The issue is not quantity of leads, but quality. If quantity is the goal then open the phone book—all your customers are in there.

So, just follow the principle of "entertainment with direct relevance" to build a more effective tradeshow presentation. If you can provide an enlightening and entertaining experience, you will create a lasting impression with your audience.

The best way to provide a memorable show is to concentrate on a few logistics. First of all, rehearse the presentation so that you know it lasts the 20 or 30 minutes you planned for it to last. Second, make sure your visuals are extremely simple. Don't use a lot of text; use plenty of graphics and photos. Visual presentations attract people from a distance to get closer and keep those seated from being distracted by the constant activity in the surrounding area. If you are presenting software or a Web site or anything that requires a computer-looking interface, keep in mind that readability from a distance will be more difficult. It is best to concentrate on key features and benefits, rather than teaching unique details that are difficult for an easily distracted audience to grasp.

Regarding the position of your "stage," try to face out to a cross-aisle. In other words, if you anchor your presentation area to a corner of your booth, perhaps you can be seen from two different aisles at the same time. This will increase the chances of attracting people walking from two different directions. When presenting, make sure your eye contact, your voice, and your gestures reach to the back of the group and beyond to increase the chances of others stopping to listen to your story.

Some of the most distracting elements at a tradeshow are light and noise. Without a canopy or enclosed space, the light from the exhibit hall can wash out your display screen. To offset this, your visuals should have a lot of contrast between backgrounds and foregrounds. When it comes to noise, expect a lot of it. Get used to the noises immediately around your booth. Sometimes you can detect a pattern from other presentations or activities. If your timing is good, you can make your key phrases heard at the least distracting moments.

Finally, make sure you get your captured audience to do something at the end of the presentation. You must get their contact information because they represent a more qualified opportunity. After all, if the average person stays two minutes at a booth and these people sat for twenty minutes, you can safely assume they have greater interest—unless, of course, they only sat there to get a prize. In that case, you made the mistake of attracting the wrong people for the wrong reason at the wrong time. Anyway you look at it—you're wrong! My son seems to mention that to me more and more often as he gets older, hmmmm.

29

The Wrong People

I remember one of the tradeshows I coordinated back in the early 1980s. The show, Comdex, was a week long gathering of manufacturers displaying their wares to mostly resellers and some corporate end-users. We had about 20 people working our booth—our entire national sales force of 15 people and the rest from marketing and engineering. Just from sales quotas alone, I think we had over 1 million dollars of employee time value in that 40×40 booth!

The night before the show officially opened, I decided to walk around the tradeshow floor and take a look at some of the other booths. Some call this spying; I call it market research! I walked up and down several aisles and then it hit me. I was dumbfounded by what was staring me in the face. It was the booth of death to anyone even remotely involved in marketing. I could only gaze with my mouth open as I glanced at a 60×60 booth space filled with about 25 computers on pedestals. Next to each pedestal was a life-size cardboard cutout of a person in a business suit, holding a printed sign with the words "Our salespeople are out selling. Where are yours?"

It turned out that by using a booth full of computers running repeated demos of accounting software and staffed by a few marketing people who could answer most questions, that company had a cost-effective way of gathering the necessary leads from the show. You can't always do something like that, but it makes you think about the right people to staff a tradeshow.

I certainly knew who the wrong people were. I realized we made a big mistake by taking our sales force out of action. From that show on, we only brought local sales people in to support the show, locally. Any leads generated from a national perspective were sent to the salesperson responsible for the area.

I learned that to enlighten people with information at a tradeshow, you don't need your entire national sales force. You just need people who know the sound bites and people who have rehearsed their presentations.

Tradeshow interaction needs to be planned and practiced. Whether you are in a conversation or presentation, if you focus on working around the distractions at a tradeshow, you can make the time spent on your feet worthwhile. The only thing that doesn't change is that after you work your first big show, you never look forward to working another one!

TIP

> If you ever have a tradeshow in Las Vegas, be careful! In Vegas the food is cheap, the air is dry, there are no windows or clocks, and everywhere you turn there's another machine waiting to eat your paycheck. So you might end up eating, drinking, staying up late, and emptying your pockets. By the third day, you will be useless to everyone, including yourself. My advice is to wear a watch, eat a full meal before 7:30 p.m., and walk past the casinos. Go back to your room, and I guarantee that after standing on your feet all day, the minute your head hits the pillow you will be out! That is the only way to keep your energy level high for the rest of the show in a city like Vegas that offers a wealth of entertaining distractions. I'll lay you seven to one odds that I'm right!

PICTURING YOURSELF ON TV

Before your career ends, you will not be typing to people anymore. You will be seeing them, just like you see people on TV. It won't exactly be face-to-face, but it will be very close. One reason communication will have to be more visual is the fact that the baby

29

boomers are past the age of 50. As our bodies get older, the dexterity in our fingers diminishes. As a maturing society we will demand an easier way to electronically converse than using a verbal banter of email messages. This evolution is inevitable. To prepare for the new age of visual communication, you need to have a better understanding of:

- Playing to the camera
- Using videoconferencing technology
- Interacting in a visual world

PLAYING TO THE CAMERA

Maybe you're already communicating on camera for occasional teleconferences, to produce videotapes, for image magnification at large conferences, or even when speaking to the media. When on camera, you need to reinforce your message using your voice, positioning, and movement.

VOICE

When you are on camera, you have to learn to relax and breathe normally. When you talk through a lens, even though you feel rushed and think you're speaking too slowly, fight the tendency to speed up. You must learn to phrase and pause naturally. Enunciate clearly and be careful to pronounce every syllable. When you're on camera, chances are you are wearing a small lapel microphone. These microphones are sensitive devices that pick up every sound in your voice. Be aware that certain consonants may cause problems. For example, the letter P can create a popping sound, and the letter S can cause a hissing sound. The microphone will pick up a lot of distracting sounds. Avoid mumbling, sniffing, clearing your throat, or using fillers (such as um, er…). Just be sure to keep your all your comments directed at the camera. If you make minor mistakes, keep going. Don't add unnecessary information by apologizing or by whispering some short, frustrated phrase insulting yourself for not being perfect.

POSITIONING

Positioning yourself to the camera and your audience has as much to do with your physical presence as it does with your personal image. You just have to be yourself. Even though you are under the scrutiny of the camera, you should feel comfortable and act appropriately in everything you say and do. It's easy to forget this when you are alone in front of the lens without a live audience watching you. You need to present yourself as credible and confident.

Given the choice, standing is preferred to sitting because it is easier to breathe when standing. In addition, being on your feet tends to keep your more alert. Sitting may be necessary for longer sessions. Keep in mind that when the camera projects your image, any movements you make look much more pronounced to the viewer. So, when seated, choose a solid chair that doesn't swivel. If you wear a jacket, sit on the back hem and you'll actually sit up straighter. This also keeps your coat from bunching up in front. If you tilt your head slightly downward or slightly to one side every now and then, you will appear more relaxed.

Naturally, in well-planned environments, someone will play the role of stage manager or production director and make sure the set looks "just right." But you need to be prepared for the local communication that becomes visual. You will play the role of producer, director, and actor—in much the same way that you play the role of publisher, editor, and author when you create your own email messages. Before the cameras start "rolling," check directly behind you. Pay attention to your backdrop. Is a disorganized bookshelf or a leftover lunch plate the image you want to portray? Assume the camera is always running and don't show or say anything that distracts from your message. Don't be distracted by items or other people in the room; you'll appear detached and uncertain.

MOVEMENT

Remember that we've been talking about the triangle since Chapter 26. The basic choreography used for stand-up presentations, whether in large or small settings, applies to working on camera—the smallest setting of all. The real difference between the environments is the proximity of the audience. In live situations you tend to be farther from the audience when you speak, and your movements need to be bigger to be seen from a greater distance. Through the camera, especially when the image is a close-up, the triangle is magnified for the viewer, and the movements need to be much smaller. You establish the triangle positions with a slight tilt of the head rather than full body movement. Take the basics of body movement and translate them to the sensitivity of the camera.

The three positions of the triangle are still used. You can establish intimacy with the audience by tilting your head forward. Technically, you are in the front of the triangle. You can create neutrality by not tilting your head at all, and you will be in the center of the triangle. You can tilt your head back to reach the back of the triangle and appear to present the larger view of the topic. On camera, the simple tilting of your head creates movement, inflection, meaning, and interest. Former U.S. President Ronald Reagan was a master at using subtle head movement to communicate his views. He was a film actor before he was a politician. He knew how to take advantage of the camera.

You can also make adjustments in the angle of your body. Position your shoulders at a 45-degree angle to the camera to establish a "rest" position. By doing this, you can, when necessary, shift the upper part of your body and "square off" to the camera to evoke power and emphasis.

One of the other issues unique to the camera is the degree to which you exist in the frame. In a live event, your view of the presenter is a function of where you sit. Obviously the camera has the ability to zoom in or pull back to create a completely different view for the audience. That is why you need to know how close the camera is set at any particular moment. If you know your "frame" of reference, you can decide what movements, if any, are available to you. Depending on the camera setting, you may have to limit your expressions and gestures.

You'll have to learn to concentrate on both your topic and your movements. If you accidentally move out of the frame, those watching won't be able to see you. If you're operating the camera yourself, you will make the choice to change the zoom level or the camera angle. In many videoconferencing sessions, either you or someone sitting with you in the conference usually controls the camera. If someone else is controlling the camera, you should talk with that person in advance and discuss any movements you expect in which the camera will have to be adjusted. In fact, if your presentation hits a particularly emotional point, you may want to cue the camera to move to a close-up.

Now, unless the event is highly choreographed, chances are the camera will stay in a relatively fixed position and capture you from the waist up. In a videoconference, the technology can usually be preset to certain angles, and many systems are voice activated so that the camera automatically shifts to the person speaking. As technology evolves toward more sophistication, you will be less concerned about the technical aspects of the visual communication. But for now, the camera angles and close-ups are controlled decisions. The timing of those decisions influences the viewer because the camera lens is the link between the presenter and the audience.

USING VIDEOCONFERENCING TECHNOLOGY

Technology is driving communication. The power of telecommunication and personal computers will soon have us all videoconferencing with the same ease and confidence that we currently use to pick up the phone. Okay, maybe not that easy, but video as the vehicle will be more the norm than the exception.

The current evolution in visual communication is toward videoconferencing, whether it is personal or group. When the videoconference is personal, it is conducted from your desktop. When a group delivers the session, it takes place in a larger setting like a conference room. In either case, this technology is ever changing. From the moment I write this to the time you read it, there will have been several changes to the systems available and already in use. Such is the nature of our fast-paced world. I don't want to talk a lot about features or limitations; instead, I want to cover the challenges posed by the nature of the technology itself.

NOTE

> *Personal Videoconferencing*, by Evan Rosen, is an excellent reference on this topic. Although personal videoconferencing refers to the individual desktop, many of the same issues apply to group videoconferencing, as well.

I think the best way to explain videoconferencing is to think of it as combining the power of television with the intimacy of face-to-face communication while bridging the gaps of distance, time, and relationships. How's that for a mouthful? It's important to understand the challenges of distance and time, especially to a growing world of visual creatures.

THE DISTANCE FACTOR

Face-to-face meetings require your physical presence. Although a lot can be accomplished through email and voice, the ability to be in the presence of another person is the highest form of communication. Sometimes you have to travel to create a face-to-face meeting. When you think about attending meetings that require travel, distance influences your plans. For example, if you work in San Francisco and need to attend a meeting in Atlanta, you already know that much of your time will be spent travelling to and from the meeting. Typically, you'll try to arrange other appointments to help "justify" the trip, the expense, and the inconvenience of being away from the office for so long. However, if the meeting were on site you would not create additional activity with nearby departments just because you happen to be going all the way to the other side of the building. But when travel distance is involved, the need to get other things accomplished while in the area becomes a priority.

So, as you plan your trip to Atlanta, you call two other contacts in the Atlanta vicinity, and you request a brief meeting because you plan "to be in the area." The others may agree to meet with you but more likely out of courtesy rather than real need. After all, they didn't call you, and they may not be as ready as you are to discuss things or make decisions. Some meetings are called because distance dictates the availability of one or more of the parties involved.

Videoconferencing tries to bridge the gap of distance while offering some of the benefits of face-to-face. It may be easier to coordinate mutually convenient schedules for a videoconference meeting if all parties need only travel a short walking distance to the visual meeting. You may be able to offer the other people two or three optional times, rather than let the airlines dictate the time and place for the event.

THE TIME FACTOR

Although convenience of scheduling is time related, the real factor here is length of time for a meeting. Today, most meetings that take place in company conference rooms are based around the convenience of the clock. Typically, conference room charts are filled with one-hour meetings, even though these meetings may not really need to be one hour. But, it is not feasible to schedule a 23-minute meeting and then another 18-minute meeting and so on.

But our other forms of communication are much more to the minute, especially when you think of phone conversations. Even a telephone conference call among distant parties offers a start time, but rarely a stop time other than an approximation. Why? Because the parties involved are private phones, separated from one another. If some of the people on the call were occupying a conference room to place the call, then the time for the call may be more limited to make the conference room available for others.

Today, videoconferencing equipment is not on everyone's desk as is a telephone or a personal computer. So the availability of the technology from a time factor is still limited by appointment. However, when the technology is on each desktop, the length of meetings will be determined by the objectives of the conversation, not the availability of space.

29

Current videoconferencing technology has a higher cost of connect time than a simple voice phone call. From an expense standpoint, companies need to limit the length of each call. This has a benefit because when you pay "by the minute," you will likely make more prudent use of the time during a videoconference session than you might in a typical face-to-face meeting in the conference room.

THE RELATIONSHIP FACTOR

Many projects involve assembling a team of experts from within an organization or even across organizations. Too often, people in different departments, in different companies, and even in different cities don't have the time or resources to meet face-to-face and yet, they somehow are required to complete a task as a team. When face-to-face meetings are not possible, it is more difficult to get a group of diverse personalities to perform as a team.

A lot of our time during business communication is spent imagining what the people we haven't met really look like. Every moment we interact without seeing a person, we are communicating with the mental image of the person, which we create. This is a natural process. The beauty of face-to-face communication is the chance to meet and greet others. This is how relationships are formed. Relationships are a huge part of the team concept.

Videoconferencing gives separated parties the chance to see and hear others who may be brought together for only a short time to accomplish a task. Although everyone can't shake hands, at least they can remove the task of imagining what the other people look like because they can see and interact through the technology of videoconferencing.

THE POWER OF TELEVISION

Television. Chances are that you grew up on it. How much money would you have if you were paid $5 dollars for each hour of TV you watched in your life? Even if you averaged 40 hours a week, and you've been watching TV for 20 years, you would have amassed more than $200,000 by now—and that's assuming you never put the money in any investment plan!

Regardless of how much TV you really do watch, the point is that no one can deny the influence of TV over the generations of the past 25 years. Figure 29.13 summarizes the most obvious features of television that keep us glued endlessly to a variety of channels sometimes offering little content.

Television is a highly produced, action-driven medium. You thrive on visual images, and you have become highly critical of those writing, producing, and performing for television. Although you are comfortable with the media as you watch the screen or talk into the lens of a home video camera, you have much higher expectations of those performing professionally on TV. It doesn't take a great stretch of the imagination to wonder what your expectations will be of those who communicate using videoconferencing technology. Maybe you won't expect TV personalities, but you might expect talent to be something better than what you have recorded on your home video camera!

Figure 29.13
The major features of television are what really keep us entertained. Without these instantly available attributes, TV would not be as powerful a presence in our everyday lives.

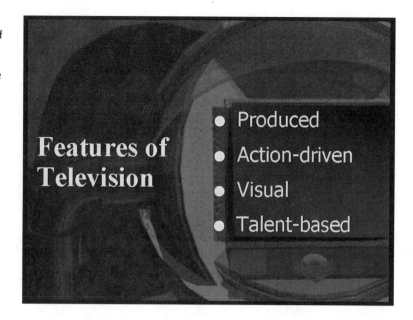

29

From a business perspective, the power of television is used most often as a "store and forward" medium, rather than a real-time one. You may have been asked to view tapes in the workplace for training, informational, or motivational reasons. This is more private and mostly one-sided—you are receiving information but not interacting. The good news is that these video productions are usually done well. They are produced using professional talent, and they are highly visual. You don't read a lot when experiencing video. We are content to use the medium of TV to serve our purposes both in business and at home. Until television is two-way and more interactive, it will continue to serve a much more passive and entertaining role in our daily life.

THE BEAUTY OF FACE-TO-FACE

Television has its place in business, similar to home, but it can't compete when a situation requires a face-to-face encounter.

Figure 29.14 summarizes the aspects of face-to-face communication. The ability to engage in real-time conversation in the same room with another person is clearly important to all of us. But the whole interpersonal experience is a very natural one when it comes to using your five senses. Just the handshake as a greeting tells you so much about another person. A casual stroll past a freshly brewing pot of coffee can change the perspective of almost any conversation.

Figure 29.14
The attributes of face-to-face communication support the need for personal contact. With its real-time intimacy and natural interaction, the face-to-face meeting is the essence of interpersonal communication.

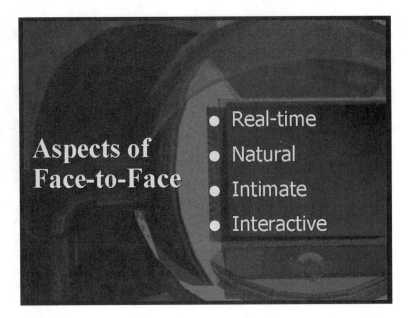

A heightened level of intimacy or closeness exists when people share face-to-face communication. The fact that people share the same moments at the same location allows them to cement a memory beyond what any other form of communication can offer. It's that closeness, that friendship, which helps develop business relationships over the course of time. Even the degree to which you can be truly interactive in a meeting makes you want to use the face-to-face process wherever and whenever you can. After all, you can tell right away if you need to change direction in a discussion or bring up additional data to support your point. In many cases you know these things by simply being in the same space as the other person.

THE IDEAL COMMUNICATION CHANNEL

If any medium could harness the best of both television and face-to-face communication, it would be the ideal communication channel. Figure 29.15 shows the elements of the ultimate medium, if it really existed. Even at this stage in the development of this technology, videoconferencing possesses many of these attributes and comes close to being the ideal communication channel.

When you think about it, videoconferencing is definitely action-driven and highly visual. Videoconferencing happens in real-time, give or take a second for transmission of the signal. In addition, it's intimate and interactive.

But of the eight elements of the ideal medium, videoconferencing falls short in some areas. Figure 29.16 shows where the technology misses, specifically in the areas of production, talent and naturalness.

Figure 29.15
By combining the features of television and the aspects of face-to-face, you can create the ideal communication channel.

Figure 29.16
Although it certainly offers a lot, video-conferencing currently falls short of meeting all the requirements of the ideal communication channel. Yet there are ways to work on some of the deficiencies.

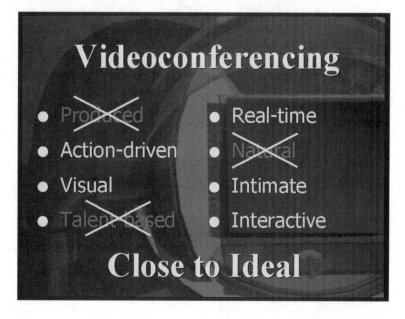

As far as being produced and talent-based, videoconferencing requires specific skills to make the event and the participants more effective. Acquiring these skills will put you on the fast track for decision making, problem solving, and getting noticed. You can't escape the eventual need to become a video communicator and screen-to-screen collaborator.

N O T E

Evan Rosen, author of *Personal Videoconferencing*, uses the term collabicator to identify those "collaborators who use video as well as application sharing and document conferencing." In the near future, we will all be called upon to "collabicate" at one time or another.

As far as the technology allowing completely natural interaction, just like face-to-face—well, let's just say that kind of virtual reality is getting closer but it is far from here. So let's take a look at what you can do to make videoconferencing look more produced and more talented than it is now.

THE PRODUCTION ASPECT

The only way to make videoconferencing more like TV is to produce a simple production. Videoconferencing allows you to incorporate a few of television's powerful elements. The effectiveness of TV stems from its capability to tap emotions. The medium leaves little to the imagination as images, graphics, voices, and music provide every detail of the stories it tells. You can enhance the visual effectiveness of videoconferencing through your setting, screenplay, and special effects.

One thing you can do is control the setting by enhancing the layout of the room where you conduct your conferences. Whether you are using personal or group videoconferencing, pay attention to the positioning of the equipment in relationship to the seating and doorways. In a group setup, the camera and codec (coding/decoding or compressing/decompressing) unit usually sit on top of the monitor to allow for the most meaningful eye-contact between the sites. Make sure the distance between the equipment and seats allows for a complete group shot, as well as appropriate close-up views of the individuals. The system's microphone should be equidistant from all participants and, if possible, positioned on a separate table to eliminate noises from shuffling and vibrations. Doorways should allow for people to enter and exit the room with minimal distraction in front of the camera.

Backdrops allow you to manipulate the audience's perception of you and your environment. The backdrops you see on television are chosen to provide details in the story being told. They are used to create an effect. This approach may be overkill for the business world, but remember that your image is everything and understanding the power of the visual image can give you an edge. For best results, choose a backdrop (or wall paint) that is about 17% gray. This ensures a flattering and smoothly transmitted backdrop.

The typical conference room is lit with fluorescent and incandescent lights. These are unflattering and provide little control. If you are creating a videoconferencing room, rely on professionals to design a lighting system that highlights each seat with quality lighting. If you will be conducting a lot of videoconferencing from your office, pay attention to how your face is lit and consider aiming one or two spotlights at your chair.

When choosing the clothes you'll wear on camera, you need to consider both technical and personal image issues. From a technical standpoint, avoid white because it washes out the

29

picture and reflects harshly to the viewers on the other side of the video transmission (also known as the "far side"). Also avoid narrow stripes and houndstooth prints because they tend to "vibrate" on the screen. Large prints and plaids also tend to distract from the communication because there are more colors and patterns that need to be transmitted through the system. Your best choice is solid blue or gray, but make sure you don't become camouflaged by your background. These colors evoke credibility and authority. Lavender and yellow are also good choices, but be careful with light pink because it tends to transmit as white and it becomes too bright from the far side view.

Another way to make a videoconference appear more "produced" is to write a screenplay. Like meetings, effective videoconferences require a bit of advance planning and a shared set of assumptions as to who does what and what rules are followed. Remember, the more the videoconference is structured around some type of plan, the better it will be for everyone.

An agenda is crucial and should be shared in advance with both parties so that the participants can be prepared for the discussion and tasks at hand. The agenda should note any visual presentations and video that may be used and which site will be responsible for the delivery. In addition, make sure that both sites are equipped and prepared to use the videoconference technology. You don't want to waste valuable meeting time teaching people how to work with the equipment.

Decide who will be facilitating or leading the meeting and who at your site will be taking responsibility for the equipment and any media used. If you divide these responsibilities in advance, the meeting will run more smoothly, and if any troubleshooting is necessary, it can be addressed quickly. With the latest advancements in videoconferencing equipment, one person can easily manage to lead the discussion while controlling the technology through a simple remote, with a few touches of a button!

Before you begin, make sure the first-time users understand that there might be a slight delay in the audio transmission. Naturally, as the bandwidth increases, the transmission of audio and video signals will be closer to the broadcast levels we get with TV. For now, the equipment may have some limitations. Just let everyone know that their brains will adjust quickly to any sound delays and that, after a while, they will learn to pick up the cues of a video conversation. At the start, introduce everyone at each site. If someone has to leave in the middle of the conference and the camera doesn't make their departure apparent to the far side, be sure to let them know that someone left the room. In a face-to-face meeting this would not be necessary, but in a videoconference the only view you have to the other side is through the eye of the camera.

The fact that you have control of the camera can add value to the production aspect of the event. Your equipment probably allows for the camera to pan and zoom, giving you a unique ability to change the perspective on the meeting. With a little practice (or a system that can program preset camera positions) you can bring the camera in close when you want to make a strong point or pan the room for individual reactions.

In fact, some systems allow you to control the camera in your room as well as that at the far side. You can pan around the room on the far side, zoom in on individuals as they speak, and pull back to view a group reaction. Just be aware that a picture-in-picture function on the far side may allow them to see what you're seeing!

Your system may also allow you to incorporate an electronic presentation, videotape, or dataconferencing into your remote meeting. You can even audioconference outgoing and incoming phone calls if you need to access the expertise of a colleague. If you choose to use these media, be sure that you rehearse the order and switching to ensure that you can move smoothly between the different devices. The power of these tools can be diminished when you begin fumbling with the technology. No matter how simple the equipment is to operate, take the time for a technical run-through.

Finally, keep in mind that a videoconference can also be videotaped for archival or review purposes. All it takes is a VCR connected to the videoconferencing system. Although the replay will only be the action from the far side, the audio will be two sided, similar to what it may have looked like had you attended the meeting. The only thing you won't see is any interaction that may have happened in the room on your side of the conference. Keep in mind that if your interactive sessions are archived, there will be compelling visual evidence available in case you change or need to defend your position on a particular topic. This is true of email and voice mail messages, but a videotape is much more impressive. Of course, a videotape recording can be blessing or a curse, depending on the nature of the content.

Those are just some of the things you can consider if you want a videoconference to appear more like a TV production. This is not much different than the effort it takes to make an average presentation look extremely professional. The more you become aware of what to work on, the easier it becomes to accomplish the task.

BOOSTING YOUR TALENT

It goes without saying that a talent-based medium requires talent. The people embracing videoconferencing are developing a unique set of skills that is setting them apart as communicators. The skill set goes beyond the ability to write well and speak comfortably in public. This technology is quick, interactive, and intimate. It requires that you constantly assess what your saying, how you are saying it, and what you look like all the while.

Earlier in this chapter we talked about playing to the camera, and a videoconference is a prime example of a situation in which your voice, positioning, and movement are most noticeable. Some other unique issues related to videoconferencing also come into play.

From a vocal standpoint, avoid the rudeness of side conversations. People may see you whispering but may not hear your comments. However, in negotiations, asides can be your ally. Many videoconferencing systems have a "mute button" on the microphone that allows you to pause the audio transmission temporarily. If you first get an agreement that both parties will be using this function to discuss items among themselves, negotiations can proceed more quickly. Just be aware that the video may still be running, allowing the other party to read your expressions and body language.

As I mentioned before, when you are using a system that has a slight audio delay, it's important to wait until an individual has completely finished a sentence before replying. Because in normal conversation, we tend to interrupt each other a lot, many experts believe that the patience required by videoconferencing users may finally teach us to wait for the other person to finish. This more "formal" timing will actually put us in line with the communication styles of our European and Asian partners and could lead to more effective communication overall. Of course, after all systems are up to real-time broadcast quality speed (like telephones), there won't be any audio delays. Then we'll go back to stepping on each other's sentences again. Some things just never change!

From a physical delivery perspective, facial expressions are critical to the communication process. By reading the faces of the other party, you may be able to tell if they are confused or supportive, eager or bored, trustworthy or lying. Likewise, your face will communicate information about how you are thinking and feeling. Remember that even though you may not be the person speaking, you are still on camera and, therefore, are still communicating. Try to manage the messages you are sending through body language, and you will be much more effective.

NOTE

> *How to Read a Person Like a Book*, by Gerald Nierenberg and Henry Calero (Pocket Books), offers some interesting insights into the role body language plays in interpersonal communication. Understanding nonverbal cues can be extremely useful in any small group environment, including a videoconference.

Eye contact is still a dilemma in videoconferencing. You can't make direct eye contact with the camera and the person on the screen simultaneously, unless you are sitting back far enough from the camera lens that you appear to be looking directly back at someone. Figures 29.17 and 29.18 demonstrate this line of sight issue. As I was typing this I decided to take some quick photos of myself with my small digital camera attached to my PC. Imagine you are looking at me during a videoconference. Figure 29.17 shows how I appear to you when I look directly into the camera lens. Notice I am looking right at you. But, if I wanted to look at your image on my end of the conference and my viewing screen is set much lower than the position of the camera, then Figure 29.18 shows how I appear to you. The only reason you notice this is because I am so close to the camera. I would have to sit farther back from the camera to give you the appearance of direct eye contact as I look at your image on my screen.

That is why most videoconference systems use a 27-inch or 32-inch TV screen with the camera mounted on top of the set and the participants seated about 10 to 12 feet away. From that distance you really can't tell that the person you're looking at is really looking slightly below their camera lens at your image on their screen. Of course, if the camera could be mounted into the middle of the TV screen then you would always appear to be looking into the lens regardless of how close you were to the screen.

Figure 29.17
If you were watching me over a videoconference and I looked straight into the camera lens mounted on top of my viewing screen, it would appear as if I am looking directly at you.

Figure 29.18
So it doesn't seem that I'm looking down all the time, I need to be sitting farther from the camera to make the eye contact appear more direct.

If you were on TV, you would always be looking directly into the camera lens because it's still a one-way communication tool. This line-of-sight problem between where the camera is mounted and where the display screen is situated is most apparent in personal videoconferencing and close-up views. Until the technology is perfected (and many solutions are being researched), you must learn to look into the camera when speaking or adjust to any differences.

Look at Me When I Talk to You!

When you watch television, there is no reciprocal eye contact. The transmission of the signal is one-way. As the viewer, you are are not sending your image back to the person in the studio, so that person only has to look into the camera lens and know that eye contact is being made with you watching from home.

Unlike television, group and desktop videoconferencing systems, today, face the challenge of absolute direct eye contact. Videoconferencing is interactive, and the two-way communication means eye contact is important on both ends of the transmission. Because the lens is outside the viewing area of the screen, maintaining absolute eye-to-eye contact is impossible. To reduce this distraction, experts suggest reducing the angle by which the eyes are averted from the lens. Adjusting the distance people sit from the screen (TV or monitor) and/or using a smaller screen size can help with direct eye contact issues.

As the screen size gets larger, you must increase the distance participants sit from the screen. The goal is to have the angle between the camera lens and the person's foveal point (the spot focused on with the eyes) to be 10 degrees or less. 10 degrees—you'll need to use your handy protracter! Oh, you don't carry a protracter? Neither do I. Okay, so here's a suggestion. Mount the camera on top of the monitor and center it. Then, make sure the monitor is at a height such that when you're sitting you're looking straight into the top third of the monitor. This reduces the angle that those on the other end (looking at you) have between your image and their camera lens.

To minimize the angle between your camera and the image of those you are looking at on your monitor, frame the shot of the other people so there is only a small amount of "unused space" above their heads. This way, your eyes have to drop down only a short distance when you look at them on your monitor, and it appears you are looking more directly into the camera lens.

Of course, the simplest way to know if your eye contact is a distraction is to ask those on the other end if it seems like you are looking directly at them or somewhat downward. If you appear to be looking down, from their perspective, then sit farther back from the monitor to reduce the distraction.

If you plan to move around at all, one way to stay within the frame of the camera is to test the camera positions in advance and plan your movement. If your videoconferencing equipment allows you to preset camera positions, you'll also be able to change from a wide shot to a close-up with the touch of a button.

Of course, real talent develops with experience. The more you use videoconferencing, the less your viewers notice the technology, and the more comfortable and natural you'll feel. Be an early-adapter and as the technology becomes more common, you can share your expertise to introduce others to the power of the media. In the beginning, it may feel like the technology is controlling you, but eventually you will use videoconferencing with the ease that you currently use your computer, fax machine, and phone.

NOT QUITE NATURAL

Although videoconferencing falls short of being the ideal communication channel, the efforts on your part concerning production and talent can bring the technology much closer to the ideal. Figure 29.19 lists all the components of videoconferencing that can be achieved, with some degree of effort—with the exception of one element: naturalness.

29

Figure 29.19
With effort you can bring video-conferencing to nearly match the elements of the ideal communication channel, with the exception of the one element circled here. As close as it might get to being a relationship medium, videoconferencing still can't attain the total natural qualities of face-to-face contact.

Current videoconferencing cannot duplicate the natural aspects of face-to-face communication. You still can't fill the coffee cups of the person at the far side. You can't smell colognes or shake hands. You can't see the subtle expression in their eyes or hear the faint pronunciation of their words. You can't casually notice the small actions of the group unless the camera picks it up for you. You can't do these things because you aren't there, on site. This limitation of videoconferencing may never be overcome.

But technology advances as we speak and perhaps, over the course of time, virtual reality will allow for seamless workplaces that simulate very real and natural interactions among people. Regardless, it is more likely that we will sacrifice the five senses for the sake of just two or three, rather than not use videoconferencing as the new age communication medium.

INTERACTING IN A VISUAL WORLD

I really think the shift to a more visual society is already upon us. Look around—the evidence is everywhere, from the workplace to the home. We have met the visual creatures, and they are us! This new millenium can be dubbed the Visual Age, and its effect will be massive.

NOTE

There has been much research about the relationship between people and media. A superb source is *The Media Equation*, by Byron Reeves and Clifford Nass (Cambridge University Press). The book is about how people treat computers, television, and new media as real people. The studies done by the authors suggest that the design of media technologies, including computer devices, applications and Web sites, be considered from a social perspective. I highly recommend this book.

The Visual Age will bring us closer together as a global society because we will be able to see one another on a more frequent basis. Realizing that, here are my forecasts for the new millennium regarding the effect a visual way of life will have on individuals and society.

THE EFFECT ON INDIVIDUALS

Let's look at age groups. Anyone under 10 probably already has the words "visual creature" stamped on the inside of their head. That age group will not have any problem adapting to an interactive and visual world. When they finally begin working for a living, I expect them to one day walk through a flea market, pick up a computer mouse, and ponder what its use might have been!

Those between 10 and 20 years old are still well developed visual creatures. When they finally embark on their journey into the business world, using visual communications will be as simple as touching a keyboard. People between 20 and 30 will be on the cusp of the changing technology. The good news is that this age group already knows that to adapt is to succeed and being in their high-spirited 20s, this crowd will lead the way to a host of major technology changes in the workplace.

Okay, now lets discuss the problem groups. Those between 30 and 40 will accept the new world of visual communications, but will resist direct participation mostly for vanity reasons. After all, knowing the camera adds ten pounds will not appeal to the Generation Xers at all. These are the people that cut their teeth on Internet chat rooms where remaining anonymous was the standard level of interaction. It is unlikely to believe this group will welcome a visual conversation while sitting around in a bathrobe eating a Pop Tart.

People between 40 and 50, the tail end of the baby boomers, will mostly resist all forms of visual communication, some for vanity reasons and others because they will be fed up with the years of email and voice mail inundation. People in this age group are already growing tired of being accessible through every other form of communication and will see the visual process as a real intrusion into the only remaining personal space in their lives. Little do they know that by adapting to a more visual world, this age group holds the life experience and maturity to lead the up and coming companies of the future. Expect only those who adapt to the new technology to come out ahead and the rest to lag behind or fall by the wayside.

Age Before Beauty?
Believe it or not, those over 50, the original baby boomers, will adapt to the world of visual communications because their biggest priority will involve nurturing. That's right. After 50 you begin to think about winding down your career, even though you may still work another 20 years. The point is that when you start thinking about retirement you wonder who will take care of you when you get older. It's not all you think about, but it certainly becomes an issue. Therefore, when a huge segment of the population ages toward retirement, long-term care becomes a priority. Women hold an advantage because they have played the role of both nurturers and decision-makers in our society. Over the past 25 years, women have proven they can handle nearly every pressure situation, whether at home or in business.

29

For these reasons, expect women to gain a much stronger hold on key business leadership positions in the future. Why? Because the "nurturer" will place more emphasis on the needs of the aging population, and the "decision-maker" will appeal to the financial goals of the same group—which, by the way, will control the vast amount of the wealth in the nation.

Invariably, the over 50 age group will welcome visual communication with open arms because, as people age, they are more honest about adopting new habits that reduce stress on the body. Visual interaction will allow for less travel and less wear and tear on the body. Remember that these people grew up on face-to-face communications, and the visual technology will help simulate that experience more than a phone conversation or an email ever could. The good news is they won't have to travel to make the face-to-face interaction happen.

So there you have it! The very young and the very old adapt, and the middle groups have some big decisions to make. I believe that anyone between 30 and 50 years old will truly have no choice but to adapt to the most current visual technology. If not, they will find themselves unable to adjust to the younger crowd sneaking up from behind and the older crowd looking back for support.

This doesn't mean people will lose their jobs, but it does mean that by avoiding the changes in the workplace, some people will experience limited advancement. It's hard to see just how rapidly things advance, but here's an interesting piece of information. Current high school graduates have virtually no frame of reference to a TV set without a remote control. Some of us still remember getting up to change the channel! The technology changes as you sleep! I'm 46, so I happen to be one of those who already realizes the world of visual communication is inevitable, and I have been embracing the concept for several years. I expect to be changing as rapidly as the technology—and only for my own sake!

THE EFFECT ON SOCIETY

You also have to look at the social benefits of a more visual world. You will be seeing people of different cultures and backgrounds more visually and more frequently than ever before. There will be a greater acceptance of diverse audiences. You can expect a more visual world to be one that welcomes our visual differences.

I really think that when you see another person, any fears, inhibitions, prejudices, concerns, ignorance, or other negative feelings can disappear faster. It's when we can't experience the whole person that we sometimes create false impressions. I was lucky enough to grow up in New York City where interaction among many cultures was the norm. No matter what the prejudices, you still had to interact with different people on a daily basis. When you ride the bus and subway with different people every single day, you just learn to get along. You don't have much choice. I'm not saying we lived in perfect harmony, but to this day I find it easy to accept people whose lifestyles and backgrounds are much different than my own. If I can't, then it's my problem, not theirs.

A world of visual communicators will offer more direct contact with more people, more frequently, resulting in a greater acceptance of diverse opinions. The good news is that a more visual world will be better for our children. After all, kids aren't born with a natural fear or dislike of others. They can only learn it. A visual world will provide more evidence as to why those who look or think differently have so much in common. Okay, so you can tell I grew up in the sixties. The point is that, the more we see one another, the more we understand one another. Visual interaction will bring us closer together, globally.

The growth of visual communications will place you in view, mainly through the eyes of a camera. The more you adapt to the changing technology, the better the chances of your success. But keep in mind that to prepare for the visual changes ahead, you will have to develop your current skills and become a more visual presenter. Everything we discussed in the earlier chapters—from messaging to media to mechanics—consistently follows the path of a visual presenter. After you add-in the latest technology, you'll be able to demonstrate your skills to the world.

So, what are you waiting for? Get used to picturing yourself on TV and before you know it you'll be staring straight into the camera lens saying, "I'm ready for my close-up, Mr. DeMille!"

TROUBLESHOOTING

Regardless of the setting, are there any general recommendations that you have for covering all the bases when preparing presentations?

Maybe the best way to approach this is to provide a presenter's checklist. These are some of the more important questions you might ask yourself when preparing for a presentation. Of course, not every question applies to every situation, but this is a pretty good list to check.

Presenter's Checklist:

- What is the topic of the presentation?
- How long is the presentation?
- What is the format? Lecture? Panel? Q&A?
- Do you need an outline of the presentation in advance of the event?
- What is the objective of the meeting? Call to action?
- When is the meeting scheduled? Date? Time?
- Where will the meeting be held? Directions?
- Is the event sponsored by an individual or an organization? Do they need to be recognized?
- Who will be attending?
- What is the anticipated size of the audience?
- What is the average age of the audience? Gender ratio?
- What cultural issues (language, customs, humor) exist?

- What is arranged for staging and A/V?
- Is the proper media (overhead, slide, or LCD projector) available?
- Is a microphone necessary and available?
- When are rehearsals and A/V checks scheduled?
- Will the meeting be video- or audiotaped?
- Is a speaker's lounge or "ready room" available?
- Will any other speakers be sharing the platform? Names? Topics?
- Who will be making introductions?
- What are the arrangements for housing and travel?
- What are the arrangements for hotel check out and return travel?
- Are any additional events planned on-site? Dress code?
- Can arrangements be made to sell/distribute support materials on-site?
- Will evaluation forms be used, and will results be available?

If you present outdoors and you still want to do a PowerPoint presentation, how do you cope with the elements of nature?

Sometimes presenting outdoors can involve the use of a screen and visual support. Assuming it's not inclement weather, lighting and sound become the major issues. Ambient (natural) light as well as background noises are controlled by nature when you present outdoors, so you have to cope with what nature provides you at the moment. I have found that most outdoor presentations that use visual support are linked to a greater outdoor activity or event. The presentation itself is the not the main component of the day.

I remember designing a presentation for the president of a company to deliver at the company picnic. It was a short presentation supported by a few visuals. The visual content was really required to help the president of the company remember everything. But let's not go there!

The presentation took place inside a big tent and all the sides of the tent were open, so there was a lot of light spilling into the space. With a lot of light hitting the screen, any dark color backgrounds tended to wash out and the related foreground elements were hard to see. The only way to create contrast was to reverse the normal design of the visuals. I had to consider light-color backgrounds and dark foreground elements. In fact, because the sun was shining so brightly, pure black and white ended up being my only choice for best readability from distance.

Another issue I had to deal with was sound. Because the sides of the tent were open, there were no walls for sound to bounce off. The microphone setup was adequate for the size of the space, but a number of background noises were drowning out the sound as I tested the microphone. It was breezy that day, and the wind was causing the hanging edges of the canvas tent to flap. Outside the tent, there were lots of kids running around, playing games and making noise, as you would expect at a picnic.

Before the presentation started, I suggested to the president of the company to invite some of the people standing at the back to move up along the sides. This created a "wall" of people in a sort of semi-circle around those seated. The "people-wall" helped localize the sound by keeping it inside the tent. In addition, those standing reduced the amount of ambient light giving the visuals higher contrast. The semi-circle of people also cut down on the wind and the noises from outside the tent.

All in all, the outdoor presentation was easier to see and hear after coping with the elements of nature that seemed like huge obstacles from the beginning.

What's on the WOPR CD

This book includes a fully licensed copy of Woody's Office POWER Pack 2003, the legendary collection of Office add-ins that will help you work faster, smarter, and more productively. This latest version of WOPR includes updates of your favorite features from previous versions, plus a handful of indispensable new tools that you'll use every day.

The copy of WOPR 2003on the CD is fully licensed at no additional cost to you. This isn't shareware, freeware, trialware, demoware, or limited in any other way. Previous versions of WOPR cost more than the price of this book, and now you are getting WOPR and this book for less than the cost of the software.

As with any other software, however, WOPR 2003 has a license agreement. Be sure to read and agree to the agreement before using the software.

What Is WOPR?

For more than a decade, WOPR (pronounced "whopper") has led the way with incredibly useful extensions to Office—in fact, many of the features you see in Office today originated as WOPR utilities. If you rely on Office, you should be using WOPR, the one truly indispensable addition to your Office bag of tricks.

WOPR 2003 brings dozens of new capabilities to Office 2003:

WOPR Commander

In order to reduce the user interface clutter normally associated with having such a large and complex add-on package such as WOPR installed into Microsoft Word, we've created the WOPR Commander. The WOPR Commander removes all of WOPR's user interface elements out of Microsoft Word's menus, toolbars, and so on and places them on one convenient pop-up menu that is accessed via clicking the WOPR Commander icon in the Microsoft Windows Taskbar's system tray area (that is, the tray notification area located by your system clock).

Each time Microsoft Word is started, the WOPR Commander's icon is automatically placed into your system tray. To access any of the WOPR utilities, simply right or left mouse-click on the WOPR Commander's icon (or use the Ctrl+Alt+W hot key), and a pop-up menu will appear allowing you to control all aspects of the WOPR program (such as displaying the WOPR Tools or Lil' WOPR Tools toolbars, adding or removing the various WOPR components, running each of the WOPR utilities, and so on).

ENVELOPER

Replace that wimpy Word envelope printer with an industrial-strength, one-click wonder. Enveloper works in Excel, Access, and Outlook, too.

Print logos, graphics, notes, and bar codes on your envelopes. Maintain multiple customized envelopes. Each envelope can be customized for a different situation: envelope size, return address, note, logo, fonts, and so on.

Enveloper lets you create custom envelopes and call them up when you need them. You can position the return address, addressee, bar code—even a logo or a note line—with a simple click and drag. One more click sets the font, and the whole process unfolds right before your eyes, so you can see how your envelopes will look before you print them. Most of all, Enveloper fits right into Office. There's no need to shell out to another program, or futz around with copying and pasting—Enveloper "grabs" addresses from your documents, worksheets, or Outlook Contacts and churns out gorgeous envelopes in no time at all. You can pull addresses from Outlook or the address book of your choice, and even look up ZIP+4 codes on the U.S. Postal Service Web site, with a couple of clicks. Whether you print one envelope at a time, churn out thousands of envelopes for mass mailings, or just run the occasional holiday card mail merge, Enveloper helps every step of the way.

WORKBAR

WorkBar gives you a one-click listing of your key working documents right on Word's menu bar (or on a toolbar—it's your choice), automatically sorts the document list as you add documents, supports a variety of file formats (it will launch a file's parent application for you automatically so that you're not limited to only Word documents on your WorkBar), and gives you control over how the document is opened in Word.

FILENEW POP-UP

This feature displays a list of useful commands that help you create new documents and interact with those documents' parent templates. It can

- Display the fully qualified filename of the current document's parent template and allow you to open it with just a click.
- Create new documents or templates based on the current document, the current document's template, Word's global template (Normal.dot), or any existing user or workgroup template.
- Quickly find and open any user or workgroup template.

FLOPPYCOPY

Working with documents on removable media (such as a floppy or Zip disk) can be a real pain—it's just plain slow. WOPR FloppyCopy makes working with documents on removable media easy. FloppyCopy steps in after you open a document from a removable media disk with Word's open file dialog box, and gives you the option of copying the document to your hard drive during editing. When you close the document, it is copied back to the removable media drive. You also have the option of keeping a copy on your hard drive for future editing.

LOOKUP ZIP+4

This utility looks up ZIP+4 codes from the United States Postal Service (USPS) Web Site. Have you ever sent a letter only to have it returned because of no ZIP Code or an incorrect ZIP Code? Have you ever wondered what the ZIP Code for a particular city is or just wanted to find the ZIP+4 code for your own or someone else's address? Well wonder no more; WOPR Lookup ZIP+4 comes to the rescue! WOPR Lookup ZIP+4 is a unique "ZIP Finding" utility that was designed to run exclusively from within Word. Simply enter an address (or partial address) into your document, fire up WOPR Lookup ZIP+4, and it will automatically grab the address, start your Dial-Up Internet Connection, retrieve the correct ZIP+4 code, and insert it into your document. WOPR Lookup ZIP+4 will even automatically disconnect from your Internet provider after a set amount of time, or you can choose to remain connected. WOPR Lookup ZIP+4 has also been hooked into Enveloper's "Find Zip" button for easy access from within your envelopes.

INSERT PICTURE

This gives you quick access to all of your graphic images, with more options and flexibility than Word's insert picture as well. With WOPR Insert Picture, you can

- Insert an image in its original size.
- Specify an exact size for the image before inserting it.
- Scale an image by any percentage before inserting it.
- Insert an image into the drawing layer, where you can float behind or on top of your text.
- Insert multiple images by telling Insert Picture to remain open on your screen after each insertion.

TASK PANE CUSTOMIZER

This powerful tool lets you customize the New Document, New Workbook, New Presentation, New File, and New Page or Web Task Panes in Microsoft Word, Excel, PowerPoint, Access, and FrontPage. With the Task Pane Customizer, you can add files or hyperlinks to, or remove files or hyperlinks from, any of the host Office application's New... Task Panes, rename existing files or hyperlinks, quickly move your files or hyperlinks to any of the four different Task Pane sections, and even clear the Task Pane's most recently used (MRU) document and template lists.

A

A

IMAGE EXTRACTOR/EDITOR

Ever want to grab the small 16×16 pixel icon out of an EXE file, DLL file, or from an Office application's command bar or toolbar? WOPR Image Extractor lets you do just that. With Image Extractor, you can extract the small icons from any EXE, DLL, ICO, or BMP file—or from any Office command bar (toolbar or menu)—and then edit and use them in any Office application such as Word, Excel, PowerPoint, Access, FrontPage, and Outlook.

DOCUMENT NOTES

These are the electronic equivalent of paper sticky notes for all of your Word documents. The notes travel along with each of your documents and can even be password protected.

DATE AND TIME TOOLS

These tools insert monthly calendars into your documents—calculate any date by selecting a start date and adding days, weeks, months, or years. They contain a menu bar alarm/timer and much more.

POP-UP CONTACTS LIST

This lets you access all of your Microsoft Outlook contacts from within Microsoft Word and insert various information about the contacts (such as their addresses, phone numbers, and so on) into your documents with just a couple of mouse clicks.

QUICKMARKS

This is a one-key navigator for big documents. QuickMarks turns your number key pad into an instant document navigator.

SHOW/HIDE ALL

This transforms Word's built-in Show/Hide command found on the Standard toolbar in to a fully customizable Show Whatever You Want powerhouse. Without having to write a single line of code, WOPR Show/Hide All allows you to choose which View options to show or hide and which View State to display when Show/Hide All is toggled on or off.

FORMATTING TOOLBAR

The WOPR Formatting toolbar is simply a better way to access your most used formatting tools. The WOPR Formatting toolbar features are

- **Enhanced Styles Menu**—Gives you quick access (via a plain text preview) to all available styles, plus organizational fly-outs for Recently Used Styles, User Defined Styles, In Use Styles, Built-In Styles, and All Styles. You can even manage your styles.

- **FastFonts**—Makes it fast and easy to find just the right font for your documents. FastFonts displays all available fonts on your system, with the font name in its actual typeface. You can even generate a printed example of every available font. Very slick!

- **Format Font and Format Paragraph Menus**—Makes it easy to access commonly used font or paragraph formatting attributes.

- **Insert Symbol Menu**—Instant access to any available symbol. With just a couple of clicks, you can insert math, Greek, Wingdings, and international symbols. There's also a Miscellaneous Symbols library that includes currency symbols (and the new Euro currency symbol as well), dots and daggers, publishers quotes, em and en dashes, trademarks and copyright symbols, and much, much more.

- **SuperSub**—Makes working with superscripts and subscripts fast and easy.

MODULE TOOLS

A custom toolbar contains a collection of tools for working with forms, modules, and macros in Microsoft Word. Features of WOPR Module Tools are

- **All Keys**—Generates a table of all available key assignments.

- **Rebuild File**—Rebuilds corrupted documents or templates. A real lifesaver!

- **Import/Export**—Imports or exports multiple VBA project components (forms, classes, and modules) in a single shot!

- **All Command Bars**—Generates a table of all available command bar controls (that is, menu bars, toolbars, and toolbar buttons).

- **FixXlate**—Fixes line continuation characters problems in WordBasic macros that have been translated into VBA by Microsoft Word.

- **Button Face IDs**—Displays all available button images for the built-in face ID numbers. You can copy the images to the clipboard or print them out in a document.

CITY2AIRPORT SMART TAGS

They recognize common city names as you type them into your documents and present you with a pop-up menu that allows you to insert the city's airport name or code into your document, view an online map of the city or the city's airport region, get driving directions TO or FROM the city's airport, and much more!

WOPR UPDATER!

This is the absolutely easiest way to make sure that you have the latest and most up-to-date version of WOPR.

LITTLE WOPRs LIBRARY

These are small, fast tools that you'll use everyday:

- **Active File Manager**—Gives you quick file-management tools for working with the active document or template—move, copy, rename, or delete the active document or template with a few clicks. You can even create a shortcut to the active document/template on your desktop, Start menu, favorites folder, and more.

A

- **Digital Signatures**—Provides easy access for working with digital signatures in the active document or template. You can quickly add digital signatures to or remove digital signatures from the active document or template, and easily import digital certificate files (using Microsoft's PVK Import tool) for use in signing your documents/templates.

- **Print Selector**—Gives you quick access to all of your printer's settings and makes printing only the portions of your documents that you want a snap.

- **Calculator**—Takes whatever values are currently selected, calculates a result, and places the result immediately after the selection in your document. A standalone toolbar-based calculator will even paste the calculation result into your document in a variety of different formats.

- **Normal Quotes**—Converts Microsoft Word's "smart quotes" back into "normal quotes."

- **Fix Line Breaks**—Removes extra line breaks from imported ASCII text files.

- **Duplicate Style**—Lets you quickly make an exact copy of any existing style in the active document or template.

- **View Characters**—Tells you exactly what ASCII codes lie behind your inscrutable characters.

- **View Header/Footer**—Brings back the old Word 2.0 header/footer functionality.

- **Remove Personal Information**—Provides easy access to Microsoft Word's Remove Personal Information feature that removes all personal information from the active document or template's comments, revisions, and File Properties dialog box.

- **Change Date/Time Stamp**—Provides a quick and easy way to change any file's creation, last modified, and last accessed date and time stamps.

- **Toggle Showing Windows in Taskbar**—Provides easy access to toggling on or off Microsoft Word's Show Windows in Taskbar feature that displays a separate icon on the Microsoft Windows taskbar for each open window in Microsoft Word.

- **Edit Replace**—Allows you to kick off the find and replace process with the currently selected text.

- **Fast Find**—Finds the current selection *quickly*; just highlight your text and press the quick keys.

INSTALLING WOPR 2003

To install WOPR 2003, make sure that you have Office 2003 installed, shut down all Office 2003 applications, insert this book's CD into your CD drive, and run the WOPR2003.EXE program directly from the CD.

You must run the installer directly from the CD. If you copy all the CD files to your hard drive and run WOPR2003.EXE from your hard drive, you will need to insert the original CD into your CD drive before the installer will proceed.

The installer asks you to select which WOPR components you want to install. By default, all options are selected. (You might want to go ahead and install all WOPR tools because you can easily remove any unneeded components later.) Click Next to finish the first stage of the installation.

The Install Wizard starts Word to finish the installation. After it has completed the installation, Word will close. Most of the WOPR components install with no further prompts, but some, such as Enveloper, have their own additional installers, which run when you first attempt to use them.

If you have an Internet connection active, WOPR 2003 can automatically check to see whether there are any updates at the end of the installation.

If you performed a partial installation and you want to install any component that you missed, select Add/Remove WOPR Components from the WOPR Commander's system tray menu (down by the Windows system clock). Select any component that wasn't installed and follow the prompts.

If you want to install WOPR on multiple PCs, send an email to `mike@wopr.com` for site licensing terms.

SECURITY CONSIDERATIONS

Because of the security model in Microsoft Office 2003, it is possible that the security settings in Office might prevent some of the WOPR applications from running. Many of these applications are based on macros in templates. Although all the macros and templates on the CD are virus free, Office security settings might prevent them from running anyway. If your Office security settings are set to High, unsigned macros will not run and you will not be given a prompt to change them. You can change this option by following the directions discussed in this book. If your company has "locked" your copy of Office to prevent you from changing this setting, you will need to contact your Office 2003 administrator to change this setting to allow these to run.

CAUTION

Some of the macros have been signed with a digital certificate to authenticate who the creator is. With these, you might be prompted whether to run them and asked whether you "trust" the signer. You should accept the prompt to allow the template or macro to work correctly.

To uninstall WOPR 2003:

1. Close all the host Office applications (Word, Excel, PowerPoint, Access, FrontPage, and Outlook).
2. Select the Add or Remove Programs applet from the Windows Control Panel.
3. Scroll down to WOPR 2003 and click the Add/Remove or Change/Remove button. Follow the onscreen prompts.

TECH SUPPORT

NOTE

The technical support options listed here are for WOPR 2003 only. For support with the other items on this book's CD, contact support@quepublishing.com.

For technical support

- Visit the FAQ (Frequently Asked Questions) page on our Web site at http://www.wopr.com/wopr-xp/support/woprsupportfaq.htm, and you will likely find your answer.
- Visit our Online Technical Support page at http://www.wopr.com/wopr-xp/support/woprsupport.shtml.
- Post a message to your WOPR using peers on the WOPR Peer-to-Peer forum in the WOPR Lounge located at http://www.wopr.com/lounge.

INDEX

emphatic headlines, 563

enabling
application sharing for online
meetings, 394
Indexing Service, 20

Encapsulated PostScript
(EPS), 258

End Meeting button (Online
Meeting toolbar), 395

End the show (slideshow
action), 188

ending
online meetings, 395
presentation broadcasts, 390

engines, speech recognition,
165-166

Enter button (Writing
Pad/Write Anywhere), 168

Entrance option (custom animations), 325

Enveloper (WOPR 2003 CD),
722

environment (presentations),
649
display screens, 654-656
lighting/sound, 650-652, 654
risers, 649-650
seating arrangements ,
656-657

EPS (Encapsulated
PostScript), 258

equipment (presentations),
660
laptops, 662-665
multimedia, 665-669
projectors, 660-662

Erase screen drawing made
with pen (slideshow action),
188

Eraser button (Table and
Borders toolbar), 88

error messages, handling, 482

event handlers, creating
(Microsoft Script Editor),
373-374

Excel
data
importing for chart
datasheets, 228
lost formatting, 414
objects, embedding in presentations, 409

exceptions, specifying
(AutoCorrect), 449

Exclude Row/Col command
(Data menu), 231

executing macros from toolbar, 425-426

Existing File or Web Page
button, 347

existing objects, embedding in
presentations, 410-411

existing presentations as basis
for new presentation cre-
ation, 46, 51-52

Exit option (custom animations), 325

Expand All button (Outlining
toolbar), 102

Expand All button (Standard
toolbar), 13

Expand button (Outlining
toolbar), 102

Expand button (Writing
Pad/Write Anywhere), 168

expanding
folders, 20
points in outlines, 104-106

expertise level, 519

exporting Word outlines to
PowerPoint, 109

extreme conditions (presentations), 691
dark shadows, 691-692
hearing difficulties, 692-694
language barriers, 694-695

eye movement
contact, 598-599, 618
anchored, 599
direct, 599

controlling, 552
arrows, 565
build sequences, 558-559
choosing typefaces and
fonts, 555-558
establishing anchors,
553-555
headlines, 563-565
overlays, 559, 562-563

F

face-to-face meetings, 703

fax machines, printing presentations to, 207

fears (presentations), 586
attacking causes of fear,
587-590
relaxation methods, 591-592

File menu commands
Add Clips to Organizer,
Automatically, 270
Add Clips to Organizer,
From Scanner or Camera,
271
Add Clips to Organizer, On
My Own, 270
Close and Return to
Microsoft PowerPoint, 421
New Collection, 274
Pack and Go, 193
Print Preview, 203
Properties, 463
Save as Web Page, 355-356,
367
Search, 16, 19
Send To, Mail Recipient, 138
Send To, Microsoft Word,
210
Send To, Original Sender,
143
View in Browser, 370

File Name property (advanced
searches), 22

FileNew Pop-Up (WOPR
2003 CD), 722

files
hyperlinks, creating, 347
presentations, missing, 362

How can we make this index more useful? Email us at indexes@quepublishing.com

Properties command (File menu), 463

Properties pane (Microsoft Script Editor), 370

Properties window (recording macros), 421

Publish as Web Page dialog box, 356-360

publishing presentations to Web, 354

punctuation and dictation mode (speech recognition), 158-159

pyramid charts, 225

Q - R

question and answer scripts, 510

QuickMarks (WOPR 2003 CD), 724

radar charts, 225

readability distance (presentations), 548-549

real-time chat (broadcasts), 386

rearranging
objects, layer order, 307
slides in presentations (Slide Sorter view), 115-116
toolbars, 37-38

recognition
handwriting, 166-167
hardware, 148
installing, 149-150
options, 169-170
software, 148
tools, 167
troubleshooting, 169
Write Anywhere, 169
writing pad, 167-168
speech, 157
audio input settings, 166
customizing, 161-162
dictation mode, 157-160
engines, 165-166
hardware, 148
installing, 149-150

profiles, 162-166
software, 148
speech recognition dictionary, 165
voice command mode, 160-161
voice training, 164

Recognition Profile Settings dialog box, 163

Recognize Now button (Writing Pad/Write Anywhere), 168

Recolor Picture button (Picture toolbar), 276-277

Recolor Picture dialog box, 277

recoloring
clip art, 277-278
pictures, 277-278

reconciling reviews, collaborative projects, 143

Record Macro dialog box, 420

Record Narration command (Slide Show menu), 181, 264

Record New Macro command (Macro menu), 420

Record Presentation Broadcast dialog box, 380

Record Sound dialog box, 263

recording
macros, 419-420
narrations, 180-182
presentation broadcasts, 379-383
sound clips, 264-265

Rectangle button (Drawing toolbar), 282, 286

rectangles, presentations, adding, 286

red/green color deficiency, 574

Redo button (Standard toolbar), 13

Reduce button (Writing Pad/Write Anywhere), 168

redundancy in presentations, 496

Regression analysis (chart trendlines), 239-240

Rehearse Timings command (Slide Show menu), 179, 188

rehearsing presentations, slide timings, 179-180

remote controls (Pro Presenter), 663

removing
buttons
Customize dialog box, 435-437
toolbars, 434-435
links, 407
menu buttons from toolbars, 437
shadows, 304
text services, 155

Rename Collection command (Edit menu), 274

Rename command (Tools menu), 58

Rename Master button (Slide Master View toolbar), 469

renaming
collections of clips, 274
presentations, 58

reordering animation effects, 332

Repeat option (Timing dialog box), 329

Replace Fonts command (Format menu), 69

Replace Text as You Type check box, 448

replacing fonts, 66, 69

Replay Broadcast button, 383

replaying presentation broadcasts, 383-384

repositioning toolbars, 432

rescaling objects, troubleshooting, 316

Reschedule Presentation Broadcast dialog box, 387

rescheduling presentation broadcasts, 387

Research command (Tools menu), 80

U - V

How can we make this index more useful? Email us at indexes@quepublishing.com

informIT

www.informit.com

Your Guide to Information Technology Training and Reference

Que has partnered with **InformIT.com** to bring technical information to your desktop. Drawing on Que authors and reviewers to provide additional information on topics you're interested in, **InformIT.com** has free, in-depth information you won't find anywhere else.

Articles

Keep your edge with thousands of free articles, in-depth features, interviews, and information technology reference recommendations – all written by experts you know and trust.

Online Books

Answers in an instant from **InformIT Online Books'** 600+ fully searchable online books. Sign up now and get your first 14 days **free**.

POWERED BY

Catalog

Review online sample chapters and author biographies to choose exactly the right book from a selection of more than 5,000 titles.

As an **InformIT** partner, **Que** has shared the knowledge and hands-on advice of our authors with you online. Visit **InformIT.com** to see what you are missing.

   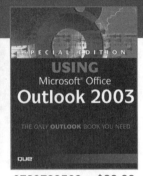

Windows Installation Instructions

1. Insert the disc into your CD-ROM drive.
2. From the Windows desktop, double-click the My Computer icon.
3. Double-click the icon representing your CD-ROM drive.
4. Double-click start.exe. Follow the on-screen prompts to access the CD content.

NOTE

> If you have the AutoPlay feature enabled, start.exe will be launched automatically whenever you insert the disc into your CD-ROM drive.

License Agreement

By opening this package, you are also agreeing to be bound by the following agreement:

You may not copy or redistribute the entire CD-ROM as a whole. Copying and redistribution of individual software programs on the CD-ROM is governed by terms set by individual copyright holders.

The installer and code from the author(s) are copyrighted by the publisher and the author(s). Individual programs and other items on the CD-ROM are copyrighted or are under an Open Source license by their various authors or other copyright holders.

This software is sold as-is without warranty of any kind, either expressed or implied, including but not limited to the implied warranties of merchantability and fitness for a particular purpose. Neither the publisher nor its dealers or distributors assumes any liability for any alleged or actual damages arising from the use of this program. (Some states do not allow for the exclusion of implied warranties, so the exclusion may not apply to you.)